PSAT/ NMSQT*

How to Prepare for the Preliminary Scholastic Aptitude Test/ National Merit Scholarship Qualifying Test

Seventh Edition

Samuel C. Brownstein
Formerly Chairman, Science Department
George W. Wingate High School, Brooklyn, N.Y.

Mitchel Weiner
Formerly Member, Department of English
James Madison High School, Brooklyn, N.Y.

Sharon Weiner Green
Formerly Instructor in English
Merritt College, Oakland, California

BARRON'S

Barron's Educational Series, Inc.
New York • London • Toronto • Sydney

*PSAT/NMSQT is a registered trademark of the College Entrance Examination Board, which does not endorse this book.

Formerly published as *How to Prepare for the PSAT*

All inquiries should be addressed to:
Barron's Educational Series, Inc.
250 Wireless Boulevard
Hauppauge, New York 11788

Library of Congress Catalog Card No. 89-299

International Standard Book No. 0-8120-4191-7

Library of Congress Cataloging-in-Publication Data

Brownstein, Samuel C., 1909-
Barron's how to prepare for the PSAT/NMSQT, Preliminary scholastic aptitude test/National merit scholarship qualifying test / Samuel C. Brownstein, Mitchel Weiner, Sharon Weiner Green. — 7th ed.
p. cm.
1. Preliminary Scholastic Aptitude Test—Study guides.
2. National merit scholarship qualifying test—Study guides.
I. Weiner, Mitchel, 1907- . II. Green, Sharon. III. Title.
IV. Title: How to prepare for the PSAT/NMSQT, Preliminary scholastic aptitude test/National merit scholarship qualifying test.
LB2353.56.B76 1989 371.2'64—dc19 89-299
ISBN 0-8120-4191-7 CIP

PRINTED IN THE UNITED STATES OF AMERICA

901 100 987654321

Contents

Preface vi
Acknowledgments vi

1 The Preliminary Scholastic Aptitude Test/ National Merit Scholarship Qualifying Test 1

Some Basic Questions Answered 1
PSAT Questions Sample 3
Answer Key 9
Answer Explanations 9

2 A Study Program 12

DIAGNOSE YOUR PROBLEM

3 A Diagnostic Test 19

Examination 20
Answer Key 29
Scoring Chart 30
Identify Your Weaknesses 31
Answer Explanations 32

CORRECT YOUR WEAKNESSES

Verbal Aptitude

4 The Antonym Question 41

Long-range Strategy 41
Tips to Help You Cope with Antonym Questions 41
Antonym Exercises A through D 42
Answer Key 49
Answer Explanations 49

5 The Sentence Completion Question 52

Tips for Handling the Sentence Completion Question 52
Sentence Completion Tests A and B 54
Answer Key 60

6 The Analogy Question 61

Long-range Strategy 61
Tips to Help You Cope with Analogy Questions 61
Analogy Exercises A through D 64
Answer Key 68
Answer Explanations 69

7 Improving Reading Comprehension 71

Long-range Strategy 71
Tips To Help You Cope with the Reading Comprehension Question 71
Reading Techniques 72
Finding the Central Thought 72
Finding Specific Detail 75
Finding Implications and Drawing Inferences 76
Determining the Meanings of Unfamiliar Words 77
Determining the Mood of the Writer 78
Determining Special Techniques Used by the Author 79

Reading Exercises A through E 83
Answer Key 99

8 Building Your Vocabulary 100

Long-range Strategy 100
A Plan for Using the Word List 100
PSAT High-Frequency Word List 101
Basic Word List with Etymologies and Tests 101

Mathematical Aptitude

9 Reviewing Mathematics 153

Tips for Handling Regular Mathematics Questions 153
A Suggested Study Program 154
Basic Mathematics 155
Algebra 157
Geometry 165
Typical Examination Problems by Topic 176
Answer Key 188

10 The Quantitative Comparison Question 189

Tips for Handling Quantitative Comparison Questions 189
Practice Exercises 190
Answer Key 192

TEST YOURSELF

11 Ten Typical Tests 195

Test A
Examination 199
Answer Key 208
Scoring Chart 208
Answers Explained 209

Test B
Examination 217
Answer Key 225
Scoring Chart 226
Answers Explained 227

Test C
Examination 235
Answer Key 243
Scoring Chart 244
Answers Explained 245

Test D
Examination 255
Answer Key 263
Scoring Chart 263
Answers Explained 264
Test E
Examination 273
Answer Key 282
Scoring Chart 282
Answers Explained 283
Test F
Examination 291
Answer Key 299
Scoring Chart 300
Answers Explained 300
Test G
Examination 309
Answer Key 317
Scoring Chart 318
Answers Explained 318
Test H
Examination 329
Answer Key 338
Scoring Chart 339
Answers Explained 339
Test I
Examination 349
Answer Key 357
Scoring Chart 358
Answers Explained 358
Test J
Examination 367
Answer Key 376
Scoring Chart 376
Answers Explained 377
Test Questions By Topic 383

Preface

For most college-bound students the PSAT/NMSQT is the first experience with a series of important examinations. A good score on the PSAT/NMSQT will help you approach the next hurdle, the Scholastic Aptitude Test (SAT), with confidence. It may also make you the winner of a college scholarship.

It is now generally agreed that one should prepare for college entrance examinations. One should not walk in cold. Nor should one cram for the test just before the test. This book is designed to help you cope with the problems of test-taking in general and with the problems of this examination in particular. Beginning with a general description of the structure of the test questions, the book then presents a diagnostic test which will quickly reveal your strengths and weaknesses. The authors give you more than the correct answers for they analyze the correct and wrong choices. They demonstrate how to attack a question, how to use time efficiently, and how to make an educated guess by using partial knowledge.

Adequate drill is provided for the various phases of the test. The important mathematical principles are reviewed with clear-cut examples followed by practice exercises. The verbal section has material to help build a more powerful vocabulary, to improve reading comprehension, and to attain skill in handling antonym, analogy, and sentence completion questions. Simulated tests with the exact number of questions and with the same level of difficulty as the actual test questions allow you to have several dress rehearsals for this important test. Going over the errors made with the analysis of explanations furnished is a valuable learning experience. As you follow this procedure, you will find that your performance improves and you will reach the point where you feel ready to walk into the examination room with confidence.

The authors are indebted to several people for the appearance and content of this revised edition. We thank our publisher, Mr. Manuel H. Barron, for putting at our disposal the talents of the members of the Production and Editorial Staffs.

Acknowledgments

The authors gratefully acknowledge all those sources who granted permission to use materials from their publications:

PSAT™ test directions are reprinted by permission of Educational Testing Service, the copyright owner. However, the test questions and other testing information are provided in their entirety by Barron's Educational Series, Inc. No endorsement of this publication by Educational Testing Service or the College Board should be inferred.

Pages 5–6: Reprinted by permission of the University of Tennessee Press from John B. Kirby's *Black Americans in the Roosevelt Era*. Copyright © 1980 by the University of Tennessee Press.

Page 22: From "Ruin," in *A Dove of the East and Other Stories*, © 1969, 1973, 1974, 1975 by Mark Helprin, Alfred A. Knopf, Inc., pp. 41–2.

Page 22: From Life Nature Library: *The Forest* (Revised Edition) by Peter Farb and the Editors of Time-Life Books, © 1980 by Time-Life Books, Inc. Reprinted by permission of the publisher.

Page 23: From *Bury My Heart at Wounded Knee: An Indian History of the American West* by Dee Brown. Copyright © 1970 by Dee Brown. Reprinted by permission of Henry Holt and Company, Inc.

Pages 24–25: From "The Tornado," by John T. Snow, April 1984, p. 86. Copyright © 1984 by *Scientific American*, Inc. All rights reserved.

Page 201: From "Lessons from Biology" by Francis Crick, *Natural History*, November 1988, p. 32.

Page 202: From *Metropolitan Museum Bulletin*, Spring 1987.

Page 203: From *From Slavery to Freedom: A History of Negro Americans*, Fifth Edition, by John Hope Franklin. Copyright © 1947, 1956, 1967, 1974, 1980 by Alfred A. Knopf, Inc. Reprinted by permission of the publisher.

Page 219: From *The English Novel: Form and Function* by Dorothy Van Ghent. Copyright 1953 by Dorothy Van Ghent. Reprinted by permission of Harper & Row, Publishers, Inc.

Page 219: From *The Soul of the Night* by Chet Raymo, © 1985. Reprinted by permission of the publisher, Prentice-Hall, Inc., Englewood Cliffs, New Jersey.

Page 220: From "W.E.B. DuBois: Protagonist of the Afro-American Protest" by Elliot Rudwick, in *Black Leaders of the Twentieth Century*, edited by John Hope Franklin and August Meier, © 1982 by the Board of Trustees of the University of Illinois, University of Illinois Press, pp. 64-5. Reprinted by permission.

Pages 221–222: From "An Occurrence at Owl Creek Bridge" by Ambrose Bierce.

Page 237: From "Medicine's Home Front," in *The Economist*, June 1987, © 1987, The Economist Newspaper Limited. Reprinted by permission.

Page 237: From "So Many Female Rivals" by Christine Froula, *The New York Times Book Review*, February 7, 1988. Copyright © 1988 by The New York Times Company. Reprinted by permission.

Page 238: From "The Birth of Massive Stars," by Michael Zeilik, April 1978, p. 110. Copyright © 1978 by *Scientific American*, Inc. All rights reserved.

Pages 238–239: From *Eyes on the Prize* by Juan Williams. Copyright © 1987 by Blackside, Inc. All rights reserved. Reprinted by permission of Viking Penguin, a division of Penguin Books USA, Inc.

Page 257: From "Yonder Peasant, Who is He?" in *Memories of a Catholic Girlhood*, copyright 1948 and renewed 1975 by Mary McCarthy, p. 33. Reprinted by permission of Harcourt Brace Jovanovich, Inc. First published in *The New Yorker*.

Pages 257–258: From *King Solomon's Ring* by Konrad Z. Lorenz. Translated by M.K. Wilson. Copyright 1952 by Konrad Z. Lorenz. Reprinted by permission of Harper & Row, Publishers, Inc.

Page 258: From "The Subduction of the Lithosphere," by M. Nafi, November 1975, p. 88. Copyright © 1975 by *Scientific American*, Inc. All rights reserved.

Page 259: From *Black History and the Historical Profession, 1915–1980*, by August Meier and Elliot Rudwick, © 1986 by the Board of Trustees of the University of Illinois. Reprinted by permission of the University of Illinois Press.

Page 275: From *Pride and Prejudice* by Jane Austen.

Page 276: From "The Odds Are You're Innumerate," by John Allen Paulos, *The New York Times Book Review*, Jan. 1, 1989, pp. 16–7. Copyright © 1989 by The New York Times Company. Reprinted by permission.

Pages 276–277: From *Century of Struggle* (Revised Edition) by Eleanor Flexnor, © 1959, 1975, Harvard University Press, pp. 222–3.

Pages 277–278: From "Huge Conservation Effort Aims to Save Vanishing Architect of the Savanna," by William K. Stevens, *The New York Times*, February 28, 1989, pp. C1, C15, Copyright © 1989 by The New York Times Company. Reprinted by permission.

Page 312: From *Rodents: Their Lives and Habits*, © 1975 by Peter W. Hanney, pp. 103–4. Reprinted by permission of Taplinger Publishing Co., Inc.

Page 313: From "Symbiotic Stars," by Minas Kafatos and Andrew G. Michalitsianos, July 1984, p. 84. Copyright © 1984 by *Scientific American*, Inc. All rights reserved.

Pages 331–332: From Life Nature Library: *The Forest* (Revised Edition) by Peter Farb and the Editors of Time-Life Books, © 1980 by Time-Life Books, Inc. Reprinted by permission of the publisher.

Page 333: Elaine Showalter, *A Literature of Their Own: British Women Novelists from Brontë to Lessing*. Copyright © 1977 by Princeton University Press. Excerpt, pp. 10–12, reprinted by permission of Princeton University Press.

Page 352: From *Athabasca* by Alistair MacLean, copyright © 1980 by Alistair MacLean. Used by permission of Doubleday, a division of Bantam, Doubleday, Dell Publishing Group, Inc.

Page 353: From *As They Were* by M.F.K. Fisher. Copyright 1983 by Alfred A. Knopf, Inc. Reprinted by permission of the publisher.

Page 371: From *The Panda's Thumb*, More Reflections in Natural History, by Stephen Jay Gould. Reprinted by permission of W.W. Norton & Company, Inc. Copyright © 1980 by Stephen Jay Gould.

Sample Timetable for the PSAT/NMSQT*

TOTAL TIME: 2 HOURS 20 MINUTES
ACTUAL TEST TIME: 1 HOUR 40 MINUTES

9:00 to 9:30	Seating of applicants, distribution of test booklets, other administrative details	
9:30 to 10:20	Section I Verbal Aptitude Test	65 Questions— antonyms, sentence completions, analogies, reading comprehension
10:20 to 10:30	Break	
10:30 to 11:20	Section II Mathematical Aptitude Test	50 Questions— 33 multiple-choice, 17 quantitative comparison

*NOTE: Actual times will vary in accordance with the time the proctor completes the preliminary work and begins the actual test. Format and timing are subject to change.

1

The Preliminary Scholastic Aptitude Test/ National Merit Scholarship Qualifying Test

Your plan to take the PSAT/NMSQT is perhaps your first concrete step toward planning a college career. PSAT/NMSQT, SAT—what do they mean to you? When? Where? What? How do these tests differ from the tests you ordinarily encounter in school? In this chapter these basic questions are answered so that you will be able to proceed to the subsequent chapters and adequately prepare yourself for this test.

SOME BASIC QUESTIONS ANSWERED

What is the PSAT/NMSQT?

The PSAT/NMSQT is a standardized test that measures verbal and mathematical ability. It is taken by high school students, usually in their junior year. The test consists of two parts, one testing verbal skills and one testing mathematical skills. Fifty minutes is allowed for answering the verbal questions; another 50 minutes, for the mathematical section.

Why is the test called the PSAT/NMSQT?

This preliminary college board examination is also the qualifying test for the scholarship competitions conducted by National Merit Scholarship Corporation (NMSC). NMSC used to offer a separate examination, but began co-sponsoring this test in 1971.

What are Merit Scholarships?

Merit Scholarships are prestigious national awards that carry with them a chance for solid financial aid. Conducted by NMSC, an independent, nonprofit organization with offices at One American Plaza, Evanston, Illinois 60201, the Merit Program today is supported by grants from over 600 corporations, private foundations, colleges and universities, and other organizations. The top-scoring PSAT/NMSQT participants in every state are named Semifinalists. Those who advance to Finalist standing by meeting additional requirements compete for one-time National Merit $2000 Scholarships and renewable, four-year Merit Scholarships, which may be worth as much as $8000 a year for four years.

What is the National Achievement Scholarship Program for Outstanding Negro Students?

This is a program aimed at honoring and assisting promising black high school students throughout the nation. It is also administered by NMSC. Students who enter the Merit Program by taking the PSAT/NMSQT and who are also eligible to participate in the Achievement Program mark a space on their test answer sheets asking to enter this competition as well. Top-scoring black students in each of the regions established for the competition compete for nonrenewable National Achievement $2000 Scholarships and for four-year Achievement Scholarships supported by over 175 sponsor organizations. To be considered for this program, you *must* mark the appropriate space on your answer sheet.

How can the PSAT/NMSQT help me?

If you are a high school junior it will help you see just how able you are to do college work. It will give you some idea of which colleges you should apply to in your senior year. It will give you access to scholarship competitions. It will definitely give you practice in answering multiple-choice questions where timing is an important factor.

In addition, you may choose to take advantage of the College Board's Student Search Service. This service is free for students who fill out the biographical section of the PSAT/NMSQT. If you fill out this section, you will receive mail from colleges and scholarship programs.

Ho do I apply for this test?

You apply through your school. Fees, when required, are collected by your school. The test is given in October. In December the results are sent to your school and to the scholarship program that you indicated on your answer sheet in the examination room.

How do scholastic aptitude tests differ from other tests?

These tests try to measure your ability to reason using facts that are part of your general knowledge or facts that are included in your test booklet. You're not required to recall great chunks of history or literature or science. You're not even required to recall most math formulas—they're printed right on the test.

Aptitude tests are multiple-choice tests. Your score depends upon how many correct answers you get within a definite period of time. Speed is important. So is accuracy. You have to pace yourself so that you don't sacrifice speed to gain accuracy (or sacrifice accuracy to gain speed).

How does the PSAT differ from the SAT?

It's shorter by an hour. The PSAT consists of two 50-minute sections; the SAT, of six half-hour ones. You have to answer fewer questions on the PSAT; however, some of them are real stumpers. Some students feel the PSAT is tougher than the SAT they take in their senior year.

Is it wise to leave answers blank?

Wild guessing will lower your score since a fraction of your wrong answers is subtracted from the number of correct answers. Since wrong answers count against you on the test, you may think that you should never guess if you aren't sure of the right answer to a question. But even if you guessed wrong four times for every time you guessed right, you would still come out even. A wrong answer costs you only $1/4$ of a point ($1/3$ on the quantitative comparison questions). The best advice is to guess if you can eliminate one or two of the answers. You have a better chance of hitting the right answer when you make this sort of "educated" guess.

As you go through this book, try this experiment to find out what kind of guesser you are. First, take part of any test that you have not taken before. You don't have to take an entire test section, but you should take at least 25 questions. Answer only those questions to which you definitely know the answers. See what your score is.

Next, take the same test section. Do not change any of your original answers, but whenever you can make an educated guess on one of the questions you originally passed, do so. See what your score is now. Finally, take the same test section, this time guessing blindly to answer all the remaining questions.

Compare your scores from the three different approaches to the test. For most people, the second score will be the best one. But you may be different. Maybe you are such a poor guesser that you should never guess at all. Or maybe you are such a good guesser that you should try every question.

What tactics can help me get ready for the PSAT?

1. Memorize the directions for each type of question. These don't change. The test time you would normally spend reading directions can be better spent answering questions.

2. Know the test. It has two sections; they will always be organized into subsets as follows:

<u>65-Question Verbal Section</u>
20 antonym questions
10 sentence completion questions
15 analogy questions
20 reading comprehension questions
<u>50-Question Mathematics Section</u>
15 standard multiple-choice questions
17 quantitative comparison questions
18 standard multiple-choice questions

3. Expect easy questions at the beginning of each set of the same question type. Within each set (except for the reading comprehension questions), the questions progress from easy to difficult. In other words, the first antonym question in a set will be easier than the last antonym question in that set; the first quantitative comparison question will be easier than the last quantitative comparison question.

4. Take advantage of the easy questions to boost your score. Remember: each question is worth the same number of points. Whether it was easy or difficult, whether it took you 10 seconds or 2 minutes to answer, you get the same number of points for each question you answer correctly. Your job is to answer as many questions as you possibly can without rushing ahead so fast that you make careless errors or lose points for failing to give some questions enough thought. Take enough time to get those easy questions right!

5. *First* answer all the easy questions on the test; *then* tackle the hard ones if you have time. You know that the questions in each segment of the test get harder as you go along (except for the reading comprehension questions). But each new segment starts with easy questions. Don't get bogged down on a difficult antonym question when only three questions away the easy sentence completion questions begin.

6. Eliminate as many wrong answers as you can. Deciding between two choices is easier than deciding among five. Even if you have to guess, every answer you eliminate improves your chances of guessing correctly.

7. Change answers only if you have a reason for doing so. Don't give in to last-minute panic. It's usually better not to change an answer on a sudden hunch or whim.

8. Write in your test book: mark questions you want to take a second look at; circle ones you have to skip. Then if you have time at the end of the section, you will be able to locate them quickly. You can and you should do your math computations in the test book. There is absolutely no need for you to try to do them in your head. And if it helps you to doodle while you think, then doodle away. The test booklet is yours. Use it.

9. Be careful not to make any stray marks on your answer sheet. This test is graded by a machine, and a machine cannot tell the difference between an accidental mark and a filled-in answer. When the machine sees two marks instead of one, it calls the answer wrong.

10. Check frequently to make sure you are answering the questions in the right spots. No machine is going to notice that you made a mistake early in the test, answered question 4 in the space for question 5, and all your following answers are in the wrong place. (One way to avoid this problem is to mark your answers in your test booklet and transfer them to your answer sheet in blocks.)

11. Line up your test book with your answer sheet. Whether you choose to fill in the answers question by question or in blocks, you will do so most efficiently if you keep your test book and your answer sheet aligned.

12. Don't get bogged down on any one question. By the time you get to the actual PSAT, you should have a fair idea of how much time to spend on each question. If a question is taking too long, leave it and go on to the next. This is no time to try to show the world that you can stick to a job no matter how long it takes. All the machine that grades the test will notice is that after a certain point you didn't have any correct answers.

How can I prevent PSAT anxiety from setting in?

1. The best way to prepare for any test you ever take is to get a good night's sleep before the test so you are well rested and alert.

2. Eat a good breakfast for once in your life. You have a full morning ahead of you. You should have a full stomach as well.

3. Allow plenty of time for getting to the test site. Taking a test is pressure enough. You don't need the extra tension that comes from worrying about whether you will get there on time.

4. Recognize how long taking the test is going to take. There are two sections on the test. Each one is 50 minutes long, and there is supposed to be a 10-minute break between sections. Add to that half an hour for paper-pushing. If you are scheduled to start the PSAT at 9 A.M., don't make a dentist appointment for 11 A.M. You can't possibly get there on time, and you'll just spend the last half hour of the test worrying about it.

5. The College Board tells you to bring two sharpened number 2 pencils to the test. Bring four. They don't weigh much, and this might be the one day in the decade when two pencil points decide to break. And bring full-size pencils, not little stubs. They are easier to write with, and you might as well be comfortable.

6. Speaking of being comfortable, wear comfortable clothes. This is a test, not a fashion show. Aim for the layered look. Wear something light, but bring a sweater. The test room may be hot, or it may be cold. You can't change the room, but you can put on the sweater.

7. Bring an accurate watch. Not a fancy watch alarm or a calculator model—the Test Center people won't let you bring it in. But you need a watch. The room in which you take the test may not have a clock, and some proctors are not very good about posting the time on the blackboard. Don't depend on them. Each time you begin a test section, write down in your booklet the time according to your watch. That way you will always know how much time you have left.

8. Smuggle in some quick energy in your pocket—trail mix, raisins, a candy bar. Even if the proctors don't let you eat in the test room, you can grab a bite en route to the rest rooms during the 10-minute break. Taking the test can leave you feeling drained and in need of a quick pickup—bring along your favorite comfort food.

9. Between sections, stretch. Use your rest break to clear your thoughts. Do breathing exercises, or close your eyes and imagine yourself floating or sun-bathing. In addition to being under mental pressure, you're under physical pressure from sitting so long in an uncomfortable seat with a No. 2 pencil clutched in your hand. Anything you can do to loosen up and get the kinks out will ease your body and help the oxygen get to your brain.

SAMPLE PSAT QUESTIONS

The purpose of this section is to familiarize you with the kinds of questions that appear on the PSAT by presenting questions like those on recent PSATs. Knowing what to expect when you take the examination is an important aid in preparing for the test and succeeding in it.

The directions that precede the various types of sample questions are the same as those on the PSAT. For all questions, you are to choose the best answer and fill in the corresponding oval on the answer sheet.

Verbal Aptitude Section

The verbal aptitude section consists of 65 questions to be completed in 50 minutes. A typical test is made up of 20 antonym questions, 10 sentence completion questions, 15 analogy questions, and 20 questions testing reading comprehension.

Antonyms (Opposites)

The antonym question tests your knowledge of vocabulary.

> Each question below consists of a word in capital letters, followed by five lettered words or phrases. Choose the word or phrase that is most nearly opposite in meaning to the word in capital letters. Since some of the questions require you to distinguish fine shades of meaning, consider all the choices before deciding which is best.
>
> Example:
>
> GOOD: (A) sour (B) bad (C) red (D) hot (E) ugly
>
> (A) ● (C) (D) (E)

1. FALTER: (A) answer rudely (B) move surely (C) observe closely (D) wish deeply (E) return unwillingly
2. UNSIGHTLY: (A) visible (B) massive (C) authentic (D) conscious (E) appealing
3. DISCLAIM: (A) admonish (B) penalize (C) acknowledge (D) qualify (E) remind
4. CURSORY: (A) exceptional (B) dispassionate (C) disdainful (D) admiring (E) meticulous
5. EFFRONTERY: (A) posterity (B) independence (C) timidity (D) coherence (E) inferiority

Sentence Completions

The sentence completion question tests your ability to use words in context and is in part a test of reading comprehension.

> Each sentence below has one or two blanks, each blank indicating that something has been omitted. Beneath the sentence are five lettered words or sets of words. Choose the word or set of words that, when inserted in the sentence, best fits the meaning of the sentence as a whole.
>
> Example:
>
> Although its publicity has been ----, the film itself is intelligent, well-acted, handsomely produced, and altogether ----.
>
> (A) tasteless . . respectable (B) extensive . . moderate (C) sophisticated . . amateur (D) risque . . crude (E) perfect . . spectacular
>
> ● (B) (C) (D) (E)

6. Folk dancing is ---- senior citizens, and it is also economical; they need neither great physical agility nor special accoutrements to enjoy participating in the dance.
(A) bewildering to (B) costly for (C) foreign to (D) appropriate for (E) impracticable for
7. The author contended that his insights were not ----, but had been made independently of others.
(A) derivative (B) esoteric (C) fallacious (D) hypothetical (E) superficial
8. Although Roman original contributions to government, jurisprudence, and engineering are commonly acknowledged, the artistic legacy of the Roman world continues to be judged widely as ---- the magnificent Greek traditions that preceded it.
(A) an improvement on (B) an echo of (C) a resolution of (D) a precursor of (E) a consummation of
9. ---- though she appeared, her journals reveal that her outward maidenly reserve concealed a passionate nature unsuspected by her family and friends.
(A) Effusive (B) Suspicious (C) Tempestuous (D) Domineering (E) Reticent
10. Crabeater seal, the common name of *Lobodon carcinophagus*, is ----, since the animal's staple diet is not crabs, but krill.
(A) a pseudonym (B) a misnomer (C) an allusion (D) a digression (E) a compromise

Analogies (Word Relationships)

The analogy question tests your ability to see relationships between words. These relationships may be cause and effect, degree, synonyms, antonyms, or others which are discussed fully in Chapter 6.

> Each question below consists of a related pair of words or phrases, followed by five lettered pairs of words or phrases. Select the lettered pair that best expresses a relationship similar to that expressed in the original pair.
>
> Example:
>
> YAWN : BOREDOM : : (A) dream : sleep (B) anger : madness (C) smile : amusement (D) face : expression (E) impatience : rebellion
>
> (A) (B) ● (D) (E)

11. WOLF : PACK : : (A) horse : saddle (B) goose : flock (C) fox : lair (D) pig : sow (E) lion : cub
12. BRANCH : TREE : : (A) lid : eye (B) strap : sandal (C) sand : beach (D) frame : picture (E) wing : building
13. FLIMSY : PRETEXT : : (A) frail : illness (B) shaky : alibi (C) apprehensive : risk (D) sorrowful : confession (E) final : judgment
14. FOIL : SCHEME : : (A) alter : decision (B) conceal : weapon (C) sketch : blueprint (D) block : passage (E) lose : competition

15. QUACK : CHARLATANRY : :
(A) miser : extravagance (B) braggart : flattery
(C) insurgent : revelry (D) ascetic : misanthropy
(E) blackguard : knavery

Reading Comprehension

Your ability to read and understand the kind of material found in college texts and the more serious magazines is tested in the reading comprehension section of the PSAT/NMSQT. You may be asked to find the central thought of a passage, find specific detail mentioned in the passage, draw inferences, determine the meaning of unfamiliar words as used in the text, analyze the mood of the author, or determine the special techniques used by the author to achieve his or her effects.

> Each passage below is followed by questions based on its content. Answer the questions following each passage on the basis of what is stated or implied in that passage.

Unlike the carefully weighed and planned compositions of Dante, Goethe's writings have always the sense of immediacy and enthusiasm. He was a constant experimenter with life, with ideas, and with forms of writing. For the same reason, his works seldom have the qualities of finish or formal beauty which distinguish the masterpieces of Dante and Virgil. He came to love the beauties of classicism, but these were never an essential part of his make-up. Instead, the urgency of the moment, the spirit of the thing, guided his pen. As a result, nearly all his works have serious flaws of structure, of inconsistencies, of excesses and redundancies and extraneities.

In the large sense, Goethe represents the fullest development of the romanticist. It has been argued that he should not be so designated because he so clearly matured and outgrew the kind of romanticism exhibited by Wordsworth, Shelley, and Keats. Shelley and Keats died young; Wordsworth lived narrowly and abandoned his early attitudes. In contrast, Goethe lived abundantly and developed his faith in the spirit, his understanding of nature and human nature, and his reliance on feelings as man's essential motivating force. The result was an all-encompassing vision of reality and a philosophy of life broader and deeper than the partial visions and attitudes of other romanticists. Yet the spirit of youthfulness, the impatience with close reasoning or "logic-chopping," and the continued faith in nature remained his to the end, together with an occasional waywardness and impulsiveness and a disregard of artistic or logical propriety which savor strongly of romantic individualism. Since so many twentieth-century thoughts and attitudes are similarly based on the stimulus of the Romantic Movement, Goethe stands as particularly the poet of the modern man as Dante stood for medieval man and as Shakespeare for the man of the Renaissance.

16. A main concern of the passage is to
(A) describe the history of Romanticism until its decline
(B) suggest that romantic literature is similar to Shakespearean drama
(C) argue that romantic writings are more fully developed than classical works
(D) compare Goethe with twentieth-century writers and poets
(E) explain the ways in which Goethe embodied the romantic spirit

17. A characteristic of romanticism NOT mentioned in this passage is its
(A) elevation of nature
(B) preference for spontaneity
(C) modernity of ideas
(D) unconcern for artistic decorum
(E) simplicity of language

18. It can be inferred from the passage that classicism has which of the following characteristics?
I. Sensitivity toward emotional promptings
II. Emphasis on formal aesthetic standards
III. Meticulous planning of artistic works
(A) II only
(B) III only
(C) I and II
(D) II and III
(E) I, II, and III

19. The author's attitude toward Goethe's writings is best described as
(A) unqualified endorsement (B) lofty indifference
(C) reluctant tolerance (D) measured admiration
(E) undisguised contempt

Like her white friends Eleanor Roosevelt and Aubrey Williams, Mary Bethune believed in the fundamental commitment of the New Deal to assist the black American's struggle and in the need for blacks to assume responsibilities to help win that struggle. Unlike those of her white liberal associates, however, Bethune's ideas had evolved out of a long experience as a "race leader." Founder of a small black college in Florida, she had become widely known by 1935 as an organizer of black women's groups and as a civil and political rights activist. Deeply religious, certain of her own capabilities, she held a relatively uncluttered view of what she felt were the New Deal's and her own people's obligations to the cause of racial justice. Unafraid to speak her mind to powerful whites, including the President, or to differing black factions, she combined faith in the ultimate willingness of whites to discard their prejudice and bigotry with a strong sense of racial pride and commitment to Negro self-help.

More than her liberal white friends, Bethune argued for a strong and direct black voice in initiating and shaping government policy. She pursued this in her conversations with President Roosevelt, in numerous memoranda to

Aubrey Williams, and in her administrative work as head of the National Youth Administration's Office of Negro Affairs. With the assistance of Williams, she was successful in having blacks selected to NYA posts at the national, state, and local levels. But she also wanted a black presence throughout the federal government. At the beginning of the war she joined other black leaders in demanding appointments to the Selective Service Board and to the Department of the Army; and she was instrumental in 1941 in securing Earl Dickerson's membership on the Fair Employment Practices Committee. By 1944, she was still making appeals for black representation in "all public programs, federal, state, and local," and "in policy-making posts as well as rank and file jobs."

Though recognizing the weakness in the Roosevelt administration's response to Negro needs, Mary Bethune remained in essence a black partisan champion of the New Deal during the 1930s and 1940s. Her strong advocacy of administration policies and programs was predicated on a number of factors: her assessment of the low status of black Americans during the Depression; her faith in the willingness of some liberal whites to work for the inclusion of blacks in the government's reform and recovery measures; her conviction that only massive federal aid could elevate the Negro economically; and her belief that the thirties and forties were producing a more self-aware and self-assured black population. Like a number of her white friends in government, Bethune assumed that the preservation of democracy and black people's "full integration into the benefits and the responsibilities" of American life were inextricably tied together. She was convinced that, with the help of a friendly government, a militant, aggressive "New Negro" would emerge out of the devastation of depression and war, a "New Negro" who would "save America from itself," who would lead America toward the full realization of its democratic ideas.

20. The author's primary goal in the passage is to do which of the following?

(A) Criticize Mary Bethune for adhering too closely to New Deal policies
(B) Argue that Mary Bethune was too optimistic in her assessment of race relations
(C) Demonstrate Mary Bethune's influence on black progress during the Roosevelt years
(D) Point out the weaknesses of the white liberal approach to black needs
(E) Summarize the attainments of blacks under the auspices of Roosevelt's New Deal

21. It can be inferred from the passage that Aubrey Williams was which of the following?

I. A man with influence in the National Youth Administration
II. A white liberal
III. A man of strong religious convictions

(A) I only
(B) II only
(C) I and II only
(D) II and III only
(E) I, II, and III

22. The author mentions Earl Dickerson (paragraph 2) primarily in order to

(A) cite an instance of Bethune's political impact
(B) contrast his career with that of Bethune
(C) introduce the subject of a subsequent paragraph
(D) provide an example of Bethune's "New Negro"
(E) show that Dickerson was a leader of his fellow blacks

Mathematical Aptitude Section

The mathematical aptitude section consists of 50 questions to be completed in 50 minutes. Some questions in the mathematical section require you to apply graphic, spatial, numerical, symbolic, and logical techniques to situations already familiar to you; these may be similar to exercises in your textbooks. In other questions you are presented with novel situations and are called upon to do original thinking and to solve problems. You will not be expected to use mathematical knowledge beyond elementary algebra and geometry.

Sample test directions and reference formulas for the mathematical section of the PSAT/NMSQT follow.

The following information is for your reference in solving some of the problems.

Circle of radius r: Area $= \pi r^2$ Circumference $= 2\pi r$
The number of degrees of an arc in a circle is 360.
The measure in degrees of a straight angle is 180.

Definitions of symbols:

$=$ is equal to	$\leqq$ is less than or equal to
$\neq$ is unequal to	$\geqq$ is greater than or equal to
$<$ is less than	$\parallel$ is parallel to
$>$ is greater than	$\perp$ is perpendicular to

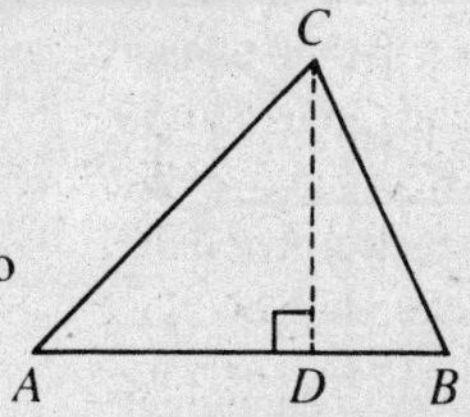

Triangle: The sum of the measures in degrees of the angles of a triangle is 180.

If $\angle CDA$ is a right angle, then

(1) area of $\triangle ABC = \dfrac{AB \times CD}{2}$

(2) $AC^2 = AD^2 + DC^2$

Note: Figures that accompany problems in this test are intended to provide information useful in solving the problems. They are drawn as accurately as possible EXCEPT when it is stated in a specific problem that its figure is not drawn to scale. All figures lie in a plane unless otherwise indicated. All numbers used are real numbers.

23. What is the exact quotient when 133,578 is divided by 543?
(A) 243 (B) 244 (C) 245 (D) 246 (E) 247

24. What part of an hour elapses from 11:55 A.M. to 12:15 P.M.?
(A) $\frac{1}{3}$ (B) $\frac{1}{4}$ (C) $\frac{1}{5}$ (D) $\frac{1}{6}$ (E) $\frac{2}{3}$

25. The enrollment at the North Shore Academy is b boys and g number of girls. What part of the academy student body is composed of girls?
(A) $\dfrac{b}{b+g}$ (B) $\dfrac{g}{b}$ (C) $\dfrac{g}{bg}$ (D) $\dfrac{g}{b+g}$ (E) b

26. In isosceles right triangle ABC, $AB = BC$ and $AC = 10$. What is the area of $\triangle ABC$?
(A) $5\sqrt{2}$ (B) $2\sqrt{5}$ (C) 5
(D) $\sqrt{25}$ (E) 25

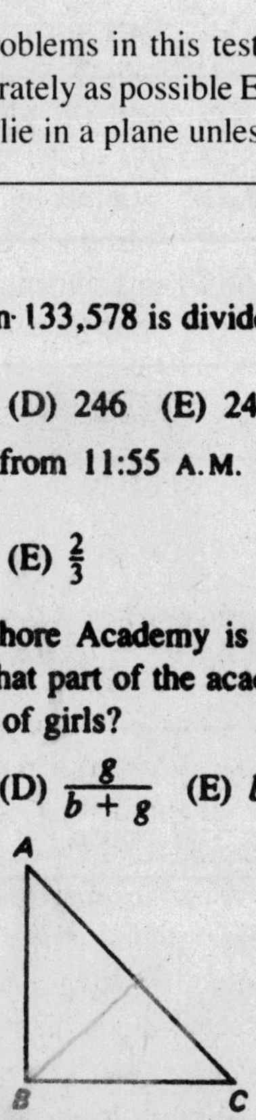

27. If the sum of the lengths of three sides of a square is r, then the perimeter of this square is
(A) $\dfrac{3}{r} + 1$ (B) $\dfrac{r}{3} + 4$ (C) $\dfrac{4r}{3}$ (D) $\dfrac{r}{3} + 1$
(E) $\dfrac{3}{r} + r$

28. When the rate for first-class postage was increased from 18¢ to 20¢, the percent of increase was
(A) 1.1% (B) 2% (C) 9% (D) 10% (E) 11.1%

29. If the angles of a triangle are in the ratio 3:4:5, then one of these angles must have a measure in degrees of
(A) 30 (B) 60 (C) 90 (D) 100 (E) 120

30. For which figure is the area equal to the product of two of its sides?
(A) right triangle (B) isosceles triangle
(C) trapezoid (D) rectangle (E) parallelogram

31. What is the average measure of the angles of a triangle?
(A) 30° (B) 45° (C) 60° (D) 90°
(E) cannot be determined from the information furnished

32. If $\dfrac{a+b}{c+2b}$ equals 1, then b equals
(A) $\dfrac{a}{c+2}$ (B) $a - c$ (C) $a + c$ (D) $\dfrac{a-c}{2}$
(E) $\dfrac{a+c}{3}$

33. If the perimeter of ΔABC is 29 meters, then the length (in meters) of the shortest side is
(A) 3 (B) 5 (C) 7
(D) 10 (E) 12

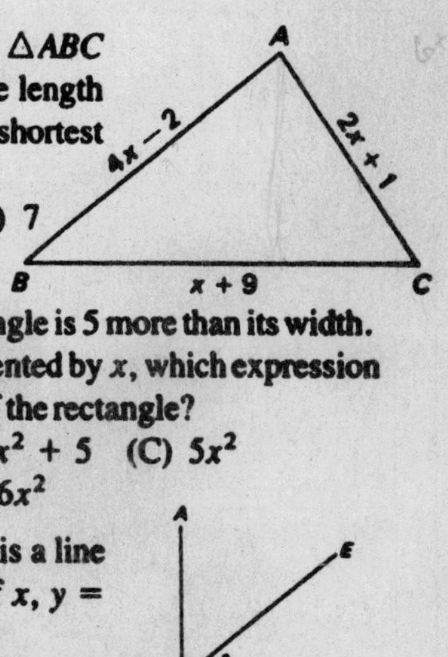

34. The length of a rectangle is 5 more than its width. If the width is represented by x, which expression represents the area of the rectangle?
(A) $x^2 + 5x$ (B) $x^2 + 5$ (C) $5x^2$
(D) $4x + 10$ (E) $6x^2$

35. $AB \perp BC$ and DBE is a line segment. In terms of x, $y =$
(A) x (B) $x - 90$
(C) $90 - x$ (D) $180 - x$
(E) $x - 180$

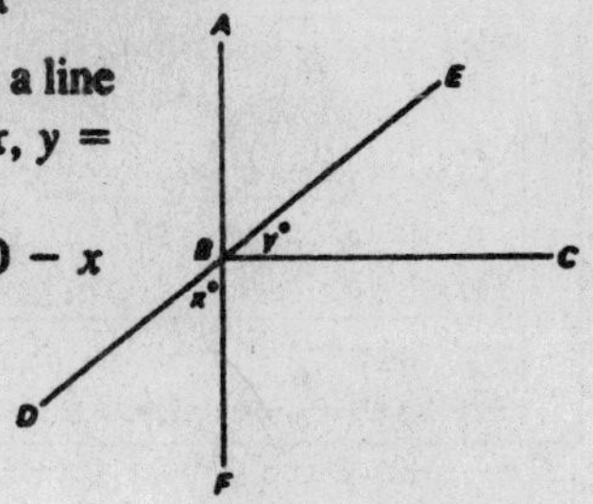

36. What is the value of z, if $x = 100$, $y = 30$, and AB is a line segment?
(A) 30 (B) 80 (C) 100
(D) 110 (E) 120

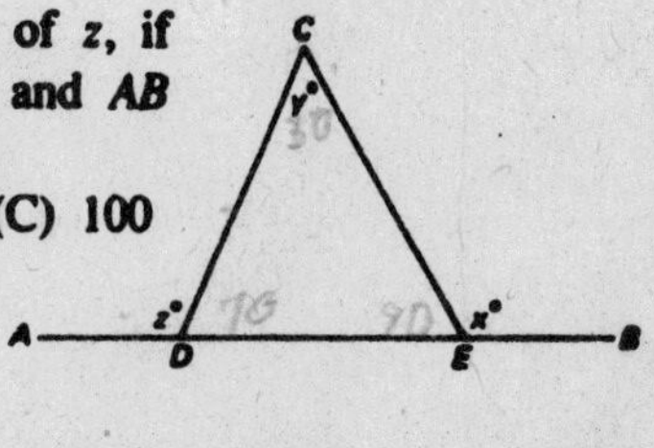

37. **In rectangle *DEBC*, *CA* is drawn, forming $\triangle ABC$. In terms of *x*, *y*, and *z*, what is the area of *ACDE*?**

(A) $xy - yz$ **(B)** $yz - xy$
(C) $xy - z$ **(D)** $y(x - z)$
(E) $xy - \frac{yz}{2}$

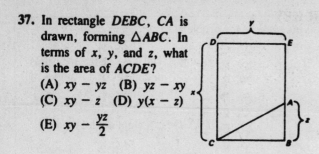

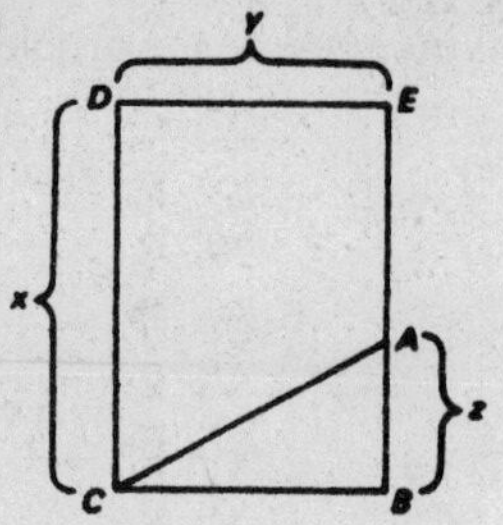

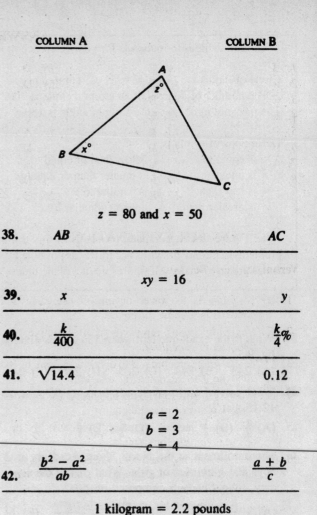

Another type of question you can expect to encounter is the type known as quantitative comparison. Questions 38 to 43 are examples of quantitative comparisons. There are only four choices from which to select an answer. The following instructions are given for these questions.

Questions 38-43 each consist of two quantities, one in Column A and one in Column B. You are to compare the two quantities and on the answer sheet fill in oval

A if the quantity in Column A is greater;
B if the quantity in Column B is greater;
C if the two quantities are equal;
D if the relationship cannot be determined from the information given.

Notes:
1. In certain questions, information concerning one or both of the quantities to be compared is centered above the two columns.
2. In a given question, a symbol that appears in both columns represents the same thing in Column A as it does in Column B.
3. Letters such as *x*, *n*, and *k* stand for real numbers.

EXAMPLES

	Column A	Column B	Answers
E1.	2×6	$2 + 6$	● B C D
	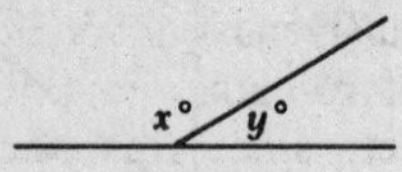		
E2.	$180 - x$	y	A B ● D
E3.	$p - q$	$q + p$	A B C ●

COLUMN A | **COLUMN B**

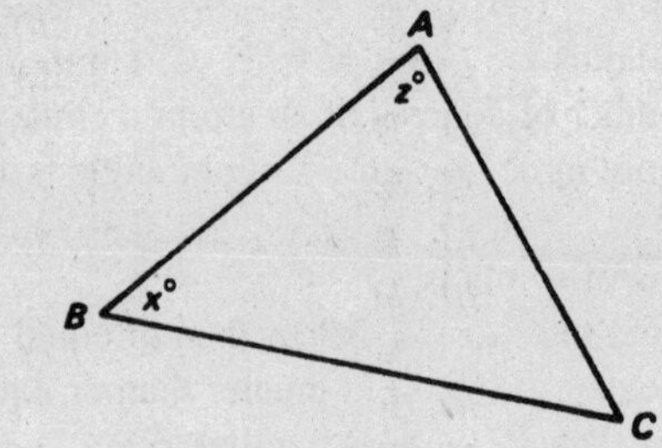

$z = 80$ and $x = 50$

	Column A	Column B
38.	***AB***	***AC***
	$xy = 16$	
39.	x	y
40.	$\frac{k}{400}$	$\frac{k}{4}\%$
41.	$\sqrt{14.4}$	0.12
	$a = 2$, $b = 3$, $c = 4$	
42.	$\frac{b^2 - a^2}{ab}$	$\frac{a + b}{c}$
	1 kilogram = 2.2 pounds	
43.	1 pound	0.33 kilogram

ANSWER KEY

1. B	9. E	18. D	27. C	36. D
2. E	10. B	19. D	28. E	37. E
3. C	11. B	20. C	29. B	38. C
4. E	12. E	21. C	30. D	39. D
5. C	13. B	22. A	31. C	40. C
6. D	14. D	23. D	32. B	41. A
7. A	15. E	24. A	33. C	42. B
8. B	16. E	25. D	34. A	43. A
	17. E	26. E	35. C	

ANSWER EXPLANATIONS

Verbal Aptitude Section

1. **B** To *falter* is to waver or move unsteadily. Its opposite is to *move surely*.

2. **E** *Unsightly* means repulsive or unattractive. Its opposite is *appealing*.

3. **C** To *disclaim* something is to disavow or deny it. Its opposite is to *acknowledge* or admit.

4. **E** *Cursory* means superficial and hasty. Its opposite is *meticulous* or painstaking.

5. **C** *Effrontery* means impudent boldness. Its opposite is *timidity* or shyness.

6. **D** *Because* senior citizens don't need great physical agility to enjoy folk dancing, it is an *appropriate* activity for them.

7. **A** If the author got his insights independently, then he did not obtain or derive them from the insights of other people. In other words, his insights were not *derivative*.

8. **B** The view of Rome's contributions to government, law, and engineering is wholly positive: these original additions to human knowledge are generally acknowledged or recognized. *In contrast*, Rome's original contributions to art are *not* recognized: they are seen as just an *echo* or imitation of the art of ancient Greece.
Note that *Although* sets up the contrast here.

9. **E** Her outward appearance was one of "maidenly reserve" (self-restraint; avoidance of intimacy). Thus, she seemed to be *reticent* (reserved; disinclined to speak or act freely), even though she actually felt things passionately.

10. **B** Because these seals eat far more krill than crabs, it *misnames* them to call them crabeater seals. The term is thus a *misnomer*, a name that's wrongly applied to someone or something.
Beware of eye-catchers. Choice **A** is incorrect. A *pseudonym* isn't a mistaken name; it's a false name that an author adopts.

11. **B** A *wolf* belongs to a *pack*. A *goose* belongs to a *flock*. (Group and Member)

12. **E** A *branch* is an offshoot from the main part of a *tree*. A *wing* is an extension from the main part of a *building*. (Part to Whole)

13. **B** A *flimsy pretext* (pretended reason) is by definition too weak to stand up to close examination. A *shaky alibi* (excuse to avoid blame) is likewise too weak to stand up to close examination.
Beware of eye-catchers. Choice **A** is incorrect. While illness may make someone frail, an illness can't be described as being frail.
(Defining Characteristic)

14. **D** To *foil* a *scheme* is to hinder or obstruct it. To *block* a *passage* is to close or obstruct it. (Function)

15. **E** A *quack* (imposter; fraud) is noted for *charlatanry* (making fradulent claims). A *blackguard* (scoundrel; rogue) is noted for *knavery* (behaving villainously). (Defining Characteristic)

16. **E** The opening sentence of the second paragraph states that "Goethe represents the fullest development of the romanticist." By providing examples of ways in which Goethe sustained his early romantic temper, the passage refutes the notion that he outgrew his romanticism and explains how he embodied this romantic spirit.

17. **E** The author never mentions *simplicity of language* as a characteristic of romanticism.
Choice **A** is incorrect. The passage refers to a "continued faith in nature" as one aspect of Goethe's romanticism. Choice **B** is incorrect. The passage refers to impulsiveness or *spontaneity* as savoring strongly of romantic individualism. Choice **C** is incorrect. Since romanticism has *formed* so many modern attitudes, one finds in romanticism ideas that seem noteworthy for their modernity. Choice **D** is incorrect. The passage refers to "a disregard of artistic or logical propriety" as characteristic of romanticism.

18. **D** You can arrive at the correct answer by the process of elimination.
Sensitivity toward emotional promptings is characteristic of romanticism; it is an unlikely characteristic of classicism. Therefore, you can eliminate Choices **C** and **E**.
Emphasis on formal aesthetic standards is a likely characteristic of classicism. The passage talks

of the formal beauty that distinguishes the classical works of Dante and Virgil. Therefore, you can eliminate Choice B.
Meticulous planning of artistic works is a likely characteristic of classicism. The passage talks of the carefully planned compositions of the classicist Dante; it also tells of the structurally flawed compositions of the romantic Goethe. Therefore, you can eliminate Choice **A**.
Only choice **D** is left. It is the correct answer.

19. **D** The author both admires Goethe's writings and notes their flaws; his attitude is one of *measured admiration*.

20. **C** The entire passage shows Bethune's impact on her people's progress.

21. **C** You can arrive at the correct answer by the process of elimination.
Williams assisted Bethune in influencing the advancement of blacks within the NYA. Therefore, you can eliminate Choices **B** and **D**.
The opening sentence of the first paragraph indicates that Williams was one of Bethune's white friends; references to him in the second paragraph suggest he was a liberal. Therefore, you can eliminate Choice **A**.
Nothing in the passage suggests Williams was religious. Therefore, you can eliminate Choice **E**.
Only Choice **C** is left. It is the correct answer.

22. **A** Bethune's success in getting Dickerson's appointment is a clear example of her impact.
Choice **B** is incorrect. The author stresses how helpful Bethune was to Dickerson, not how different Bethune's career was from Dickerson's. Choice **C** is incorrect. Dickerson is not the subject of the paragraph that follows. Choice **D** is incorrect. The author brings up Bethune's belief in the "New Negro" well after he mentions her assistance to Dickerson. He draws no connection between Dickerson and the "New Negro." Also Choice **E** is incorrect. The author is making a point about Bethune, not about Dickerson.

Mathematical Aptitude Section

23. **D** This is not an arithmetic test. Also, time does not permit using the standard method of long division. Observe that the dividend ends with the digit 8 and the divisor ends with the digit 3. The quotient must end with the digit 6.

$$\begin{array}{r} \text{quotient} \\ \text{divisor}\,\overline{)\text{dividend}} \end{array}$$

24. **A** Time elapsed is 20 minutes.
$\frac{20}{60}$ is $\frac{1}{3}$ of an hour.

25. **D** The entire student body = $b + g$.
$\frac{g}{b+g}$ = part of entire student body composed of girls

26. **E** Let $x = BC = AB$.
Using the Pythagorean Theorem,
$(x)^2 + (x)^2 = (10)^2$
or $2x^2 = 100$, *or* $x^2 = 50$.
Area of $\triangle ABC = \frac{1}{2}(AB)(BC)$, *or* $\frac{1}{2}(x)(x)$, *or* $\frac{1}{2}(x)^2$, *or* $\frac{1}{2}(50) = 25$

27. **C** If the sum of the lengths of 3 sides of a square = r, then each side = $\frac{r}{3}$ and 4 sides = $\frac{4r}{3}$.

28. **E** The increase was 2¢.
$\frac{\text{increase}}{\text{original}} \times 100 = \text{percent increase}$
$\frac{2¢}{18¢} = \frac{1}{9} = 11.1\%$

29. **B** $3x + 4x + 5x = 180°$
$12x = 180°$
$x = 15°$
$\therefore$ measure of angles = 45°, 60°, and 75°

30. **D** In a rectangle the length is perpendicular to the width. The area of the rectangle equals the product of the length (one of the sides) and the width (the other side).

31. **C** The sum of the measure of the angles of a triangle equals 180°: 180° ÷ 3 = 60°.

32. **B** If the value of a fraction is 1, the numerator equals (has the same value as) the denominator.
$a + b = c + 2b$
$a - c = b$

33. **C** $4x - 2 + 2x + 1 + x + 9 = 29$
$7x + 8 = 29$
$7x = 21$
$x = 3$
Thus, side $4x - 2 = 10$
side $x + 9 = 12$
side $2x + 1 = 7$ [answer]

34. **A** x = width [given]
$\therefore x + 5$ = length
$x(x + 5)$ = area, *or* area = $x^2 + 5x$

35. **C** $\angle ABE = \angle DBF$ [vertical angles]
$\angle DBF = x°$ [given]
$\therefore ABE = x°$
$\angle ABC = 90°$ [$AB \perp BC$]
$\therefore EBC = 90° - x°$
$y° = 90° - x°$
$y = 90 - x$

36. **D** $\angle CED \stackrel{\circ}{=} 80$
$\angle CDE \stackrel{\circ}{=} 180 - (80 + 30)$ *or* 70
$z° = 180 - 70$ *or* 110

37. **E** The area of $ACDE$ = area of rectangle $BCDE$ − area of $\triangle ABC$.
Area of $BCDE = xy$
Area of $\triangle ABC = \frac{yz}{2}$
Area of $ACDE = xy - \frac{yz}{2}$

38. **C** $\angle ACB \stackrel{\circ}{=} 180 - (80 + 50)$ *or* 50
$\therefore AB = AC$ [If 2 angles of a $\triangle$ are equal, the sides opposite those angles are equal.]

39. **D** x and/or y may have negative values.

40. **C** % means $\frac{}{100}$.

$\frac{k}{4}\% = \left(\frac{k}{4}\right)\left(\frac{1}{100}\right)$ or $\frac{k}{400}$

41. **A** $\sqrt{14.4} = 3+$

$3+ > 0.12$

42. **B** $\frac{9-4}{6} = \frac{5}{6}$ [Column A]

$\frac{2+3}{4} = \frac{5}{4}$ [Column B]

$\frac{5}{4} > \frac{5}{6}$

43. **A** 0.33 kilogram is about $\frac{1}{3}$ of a kilogram or $\frac{1}{3}$ of 2.2 pounds, which is 0.7 pound. Column A is 1 pound.

How are the results of your PSAT/NMSQT reported?

About six to eight weeks after the test, you will receive, through your school, the following:

(1) a Report of Student Answers with your scores
(2) a copy of the answers you gave
(3) a copy of the correct answers
(4) a Selection Index, which identifies those eligible for NMSC programs
(5) a copy of the original test booklet which you used in the examination room
(6) a booklet entitled "About Your PSAT/NMSQT Scores," which helps you interpret your scores and gives you advice about college planning.

After the PSAT/NMSQT

After the scores of the PSAT/NMSQT are received, you, your parents, and your guidance counselor can begin to make plans for college. Some references follow:

BARRON'S HOW TO PREPARE FOR COLLEGE ENTRANCE EXAMINATIONS (SAT), by Samuel C. Brownstein, Mitchel Weiner, and Sharon Weiner Green. *This classic of college entrance examinations now includes a diagnostic test as well as six complete simulated exams that enable you to practice under exact* SAT *format and test conditions; all model tests have answer keys and answer explanations. Verbal aptitude practice includes selected and graded word lists, definitions, and vocabulary tests. Mathematical aptitude practice reviews necessary math from arithmetic through high school algebra and geometry, and features the quantitative comparison questions included on the* SAT. *Practice is given with elements of grammar and usage, including concise review of grammar rules for the Test of Standard Written English. Testing tactics and strategies are featured.* 1989, 15th Edition.

VOCABULARY BUILDER (A Systematic Plan for Building a Vocabulary, Testing Progress, and Applying Knowledge), by Samuel C. Brownstein and Mitchel Weiner. *This procedure will enable students to acquire the vocabulary required to comprehend high school and college texts and outside reading. Offers instruction on how to answer vocabulary sections on college admission and similar tests. Contains 3000 word entries, divided into 40 word study groups, each followed by a brief test.* 1984, 9th Edition.

BARRON'S MATHEMATICS WORKBOOK FOR COLLEGE ENTRANCE EXAMINATIONS, by Samuel C. Brownstein. *Tremendous addition to practice material in math texts—280 exercises, 562 verbal problems, 20 complete tests with a total of 650 problems. A vital need for individual or class review. All fundamentals, problem areas through 12th-grade math.* 1987, 5th Edition.

BARRON'S VERBAL APTITUDE WORKBOOK FOR COLLEGE ENTRANCE EXAMINATIONS (SAT), by Mitchel Weiner and Sharon Weiner Green. *A companion to the Math Workbook—it provides hundreds of practice exercises and diagnostic tests for intensive review of vocabulary, sentence completion, word relationships, and reading comprehension. 1000 questions plus 10 complete model verbal aptitude tests prepare students to score high on college boards, admission, placement, and scholarship examinations where word usage and understanding are tested.* 1987, 6th Edition

BARRON'S PROFILES OF AMERICAN COLLEGES. *Searching studies of more than 1500 regionally accredited four-year American colleges and universities that will give the prospective student a preview of his or her relationship to a particular college—based on its facilities, outstanding features and programs, admission requirements, costs, available financial aid, extracurricular activities, programs and major offerings, degrees awarded, enrollment, religious affiliation, housing facilities, social or honorary societies, religious or other regulations for student life. The comprehensive and detailed information on each college will be of tremendous help to guidance counselors, college-bound students, and their families.* 1988, 16th Edition, 2 Volumes.

2

A Study Program

No matter how little time you have to prepare for the PSAT, it can be put to good use. To help you organize your study plans for the PSAT, we offer three study programs—one a two-day crash program, one a two-week concentrated program, and one a comprehensive program covering six weeks or more.

Choose the plan that is best for you, but remember that these plans are only suggestions. If you find that you are weak in one particular area, you should concentrate on that area, spending more time on it.

THE TWO-DAY CRASH PROGRAM

It's Wednesday and you are taking the PSAT on Saturday and you are starting to panic. You just became acquainted with this guide for preparing for the PSAT. Follow this crash program. It's not the ideal way to prepare but intensive preparation with this book is better than walking in cold.

Day 1: Do the Sample Questions in Chapter 1, page 4. Make sure you know how to do each type. Take the Diagnostic Test (page 19). Score your test. Study the analysis of answers for all questions you missed or omitted, so you understand where you went wrong.

Day 2: Study the hints for handling the different types of verbal and mathematics questions. These hints are provided at the beginning of each of the review/practice chapters (Chapters 4–10). Pay particular attention to the types of questions that gave you trouble on the Diagnostic Test. Make sure you know the directions for the different types of questions that will appear on the PSAT. Then, spend as much time as you can reviewing high-frequency words on the Word List (pages 101–148) and Basic Mathematics Facts (pages 153–192). Finally, take a complete model test (page 199) so that you will be completely familiar with the examination.

THE TWO-WEEK CONCENTRATED PROGRAM

This is the program to follow when you haven't waited until the very last minute, but you've procrastinated enough that time is getting tight.

Session	Topic	Activity
1.	The PSAT	Study the test format and do the sample questions in Chapter 1. Check your answers.
2.	The Trial Run	Under simulated test conditions, take the Diagnostic Test (page 19).
3.	Self-Evaluation	Score and evaluate the results of your Diagnostic Test. Make a list of your weak areas to use later in doing practice exercises. Carefully study the explanations of correct answers for the questions you missed.
4.	Vocabulary Building and Antonyms	Study the High-Frequency Word List in Chapter 8 and do the antonym exercises in Chapter 4. Compare your answers with the correct ones.
5.	Basic Mathematics and Algebra	Study the first part of Chapter 9. Do the practice exercises in algebra. Concentrate on areas of weakness discovered in the Diagnostic Test.
6.	Vocabulary Building and Sentence Completion	Continue studying the Word List. Study the tips for handling sentence completion questions in Chapter 5. Do the exercises and compare your answers with the correct ones.
7.	Plane Geometry	Review geometry facts (Chapter 9, pages 165–176). Do the geometry exercises, and study the correct answers.
8.	Analogies	Study the tips to help you cope with analogy questions (pages 61–62). Do the exercises and check your answers.

Session	Topic	Activity
9.	Reading Comprehension	Study the hints in Chapter 7. Do the first half of the reading comprehension exercises. Compare your answers with the correct ones. Go over the questions you missed.
10.	Fractions, Percent, Averages, Motion, Ratio, Data Interpretation, Quantitative Comparison	Study the rest of Chapter 9: Fractions (page 176), Percent (page 178), Averages (page 180), Motion (page 182), Ratio and Proportion (page 183), Work (page 185), and Data Interpretation (page 187). Review Chapter 10.
11.	Reading Comprehension	Finish the exercises in Chapter 7. Compare your answers with the correct ones. Go over the questions you missed.
12.	Getting Ready	Establish test conditions and take Model Test A. Score your results. Study the answer explanations for questions you missed. Note your areas of weakness.
13.	Getting Set	Take a few additional Model Tests, paying particular attention to your areas of weakness.
14.	Final Dress Rehearsal	Complete as many Model Tests as you can in the time you have left. Score your results. Study the answer explanations for questions you missed.

Note: Sessions 4 through 11 need not be followed in this sequence. Concentrate on the areas that give you trouble. Don't spend your time reviewing material you already know well. Do as many of the exercises as you can in your problem areas.

THE COMPREHENSIVE STUDY PROGRAM

This is the plan to use when you have 7 weeks or more to study for the PSAT. It allows you to work slowly and steadily, building on what you have already learned, which is the best way to prepare for this or any other test.

The study program includes 10 math sessions and 10 verbal sessions. Together, the 20 sessions total approximately 20 hours of work. The sessions are keyed to specific review material and practice exercises in the verbal and mathematical parts of this book.

The verbal section covers antonym, sentence completion, analogy, and reading comprehension questions. Each session will require 30 to 45 minutes of your time, though this will vary according to individual needs.

The math section of this study program covers the material expected of a high school junior. Each session will require approximately 90 minutes of your time, though, again, this will vary. You may find that you can complete several sessions in that time, and you may find sessions on which you need to spend more time.

Take the Diagnostic Test before you begin this study program. Use the diagnostic procedures to discover which topics and/or types of questions are troublesome for you. Adjust the study program, if necessary, so that you concentrate on the areas that give you trouble.

Work out a suitable time schedule and carefully follow it until you have completed the study program. In planning your schedule, find time to work on vocabulary in addition to working with the topics covered in the study program given here. In particular, review the high-frequency words listed on page 101. After you finish your review, take the ten Model Tests in Chapter 11. Each test will provide you with valuable test-taking experience. Though you may decide to work on these section-by-section rather than as complete tests, you should make time to take at least one or two of the two-hour tests in one sitting, under test conditions.

VERBAL

Session	Topic	Activity
1.	Antonyms	Study the tips in Chapter 4 (pages 41–42). Do Exercises A and B, and check your answers.
2.	Sentence Completion	Study the tips in Chapter 5. Do Sentence Completion Test A (page 52). Check your answers.
3.	Analogies	Study the tips in Chapter 6 (pages 61–62). Do Exercises A and B, and check your answers.
4.	Reading Comprehension	Study the tips in Chapter 7 (pages 71–72).

Session	Topic	Activity
5.	Reading Comprehension	Do Reading Exercise A in Chapter 7. Compare your answers with the correct ones. Go over the questions you missed.
6.	Antonyms	Do Exercises C and D in Chapter 4. Check your answers.
7.	Sentence Completion	Do Sentence Completion Test B (Chapter 5, page 57). Check your answers.
8.	Analogies	Do Exercises C and D (Chapter 6, pages 66–68). Check your answers.
9.	Reading Comprehension	Do Reading Exercises B and C in Chapter 7. Compare your answers with the correct ones. Go over the questions you missed.
10.	Reading Comprehension	Do Reading Exercises D and E in Chapter 7. Compare your answers with the correct ones. Go over the questions you missed.

Note: Answers to all exercises and tests appear at the end of each chapter.

MATHEMATICS

Session	Topic	Activity
1.	Basic Math and Algebra	Study the tips in Chapter 9. Study whole numbers, real numbers, fundamental operations, the language of algebra, and fundamental algebraic operations on pages 155–159.
2.	Algebra	Study factoring, roots, and solving equations on pages 159–161, and do the practice exercises on pages 161–162.
3.	Algebra	Study solving problems by equations on pages 162–163, and inequalities on page 164. Do the practice exercises on pages 164–165.
4.	Geometry	Study pages 165–176, and do the practice exercises.
5.	Fractions	Study the sections on solving fractional equations and problems involving fractions (pages 176–177). Do the practice exercises.
6.	Percent and Averages	Study the facts involving percent (pages 178–179) and averages (page 180). Do the practice exercises.
7.	Motion and Ratio and Proportion	Study the definitions, principles, and problem-solving hints on pages 182–184. Do the practice exercises.
8.	Work	Study the facts and problem-solving hints on page 185. Do the practice exercises.
9.	Data Interpretation	Study the definitions on page 187, and do the practice exercises.
10.	Quantitative Comparison	Study the tips in Chapter 10, and do the exercises.

Note: Answers to all exercises appear at the end of the chapters.

DIAGNOSE YOUR PROBLEM

PSAT/NMSQT Answer Sheet

DIAGNOSTIC TEST

Verbal Aptitude Section

1 (A) (B) (C) (D) (E)
2 (A) (B) (C) (D) (E)
3 (A) (B) (C) (D) (E)
4 (A) (B) (C) (D) (E)
5 (A) (B) (C) (D) (E)
6 (A) (B) (C) (D) (E)
7 (A) (B) (C) (D) (E)
8 (A) (B) (C) (D) (E)
9 (A) (B) (C) (D) (E)
10 (A) (B) (C) (D) (E)
11 (A) (B) (C) (D) (E)
12 (A) (B) (C) (D) (E)
13 (A) (B) (C) (D) (E)
14 (A) (B) (C) (D) (E)
15 (A) (B) (C) (D) (E)
16 (A) (B) (C) (D) (E)
17 (A) (B) (C) (D) (E)
18 (A) (B) (C) (D) (E)
19 (A) (B) (C) (D) (E)
20 (A) (B) (C) (D) (E)
21 (A) (B) (C) (D) (E)
22 (A) (B) (C) (D) (E)
23 (A) (B) (C) (D) (E)
24 (A) (B) (C) (D) (E)
25 (A) (B) (C) (D) (E)
26 (A) (B) (C) (D) (E)
27 (A) (B) (C) (D) (E)
28 (A) (B) (C) (D) (E)
29 (A) (B) (C) (D) (E)
30 (A) (B) (C) (D) (E)
31 (A) (B) (C) (D) (E)
32 (A) (B) (C) (D) (E)
33 (A) (B) (C) (D) (E)
34 (A) (B) (C) (D) (E)
35 (A) (B) (C) (D) (E)
36 (A) (B) (C) (D) (E)
37 (A) (B) (C) (D) (E)
38 (A) (B) (C) (D) (E)
39 (A) (B) (C) (D) (E)
40 (A) (B) (C) (D) (E)
41 (A) (B) (C) (D) (E)
42 (A) (B) (C) (D) (E)
43 (A) (B) (C) (D) (E)
44 (A) (B) (C) (D) (E)
45 (A) (B) (C) (D) (E)
46 (A) (B) (C) (D) (E)
47 (A) (B) (C) (D) (E)
48 (A) (B) (C) (D) (E)
49 (A) (B) (C) (D) (E)
50 (A) (B) (C) (D) (E)
51 (A) (B) (C) (D) (E)
52 (A) (B) (C) (D) (E)
53 (A) (B) (C) (D) (E)
54 (A) (B) (C) (D) (E)
55 (A) (B) (C) (D) (E)
56 (A) (B) (C) (D) (E)
57 (A) (B) (C) (D) (E)
58 (A) (B) (C) (D) (E)
59 (A) (B) (C) (D) (E)
60 (A) (B) (C) (D) (E)
61 (A) (B) (C) (D) (E)
62 (A) (B) (C) (D) (E)
63 (A) (B) (C) (D) (E)
64 (A) (B) (C) (D) (E)
65 (A) (B) (C) (D) (E)

Mathematical Aptitude Section*

1 (A) (B) (C) (D) (E)
2 (A) (B) (C) (D) (E)
3 (A) (B) (C) (D) (E)
4 (A) (B) (C) (D) (E)
5 (A) (B) (C) (D) (E)
6 (A) (B) (C) (D) (E)
7 (A) (B) (C) (D) (E)
8 (A) (B) (C) (D) (E)
9 (A) (B) (C) (D) (E)
10 (A) (B) (C) (D) (E)
11 (A) (B) (C) (D) (E)
12 (A) (B) (C) (D) (E)
13 (A) (B) (C) (D) (E)
14 (A) (B) (C) (D) (E)
15 (A) (B) (C) (D) (E)
16 (A) (B) (C) (D) (E)
17 (A) (B) (C) (D) (E)
18 (A) (B) (C) (D) (E)
19 (A) (B) (C) (D) (E)
20 (A) (B) (C) (D) (E)
21 (A) (B) (C) (D) (E)
22 (A) (B) (C) (D) (E)
23 (A) (B) (C) (D) (E)
24 (A) (B) (C) (D) (E)
25 (A) (B) (C) (D) (E)
26 (A) (B) (C) (D) (E)
27 (A) (B) (C) (D) (E)
28 (A) (B) (C) (D) (E)
29 (A) (B) (C) (D) (E)
30 (A) (B) (C) (D) (E)
31 (A) (B) (C) (D) (E)
32 (A) (B) (C) (D) (E)
33 (A) (B) (C) (D) (E)
34 (A) (B) (C) (D) (E)
35 (A) (B) (C) (D) (E)
36 (A) (B) (C) (D) (E)
37 (A) (B) (C) (D) (E)
38 (A) (B) (C) (D) (E)
39 (A) (B) (C) (D) (E)
40 (A) (B) (C) (D) (E)
41 (A) (B) (C) (D) (E)
42 (A) (B) (C) (D) (E)
43 (A) (B) (C) (D) (E)
44 (A) (B) (C) (D) (E)
45 (A) (B) (C) (D) (E)
46 (A) (B) (C) (D) (E)
47 (A) (B) (C) (D) (E)
48 (A) (B) (C) (D) (E)
49 (A) (B) (C) (D) (E)
50 (A) (B) (C) (D) (E)

*If there are more answer spaces than you need, leave them blank.

3

A Diagnostic Test

This chapter offers a simulated 100-minute PSAT/NMSQT test. The purpose is to provide you with a fairly accurate evaluation of what your score would be without any special preparation. Take this test, following directions for time allowances for each of the two sections. Then score your answers and evaluate the results, using the self-rating guides provided. Consult the explanations of answers for all test items that you failed to answer correctly.

You will then be in a position to approach your review program realistically and allot your time for study. You will know which topics in mathematics require your review and drill and which of your verbal skills require concentrated study.

Simulate Test Conditions **TOTAL TIME: 100 MINUTES**

Find a quiet place to work, in order to simulate examination conditions. Keep an accurate record of your time. If you complete the verbal section before the suggested time has elapsed, check your work over rather than start the math section. Don't be worried, however, if you are not able to answer all questions in the allotted time. This may also occur on the actual test. No one is expected to know the answers to all questions on an aptitude test. Read the questions carefully. Work carefully and rapidly. Do not spend too much time on questions that seem difficult for you. If time permits, go back to the ones you left out.

The questions are all of the objective type with a penalty imposed for guessing. The score is determined by the number of correct answers minus a fraction of the number of incorrectly marked answers. Omitted answers do not count. Economy of time is of utmost concern. It is best to work rapidly and carefully and not to waste time on questions that contain difficult or unfamiliar material. Whereas wild guessing is inadvisable, educated or "shrewd" guessing is to be encouraged. You may sometimes eliminate certain possible answers to a question because of your general knowledge, and, despite your inability to explain by good reasoning why you choose a specific answer, you may feel that it is the correct one. Such a shrewd guess may be right and you should therefore give that answer.

DIAGNOSTIC TEST

SECTION 1	Time—50 minutes 65 Questions	For each question in this section, choose the best answer and fill in the corresponding circle on the answer sheet.

Each question below consists of a word in capital letters, followed by five lettered words or phrases. Choose the word or phrase that is most nearly opposite in meaning to the word in capital letters. Since some of the questions require you to distinguish fine shades of meaning, consider all the choices before deciding which is best.

Example:

GOOD: (A) sour (B) bad (C) red (D) hot (E) ugly

Ⓐ ● Ⓒ Ⓓ Ⓔ

1. DRAB: (A) plentiful (B) perplexed (C) weary (D) glamorous (E) friendly
2. CRUMPLE: (A) make smooth (B) mix together (C) soften (D) discard (E) rip apart
3. IMPROPER: (A) intense (B) correct (C) awkward (D) restless (E) definite
4. RAZE: (A) build (B) choose (C) trim (D) acquire (E) decrease
5. MOBILE: (A) loose (B) fragile (C) compact (D) passive (E) stationary
6. RECIPIENT: (A) tenant (B) donor (C) truant (D) guest (E) servant
7. BOISTEROUS: (A) ferocious (B) solitary (C) ungenerous (D) quiet (E) wise
8. INSUBORDINATION: (A) neatness (B) indifference (C) agitation (D) vitality (E) submissiveness
9. DORMANT: (A) voluntary (B) awake (C) cryptic (D) adaptable (E) widespread
10. RENEGADE: (A) adversary (B) loyal follower (C) absent friend (D) false leader (E) mediator
11. COHERE: (A) shrivel (B) transform (C) become active (D) fall apart (E) convince
12. VOLATILITY: (A) stability (B) finiteness (C) measurability (D) dilution (E) dependency
13. SOLICITOUS: (A) indifferent (B) legalistic (C) uncomfortable (D) indolent (E) unnecessary
14. ENCUMBER: (A) forget (B) assist (C) limit (D) attract (E) distort
15. DEARTH: (A) excess (B) turbulence (C) coarseness (D) inexpensiveness (E) efficiency
16. INGRATIATING: (A) perceptive (B) displeasing (C) obedient (D) thankful (E) vulnerable
17. LICENTIOUS: (A) unauthorized (B) functioning poorly (C) observant of morality (D) truthful in speech (E) narrow in scope
18. FLUX: (A) health (B) obscurity (C) stagnation (D) catalyst (E) asymmetry
19. EXUDE: (A) elude (B) incite (C) respond slowly (D) shine brightly (E) absorb
20. APLOMB: (A) discomposure (B) righteousness (C) temerity (D) disapprobation (E) parsimoniousness

Each sentence below has one or two blanks, each blank indicating that something has been omitted. Beneath the sentence are five lettered words or sets of words. Choose the word or set of words that, when inserted in the sentence, best fits the meaning of the sentence as a whole.

Example:

Although its publicity has been ----, the film itself is intelligent, well-acted, handsomely produced, and altogether ----.

(A) tasteless . . respectable (B) extensive . . moderate (C) sophisticated . . amateur (D) risque . . crude (E) perfect . . spectacular

● Ⓑ Ⓒ Ⓓ Ⓔ

21. Normally an individual thunderstorm lasts about 45 minutes, but under certain conditions the storm may ----, becoming ever more severe, for as long as four hours.
(A) wane (B) moderate (C) persist (D) vacillate (E) disperse
22. For Miro, art became a ---- ritual: paper and pencils were holy objects to him, and he worked as though he were performing a religious rite.
(A) superficial (B) sacred (C) banal (D) cryptic (E) futile
23. The newest fiber-optic cables that carry telephone calls cross-country are made of glass so ---- that a piece 100 miles thick is clearer than a standard windowpane.
(A) fragile (B) immaculate (C) tangible (D) transparent (E) iridescent

24. Any numerical description of the development of the human population cannot avoid ----, simply because there has never been a census of all the people in the world.
(A) analysis (B) conjecture
(C) disorientation (D) corroboration
(E) statistics

25. Her employers could not complain about her work because she was ---- in the ---- of her duties.
(A) derelict . . performance
(B) importunate . . observance
(C) meticulous . . postponement
(D) assiduous . . execution
(E) hidebound . . conception

26. Despite an affected ---- which convinced casual observers that he was indifferent about his painting and enjoyed only frivolity, Warhol cared deeply about his art and labored at it ----.
(A) nonchalance . . diligently
(B) empathy . . methodically
(C) fervor . . secretly
(D) gloom . . intermittently
(E) hysteria . . sporadically

27. Soap operas and situation comedies, though given to distortion, are so derivative of contemporary culture that they are inestimable ---- the attitudes and values of our society in any particular decade.
(A) contradictions of (B) antidotes to
(C) indices of (D) prerequisites for
(E) determinants of

28. Alec Guinness has few equals among English-speaking actors, and now in his autobiography he reveals himself to be an uncommonly ---- prose stylist as well.
(A) ambivalent (B) infamous
(C) supercilious (D) felicitous (E) pedestrian

29. Although eighteenth-century English society as a whole did not encourage learning for its own sake in women, nonetheless it illogically ---- women's sad lack of education.
(A) palliated (B) postulated
(C) decried (D) brooked (E) vaunted

30. Compromise is ---- to passionate natures because it seems a surrender; and to intellectual natures because it seems a ----.
(A) odious . . confusion
(B) inherent . . fabrication
(C) welcome . . fulfillment
(D) unsuited . . submission
(E) intimidating . . dichotomy

Each question below consists of a related pair of words or phrases, followed by five lettered pairs of words or phrases. Select the lettered pair that best expresses a relationship similar to that expressed in the original pair.

Example:

YAWN : BOREDOM : : (A) dream : sleep
(B) anger : madness (C) smile : amusement
(D) face : expression (E) impatience : rebellion

Ⓐ Ⓑ ● Ⓓ Ⓔ

31. MINNOW : FISH : : (A) poodle : dog
(B) flock : sheep (C) marrow : bone
(D) snare : rabbit (E) fang : snake

32. CHIP : PLATE : : (A) scour : pot
(B) snag : sweater (C) scoop : spoon
(D) fold : napkin (E) peel : carrot

33. TANK : OXYGEN : : (A) automobile : gasoline
(B) carton : milk (C) salt : sodium
(D) metal : iron (E) molecule : atom

34. SAGE : HERB : : (A) leaf : tree
(B) bud : flower (C) rocker : chair
(D) salt : meal (E) rose : bouquet

35. GIRDER : SUPPORT : : (A) stocking : mend
(B) card : shuffle (C) axe : sharpen
(D) winch : hoist (E) ladder : lean

36. BRIDGE : GAP : : (A) cleanse : wound
(B) reconcile : estrangement
(C) construct : hypothesis (D) enter : doorway
(E) return : favor

37. EGGSHELL : FRAGILITY : :
(A) dewdrop : grief (B) peapod : variety
(C) rainbow : mobility (D) barbell : weight
(E) packrat : discrimination

38. HOSTILE : FRIENDSHIP : :
(A) inimical : opposition (B) traitorous : loyalty
(C) intolerant : bias (D) magnificent : delicacy
(E) bombastic : grandiloquence

39. STAMPS : PHILATELY : :
(A) paintings : museum (B) words : lexicon
(C) coins : numismatics (D) countries : alliance
(E) rockets : pyrotechnics

40. CIRCUMSPECT : WARINESS : :
(A) meaningful : inanity
(B) respectful : pertinence
(C) detrimental : misapprehension
(D) reckless : foolhardiness
(E) wicked : abstinence

41. PARAGON : STANDARD : :
(A) colleague : rival (B) painting : landscape
(C) heredity : environment (D) author : publisher
(E) imitation : copy

42. PULVERIZE : DUST : : (A) analyze : argument (B) vaporize : mist (C) petrify : fear (D) permeate : odor (E) solidify : fluid

43. PLEAD : SUPPLIANT : : (A) disperse : rioter (B) shun : outcast (C) revere : elder (D) beg : philanthropist (E) translate : interpreter

44. LUMINARY : ILLUSTRIOUS : : (A) zealot : intense (B) miser : prodigal (C) atheist : radical (D) dignitary : conceited (E) celebrity : wealthy

45. APOCRYPHAL : AUTHENTICITY : :
(A) nefarious : wickedness
(B) dogmatic : plausibility
(C) hypocritical : integrity
(D) perspicacious : industry
(E) deceptive : artifice

Each passage below is followed by questions based on its content. Answer the questions following each passage on the basis of what is stated or implied in that passage.

My father was a cattle rancher in Jamaica. One day after the war he had become sick after eating a bad piece of frozen meat, and that was it. Suddenly all our cane went down and men began putting up fences. By himself my father took the Oracabessa launch to Cuba, went up into the mountains he said, and came back a week later with a Cuban he had known during the war in North Africa. Pappy was his name, and he had two teeth in his mouth and looked thin and stupid, but knew cattle.

It was a risk for my father to take the Oracabessa launch across the straits in September. It was only ninety miles, but September in Jamaica is the time for bad storms; they come up quickly. He was very daring, my mother told me, after the war, and I remember it a bit myself. All the men were a little like that. My mother said that after Al Alamain my father thought he could do anything. He was impetuous, like a young boy, the war having taught him both how temporary life is, and how valuable.

He had been a cane grower all his life, that was what he knew, but he was willing to learn cattle. He put every penny, every quattie of what we had, into a small herd, and a prize black bull that came from Corpus Christi in October and was lowered from the freighter to the dock, hung from a bright yellow sling. When the yellow sash was dropped away and we could see the bull's blackness and the rotations of green that were its eyes, my father was a proud man. The bull looked up and snorted, its eyes fixed on the mountain, and Pappy said with a hideous gentle smile that it smelled the herd, and that the sea voyage had done it no good.

46. The narrator states all of the following about his father EXCEPT:
(A) He was audacious and impulsive.
(B) He had resented his military service.
(C) He had not started out as a cattle rancher.
(D) His journey to Cuba was potentially dangerous.
(E) He was aware of life's impermanence.

47. The author most likely uses the phrase "and that was it" (sentence 2) to pinpoint the moment that
(A) his father first ate frozen meat
(B) he understood his father's weakness
(C) his father left home for good
(D) Pappy first entered his life
(E) his father decided to try raising cattle

48. It can be inferred from the passage that the father most likely sought out Pappy
(A) because he missed his days in North Africa
(B) out of pity for Pappy's poverty
(C) to find a cure for his food-poisoning
(D) because he needed Pappy's guidance
(E) because he knew how to navigate a launch

The problems of living in the dark rain forest, and the unusual efforts made to rise into the sun, are best symbolized by the strangler trees. They achieve their place in the sun by stealth. The strangler begins life as an epiphyte, its seed germinating high up in the fork of a large tree. The seedling puts out two kinds of roots: one seizes the branch and serves as a grapple to hold the plant in place, and the other dangles like a cable, growing steadily closer to the soil. Until it makes contact with the ground, the strangler grows like any other epiphyte, obtaining small quantities of water and nutrients from the debris in the tree crevice. But once the descending root reaches the soil its source of supply is increased enormously and the plant's growth quickens. It sprouts more leaves high in the canopy and grows upward toward a sunlit window between the leaves; a maze of additional feeding cables descends to the soil and eventually the supporting tree is encased in a network of them. It was once thought that the strangler kills the forest giant by the simple process of enwrapping it and preventing its trunk from expanding, but it is now known that it actually squeezes its host to death. As the hold tightens, the strangler's roots thicken markedly, preparing for the time when it will need props to stand by itself in the sunlight it has captured. The host finally expires, thoroughly encased inside the "trunk" (actually the fused roots) of the strangler tree which now stands on its own pedestal as a member of the high forest canopy.

49. Which of the following would be the most suitable title for the passage?
(A) Newly Discovered Varieties of Epiphytes
(B) The Invisible Strangler Tree
(C) Cultivating the Rare Strangler Tree
(D) Growth of the Strangler Tree
(E) A Study of the Epiphytes of the Rain Forest

MARIKKA HOPKINS

50. The author states all of the following about the strangler tree EXCEPT
(A) It eventually becomes self-supporting.
(B) Its feeding cables ascend toward the forest canopy.
(C) Its roots extend far from its point of germination.
(D) It undergoes a rapid growth spurt.
(E) Its roots become conspicuously larger.

51. Which of the following can be inferred from the passage about the strangler tree?
(A) It needs only a small supply of nutrients for full growth.
(B) All its roots seek the forest floor.
(C) It outgrows its need for its host.
(D) It is killed by the forest giant that supports it.
(E) It eventually sheds its feeder cables.

Yet they are not all lost, those Indian voices of the past. A few authentic accounts of American western history were recorded by Indians either in pictographs or in translated English, and some managed to get published in obscure journals, pamphlets, or books of small circulation. In the late nineteenth century, when the white man's curiosity about Indian survivors of the wars reached a high point, enterprising newspaper reporters frequently interviewed warriors and chiefs and gave them an opportunity to express their opinions on what was happening in the West. The quality of these interviews varied greatly, depending upon the abilities of the interpreters, or upon the inclination of the Indians to speak freely. Some feared reprisals for telling the truth, while others delighted in hoaxing reporters with tall tales and shaggy-dog stories. Contemporary newspaper statements by Indians must therefore be read with skepticism, although some of them are masterpieces of irony and others burn with outbursts of poetic fury.

Among the richest sources of first-person statements by Indians are the records of treaty councils and other formal meetings with civilian and military representatives of the United States government. Isaac Pitman's new stenographic system was coming into vogue in the second half of the nineteenth century, and when Indians spoke in council a recording clerk sat beside the official interpreter.

Even when the meetings were in remote parts of the West, someone usually was available to write down the speeches, and because of the slowness of the translation process, much of what was said could be recorded in longhand. Interpreters quite often were half-bloods who knew spoken languages but seldom could read or write. Like most oral peoples they and the Indians depended upon imagery to express their thoughts, so that the English translations were filled with graphic similes and metaphors of the natural world. If an eloquent Indian had a poor interpreter, his words might be transformed to flat prose, but a good interpreter could make a poor speaker sound poetic.

Most Indian leaders spoke freely and candidly in councils with white officials, and as they became more sophisticated in such matters during the 1870's and 1880's, they demanded the right to choose their own interpreters and recorders. In this latter period, all members of the tribes were free to speak, and some of the older men chose such opportunities to recount events they had witnessed in the past, or sum up the histories of their peoples. Although the Indians who lived through this doom period of their civilization have vanished from the earth, millions of their words are preserved in official records. Many of the more important council proceedings were published in government documents and reports.

Out of all these sources of almost forgotten oral history, I have tried to fashion a narrative of the conquest of the American West as the victims experienced it, using their own words whenever possible. Americans who have always looked westward when reading about this period should read this book facing eastward.

52. A main concern of the author in this passage is to
(A) denounce the white man for his untrustworthiness and savagery
(B) evaluate the effectiveness of the military treaty councils
(C) argue for the improved treatment of Indians today
(D) suggest that Indian narratives of the conquest of the West are similar to white accounts
(E) introduce the background of the original source materials for his text

53. According to the passage, nineteenth-century newspaper accounts of interviews with Indians may contain inaccuracies for which of the following reasons?
I. Lack of skill on the part of the translators
II. The tendency of the reporters to overstate what they were told by the Indians
III. The Indians' misgivings about possible retaliations
(A) I only
(B) III only
(C) I and II only
(D) I and III only
(E) I, II, and III

54. The author's tone in describing the Indian survivors can best be described as
(A) skeptical (B) detached (C) elegiac
(D) obsequious (E) impatient

55. The author is most impressed by which aspect of the English translations of Indian speeches?
(A) Their vividness of imagery
(B) Their lack of frankness
(C) The inefficiency of the process
(D) Their absence of sophistication
(E) Their brevity of expression

56. The author most likely suggests that Americans should read this book facing eastward
(A) in an inappropriate attempt at levity
(B) out of respect for Western superstitions
(C) in order to read by natural light
(D) because the Indians came from the East
(E) to identify with the Indians' viewpoint

James's first novels used conventional narrative techniques: explicit characterization, action which related events in distinctly phased sequences, settings firmly outlined and specifically described. But this method gradually gave way to a subtler, more deliberate, more diffuse style of accumulation of minutely discriminated details whose total significance the reader can grasp only by constant attention and sensitive inference. His later novels play down scenes of abrupt and prominent action, and do not so much offer a succession of sharp shocks as slow piecemeal additions of perception. The curtain is not suddenly drawn back from shrouded things, but is slowly moved away.

Such a technique is suited to James's essential subject, which is not human action itself but the states of mind which produce and are produced by human actions and interactions. James was less interested in what characters do, than in the moral and psychological antecedents, realizations, and consequences which attend their doings. This is why he more often speaks of "cases" than of actions. His stories, therefore, grow more and more lengthy while the actions they relate grow simpler and less visible; not because they are crammed with adventitious and secondary events, digressive relief, or supernumerary characters, as overstuffed novels of action are; but because he presents in such exhaustive detail every nuance of his situation. Commonly the interest of a novel is in the variety and excitement of visible actions building up to a climactic event which will settle the outward destinies of characters with storybook promise of permanence. A James novel, however, possesses its characteristic interest in carrying the reader through a rich analysis of the mental adjustments of characters to the realities of their personal situations as they are slowly revealed to them through exploration and chance discovery.

57. The passage supplies information for answering which of the following questions?
(A) Did James originate the so-called psychological novel?
(B) Is conventional narrative technique strictly chronological in recounting action?
(C) Can novels lacking overtly dramatic incident hold the reader's interest?
(D) Were James's later novels more acceptable to the general public than his earlier ones?
(E) Is James unique in his taste for exploring psychological nuances of character?

58. According to the passage, James's later novels differ from his earlier ones in their
(A) preoccupation with specifically described settings
(B) ever-increasing conciseness and tautness of plot
(C) levels of moral and psychological complexity
(D) development of rising action to a climax
(E) subordination of psychological exploration to dramatic effect

59. The author's attitude toward the novel of action appears to be one of
(A) pointed indignation (B) detached neutrality
(C) scathing derision (D) strong partisanship
(E) clear disapprobation

60. The author's primary purpose in this passage is to
(A) discount James's tendency toward psychological exploration
(B) decide whether or not James's earlier novels surpass his later works
(C) prove that Jamesian psychological analysis has a place in literary tradition
(D) evaluate and discuss the nature of James's subject matter and technique
(E) attack the standard position on James's place in literary history.

A tornado is the product of a thunderstorm, specifically of the interaction of a strong thunderstorm with winds in the troposphere (the active layer of the atmosphere that extends nine to 17 kilometers up from the ground). The process by which a tornado is formed is one in which a small fraction of the tremendous energy of the thunderstorm, whose towering cumulonimbus cloud can be 10 to 20 kilometers across and more than 17 kilometers high, is concentrated in an area no more than several hundred meters in diameter. Before going into the process in detail let me first describe the phenomenon itself.

A tornado is a vortex; air rotates around the tornado's axis about as fast as it moves toward and along the axis. Drawn by greatly reduced atmospheric pressure in the central core, air streams into the base of the vortex from all directions through a shallow layer a few tens of meters deep near the ground. In the base the air turns abruptly to spiral upward around the core and finally merges, at the hidden upper end of the tornado, with the airflow in the parent cloud. The pressure within the core may be as much as 10 percent less than that of the surrounding atmosphere; about the same difference as that between sea level and an altitude of one kilometer. Winds in a tornado are almost always cyclonic, which in the Northern Hemisphere means counterclockwise.

The vortex frequently—not always—becomes visible as a funnel cloud hanging part or all of the way to the ground from the generating storm. A funnel cloud forms only if the pressure drop in the core exceeds a critical value that depends on the temperature and the humidity of the inflowing air. As air flows into the area of lower pressure, it expands and cools; if it cools enough, the water vapor in it condenses and forms droplets. The warmer and drier the inflowing air is, the greater the pressure drop must be for condensation to occur and a cloud to form. Sometimes no condensation funnel forms, in which case the tornado reveals itself only through the dust and debris it carries aloft.

A funnel can be anywhere from tens of meters to several kilometers long, and where it meets the parent cloud its diameter ranges from a few meters to hundreds of meters. Usually it is coneshaped, but short, broad, cylindrical pillars are formed by very strong tornadoes, and long, ropelike tubes that trail off horizontally are also common. Over a tornado's brief lifetime (never more than a few hours) the size and shape of the funnel may change markedly, reflecting changes in the intensity of the winds or in the properties of the inflowing air. Its color varies from a dirty white to gray to dark blue gray when it consists mostly of water droplets, but if the core fills with dust, the funnel may take on a more exotic hue, such as the red of west Oklahoma clay. Tornadoes can also be noisy, often roaring like a freight train or a jet engine. This may result from the interaction of the concentrated high winds with the ground.

61. Tornadoes are characterized by which of the following?

I. Brevity of duration
II. Intense concentration of energy
III. Uniformity of shape

(A) I only
(B) II only
(C) I and II only
(D) II and III only
(E) I, II, and III

62. Which of the following titles best summarizes the content of this passage?

(A) The Composition and Nature of Tornadoes
(B) Predicting the Tornado's Path
(C) The Destructive Impact of Tornadoes
(D) Harnessing the Tornado's Energy
(E) Facts and Fictions About Tornadoes

63. It can be inferred that which of the following is true of a tornado?

(A) Its winds are invariably counterclockwise.
(B) It can last for days at a time.
(C) Its funnel cloud will not form if the air is cool and dry.
(D) It exceeds its parent cloud in size.
(E) It responds to changes in temperature and humidity.

64. According to the author, a direct relation may exist between the color a tornado takes on and

(A) the composition of the terrain it passes over
(B) the intensity of the winds it concentrates
(C) the particular shape of funnel it forms
(D) the direction in which its winds rotate
(E) the degree of noise involved

65. In the final paragraph the author does all of the following EXCEPT

(A) suggest a hypothesis
(B) provide a concrete example
(C) indicate a time span
(D) argue a viewpoint
(E) use a simile

DIAGNOSTIC TEST

SECTION 2 **Time—50 minutes 50 Questions**

In this section solve each problem, using any available space on the page for scratchwork. Then decide which is the best of the choices given and fill in the corresponding circle on the answer sheet.

The following information is for your reference in solving some of the problems.

Circle of radius r: Area $= \pi r^2$ Circumference $= 2\pi r$
The number of degrees of arc in a circle is 360.
The measure in degrees of a straight angle is 180.

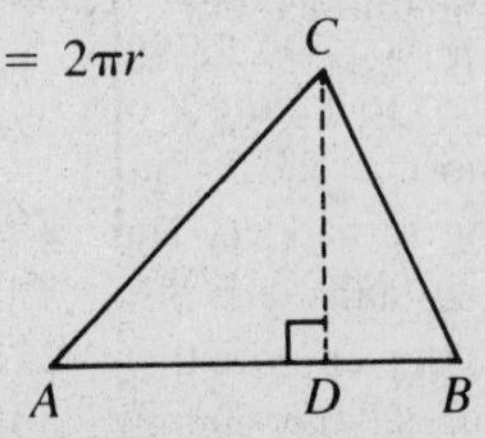

Triangle: The sum of the measures in degrees of the angles of a triangle is 180.

If $\angle CDA$ is a right angle, then

(1) area of $\triangle ABC = \frac{AB \times CD}{2}$

(2) $AC^2 = AD^2 + DC^2$

Definitions of symbols:

$=$ is equal to	$\leqq$ is less than or equal to
$\neq$ is unequal to	$\geqq$ is greater than or equal to
$<$ is less than	$\parallel$ is parallel to
$>$ is greater than	$\perp$ is perpendicular to

Note: Figures that accompany problems in this test are intended to provide information useful in solving the problems. They are drawn as accurately as possible EXCEPT when it is stated in a specific problem that its figure is not drawn to scale. All figures lie in a plane unless otherwise indicated. All numbers used are real numbers.

1. 104% of 25 =
(A) 1 (B) 26 (C) 100 (D) 260 (E) 325

2. 64 is $\frac{2}{7}$ of what number?
(A) $18\frac{2}{7}$ (B) 48 (C) 128 (D) 224 (E) 448

3. $\frac{87955936}{284}$ equals exactly
(A) 309701 (B) 309702 (C) 309703
(D) 309704 (E) 309705

4. When $N = 0$ the value of $\frac{(2K)(NB)}{K + B}$ equals
(A) 0 (B) 1 (C) $\frac{2K}{K + B}$ (D) $K + B$
(E) $\frac{1}{K + B}$

5. If Δ represents an odd integer, which of the following represents an even integer?
(A) $2\Delta + 1$ (B) $2(\Delta + 2)$ (C) $\Delta + \Delta - 1$
(D) $(\Delta - 2)(\Delta + 2)$ (E) 3Δ

6. How many posts are needed for a fence 144 feet long, if the posts are placed 12 feet apart?
(A) 11 (B) 12 (C) 13 (D) 14 (E) 15

7. To get to school, a pupil must spend $\frac{1}{5}$ of an hour walking to the bus and $\frac{1}{3}$ of an hour riding in the bus, and then walk for $\frac{1}{6}$ of an hour to the school. What part of an hour does this pupil spend getting to school?
(A) $\frac{1}{14}$ (B) $\frac{7}{30}$ (C) $\frac{7}{10}$ (D) $\frac{3}{10}$ (E) $\frac{7}{20}$

8. It took Sam 200 minutes to complete the difficult *Sunday Times* crossword puzzle. Stanley did the same puzzle in 160 minutes. By what fraction of an hour was Sam's time longer than Stanley's?
(A) $\frac{1}{5}$ (B) $\frac{1}{4}$ (C) $\frac{2}{5}$ (D) $\frac{1}{2}$ (E) $\frac{2}{3}$

9. R and T are points on straight line PQ on which $PR = RT = TQ$. What percent of PT is PQ?
(A) $1\frac{1}{2}$% (B) 50% (C) $66\frac{2}{3}$% (D) $33\frac{1}{3}$%
(E) 150%

10. If 20 teachers in a faculty of 80 are transferred, what percent of the original faculty remains?
(A) 4% (B) 16% (C) 25% (D) 60%
(E) 75%

11. SHURGRO fertilizer contains 18% ammonia plus carbon compounds. If 80% of the ammonia contains the chemical element nitrogen, what percent of this fertilizer is nitrogen?
(A) 14.4% (B) 18% (C) 38% (D) 40%
(E) 62%

12. The enrollment in a university is now 52,500, an increase of 5% over the enrollment last year. By how many students did the enrollment increase this year?
(A) 2500 (B) 47,500 (C) 50,000
(D) 55,000 (E) 57,750

13. When inserted in the parentheses, which of the symbols (+, −, ×, ÷ or =) will make the following a true statement?

$$12t(?)\frac{3t}{\frac{1}{4}} = \frac{4t^2}{\frac{t}{3}}$$

(A) + (B) − (C) × (D) ÷ (E) =

14. If $2^{n+2} = 8$, then $n =$
(A) -1 (B) $+1$ (C) 2 (D) 3 (E) 4

15. $\sqrt{\frac{1}{16} + \frac{1}{9}}$ equals
(A) $\frac{1}{7}$ (B) $\frac{2}{7}$ (C) $\frac{5}{12}$ (D) $\frac{7}{12}$ (E) $\frac{25}{144}$

Questions 16-32 each consist of two quantities, one in Column A and one in Column B. You are to compare the two quantities and on the answer sheet fill in circle

A if the quantity in Column A is greater;
B if the quantity in Column B is greater;
C if the two quantities are equal;
D if the relationship cannot be determined from the information given.

Notes:
1. In certain questions, information concerning one or both of the quantities to be compared is centered above the two columns.
2. In a given question, a symbol that appears in both columns represents the same thing in Column A as it does in Column B.
3. Letters such as x, n, and k stand for real numbers.

EXAMPLES

	Column A	Column B	Answers
E1.	2×6	$2 + 6$	● Ⓑ Ⓒ Ⓓ
	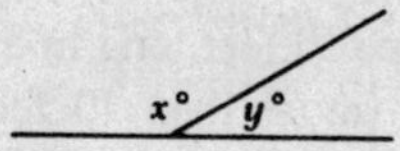		
E2.	$180 - x$	y	Ⓐ Ⓑ ● Ⓓ
E3.	$p - q$	$q - p$	Ⓐ Ⓑ Ⓒ ●

COLUMN A | **COLUMN B**

In $\triangle ABC$,
$\angle B \doteq 30$
and $AB = AC$

16. The measure of $\angle A$ — The measure of $\angle C$

$a > 1$

17. $(a + 1)^2$ — $a(a + 2)$

$a > 1$

18. $(a)\left(\frac{1}{17}\right)(48)(6)$ — $(48)\left(\frac{a}{17}\right)(12)$

$x \neq y$ and $x > 1$
and $y > 1$
$4x = 2y$

19. y — $2x$

COLUMN A | **COLUMN B**

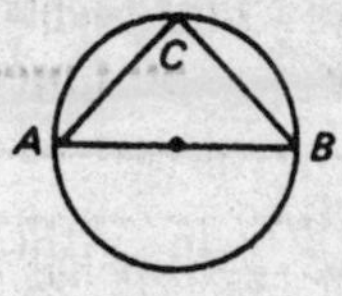

Diameter $AB = 10$
$AC = BC$

20. Area of ABC — $\sqrt{50}$

21. The area of a triangle with base $\frac{x}{2}$ and height y — The area of a square with side $\frac{\sqrt{xy}}{2}$

$x + 5 = y$
$x = \frac{y}{2}$

22. $2y$ — 10

23. $a - b$ — $b - a$

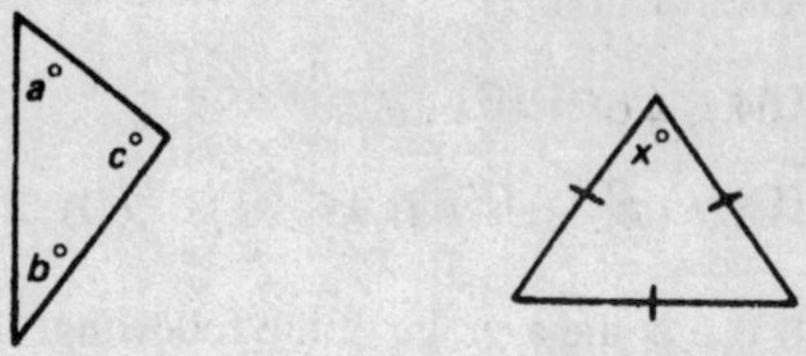

24. Average of a, b, and c — x

25. The sum of $2\frac{1}{2}$ and its reciprocal — 2.5

$z > 0$

26. $2z^3$ — $3z^2$

$5b = 12.5$
$3a + 2b = 12.5$

27. a — b

$\frac{x}{6} = \frac{y}{4}$

28. $2x$ — $3y$

$\frac{2}{5} + \frac{x}{y} = \frac{7}{5}$

29. x — y

$3x - 2 < 0$

30. $3x$ — 2

	COLUMN A	COLUMN B
	$\frac{3}{x} = 2$ and $\frac{5}{y} = 2$	
31.	x	y
	In $\triangle ABC$, side $AB = 9$ units and side $BC = 4$ units	
32.	Area of ABC	18 square units

> Solve each of the remaining problems in this section using any available space for scratchwork. Then decide which is the best of the choices given and fill in the corresponding circle on the answer sheet.

33. What is $a\%$ of b divided by $b\%$ of a?
(A) a (B) b (C) 1 (D) 10 (E) 100

34. Which of the following is next smaller than one-half?
(A) $\frac{1}{5}$ (B) $\frac{1}{4}$ (C) $\frac{2}{5}$ (D) $\frac{16}{25}$ (E) $\frac{3}{10}$

35. The fraction $\frac{t+n}{n} =$
(A) $\frac{t}{n} + n$ (B) $\frac{t+n}{t}$ (C) $\frac{t}{n} + 1$
(D) $t^2 + 1$ (E) t

36. If 0.6 is the average of the following: 0.2, 0.8, 1.0, and x, what is the numerical value of x?
(A) 0.2 (B) 0.4 (C) 0.67 (D) 1.3 (E) 2.4

37. $\frac{a^2 - b^2}{(a-b)^2}$ is equal to
(A) $a + b$ (B) $a - b$ (C) $\frac{a+b}{a-b}$ (D) $\frac{a-b}{a+b}$
(E) 1

38. If two items cost c¢, how many items can be purchased for x¢?
(A) $\frac{x}{2c}$ (B) $\frac{2c}{x}$ (C) $\frac{2x}{c}$ (D) $\frac{cx}{2}$ (E) $2cx$

39. Four similar glass tumblers just fit into a cubical box. The area of the top of the circular cover of any one of the tumblers is 4π. The area of each side of the box is
(A) 16 (B) 32 (C) 32π (D) 64 (E) 64π

40. $AB = AC$, $FD = FC$, the measure of $\angle DEB \stackrel{\circ}{=} 120$.
What is the measure of $\angle DFC$?
(A) 10°
(B) 20°
(C) 30°
(D) 50°
(E) 80°

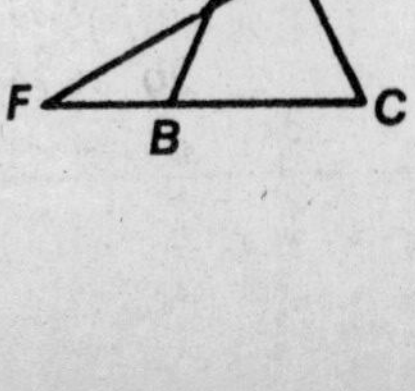

41. The area of square $EFGH$ is equal to the area of rectangle $ABCD$. $GH = 6$ feet, $AD = 4$ feet.

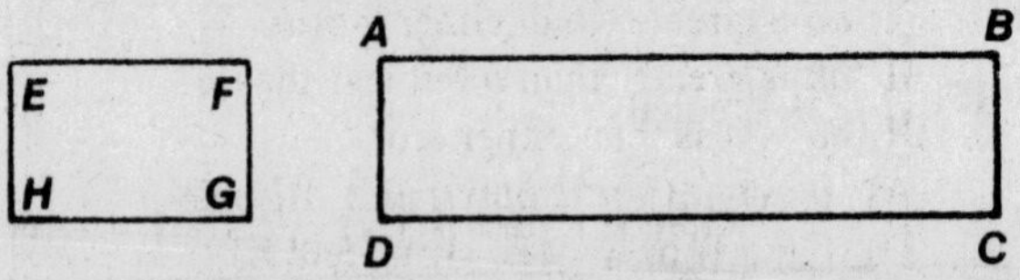

The perimeter of the rectangle (in feet) is
(A) 13 (B) 16 (C) 24 (D) 26 (E) 36

42. Circle I represents all students in a certain high school who are taking mathematics, Circle II represents all who are taking chemistry, and Circle III represents all who are taking physics. Which of the following represents all students who are taking both mathematics and chemistry but not physics?
(A) Region 4 + Region 5 − Region 6
(B) Circle I + Circle II − Circle III
(C) Region 4 + Region 8 + Region 5
(D) Region 8
(E) Circle I + Circle II − Region 10

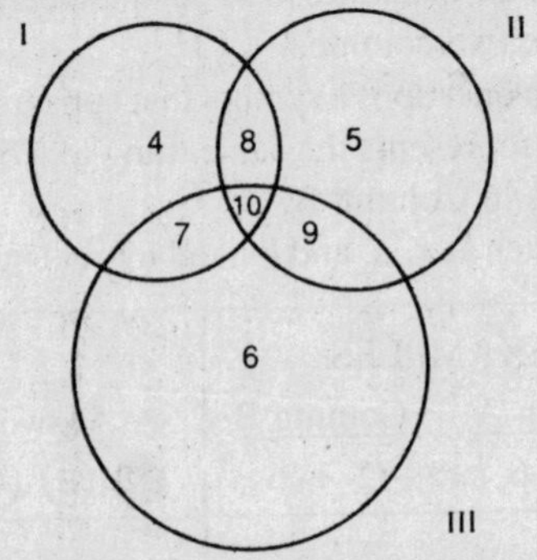

43. A cow is attached to a rope 10 feet long in a pasture bordered by two fences (more than 10 feet long) meeting at an angle of 60°. What is the area of the space in which the cow is grazing?
(A) 20π (B) $\frac{5\pi}{3}$
(C) $\frac{20\pi}{3}$ (D) $\frac{50\pi}{3}$
(E) 100π

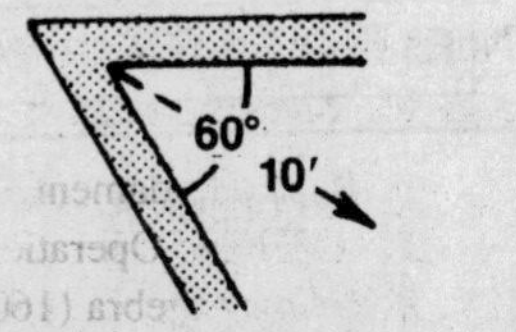

44. If the operation ϕ is defined by the equation $x \phi y = 2x + y$, what is the value of a in the equation $2 \phi a = a \phi 3$?
(A) 0 (B) −1 (C) 1 (D) 1.5 (E) −1.5

45. AB is parallel to CD. Line segment CD is divided into six equal segments.

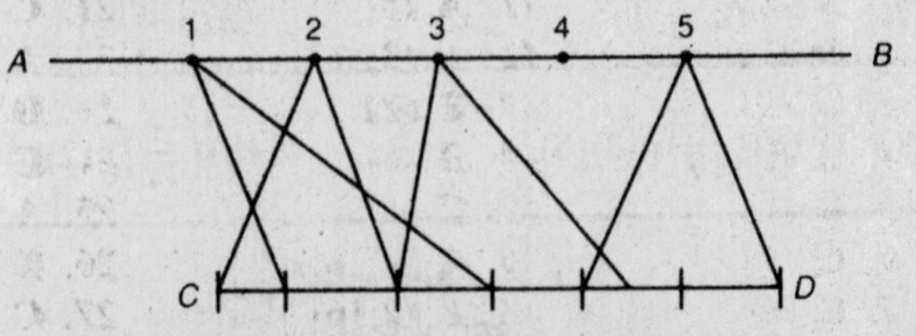

Of the triangles labeled by the numerals 1–5 on their vertices, the triangle with the greatest area is
(A) 1 (B) 2 (C) 3 (D) 4 (E) 5

46. If a and b are both positive numbers, and $a > b$, which of the following could be true?
I. ab is greater than either a or b.
II. ab is greater than b but less than a.
III. ab is less than either a or b.
(A) I only (B) II only (C) III only
(D) I and II only (E) I, II, and III

47. A secondhand book is sold for \$1.20, which is $\frac{2}{3}$ of its original price. What was the original price?
(A) \$1.80 (B) \$.80 (C) \$1.60 (D) \$2.00
(E) \$3.80

48. The distance between two points is correctly expressed as 720 statute miles or 630 nautical miles. Which of the following most closely approximates the value of one statute mile in terms of nautical miles?
(A) 0.88 (B) 0.89 (C) 0.90 (D) 1.14
(E) 1.25

49. The average of P numbers is x and the average of N numbers is y. What is the average of all the $(P + N)$ numbers?
(A) $\frac{x + y}{2}$ (B) $x + y$ (C) $\frac{Py + Nx}{xy(P + N)}$
(D) $\frac{x + y}{P + N}$ (E) $\frac{Px + Ny}{P + N}$

50. In this figure K is the vertex of square $KLMN$, not shown. Side KL is parallel to either the x- or y-axis. If the area of $KLMN$ is 16, each of the following could be the coordinates of L EXCEPT
(A) (2,6)
(B) (6,2)
(C) (2, −2)
(D) (−2,2)
(E) (4,4)

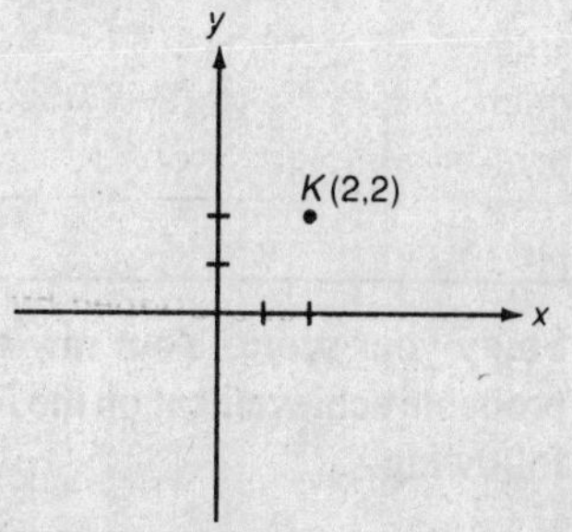

ANSWER KEY

Verbal Aptitude Section

1. **D**	11. **D**	21. **C**	31. **A**	41. **E**	51. **C**	61. **C**
2. **A**	12. **A**	22. **B**	32. **B**	42. **B**	52. **E**	62. **A**
3. **B**	13. **A**	23. **D**	33. **B**	43. **E**	53. **D**	63. **E**
4. **A**	14. **B**	24. **B**	34. **C**	44. **A**	54. **C**	64. **A**
5. **E**	15. **A**	25. **D**	35. **D**	45. **C**	55. **A**	65. **D**
6. **B**	16. **B**	26. **A**	36. **B**	46. **B**	56. **E**	
7. **D**	17. **C**	27. **C**	37. **D**	47. **E**	57. **C**	
8. **E**	18. **C**	28. **D**	38. **B**	48. **D**	58. **C**	
9. **B**	19. **E**	29. **C**	39. **C**	49. **D**	59. **E**	
10. **B**	20. **A**	30. **A**	40. **D**	50. **B**	60. **D**	

Mathematical Aptitude Section

Note: Each correct answer to the mathematics questions is keyed by number to the corresponding topic in Chapters 9 and 10. These numerals refer to the topics listed below, with specific page references in parentheses.

1. Basic Fundamental Operations (155–157)
2. Algebraic Operations (157–160)
3. Using Algebra (160–164)
4. Exponents, Roots and Radicals (159–160)
5. Inequalities (164–165)
6. Fractions (176–178)
7. Decimals (176)
8. Percent (178–180)
9. Averages (180–181)
10. Motion (182–183)
11. Ratio and Proportion (183–185)
12. Mixtures and Solutions (177–178)
13. Work (185–186)
14. Coordinate Geometry (172–173)
15. Geometry (165–172, 173–176)
16. Quantitative Comparisons (189–192)

1. **B** (8)	11. **A** (8)	21. **C** (15,16)	31. **B** (2,6,16)	41. **D** (15)
2. **D** (3)	12. **A** (3,8)	22. **A** (2,16)	32. **D** (15,16)	42. **D** (15)
3. **D** (1)	13. **E** (2)	23. **D** (2,16)	33. **C** (2,8)	43. **D** (15)
4. **A** (2)	14. **B** (4)	24. **C** (9,15,16)	34. **C** (6)	44. **C** (2)
5. **B** (1)	15. **C** (4)	25. **A** (1,6,16)	35. **C** (2,6)	45. **C** (15)
6. **C** (1)	16. **A** (15,16)	26. **B** (2,16)	36. **B** (9)	46. **E** (1)
7. **C** (6)	17. **A** (2,16)	27. **C** (2,16)	37. **C** (2,4)	47. **A** (3,7)
8. **E** (6)	18. **B** (1,16)	28. **C** (2,6,16)	38. **C** (11)	48. **A** (11)
9. **E** (6,8)	19. **C** (2,16)	29. **C** (2,6,16)	39. **D** (15)	49. **E** (9)
10. **3** (8)	20. **A** (15,16)	30. **B** (5,16)	40. **B** (15)	50. **E** (14)

SCORING CHART—DIAGNOSTIC TEST

Verbal Section		Mathematical Section *		
No. correct	________	No. correct	(A)	________
No. omitted	________	No. incorrect (# 1-15, 33-50)	(B)	________
No. incorrect	________	No. incorrect (# 16-32)	(C)	________
¼ no. incorrect	________	¼ (B) + ⅓ (C)	(D)	________
Raw Score: (no. correct minus ¼ no. incorrect)	________	*Raw Score* = (A) − (D)		________

* (In the Mathematical section, deduct ¼ of a point for each five-choice question answered incorrectly and ⅓ of a point for each four-choice question answered incorrectly).

EVALUATION CHART

Study your score. Your raw score on the Verbal and Mathematical Aptitude Sections is an indication of your probable achievement on the PSAT/NMSQT. As a guide to the amount of work you need or want to do, study the following.

Raw Score		Self-rating
Verbal	*Mathematical*	
58-65	41-50	Superior
46-57	25-40	Very good
40-45	20-24	Satisfactory
36-39	16-19	Average
30-35	10-15	Needs further study
20-29	7-9	Needs intensive study
0-19	0-6	Probably inadequate

The Identify Your Weaknesses chart will help you identify those areas in which you are weak and should concentrate your study efforts. After checking the Answer Key, circle the question numbers you got wrong. You will probably find that most of your errors fall under two or three topics—geometry and fractions, for example. You should then plan to spend most of your time reviewing material under that topic.

IDENTIFY YOUR WEAKNESSES

Skills	Page References	Question Numbers
Verbal Aptitude		
Vocabulary Sentence Completion Analogies Reading Comprehension	41–51, 100–150 52–60 61–70 71–99	1-20 21-30 31-45 46-65
Mathematical Aptitude		
Basic Fundamental Operations	155–157	3,5,6,17,18,25,46
Algebraic Operations	157–160	4,13,19,22,23,26,27,28,29,31,33,35,37,44
Using Algebra	160–164	1,2,12,47,48
Exponents, Roots, and Radicals	159–160	14,15,37
Inequalities	164–165	30
Fractions	176–178	7,8,9,25,28,29,31,34,35,47,50
Decimals	176	25,47
Percent	178–180	1,9,10,11,12,33
Mixtures, Motion, and Work	177–178, 182–183, 185–186	
Averages	180–181	24,36,49
Ratio and Proportion	183–185	38,48
Geometry	165–176	16,20,21,24,32,39,40,41,42,43,45,50
Quantitative Comparisons	189–192	16,17,18,19,20,21,22,23,24,25,26,27,28, 29,30,31,32

ANSWER EXPLANATIONS

Verbal Aptitude Section

1. **D** The opposite of *drab* (colorless) is *glamorous.* Think of "dull, drab clothing."
2. **A** The opposite of to *crumple* (wrinkle) is to *make smooth*. Think of "crumpling a sheet of paper."
3. **B** The opposite of *improper* (unsuitable; inappropriate) is *correct*. Think "wearing improper clothes" for an occasion.
4. **A** The opposite of to *raze* or destroy is to *build.* Think of a wrecking crew "razing a building."
5. **E** The opposite of *mobile* (capable of moving) is *stationary* (motionless; fixed in place). Think of traveling "mobile homes."
6. **B** The opposite of a *recipient* (person who receives) is a *donor* (person who gives). Think of "a transplant recipient" (as opposed to an organ donor).
7. **D** The opposite of *boisterous* (loud and noisy) is *quiet*. Think of "a boisterous party."
8. **E** The opposite of *insubordination* (defiance; disobedience) is *submissiveness*. Think of "being court-martialed for insubordination."
9. **B** The opposite of *dormant* (inactive; sleeping) is *awake*. Think of hibernating animals "lying dormant."
10. **B** The opposite of a *renegade* or traitor is a *loyal follower*. Think of "a treacherous renegade."
11. **D** The opposite of to *cohere* (hold together) is to *fall apart*. "The hollandaise sauce separated; it would not cohere."
12. **A** The opposite of *volatility* or changeableness is *stability*. Think of "emotional volatility."
13. **A** The opposite of *solicitous* (concerned) is *indifferent* (uncaring). Think of being "solicitous about someone's health."
14. **B** The opposite of to *encumber* (burden or hinder) is to *assist*. Think of "being encumbered by red tape."
15. **A** The opposite of *dearth* (lack or scarcity) is *excess*. "Disappointed skiers complained about the dearth of snow."
16. **B** The opposite of *ingratiating* (agreeable; trying to please) is *displeasing*. Think of "an ingratiating smile."
17. **C** The opposite of *licentious* (unrestrained by rules of conduct) is *observant of morality*. Think of "lewd and licentious."
18. **C** The opposite of *flux* (constant change, fluctuation) is *stagnation* (inactivity). Think of "the constant flux of stock prices."
19. **E** The opposite of to *exude* (ooze out or emit) is to *absorb* or soak up. Think of "exuding beads of sweat."
20. **A** The opposite of *aplomb* (equanimity or poise) is *discomposure* or agitation. Think of "the aplomb of a diplomat."
21. **C** *But* signals a contrast. Normally thunderstorms last for a short time. However, sometimes they last or *persist* for a long time. Note the effect of the phrase "becoming ever more severe." If the storm keeps on getting worse, it is not *waning* (declining), *moderating* (becoming less severe), *vacillating* (wavering), or *dispersing* (being scattered).
22. **B** For Miro, art was holy or *sacred*. Note how the second clause clarifies what kind of ritual art became for Miro.
23. **D** Why is this 100-mile-thick piece of glass clearer than a standard windowpane? *Because* the glass is exceptionally *transparent*. The "so...that" structure signals cause and effect.
24. **B** There has never been a census or numerical count of all the people in the world. *Therefore*, any attempt to describe the world's population numerically must involve guesswork or *conjecture*.
25. **D** The *assiduous* or diligent *execution* (performance) of one's job would give one's employer no cause for complaint. Again, note the sentence's cause and effect structure.
26. **A** *Despite* signals a contrast. Although Warhol seemed *nonchalant* (coolly unconcerned; casual), he was not. Instead, he cared deeply about his art, laboring at it *diligently*.
27. **C** Because these shows are highly derivative of (stem from) our culture, they reflect what our culture is like. Thus, they are good *indices* (indicators or signs) of our culture's attitudes and values. *Indices* is the plural form of *index*.
28. **D** *And* is a support signal. The opening clause states something positive about Guinness. The conclusion of the sentence must support that idea: it must also say something positive about him. In this case, it says he's a good writer: an unusually *felicitous* prose stylist, one who has a special talent for finding exactly the right words.
29. **C** Given that English society didn't encourage women to get an education, you would expect it not to care that women were uneducated. However, English society was illogical: it *decried* or expressed its disapproval of women's lack of education.
30. **A** A passionate nature hates compromise (finds it *odious*) because it seems a surrender. An intellectual nature hates compromise because it seems a *confusion*, mixing together things that to the intellect are inherently distinct.
31. **A** A *minnow* is a kind of *fish*. A *poodle* is a kind of *dog*. (Class and Member)
32. **B** To *chip* a *plate* is to damage it. To *snag* a *sweater* is to damage it. (Cause and Effect)
33. **B** *Oxygen* is stored in a *tank*. *Milk* is stored in a *carton*. (Function)

34. **C** *Sage* is a kind of *herb*. A *rocker* is a kind of *chair*. (Class and Member)

35. **D** A *girder* is used to *support* things. A *winch* is used to *hoist* or lift them. (Function)

36. **B** *Bridging a gap* spans a physical distance between two sides, making a connection between them. *Reconciling* (setting right) *an estrangement* (loss of affection, separation) spans an emotional distance between two sides, making a connection between them. (Function)

37. **D** An *eggshell* is characterized by delicacy or *fragility*. A *barbell* is characterized by *weight*. (Defining Characteristic)

38. **B** *Hostile* (antagonistic; unfriendly) by definition means lacking *friendship*. *Traitorous* (disloyal) by definition means lacking *loyalty*. (Antonym Variant)

39. **C** *Philately*, by definition, is the study and collection of *stamps*. *Numismatics*, by definition, is the study and collection of *coins*. (Definition)

40. **D** Someone *circumspect* (cautious) is characterized by *wariness* (carefulness). Someone *reckless* (heedless; daring) is characterized by *foolhardiness* (rashness). (Defining Characteristic)

41. **E** *Paragon* (model of excellence) and *standard* or ideal are synonyms. Similarly, *imitation* and *copy* are synonyms. (Synonym)

42. **B** To *pulverize* something is to convert it to powder or *dust*. To *vaporize* something is to convert it to vapor or *mist*. (Definition)

43. **E** A *suppliant* (humble petitioner), by definition, *pleads*. An *interpreter*, by definition, *translates*. (Definition)

44. **A** A *luminary* (notable person) is by definition *illustrious* (renowned). A *zealot* (fanatic; extremist) is by definition *intense*. (Defining Characteristic)

45. **C** Something *apocryphal* (doubtful; unverified) lacks *authenticity* (genuineness). Something *hypocritical* (insincere) lacks *integrity* (honesty). (Antonym Variant)

46. **B** The narrator never indicates that his father felt bitter about his army service. Choice **A** is incorrect. The narrator describes his father as "daring" and "impetuous." Choice **C** is incorrect. The narrator indicates that his father had been a sugarcane grower before he took up cattle ranching. Choice **D** is incorrect. Paragraph 2 stresses the riskiness of the trip during the stormy season. Choice **E** is incorrect. The narrator states his father had learned from the war that life was temporary.

47. **E** Look at the context of the phrase. The very next words are "Suddenly all our cane went down and men began putting up fences." Why? They are putting up fences in order to be ready to enclose the cattle the father is about to buy. The father has sensed there is a market for good, fresh, untainted meat, and has immediately decided to try his hand at raising cattle.

48. **D** Pappy "knew cattle." The father knew cane-growing, but wanted to learn cattle. This suggests that the father sought out Pappy *because he needed Pappy's guidance*.

49. **D** Throughout the passage the author describes the various stages of the growth of the strangler tree.

50. **B** The strangler tree's feeding cables do not ascend toward the canopy; they descend to the forest floor. You can double-check your answer by using the process of elimination. The strangler tree eventually stands on its own pedestal or supports itself. You can eliminate Choice **A**.
One set of the strangler tree's roots (the "feeding cable") extends all the way from high up in the fork of the host tree down to the forest floor. You can eliminate Choice **C**.
When the feeder cable reaches the soil, the plant's growth quickens. You can eliminate Choice **D**.
The strangler's roots "thicken markedly," becoming *conspicuously larger*. You can eliminate Choice **E**.
Only Choice **B** is left. It is the correct answer.

51. **C** The concluding sentence states that the host expires and the strangler tree stands on its own pedestal of thickened roots (its original feeding cables, now fused together). Thus, the strangler tree has *outgrown its need for its host*.)

52. **E** Throughout the passage the author presents and comments on the nature of the original documents that form the basis for his historical narrative. Thus, it is clear that a major concern of his is to *introduce* these "sources of almost forgotten oral history" to his readers.
Choice **A** is incorrect. The author clearly regrets the fate of the Indians. However, he does not take this occasion to denounce or condemn the white man. Choice **B** is incorrect. While the author discusses the various treaty councils, he does not evaluate or judge how effective they were. Choice **C** is incorrect. The author never touches on the current treatment of the Indians. Choice **D** is incorrect. The author indicates no such thing.

53. **D** You can arrive at the correct choice by the process of elimination.
Statement I is true. The passage states that the quality of the interviews depended on the interpreters' abilities. Inaccuracies could creep in because of the translators' lack of skill. Therefore, you can eliminate Choice **B**.
Statement II is untrue. The passage indicates that the Indians sometimes exaggerated, telling the reporters tall tales. It does not indicate that the reporters in turn overstated what they had been told. Therefore, you can eliminate Choices **C** and **E**.
Statement III is true. The passage indicates that the Indians sometimes were disinclined to speak the whole truth because they feared reprisals (retaliation) if they did. Therefore, you can eliminate Choice **A**.
Only Choice **D** is left. It is the correct answer.

54. **C** The author speaks of the Indians who lived through the "doom period of their civilization," the victims of the conquest of the American West. In doing so, his tone can best be described as *elegiac*, expressing sadness about their fate and lamenting their vanished civilization.

55. **A** In paragraph 3 the author comments upon the "graphic similes and metaphors of the natural world" found in the English translations of Indian speeches. Thus, he is impressed by their *vividness of imagery*.

56. **E** The author has tried to create a narrative of the winning of the West from the victims' perspective. This suggests that, in asking his readers to read the book facing eastward (the way the Indians would have been looking when they first saw the whites headed west), he is asking them metaphorically to look at things from the Indians' point of view.

57. **C** The author states that the later novels of James play down prominent action. Thus they lack *overtly (openly) dramatic incident*. However, the author goes on to state that James's novels *do* possess interest; they carry the reader through "a rich analysis of the mental adjustments of the characters to the realities of their personal situations." It is this dramatic psychological revelation that holds the reader's interest.
Question **A** is unanswerable on the basis of the passage. It is evident that James wrote psychological novels; it is nowhere stated that he originated the genre. Question **B** is unanswerable on the basis of the passage. Although conventional narrative technique relates "events in distinctly phased sequences," clearly separating them, it does not necessarily present action in *strictly* chronological order. Question **D** is unanswerable on the basis of the passage. The passage does not deal with the general public's reaction to James. Question **E** is unanswerable on the basis of the passage. The passage talks of qualities in James as a novelist in terms of their being *characteristic*, not in terms of their making him *unique*.

58. **C** While the stories themselves grow simpler, their moral and psychological aspects become increasingly complex.
Choice **A** is incorrect. The passage mentions the specific description of settings as characteristic of James's early, conventional novels, not of his later works. Choice **B** is incorrect. In his later novels James grew less concerned with plot and more concerned with psychological revelation. Choice **D** is incorrect. The "excitement of visible actions building up to a climactic event" (next-to-last sentence) is characteristic of the common novel, not of the Jamesian psychological novel. Choice **E** is incorrect. The later novels tend instead to subordinate dramatic effect, making it secondary to psychological exploration and revelation.

59. **E** The author is being somewhat negative: he refers to novels of action as "overstuffed" and describes them as "crammed with *adventitious* events"—events that are not built in to the situation, but are added, possibly irrelevantly, to the general story. However, these comments are merely made in passing: the author is not launching a full-scale attack against the novel of action. Thus, his attitude is best described as one of *clear disapprobation* or disapproval.
Choice **A** is incorrect. The author is not *pointedly indignant* or deeply resentful in tone. He is merely making mildly critical remarks in passing. Choice **B** is incorrect. The author does make passing comments that disparage (belittle) the novel of action. He is not wholly *neutral* on the topic. Choice **C** is incorrect. While the author does slightly disparage the novel of action, he does not ridicule or *deride* it sharply. Choice **D** is incorrect. The author is certainly not a *strong partisan* or advocate of the novel of action.

60. **D** Throughout the passage the author discusses and makes judgments about James's subject matter (the moral and psychological responses of people to their personal situations) and technique (the accumulation of details; the increasing simplicity of action).

61. **C** You can arrive at the correct choice by the process of elimination.
Statement I is true. The passage states that the tornado's lifetime is never more than a few hours. Therefore, you can eliminate Choices **B** and **D**.
Statement II is true. The first paragraph indicates that a fraction of the thunderstorm's tremendous energy "is concentrated into an area no more than several hundred meters in diameter." A later portion of the passage refers to the tornado's "concentrated high winds." Therefore, you can eliminate Choice **A**.
Statement III is untrue. The passage indicates that tornadoes may vary markedly in size and shape. Therefore, you can eliminate Choice **E**.
Only Choice **C** is left. It is the correct answer.

62. **A** The passage describes tornadoes as the product of thunderstorms and goes on to discuss various aspects of their nature (energy concentration, pressure drops, intense winds, funnel clouds, etc.).

63. **E** Paragraph 3 states that the "warmer and drier the inflowing air is, the greater the pressure drop must be for condensation to occur and a cloud to form." This suggests that temperature and humidity affect the tornado, and that it *responds to changes in temperature and humidity*.
Choice **A** is incorrect. The passage indicates that in the Northern Hemisphere a tornado's winds may be counterclockwise; it never suggests that a tornado's winds are *invariably* counterclockwise. Choice **B** is incorrect. Paragraph 4 states that a tornado's lifetime is never more than a few hours. Choice **C** is incorrect. The *warmer* and *drier* the

air is, the greater the pressure drop has to be for the funnel cloud to form. This does not suggest that the cloud will not form if the air is cool and dry. Choice **D** is incorrect. A thunderstorm's cumulonimbus cloud can be more than 17 kilometers high. A tornado's funnel cloud is described as smaller than this.

64. **A** The author states (paragraph 4) that "if the core fills with dust, the funnel may take on a more exotic hue, such as the red of west Oklahoma clay." The hue or color of the funnel thus depends on what the soil in the region is made of.

65. **D** The author suggests a hypothesis (tornado noise "may result from the interaction of the concentrated high winds with the ground"). He provides a concrete example ("the red of west Oklahoma clay"). He indicates a time span ("never more than a few hours"). He uses similes ("roaring like a freight train or a jet engine"). He does not, however, argue a particular point of view.

Mathematical Aptitude Section

1. **B** 100% of 25 = 25. We are required to find an additional 4% of 25, which would make the correct answer *slightly* more than 25. Glance at the answers—a very good habit to develop. Note that only one possible answer is slightly more than 25. The more time-consuming method would be to compute (25)(104%) or (25)(1.04) to get 26.

2. **D** Algebraically, if x is the number required, then

$$\frac{2}{7}x = 64$$

$$\left(\frac{7}{2}\right)\left(\frac{2}{7}x\right) = \left(\overset{32}{64}\right)\left(\frac{7}{2}\right)$$

$$x = 224$$

An alternate method using simple reasoning is to consider that if $\frac{2}{7}$ of the number is 64, then $\frac{1}{7}$ of the number is 32 and $\frac{7}{7}$ of the number is 224.

3. **D** This is not a test in fundamentals of arithmetic. Besides, too much time would be spent with long division. Glance at the answers given. Observe that they differ only in their last digits. Since the dividend ends with the digit 6 and the divisor with 4, then the quotient must end with the digit 4, since there is no remainder. Note the "equals exactly."

4. **A** This question should be done in seconds. Since the value of the numerator is zero, the value of the fraction is zero.

5. **B** Twice an odd integer yields an even integer. When 1 is added, an odd integer results (A). If 2 is added to an odd integer, an odd integer results. When this is doubled, an even integer results (B). An odd integer plus an odd integer yields an even integer, but when 1 is subtracted, an odd integer results (C). $\Delta^2 - 4$ is odd − even = odd (D). 3Δ is the product of three odds, which is odd (E).

6. **C** $144 \div 12 = 12$ spaces. We must place a post where the fence begins, so that at the first space we have 2 posts, at the end of the second space we have 3 posts . . . and at the end of the last (twelfth) space we have 13 posts.

7. **C** Since all units are in hours, do not convert to minutes, but simply add fractions. Recall that to add fractions they must all have common denominators.

$$\frac{1}{5} + \frac{1}{3} + \frac{1}{6} =$$

$$\frac{6}{30} + \frac{10}{30} + \frac{5}{30} = \frac{21}{30} = \frac{7}{10}$$

8. **E** Sam took 40 minutes longer than Stanley.

$$\frac{40}{60} = \frac{2}{3}.$$

9. **E** For problems using PART OF or PERCENT OF, the expression following OF is the denominator.

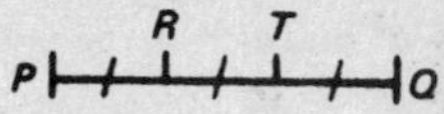

$$\frac{PQ}{PT} = \frac{3 \text{ equal units}}{2 \text{ equal units}} = 1\frac{1}{2} = 150\%$$

10. **E** We are concerned with the 60 teachers who were NOT transferred.

$$\frac{60}{80} = \frac{3}{4} = 75\%$$

11. **A** No computation is necessary. Part (80%) of the ammonia contains nitrogen. Therefore the correct answer must be less than 18%, which is the entire ammonia content of the fertilizer. Observe that only one choice is less than 18%. The more time-consuming method is to take 80% of 18%, (.8)(18%) or 14.4%.

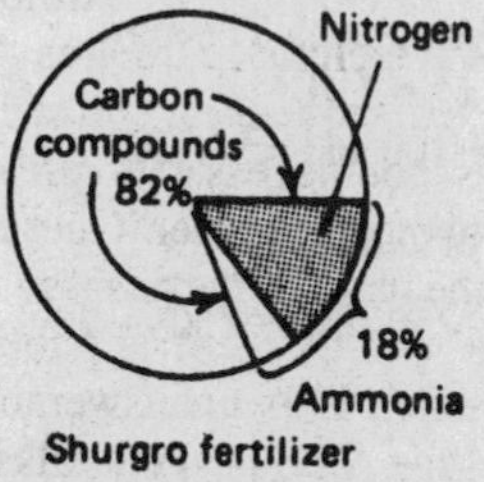

Shurgro fertilizer

12. **A** This question illustrates that often it is advisable to work back from the answers given. Bear in mind that 5% of one of the answers represents an increase that will yield 52,500. Choices (D) and (E) are unreasonable since they are each more than 52,500 and cannot express the change between the original and the present enrollment of 52,500. Choice (C) evidently gives the original enrollment, which is not asked for in this question. Choice (B) should be rejected because it represents a large increase, while we are concerned with a 5% increase. To do this algebraically, let x be the original enrollment.

$$x + .05x = 52{,}500$$
$$100x + 5x = 5{,}250{,}000$$
$$105x = 5{,}250{,}000$$
$$x = 50{,}000 \text{ (one of the incorrect choices)}$$

Since we are asked to find the *increase* in number of students,

$$52{,}500 - 50{,}000 = 2500$$

13. **E** $3t \div \frac{1}{4} = (3t)(4) = 12t$

$4t^2 \div \frac{t}{3} = (4t^2)\left(\frac{3}{t}\right) = 12t$

14. **B** $(2)^? = 8$

$(2)^3 = 8$

Therefore $n + 2 = 3$

and $n = 1$.

15. **C** $\sqrt{\frac{1}{16} + \frac{1}{9}} = \sqrt{\frac{9}{144} + \frac{16}{144}} = \sqrt{\frac{25}{144}} = \frac{5}{12}$

Note: $\sqrt{\frac{1}{16} + \frac{1}{9}}$ is NOT equivalent to

$\sqrt{\frac{1}{16}} + \sqrt{\frac{1}{9}}$.

16. **A**

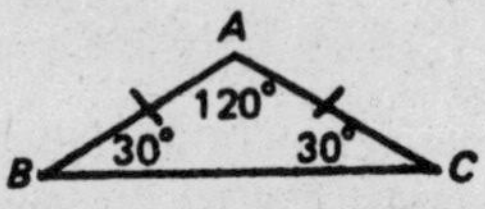

17. **A** $(a + 1)^2 = a^2 + 2a + 1$

$a(a + 2) = a^2 + 2a$

18. **B** Eliminate the terms common to both expressions:

$(a)\left(\frac{1}{17}\right)(48)(6) \qquad (48)\left(\frac{a}{17}\right)(12)$

19. **C** $4x = 2y$. Divide by 2 and $2x = y$.

20. **A**

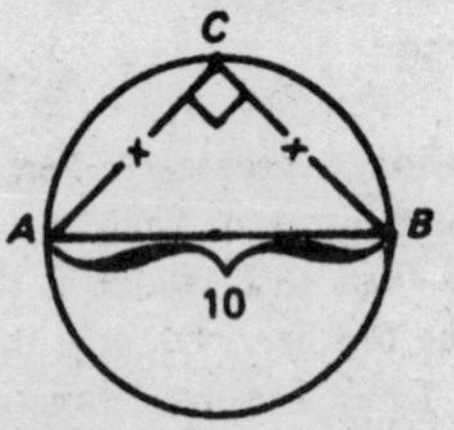

$\angle C$ inscribed in a semicircle is a right angle. Using the Pythagorean Theorem,

$x^2 + x^2 = (10)^2$

$2x^2 = 100$ and $x^2 = 50$.

Area of $\triangle ABC = \frac{(x)(x)}{2} = 25$

$25 > \sqrt{50}$ since $\sqrt{50} = 7+$

21. **C** Area of triangle $= \frac{bh}{2} = \frac{\left(\frac{x}{2}\right)(y)}{2} = \frac{\frac{xy}{2}}{2} =$

$\left(\frac{xy}{2}\right)\left(\frac{1}{2}\right) = \frac{xy}{4}$

Area of square $= (\text{side})^2 = \left(\frac{\sqrt{xy}}{2}\right)^2 = \frac{xy}{4}$

22. **A** Substitute: $x = \frac{y}{2}$

$\frac{y}{2} + 5 = y$

$y + 10 = 2y$

$y = 10$ and $2y = 20$

23. **D** a may be a negative quantity or have a value of zero. The same is true for b.

24. **C** Since $a + b + c = 180$, the average is 60. Since the triangle in Column B is equilateral, $x = 60$.

25. **A** $2\frac{1}{2} = \frac{5}{2}$; Reciprocal $= \frac{2}{5}$

$\frac{5}{2} + \frac{2}{5} = \frac{25}{10} + \frac{4}{10} = \frac{29}{10} = 2.9$

$2.9 > 2.5$

26. **B** Since z is negative, z^3 is negative, but z^2 is positive. Therefore $3z^2 > 2z^3$.

27. **C** $3a + 2b = 5b$ (they are each equal to 12.5)

$3a = 3b$

$a = b$

28. **C** Cross multiply: $\frac{x}{6} = \frac{y}{4}$

$4x = 6y$

Divide by 2: $2x = 3y$

29. **C** $\frac{2}{5} + \frac{x}{y} = \frac{7}{5}$ (subtract $\frac{2}{5}$)

$\frac{x}{y} = \frac{5}{5} = 1$

$x = y$

30. **B** $3x - 2 < 0$

$3x < 2$ (add 2 to each side of the inequality)

or, $2 > 3x$

31. **B** $\frac{3}{x} = 2$

$2x = 3$

$x = \frac{3}{2} = 1\frac{1}{2}$

$\frac{5}{y} = 2$

$2y = 5$

$y = \frac{5}{2} = 2\frac{1}{2}$

32. **D** We may not assume that ABC is a right triangle.

33. **C** $a\% = \frac{a}{100}$ and $b\% = \frac{b}{100}$

$\left(\frac{a}{100}\right)(b) \div \left(\frac{b}{100}\right)(a)$ or, $\frac{ab}{100} \div \frac{ba}{100} = 1$

34. **C** Apply the principle of percentage. Recall that percent means $\frac{?}{100}$.

$\frac{1}{5} = \frac{20}{100} = 20\%$

$\frac{1}{4} = \frac{25}{100} = 25\%$

$\frac{2}{5} = \frac{40}{100} = 40\%$ (next smaller than 50%)

$\frac{16}{25} = \frac{64}{100} =$ (more than 50%)

$\frac{3}{10} = \frac{30}{100} = 30\%$

35. **C** $\frac{t + n}{n} = \frac{t}{n} + \frac{n}{n}$ or $\frac{t}{n} + 1$

36. **B** $\frac{\text{sum of numbers}}{\text{quantity of numbers}} = \text{average}$

$\frac{2 + x}{4} = 0.6$

$2 + x = 2.4$

$x = 0.4$

37. **C** Factor $\frac{(a+b)\cancel{(a-b)}}{(a-b)\cancel{(a-b)}} = \frac{a+b}{a-b}$

38. **C** Many problems involve ratio and proportion. Set up a ratio. Substitute. (Watch units!)

$$\frac{\text{number of items}}{\text{cost in ¢}} = \frac{2}{c} = \frac{?}{x}$$

$$(c)(?) = 2x$$

$$? = \frac{2x}{c}$$

39. **D** Since the area of the top of each circular cover $= 4\pi$, use the formula for the area of a circle, $\pi r^2 =$ Area, substitute values $\pi r^2 = 4$, and divide by π: $r^2 = 4$ and $r = 2$.

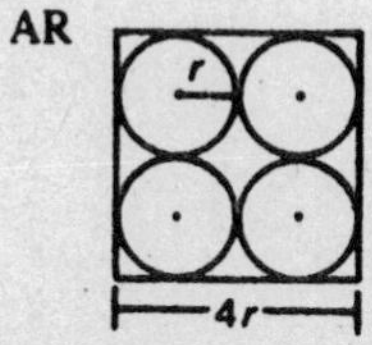

The length of each side of the box consists of $4r$ or 8 units. Therefore, the area of each side of the box $= 8 \times 8$ or 64.

40. **B** Since $AB = AC$,
m $\angle 1 =$ m $\angle 2$.
Since $FD = FC$,
m $\angle 3 =$ m $\angle 2$.
$\therefore$ m $\angle 1 =$ m $\angle 2 =$ m $\angle 3$.
The sum of the measure of the angles of $BCDE = 360°$.
m$\angle 1$ + m$\angle 2$ + m$\angle 3$ = 360° − 120° or 240°, or each of these angles has a measure of 80°. Consider $\triangle FDC$.
Since $\angle 2 + \angle 3 \overset{\circ}{=} 160$, then $\angle DFC \overset{\circ}{=} 20$.

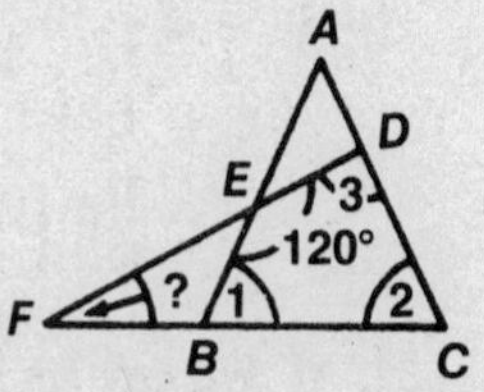

41. **D** Area of $EFGH = 6$ feet $\times$ 6 feet $= 36$ feet^2

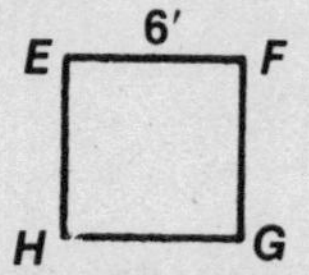

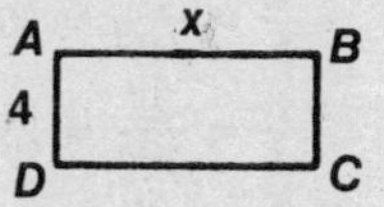

Area of $ABCD = 36$ feet^2
Let $x = AB$.
Area of $ABCD = 4x = 36$
$x = 9$ feet (AB)
Since $DC = AB$,
perimeter $= 9' + 9' + 4' + 4' = 26$ feet.

42. **D** Students taking both mathematics and chemistry are represented by the regions in which Circle I and Circle II overlap, that is, Region 8 + Region 10. But Region 10 also lies in Circle III and therefore represents some who are taking physics as well. Those who are taking both mathematics and chemistry but not physics are represented by Region 8 alone.

43. **D** Without the borders formed by the two fences the cow would be able to graze in a circular area with the 10-foot rope as a radius. That area would be 100π square feet (one of the incorrect answers). The fences, which are longer than the rope, form an angle of 60°, so that the available area for grazing is $\frac{60}{360}$ or $\frac{1}{6}$ of the area of the circle or $\left(\frac{1}{6}\right)(100\,\pi)$ or $\frac{100\pi}{6} = \frac{50\pi}{3}$.

44. **C**

$$2\,\phi\,a = a\,\phi\,3$$
$$2(2) + a = 2(a) + 3$$
$$4 + a = 2a + 3$$
$$1 = a$$

45. **C** Since AB is parallel to CD, the altitude is the same for all five triangles. Triangle #3 is the only one that has more than 2 units as a base.

46. **E** If a and b are both greater than 1, the product, ab, will be greater than either a or b; for example, $2 \times 3 = 6$ and $6 > 2$ or 3. If b is a fraction less than 1 and a is greater than 1, ab will be greater than b but less than a; for example, $3 \times \frac{1}{2} = 1\frac{1}{2}$. If a and b are both positive fractions less than 1, their product, ab, will be less than either a or b; for example,

$$\frac{1}{5} \times \frac{1}{10} = \frac{1}{50} \quad \text{and} \quad \frac{1}{50} < \frac{1}{5} \text{ or } \frac{1}{10}.$$

Thus, I, II, or III could each be true, depending on the values of a and b.

47. **A** $\frac{2}{3}$ of one of the answers given is \$1.20. Work back from the answers. Often it is advisable to first reject the unreasonable choices as in (B), which is less than \$1.20. Try the one that is easiest to test. In the case of (A), $\left(\frac{2}{3}\right)$ (\$1.80) = \$1.20 or algebraically, $\frac{2}{3}x =$ \$1.20 and $x =$ (\$1.20)$\left(\frac{3}{2}\right)$ = \$1.80. Also, if $\frac{2}{3}$ is \$1.20, then $\frac{1}{3}$ is \$0.60. $\frac{2}{3} + \frac{1}{3}$ is the total original price: \$1.20 + \$0.60 = \$1.80.

48. **A** Examples of conversion of units are similar to #38.

$$\frac{\text{nautical miles}}{\text{statute miles}} = \frac{630}{720} = \frac{x}{1}$$

$$x = \frac{630}{720} = \frac{63}{72} = \frac{7}{8} = 0.875 \text{ or } 0.88$$

49. **E** This example involves the combination of the averages of two different sets of numbers. They must be weighted in proportion to the numbers of members of each set. If x is the average of P numbers, then the sum of these numbers is Px. If y is the average of N numbers, the sum of these numbers is Ny. Therefore $Px + Ny$ is the sum of both sets of numbers. The average of these $(P + N)$ numbers is $\frac{Px + Ny}{P + N}$.

50. **E** Since the area of square *KLMN* is 16, each side must equal 4 units. Note that *KL* equals 4 units in all choices but (E).

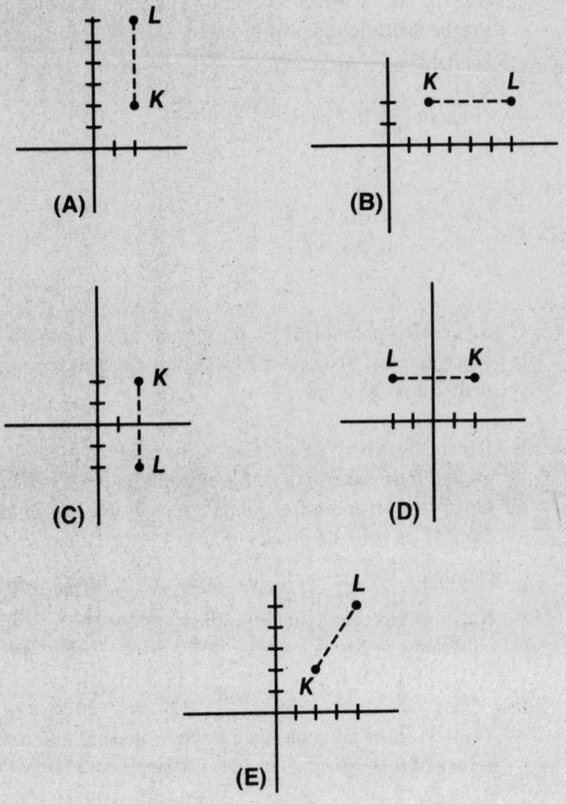

CORRECT YOUR WEAKNESSES

Verbal Aptitude

4

The Antonym Question

The antonym questions on the PSAT primarily test the extent of your vocabulary. The 20 antonym questions are always the first group of questions in the verbal test, and they are the most straightforward vocabulary questions on the test. You are given a word and must choose, from the five choices that follow it, the best antonym (opposite). The vocabulary in this section includes many words that you have probably seen in your reading, although you may never have used or even heard them in everyday conversations. It also includes some difficult words (generally the last five or six in the group) that most students are highly unlikely to know, and that only students actively competing for National Merit Scholarships need to know at this stage of their careers.

LONG-RANGE STRATEGY

The key strategy for learning antonyms is (as always): READ. However, there are some helpful things you can do using the High-Frequency and Basic Word Lists (Chapter 8).

Use the Word Lists as a guide in making flash cards. Scan a list looking for words you don't quite know—not words you are totally unfamiliar with, but words you are on the brink of knowing. Look for words you have heard or seen before but can't use in a sentence or define. Effort you put into mastering such "borderline" words will pay off—soon!

Be brief, but include all the information you need. On one side write the word. On the other side write *concise* definitions—two or three words at most—for each major meaning of the word you want to learn. Include an antonym, too: the synonym-antonym associations can help you remember both words. To fix the word in your mind, use it in a short phrase. Then write that phrase down.

Carry a few of your flash cards with you every day. Look them over whenever you have a spare moment or two. Work in short bursts. Try going through five flash cards at a time, shuffling through them rapidly so that you can build up your rapid sight recognition of the words for the test. You want these words and their antonyms to spring to your mind instantaneously, so that you can speed through the antonym section of the PSAT.

TIPS TO HELP YOU COPE WITH ANTONYM QUESTIONS

1. Think of a context for the capitalized word. Take a quick look at the word. If you don't recollect its meaning right away, try to think of a phrase or sentence in which you have heard it used. The context may help you come up with the meaning.

2. Before you look at the choices, think of antonyms for the capitalized word. If the capitalized word is a word you know, try quickly to come up with opposites for it before you look at the answer choices. Even if you don't find any of your opposites in the answers, you may find it easier to spot a similar word.

3. Read all the choices before you decide which is best. A possible answer is not always the *best* answer.

4. Choose an answer as *extreme* as the capitalized word. Words have shades of meaning. In matching a word with its opposite, you must pay attention to these shades of meaning. Check to see whether the capitalized word and your answer have the same degree of intensity. Suppose that the capitalized word is *adore* and the answer choices include both *dislike* and *loathe*. The second would be a much better answer, since *dislike* is a much milder term. But if the capitalized word were *approve* rather than *adore*, then *dislike* would be the better answer. *Loathe* would be too strong.

5. Look at the answer choices for clues to the main word's part of speech. A word may have more than one part of speech. If you don't know whether you're dealing with the common noun *contract* (a binding agreement) or the less common verb *contract* (make smaller), look at the answer choices. They'll all have the same part of speech.

6. Consider secondary meanings of the capitalized word as well as its primary meaning. If none of the answer choices seems right to you, take another look at the capitalized word. It may have more than one meaning.

The PSAT often contains questions that make use of secondary, less well-known meanings of deceptively familiar words.

7. Break down unfamiliar words into recognizable parts. When you come upon a totally unfamiliar word, don't give up. Break it down and see if you recognize any of its parts. Pay particular attention to prefixes—word parts added to the beginning of a word—and to roots, the building blocks of the language. For example, if you know the root *ver* in the word *verify* means truth, you can figure out that *veracity*, *veracious*, and *verisimilitude* must all have something to do with truth.

8. When you encounter an unfamiliar word, see whether it looks more familiar if you change its part of speech. If the noun *opacity* is unfamiliar to you, think of the adjective *opaque* (not transparent). If the adjective *intrusive* is unfamiliar, think of the common verb *intrude* (to butt in).

9. Test words for their positive or negative connotations. If you are dealing with a *partly* unfamiliar word, a word that you cannot define or use in a sentence but that you think you have seen before, try to remember the *general* context in which you saw the word. Ask yourself whether it had a positive feeling to it, or whether it had a negative feel. If you are sure the capitalized word had a positive connotation, then, since you are looking for an antonym, you *know* the correct answer must have a negative one. Thus, you can toss out answer choices that have positive feelings and guess among the answer choices that are negative in tone.

ANTONYM EXERCISES

To develop your ability to handle antonym questions, work your way through the following four exercises. *Warning:* These exercises are graded in difficulty. The further you go, the harder the items get, just as on a video game. Go all the way. Even if you do less well on Exercise D than you did on Exercise A, look on every error as an opportunity to learn. Study all the words you found difficult. Remember, these are *all* typical PSAT words.

After completing each exercise, see how many questions you answered correctly. (The correct answers are given on page 49.) Then *read the answer explanations* for questions you answered incorrectly, questions you omitted, and questions you answered correctly but found difficult.

> Each question below consists of a word in capital letters, followed by five lettered words or phrases. Choose the word or phrase that is most nearly <u>opposite</u> in meaning to the word in capital letters. Since some of the questions require you to distinguish fine shades of meaning, consider all the choices before deciding which is best.
>
> Example:
>
> GOOD: (A) sour (B) bad (C) red (D) hot (E) ugly
>
> Ⓐ ● Ⓒ Ⓓ Ⓔ

EXERCISE A

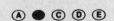

25 questions—12 minutes

1. ALLY:
(A) prisoner
(B) fugitive
(C) enemy
(D) sage
(E) mediator

2. PROTECT:
(A) challenge
(B) accuse
(C) respect
(D) damage
(E) reward

3. BRITTLE:
(A) aggressive
(B) angry
(C) curious
(D) pliant
(E) genuine

4. APPREHEND:
(A) release
(B) cringe
(C) defend
(D) enforce
(E) accelerate

5. BLUNDER:
(A) pack tightly
(B) denounce vehemently
(C) act intelligently
(D) await anxiously
(E) work diligently

6. SOOTHE:
(A) annoy
(B) refute
(C) prescribe
(D) defend
(E) isolate

7. CONTAMINATE:
(A) evaluate
(B) purify
(C) persuade
(D) energize
(E) disrupt

8. LENIENCY:
(A) strength
(B) concern
(C) justification
(D) defense
(E) severity

9. DEBASE:
(A) work alone
(B) expose to danger
(C) conclude
(D) incense
(E) enhance

10. CALAMITY:
(A) outcome
(B) evasion
(C) occurrence
(D) pipe dream
(E) good fortune

11. CLAMOR:
(A) tolerance
(B) meekness
(C) innocence
(D) tranquillity
(E) ambition

12. COMPLIANCE:
(A) disobedience
(B) commitment
(C) detachment
(D) decisiveness
(E) honesty

13. AGITATION:
(A) criticism
(B) calmness
(C) devotion
(D) authority
(E) diversity

14. CHAOS:
(A) courage
(B) opinion
(C) praise
(D) order
(E) behavior

15. COMPLEX:
(A) simple
(B) boring
(C) conclusive
(D) trivial
(E) unique

16. DRAWBACK:
(A) evidence
(B) benefit
(C) contraction
(D) essential act
(E) grudging acceptance

17. GRIM:
(A) modern
(B) skillful
(C) cheerful
(D) conclusive
(E) discreet

18. HUMANE:
(A) attentive
(B) vulnerable
(C) spontaneous
(D) reticent
(E) cruel

19. IMPROVE:
(A) impair
(B) contend
(C) deny
(D) borrow
(E) comply

20. CLARITY:
(A) loudness
(B) certainty
(C) ambiguity
(D) persistence
(E) tenderness

21. HUMDRUM:
(A) conclusive
(B) futile
(C) interesting
(D) mournful
(E) disappointing

22. INDISPUTABLE:
(A) unjust
(B) questionable
(C) indelicate
(D) indescribable
(E) unconcerned

23. ADORATION:
(A) absolution
(B) strength
(C) abhorrence
(D) malaise
(E) villification

24. CONVENTIONAL:
(A) useful and pleasing
(B) foolish and untrustworthy
(C) kindly and warm
(D) extraordinary
(E) obvious

25. SOPHISTICATED:
(A) ingenuous
(B) clever
(C) partial
(D) integrated
(E) cordial

EXERCISE B

25 questions—12 minutes

1. AFFLUENCE:
(A) neutrality
(B) sentimentality
(C) poverty
(D) beauty
(E) evil

2. REPREHENSIBLE:
(A) distracting
(B) praiseworthy
(C) conclusive
(D) frightening
(E) irrevocable

3. INSCRUTABLE:
(A) disorderly
(B) shallow
(C) unwritten
(D) painful
(E) obvious

4. TENTATIVE:
(A) forgotten
(B) fabricated
(C) concerned
(D) permanent
(E) absent

5. RELENTLESS:
(A) unwise
(B) fearless
(C) straightforward
(D) bizarre
(E) yielding

6. ABUSIVE:
(A) flawed
(B) pliant
(C) flexible
(D) cordial
(E) intricate

7. PUNY:
(A) strong
(B) humorous
(C) quarrelsome
(D) studious
(E) innocent

8. FACILITATE:
(A) overestimate
(B) copy
(C) obstruct
(D) offend
(E) decorate

9. INTANGIBLE:
(A) incomplete
(B) individual
(C) concrete
(D) uninjured
(E) careless

10. SAVORY:
(A) improvident
(B) wise
(C) unappetizing
(D) warm
(E) uncivilized

11. CANDID:
(A) hasty
(B) shining
(C) insincere
(D) critical
(E) sufficient

12. STAMINA:
(A) flatness
(B) darkness
(C) haste
(D) weakness
(E) reliability

13. INANIMATE:
(A) emotional
(B) cruel
(C) alive
(D) scrupulous
(E) ridiculous

14. ENHANCE:
(A) sympathize
(B) emote
(C) resist
(D) weaken
(E) fascinate

15. DISREPUTABLE:
(A) polite
(B) certain
(C) argumentative
(D) amendable
(E) praiseworthy

16. CONCISE:
(A) inaccurate
(B) lengthy
(C) sudden
(D) painful
(E) extraneous

17. MAMMOTH:
(A) modern
(B) impotent
(C) constructive
(D) dramatic
(E) minute

18. INCITE:
(A) exclude
(B) destroy
(C) perceive
(D) subdue
(E) vindicate

19. ANTIQUATED:
(A) limited
(B) active
(C) prophetic
(D) inevitable
(E) contemporary

20. ERRATIC:
(A) indifferent
(B) obvious
(C) constant
(D) suspicious
(E) harmless

21. BEWAIL:
(A) consider thoughtfully
(B) feel joyous
(C) shine brightly
(D) abandon hope
(E) make effective

22. EXOTIC:
(A) unnecessary
(B) ambiguous
(C) involved
(D) ordinary
(E) emotional

23. INAPPROPRIATE:
(A) slanted
(B) absolute
(C) opposed
(D) encouraging
(E) suitable

24. ADJACENT:
(A) essential
(B) understanding
(C) approximately equal
(D) far apart
(E) at odds with

25. ADVISABLE:
(A) formidable
(B) appropriate
(C) inconsiderate
(D) imprudent
(E) improvident

EXERCISE C

25 questions—12 minutes

1. AMENABLE:
(A) religious
(B) feminine
(C) proud
(D) unfriendly
(E) intractable

2. ADULTERATE:
(A) grow up
(B) push ahead
(C) make pure
(D) send away
(E) turn loose

3. DISAPPROBATION:
(A) inquiry
(B) indolence
(C) neglect
(D) permanence
(E) approval

4. IMPRUDENT:
(A) careful
(B) excitable
(C) domineering
(D) wealthy
(E) powerful

5. DISSENSION:
(A) harmony
(B) analysis
(C) accolade
(D) slyness
(E) mischief

6. SEDATE:
(A) flighty
(B) erect
(C) buried
(D) timid
(E) turbid

7. LUCRATIVE:
(A) indolent
(B) refined
(C) unprofitable
(D) disconsolate
(E) somber

8. ORNATE:
(A) plain
(B) original
(C) systematic
(D) unbecoming
(E) obsolete

9. UNOBTRUSIVE:
(A) flawed
(B) faulty
(C) mediocre
(D) fastidious
(E) conspicuous

10. MARTIAL:
(A) blessed
(B) demonstrated
(C) peaceful
(D) rejected
(E) abominated

11. ACCLAMATION:
(A) condemnation
(B) negotiation
(C) imitation
(D) vexation
(E) nepotism

12. DEBILITATE:
(A) inebriate
(B) fascinate
(C) decipher
(D) invigorate
(E) persuade

13. ADHERENT:
(A) conspirator
(B) dissenter
(C) anarchist
(D) predecessor
(E) fledgling

14. OBSCURE:
(A) unique
(B) prominent
(C) superficial
(D) essential
(E) generous

15. AVARICE:
(A) generosity
(B) acquiescence
(C) agreement
(D) inflexibility
(E) persistence

16. VIVACIOUS:
(A) languid
(B) obstinate
(C) articulate
(D) amorous
(E) decorous

17. BANKRUPT:
(A) fiduciary
(B) quantitative
(C) embezzled
(D) solvent
(E) bereft

18. ACQUIESCE:
(A) deplete
(B) object
(C) expedite
(D) isolate
(E) prolong

19. PRODIGAL:
(A) frugal
(B) loyal
(C) deceitful
(D) amorous
(E) ignorant

20. PLETHORA:
(A) displeasure
(B) arrogance
(C) paucity
(D) inequality
(E) exaggeration

21. SANCTIFY:
(A) harrow
(B) embalm
(C) procure
(D) relate
(E) profane

22. SUBSERVIENT:
(A) superlative
(B) prolific
(C) domineering
(D) overcoming
(E) magnificent

23. ASSIMILATE:
(A) pretend
(B) reject
(C) penetrate
(D) imitate
(E) anticipate

24. RIGOR:
(A) padding
(B) mold
(C) litigation
(D) excavation
(E) laxity

25. IRREVERENT:
(A) logical
(B) unimportant
(C) violent
(D) respectful
(E) unafraid

EXERCISE D

25 questions—12 minutes

1. NOXIOUS:
(A) healthful
(B) lively
(C) uncertain
(D) unprepared
(E) calming

2. GARRULOUS:
(A) laconic
(B) fascinating
(C) literate
(D) bestial
(E) credulous

3. LUGUBRIOUS:
(A) infinitesimal
(B) insignificant
(C) jovial
(D) profitable
(E) weakening

4. INNOCUOUS:
(A) noticeable
(B) harmful
(C) weak
(D) zealous
(E) prejudiced

5. LETHARGY:
(A) alertness
(B) caution
(C) censure
(D) persistence
(E) foolishness

6. ENIGMATIC:
(A) obvious
(B) extraordinary
(C) extraneous
(D) covert
(E) blasphemous

7. TEMERITY:
(A) caution
(B) encouragement
(C) destitution
(D) candor
(E) altruism

8. CACOPHONY:
(A) censure
(B) evasion
(C) selfishness
(D) harmony
(E) futility

9. TRACTABLE:
(A) frantic
(B) unruly
(C) indefinable
(D) inept
(E) experienced

10. VILIFY:
(A) eulogize
(B) analyze
(C) magnify
(D) violate
(E) prevaricate

11. ERUDITE:
(A) illiterate
(B) ill-mannered
(C) illegible
(D) improper
(E) immaterial

12. PUSILLANIMOUS:
(A) firmly convinced
(B) approximately equal
(C) authentic
(D) parsimonious
(E) courageous

13. PROPITIOUS:
(A) antagonistic
(B) ambitious
(C) unappetizing
(D) unfavorable
(E) innocuous

14. STEADFAST:
(A) scrupulous
(B) capricious
(C) ancillary
(D) equitable
(E) objective

15. VINDICTIVE:
(A) forgiving
(B) courageous
(C) integrated
(D) figurative
(E) passive

16. ABSTRACT:
(A) concrete
(B) apathetic
(C) diligent
(D) disreputable
(E) cooperative

17. SPURIOUS:
(A) comprehensive
(B) incandescent
(C) predictable
(D) magnanimous
(E) authentic

18. GALVANIZE:
(A) acquiesce
(B) restrict
(C) deaden
(D) disapprove
(E) coalesce

19. EVANESCENT:
(A) permanent
(B) sparkling
(C) turgid
(D) frantic
(E) segregated

20. ANTISOCIAL:
(A) formal
(B) gregarious
(C) impending
(D) postponing
(E) corrective

21. FORTUITOUS:
(A) intended
(B) disastrous
(C) beneficial
(D) uncanny
(E) sagacious

22. DESULTORY:
(A) bland
(B) content
(C) agreeable
(D) methodical
(E) honorable

23. ABROGATE:
(A) punish
(B) institute
(C) discharge
(D) commiserate
(E) launch

24. AMITY:
(A) hostility
(B) exhaustion
(C) verification
(D) orientation
(E) innovativeness

25. TRAVAIL:
(A) ineffectiveness
(B) inelasticity
(C) sedation
(D) suffrage
(E) relaxation

ANSWER KEY

EXERCISE A

1. C	6. A	11. D	16. B	21. C
2. D	7. B	12. A	17. C	22. B
3. D	8. E	13. B	18. E	23. C
4. A	9. E	14. D	19. A	24. D
5. C	10. E	15. A	20. C	25. A

EXERCISE B

1. C	6. D	11. C	16. B	21. B
2. B	7. A	12. D	17. E	22. D
3. E	8. C	13. C	18. D	23. E
4. D	9. C	14. D	19. E	24. D
5. E	10. C	15. E	20. C	25. D

EXERCISE C

1. E	6. A	11. A	16. A	21. E
2. C	7. C	12. D	17. D	22. C
3. E	8. A	13. B	18. B	23. B
4. A	9. E	14. B	19. A	24. E
5. A	10. C	15. A	20. C	25. D

EXERCISE D

1. A	6. A	11. A	16. A	21. A
2. A	7. A	12. E	17. E	22. D
3. C	8. D	13. D	18. C	23. B
4. B	9. B	14. B	19. A	24. A
5. A	10. A	15. A	20. B	25. E

ANSWER EXPLANATIONS

EXERCISE A

1. **(C)** An *ally* is one who helps. An *enemy* is one who seeks to harm.
2. **(D)** To *protect* is to shield from injury or distruction. To *damage* is to inflict injury or to destroy.
3. **(D)** *Brittle* means easily shattered. *Pliant* means flexible.
4. **(A)** To *apprehend* is to arrest; to *release* is to set free.
5. **(C)** To *blunder* is to make an error, the opposite of to *act intelligently*.
6. **(A)** To *soothe* is to relieve or comfort; to *annoy* is to irritate or disturb.
7. **(B)** *Contaminate* means pollute. *Purify* means cleanse.
8. **(E)** *Leniency* is tolerance or permissiveness; *severity* is strictness or harshness.
9. **(E)** To *debase* is to lower in quality or value, while *enhance* means to raise in quality or value.
10. **(E)** A *calamity* is a disaster; its opposite is *good fortune*.

11. **(D)** *Clamor* means noise; *tranquillity* means free of disturbance.
12. **(A)** *Compliance* means yielding to the demands of others. Its opposite is *disobedience*, the refusal to obey.
13. **(B)** *Agitation* means disturbance. *Calmness* means lack of disturbance.
14. **(D)** *Chaos* is utter disorder. Its antonym is *order*.
15. **(A)** *Complex* means complicated. *Simple* means plain, uncomplicated.
16. **(B)** *Drawback* is an objectionable feature. Its opposite, *benefit*, is a useful feature.
17. **(C)** *Grim* means stern, harsh, the opposite of *cheerful*.
18. **(E)** *Humane* means kind; its antonym is *cruel*.
19. **(A)** *Improve* is to make better; *impair* is to make worse.
20. **(C)** *Ambiguity* (obscurity) is the opposite of *clarity*.
21. **(C)** *Humdrum* means monotonous or boring, not *interesting*.
22. **(B)** Something *indisputable* cannot be denied. It is not *questionable*.
23. **(C)** *Adoration* (love) and *abhorrence* (hatred) are opposites.
24. **(D)** Something *conventional* is typical. It has become commonplace or ordinary. Its opposite is *extraordinary*.
25. **(A)** *Sophisticated* (worldly) is the opposite of *ingenuous* (naive).

EXERCISE B

1. **(C)** *Affluence* means wealth; *poverty* means lack of wealth.
2. **(B)** *Reprehensible* (deserving disapproval) is the opposite of *praiseworthy*.
3. **(E)** *Inscrutable* describes something that cannot be easily grasped; it is, therefore, not *obvious*.
4. **(D)** Something that is *tentative* is done as a trial or experiment; it is not *permanent*.
5. **(E)** *Relentless* means unyielding.
6. **(D)** *Abusive* (characterized by verbal or physical abuse) is the opposite of *cordial* (warm and pleasant).
7. **(A)** *Puny* (tiny, weak) is the opposite of *strong*.
8. **(C)** *Facilitate* (make easier) and *obstruct* (make more difficult) are opposites.
9. **(C)** *Intangible* (imperceptible to the sense of touch) and *concrete* (definite, perceptible) are antonyms.
10. **(C)** *Savory* (tasty) is the opposite of *unappetizing*.
11. **(C)** A *candid* (frank, sincere) person is not *insincere*.
12. **(D)** *Stamina* (vigor, power to endure suffering) is the opposite of *weakness*.
13. **(C)** *Inanimate* (not alive) and *alive* are opposites.
14. **(D)** *Enhance* (improve in quality, strengthen) and *weaken* are opposites.
15. **(E)** *Disreputable* (having a bad reputation) and *praiseworthy* are opposites.
16. **(B)** *Concise* (expressing much in few words) is the opposite of *lengthy*.
17. **(E)** *Mammoth* (large, huge) is the opposite of *minute* (extremely small).
18. **(D)** *Incite* (stir-up, provoke) and *subdue* (tone down) are opposites.
19. **(E)** *Antiquated* means old. *Contemporary* means modern.
20. **(C)** *Erratic* means inconsistent, irregular; its opposite is *constant*, which means unchanging.
21. **(B)** To *bewail* is to express sorrow, not joy.
22. **(D)** *Exotic* (strikingly unusual) and *ordinary* are opposites.
23. **(E)** *Suitable* means pertinent and appropriate.
24. **(D)** *Adjacent* means next to, not *far apart*.
25. **(D)** *Imprudent* means not expedient or *advisable*.

EXERCISE C

1. **(E)** An *amenable* person is yielding and submissive. An *intractable* person refuses to be managed or led.
2. **(C)** *Adulterate* means to make impure by adding something inferior.
3. **(E)** *Disapprobation* is disapproval, not *approval*.
4. **(A)** *Imprudent* (not prudent or careful) is the opposite of *careful*.
5. **(A)** *Dissension* (strong disagreement) is the opposite of *harmony*.
6. **(A)** *Sedate* (undisturbed, calm) and *flighty* (giddy) are antonyms.
7. **(C)** *Lucrative* means profitable.
8. **(A)** *Ornate* (elaborately decorated) and *plain* are antonyms.
9. **(E)** *Unobtrusive* (not conspicuous) is the opposite of *conspicuous*.
10. **(C)** *Martial* (warlike) and *peaceful* are opposites.
11. **(A)** *Acclamation* (demonstration of approval) and *condemnation* (expression of disapproval) are antonyms.
12. **(D)** *Debilitate* (to weaken, enfeeble) is the opposite of *invigorate*.
13. **(B)** An *adherent* is a follower or believer, the opposite of a *dissenter*.
14. **(B)** Something *obscure* is shrouded or hidden, the opposite of noticeable or *prominent*.
15. **(A)** *Avarice*, or greed, is the antonym of *generosity*.
16. **(A)** *Vivacious* (animated, spirited) and *languid* (listless) are antonyms.
17. **(D)** A person who is *bankrupt* is not *solvent*.
18. **(B)** To *acquiesce* is to agree or comply, while *object* means to oppose.

19. **(A)** *Prodigal* means extravagant. *Frugal* means economical.
20. **(C)** *Plethora* (overabundance) is the opposite of *paucity* (scarcity).
21. **(E)** *Sanctify* (make holy) and *profane* (desecrate) are opposites.
22. **(C)** *Subservient* (servilely submissive) is the opposite of *domineering* (overbearing).
23. **(B)** *Assimilate* (take in as one's own) is the opposite of *reject*.
24. **(E)** *Rigor* (strictness, severity) and *laxity* (lack of strictness) are antonyms.
25. **(D)** *Irreverent* (showing disrespect) is the opposite of *respectful*.

EXERCISE D

1. **(A)** *Noxious* (harmful to health) and *healthful* are antonyms.
2. **(A)** *Garrulous* (ramblingly talkative) and *laconic* (brief, curt) are antonyms.
3. **(C)** *Lugubrious* (melancholy) and *jovial* (joyful) are antonyms.
4. **(B)** *Innocuous* means harmless.
5. **(A)** *Lethargy* (sluggishness, drowsiness) and *alertness* are antonyms.
6. **(A)** That which is *enigmatic* (puzzling) cannot be *obvious*.
7. **(A)** *Temerity* (reckless boldness) and *caution* are antonyms.
8. **(D)** *Cacophony* (discord) and *harmony* are opposites.
9. **(B)** *Tractable* (manageable) and *unruly* (difficult to manage) are opposites.
10. **(A)** To *vilify* is to make abusive and slanderous statements; to *eulogize* is to praise.
11. **(A)** *Erudite* (learned) and *illiterate* are antonyms.
12. **(E)** *Pusillanimous* (cowardly) is the opposite of *courageous*.
13. **(D)** *Propitious* (favorable) is the opposite of *unfavorable*.
14. **(B)** *Steadfast* (firm, unwavering) and *capricious* (changing) are antonyms.
15. **(A)** *Vindictive* (revengeful) is the opposite of *forgiving*.
16. **(A)** *Abstract* means nonspecific and detached; *concrete* means specific and tangible.
17. **(E)** *Spurious* means false, not genuine.
18. **(C)** *Galvanize* is to stir up or stimulate by shock, as opposed to *deaden* or lose life.
19. **(A)** *Evanescent* means vanishing, not lasting.
20. **(B)** *Gregarious* means sociable, fond of the company of others.
21. **(A)** *Fortuitous* (happening by chance) and *premeditated* (planned in advance) are opposites.
22. **(D)** *Desultory* means lacking in method or organization.
23. **(B)** *Abrogate* is to abolish; *institute* is to begin.
24. **(A)** *Amity* is friendliness, the opposite of *hostility*.
25. **(E)** *Travail* is painful, arduous labor, the antonym of *relaxation*.

5

The Sentence Completion Question

The sentence completion questions ask you to choose the best way to complete a sentence from which one or two words have been omitted. These questions test a combination of reading comprehension skills and vocabulary. You must be able to recognize the logic, style, and tone of the sentence, so that you can choose the answer that makes sense in this context. You must also be able to recognize the way words are normally used. At some time in your schooling, you have probably had a vocabulary assignment in which you were asked to define a word and use it in a sentence of your own. In this part of the PSAT, you have to use the words in sentences that are given to you. Once you understand the implications of a sentence, you should be able to choose the answer that will make the sentence clear, logical, and stylistically consistent.

The sentences cover a wide variety of topics of the sort you have probably encountered in your general reading. However, this is not a test of your general knowledge. You may feel more comfortable if you are familiar with the topic the sentence is discussing, but you should be able to handle any of the sentences using your understanding of the English language.

TIPS FOR HANDLING THE SENTENCE COMPLETION QUESTION

1. Before you look at the answer choices, read the sentence and think of words you know that might make sense in the context. You may not come up with the exact word, but you *may* come up with a synonym.
2. Don't be hasty in picking an answer. Test each answer choice, substituting it for the missing word. That way you can satisfy yourself that you have selected the answer that best fits.
3. In double-blank sentences, eliminate answer pairs by testing their first words. Read through the entire sentence. Then insert the first word of each answer pair in the first blank of the sentence. Ask yourself whether this particular word makes sense in this blank. If the initial word of an answer pair makes no sense in the sentence, you can eliminate that answer pair.
4. If you're having vocabulary trouble, look for familiar parts—prefixes, suffixes, and roots—in unfamiliar words.
5. Watch out for negative words and words telling how long something lasts. Only a small change makes these two sentences very different in meaning:

   They were not lovers.
   They were not often lovers.
6. Look for words or phrases which indicate a contrast between one idea and another—words like *although, however, despite,* or *but.* In such cases an antonym or near-antonym for another word in the sentence may provide the correct answer.
7. Look for words or phrases which indicate similarities—words like *in the same way, in addition,* and *also.* In such cases, a synonym or near-synonym for another word in the sentence may provide the correct answer.
8. Look for words or phrases which indicate that one thing causes another—words like *because, since, therefore,* or *thus.*

EXAMPLE 1

See how the first tip works in dealing with the following sentence:

The psychologist set up the experiment to test the rat's ----; he wished to see how well the rat adjusted to the changing conditions it had to face.

Even before you look at the answer choices, you can figure out what the answer *should* be.

Look at the sentence. A psychologist is trying to test some particular quality or characteristic of a rat. What quality? How do you get the answer?

Look at the second part of the sentence, the part following the semicolon (the second clause, in technical terms). This clause defines or clarifies what the psychologist is trying to test. He is trying to see how well the rat *adjusts*. What words does this suggest to you? *Flexibility*, possibly, or *adaptability* comes to mind. Either of these words could logically complete the sentence's thought.

Here are the five answer choices given:
(A) reflexes (B) communicability (C) stamina
(D) sociability (E) adaptability

The best answer clearly is *adaptability*, Choice **E**.

EXAMPLE 2

When you're racing the clock, you feel like marking down the first correct-sounding answer you come across. *Don't*. You may be going too fast.

Because the enemy had a reputation for engaging in sneak attacks, we were ---- on the alert.
(A) frequently (B) furtively (C) evidently
(D) constantly (E) occasionally

A hasty reader might be content with Choice **A**, *frequently*, but *frequently* is not the best fit. The best answer is Choice **D**, *constantly*, because "frequent" periods of alertness would not be enough to provide the necessary protection against sneak attacks that could occur at any time. "Constant" vigilance is called for: the troops would have to be always on the alert.

EXAMPLE 3

Dealing with double-blank sentences can be tricky. It helps to test the first word of each answer pair when you're narrowing things down.

The opossum is ---- the venom of snakes in the rattlesnake subfamily and thus views the reptiles not as ---- enemies but as a food source.
(A) vulnerable to . . natural (B) indicative of . . mortal
(C) impervious to . . lethal (D) sensitive to . . deadly
(E) defenseless against . . potential

Look at the first word of each answer pair. Do any of these words make no sense in the context? The sentence is talking about the way opossums react to rattlesnake poison. What words seem possible? Opossums could be *vulnerable* to this poison, capable of being hurt by it. They could be *sensitive* to it, excessively affected by it. They could be *defenseless* against it, wholly unable to protect themselves from the poison. They could even be *impervious* to it, unaffected by it. But *indicative* of it? The word makes no sense. You can eliminate Choice **B**.

Now examine the second half of the sentence. Opossums look on rattlesnakes as a food source; they eat rattlers. What makes it possible for them to do so? They can do so *because* they're *impervious* to the poison (that is, unharmed by it). That's the reason they can treat the rattlesnake as a potential source of food and not as a *lethal* or deadly enemy. The correct answer is Choice **C**.

Note the cause-and-effect signal *thus*. The nature of the opossum's response to the venom explains *why* it can look on a dangerous snake as an easy prey.

EXAMPLE 4

After a tragedy, many people claim to have had a ---- of disaster.
(A) taste (B) dislike (C) presentiment
(D) context (E) verdict

Use your knowledge of word parts to enable you to deal with unfamiliar words in sentence completion questions.

Take the unfamiliar word *presentiment*. Break it down into parts. A sentiment is a *feeling* (the root *sens* means *feel*). *Pre-* means *before*. A *presentiment* is something you *feel before* it happens, a foreboding. Your best answer is Choice **C**.

EXAMPLE 5

Watch out for *not:* it's easy to overlook, but it's a key word.

Madison was not ---- person and thus made few public addresses; but those he made were memorable, filled with noble phrases.
(A) a reticent (B) a stately (C) an inspiring
(D) an introspective (E) a communicative

What would happen if you overlooked *not* in this question? Probably you'd wind up choosing Choice **A**: Madison was a *reticent* (quiet; reserved) man. *For this reason* he made few public addresses.

Unfortunately, you'd have gotten things backward. The sentence isn't telling you what Madison was like. It's telling you what he was *not* like. And he was not a *communicative* person; he didn't express himself feeely. However, when he did get around to speaking in public, he had valuable things to say.

EXAMPLE 6

We expected him to be jubilant over his victory, but he was ---- instead.
(A) triumphant (B) adult (C) morose
(D) talkative (E) culpable

Watch for words that indicate contrast: *although, however, despite,* or *but.*

But suggests that the winner's expected reaction contrasts with his actual one. Instead of being *jubilant* (extremely joyful), he is sad. The correct answer is Choice **C**, *morose*.

EXAMPLE 7

The simplest animals are those whose bodies are least complex in structure and which do the things done by all animals, such as eating, breathing, moving, and feeling, in the most ---- way.
(A) haphazard (B) bizarre (C) advantageous
(D) primitive (E) unique

The transition word *and* signals you that the writer intends to develop the concept of simplicity introduced in the sentence. You should know from your knowledge of biology that *primitive* life forms were simple in structure and that the more complex forms evolved later. Choice **C** may seem possible. However, to secure the most *advantageous* way of conducting the activities of life, the animal would have to become specialized and complex. Thus, Choice **D** (*primitive*) is best, because it is the only choice which develops the idea of simplicity.

EXAMPLE 8

Because his delivery was ----, the effect of his speech on the voters was nonexistent.
(A) halting (B) plausible (C) moving
(D) respectable (E) audible

Watch for words that show a cause-and-effect relationship: *because, since, therefore,* or *thus.*

What sort of delivery would cause a speech to have no effect? Obviously, you would not expect a moving or eloquent delivery to have such a sorry result. A *halting* or stumbling speech, however, would normally have little or no effect. Thus, Choice **A** is best.

The two tests that follow will give you an indication of your ability to handle these sentence completion questions. Scoring may be interpreted as follows:

43 TO 50—EXCELLENT
35 TO 43—SUPERIOR
27 TO 34—SATISFACTORY
21 TO 26—AVERAGE
20 TO 0—UNSATISFACTORY

SENTENCE COMPLETION TEST A

TIME: 30 MINUTES

Each sentence below has one or two blanks, each blank indicating that something has been omitted. Beneath the sentence are five lettered words or sets of words. Choose the word or set of words for each blank that best fits the meaning of the sentence as a whole.

1. Although the play was not praised by the critics, it did not ---- thanks to favorable word-of-mouth comments.
(A) succeed (B) translate (C) function
(D) close (E) continue

2. Perhaps because something in us instinctively distrusts such displays of natural fluency, some readers approach John Updike's fiction with ----.
(A) indifference (B) suspicion (C) veneration
(D) recklessness (E) bewilderment

3. We lost confidence in him because he never ---- the grandiose promises he had made.
(A) forgot about (B) reneged on (C) tired of
(D) delivered on (E) retreated from

4. Because the hawk is ---- bird, farmers try to keep it away from their chickens.
(A) a migratory (B) an ugly (C) a predatory
(D) a reclusive (E) a huge

5. We were amazed that a man who had been heretofore the most ---- of public speakers could, in a single speech, electrify an audience and bring them cheering to their feet.
(A) enthralling (B) accomplished
(C) pedestrian (D) auspicious (E) masterful

6. If you are trying to make a strong impression on your audience, you cannot do so by being understated, tentative, or ----.
(A) hyperbolic (B) restrained (C) argumentative
(D) authoritative (E) passionate

7. Despite the mixture's ---- nature, we found that by lowering its temperature in the laboratory we could dramatically reduce its tendency to vaporize.
(A) resilient (B) volatile (C) homogeneous
(D) insipid (E) acerbic

8. No other artist rewards the viewer with more sheer pleasure than Miro: he is one of those blessed artists who combine profundity and ---- .
(A) education (B) wisdom (C) faith
(D) fun (E) depth

9. Some Central Intelligence Agency officers have ---- their previous statements denying any involvement on their part with the contra aid network and are now revising their earlier testimony.
(A) justified (B) recanted (C) repeated
(D) protracted (E) heeded

10. New concerns about growing religious tension in northern India were ---- this week after at least fifty people were killed and hundreds were injured or arrested in rioting between Hindus and Moslems.
(A) lessened (B) invalidated (C) restrained
(D) dispersed (E) fueled

11. In a happy, somewhat boisterous celebration of the origins of the United States, the major phase of the Constitution's Bicentennial got off to ---- start on Friday.
(A) a slow (B) a rousing (C) a reluctant
(D) an indifferent (E) a quiet

12. In a revolutionary development in technology, several manufacturers now make biodegradable forms of plastic: some plastic six-pack rings, for example, gradually ---- when exposed to sunlight.
(A) harden (B) stagnate (C) inflate
(D) propagate (E) decompose

13. To alleviate the problem of contaminated chicken, the study panel recommends that the federal government shift its inspection emphasis from cursory bird-by-bird visual checks to a more ---- random sampling for bacterial and chemical contamination.
(A) rigorous (B) perfunctory (C) symbolic
(D) discreet (E) dubious

14. To the dismay of the student body, the class president was ---- berated by the principal at a school assembly.
(A) ignominiously (B) privately
(C) magnanimously (D) fortuitously
(E) inconspicuously

to disgrace

15. Although Barbara Tuchman never earned a graduate degree, she nonetheless ---- a scholarly career as a historian noted for her vivid style and ---- erudition.
(A) interrupted . . deficient
(B) relinquished . . immense
(C) abandoned . . capricious
(D) pursued . . prodigious
(E) followed . . scanty

16. When Frazer's editors at Macmillan tried to ---- his endless augmentations, he insisted on a type size so small and a page so packed as to approach illegibility; and if that proved ----, thinner paper.
(A) protract . . unwarranted
(B) expurgate . . satisfactory
(C) reprimand . . irrelevant
(D) restrict . . insufficient
(E) revise . . idiosyncratic

17. Baldwin's brilliant *The Fire Next Time* is both so eloquent in its passion and so searching in its ---- that it is bound to ---- any reader.
(A) bitterness . . embarrass
(B) romanticism . . appall ← to deeply wonder / grievous word
(C) candor . . unsettle
(D) indifference . . disappoint
(E) conception . . bore

18. Unlike other examples of ---- verse, Milton's *Lycidas* does more than merely mourn for the death of Edward King; it also denounces corruption in the Church in which King was ordained.
(A) satiric (B) elegiac (C) free
(D) humorous (E) didactic

19. We now know that what constitutes practically all of matter is empty space: relatively enormous ---- in which revolve infinitesimal particles so small that they have never been seen or photographed.
(A) crescendos (B) enigmas (C) conglomerates
(D) abstractions (E) voids

20. The officers threatened to take ---- if the lives of their men were ---- by the conquered natives.
(A) liberties . . irritated (B) measures . . enhanced
(C) pains . . destroyed (D) reprisals . . endangered
(E) affront . . enervated

21. Despite his ---- appearance, he was chosen by his employer for a job which required neatness and polish.
(A) unkempt (B) impressive (C) prepossessing
(D) aloof (E) tardy

22. The ---- remarks of the speaker annoyed the audience because they were lengthy as well as meaningless.
(A) lugubrious (B) sarcastic (C) pithy
(D) inane (E) pungent

23. He was so ---- in meeting the payments on his car that the finance company threatened to seize the automobile.
(A) dilatory (B) mercenary (C) solvent
(D) diligent (E) compulsive

24. The earthquake created some damage, but the tidal wave that followed was more devastating because it ---- many villages.
(A) bypassed (B) absorbed (C) desiccated
(D) congested (E) inundated

25. The insurance company rejected his application for accident insurance because his ---- occupation made him a poor risk.
(A) desultory (B) haphazard (C) esoteric
(D) hazardous (E) peripatetic

26. Since we had been promised a definite answer to our proposal, we were ---- by his ---- reply.
(A) pleased . . equivocal (B) vexed . . negative
(C) annoyed . . noncommital
(D) delighted . . dilatory (E) baffled . . decided

27. Because she had a reputation for ----, we were surprised and pleased when she greeted us so ----.
(A) insolence . . informally
(B) insouciance . . cordially
(C) graciousness . . amiably
(D) arrogance . . disdainfully
(E) querulousness . . affably

28. The child was so spoiled by her indulgent parents that she pouted and became ---- when she did not receive all of their attention.
(A) discreet (B) suspicious (C) elated
(D) sullen (E) tranquil

29. Just as disloyalty is the mark of the renegade, ---- is the mark of the ----.
(A) timorousness . . hero (B) temerity . . coward
(C) avarice . . philanthropist
(D) cowardice . . craven (E) vanity . . flatterer

30. He became quite overbearing and domineering once he had become accustomed to the ---- shown to soldiers by the natives; he enjoyed his new sense of power and self-importance.
(A) disrespect (B) apathy (C) deference
(D) culpability (E) enmity

31. The ---- of time had left the castle ----; it towered above the village, looking much as it must have done in Richard the Lion-Hearted's time.
(A) repairs . . destroyed (B) remoteness . . alone
(C) lack . . defended (D) status . . lonely
(E) ravages . . untouched

32. One of the most ---- educators in New York's history, Dr. Shalala ignited a controversy in 1984 by calling the city public schools a "rotten barrel" in need of ---- reform.
(A) disputatious . . little (B) outspoken . . systemic
(C) caustic . . partial (D) indifferent . . pretentious
(E) sycophantic . . superficial

33. The reasoning in this editorial is so ---- that we cannot see how anyone can be deceived by it.
(A) coherent (B) astute (C) cogent
(D) specious (E) dispassionate

34. The ---- of evidence was on the side of the plaintiff since all but one witness testified that his story was correct.
(A) paucity (B) propensity (C) accuracy
(D) brunt (E) preponderance

35. Because Inspector Morse could not contain his scorn for the police commissioner, he was imprudent enough to make ---- remarks about his superior officer.
(A) ambiguous (B) dispassionate
(C) unfathomable (D) interminable (E) scathing

36. Modern architecture has discarded ---- trimming on buildings and has concentrated on an almost Greek simplicity of line.
(A) flamboyant (B) austere (C) inconspicuous
(D) aesthetic (E) derivative

37. If you are seeking ---- that will resolve all our ailments, you are undertaking an impossible task.
(A) a precedent (B) a panacea
(C) an abstraction (D) a direction
(E) a contrivance

38. I have no ---- motive in offering this advice; I seek no personal advantage or honor.
(A) nominal (B) altruistic (C) incongruous
(D) disinterested (E) ulterior

39. This park has been preserved in all its ---- wildness so that visitors in future years may see how people lived during the eighteenth century.
(A) hedonistic (B) prospective (C) esoteric
(D) untrammeled (E) pristine

40. Though she was theoretically a friend of labor, her voting record in Congress ---- that impression.
(A) implied (B) created (C) confirmed
(D) belied (E) maintained

41. The orator was so ---- that the audience became ----.
(A) soporific . . drowsy (B) inaudible . . elated
(C) pompous . . bombastic (D) dramatic . . affable
(E) convincing . . moribund

42. If you carry this ---- attitude to the conference, you will ---- any supporters you may have at this moment.
(A) belligerent . . delight
(B) truculent . . alienate
(C) conciliatory . . defer
(D) supercilious . . attract
(E) flippant . . consolidate

43. The ---- pittance the widow receives from the government cannot keep her from poverty.
(A) magnanimous (B) indulgent
(C) meticulous (D) munificent (E) scanty

44. Harriman, Kennan, and Acheson were part of that inner ---- of the American diplomatic establishment whose distinguished legacy ---- U.S. foreign policy to this day.
(A) circle . . grieves (B) sanctum . . absorbs
(C) core . . dominates (D) life . . biases
(E) coterie . . exacerbates

45. The young man was quickly promoted when his employers saw how ---- he was.
(A) indigent (B) indifferent (C) assiduous
(D) lethargic (E) cursory

46. Because it arrives so early in the season, before many other birds, the robin has been called the ---- of spring.
(A) hostage (B) autocrat (C) compass
(D) newcomer (E) harbinger

47. Shy and hypochondriacal, Madison was uncomfortable at public gatherings; his character made him a most ---- lawmaker and practicing politician.
(A) conscientious (B) unlikely (C) fervent
(D) gregarious (E) effective

48. The tapeworm is an example of ---- organism, one that lives within or on another creature, deriving some or all of its nutriment from its host.
(A) a hospitable (B) an exemplary
(C) a parasitic (D) an autonomous
(E) a protozoan

49. In place of the more general debate about abstract principles of government that most delegates probably expected, the Constitutional Convention put ---- proposals on the table.
(A) theoretical
(B) vague
(C) concrete
(D) tentative
(E) redundant

50. Overindulgence ---- character as well as physical stamina.
(A) strengthens
(B) stimulates
(C) debilitates
(D) maintains
(E) provides

SENTENCE COMPLETION TEST B

TIME: 30 MINUTES

> Each sentence below has one or two blanks, each blank indicating that something has been omitted. Beneath the sentence are five lettered words or sets of words. Choose the word or set of words for each blank that best fits the meaning of the sentence as a whole.

51. The scientist maintains that any hypothesis must explain what has already been discovered and must be constantly ---- by future findings.
(A) confirmed (B) invalidated (C) disregarded
(D) equaled (E) reversed

52. Being cynical, he was reluctant to ---- the ---- of any kind act until he had ruled out all possible secret, uncharitable motives.
(A) question . . benevolence
(B) acknowledge . . wisdom
(C) credit . . unselfishness
(D) endure . . loss
(E) witness . . outcome

53. In view of the interrelationships among a number of the African-American leaders treated in this anthology, there is inevitably a certain amount of ---- among some of the essays presented here.
(A) overlapping (B) inaccuracy (C) pomposity
(D) exaggeration (E) objectivity

54. Hellman was not an ---- woman and thus was hard to get to know; nevertheless, many made the attempt, attracted by her wit and celebrity.
(A) enigmatic (B) eccentric (C) astute
(D) extroverted (E) eminent

55. Most Antarctic animals ---- depend on the tiny shrimplike krill, either feeding on them directly, like the humpback whale, or consuming species that feed on them.
(A) seldom (B) ultimately (C) preferably
(D) immediately (E) marginally

56. Truculent in defending their rights of sovereignty under the Articles of Confederation, the newly formed states ---- constantly.
(A) apologized (B) digressed (C) conferred
(D) acquiesced (E) squabbled

57. If the Titanic had hit the iceberg head on, its watertight compartments might have saved it from ----, but it swerved to avoid the iceberg, and in the collision so many compartments were opened to the sea that disaster was ----.
(A) foundering. . inevitable
(B) sinking . . escaped
(C) damage . . limited
(D) buoyancy . . unavoidable
(E) collapse . . averted

58. Written in an amiable style, the book provides a comprehensive overview of European wines that should prove inviting to both the virtual ---- and the experienced connoisseur.
(A) prodigal (B) novice (C) zealot
(D) miser (E) glutton

59. The sugar dissolved in water ----; finally all that remained was an almost ---- residue on the bottom of the glass.
(A) quickly . . lumpy
(B) immediately . . fragrant
(C) gradually . . imperceptible
(D) subsequently . . glassy
(E) spectacularly . . opaque

60. Traffic speed limits are set at a level that achieves some balance between the danger of ---- speed and the desire of most people to travel as quickly as possible.
(A) marginal (B) normal (C) prudent
(D) inadvertent (E) excessive

61. Although the economy suffers downturns, it also has strong ---- and self-correcting tendencies.
(A) unstable (B) recidivist (C) inauspicious
(D) recuperative (E) self-destructive

62. Since Cyrano de Bergerac did not wish to be under an obligation to any man, he refused to be a ---- of Cardinal Richelieu.
(A) skeptic (B) mentor (C) protege
(D) benefactor (E) predecessor

63. The members of the religious sect ostracized the ---- who had abandoned their faith.
(A) coward (B) suppliant (C) litigant
(D) recreant (E) proselyte

64. I am not attracted by the ---- life of the ----, always wandering through the countryside, begging for charity.
(A) proud . . almsgiver
(B) noble . . philanthropist
(C) affluent . . mendicant
(D) natural . . philosopher
(E) peripatetic . . vagabond

65. They fired upon the enemy from behind trees, walls, and any other ---- point they could find.
(A) conspicuous (B) definitive (C) vantage
(D) exposed (E) indefensible

66. We need more men and women of culture and enlightenment; we have too many ---- among us.
(A) visionaries (B) students (C) philistines
(D) pragmatists (E) philosophers

67. It is foolish to vent your spleen on ---- object; still, you make ---- enemies that way.
(A) an inanimate . . fewer
(B) an immobile . . bitter
(C) an interesting . . curious
(D) an insipid . . dull
(E) a humane . . more

68. After the Japanese attack on Pearl Harbor on December 7, 1941, Japanese-Americans were ---- of being spies for Japan, although there was no ---- to back up this viewpoint.
(A) acquitted . . buttress
(B) tired . . witness
(C) reminded . . reason
(D) suspected . . evidence
(E) exonerated . . money

69. More than one friendly whale has nudged a boat with such ---- that passengers have been knocked overboard.
(A) enthusiasm (B) lethargy (C) hostility
(D) serenity (E) animosity

70. Chaotic in conception but not in ----, Kelly's canvases are as neat as the proverbial pin.
(A) conceit (B) theory (C) execution
(D) origin (E) intent

71. After having worked in the soup kitchen feeding the hungry, the volunteer began to see her own good fortune as ---- and her difference from the ---- as chance rather than destiny.
(A) an omen . . homeless
(B) a fluke . . impoverished
(C) a threat . . destitute
(D) a reward . . indigent
(E) a lie . . affluent

72. Some students are ---- and want to take only the courses for which they see immediate value.
(A) theoretical (B) impartial (C) pragmatic
(D) idealistic (E) opinionated

73. Unlike the Shakespearean plays that lit up the English stage, the "closet dramas" of the nineteenth century were meant to be ---- rather than ----.
(A) seen . . acted (B) read . . staged
(C) quiet . . raucous (D) sophisticated . . urbane
(E) produced . . performed

74. Japan's industrial success is ---- in part to its tradition of group effort and ----, as opposed to the emphasis on personal achievement that is a prominent aspect of other industrial nations.
(A) responsive . . independence
(B) related . . introspection
(C) equivalent . . solidarity
(D) subordinate . . individuality
(E) attributed . . cooperation

75. I was so bored with the verbose and redundant style of Victorian novelists that I welcomed the change to the ---- style of Hemingway.
(A) prolix (B) consistent (C) terse
(D) logistical (E) florid

76. As ---- head of the organization, he attended social functions and civic meetings but had no ---- in the formulation of company policy.
(A) titular . . voice (B) hypothetical . . vote
(C) former . . pride (D) nominal . . competition
(E) actual . . say

77. Her listeners enjoyed her ---- wit but her victims often ---- at its satire.
(A) lugubrious . . suffered (B) caustic . . laughed
(C) kindly . . smarted (D) subtle . . smiled
(E) trenchant . . winced

78. It is only to the vain that all is vanity; and all is ---- only to those who have never been ---- themselves.
(A) arrogance . . proud of
(B) deception . . sincere with
(C) cowardice . . afraid for
(D) indolence . . bored by
(E) solitude . . left to

79. No act of ---- was more pronounced than his refusal of any rewards for his discovery.
(A) abeyance (B) submission (C) egoism
(D) denunciation (E) abnegation

80. The evil of class and race hatred must be eliminated while it is still in an ---- state; otherwise it may grow to dangerous proportions.
(A) amorphous (B) embryonic (C) uncultivated
(D) overt (E) independent

81. She is a pragmatist, as ---- to base her future on impractical dreams as she would be to build a castle on shifting sand.
(A) determined (B) disinclined (C) quick
(D) apt (E) diligent

82. Aimed at curbing European attempts to seize territory in the Americas, the Monroe Doctrine was a warning to ---- foreign powers.
(A) pertinacious (B) credulous (C) remote
(D) overt (E) predatory

83. Although Josephine Tey is arguably as good a mystery writer as Agatha Christie, she is clearly far less ---- than Christie, having written only six books in comparison to Christie's sixty.
(A) coherent (B) prolific (C) equivocal
(D) pretentious (E) gripping

84. The systems analyst hesitated to talk to strangers about his highly specialized work, fearing it was too ---- for people uninitiated in the computer field to understand.
(A) intriguing (B) derivative (C) frivolous
(D) esoteric (E) rudimentary

85. Through her work at the Center for the Family in Transition, Wallerstein has come to see divorce not as a single circumscribed event but as ---- of changing family relationships—as a process that begins during the failing marriage and extends over many years.
(A) a continuum (B) an episode (C) a parody
(D) a denial (E) a curtailment

86. A code of ethics governing the behavior of physicians during epidemics did not exist until 1846, when it was ---- by the American Medical Association.
(A) rescinded (B) promulgated (C) presupposed
(D) depreciated (E) implied

87. Both *China Beach* and *Tour of Duty* reflect the way dissent has become ---- in America; what were radical antiwar attitudes in the 1960s are now ---- TV attitudes.
(A) domesticated . . mainstream
(B) obsolete . . militant
(C) meaningful . . unfashionable
(D) sensationalized . . trite
(E) troublesome . . conventional

88. MacDougall's former editors remember him as a ---- man whose ---- and exhaustive reporting was worth the trouble.
(A) domineering . . wearisome
(B) congenial . . pretentious
(C) popular . . supercilious
(D) fastidious . . garbled
(E) cantankerous . . meticulous

89. Americans have always been rightfully ---- unnecessary government coercion, feeling that the government should use its powers sparingly.
(A) disarmed by (B) chary about
(C) dependent on (D) amenable to
(E) enthusiastic about

90. Lavish in visual beauty, the film *Lawrence of Arabia* also boasts ---- of style: it knows how much can be shown in a shot, how much can be said in a few words.
(A) nonchalance (B) economy (C) autonomy
(D) frivolity (E) arrogance

91. We must try to understand his momentary ----, for he has ---- more strain and anxiety than any among us.
(A) outcry . . described (B) senility . . understood
(C) vision . . forgotten (D) generosity . . desired
(E) aberration . . undergone

92. He is ---- opponent; you must respect and fear him at all times.
(A) a redoubtable (B) a disingenuous
(C) a pugnacious (D) an insignificant
(E) a craven

93. Your ---- tactics may compel me to cancel the contract as the job must be finished on time.
(A) dilatory (B) offensive (C) repugnant
(D) infamous (E) confiscatory

94. The mind of a bigot is like the pupil of the eye: the more light you pour upon it, the more it will ----.
(A) blink (B) veer (C) stare
(D) reflect (E) contract

95. In the North American tribes, men were the representational artists; women, on the other hand, traditionally ---- abstract, geometrical compositions.
(A) decried (B) shunned (C) devised
(D) impaired (E) prefigured

96. By its very nature, printmaking was judged ---- the aims of most Impressionist painters, who believed that its technical procedures ---- spontaneity and failed to render the transient appearance of nature.
(A) antithetical to . . defeated
(B) indicative of . . enhanced
(C) conducive to . . increased
(D) warranted by . . encouraged
(E) incumbent on . . bypassed

97. Breaking with established artistic and social conventions, Dali was ---- genius whose heterodox works infuriated the traditionalists of his day.
(A) a derivative (B) an iconoclastic
(C) an uncontroversial (D) a venerated
(E) a trite

98. Dr. Smith cautioned that the data so far are not sufficiently ---- to warrant dogmatic assertions by either side in the debate.
(A) hypothetical (B) tentative (C) controversial
(D) unequivocal (E) imponderable

99. Mr. Wilson sets out only the broad contours of a new policy agenda, leaving it to others to ---- specific initiatives.
(A) ignore
(B) mold
(C) apprehend
(D) forestall
(E) regret

100. The concept of individual freedom grew from political and moral convictions that were to ---- the closed and ---- world of feudalism into a more open and dynamic society.
(A) galvanize . . vibrant (B) convert . . irreverent
(C) transform . . hierarchical (D) recast . . vital
(E) merge . . unregulated

ANSWER KEY

Test A

1. D	11. B	21. A	31. E	41. A
2. B	12. E	22. D	32. B	42. B
3. D	13. A	23. A	33. D	43. E
4. C	14. A	24. E	34. E	44. C
5. C	15. D	25. D	35. E	45. C
6. B	16. D	26. C	36. A	46. E
7. B	17. C	27. E	37. B	47. B
8. D	18. B	28. D	38. E	48. C
9. B	19. E	29. D	39. E	49. C
10. E	20. D	30. C	40. D	50. C

Test B

51. A	61. D	71. B	81. B	91. E
52. C	62. C	72. C	82. E	92. A
53. A	63. D	73. B	83. B	93. A
54. D	64. E	74. E	84. D	94. E
55. B	65. C	75. C	85. A	95. C
56. E	66. C	76. A	86. B	96. A
57. A	67. A	77. E	87. A	97. B
58. B	68. D	78. B	88. E	98. D
59. C	69. A	79. E	89. B	99. B
60. E	70. C	80. B	90. B	100. C

6

The Analogy Question

In the PSAT/NMSQT, the analogy question presents a pair of words followed by five additional pairs of words. You must select the pair of words from among the five choices which best matches the relationship existing between the first two words.

These are the questions that people seem to think of most often when they think about the PSAT. Analogies may well be the most difficult kind of question on the test, but they aren't impossible, and at least some of them will be fairly easy. Questions of this kind test your understanding of the relationships among words and ideas. You are given one pair and must choose another pair that is related in the same way. Many relationships are possible. The two terms in the pair can be synonyms; one term can be a cause, the other the effect; one can be a tool, the other the user.

LONG-RANGE STRATEGY

Continue to build up your vocabulary and to study the connotations as well as the literal meanings of words. Read in a wide variety of fields. Pay particular attention to specialized technical words for things people use (*mortar, vise, blueprint*) and for natural phenomena (*foliage, chaff, eddy*). Also, be sure you know the terms for the common types of relationships that exist among people and animals (*sister* and *sibling*; *mare* and *foal*; *lion* and *pride*).

TIPS TO HELP YOU COPE WITH ANALOGY QUESTIONS

1. Consider the first pair in each question carefully, and try to make a clear sentence using the two terms. Then look at the other pairs. It should be possible to substitute the correct answer (and only the correct answer) into your sentence and still have the sentence make sense.

2. Do not be misled if the choices are from different fields or areas, or seem to deal with different items, from the given pair. Study the capitalized words until you see the connection between them; then search for the same relationship among the choices.
BOTANIST : MICROSCOPE : : CARPENTER : HAMMER, even though the two workers may have little else in common besides their use of tools.

3. If more than one answer choice fits, try making your sentence more specific. Example:

> **MITTEN : HAND : :**
> **(A) bracelet : wrist (B) belt : waist**
> **(C) muffler : neck (D) ring : finger**
> **(E) sandal : foot**

You make up the sentence, "You wear a mitten on your hand." Unfortunately, *all* the answer choices will fit that sentence, so you say to yourself, "Why do you wear a mitten? You wear a mitten to keep your hand warm." Now when you try to substitute, only Choice **C** works, so you have your answer.

4. Beware of words that can have more than one meaning. A simple word like *lie* can mean either recline or fib. If you get one meaning fixed too firmly in your mind, you may miss the point of the analogy.

5. Be particularly careful of words that have different meanings when they are pronounced differently. Suppose you are given the analogy SOW : SEED. If you keep thinking of *sow* as a female pig, the analogy makes no sense. But if you change your pronunciation, you will remember that *sow* also means to plant. Try to keep flexible.

6. Be guided by what you know about parts of speech. If the capitalized words are a noun and a verb, each of your answer pairs will be a noun and a verb. If the capitalized words are an adjective and a noun, each of your answer pairs will be an adjective and a noun. Even if you don't recognize the parts of speech of the capitalized words, you can still work things out: if you can recognize the parts of speech in a single answer pair, you know the parts of speech of all the other answer pairs, and of the original pair as well. This information can help you recognize analogy types and spot the use of unfamiliar or secondary meanings of words.

7. Watch out for errors caused by eye-catchers. These are incorrect answer choices *designed* to catch your eye. Eye-catchers grab your attention because they somehow remind you of one of the capitalized words. For example, if the original pair of words is ARMOR : BODY (armor *protects* the body), a good eye-catcher would be HELMET : STEEL (a helmet *is made of* steel).

8. Eliminate answer choices whose terms are only casually linked. In your capitalized pair of words (and in your correct answer choice), the words are always clearly linked:

Armor *protects* the body.
A shepherd *is someone who* herds sheep.
A chapter *is a division of* a book.

In the answer pairs, the relationship between the words can be pretty vague. There's a clear dictionary relationship between *chapter* and *book*. There's no necessary relationship between *chapter* and *pencil*.

9. Watch out for errors stemming from grammatical reversals. Ask yourself *who* is doing what to whom. FUGITIVE : FLEE is not the same as LAUGHINGSTOCK : MOCK. A fugitive is the person who flees. A laughingstock is the person who *is mocked*.

10. Remember that the test-makers usually place more difficult analogies toward the end of the analogy section. Therefore, if one of the final analogy questions in a set looks simple, *suspect a trap*.

11. Be familiar with the whole range of common analogy types. Know the usual ways in which pairs of words on the PSAT are linked.

Common Analogy Types

Synonyms
DAUNTLESS : COURAGEOUS
Dauntless (fearless) and *courageous* are synonyms.

Synonym Variant
DAUNTLESS : COURAGE
Someone *dauntless* shows *courage*.

Antonyms
DAUNTLESS : COWARDLY
Dauntless and *cowardly* are antonyms.

Antonym Variant
DAUNTLESS : COWARDICE
Someone *dauntless* does not exhibit *cowardice*.

Worker and Work Created
POET : SONNET
A *poet* creates a *sonnet*.

Worker and Tool
PAINTER : BRUSH
A *painter* uses a *brush*.

Tool and Object Worked On
SAW : WOOD
A *saw* cuts *wood*.

Function
CROWBAR : PRY
A *crowbar* is a tool used to *pry*.

Action and Its Significance
NOD : ASSENT
A *nod* is a sign of *assent* (agreement).

Manner
STAMMER : TALK
To *stammer* is to *talk* in a halting manner.

Degree of Intensity
LUKEWARM : BOILING
Lukewarm is less intense than *boiling*.

Class and Member
MAMMAL : WHALE
A *whale* is a member of the class known as *mammal*.

Defining Characteristic
TIGER : CARNIVOROUS
A *tiger* is by definition a *carnivorous* (meat-eating) animal.

Part to Whole
ISLAND : ARCHIPELAGO
An *archipelago* (chain of islands) is made up of many *islands*.

Sex
DOE : STAG
A *doe* is a female deer; a *stag*, a male deer.

Age
DEER : FAWN
A *fawn* is a young *deer*.

Symbol and Abstraction It Represents
DOVE : PEACE
A *dove* is the symbol of *peace*.

Use these tips to help you with the following examples.

EXAMPLE 1

CONSTELLATION : STARS : :
(A) prison : bars (B) assembly : speaker
(C) troupe : actors (D) mountain : peak
(E) flock : shepherds

A *constellation* is made up of *stars*. A *troupe* (not *troop* but *troupe*) is made up of *actors* (and actresses, of course). Choice **C** is correct.

Note, by the way, the characteristics of the analogy you have just analyzed. The relationship between the words in CONSTELLATION : STARS is built-in: if you look up *constellation* in a dictionary, you will see that a constellation is a group of stars. The words are related *by definition*. The relationship is clear. You can phrase your linking sentence in several ways:

"A *constellation* is made up of *stars*."

"A *constellation* is a group of *stars*."

"A *constellation* is composed of *stars*."

"The specific term for a group of *stars* is *constellation*."

However, the essential relationship between the words is unchanged.

Your correct answer choice must have the same characteristics as the original pair. The words must have a clear relationship. They must be related *by definition*. If you substitute them in your linking sentence, they have got to fit—*tight*.

EXAMPLE 2

SKYCAP : AIRPORT : :
(A) stenographer : office (B) cashier : box office
(C) waitress : restaurant (D) actress : theater
(E) typist : paper

If you word your sentence "A *skycap* works at an *airport*," you will find that Choices **A, B, C,** and **D** are all good analogies. At this point, take a second look at the original relationship. A skycap works at an airport, true. What else do you know about a skycap's work? For one, he carries things for people. What's more, when he works at the airport, he relies on tips.

Refine your original sentence to include these additional facts. "A *skycap* carries bags for travelers at the *airport* in the hope of earning tips." Now test the answers. Only one answer fits: "A *waitress* carries food for patrons at a *restaurant* in the hope of earning tips." Choice **C** is the correct answer.

Your sentence should reflect the relationship between the two capitalized words *exactly*. If it doesn't, try, try again.

EXAMPLE 3

COMPOSER : SYMPHONY : :
(A) porter : terminal (B) writer : plagiarism
(C) coach : team (D) painter : mural
(E) doctor : stethoscope

A composer creates a symphony. You therefore are looking for a relationship between a worker and a work he or she has created. You can easily eliminate Choices **A** and **E**; a porter works *at* a terminal; a doctor works *with* a stethoscope. You can also eliminate Choice **C**: no coach literally *creates* a team in the same way that a composer creates a symphony.

Writers and painters, however, both create works of art. Which answer is correct, **B** *or* **D**?

If you do not know the meanings of *plagiarism* and *mural*, think of a context for one (or both) of them. Someone is "accused of plagiarism." From this you can infer that *plagiarism* is a crime (passing off someone else's work as one's own), not a created work. A *mural* is a picture painted on a wall. The correct answer is Choice **D**.

EXAMPLE 4

EROSION : ROCKS : :
(A) flatness : landscape (B) fatigue : task
(C) fasting : food (D) dissipation : character
(E) forgery : signature

The idea of a wearing away of a substance (the *erosion* of *rocks*) is repeated in Choice **D**. *Dissipation* implies a wasting away of energies, which results in a loss of *character*.

Note that you are dealing with a secondary meaning. *Character* is not used here as a synonym for *nature*. It is used instead with the meaning of a person's *moral constitution*.

EXAMPLE 5

CAMPAIGN : OBJECTIVE : :
(A) motivation : goal (B) misdeed : consequence
(C) victory : triumph (D) talent : success
(E) voyage : destination

Just as the goal of a *campaign* is defined as its *objective*, the goal of a *voyage* is defined as its *destination*. Choice **E** is correct.

Note that, while a *misdeed* may have *consequences*, these consequences are not its intended goal.

ANALOGY EXERCISES

To develop your ability to handle analogy questions, work your way through the following four exercises. *Warning:* These exercises are graded in difficulty. The further you go, the harder the items get, just as on a video game. Go all the way. Even if you do less well on Exercise D than you did on Exercise A, look on every error as an opportunity to learn. Study all the analogies you found difficult. Remember these are *all* typical PSAT analogy types.

After completing each exercise, see how many questions you answered correctly. (The correct answers are given on page 68.) Then *read these answer explanations*. Pay particular attention to the way the analogies are expressed in clear, concise sentences. Your job is to learn to express these relationships in sentences just as concise and clear.

Each question below consists of a related pair of words or phrases, followed by five lettered pairs of words or phrases. Select the lettered pair that best expresses a relationship similar to that expressed in the original pair.

Example:

YAWN : BOREDOM ::
(A) dream : sleep
(B) anger : madness
(C) smile : amusement
(D) face : expression
(E) impatience : rebellion

Ⓐ Ⓑ ● Ⓓ Ⓔ

EXERCISE A

1. MASON : WALL ::
(A) artist : easel
(B) fisherman : trout
(C) author : book
(D) congressman : senator
(E) sculptor : museum

2. STUDENT : KNOWLEDGE ::
(A) hypocrite : truth
(B) prospector : gold
(C) disciple : discipline
(D) hermit : society
(E) actor : rehearsal

3. FIRE : ASHES ::
(A) accident : delay
(B) wood : splinters
(C) water : waves
(D) regret : melancholy
(E) event : memories

4. GOOSE : GANDER ::
(A) duck : drake
(B) hen : chicken
(C) sheep : flock
(D) dog : kennel
(E) horse : bridle

5. PREDICT : FORETELL ::
(A) procrastinate : expedite
(B) lie : prevaricate
(C) prophesy : vindicate
(D) anticipate : participate
(E) magnify : diminish

6. CARPENTER : SAW ::
(A) stenographer : typewriter
(B) painter : brush
(C) lawyer : brief
(D) seamstress : scissors
(E) runner : sneakers

7. CAPTAIN : SHOALS ::
(A) lawyer : litigation
(B) pilot : radar
(C) soldier : ambush
(D) doctor : hospital
(E) corporal : sergeant

8. WARM : FEVERISH ::
(A) tepid : lukewarm
(B) industrious : indolent
(C) tepid : frozen
(D) angry : irate
(E) moist : soaked

9. RAZOR : BEARD ::
(A) scythe : time
(B) sickle : grass
(C) carburetor : gasoline
(D) student : class
(E) barber : hair

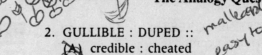

10. HORNS : BULL ::
(A) mane : lion
(B) wattles : turkey
(C) antlers : stag
(D) hoofs : horse
(E) wings : eagle

11. TIGER : ZOOLOGY ::
(A) insect : etymology
(B) tiger lily : botany
(C) granite : biology
(D) butterfly : anthropology
(E) essay : prosody

12. CHAIRPERSON : BOARD ::
(A) mascot : gang
(B) captain : team
(C) wolf : pack
(D) foe : battle
(E) politician : platform

13. FROG : AMPHIBIAN ::
(A) whale : mammalian
(B) otter : crustacean
(C) cow : herbivorous
(D) dog : loyal
(E) trout : reptilian

14. JUDGE : COURTHOUSE ::
(A) carpenter : bench
(B) lawyer : brief
(C) architect : blueprint
(D) surgeon : hospital
(E) landlord : studio

15. PAUPER : MONEY ::
(A) banker : debtors
(B) teacher : school
(C) author : publisher
(D) pugilist : ring
(E) moron : intelligence

EXERCISE B

1. HELMET : HEAD ::
(A) pedal : foot
(B) gun : hand
(C) breastplate : chest
(D) pendant : neck
(E) knapsack : back

2. GULLIBLE : DUPED ::
(A) credible : cheated
(B) careful : cautioned
(C) malleable : molded
(D) myopic : diagnosed
(E) articulate : silenced

3. FOLLY : SENSE ::
(A) insolvency : funds
(B) plagiarism : books
(C) beauty : beholder
(D) piety : religion
(E) anxiety : care

4. MOCK : CONTEMPT ::
(A) falsify : mimicry
(B) scold : disapproval
(C) imitate : respect
(D) anticipate : fear
(E) atone : retribution

5. CONDIMENT : FOOD ::
(A) additive : milk
(B) wit : conversation
(C) tenement : building
(D) prescription : patient
(E) brochure : book

6. DUNGEON : CONFINEMENT ::
(A) church : chapel
(B) school : truant
(C) asylum : refuge
(D) hospital : mercy
(E) courthouse : remorse

7. GRIDIRON : FOOTBALL ::
(A) net : tennis
(B) saddle : racing
(C) round : boxing
(D) puck : hockey
(E) diamond : baseball

8. HERMIT : GREGARIOUS ::
(A) miser : penurious
(B) ascetic : hedonistic
(C) coward : pusillanimous
(D) scholar : literate
(E) crab : crustacean

9. CLANDESTINE : OVERT ::
(A) thorough : complete
(B) limited : unrestrained
(C) warm : feverish
(D) circular : oval
(E) vacillating : tentative

10. PINE : YEARN ::
(A) amaze : astonish
(B) whisper : shout
(C) meander : march
(D) strive : prosper
(E) collect : scatter

11. WINE : VINTNER ::
(A) tobacco : smoker
(B) meat : packer
(C) water : plumber
(D) beer : brewer
(E) oil : masseur

12. MENDACITY : HONESTY ::
(A) courage : cravenness
(B) truth : beauty
(C) strength : fortitude
(D) unsophistication : ingenuousness
(E) hirsuteness : hair

13. PREFACE : BOOK ::
(A) prologue : play
(B) presage : folly
(C) preamble : poem
(D) appendix : text
(E) couplet : sonnet

14. LAUREL : VICTORY ::
(A) black cat : defeat
(B) fig leaf : license
(C) olive branch : peace
(D) lantern : caution
(E) flag : triumph

15. EXPERIENCE : KNOWLEDGE ::
(A) purgative : disease
(B) poison : death
(C) growth : investment
(D) beauty : cosmetics
(E) truth : memory

EXERCISE C

1. MARATHON : STAMINA ::
(A) relay : independence
(B) hurdle : perseverance
(C) sprint : celerity
(D) jog : weariness
(E) ramble : directness

2. NAIVE : INGENUE ::
(A) ordinary : genius
(B) venerable : celebrity
(C) urbane : sophisticate
(D) crafty : artisan
(E) modest : braggart

3. HULKING : MASSIVE ::
(A) pert : polite
(B) brutal : compulsive
(C) raucous : harsh
(D) furtive : ironic
(E) trite : remarkable

4. DISASTER : LUGUBRIOUS ::
(A) fruition : satisfied
(B) success : saturnine
(C) catastrophe : fatal
(D) tragedy : complacent
(E) failure : gay

5. ASSEMBLE : GATHER ::
(A) dismiss : hasten
(B) proclaim : confide
(C) garner : squander
(D) select : collect
(E) feign : dissemble

6. RETOUCH : PHOTOGRAPH ::
(A) hang : painting
(B) finger : fabric
(C) retract : statement
(D) compose : melody
(E) refine : style

7. HONESTY : HYPOCRISY ::
(A) pacifism : belligerence
(B) treachery : duplicity
(C) pugnacity : intolerance
(D) integrity : righteousness
(E) magnanimity : greatness

8. INDIGENT : WEALTH ::
(A) contented : happiness
(B) aristocratic : stature
(C) smug : complacency
(D) emaciated : nourishment
(E) variegated : variety

9. SHALE : GEOLOGIST ::
(A) catacombs : entomologist
(B) aster : botanist
(C) obelisk : fireman
(D) love : philologist
(E) reef : astrologer

10. FLEETING : DURATION ::
(A) glancing : distance
(B) concise : length
(C) rapid : leisure
(D) grim : manner
(E) fragrant : smell

11. DIDACTIC : TEACH ::
(A) sophomoric : learn
(B) satiric : mock
(C) reticent : complain
(D) chaotic : rule
(E) apologetic : deny

12. SOPORIFIC : SLEEP ::
(A) calorific : hunger
(B) insipid : flavor
(C) honorific : embarrassment
(D) worrisome : anxiety
(E) obtuse : insight

13. HACKNEYED : ORIGINAL ::
(A) mature : juvenile
(B) trite : morbid
(C) withdrawn : reserved
(D) evasive : elusive
(E) derivative : traditional

14. AUGER : CARPENTER ::
(A) studio : sculptor
(B) awl : cobbler
(C) seam : seamstress
(D) cement : mason
(E) apron : chef

15. MUSTER : CREW ::
(A) convene : committee
(B) demobilize : troops
(C) dominate : opposition
(D) cheer : team
(E) dismiss : jury

EXERCISE D

1. DWELL : DENIZEN ::
(A) shun : outcast
(B) inherit : heir
(C) squander : miser
(D) obey : autocrat
(E) patronize : protege

2. HAZARDOUS : PERIL ::
(A) supercilious : modesty
(B) innovative : novelty
(C) venerable : immaturity
(D) antagonistic : apathy
(E) competitive : pride

3. LAUDABLE : PRAISE ::
(A) imperturbable : agitation
(B) fragile : stability
(C) contemptible : scorn
(D) enamored : love
(E) fastidious : taste

4. OPHTHALMOLOGIST : EYES ::
(A) podiatrist : feet
(B) cardiologist : brain
(C) bacteriologist : atoms
(D) numismatist : nerves
(E) pediatrician : bones

5. MEANDERING : DIRECT ::
(A) menacing : ambitious
(B) affable : permissive
(C) digressive : concise
(D) circuitous : roundabout
(E) aboveboard : open

6. IRON : RUST ::
(A) yeast : mold
(B) bronze : patina
(C) cake : icing
(D) stone : gravel
(E) coal : dust

7. EPHEMERAL : LAST ::
(A) competitive : contend
(B) indispensable : suffice
(C) perishable : die
(D) insignificant : matter
(E) transient : travel

8. DONOR : GIFT :
(A) prophet : prediction
(B) zealot : detachment
(C) advisee : counsel
(D) braggart : attention
(E) mourner : sympathy

9. ACT : DRAMA ::
(A) chapter : essay
(B) aria : opera
(C) platoon : company
(D) grade : course
(E) blueprint : building

10. CEMENT : TROWEL ::
   (A) lawn : rake
   (B) conflagration : match
   (C) paint : brush
   (D) floor : polish
   (E) wallpaper : ladder

11. PIGHEADED : YIELD ::
   (A) lionhearted : retreat
   (B) lilylivered : flee
   (C) dogged : pursue
   (D) featherbrained : giggle
   (E) eagle-eyed : discern

12. UNCTUOUS : SINCERITY ::
   (A) fatuous : ambivalence
   (B) unclean : impunity
   (C) avuncular : benevolence
   (D) frivolous : gravity
   (E) hypocritical : virtue

13. PIRATE : BUCCANEER ::
   (A) sailor : beachcomber
   (B) puritan : virtuoso
   (C) captain : admiral
   (D) wanderer : nomad
   (E) cynic : flatterer

14. ALARM : TRIGGER ::
   (A) prison : escape
   (B) tunnel : dig
   (C) criminal : corner
   (D) fright : allay
   (E) trap : spring

15. QUOTATION : QUOTATION MARKS ::
   (A) remark : colon
   (B) sentence : period
   (C) aside : parentheses
   (D) clause : semicolon
   (E) interjection : exclamation point

ANSWER KEY

EXERCISE A

1. C	4. A	7. C	10. C	13. A
2. B	5. B	8. E	11. B	14. D
3. E	6. D	9. B	12. B	15. E

EXERCISE B

1. C	4. B	7. E	10. A	13. A
2. C	5. B	8. B	11. D	14. C
3. A	6. C	9. B	12. A	15. B

EXERCISE C

1. C	4. A	7. A	10. B	13. A
2. C	5. E	8. D	11. B	14. B
3. C	6. E	9. B	12. D	15. A

EXERCISE D

1. B	4. A	7. D	10. C	13. D
2. B	5. C	8. A	11. A	14. E
3. C	6. B	9. C	12. E	15. C

ANSWER EXPLANATIONS

EXERCISE A

1. **(C)** A *mason* (stoneworker) creates a *wall*. An *author* creates a *book*.
2. **(B)** A *student* seeks *knowledge*. A *prospector* seeks *gold*.
3. **(E)** A *fire* leaves behind *ashes*. An *event* leaves behind *memories*.
4. **(A)** A *gander* is a male *goose*. A *drake* is a male *duck*.
5. **(B)** Someone who can *predict* the future can be said to *foretell* it. Someone who is known to *lie* can be said to *prevaricate* or speak falsely.
6. **(D)** A *carpenter* uses a *saw* to cut things. A *seamstress* uses *scissors* to cut things.
7. **(C)** A *captain* must beware of *shoals*, shallow areas or sandbanks in the water. A *soldier* must beware of an *ambush*.
8. **(E)** *Warm* is less extreme in heat than *feverish*. *Moist* is less extreme in wetness than *soaked*.
9. **(B)** One uses a *razor* to cut a *beard*. One uses a *sickle*, a farm tool, to cut *grass* or grain.
10. **(C)** A *bull* has sharp *horns* on his head. A *stag* (male deer) has sharp *antlers* on his head.
11. **(B)** *Zoology*, the study of animals, would include a particular animal, the *tiger*. *Botany*, the study of plants, would include a particular plant, the *tiger lily*.
12. **(B)** The *chairperson* is the head of the *board*. The *captain* is the head of the *team*.
13. **(A)** The *frog* is a member of the *amphibian* class, adapted to live both on the land and in the water. The *whale* is a member of the *mammalian* class, adapted to feed its young with milk from the mother.
14. **(D)** A *judge* works in a *courthouse*. A *surgeon* works in a *hospital*.
15. **(E)** A *pauper* has very little *money*. A *moron* has very little *intelligence*.

EXERCISE B

1. **(C)** A *helmet* protects one's *head*. A *breastplate*, a piece of armor, protects one's *chest*.
2. **(C)** A person who is *gullible* is easily fooled or *duped*. A person who is *malleable* (impressionable) is easily influenced or *molded*.
3. **(A)** A person engaged in *folly* or foolishness lacks *sense*. A person in a state of *insolvency* or bankruptcy lacks *funds*.
4. **(B)** A person who *mocks* shows *contempt*. A person who *scolds* shows *disapproval*.
5. **(B)** A *condiment* enhances *food*. *Wit* enhances *conversation*.
6. **(C)** A *dungeon* by definition is a place of *confinement*. An *asylum* by definition is a place of *refuge*.
7. **(E)** People play *football* on a field called a *gridiron*. People play *baseball* on a field called a *diamond*.
8. **(B)** A *hermit*, who chooses to live alone, is by definition not *gregarious* (companionable and outgoing). An *ascetic*, who chooses a life of self-denial, is by definition not *hedonistic* (devoted to pleasure).
9. **(B)** An activity which is *clandestine* (secret) is not *overt* or unconcealed. An activity which is *limited* (within boundaries) is not *unrestrained* or free of restrictions.
10. **(A)** To *pine* (to long for or to languish) means to *yearn*. To *amaze* (to astound) means to *astonish*.
11. **(D)** A *vintner* is a person who makes *wine*. A *brewer* is a person who makes *beer*.
12. **(A)** *Mendacity* or untruthfulness is the opposite of *honesty*. *Courage* is the opposite of *cravenness* or cowardice.
13. **(A)** A *preface* is an introduction at the beginning of a *book*. A *prologue* is an introduction at the beginning of a *play*.
14. **(C)** A wreath made from the *laurel* tree symbolizes *victory*. An *olive branch* symbolizes *peace*.
15. **(B)** *Experience* leads to *knowledge*. *Poison* leads to *death*.

EXERCISE C

1. **(C)** A *marathon* (very long race) requires *stamina* or endurance. A *sprint* (very short race) requires *celerity* or speed.
2. **(C)** An *ingenue* or inexperienced young person is *naive* (innocent, frank). A *sophisticate* or worldly person is *urbane* (suave, elegantly polite).
3. **(C)** *Hulking* means bulky or *massive*. *Raucous* means grating or *harsh*.
4. **(A)** A person is *lugubrious* or mournful after a *disaster*. A person is *satisfied* after the *fruition* (attainment or completion) of something desired.
5. **(E)** To *assemble* things is to *gather* them. To *feign* or deceive is to *dissemble*.
6. **(E)** To *retouch* a *photograph* is to alter its appearance, to free it from imperfections. To *refine* a *style* is to free it from imperfections as well.
7. **(A)** *Honesty* is the opposite of *hypocrisy* (pretending to be what one isn't). *Pacifism*, a policy of peace, is the opposite of *belligerence* (being warlike, eager to fight).
8. **(D)** Someone who is *indigent* or poor lacks *wealth*. Someone who is *emaciated* or abnormally thin lacks *nourishment*.
9. **(B)** A *geologist*, who studies rocks, deals with *shale*, a particular kind of rock. A *botanist*, who studies plants, deals with the *aster*, a particular flower.

10. **(B)** Something *fleeting* is brief in *duration*. Something *concise* is brief in *length*.
11. **(B)** *Didactic* by definition means inclined to *teach*. *Satiric* by definition means inclined to *mock*.
12. **(D)** *Soporific* means inducing or causing *sleep*. *Worrisome* means inducing or causing *anxiety*.
13. **(A)** *Hackneyed* (worn, trite) is the opposite of *original* or novel. *Mature* is the opposite of *juvenile*.
14. **(B)** An *auger* or bit is a tool used by a *carpenter*. An *awl* (tool for piercing holes in leather) is a tool used by a *cobbler* or shoemaker.
15. **(A)** To *muster* a ship's *crew* is to assemble or gather the members together. To *convene* a *committee* is to assemble or gather its members together.

EXERCISE D

1. **(B)** A *denizen* (resident) by definition *dwells* or resides in a region. An *heir* by definition *inherits* or receives a legacy from someone who has died.
2. **(B)** Something *hazardous* (dangerous) is characterized by *peril* (danger). Something *innovative* (new in form or design) is characterized by *novelty* (newness, originality).
3. **(C)** *Laudable* means praiseworthy or deserving *praise*. *Contemptible* means despicable or deserving *scorn*.
4. **(A)** An *ophthalmologist* specializes in the care of the *eyes*. A *podiatrist* specializes in the care of the *feet*.
5. **(C)** *Meandering* (proceeding by an indirect course) and *direct* are antonyms. *Digressive* (departing from the main subject) and *concise* (keeping brief and to the point) are antonyms.
6. **(B)** The covering of *iron* caused by oxidation is called *rust*. The covering of *bronze* is called a *patina*.
7. **(D)** Something *ephemeral* by definition does not *last*. Something *insignificant* by definition does not *matter*.
8. **(A)** A *donor* or benefactor makes a *gift*. A *prophet* or seer makes a *prediction*.
9. **(C)** A *drama* or play is divided into *acts*. A military *company* is divided into *platoons*.
10. **(C)** *Cement* is applied with a *trowel*. *Paint* is applied with a *brush*.
11. **(A)** Someone *pigheaded* or stubborn is disinclined to *yield* (give in). Someone *lionhearted* or brave is disinclined to *retreat*.
12. **(E)** An *unctuous* or excessively pious manner is affected, having a false appearance of *sincerity*. A *hypocritical* or dissembling manner is feigned, having a false appearance of *virtue*.
13. **(D)** *Pirate* and *buccaneer* are synonyms, as are *wanderer* and *nomad*.
14. **(E)** To *trigger* an *alarm* is to release it or set it off. To *spring* a *trap* is to release it or set it off.
15. **(C)** The beginning and the end of a *quotation* (group of words repeated from a book or speech) are indicated by *quotation marks*. The beginning and the end of an *aside* (parenthetical remark; temporary digression from the main subject) are indicated by *parentheses*.

7

Improving Reading Comprehension

Doing well on the reading comprehension questions often makes the difference between success and failure on the PSAT. The last questions on the exam, they are also the most time-consuming and the ones most likely to bog you down. However, you can handle them, and this chapter will show you how.

LONG-RANGE STRATEGY

Read, read, read!

Just do it.

There is no substitute for extensive reading as a preparation for the PSAT and for college work. The only way to gain proficiency in reading is by reading books of all kinds. As you read, you will develop speed, stamina, and the ability to comprehend the printed page. But if you want to turn yourself into the kind of reader the colleges are looking for, you must develop the habit of reading every day.

Challenge yourself. Don't limit your reading to light fiction and biography as so many high school students do. Branch out a bit. Try to develop an interest in as many fields as you can. Sample some of the quality magazines: *The New Yorker, Smithsonian, Scientific American, National Geographic, Newsweek, Time*. In these magazines you'll find articles on literature, music, science, philosophy, history, the arts—the whole range of fields touched on by the PSAT. If you take time to acquaint yourself with the contents of these magazines, you won't find the subject matter of the reading passages on the examination so strange.

TIPS TO HELP YOU COPE WITH READING COMPREHENSION QUESTIONS

1. Tackle passages with familiar subjects before passages with unfamiliar ones. It is hard to concentrate when you read about something wholly unfamiliar to you. Give yourself a break. First tackle the reading passages that interest you or that deal with topics you are well grounded in. You'll do better on them.

2. First read the passage; then read the questions. Reading the questions before you read the passage will not save you time. It will cost you time. If you read the questions first, when you turn to the passage you will have a number of question words and phrases dancing around in your head. You will be so involved in trying to spot the places they occur in the passage that you'll be unable to concentrate on comprehending the passage as a whole.

3. Read as rapidly as you can with understanding, but do not force yourself. Do not worry about the time element. If you worry about not finishing the test, you will begin to take shortcuts and miss the correct answer in your haste.

4. As you read the opening sentences, try to anticipate what the passage will be about. Ask yourself who or what the author is talking about.

5. As you continue reading, try to remember in what part of the passage the author makes major points. In that way, when you start looking for the phrase or sentence which will justify your choice of answer, you will be able to save time by going to that section of the passage immediately rather than having to reread the entire selection.

6. When you tackle the questions, *go back to the passage* to verify your answer choices. Do not rely on your memory, and, above all, do not ignore the passage and just answer questions on the basis of your own knowledge. Remember, the questions are asking you about what *this* author has to say about the subject, not about what some other author you once read said about it in another book.

7. When the questions ask about specific information in the passage, do not expect to find it stated in exactly the same words. If the question is:

> According to the passage, widgets are
> (A) good (B) bad (C) indifferent
> (D) pink (E) purple Ⓐ Ⓑ Ⓒ Ⓓ Ⓔ

do not expect to find a sentence in the reading that says, "Widgets are bad." However, you may well find a sentence that says, "Widgets are totally undesirable and have a negative influence." That is close enough to tell you that the answer must be **B**.

8. When you read, watch for key words that indicate how a passage is being developed.
Equality or continuity of ideas: *again, also, and, another, as well as, besides, first, furthermore, likewise, moreover, in addition*
Contrast or change of topic: *although, despite, in spite of, instead of, notwithstanding, regardless, nevertheless, on the other hand, however*
Conclusion: *accordingly, as a result, hence, in conclusion, in short, therefore, thus, consequently*

9. Be on the alert for *all-inclusive words*, such as *always, at all times*, and *entirely*, and for negative or limiting words, such as *only, never, no, none*, and *but*.

10. Watch out for words or phrases in the question that can alert you to the kind of question being asked. Just as it will help you to know the directions for the antonym, analogy, and sentence completion questions on the PSAT, it will also help you to familiarize yourself with the major types of reading questions on the test. If you can recognize just what a given question is asking for, you'll be better able to tell which particular reading tactic to apply.

PSAT READING COMPREHENSION QUESTIONS TEST YOUR ABILITY TO

- **find the central thought of a selection**
- **find specific detail mentioned in the passage**
- **find implications and draw inferences from the text**
- **determine the meaning of strange words as used in the text**
- **determine the mood of the writer**
- determine the special techniques used by the author to achieve his or her effects

Each of these kinds of questions will be analyzed in detail in the following exercises. At first, only one kind of question will be treated in each reading selection. Read each selection carefully; then read the question and decide which answer you think is best. Compare your answer and your reasoning with the explanation which follows each exercise. After you have done the first group of exercises, you will be provided with more difficult passages taken from the fields of literature, social studies, philosophy, fine arts, and science.

FINDING THE CENTRAL THOUGHT OF A PASSAGE

Questions testing ability to find the central thought often take the following forms:

1. **The title that best expresses the ideas of the passage is . . .**
2. **The main idea of this selection may be best expressed as . . .**
3. **Which of the following best states the theme of the passage?**
4. **This passage illustrates . . .**
5. **The author's purpose in writing this passage is . . .**

Since a paragraph has been defined as a group of sentences revolving about a central theme, any title that is appropriate must include the thought that each of the sentences in the paragraph is developing. It should be neither too broad nor too narrow in its scope; it should be specific and yet comprehensive enough to include all the essential ideas presented by the sentences. A good title for a passage of two or more paragraphs should include the thoughts of all the paragraphs.

Very frequently, authors provide the reader with a sentence which expresses the main idea succinctly. Such *topic sentences* may appear anywhere in the paragraph, although we are accustomed to looking for them in the opening or closing sentences. However, in the kind of reading that college-bound students are expected to be able to handle, topic sentences are often implied rather than stated.

To develop proficiency in selecting the main idea of a passage, read the five passages that follow. In each case, select the best answer to the question. Then read the analysis provided.

PASSAGE 1

Your mind, like your body, is a thing whereof the powers are developed by effort. That is a principal use, as I see it, of hard work in studies. Unless you train your body you cannot be an athlete, and unless you train your mind you cannot be much of a scholar. The four miles an oarsman covers at top speed is in itself nothing to the good, but the physical capacity to hold out over the course is thought to be of some worth. So a good part of what you learn by hard study may not be permanently retained, and may not seem to be of much final value, but your mind is a better and more powerful instrument because you learned it. "Knowledge is power," but still more the faculty of acquiring and using knowledge is power. If you have a trained and powerful mind, you are bound to have stored it with something, but its value is more in what it can do, what it can grasp and use, than in what it contains; and if it were possible, as it is not, to come out of college with a trained and disciplined mind and

nothing useful in it, you would still be ahead, and still, in a manner, educated.

The title that best expresses the ideas of this passage is
(A) "Knowledge Is Power"
(B) How to Retain and Use Facts
(C) Why Acquire Knowledge
(D) Physical and Mental Effort
(E) The Trained Mind

ANALYSIS OF PASSAGE 1

Look at the opening and summary sentences of the paragraph: "Your *mind*, like your body, is a thing whereof the powers are developed by effort . . . if it were possible, as it is not, to come out of college with *a trained and disciplined mind* and nothing useful in it, you would still be ahead, and still, in a manner, educated." Note the italicized phrases.

In this passage, the author stresses the need for hard work in studies. He compares the training the athlete gets to the training the scholar needs. He concedes that you may forget much that you learn, but he stresses the value of knowing how to get and use knowledge. This comes from training. It is not the knowledge that you get from college that is valuable, but the training of your mind.

Now go through the choices. You may eliminate Choice **A** ("Knowledge Is Power"): the author states that the faculty of acquiring knowledge is more important than the knowledge itself. You may eliminate Choice **B** (How to Retain and Use Facts): the passage is not a "how-to" guide. Choice **C** (Why Acquire Knowledge) may be supported by the quotation that "Knowledge Is Power," but you can see that the author is under-cutting this statement in the sentence in which he quotes it. You may argue in favor of Choice **D** (Physical and Mental Effort) because you recognize that the author is making an analogy between the training of the athlete and the training of the scholar. However, Choice **D** is not as good as Choice **E** (The Trained Mind) because *throughout the passage* the author is stressing that the trained mind is something that must be developed and that is in itself a valuable and important faculty.

NOTE: In readings that occur on the PSAT, topic sentences are sometimes implied rather than stated directly. If you cannot find a topic sentence, ask yourself these questions.

1. Who or what is this passage about?
2. What aspect of this subject is the author talking about?
3. What is the author trying to get across about this aspect of the subject?

PASSAGE 2

But there is more to the Library of Congress for the American dream than merely the wise appropriation of public money. The Library of Congress could not have become what it is today, with all the generous aid of Congress, without such a citizen as Dr. Herbert Putnam at the directing head of it. He and his staff have devoted their lives to making the four million and more books and pamphlets serve the public to a degree that cannot be approached by any similar great institution in the Old World. Then there is the public that uses these facilities. As one looks down on the general reading room, which alone contains ten thousand volumes that may be read without even the asking, one sees the seats filled with silent readers, old and young, rich and poor, black and white, the executive and the laborer, the general and the private, the noted scholar and the schoolboy, all reading at their own library provided by their own democracy.

The title that best expresses the ideas of this passage is
(A) Wise Use of Public Funds
(B) An Institution of Democracy
(C) Dr. Herbert Putnam, Director
(D) Intelligent Use of Books
(E) Libraries in the Old World and the New

ANALYSIS OF PASSAGE 2

When you are trying to select the best title for a passage, watch out for words or phrases that come straight out of the passage. They may not always be your best choice. A more careful reading will reveal shortcomings in most of them. Consider Choice **A**. In the first sentence, the author talks of the "wise appropriation of public money." This is not the same as "wise use." Likewise, although the passage mentions Dr. Herbert Putnam, Choice **C** (Dr. Herbert Putnam, Director) is too narrow in scope to be a good title for this text.

Choices **D** and **E** also have flaws. The passage does not describe the use of books in general; instead, it describes the public's use of books at one particular institution. Thus Choice **D** is poor. Again, while the passage refers to libraries in the Old World, it does so only to contrast them with our own Library of Congress. This contrast is too limited to justify the very broad implications of Choice **E**.

The best of the titles is Choice **B** (An Institution of Democracy). This choice of title is supported by the author's emphasis on the varied and contrasting groups using the facilities of the library provided (through *democratic* processes) for the use of all.

PASSAGE 3

Today in America vast numbers of youth are flocking to our colleges, eager for something, just what they do not know. It makes much difference what they get. They will be prone to demand something they can immediately use; the tendency is strong to give it to them: science, economics, business administration, law in its narrower sense. I submit that the shepherds should not first feed the flock with these. I argue for the outlines of what used to go as a liberal education—not necessarily in the sense that young folks should waste precious years in efforts, unsuccessful for some reason I cannot understand, to master ancient tongues; rather, I speak for an introduction into the thoughts and deeds of persons who have lived before them, in other countries than their own, with other strifes and other needs. This I maintain, not in the interest of that general cultural background which is so often a cloak for the superior person, the prig, the snob and the pedant. But I submit to you that in some such way alone can we meet and master the high-power vendor of political patent medicines.

The title that best expresses the ideas of this passage is
(A) Why Students Go to College
(B) Foreign Languages for Culture
(C) The Need for Vocational Training
(D) The Shepherd and His Student Flock
(E) The Importance of a Liberal Education

ANALYSIS OF PASSAGE 3

The author maintains that the young people flocking to our colleges do not know exactly what they are seeking. They often desire materials which they can put to immediate use; they seek subjects which have practical application. The author urges a study of the ideas and actions of persons in other countries and other times. This liberal education is valuable not for its snobbishness or pedantry but for the insight it gives the student which will enable him or her to meet the problems of current society.

By paraphrasing the ideas of the passage in some such manner, the student can see that the writer is stressing "the importance of a liberal education." Thus, Choice **E** is best. Choice **A** is inadequate because it is not discussed in the passage. We are told that students are flocking to the colleges but we are not told why. Choice **B** is mentioned only by indirection. The author talks of mastering ancient tongues. He does not mention the study of contemporary foreign languages in this passage. Similarly, the author does not discuss the need for vocational training. Instead he implies that students, mistakenly, often seek vocational training because of its immediacy of application. Choice **D** is so broad that it becomes vague. The author is more interested in what the teacher gives his or her pupils than in the general idea of teacher and pupil.

PASSAGE 4

Too often we retire people who are willing and able to continue working, according to Federal Security Agency Administrator Oscar R. Ewing in addressing the first National Conference on Aging to point up the fact that chronological age is no longer an effective criterion in determining whether or not an individual is capable of working. World War II proved this point when it became necessary to hire older, experienced people to handle positions in business and industry vacated by persons called to serve their country. As shown by production records set during the war period, the employment of older people helped us continue, and even better, our high level of production.

It was also pointed out at the conference that our life expectancy is increasing and that the over-65 group will jump from 11,500,000 now to twenty million within ten years. A good many of these people are capable of producing and have a desire to work, but they are kept from gainful employment by a short-sightedness on the part of many employers which leads them to believe that young people alone can give them adequate service. It is true that the young person has greater agility and speed to offer, but on the other hand there is much to be gained from the experience, steadfastness, and maturity of judgment of the elderly worker.

The title that best expresses the ideas of this passage is
(A) Increased Efficiency of Elderly Workers
(B) Misjudging Elderly Workers
(C) Lengthening the Span of Life
(D) New Jobs for the Aged
(E) Production during World War II

ANALYSIS OF PASSAGE 4

The author does not discuss the *increased* efficiency of elderly workers. He describes the useful and effective job they did during World War II. He does not maintain that their efficiency increased. Similarly, the author does not discuss *new* jobs for the aged. He discusses the inadvisability of dropping experienced and qualified workers because of age. Thus, Choices **A** and **D** introduce ideas not presented by the author and are, therefore, unsuitable as titles.

Choices **C** and **E** do appear in the text but only as illustrations of the major point the author is presenting. He tells us that the life span is increasing and that we will have many more qualified elderly workers in the future. He also tells us that production in World War II was maintained at a high level, but he uses this information to demonstrate that elderly people can perform satisfactorily when given the opportunity.

Throughout the passage, the author tells us that we are making a mistake when we retire elderly people. He talks of the experience, steadfastness, and maturity of judgment which these elderly workers have and which we ignore when we replace them with younger workers who can offer greater agility and speed. Thus, we are guilty of seriously misjudging elderly workers. Choice **B** is the best title for this passage.

PASSAGE 5

The characteristic American believes, first, in justice as the foundation of civilized government and society, and, next, in freedom for the individual, so far as that freedom is possible without interference with the equal rights of others. He or she conceives that both justice and freedom are to be secured through popular respect for the laws enacted by the elected representatives of the people and through the faithful observance of those laws. It should be observed, however, that American justice in general keeps in view the present common good of the vast majority, and the restoration rather than the punishment of the exceptionally malignant or defective individual. It is essentially democratic; and especially it finds suffering inflicted on the innocent unintelligible and abhorrent.

Blind obedience and implicit submission to the will of another do not commend themselves to characteristic Americans. The discipline in which they believe is the voluntary cooperation of many persons in the orderly and effective pursuit of common ends. Thus they submit willingly to any restrictions on individual liberty which can be shown to be necessary to the preservation of the public health, and they are capable of the most effective cooperation needed in business, sports and war.

The main idea of this selection may be best expressed as
(A) American Justice
(B) a plea for cooperation
(C) the American government
(D) liberty as the foundation of government
(E) the basis of American democracy

ANALYSIS OF PASSAGE 5

The author in the opening sentence couples justice and freedom of the individual as the foundations of civilized government. Any choice which does not include both aspects is incomplete. Choices **A** and **D** are inadequate for this reason.

Choice **B** is inaccurate because this passage specifically cites the American belief in cooperation. The author does not have to plead for cooperation on the part of Americans. It is already part of their basic philosophy.

Choice **C** (the American government) is not discussed in the passage. The author is discussing the factors, justice and liberty, which Americans regard as the basis of good government.

Choice **E** is best because the author is expounding on the factors which form "the basis of American democracy."

FINDING SPECIFIC DETAIL MENTIONED IN THE PASSAGE

In developing the idea of the paragraph, a writer will make statements in support of the point of view or the message which he or she is trying to convey. The most frequent question found in reading tests deals with the statements made by the author in the development of the paragraph. These take the following forms:

1. The author states...
2. The author states all of the items listed EXCEPT...
3. Which of the following statements is correct?

Students taking a reading test must be certain that the answer they select is in the passage. They must find the word or sentence or group of sentences which justifies their choice. They must not rely upon knowledge obtained elsewhere, nor must they jump to quick conclusions in their anxiety to finish the test.

The following selections will illustrate the kind of question that often appears and the reason for the choice of the correct answer.

PASSAGE 6

The reasons for the do-it-yourself movement are apparent. An ever-reduced work week means more and more leisure time, and we have to fill waking hours that might otherwise go empty. Now automation threatens us with an even greater number of idle hours. Then, the postwar housing boom, which for the first time in our history has made us really a nation of homeowners, makes us home-conscious. It is one thing to let someone else's lawn go bad, another when you yourself are the owner and the weeds are no one's but your own. There's another reason too, like that of the fellow who explained there were a hundred reasons why he didn't want to build a squash court: "The first is that a court costs $100,000 ... the other ninety-nine don't matter!" So it is with do-it-yourself—the best answer to rising costs of labor in a number of trades.

According to the author, many members of the do-it-yourself group
(A) have developed a new interest in community affairs
(B) find it hard to pay for home repairs and renovations
(C) are scientific gardeners
(D) now favor automation
(E) avoid using machine tools

The do-it-yourself movement can best be explained as being the result of
(A) a variety of postwar economic factors
(B) increased use of power tools
(C) a general relaxing of credit restrictions
(D) a trend toward a lower standard of living
(E) increased employment in specialized trades

According to the passage, which statement is true?
(A) More homes than apartment houses are being erected.
(B) Homeowners are now building squash courts.
(C) Automation will decrease the number of homeowners.
(D) Homeowners may have more leisure time in the future.
(E) The lawns of rented homes are usually neglected.

ANALYSIS OF PASSAGE 6

The careful reader will observe that the last sentence of the paragraph states that doing it yourself is the best answer to rising costs. It is in this sentence that we find the justification for Choice **B** as the answer to the first question. None of the other four statements is mentioned in the paragraph.

In the second question, Choices **B, C, D,** and **E** are not mentioned in the paragraph directly or indirectly. The author does mention a reduced work week, the increasing use of automation, and the postwar housing boom. Thus we can justify Choice **A**, "a variety of postwar economic factors."

As we examine the choices in the third question, we should realize that Choice **A** is unsatisfactory because it is not mentioned at all in the passage. Choice **B** is false because the paragraph gives reasons for NOT building squash courts. Choice **C** is not mentioned. Choice **D** is correct because the first three sentences of the paragraph inform us that all people (including homeowners) for many reasons will have shorter work weeks. Choice **E** is an unwarranted conclusion based on the fifth sentence of the passage.

PASSAGE 7

Good American English is simply good English, English that differs little in pronunciation, vocabulary, and occasionally in idiom from good English as spoken in London or South Africa, but which differs no more than our physical surroundings, our political and social institutions, and other circumstances that are reflected in language. It rests upon the same basis as that which the standard speech of England rests upon—the usage of reputable speakers and writers throughout the country. No American student of language is so provincial as to hope, or wish, that the American standard may some day be adopted in England. Nor does he or she share the views of such in England as think that we would do well to take our standard readymade from them. The American student will be content with the opinion of Henry Bradley that "the wiser sort among us will not dispute that Americans have acquired the right to frame their own standards of correct English on the usage of their best writers and speakers."

The author considers a good American English to be
- (A) proper for use in America
- (B) superior to the English spoken in South Africa
- (C) inferior to the English spoken in England
- (D) too idiomatic for general acceptance
- (E) suitable as a standard for all English-speaking countries.

According to the author, correctness in language is determined by
- (A) the majority of those who speak it
- (B) the dominant social and political institutions
- (C) geographical conditions
- (D) good speakers and writers
- (E) those who wish to standardize the language

ANALYSIS OF PASSAGE 7

The statement of Henry Bradley in the last sentence justifies the selection of Choice **A** as the answer to the first question.

The justification for Choice **D** as the best answer to the second question can be found in two sentences in the passage. Mr. Bradley's quotation mentions the usage of the "best writers and speakers." Likewise, the same thought is found in the second sentence ("the usage of reputable speakers and writers throughout the country").

FINDING IMPLICATIONS AND DRAWING INFERENCES FROM THE TEXT

A slightly more difficult type of question calls for reasoning based on the statements made by the author. The reader should be able to see the logical development of the author's statements. Thus, the good reader in this type of question demonstrates his or her ability to understand the text and to reason intelligently.

The following three paragraphs will illustrate this type of question.

PASSAGE 8

The dramatic events of December 7, 1941, plunged the nation into war. The full import of the war we can not even now comprehend, but one of the effects stands out in sharp relief—the coming of the air age. The airplane, which played a relatively minor part in World War I, has already soared to heights undreamed of save by the few with mighty vision. In wartime the airplane is the artillery on wings and the battleship that flies. To human beings in their need it symbolizes deadly extremes: friend or foe; deliverance or death. It is a powerful instrument of war—revolutionizing military strategy, but its peacetime role is just as revolutionary. This new master of time and space, fruit of human inventive genius, has come to stay, making small the earth and smoothing its surface. To all of us, then, to youth and to adult alike, comes the winged challenge to get ourselves ready—to orient ourselves for living in an age which the airplane seems destined to mold.

The author implies that aviation must play in peacetime a role that
- (A) is greater than the one it played in war
- (B) is as significant as the one it played in war
- (C) is less important than the one it played in war
- (D) orients us to the past and the present
- (E) will revolutionize military strategy

ANALYSIS OF PASSAGE 8

The justification of Choice **B** as the best answer is found in the middle sentence: "It is a powerful instrument of war—revolutionizing military strategy, but its peacetime role is just as revolutionary." Thus we see that the author eliminates Choices **A** and **C**.

Choice **D** is faulty because the orientation mentioned in the last sentence is an adustment to the present air age and not to the past. Choice **E** is irrelevant in a question dealing with *peacetime* aviation.

PASSAGE 9

Such homely virtues as thrift, hard work, and simplicity appear old-fashioned in these days, so probably we do well to remember the career of Benamin Franklin, a true American. Though he had slight formal education, he became one of the best-educated men of his day, for he discovered the simple principle that people learn only what they teach themselves. Teachers can direct and organize the search for skills and information; a few can inspire. There is no substitute for the drudgery of learning. Franklin learned a trade and began reading inspirational books. He sought self-reliance and expressed thoughts that have interested more than one generation of readers. His essays and his *Autobiography* reveal that his knowledge was useful.

This selection suggests that
(A) old-fashioned virtues should be discarded
(B) most people have homely virtues
(C) everyone can get an education
(D) learning need not be drudgery
(E) Franklin learned his trade by studying inspirational books

ANALYSIS OF PASSAGE 9

The statement "that people learn only what they teach themselves" and the reference to Benamin Franklin's limited formal education suggest that anyone who is willing to apply him- or herself can get an education (Choice **C**).

PASSAGE 10

A more significant manifestation of the concern of the community with the general welfare is the collection and dissemination of statistics. This statement may cause the reader to smile, for statistics seem to be drab and prosaic things. The great growth of statistics, however, is one of the most remarkable characteristics of the age. Never before has a community kept track from month to month, and in some cases from week to week, of how many people are born, how many die and from what causes, how many are sick, how much is being produced, how much is being sold, how many people are at work, how many people are unemployed, how long they have been out of work, what prices people pay, how much income they receive and from what sources, how much they owe, what they intend to buy. These elaborate attempts of the country to keep informed about what is happening mean that the community is concerned with how its members are faring and with the conditions under which they live. For this reason the present age may take pride in its numerous and regular statistical reports and in the rapid increase in the number of these reports. No other age has evinced such a keen interest in the conditions of the people.

The writer implies that statistics are
(A) too scientific for general use
(B) too elaborate and too drab
(C) related to the quality of living conditions
(D) frequently misinterpreted
(E) a product of the machine age

ANALYSIS OF PASSAGE 10

The opening and closing sentences of this passage tell us that statistics are collected out of consideration for the "general welfare" and are the result of a "keen interest in the conditions of the people." Thus, Choice **C** is justified. Nowhere in the passage does the author state that statistics are too scientific or misinterpreted. The author, likewise, does not state that statistics are too elaborate. He states that they may *seem* drab.

The use of the word *seem* implies that he does not believe that the statement is correct. Choice **E** is not justified by the text.

DETERMINING THE MEANINGS OF UNFAMILIAR WORDS IN THE TEXT

Every student who has ever looked into a dictionary is aware that many words have more than one meaning. A common question that appears on reading examinations tests the ability to determine the correct meaning of a word from its context. Sometimes, the word is a common one and the student must determine the exact meaning as used by the author. At other times, the word is strange. Its meaning can be determined by a careful examination of the text.

The following passages will illustrate this type of question.

PASSAGE 11

Spring comes without trumpets to a city. The asphalt is a wilderness that does not quicken overnight; winds blow gritty with cinders instead of merry with the smells of earth and fertilizer. Women wear their gardens on their hats. But spring is a season in the city and it has its own harbingers, constant as daffodils. Shop windows change their colors, people walk more slowly on the streets, what one can see of the sky has a bluer tone. Pulitzer prizes awake and sing and matinee tickets go abegging. But gayer than any of these are the carrousels, which are already in sheltered places, beginning to turn with the sound of springtime itself. They are the earliest and the truest and the oldest of all the urban signs.

In the passage, the word *harbingers* means

(A) storms
(B) noises
(C) truths
(D) virtues
(E) forerunners

ANALYSIS OF PASSAGE 11

The readers of this book who have studied the Word Lists in Chapter 8 have already encountered the word *harbinger* and they know that it means *forerunner* (Choice E). However, for those to whom the word is strange, the passage offers many clues. We can eliminate *storms* for they are not mentioned in the text. *Noises* also can be eliminated because we are told that the season comes "without trumpets." The author calls our attention to the changing shop windows, the slower gait of people, the bluer sky, etc., and tells us that these are the signs, indicators, or *forerunners* of spring.

PASSAGE 12

All museum adepts are familiar with examples of *ostrakoi*, the oystershells used in balloting. As a matter of fact, these "oystershells" are usually shards of pottery, conveniently glazed to enable the voter to express his wishes in writing. In the Agora a great number of these have come to light, bearing the thrilling name Themistocles. Into rival jars were dropped the ballots for or against his banishment. On account of the huge vote taken on that memorable day, it was to be expected that many ostrakoi would be found, but the interest of this collection is that a number of these ballots are inscribed in an *identical* handwriting. There is nothing mysterious about it! The Boss was on the job, then as now. He prepared these ballots and voters cast them—no doubt for the consideration of an obol or two. *The ballot box was stuffed.*

How the glory of the American boss is diminished! A vile imitation, he. His methods as old as Time!

An obol, as used in the passage, is evidently

(A) an oyster shell
(B) a Greek coin
(C) a promise of bread
(D) a complimentary remark
(E) an appointive public office

ANALYSIS OF PASSAGE 12

Only numismatists and scholars of Greek antiquity may reasonably be expected to know what an obol is. The rest of us may never have encountered the word until we read the passage. Yet, most of us should recognize that voters would be tempted to cast their ballots in accordance with the wishes of the Boss by a bribe of some kind, preferably money. It is therefore logical to assume that an obol is a Greek coin.

DETERMINING THE MOOD OF THE WRITER

A writer often reveals a personal attitude or emotional state in the course of his or her development of a paragraph or essay. The observant reader will recognize this emotional coloration. Frequently, questions involving this aspect appear on reading tests.

The following three passages illustrate this type of question.

PASSAGE 13

The question is whether night baseball will prove a boon or a disaster to the game. The big crowds now attending the night games, the brilliance of the spectacle, the miracle of the spinning turnstiles—all these seem sufficient evidence that what is needed is not less night ball, but more. The fact remains, however, that despite all apparent success, some of the shrewdest, most experienced men in baseball remain unconvinced of the miracle. They are steady in their preference for daytime baseball, and they view with increasing distrust the race towards more lights. It could be that these men are simply being obstinate. Yet, on the other hand, it could be that in reviewing the caliber of baseball as it is played at night, in speculating upon the future effect of night ball, they are not entirely unprophetic. It could even be, indeed, that they are dead right.

In his attitude toward the future of night baseball, the author expresses

(A) uncertainty
(B) confidence
(C) optimism
(D) sharp criticism
(E) antagonism

ANALYSIS OF PASSAGE 13

The opening sentence indicates that the author is uncertain whether night baseball is a boon or a disaster. He then proceeds to mention the large crowds that attend night games. He immediately tells us of the doubts of shrewd observers. He tells us that they may be stubborn or correct in their doubts. Throughout the passage, there is an element of uncertainty. Therefore, Choice **A** is best.

PASSAGE 14

It takes no calendar to tell root and stem that the calm days of mid-summer are here. Last spring's sprouted seed comes to fruit. None of these things depends on a calendar of the days and months. They are their own calendar, marks on a span of time that reaches far back into the shadows of time. The mark is there for all to see, in every field and meadow and treetop, as it was last year and ten years ago and when the centuries were young.

The time is here. This is that point in the great continuity when these things happen, and will continue to happen year after year. Any summer arrives at this point, only to lead on to the next and the next, and so to summer again. These things we can count on; these things will happen again and again, so long as the earth turns.

The passage indicates that the author experiences a feeling of
(A) frustration
(B) fear of the forces of nature
(C) pessimism
(D) regret at the rapid passage of time
(E) serene confidence

ANALYSIS OF PASSAGE 14

The author sees in nature a great continuity of events. Things have happened in the past and will continue "so long as the earth turns." This is a statement that is serenely confident (Choice **E**).

PASSAGE 15

The six-year-old is about the best example that can be found of that type of inquisitiveness that causes irritated adults to exclaim, "Curiosity killed the cat." To children of this age the world is a fascinating place to be explored and investigated quite thoroughly, but such a world is bounded by the environment in which they or the people they know live. It is constantly expanding through new experiences, which bring many eager questions from members of any group of first graders, as they try to figure out new relationships—to know and accept their places within the family, the school, and the community—to understand all around them. There are adults who find it quite annoying to be presented with such rank inquisitiveness. But this is no purposeless prying, no idle curiosity! It is that quality, characteristic of the successful adult, inherent in the good citizen—intellectual curiosity.

In this passage the author's attitude toward children is one of
(A) despair
(B) confidence
(C) indifference
(D) sharp criticism
(E) exaggerated optimism

ANALYSIS OF PASSAGE 15

Although the author discusses the irritation adults sometimes feel at the incessant questions asked by six-year-old children, he feels that these questions are not purposeless. He feels that this intellectual curiosity is a characteristic of the adult citizen, and he is happy and confident when children display this trait (Choice **B**).

DETERMINING SPECIAL TECHNIQUES USED BY THE AUTHOR

In developing their ideas or telling their stories, authors make use of well-known techniques. They may reason from experimental data (inductive method), they may base their reasoning on principles accepted in advance (deductive method), or they may make analogies and comparisons. They may use comparisons such as similes and metaphors to convey their thoughts and impressions.

The special technique used by an author should be recognized by the capable reader. Questions about technique may therefore appear on a reading test.

Passage 16 illustrates this type of question.

PASSAGE 16

Some analysts consider the process of automation a second industrial revolution with the potential for social upheaval that marked the birth of the factory a century and a half ago. Others insist it is just another step in industry's progress toward greater efficiency, no different in its basic attributes from any of the other technological advances that have helped raise American wages, employment totals and living standards.

Congressional investigators, puzzled about what action the government should take, have been told by union leaders that automation threatens mass unemployment and by business executives that it will bring unparalleled prosperity.

Engineers say that push-button factories may eventually permit a work schedule in which the weekend will be longer than the week. Educators see all this leisure promoting a scholastic renaissance in which cultural attainments will become the yardstick of social recognition for worker and boss alike. Gloomier observers fear the trend toward "inhuman production" will end by making human workers obsolete.

The passage is developed principally by means of
(A) cause and effect
(B) examples
(C) definition
(D) narration
(E) contrast

ANALYSIS OF PASSAGE 16

A careful examination of this passage reveals that the author is interested in presenting both sides of the question of automation. In paragraph 1, we get the contrasting views of those who regard it as having the potential for social upheaval and those who look upon it as merely another technological advance. In paragraph 2, we get the conflicting views of union and business leaders. In paragraph 3, we find the optimistic views of engineers and educators contrasted with the pessimistic outlook that human workers will become obsolete.

Thus we see that the author develops his idea throughout the passage by means of contrast (Choice **E**).

In the analysis of the sixteen passages in the preceding pages, we have considered only one type of question for each passage. Of course, on reading tests, more than one question is asked about each passage. You may expect about three questions on short paragraphs (100 to 250 words) and as many as five questions on longer passages (400 to 500 words).

The following passages have several questions and are more typical of the actual reading tests.

PASSAGE 17

OF STUDIES—Sir Francis Bacon

Studies serve for delight, for ornament, and for ability. Their chief use for delight is in privateness and retiring; for ornament, is in discourse; and for ability, is in the judgment and disposition of business. For expert men can execute, and perhaps judge of particulars, one by one; but the general counsels, and the plots and marshaling of affairs, come best from those that are learned. To spend too much time in studies is sloth; to use them too much for ornament is affectation; to make judgment wholly by their rules, is the humor of a scholar. They perfect nature, and are perfected by experience; for natural abilities are like natural plants, that need pruning by study; and studies themselves do give forth directions too much at large, except they be bounded by experience. Crafty men contemn studies, simple men admire them, and wise men use them; for they teach not their own use; but that is a wisdom without them, and above them, won by observation. Read not to contradict and confute; nor to believe and take for granted; nor to find talk and discourse; but to weigh and consider. Some books are to be tasted, others to be swallowed, and some few to be chewed and digested; that is, some books are to be read only in parts; others to be read, but not curiously; and some few to be read wholly, and with diligence and attention. Some books also may be read by deputy, and extracts made of them by others; but that would be only in the less important arguments, and the meaner sort of books; else distilled books are like common distilled waters, flashy things.

1. By *studies*, Bacon means
(A) homework
(B) reading
(C) experience
(D) experiment
(E) classwork

2. According to the passage, reading for pleasure is best done
(A) aloud
(B) by tasting
(C) alone
(D) by chewing and digesting
(E) quietly

3. *Sloth* as used in line 7 means
(A) an animal
(B) laziness
(C) showing off
(D) wisdom
(E) a weakness

4. Which of the following books should most likely be "chewed and digested"?
(A) *Poetry of the 19th Century*
(B) *The Case of the Missing Corpse*
(C) *Medical Practice and Jurisprudence*
(D) *The Small Family Cookbook*
(E) *Best Short Stories of 1980*

ANALYSIS OF PASSAGE 17

Question 1:

The entire paragraph refers to reading. It is apparent that **B** is the correct answer.

Question 2:

In the first two lines of the passage, we learn that "their chief use for delight is in privateness." That is our clue to the correct answer, **C**.

Question 3:

Let us assume that we do not know the meaning of the word in question. By examining the sentence in which the word appears and the sentences preceding and following, we can get a general impression of the author's meaning. We can eliminate Choice **C** because the author goes on to say that "to use them too much for ornament is affectation," which indicates that this is the type that shows off. All three ways mentioned in the sentence are apparently disliked by Bacon and on that basis we may eliminate **D**. *Sloth* means both an animal and laziness. The tone of the sentence seems to indicate that Bacon is using the second meaning. Hence, **B** is correct.

Question 4:

It is obvious that only serious books, which have to be mastered, should be "chewed and digested." The medical book **(C)** falls in this category. The cookbook, the volume of poetry, and the collection of short stories may be read in any order and in parts. The detective story is one that requires no thinking and may be "swallowed."

Now try to answer the questions based on this paragraph.

PASSAGE 18

There are exceptions to the rule of male insects being smaller than the females, and some of these exceptions are intelligible. Size and strength would be an advantage to the males which fight for the possession of the females, and in these cases, as with the stag beetle (Lucanus), the males are larger than the females. There are, however, other beetles which are not known to fight together, of which the males exceed the females in size. The meaning of this fact is not known, but in some of these cases, as with the huge Dynastes and Megasoma, we can at least see that there would be no necessity for the males to be smaller than the females in order to be matured before them, for these beetles are not short-lived, and there would be ample time for the pairing of the sexes.

1. According to the author, which of the following is true?
(A) Male insects are always smaller than females.
(B) In a given species nature provides differences between sexes to ensure successful reproduction.
(C) Size and strength protect females from other females.
(D) Longevity is characteristic of the Dynastes and Megasoma.
(E) In the stag beetle, females are larger than the males.

2. Where male beetles are smaller than female beetles, the reason is that
(A) the males have to fight for their mates
(B) the males are more intelligent
(C) the males are ephemeral creatures
(D) there is ample time for mating
(E) the males do not have to fight for their mates.

3. The paragraph preceding this one probably
(A) discusses a generalization about the size of insects
(B) develops the idea that male insects do not live long after maturity
(C) discusses male and female beetles
(D) emphasizes that beetles are belligerent animals
(E) discusses insect behavior

4. The male Lucanus is particularly
(A) adaptable
(B) strong
(C) large
(D) belligerent
(E) stagnant

ANALYSIS OF PASSAGE 18

Question 1:

The answer is **D**. We can eliminate Choice **A** because in line 1 we are told that "there are exceptions" to the rule. Lines 6–7 and 9–13 contain additional references to male insects that are larger than females. Incidentally, this choice illustrates one area where students should exercise caution. Whenever an answer is in the superlative (*best, worst,* etc.) or is all-inclusive *(always, all)* or all-exclusive *(none)*, be sure to reread the paragraph to make certain that the author actually makes the statement.
Choice **B** may be correct biologically and logically but the author has not stated it in the paragraph. You are adding your interpretation to the paragraph if you select this.
Choice **C** is not stated in the paragraph.
Choice **D** is found in lines 14 and 15. *Longevity* means "long life."
Choice **E** is wrong. In lines 6 and 7, the author states that males are larger.

Question 2:

The correct answer **(C)** can be supported by analyzing lines 11–16. Although the author is discussing large male beetles in these lines, we learn why other male beetles are smaller than female beetles. Male beetles are smaller (1) because they mature earlier and (2) because they are short-lived. The word *ephemeral* means short-lived.
Choice **A** is incorrect. In lines 3 and 4 we find that male beetles are larger if they have to fight for their mates.
Choice **B** is not stated in the paragraph.
Choice **D** is incorrect: Beetles grow *large* when there is ample time for mating.
Choice **E** is likewise incorrect. Size is important when males have to fight for their mates and therefore would explain the largeness of male beetles rather than the smallness.

Question 3:

This question calls for inferences. The clue lies in the first sentence. It is fair to assume that, if the author discusses exceptions to a rule, he has explained the rule in the preceding paragraph. There is no evidence in the paragraph that any of the other ideas were discussed previously. The correct answer is **A**.

Question 4:

The answer is **D**. The second sentence of this paragraph (lines 3 through 7) develops the idea that the male Lucanus is larger and stronger than the female beetle. However, we cannot accept either **B** or **C** as the answer because *strong* and *large* are relative terms. We are told in the same sentence that the males fight for the females. The word *belligerent* fits this situation. Choices **A** and **E** are not found in the paragraph.

PASSAGE 19

Most people do not think of fishes and other marine animals as having "voices," and of those who are aware of the fact that many of them can "speak," few understand that these "conversations" have significance. Actually, their talk may be as meaningful as much of our own. For example, some sea animals use their "voices" to locate their food in the ocean expanses; others, to let their fellows know of their whereabouts; and still others, as a means of obtaining mates. Sometimes, "speaking" may even mean the difference between life and death to a marine animal. It appears in some cases that when a predator approaches, the prey depends on no more than the sounds it makes to escape.

Fish sounds are important to human beings also. By listening to them we can learn a great deal about the habits of the creatures that make them, the size of the schools they form, the patterns of their migrations, and the nature of the environments in which they live. We can also apply this information to the more effective utilization of the listening posts we have set up to detect enemy submarines. A knowledge of fish sounds can avoid confusion and unneeded effort when a "new" sound is picked up and the sound sentry must decide whether or not to call an alert.

1. Which of the following statements is *best* supported by the information given?
   (A) Noises produced by fish are apparently random.
   (B) Fish noises are used by fishermen to increase their catch.
   (C) Fish noises can be utilized to tell whether or not a submarine is nearby.
   (D) Fish noises can confuse users of submarine-detection equipment.
   (E) Fish noises are inaudible under water.
2. Which of the following statements can *best* be inferred from the information given?
   (A) Fish noises cannot be transmitted through air.
   (B) Hearing is more acute in fishes than in people.
   (C) The chief use of "fish voices" is to enable one fish to communicate with another fish.
   (D) The significance of some fish noises has been studied.
   (E) Fish can be noisier than people.

ANALYSIS OF PASSAGE 19

Question 1:

The passage informs us that the noises produced by fish are "meaningful" (line 4) and therefore not apparently random. This eliminates Choice **A**. Statement **B** may be inferred from the text but is not mentioned in the passage. Choice **E** is obviously incorrect; if these fish noises were inaudible they would carry no information to other fish. Fish sounds apparently interfere with listening posts for submarines, but these sounds cannot be used to detect submarines. The listener must learn to differentiate between fish sounds and the sounds made by submarines; otherwise, he or she will be confused. Thus **D** is the best answer.

Question 2:

Go through the answer choices one by one. Remember that in answering inference questions you must go beyond the obvious, go beyond what the author explicitly states, to look for logical implications of what the author says.

Choice **A** is incorrect *as an inference*. It may or may not be true as a statement of fact. The passage never mentions anything about air transmission of fish noises; you have no basis in the paragraph for coming to this conclusion.

Similarly, Choices **B** and **E** are incorrect inferences. Don't answer inference questions on the basis of your personal opinions. Answer them on the basis of what the passage implies. Hearing in fishes may or may not be more acute than hearing in people. Fish may or may not be noisier than people. From the passage you have no way to tell.

Choices **A, B** and **E** are assumptions, not inferences. Choice **C** is an inference, but an unwarranted one. Nothing in the passage justifies the statement that the "chief" use of fish voices is for communication. From the passage, you can't tell.

The best answer is Choice **D**: the opening sentences of the second paragraph, which discuss listening to fish sounds and learning from them, obviously imply that people have been studying them.

PRACTICE EXERCISES

Having examined the six types of questions popular on reading tests, you can proceed with the reading exercises in this chapter.

On the following pages, you will find five groups of reading exercises. Allow about an hour at first for each group. The correct answers are given at the end of the chapter.

READING EXERCISE A

The chief characteristic of art today, if we are to judge by the reactions of the common man, is its obscurity. Everybody complains about obscurity in poetry, in painting, in music. I do not suggest that in some cases the complaint is unjustified. But we should remember that the really original work of art in any age seems obscure to the general public. From a certain point of view it would be true to say that no great work of art finds an appreciative public waiting for it. The work creates its own public, slowly and painfully. A work of art is born as an intellectual foundling. What is interesting to notice is that often the art specialists themselves are caught napping. It was André Gide, you remember, who first saw Proust's great novel while he was working as a reader for a firm of publishers. He turned it down without hesitation. Perhaps you remember Leigh Hunt's verdict on Blake as "an unfortunate madman whose mildness alone prevented him from being locked up." Wordsworth also thought Blake mad, and yet it was he who wrote: "Every great and original writer, in proportion as he is great and original, must himself create the taste by which he is to be judged."

1. The title that best expresses the ideas of the passage is
   (A) Gide's Blunder
   (B) Present-day Complaints of the Public
   (C) Hunt and Wordsworth as Critics
   (D) Taste in Poetry, Painting, and Music
   (E) Difficulties in Evaluating Contemporary Art

2. The passage indicates that often critics
   (A) discover genius
   (B) add to obscurity in art
   (C) create taste
   (D) misjudge a masterpiece
   (E) explain a work of art to the public

Intuition is not a quality which everyone can understand. As the unimaginative are miserable about a work of fiction until they discover what flesh-and-blood individual served as a model for the hero or heroine, so even many scientists doubt scientific intuition. They cannot believe that a blind person can see anything that they cannot see. They rely utterly on the celebrated inductive method of reasoning; the facts are to be exposed, and we are to conclude from them only what we must. This is a very sound rule—for mentalities that can do no better. But it is not certain that the really great steps are made in this plodding fashion. Dreams are made of quite other stuff, and if there are any left in the world who do not know that dreams have remade the world, then there is little that we can teach them.

3. The title that best expresses the ideas of this passage is
(A) Sound Scientific Reasoning
(B) The Limitation of Inductive Reasoning
(C) The Results of Scientific Intuition
(D) The Weakness of Dreamers
(E) The Value of Intuition

4. The writer implies that intuition depends upon
(A) induction
(B) imagination
(C) an exposition of facts
(D) good vision
(E) plodding habits

Too many parents force their children into group activities. They are concerned about the child who loves to do things alone, who prefers a solitary walk with a camera to a game of ball. They want their sons to be "good fellows" and their daughters "social mixers." In such foolish fears lie the beginnings of the blighting of individuality, the thwarting of personality, the stealing of the wealth of one's capital for living joyously and well in a confused world. What America needs is a new army of defense, manned by young men and women who, through guidance and confidence, encouragement and wisdom, have built up values for themselves by themselves and away from crowds and companies.

5. The title that best expresses the ideas of this passage is
(A) Aspiring Parents
(B) Group Activities
(C) "Good Fellows and Social Mixers"
(D) Developing Character in Solitude
(E) Parents' Fears

6. The author implies that
(A) young people need time to themselves
(B) group activities are bad
(C) parents knowingly thwart their children's personalities
(D) America needs universal military training
(E) independent thinking is of questionable value

"Sticks and stones can break my bones,
But names will never hurt me."

No doubt you are familiar with this childhood rhyme; perhaps, when you were younger, you frequently invoked whatever protection it could offer against unpleasant epithets. But like many popular slogans and verses, this one will not bear too close scrutiny. For names *will* hurt you. Sometimes you may be the victim, and find yourself an object of scorn, humiliation, and hatred just because other people have called you certain names. At other times you may not be the victim, but clever speakers and writers may, through name calling, blind your judgment so that you will follow them in a course of action wholly opposed to your own interests or principles. Name calling can make you gullible to propaganda which you might otherwise readily see through and reject.

9. The title that best expresses the ideas of this passage is
(A) An Object of Scorn
(B) An Unusual Course of Action
(C) The Foolishness of Rhymes
(D) Verbal Assassination
(E) The Clever Speaker

8. Name calling may make you more susceptible to
(A) childhood rhymes
(B) biased arguments
(C) sticks and stones
(D) invoked protection
(E) unpleasant epithets

9. The author evidently feels that slogans and verses are frequently
(A) invoked by gullible writers
(B) humiliating to their authors
(C) disregarded by children
(D) misunderstood by clever speakers
(E) an oversimplification of a problem

It takes no particular expert in foods, or even glutton, to know that no meal on the table ever is as good as the meal in the oven's roasting pan or the stove's covered kettle. There is something about the furtive lifting of the lid and the opening of the door that is better than all sauce and gravies. Call it the surprise appetizer. Call it, also, that one gesture which the proprietor of the kitchen hates above all others, which brings forth the shortest, most succinct sentences with the word "meddling" in them. Yet it is essentially a friendly gesture, one based on good will, and not on its more general misconstruction, curiosity. It is quite proper, to state the case flatly, to say that a little quiet investigation of what is cooking is simply an attempt to share the good things of life. It is possible to state that, but it will take more than a statement to convince the cook that it is not an act of interference. The kitchen has special laws.

10. The title that best expresses the ideas of this passage is
(A) The Attractions of the Kitchen
(B) The Privacy of the Kitchen
(C) Meddling in the Kitchen
(D) In Defense of Kitchen Meddling
(E) The Influence of the Kitchen in the Home

11. From the passage one can conclude that the writer is
(A) critical
(B) indifferent
(C) pessimistic
(D) uncertain
(E) genial

12. According to the author, the cook regards any investigation of what is cooking in the kitchen as
(A) furtive exploration
(B) an act of friendship
(C) gluttony
(D) a succinct sentence
(E) based on curiosity

Had Leonardo da Vinci seen the plain evidence of upward winds—the evidence of flying leaves and soaring birds—the air age might have begun in his time, and the airplane would have developed along with the sailing of gliders. A glider is nothing but a wood and fabric replica of a hawk; there is nothing in it that Leonardo could not have designed, built, and flown. It used to be that motorless airplanes could fly only over carefully selected sites, where a steep hillside faced a strong wind and deflected it upward. But today, with no new equipment but a clear mental image of these upward winds, human beings can fly without motors for hundreds of miles across country, even across flat plains, without machine power of any kind, riding on these updrafts.

13. The title that best expresses the ideas of this passage is
(A) Updrafts
(B) A Wood and Fabric Bird
(C) Da Vinci's Invention
(D) The Power of Imagination
(E) The Limitations of Gliders

14. Gliders can soar only
(A) over plateaus
(B) by riding the winds
(C) for short distances
(D) in mountainous country
(E) over carefully surveyed areas

15. The author's treatment of his material may best be described as
(A) quaintly humorous
(B) completely carefree
(C) predominantly factual
(D) utterly pessimistic
(E) bitterly sarcastic

The large college offers some distinct advantages over the small college. Large endowments are responsible for well-equipped libraries, laboratories, dormitories, and student activity facilities. Outstanding scholars are attracted to the faculty. The size also makes possible a great variety of courses and a high degree of specialization. As for the disadvantages, they are not so obvious. It has been said that large colleges seem to turn out their graduates on a production-line basis, without personalized instruction and guidance. In the small college each student is able to know almost every other student on the campus whereas in the larger college one may be lost in the thousands and at graduation may know only a few people. In a large institution a student may not meet the college president until commencement day, while in a small school students may have frequent contact with the president during their college years.

President D. C. Wedel of Bethel College, North Newton, Kansas, proudly points out that his small institution is reported to be among the fifty colleges in this country which produce more than ten scholars to each 1,000 graduates. [In these statistics a scholar is defined as a person who has earned a Ph.D. or received a fellowship in open competition.]

Using another type of educational achievement as a criterion, the editors of *Who's Who in America* reported that the small colleges contribute a higher percentage of those who merit rating than the larger institutions.

16. The title that best expresses the ideas of this passage is
(A) Choosing a College
(B) The Large University
(C) The Advantages of a Small College
(D) Scholarship
(E) Specialization

17. In a large university, a student may lack
(A) specialization
(B) friends
(C) close contact with the faculty
(D) a variety of courses from which to choose
(E) disadvantages

18. To be called a scholar, by a criterion in this passage, a student must
(A) earn an A average
(B) complete his or her doctoral studies
(C) obtain a baccalaureate degree
(D) be in the top one percent of the class
(E) attend a large university

19. *Who's Who in America*, according to the passage,
(A) rates colleges
(B) has compared the enrollments of large and small colleges
(C) has examined the educational records of those listed in their book
(D) lists the top 50 colleges in the country
(E) has studied the numbers from small and large colleges

Another example of the exercise of power by Congress was the action taken by it during the Reconstruction Period after the Civil War. It has already been noted above that President Johnson favored a lenient policy toward the South and attempted to carry out Lincoln's "10 per cent plan." He pardoned most of the Southern leaders and permitted them to restore their state governments. They were permitted to elect Senators and Representatives.

Congress, however, led by the Radical Republican Thaddeus Stevens, had other ideas about the handling of the defeated Confederacy. They favored punitive policies. The South should be treated as conquered territory, and its readmission should be handled by Congress rather than the President. They opposed the "*Johnson Governments*" and the "*Black Codes*" passed by Southern states which virtually restored former slaves to their masters. Accordingly they passed the *Reconstruction Act* of 1867. This measure divided the South into five military districts and provided that a seceded state would be readmitted into the Union only after it had ratified the *14th Amendment*, which provided that all persons born or naturalized in the United States should be citizens of the United States and of the state in which they resided, granted equality before the law to all persons, and prohibited a state from depriving any person of life, liberty, or property without due process of law. It also reduced the representation of states which barred qualified persons from voting, barred rebel leaders from federal office, and repudiated the Confederate debt. Later it adopted the *15th Amendment* guaranteeing the Negroes the right to vote.

Johnson vigorously opposed these measures. He vetoed the Reconstruction Act and others, only to see Congress repass them over his veto. After such passage of the Tenure of Office Act, Johnson, believing it unconstitutional, violated it and removed a member of his Cabinet without consulting Congress. The House of Representatives proceeded to impeach Johnson. The Senate, however, failed, by one vote, to reach the two-thirds majority necessary for his removal.

20. The title that best expresses the ideas of this passage is
(A) The Impeachment of President Johnson
(B) The Reconstruction Period
(C) A Conflict between the President and Congress
(D) A Lenient President
(E) The Reconstruction Act of 1867

21. The Reconstruction Act of 1867
(A) endorsed the "Black Codes"
(B) was vetoed by the President
(C) utilized Lincoln's "10 per cent" plan
(D) was declared unconstitutional by the President
(E) paid off the Confederate debt

22. Johnson was impeached
(A) because he opposed Congress
(B) because he did not consult Congress about the removal of a cabinet member
(C) by one vote
(D) because he vetoed many bills
(E) in 1865

I agree that Alaska faces more problems as a state than as a territory. As a territory, Alaska was under the jurisdiction of Congress and the President. The President appointed the Governor. The people had the responsibility of choosing the local legislature and delegates to the House of Representatives at Washington who had no vote there. The Governor appointed local officials and had a veto power over the acts of the local legislature. Hence, the people of Alaska had few political responsibilities. Political parties played a small part, and political activity was at a minimum. This government might be described as a paternal one, with the people looking to Washington for help, rather than relying on themselves.

As a state, Alaska can no longer look to the national capital for the solution of its problems. The people have a greater responsibility for managing the affairs of their state. Politics and political parties have suddenly become important. A new state government, consisting of an Executive Department headed by a Governor, a two-house legislature, and a system of courts have been provided, and the people must choose their own people to fill these posts. Many Alaskans having lived all their lives under a territorial system, and unused to the responsibilities of voting citizenship, must now adjust their attitudes and assume new civic responsibilities. Political leaders and groups have new tasks in educating voters, carrying on campaigns, and winning elections.

Another aspect of statehood concerns the handling of internal improvements, such as roads, bridges, public buildings, education, sanitation, health, and the many other functions of states which face the people of the state of Alaska and which were formerly the responsibility of the federal government.

23. The title that best expresses the ideas of this passage is
(A) The Good Old Days
(B) Problems of Statehood
(C) A Paternal Government
(D) The Right to Vote
(E) Alaska—the Largest State

24. As citizens of a territory, Alaskans
(A) had no vote
(B) had a paternal attitude
(C) elected delegates to Congress
(D) had no political activity
(E) paid no taxes

25. The author's attitude in writing this passage is
(A) sarcastic
(B) analytical
(C) confused
(D) skeptical
(E) feasible

READING EXERCISE B

One person's productivity, however, varies greatly from country to country. It depends on the amount of assistance the average worker is given in the form of machinery—that is to say, on the horsepower per head. It depends also—and this may be a point of growing importance—on the spirit and stamina of the workers. The industrial workers of certain countries have been working under heavy strain for many years. During that time they have been badly fed. Moreover, the countries referred to have become dependent in a significant degree on slave labor, the inefficiency of which is notorious.

26. The title that best expresses the ideas of this passage is
- (A) Machinery Makes the Difference
- (B) Horsepower per Head
- (C) Worker Productivity
- (D) Countries and Workers
- (E) The Importance of Spirit and Stamina

27. The author implies that
- (A) workers have neglected their health
- (B) slaves are weak
- (C) machinery adds one horsepower to each worker
- (D) working under strain reduces output
- (E) one person counts little

The rattler is our national snake, or would be if we had a national snake. Benjamin Franklin wanted to see it on the Great Seal. Maine, New Hampshire and Vermont seem to be the only states which are practically free of it, though rumors come down from time to time of rattlers having strayed across into southern Vermont. The rattler varies from the great diamondbacks down to pygmies no larger than garter snakes. Our local variety, the timber rattler, suns itself on the rock ledges of the mountains of Massachusetts, New York, New Jersey and Pennsylvania. To the west of us is the territory of the massasauga, a rattler which grows to two or three feet.

28. The title that best expresses the ideas of this passage is
- (A) Snakes from Maine to New York
- (B) Ben Franklin's Design for the Great Seal
- (C) A Widely Distributed Snake
- (D) Reptiles of New England and the West
- (E) Snakes Rampant

29. The paragraph implies that rattlesnakes
- (A) are on the Great Seal
- (B) are unknown in Vermont
- (C) appear in more than two sizes
- (D) of the smallest size are garter snakes
- (E) migrate by way of Vermont

As soon as you begin to take yourself seriously and imagine that your virtues are important because they are yours, you become the prisoner of your own vanity and even your best works will blind and deceive you. Then, in order to defend yourself, you will begin to see sins and faults everywhere in the actions of others. And the more unreasonable importance you attach to yourself and to your own works, the more you will tend to build up yourself by condemning other people. Some of the most virtuous people in the world are also the bitterest and most unhappy, because they have come to believe that all their happiness depends on their being more virtuous than others.

30. The title that best expresses the ideas of this passage is
- (A) The Necessity of Being Important
- (B) The Importance of Being Earnest
- (C) Evaluating One's Own Virtue
- (D) Dependence of Happiness upon Virtue
- (E) Relationship of Self-confidence to Virtue

31. One's good works may
- (A) lead one to be uncritical of others
- (B) lower one's ideas of oneself by leading one to criticize others
- (C) lead to self-righteousness
- (D) be spiritually dead to others
- (E) lead to superficiality and false values

For the sad state of criticism the writers must hold themselves much to blame. Literary artists, concerned solely in the creation of a book or story as close to perfection as their powers will permit, are generally quiet individuals, contemplative, retiring. On occasion they can be influenced to anger by some grievous social wrong which calls for desperate remedy. But mostly they are prone to sit in their towers reflecting on the absurdities of a foolish world, asking only to be left alone with their labor. Never aggressive in their own interest, seeking only peace, they lay themselves open to aggression. Thus they do not see the enemy who has stolen into the shadows at the rear of their retreat and is slowly scaling the walls. Such has been the course of events. While the artists have slept, the critical dwarfs have appeared. They have evolved a new language, written out a new set of definitions. Black is white, and white is black. The ugly and the nauseous are the beautiful; the beautiful is nightmare.

32. The title that best expresses the ideas of this passage is
- (A) Writers as Champions of Social Wrongs
- (B) Cooperation between Writer and Critic
- (C) Domination by the Critic
- (D) Progressive Standards of Criticism
- (E) Development of the Writing Profession

33. According to the passage, the critics' standards of criticism are
- (A) a development of former standards
- (B) a reversal of accepted standards
- (C) a valuable guide to the literary artist
- (D) a help in suggesting subjects to be written about
- (E) the result of the authors' neglect of good writing

34. Literary artists are inclined to
(A) be unconcerned with what is happening around them
(B) be continually aroused by wrongs
(C) slight the work of writing
(D) welcome aggression
(E) accept criticism gladly

Modern biology is a far cry from the old picture of the naturalist with the butterfly net, or the laboratory redolent of formaldehyde where earthworms and frogs were dissected. Today's laboratory fairly bristles with chemical and physical apparatus, which is used to study the nature of the living cell. The electronic microscope is one of the important new tools. The compounds that compose all living things—animals, plants, and microorganisms—are being listed. Over 2,500 different kinds of organic molecules have been identified so far, and the list is still growing. The discovery that all living things are made up of the same compounds is one of the first great generalizations from such studies.

Molecules, cells, organs, whole organisms—the units that biologists study cover a wide range. Or the subject may be the relationship of whole populations of various kinds of plants and animals to each other, the laboratory a protected square mile of virgin forest. Again, the laboratory may be hundreds of square miles of sea. For example, the NSF has given support to a study of the migration and orientation abilities of the green turtle, once an important food item in the Caribbean area but now in danger of becoming extinct; to an international research expedition to the Indian Ocean, in which oceanographers, meteorologists, and biologists are cooperating; and to an international program of studies of tropical botany, in which U.S. and Central American scientists are cooperating, where the "laboratory" will be the vegetation of Central America. Altogether, the NSF regularly supports basic research in eight branches of biology.

35. The old-fashioned biologist
(A) was a collector of specimens
(B) studied inorganic molecules
(C) roamed the seas
(D) cooperated with meteorologists
(E) covered a wide range of studies

36. The modern biologist studies
(A) virgin forests
(B) ocean life
(C) the migration of the green turtle
(D) tropical botany
(E) the nature of the living cell

37. Modern biology has succeeded in
(A) analyzing over 2,500 different living cells
(B) listing living compounds
(C) proving that all life is the same
(D) using new materials
(E) determining the compounds that make up all living things

The coastlines on the two sides of the Atlantic Ocean present a notable parallelism: the eastern most region of Brazil, in Pernambuco, has a convexity that corresponds almost perfectly with the concavity of the African Gulf of Guinea, while the contours of the African coastline between Rio de Oro and Liberia would, by the same approximation, match those of the Caribbean Sea.

Similar correspondences are also observed in many other regions of the Earth. This observation began to awaken scientific interest less than fifty years ago, when Alfred Wegener, a professor at the University of Hamburg, used it as the basis for formulating a revolutionary theory in geological science. According to Wegener, there was originally only one continent or land mass, which he called Pangea. Inasmuch as continental masses are lighter than the base on which they rest, he reasoned, they must float on the substratum of igneous rock, known as sima, as ice floes float on the sea. Then why, he asked, might continents not be subject to drifting? The rotation of the globe and other forces, he thought, had caused the cracking and, finally, the breaking apart of the original Pangea, along an extensive line represented today by the longitudinal submerged mountain range in the center of the Atlantic. While Africa seems to have remained static, the Americas apparently drifted toward the west until they reached their present position after more than 100 million years. Although the phenomenon seems fantastic, accustomed as we are to the concept of the rigidity and immobility of the continents, on the basis of the distance that separates them it is possible to calculate that the continental drift would have been no greater than two inches per year.

38. The title that best expresses the ideas of this passage is
(A) A Novel Theory
(B) Pangea
(C) Two Inches per Year
(D) Static Africa
(E) A Notable Parallelism

39. The submerged mountain range in the Atlantic
(A) runs from east to west
(B) runs from north to south
(C) is proof of Professor Wegener's theory
(D) is made up of igneous rock
(E) drifts in a westwardly direction

40. Professor Wegener's theory is
(A) an attempt to explain many geographic parallelisms
(B) based on a study of 100 million years
(C) an analysis of the lost continent
(D) unsound
(E) revolutionary

41. Sima, as described in this passage, is
(A) the basic substance of Pangea
(B) like an ice floe
(C) the submerged mountain range
(D) the continental land mass
(E) igneous rock

The recognized religion of Colonial Massachusetts was the Puritan (later called Congregationalist) branch of the Protestant faith. The Puritan Church was the officially established church. Only members of that faith were recognized as citizens; no others were tolerated there. The Church regulated the lives of the settlers very strictly. All had to pay taxes to support it. Attendance at church was compulsory. The lives, habits, and customs of all the people were very carefully regulated. The regulations were most minute, and those who violated them in the slightest were subjected to the ridicule or contempt of the community, and, at times, were punished by being forced to endure the humiliation of the stock or pillory. At Salem this persecution took the form of trials of certain women for witchcraft. In these, many were condemned to the stake and put to death.

Religion has undergone many changes in Massachusetts. The principle of religious freedom has displaced that of religious intolerance. While the Congregationalist Church is still in existence, it is no longer the only, or even the major, church. There are many faiths including various Protestant, Roman Catholic, Jewish, and other groups. There is no established church and no church tax. Citizenship is granted for other than religious reasons. A person may or may not be affiliated with a religious group. No one may expose anyone to ridicule, contempt, or punishment on grounds of religion or lack of it. Religious organizations devote themselves to religious work or other activities they choose to engage in. These are, however, private matters, and have no bearing on the lives of other citizens.

42. The title that best expresses the ideas of this passage is
- (A) Religious Intolerance in Massachusetts
- (B) Colonial Customs
- (C) The Church and State
- (D) Puritanism in America
- (E) Changes in Religious Life in Massachusetts

43. According to this passage, the penalty for witchcraft was
- (A) trivial
- (B) death
- (C) being pilloried
- (D) loss of citizenship
- (E) excommunication

44. Religion in Massachusetts today
- (A) determines citizenship
- (B) is a private matter
- (C) is democratic
- (D) is supported by the State
- (E) is forbidden by the State

45. In colonial Massachusetts, the citizens were
- (A) Puritans
- (B) tolerant
- (C) regulated
- (D) pilloried
- (E) religious

Rocks which have solidified directly from molten materials are called igneous rocks. Igneous rocks are commonly referred to as primary rocks because they are the original source of material found in sedimentaries and metamorphics. Igneous rocks compose the greater part of the earth's crust, but they are generally covered at the surface by a relatively thin layer of sedimentary or metamorphic rocks. Igneous rocks are distinguished by the following characteristics: (1) they contain no fossils; (2) they have no regular arrangement of layers; and (3) they are nearly always made up of crystals.

Sedimentary rocks are composed largely of minute fragments derived from the disintegration of existing rocks and in some instances from the remains of animals. As sediments are transported, individual fragments are assorted according to size. Distinct layers of such sediments as gravels, sand, and clay build up, as they are deposited by water and occasionally wind. These sediments vary in size with the material and the power of the eroding agent. Sedimentary materials are laid down in layers called strata.

When sediments harden into sedimentary rocks, the names applied to them change to indicate the change in physical state. Thus, small stones and gravel cemented together are known as conglomerates; cemented sand becomes sandstone; and hardened clay becomes shale. In addition to these, other sedimentary rocks such as limestone frequently result from the deposition of dissolved material. The ingredient parts are normally precipitated by organic substances, such as shells of clams or hard skeletons of other marine life.

Both igneous and sedimentary rocks may be changed by pressure, heat, solution, or cementing action. When individual grains from existing rocks tend to deform and interlock, they are called metamorphic rocks. For example, granite, an igneous rock, may be metamorphosed into a gneiss or a schist. Limestone, a sedimentary rock, when subjected to heat and pressure may become marble, a metamorphic rock. Shale under pressure becomes slate.

46. Which one of the following is a metamorphic rock?
- (A) Granite
- (B) Shale
- (C) Slate
- (D) Limestone
- (E) Gravel

47. One factor which does not cause a change in rock structure is
- (A) heat
- (B) wind
- (C) pressure
- (D) solution
- (E) interlocking grains

48. If a rock formation is stratified, we may assume that
(A) it is the result of volcanic action
(B) it is crystalline in structure
(C) it was built up over a period of years
(D) it is metamorphic
(E) it is organic in composition

49. In a granite quarry, we may expect to find
(A) strata
(B) limestone
(C) metamorphic rocks
(D) gravel beds
(E) no trace of fossils

50. The person most interested in the ideas found in this passage would most likely be a
(A) sculptor
(B) archeologist
(C) paleontologist
(D) farmer
(E) geologist

READING EXERCISE C

As a practicing warrior for many years, I am convinced of the complete futility of war. It settles only the problems of the past and creates the new problems of the future. There is no place in the world of today for the narrow, competitive nationalism that sparks the tinder of war. I am convinced that the people of this planet must ultimately and inevitably move toward a single form of world government if civilization is to survive. But it is our immediate task to see that this world government comes as a mutual federation of free peoples rather than through the ruthless domination of a master state enslaving all others.

51. The title that best expresses the ideas of this passage is
(A) Problems of the Past
(B) Why War Is Futile
(C) Dangers Concerning World Government
(D) Competition in Today's World
(E) Securing a Worthy World Government

52. The author believes that wars start chiefly because of
(A) ruthless domination of a master race
(B) slavery
(C) insufficient demands for freedom
(D) competitive nationalism
(E) unsettled problems of the past

The propaganda of a nation at war is designed to stimulate the energy of its citizens and their will to win, and to imbue them with an overwhelming sense of the justice of their cause. Directed abroad, its purpose is to create precisely contrary effects among citizens of enemy nations and to assure to nationals of allied or subjugated countries full and unwavering assistance.

53. The title that best expresses the ideas of this passage is
(A) Propaganda's Failure
(B) Designs for Waging War
(C) Influencing Opinion in Wartime
(D) The Propaganda of Other Nations
(E) Citizens of Enemy Nations and Their Allies

54. The passage implies that a nation's wartime propaganda is
(A) dangerous to its nationals
(B) useful to some of its enemies
(C) unjustified
(D) doubtful procedure
(E) varied

In the case of persons whose judgment is really deserving of confidence, how has it become so? They have kept their minds open to criticism of their opinions and conduct. It has been their practice to listen to all that could be said against them; to profit by as much of it as was just, and expound to themselves, and upon occasion to others, the fallacy of what was fallacious. They have felt that the only way in which a human being can make some approach to knowing the whole of a subject is by hearing what can be said about it by persons of every variety of opinion, and studying all models in which it can be looked at by every character of mind. No wise person ever acquired wisdom in any mode but this; nor is it in the nature of human intellect to become wise in any other manner.

55. The title that best expresses the ideas of this passage is
(A) Criticism of Ill-formed Opinion
(B) How to Form an Opinion
(C) Developing Wisdom
(D) Listen to Everything
(E) The Nature of Human Intellect

56. An intelligent person
(A) should be slow to change his or her opinion
(B) should get all views of a subject
(C) can be certain that his or her conduct is sound
(D) believes that an open mind guarantees wisdom
(E) shuts his or her mind to the notions of the uneducated

57. One may become worthy of confidence by
(A) pretending to listen to everyone
(B) expounding the falseness of every opinion
(C) welcoming and studying criticism
(D) accepting every variety of view
(E) studying the nature of the intellect

Although patience is the most important quality a treasure hunter can have, the trade demands a certain amount of courage too. I have my share of guts, but make no boast about ignoring the hazards of diving. As all good divers know, the business of plunging into an alien world with an artificial air supply as your only link to the world above can be as dangerous as stepping into a den of lions. Most of the danger rests within the diver himself.

The devil-may-care diver who shows great bravado underwater is the worst risk of all. He may lose his bearings in the glimmering dim light which penetrates the sea and become separated from his diving companions. He may dive too deep, too long, and suffer painful, sometimes fatal, bends.

He may surface too quickly and force his lungs to squeeze their supply of high pressure air into his bloodstream, causing an embolism—a bubble of air in the blood—which often kills. He may become trapped in a submarine rockslide, get lost in an underwater cave, or be chopped to bits by a marauding shark. These are not occasional dangers such as crossing a street in busy traffic. They are always with you under water. At one time or another I have faced all of them except bends and embolism, which can be avoided by common sense and understanding of human physical limits beneath the surface.

Once, while salvaging brass from the sunken hulk of an old steel ship, I brushed lightly against a huge engine cylinder which looked as if it were as solid as it was on the day the ship was launched. Although the pressure of my touch was hardly enough to topple a toy soldier, the heavy mass of cast iron collapsed, causing a chain reaction in which the rest of the old engine crumbled. Tons of iron dropped all around me. Sheer luck saved me from being crushed. I have been wary of swimming around steel shipwrecks ever since.

58. The title that best expresses the main idea of this passage is
(A) Adventuring in an Alien World
(B) The Wrong Kind of Courage
(C) Underwater Perils
(D) The Successful Skindiver
(E) Hunting Treasure the Hard Way

59. We may most safely conclude that the author is
(A) a tester of underwater equipment
(B) a professional underwater salvager
(C) a marine engineer
(D) an amateur diver
(E) an underwater fisherman

60. The author apparently assumes that the readers are *least* likely to know the meaning of the word
(A) bravado
(B) bends
(C) embolism
(D) marauding
(E) salvaging

Air Research Centers at various sites in the United States use balloons in the study of the atmosphere 50,000 to 100,000 feet above the ground. The balloons are unmanned but carry a number of instruments. They aim to find the answers to questions about wind patterns, temperatures, pressures and turbulence in the upper air regions as yet unexplored. Balloons are preset to reach specific altitudes and to remain there the desired length of time. As they are carried along with the wind stream, delicate instruments radio back—or telemeter—the pertinent data. Radio direction-finding stations track the balloon in transit and record the telemetered data concerning altitudes, identification of the particular balloon, rate of its ballast consumption, and so on. By accurately tracking and plotting the balloon in flight, it is easy to determine the direction of the wind currents carrying the balloon along.

61. The title that best expresses the ideas of this passage is
(A) Gathering Meteorological Data
(B) Weather at 50,000 Feet
(C) Plastic Technicians
(D) Real Flying Saucers
(E) Aviation Research

62. The purpose of a radio in a balloon is to
(A) relay information from other instruments to earth
(B) allow the pilot to contact the Air Research Center
(C) control the balloon's rate of ascent
(D) plot the direction of wind currents
(E) track the balloon in flight

63. The balloons of the Air Research Center
(A) are similar to rockets
(B) are valuable instruments of war
(C) may detect use of the hydrogen bomb
(D) rise to the altitudes indicated by the experimenters
(E) are launched from a central point in the United States

Although political parties are nowhere mentioned in the Constitution they have come to play an important role in the process of American government. George Washington cautioned against the growth of political factions and sought to avoid political partisanship. Nevertheless, during his administration differing political philosophies were responsible for the growth of two major political parties in the United States. The first party, the Federalists, was characterized by the philosophy of Alexander Hamilton, that only the rich and well-born were fit to govern, and its program reflected their interests. It favored the assumption of state debts by the federal government, payment of national debts at face value, payment of foreign debts, establishment of a national bank, an excise tax, a strong central government, loose interpretation of the Constitution, and sympathy with aristocratic England in foreign affairs. The second party, the Republicans, led by Thomas Jefferson, believed in government opposed to aristocracy, monarchy and privilege. It advocated strong states' rights, limited federal power and strict interpretation of the Constitution and opposed the payment of national debts at face value and the assumption of state debts. It also opposed the national bank and sympathized with revolutionary France in foreign affairs.

64. The title that best expresses the ideas of this passage is
(A) A Two-party System
(B) Hamilton and Jefferson
(C) Washington's Antipathy to Political Parties
(D) The Federalists
(E) Differing Philosophies of Government

65. Jefferson advocated
(A) a good relationship with France
(B) strict support of a national bank
(C) government of the elite
(D) the establishment of an aristocracy
(E) a return to monarchy

66. According to the passage, which of the following are characteristics of the Federalist party?
a. Belief in a privileged class
b. Support of a national bank
c. Jeffersonian democracy
d. States' rights
(A) all of the above
(B) a and b only
(C) none of the above
(D) a and c only
(E) a, b, and d only

67. The theory that only the rich are fit to govern justifies the imposition of
(A) a poll tax
(B) excise taxes
(C) states' rights
(D) a loose interpretation of the Constitution
(E) an income tax

An essay which appeals chiefly to the intellect is Francis Bacon's "Of Studies." His careful tripartite division of studies expressed succinctly in aphoristic prose demands the complete attention of the mind of the reader. He considers studies as they should be: for pleasure, for self-improvement, for business. He considers the evils of excess study: laziness, affectation, and preciosity. Bacon divides books into three categories: those to be read in part, those to be read cursorily, and those to be read with care. Studies should include reading, which gives depth; speaking, which adds readiness of thought; and writing, which trains in preciseness. Somewhat mistakenly, the author ascribes certain virtues to individual fields of study: wisdom to history, wit to poetry, subtlety to mathematics and depth to natural philosophy. Bacon's four-hundred-word essay, studded with Latin phrases and highly compressed in thought, has intellectual appeal indeed.

68. The title that best expresses the ideas of this passage is
(A) The Appeal of the Essay
(B) A Tripartite Division
(C) Francis Bacon's "Of Studies"
(D) A 400-word Essay
(E) How to Read Books

69. *Aphoristic* (line 3), as used by the writer, means
(A) abstruse
(B) pithy
(C) divided into thirds
(D) proverbial
(E) Latin

70. The value of writing lies in the fact that
(A) it is permanent
(B) it is available to the reader when he or she wants it
(C) subtlety is developed
(D) exactness is required
(E) it makes a well-rounded person

The atmosphere contains water vapor, but there is a limit to how much water can be evaporated into a given volume of air, just as there is a limit to how much sugar can be dissolved in one cupful of coffee. More sugar can be dissolved in hot coffee than in cold. A given volume of air can hold more water vapor at a higher temperature than at a lower temperature. The air is said to be *saturated* when it holds as much water vapor as it can at that temperature. At 20°C a cubic meter of air can hold about 17 gm of water vapor; at 30°C it can hold about 30 gm. Usually the atmosphere is not saturated. *Relative humidity* (expressed in per cent) is the ratio of the mass of water vapor actually present in a given volume of air to the mass which would be present in it if it were saturated. For example, if a cubic meter of air at 20°C contains 12 gm of water vapor, the relative humidity is $\frac{12\text{ gm}}{17\text{ gm}} \times 100 = 71\%$. Hygrometers are instruments for measuring relative humidity. Readings on wet and dry bulb thermometers can be compared with the aid of a chart from which one can then read off the relative humidity. The basic principle of this is that evaporation is a cooling process. The rate of evaporation from the wet bulb thermometer will be high when the relative humidity is low, and therefore on such a day the wet bulb thermometer will read considerably below the dry bulb one. There is no simple formula for converting this temperature difference to relative humidity, and therefore a chart is used.

If unsaturated air is cooled, its relative humidity goes up. If the temperature of the air drops sufficiently, saturation is reached and excess moisture precipitates out. The *dew point* is the temperature to which the air must be cooled so that it will be saturated and condensation will just form.

71. When the readings on the wet bulb thermometer and the dry bulb thermometer are similar, we may assume that
(A) we have relative humidity
(B) the air is saturated
(C) the thermometers are inefficient
(D) the temperature is going to rise
(E) the temperature is about to fall

72. When the air is saturated, it is likely to be
(A) raining
(B) windy
(C) clear
(D) getting warmer
(E) getting cooler

73. According to the passage, the dew point is most often reached
(A) early in the morning
(B) at noon
(C) late in the afternoon
(D) at dusk
(E) after midnight

74. A chart is used to determine the relative humidity after using a wet and a dry bulb thermometer because
(A) it comes with the instrument
(B) the mathematics involved is complicated
(C) there is no need to duplicate the work
(D) people do not know how to handle percent
(E) cool air makes the relative humidity rise

75. When the temperature of the air rises above the dew point,
(A) dew will form
(B) it will rain
(C) the relative humidity exceeds 100%
(D) evaporation is likely to take place
(E) the hygrometer will become inaccurate

READING EXERCISE D

Today in a time of great confusion and fierce disagreement, and also a time of great opportunity for all who are disposed to make their profit of that confusion, we who use words have a heavy responsibility. We need illimitable boldness in our seeking of truth, and great generosity of feeling and imagination in our approach to our task of giving it concrete and moving expression. But we need the greatest care in our choice of the words we use that they may first of all be accurate and fair, that they may meet the classic American test of "justice to all."

76. The title that best expresses the ideas of this passage is
(A) Taking Advantage of Confusion
(B) The Need for Disagreement
(C) A Duty of Writers and Speakers
(D) Confusion and Limitation of Words
(E) Truth-seeking Aspects of Words

77. The writer believes that
(A) most Americans lack imagination
(B) writers must be fearless
(C) all Americans stand for justice for all
(D) "Justice for All" is a classic American essay
(E) a majority wish to make a profit from confusion

In California one public utility company seeded clouds over a watershed a hundred miles square and in three successive years brought down enough rain to supply a city of 50,000 with water enough for three months. On the other hand, the Arizona Date Institute has threatened rainmakers with suits if the date crop is damaged by too much artificially produced rain. Last June Dr. Irving Langmuir warned that enthusiastic but unscientific rainmaking might actually prevent rain from falling, and his disciple, Dr. Bernard Vonnegut, has added that unless there is police regulation unrestrained cloud seeding will hamper earnest scientists who are trying to develop a new meteorological art.

78. The title that best expresses the ideas of this passage is
(A) Legislation against Rainmaking
(B) Cloud Seeding
(C) California, Pioneer in Rainmaking
(D) The Art of Meteorology
(E) The Case Against Cloud Seeding

79. Regulation of rainmaking is
(A) demanded by Arizona
(B) threatened by Dr. Langmuir
(C) opposed by California
(D) being discussed
(E) questioned by Dr. Vonnegut

By the words *public duty* I do not necessarily mean *official* duty, although it may include that. I mean simply that constant and active practical participation in the details of politics without which, upon the part of the most intelligent citizens, the conduct of public affairs falls under the control of selfish and ignorant or crafty and venal persons. I mean that personal attention—which, as it must be incessant, is often wearisome and even repulsive—to the details of politics, attendance at meetings, service upon committees, care and trouble and expense of many kinds, patient endurance of rebuffs, chagrins, ridicules, disappointments, defeats—in a word, all those duties and services which, when selfishly and meanly performed, stigmatize a person as a mere politician; but whose constant, honorable, intelligent, and vigilant performance is the gradual building, stone by stone and layer by layer, of that great temple of self-restrained liberty which all generous souls mean that our government should be.

80. The title that best expresses the ideas of this passage is
(A) The Public Duty of Intelligent Persons
(B) The Evils of Indifference
(C) Characteristics of the Mere Politician
(D) The Ideal Democracy
(E) True Patriotism

81. The maintenance of the American democratic ideal depends upon
(A) a highly educated body of citizens
(B) unification of political parties
(C) absence of dissenting ideas
(D) an easily led minority
(E) alert sharing of civic responsibilities

82. Which one of the following statements best expresses an idea found in the passage?
(A) Constant and active participation in politics perpetuates the democratic ideal
(B) Personal attention of officeholders ensures American democratic principles.
(C) Genuine public spirit demands personal sacrifice.
(D) *Public duty* is synonymous with official duty.
(E) American liberty is based upon constant legislation.

Of course, a manager's job isn't all managing. In the complex industry that major league baseball has become, a key man needs many talents. Games are won not only in the ball park but at spring training quarters, where the manager finds his steel and tempers it; in the "front office," where the team's weaknesses and strength are analyzed and players shifted, farmed out, traded, sold; in the locker room, where statistics and direct observation are brought to bear on the chinks in the armor of the opposition. In spring quarters, a manager must be a teacher; in the front office, a businessman; in the locker room, a psychologist; in the ball park, a strategist.

83. The title that best expresses the ideas of this passage is
(A) Jack-of-All-Trades
(B) Baseball Is Big Business
(C) Developing a Pennant Winner
(D) Winning the Game in the "Front Office"
(E) The Work of the Team Manager

84. The author implies that in major league baseball
(A) a majority of games are won in spring training
(B) happenings in the locker room are unimportant
(C) unfair methods are used to win
(D) there must be a boss
(E) financial ability is the most important quality

Whatever the sundry predictions on the medium's future, television's appeal to the family in the home admittedly is its peculiar strength both as entertainment and as a social force. The source of that strength lies basically in the fact that television makes it possible to be in two places at once. If the ultimate effects of such a social phenomenon are cloaked in uncertainty, there is good reason. It never happened before.

85. The title that best expresses the ideas of this passage is
(A) Television's Special Appeal
(B) Being in Two Places at Once
(C) Television's Ultimate Future
(D) A Remarkable Social Phenomenon
(E) Television's Uncertain Popularity

86. The passage implies that
(A) television's prospects are not very bright
(B) the family as a moral force is strengthened by television
(C) the social phenomenon mentioned is the television program
(D) the viewer of a television program is in effect present at the scene
(E) the author is able to predict the future of television

Windstorms have recently established a record which meteorologists hope will not be equalled for many years to come. Disastrous tornadoes along with devastating typhoons and hurricanes have cost thousands of lives and left property damage totaling far into the millions. The prominence these storms have held in the news has led many people to ask about the difference between the three. Is a typhoon the same as a hurricane? Is a tornado the same as a typhoon? Basically, there is no difference. All three consist of wind rotating counterclockwise (in the Northern Hemisphere) at a tremendous velocity around a low-pressure center. However, each type does have its own definite characteristics. Of the three, the tornado is certainly the most treacherous. The Weather Bureau can, with some degree of accuracy, forecast the typhoon and the hurricane; it is impossible to determine where or when the tornado will strike. And out of the three, if one had a choice, perhaps it would be safer to choose to withstand the hurricane.

87. The title that best expresses the ideas of this passage is
(A) Recent Storms
(B) Record-breaking Storms
(C) Predicting Windstorms
(D) Treacherous Windstorms
(E) Wind Velocity and Direction

88. Which is *not* common to all of the storms mentioned?
(A) fairly accurate forecasting
(B) violently rotating wind

(C) high property damage
(D) loss of human lives
(E) public interest

89. The author indicates that
(A) typhoons cannot be forecast
(B) the Southern Hemisphere is free from hurricanes
(C) typhoons are more destructive than hurricanes
(D) hurricanes are not really dangerous
(E) tornadoes occur around a low-pressure center

The Greek language is a member of the Aryan or Indo-European family and its various dialects constitute the Hellenic group. It was probably spoken in Europe and Asia at least 1,500 years before the Christian Era by Greeks with classical learning. Later it was a universal language among the cultured classes, just as Latin afterward became the medium of international communication. During the Dark Ages, Greek was little known to Western Europe, except in monasteries, although it remained the language of the Byzantine Empire. The emigration of the Greeks to Italy after the fall of Constantinople, and during the century preceding, gave a new impetus to the study of the Greek language, and the revival of learning gave it the place it has ever since occupied.

90. The title that best expresses the ideas of this passage is
(A) The Greek Language
(B) Greece, Past and Present
(C) Importance of the Greek Dialects
(D) Greek, the Universal Language
(E) An Interesting Language

91. A result of Greece's being the center of classical learning was that
(A) it built great schools
(B) its citizens were all cultured
(C) Greek displaced Latin
(D) Greek was the universal language among the cultured classes
(E) Greek was not important during the Dark Ages

92. The Greek language
(A) became dominant in Italy
(B) was introduced into Europe by way of Constantinople
(C) was responsible for the revival of learning
(D) was probably spoken in Europe as early as 1500 B.C.
(E) had more dialects than Latin

Men and women never stop learning. They all matriculate at the "university of hard knocks." Those who make the effort to learn are engaged in "adult education." Most adult education comes through the daily press, magazines, books, libraries, museums, the theater, concerts, the radio, motion pictures, conversation, travel and attendance at meetings and lectures. Government has touched certain parts of education very definitely through encouraging and supporting public libraries, providing classes—mostly in English—for foreign groups, arranging occasional lectures, and supervising correspondence courses. The Federal Extension Service with its farm, home and club county agents is the largest education service in rural areas. No one can tell in advance what the adult education requirements of any community will be as time goes on but the possibilities of the radio as an instrument of instruction should certainly be explored.

93. Adult education presupposes
(A) graduation
(B) leisure
(C) an effort to learn
(D) entering a university
(E) plenty of money

94. The greatest educational aid for rural districts is
(A) correspondence courses
(B) travel
(C) museums
(D) The Federal Extension Service
(E) public libraries

95. The most important possibility for future adult education is the
(A) club
(B) radio
(C) newspaper
(D) automobile
(E) lecture

96. The author's failure to mention television as an educational factor may be explained by
(A) the possibility that this passage was written before the development of television
(B) the fact that television is a "wasteland"
(C) the realization that television is used mainly for entertainment
(D) the author's aversion to the medium
(E) the fact that television sets are much more costly than radio sets

History has long made a point of the fact that the magnificent flowering of ancient civilization rested upon the institution of slavery, which released opportunity at the top for the art and literature which became the glory of antiquity. In a way, the mechanization of the present-day world produces the condition of the ancient in that the enormous development of labor-saving devices and of contrivances which amplify the capacities of humankind affords the base for the leisure necessary to widespread cultural pursuits. Mechanization is the present-day slave power, with the difference that in the mechanized society there is no group of the community which does not share in the benefits of its inventions.

97. The title that best expresses the ideas of this passage is
(A) Slavery in the Ancient World
(B) Today's Community
(C) Worthwhile Use of Leisure
(D) Ancient Culture
(E) Modern Slave Power

98. Which factor has produced more leisure time?
(A) The abolition of slavery
(B) The glory of antiquity
(C) The development of art and literature
(D) An increase in inventions
(E) The development of the community

99. The flowering of any civilization has always depended on
(A) the galley slave
(B) freedom for the working person
(C) mechanical power
(D) leisure for cultural pursuits
(E) transportation

100. The author's attitude toward mechanization is one of
(A) awe
(B) acceptance
(C) distrust
(D) fear
(E) devotion

READING EXERCISE E

Lithography is the art of drawing with a greasy substance, usually crayon, on a stone, metal, or paper surface, and then printing it. It is based on the fact that grease attracts grease and is repelled by water. It is the most direct of all the graphic arts, for in practicing it the artist first sees the exact value of each line that he draws and then has the drawing reproduced so accurately that it may truly be said to have been multiplied. In making either an etching, a process in which a drawing is engraved on a metal plate through a thin film of wax, or a woodblock, in which the drawing is carved in wood, the artist must wait for a print to estimate his work fairly. When a lithograph is made, the artist's drawing grows in definite values under his eyes and changes can be made in it as the artist works.

101. The title that best expresses the ideas of this passage is
(A) Advantages of Lithography
(B) How Etchings and Woodblocks Are Made
(C) Crayon and Stone in Art
(D) Modern Graphic Arts
(E) Basic Principles of Art

102. A great advantage of lithography as a means of reproducing drawings is that it
(A) is quicker and neater than other methods
(B) gives faithful reproductions
(C) requires a metal plate
(D) requires no special materials
(E) is less expensive than other methods

103. Many artists like to use lithography to reproduce their drawings because they
(A) know in advance the value of each picture
(B) often get unexpected results
(C) get higher prices for lithographs than for etchings
(D) can get clearer enlargements
(E) can make alterations and corrections

The American Revolution is the only one in modern history which, rather than devouring the intellectuals who prepared it, carried them to power. Most of the signatories of the Declaration of Independence were intellectuals. This tradition is ingrained in America, whose greatest statesmen have been intellectuals—Jefferson and Lincoln, for example. These statesmen performed their political function, but at the same time they felt a more universal responsibility, and they actively defined this responsibility. Thanks to them there is in America a living school of political science. In fact, it is at the moment the only one perfectly adapted to the emergencies of the contemporary world, and one which can be victoriously opposed to communism. A European who follows American politics will be struck by the constant reference in the press and from the platform to this political philosophy, to the historical events through which it was best expressed, and to the great statesmen who were its best representatives.

104. The title that best expresses the ideas of this passage is
(A) Fathers of the American Revolution
(B) Jefferson and Lincoln—Ideal Statesmen
(C) The Basis of American Political Philosophy
(D) Democracy versus Communism
(E) The Responsibilities of Statesmen

105. According to this passage, intellectuals who pave the way for revolutions are usually
(A) honored
(B) destroyed
(C) misunderstood
(D) forgotten
(E) elected to office

106. Which statement is true according to the passage?
(A) America is a land of intellectuals.
(B) The signers of the Declaration of Independence were all well educated.
(C) Adaptability is a characteristic of American political science.
(D) Jefferson and Lincoln were revolutionaries.
(E) Europeans are confused by American politics

Man is always mysterious. Primordial forces hidden in the recesses of his soul, not the economic causes that are measured by statistics or in the laboratory, determine today as they have for thousands, perhaps millions, of years the crucial acts of his life: struggles and wars, procreation, religious awe, provision of shelter, the search for leaders in peace and in war, satisfaction for his hunger. Thought, modern science, is but a slender taper burning in the depths of the night. But with this tiny flame, the fire of Prometheus or Lucifer, man begins the ordering of his world and the fabrication of those objects that sometimes help him, sometimes enslave him, as, with ever-fresh interest, he ponders his origin and his destiny.

107. the title that best expresses the ideas of this passage is
(A) The Mystery of Man
(B) The Value of Thought
(C) Statistical Studies
(D) Primordial Forces
(E) Prometheus' Contribution

108. *Primordial* means
(A) hidden
(B) existing from the beginning of time
(C) unconscious
(D) subconscious
(E) mysterious

109. The sentence "Thought, modern science, is but a slender taper . . ." is an illustration of
(A) exaggeration
(B) allusion
(C) simile
(D) metaphor
(E) personification

110. Human behavior is controlled by
(A) emotion
(B) economic forces
(C) science
(D) history
(E) hidden influences

At certain periods of our life we long to stop the inexorable ticking hand of time and meditate upon our whole destiny. But alas, in the turmoil of today it is well-nigh impossible to drop out of the line and halt awhile. Our sense of honor and duty forbids us to be laggard in the fierce race. We must live amid the noise and shouts of the world, and our houses must be open for all the world to see. And yet never was there a time when humanity more needed its moments of silent meditation.

111. The title that best expresses the ideas of this passage is
(A) The Race of Life
(B) The Need for Quiet Thought
(C) The Turmoil of Today
(D) The Sense of Honor and Duty
(E) The Inexorable Ticking Hand of Time

112. The writer implies that
(A) we may lack honor
(B) our destiny is secure
(C) ours is a competitive world
(D) our minds must be at peace
(E) we are less laggard than our ancestors

English folksingers have adopted a conventional method of singing. During the performance the eyes are closed, the head is upraised, and a rigid expression of countenance is maintained until the song is finished. A short pause follows the conclusion, and then the singer assumes a relaxed attitude and repeats in an ordinary voice the last line of the song, or its title. This is the invariable ritual on formal occasions. It does not proceed from any lack of appreciation. The English peasant is by nature shy and undemonstrative, and on ceremonious occasions, as when singing before an audience, the rustic performer becomes very nervous and restrained, and welcomes the shelter afforded by convention.

113. The title that best expresses the ideas of this passage is
(A) Country Music Festivals
(B) Traditional Music
(C) A Helpful Custom
(D) A Changing Ritual of Song
(E) An Unappreciative Audience

114. The English folksinger has adopted a conventional method of singing chiefly because of
(A) pride
(B) a relaxed attitude
(C) a dislike of customs
(D) a reserved nature
(E) a desire to please

115. The tone of this passage is best described as
(A) pleading
(B) argumentative
(C) matter-of-fact
(D) depressing
(E) ironic

No, there are far better places than a train for talk. But few places are a train's equal for reading. Not magazines or newspapers alone. They are mere canapés to the heavy meal which can follow. The classics you have always meant to read, the new books you have failed to get around to, the fat books which usually are put aside for summer, the volume you could not resist while browsing in the station bookstore, the old books you are anxious to reread to see how you and they have changed—these are the perfect companions on a journey.

116. The title that best expresses the ideas of this passage is
(A) Successful Reading
(B) Advantages of a Trip by Train
(C) Wide Reading of Periodicals and the Best Books
(D) Reading vs. Conversation
(E) Reading on the Train

117. The author implies that
(A) magazines should be read before meals in the dining car
(B) long books are more likely to be read in the summer
(C) books are frequently rewritten for later publication
(D) classics and heavy meals belong together
(E) reading is superior to browsing

Machines are demolishing the sharecropper system, a definitive answer to those who claimed that it was a vicious system designed to enslave the cropper. Sharecropping, no heaven for the tenant, was no paradise for the farmer, and he has eagerly seized upon machines to end it. When mechanization of the Delta agriculture has been completed, out into the unknown there will go about 70 percent of those presently upon the land, over 200,000 persons.

As they go, the old-time plantation goes. Under mechanization the fields march from horizon to horizon unbroken by cabins, churches, gardens, cowsheds. Scattered cabins and other structures give way to small villages as in European agriculture. Workers move to and from the fields on the self-propelled vehicles that are their tools.

118. The title that best expresses the ideas of this passage is
(A) The Machine Enslaves the Sharecropper
(B) Plantation Memories
(C) A Vicious System
(D) In Defense of Sharecropping
(E) Agricultural Trends in the South

119. The author implies that the system of sharecropping
(A) gave advantages to the tenants
(B) is desired by farm owners
(C) will be strengthened by the use of machinery
(D) caused the homes of farm workers to be separated from each other
(E) was brought to this country from Europe

The tonnage of warships is almost always given in terms of displacement, and this because they carry no cargo other than stores. Displacement, as the name indicates, is the weight of water in long tons pushed aside by the hull's own weight at a fixed draught. Since some transatlantic companies find it expedient to advertise that one of their liners is the largest afloat, they sometimes express the size of a record-breaker in displacement tons, for these are usually larger than gross tonnage. Sometimes glass-enclosed decks are included in the cubic contents to arrive at a high gross tonnage.

120. The title that best expresses the ideas of this passage is
(A) Glass-enclosed Decks and Ship Weight
(B) The Weights of Ships
(C) Ships With and Without Cargo
(D) Weighing the Great Ocean Liners
(E) Long Tons vs. Displacement

The junior college is often a salvation for high school seniors who have been rejected by their colleges of first choice and, late in spring, find themselves without a school. Junior colleges serve several functions. In the first place they offer a complete 2-year course for those who have the choice between 2 years of college and none. This is far superior to going for 2 years to an institution whose curriculum is geared to 4 years of work. Second, these schools include sufficient courses in English, history, political science, sociology, and psychology to permit students to learn the principles of human relationships. This general education makes them better members of their family and their community. Most junior colleges provide guidance to help the student in making vocational plans. Perhaps the most important purpose served is the one that prepares the student for transfer to the traditional 4-year college. Some high school graduates find that they cannot qualify for admission to a 4-year college because of certain matriculation deficiencies. By enrolling in a junior college they can remove these difficulties and in addition take other worthwhile courses. Some who do not have these problems prefer to take this 2-year course and then transfer to the traditional college. Many students who are successful in junior colleges become juniors in 4-year institutions, equipped with a firm academic background. Ordinarily they suffer no handicap in their competition with the "old residents" who have been there since freshman year.

121. The title that best expresses the ideas of this passage is
(A) The Salvation of the High School Senior
(B) Matriculation Deficiencies
(C) Two Years or Four Years of College
(D) The Function of the Junior College
(E) Transferring from Junior College to Regular School

122. A junior college is preferable to a regular college when
(A) no regular college will accept the student
(B) a student has only two years for his or her education
(C) a student has matriculation deficiencies
(D) a student wishes to learn the principles of human relationships
(E) a student wishes to transfer to a regular college

123. A subject not mentioned as aiding in understanding the principles of human relationships is
(A) French
(B) English
(C) psychology
(D) history
(E) government

124. The most important function of the junior college according to the author is
(A) to provide education for those with limited time
(B) to enable students to understand the principles of human relationships
(C) to provide vocational guidance
(D) to enable students to transfer to four-year colleges
(E) to enable students to make up deficiencies

125. The transfer from junior colleges to regular four-year colleges is
(A) limited
(B) normally made without too much difficulty
(C) resented by the "old residents"
(D) available at any time
(E) desirable because it makes the student a better member of his or her community

---

ANSWER KEY

Exercise A *(Page 83)*

1. E	4. B	7. D	10. D	13. A	16. C	18. B	20. C	22. B	24. C
2. D	5. D	8. B	11. E	14. B	17. C	19. E	21. B	23. B	25. B
3. E	6. A	9. E	12. E	15. C					

Exericse B *(Page 87)*

26. C	29. C	32. C	35. A	38. E	41. E	43. B	45. A	47. B	49. E
27. D	30. C	33. B	36. E	39. B	42. E	44. B	46. C	48. C	50. E
28. C	31. C	34. A	37. E	40. A					

Exercise C *(Page 90)*

51. E	54. E	57. C	60. C	63. D	66. B	68. C	70. D	72. A	74. B
52. D	55. C	58. C	61. A	64. E	67. A	69. B	71. B	73. E	75. D
53. C	56. B	59. B	62. A	65. A					

Exercise D *(Page 93)*

76. C	79. D	82. C	85. A	88. A	91. D	93. C	95. B	97. E	99. D
77. B	80. A	83. E	86. D	89. E	92. D	94. D	96. A	98. D	100. B
78. E	81. E	84. D	87. D	90. A					

Exercise E *(Page 96)*

101. A	104. C	107. B	110. E	113. C	116. E	118. E	120. B	122. B	124. D
102. B	105. B	108. B	111. B	114. D	117. B	119. D	121. D	123. A	125. B
103. E	106. C	109. D	112. C	115. C					

8

Building Your Vocabulary

Recognizing the meaning of words is essential to comprehending what you read. The more you stumble over unfamiliar words in a text, the more you have to take time out to look up words in your dictionary, the more likely you are to wind up losing track of what the author has to say.

To succeed in college, you must develop a college-level vocabulary. You must familiarize yourself with technical words in a wide variety of fields, mastering each field's special vocabulary. You must learn to use these words, and re-use them until they become second nature to you. The time you put in now learning vocabulary-building techniques for the PSAT will pay off later on, and not just on the PSAT.

LONG-RANGE STRATEGY

There is only one effective long-range strategy for vocabulary-building: READ.

Read—widely and well. Sample different fields—physics, art history, political science, geology—and different styles. Extensive reading is the one sure way to make your vocabulary grow.

As you read, however, take some time to acquaint yourself specifically with the kinds of words you must know to do well on the PSAT. No matter how little time you have before the test, you still can familiarize yourself with the sort of vocabulary you will be facing on the PSAT. First, look over the 151 words you will find on our PSAT High-Frequency Word List (page 101): each of these 151 words, ranging from everyday words such as *adapt* and *heed* to less commonly known ones such as *fortuitous* and *pretentious* has appeared (as answer choices or as question words) at least two or three times in PSATs during the 1980s.

Next, proceed to master these High-Frequency words. First check, off the words you think you know. Then *look up all 151 words and their definitions in our 1,200 Basic Word List* (pages 101–148). Pay particular attention to the words you thought you knew. See whether any of them are defined in an unexpected way. If they are, make a special note of them. As you know from the preceding chapters, the PSAT often stumps students with questions based on unfamiliar meanings of familiar-looking words.

Not only will looking over the High-Frequency Word List reassure you that you *do* know some PSAT-type words, but also it may well help you on the actual day of the test. These words have turned up on recent tests: some of them may appear on the test you take.

Examine the entire Basic Word List as well. Even before the College Board began publishing its own PSAT sample examinations, the Basic Word List was unique in its ability to reflect, and often predict, the actual vocabulary appearing on the PSAT. Today, thanks to our ongoing research and computer analysis of published PSAT materials, we believe our Basic Word List is the best in the field.

For this book, we have selected the most important 1,200 words of the master list. Most students preparing for the PSAT/NMSQT have little time in which to study and don't feel up to facing the 3,500-word SAT list. We want you to have a tool that will be useful to you, both now and when you study for the SAT in your senior year. We hope this compact list will be the tool you need.

A PLAN FOR USING THE WORD LIST

For those of you who wish to work your way through the word list and feel the need for a plan, we recommend that you follow the procedure described below in order to use the lists and the exercises most profitably:

1. Allot a definite time each day for the study of a list.
2. Devote at least one hour to each list.
3. First go through the list looking at the short, simple-looking words (6 letters at most). Mark those you don't know. In studying, pay particular attention to them.
4. Go through the list again looking at the longer words. Pay particular attention to words with more than one meaning and familiar-looking words which have unusual definitions that come as a surprise to you. Many tests make use of these secondary definitions.

5. List unusual words on index cards, which you can shuffle and review from time to time. (Study no more than 5 cards at a time.)

6. Use the illustrative sentences in the list as models and make up new sentences of your own.

7. Take the test which follows each list at least one day after studying the words. In this way, you will check your ability to remember what you have studied.

8. If you can answer correctly 15 of the 20 questions in the test, you may proceed to the next list; if you cannot answer this number, restudy the list.

9. Keep a record of your guesses and of your success as a guesser.

For each word, the following is provided:

1. The word (printed in heavy type).
2. Its part of speech (abbreviated).
3. A brief definition.
4. A sentence illustrating the word's use.
5. Whenever appropriate, related words are provided, together with their parts of speech.
6. Following each word list will be a group of common prefixes, suffixes and roots. Studying these can help you reinforce the impression the word has made on you. It will help you interpret other words you meet. However, remember that many words have lost their original meanings and have taken on more specific and limited meanings. Use these prefixes, suffixes, and roots as a guide when you are in doubt about the meaning of a strange word. Don't assume, however, that studying bits and pieces of words can substitute for learning the exact meaning of each word as it is used today.

The 30 Word Lists are arranged in strict alphabetical order.

PSAT HIGH-FREQUENCY WORD LIST

abstract	contentious	eccentric	impartial	obsessive	satirize
adapt	credibility	eclipse	imperceptible	opaque	scrutinize
adversary	cryptic	endorse	implication	optimist	serenity
adverse	curtail	enhance	incentive	paradox	sever
aesthetic	cynic	enterprising	incongruity	passive	shrewd
aggressor	dawdle	erratic	indict	perjury	skeptical
alienate	defiance	esoteric	indifferent	pervasive	stagnation
ambiguous	denounce	espouse	induce	pessimism	subdued
ambivalence	deny	exploit	inept	petulant	substantial
amenable	derision	feasible	inevitable	philanthropist	suppress
ample	derivative	flippant	ingenious	precedent	surpass
arrogance	detached	forthright	innovation	pretentious	symmetry
ascendancy	deterrent	fortuitous	intricacy	prologue	taciturn
authentic	digressive	foster	intuition	prophetic	termination
buttress	dilute	frail	irrelevant	provocative	transparent
candor	disclose	futile	justification	recluse	uniformity
choreography	disinterested	hamper	laud	refute	vacillation
compliance	disparage	heed	loathe	reproachful	versatile
concord	disperse	hindrance	meek	repudiate	vigor
confirm	disseminate	hostility	momentous	resentment	vivacious
conform	dissent	humble	monotony	resolution	volatile
congenial	dissuade	hypocritical	mutable	restraint	vulnerable
consistent	diverse	hypothetical	naivete	reticence	withhold
consolidation	docile	immune	nostalgia	reverence	
contempt	dogmatic	impair	obscure	sarcasm	

BASIC WORD LIST WITH ETYMOLOGIES AND TESTS

The abridged Basic Word List follows. *Do not let this list overwhelm you.* You do not need to memorize every word.

The present word list derives from our standard 3,500-word list, published in *Barron's How to Prepare for the SAT.* Ever since this list first appeared in 1954, countless students have reported that working with these words has helped them immensely in taking all kinds of college entrance and scholarship tests. The list has been used with profit by people preparing for civil service examinations, placement tests, and promotional examinations in many fields. Above all, it has been used with profit by students studying for the SAT and PSAT.

An entry preceded by a bullet (•) is a High-Frequency Word.

WORD LIST 1 abash - alleviate

abash V. embarrass. She was not at all *abashed* by his open admiration

abate V. subside; moderate. Rather than leaving immediately, they waited for the storm to *abate*. abatement, N.

abdicate V. renounce; give up. When Edward VIII *abdicated* the British throne, he surprised the entire world.

abet V. aid, usually in doing something wrong; encourage. She was unwilling to *abet* him in the swindle he had planned.

abominate V. loathe; hate. Moses *abominated* idol worship.

aboriginal ADJ. being the first of its kind in a region; primitive; native. Her studies of the primitive art forms of the *aboriginal* Indians were widely reported in the scientific journals. aborigines, N.

abrogate V. abolish. He intended to *abrogate* the decree issued by his predecessor.

abscond V. depart secretly. The teller *absconded* with the bonds.

absolve V. pardon (an offense). The father confessor *absolved* him of his sins. absolution, N.

abstemious (*-stēm'*) ADJ. temperate; sparing in drink, etc. The drunkards mocked him because of his *abstemious* habits.

•**abstract** ADJ. theoretical; not concrete; nonrepresentational. To him, hunger was an *abstract* concept; he had never missed a meal.

accelerate V. move faster. In our science class, we learn how falling bodies *accelerate*. acceleration, N.

accessory N. additional object; useful but not essential thing. The *accessories* she bought cost more than the dress. also ADJ.

accolade (*-lād'*) N. award of merit. In Hollywood, an "Oscar" is the highest *accolade*.

accommodate V. adapt to. John was a very flexible person, willing to accommodate himself to circumstances. (secondary meaning)

accomplice N. partner in crime. She was his *accomplice* in the murder

accord N. agreement. He was in complete *accord* with the just verdict.

accost V. approach and speak first to a person. The salesman *accosted* the young lady.

acknowledge V. recognize; admit. When pressed for an answer, she *acknowledged* the existence of another motive for the crime.

acoustics (*-kōōs'-*) N. science of sound; quality that makes a room easy or hard to hear in. Carnegie Hall is liked by music lovers because of its fine *acoustics*.

acquittal N. deliverance from a charge. Her *acquittal* by the jury surprised those who had thought her guilty.

acrimony N. bitterness of words or manner. The candidate attacked his opponent with great *acrimony*. acrimonious, ADJ.

actuate V. compel; motivate. I fail to understand what *actuated* you to reply to this letter so flippantly.

acumen (*-kū'-*) N. mental keenness. Her business *acumen* helped her to succeed where others had failed.

adamant (*ăd'-*) ADJ. hard; inflexible. He was *adamant* in his determination to punish the wrongdoer. adamantine, ADJ.

•**adapt** V. alter; modify. Some species of animals have become extinct because they could not *adapt* to a changing environment.

addiction N. compulsive, habitual need. His *addiction* to drugs caused his friends much grief.

adhere V. stick fast to. I will *adhere* to this opinion until proof that I am wrong is presented. adhesion, N.

adjacent ADJ. neighboring; adjoining. You will find a test on this word list located on the *adjacent* page.

admonish V. warn; reprove. He *admonished* his listeners to change their wicked ways. admonition, N.

adroit ADJ. skillful. Her *adroit* handling of the delicate situation pleased her employers.

adulation N. flattery; admiration. The rock star thrived on the *adulation* of his groupies and yes-men.

adulterate V. make impure by mixing with baser substances. It is a crime to *adulterate* foods without informing the buyer.

•**adversary** N. opponent; enemy. The young wrestler struggled to defeat his *adversary*.

•**adverse** (*-vêrse'*) ADJ. opposing; hostile. *Adverse* circumstances compelled him to close his business.

adversity N. poverty; misfortune. We must learn to meet *adversity* gracefully.

advocate V. urge; plead for. The abolitionists *advocated* freedom for the slaves. also N.

•**aesthetic** (*ĕs-thĕt'-*) ADJ. artistic; dealing with or capable of appreciation of the beautiful. Because of his *aesthetic* nature, he was emotionally disturbed by ugly things. aesthete, N.

affable ADJ. courteous; warmly polite. Although she held a position of authority in the firm, she was an *affable* individual, willing to listen to anyone with a problem or a complaint.

affected ADJ. artificial; pretended. Her *affected* mannerisms irritated many of us who had known her before her promotion. affectation, N.

affiliation N. joining; associating with. His *affiliation* with the political party was of short duration for he soon disagreed with his colleagues.

affinity N. kinship. He felt an *affinity* with all who suffered; their pains were his pains.

affirmation N. solemn avowal by one who refuses to take an oath. The Constitution of this country provides for oath or *affirmation* by officeholders.

affluence (*ăff'-*) N. abundance; wealth. Foreigners are amazed by the *affluence* and luxury of the American way of life.

aggregate ADJ. sum; total. The *aggregate* wealth of this country is staggering to the imagination. also V.

•**aggressor** N. attacker. Before you punish both boys for fighting, see whether you can determine which one was the *aggressor*.

aghast ADJ. horrified. He was *aghast* at the effrontery of the speaker who had insulted his host.

agility N. nimbleness. The *agility* of the acrobat amazed and thrilled the audience.

agitate V. stir up; disturb. Her fiery remarks *agitated* the already angry mob.

alacrity N. cheerful promptness. He demonstrated his eagerness to serve by his *alacrity* in executing the orders of his master.

alias (*ăl'-ĭ-ăs*) N. an assumed name. John Smith's *alias* was Bob Jones.

•**alienate** V. make hostile; separate. Her attempts to *alienate* the two friends failed because they had complete faith in one another.

allege V. state as a fact. It is *alleged* that he had worked for the enemy. allegation, N.

alleviate V. relieve. This should *alleviate* the pain; if it does not, we shall have to use stronger drugs.

ETYMOLOGY 1

AB, ABS (from, away from) prefix
abduct lead away, kidnap
abjure renounce (swear away from)
abject degraded (thrown away from)

ABLE, IBLE (capable of) adjective suffix
portable able to be carried
legible able to be read
interminable unable to be ended

AC, IC (like, pertaining to) adjective suffix
cardiac pertaining to heart
aquatic pertaining to water
dramatic pertaining to drama

ACR (sharp)
acrimonious bitter
acerbity bitterness of temper
acidulate to make somewhat acidy or sour

AD (to, forward) prefix
adit entrance
adjure request earnestly
admit allow entrance

Note: by assimilation, the AD prefix is changed to
AC in accord
AF in affliction
AG in aggregation
AN in annexation
AP in apparition
AR in arraignment
AS in assumption
AT in attendance

AEV (age, era)
primeval of the first age
coeval of the same age or era
medieval of the middle ages

AG, ACT (to do)
act deed
agent doer
retroactive having a backward or reversed action

AGOG (leader)
demagogue false leader of people
pedagogue teacher (leader of children)
synagogue house of worship (leading together of people)

AGRI, AGRARI (field)
agrarian one who works in the fields; farmer
agriculture cultivation of fields
peregrination wandering; going through fields

ALI (another)
alias assumed (another) name
alienate estrange (divert from another)
inalienable unable to be diverted from another

TEST—WORD LIST 1—SYNONYMS

Each of the questions below consists of a word printed in italics, followed by five words or phrases numbered 1 to 5. Choose the numbered word or phrase which is most nearly similar in meaning to the word in italics and write the number of your choice on your answer paper.

1. *adhere* 1) stick to 2) be present 3) activate 4) magnify 5) detract
2. *allege* 1) supply 2) avow 3) permit 4) maintain 5) verify
3. *adapt* 1) indoctrinate 2) activate 3) worry 4) verify 5) modify
4. *advocate* 1) break off 2) urge 3) auction 4) advise 5) plead
5. *accost* 1) maltreat 2) cheapen 3) market 4) greet 5) deny
6. *adamant* 1) weak 2) pusillanimous 3) inflexible 4) wanton 5) famous
7. *aboriginal* 1) impure 2) native 3) old 4) wild 5) illiterate
8. *abstemious* 1) absent 2) present 3) temperate 4) intemperate 5) vacant
9. *acrimonious* 1) alcoholic 2) soothing 3) sensitive 4) silly 5) stinging
10. *abash* 1) embarrass 2) dismay 3) frighten 4) frustrate 5) gratify
11. *abrogate* 1) endorse 2) wipe out 3) qualify 4) estimate 5) question
12. *abominate* 1) dwell 2) deliver 3) erect 4) cancel 5) hate
13. *agitate* 1) mollify 2) equate 3) anticipate 4) disqualify 5) disturb
14. *aghast* 1) horrified 2) open 3) at sea 4) pliable 5) spectral
15. *admonish* 1) polish 2) adorn 3) reprove 4) laud 5) repay
16. *acumen* 1) arrival 2) alertness 3) policy 4) vision 5) vengeance
17. *accomplice* 1) antecedent 2) descendant 3) assistant 4) superior 5) culprit
18. *accolade* 1) market place 2) marriage performance 3) praise 4) deceit 5) plan
19. *alacrity* 1) scarcity 2) propriety 3) fear 4) courage 5) promptness
20. *adverse* 1) opposed 2) promoted 3) hostile 4) ancient 5) ardent

Answers to this test on page 148.

WORD LIST 2 allude - appurtenances

allude V. refer indirectly. Try not to *allude* to this matter in his presence because it annoys him to hear of it.

allure V. entice; attract. *Allured* by the song of the sirens, the helmsman steered the ship toward the reef. also N.

allusion N. indirect reference. The *allusions* to mythological characters in Milton's poems bewilder the reader who has not studied Latin.

aloof ADJ. apart; reserved. He remained *aloof* while all the rest conversed.

altercation N. wordy quarrel. Throughout the entire *altercation*, not one sensible word was uttered.

altruistic ADJ. unselfishly generous; concerned for others. In providing tutorial assistance and college scholarships for hundreds of economically disadvantaged youths, Eugene Lang performed a truly *altruistic* deed. altruism, N.

•**ambiguous** (-*bĭg'*-) ADJ. doubtful in meaning. His *ambiguous* directions misled us; we did not know which road to take. ambiguity, N.

•**ambivalence** N. the state of having contradictory or conflicting emotional attitudes. Torn between loving her parents one minute and hating them the next, she was confused by the *ambivalence* of her feelings.

amble V. move at an easy pace. The horse began to *amble* almost before she could get her feet into the stirrups.

ambulatory (*ăm'*-) ADJ. walking. He was described as an *ambulatory* patient because he was not confined to his bed.

ameliorate (-*mēl'ĭ*-) V. improve. Many social workers have attempted to *ameliorate* the conditions of people living in the slums.

•**amenable** (-*mēn'*-) ADJ. readily managed; willing to be led. He was *amenable* to any suggestions which came from those he looked up to; he resented advice from his inferiors.

'**amiable** (*ām'*-) ADJ. agreeable; lovable. Her *amiable* disposition pleased all who had dealings with her.

amphitheatre N. oval building with tiers of seats. The spectators in the *amphitheatre* cheered the gladiators.

•**ample** ADJ. abundant. He had *ample* opportunity to dispose of his loot before the police caught up with him.

amputate V. cut off part of the body; prune. When the doctors decided to *amputate* his leg to prevent the spread of gangrene, he cried that he preferred death to incapacity. amputation, N.

anaesthetic (-*thĕt'*) N. substance that removes sensation with or without loss of consciousness. His monotonous voice acted like an *anaesthetic*; his audience was soon asleep. anaesthesia, N.

analogous (-*năl'*-) ADJ. comparable. He called our attention to the things that had been done in an *analogous* situation and recommended that we do the same.

analogy N. similarity; parallelism. Your *analogy* is not a good one because the two situations are not similar.

anarchy (-*ăn'*-) N. absence of governing body; state of disorder. The assassination of the leaders led to a period of *anarchy*.

anhydrous ADJ. lacking water. Certain crystalline substances are found in an *anhydrous* as well as a wet state.

animated ADJ. lively. Her *animated* expression indicated a keenness of intellect. animation, N.

animosity N. active enmity. He incurred the *animosity* of the ruling class because he advocated limitations of their power.

annals N. records; history. In the *annals* of this period, we find no mention of democratic movements.

annihilate (-*nī'-ĭ*-) V. destroy. The enemy in its vindictiveness tried to *annihilate* the entire population.

annul (-*nŭl'*) V. make void. The parents of the eloped couple tried to *annul* the marriage. annulment, N.

anomalous (-*nŏm'*-) ADJ. abnormal; irregular. She was placed in the *anomalous* position of seeming to approve procedures which she despised.

antagonism (-*tăg'*-) N. active resistance. We shall have to overcome the *antagonism* of the natives before our plans for settling this area can succeed.

anticlimax (-*clīm'*-) N. let-down in thought or emotion. After the fine performance in the first act, the rest of the play was an *anticlimax*. anticlimactic, ADJ.

antiquated ADJ. obsolete; outdated. Many young people are sure that their parents have very *antiquated* notions of behavior.

antiseptic N. substance that prevents infection. It is advisable to apply an *antiseptic* to any wound, no matter how slight or insignificant.

antithesis N. contrast; direct opposite of or to. This tyranny was the *antithesis* of all that he had hoped for, and he fought it with all his strength.

apathetic ADJ. indifferent. He felt *apathetic* about the conditions he had observed and did not care to fight against them.

aphorism (*ăf'-or-ĭzm*) N. pithy maxim. An *aphorism* differs from an adage in that it is more philosophical or scientific. aphoristic, ADJ.

aplomb N. poise. His nonchalance and *aplomb* in times of trouble always encouraged his followers.

apocryphal (-*pŏk'*-) ADJ. not genuine; sham. His *apocyphal* tears misled no one.

apostate (-*pŏs'*-) N. one who abandons his religious faith or political beliefs. Because he switched from one party to another, his former friends shunned him as an *apostate*.

apotheosis (-*ōs'*-) N. deification; glorification. The *apotheosis* of a Roman emperor was designed to insure his eternal greatness.

appellation N. name; title. He was amazed when the witches hailed him with his correct *appellation*.

append V. attach. I shall *append* this chart to my report.

apprehensive ADJ. fearful; discerning. His *apprehensive* glances at the people who were walking in the street revealed his nervousness.

apprise (*prīz*) V. inform. When he was *apprised* of the dangerous weather conditions, he decided to postpone his trip.

appurtenances N. subordinate possessions. She brought the estate and all its *appurtenances*.

ETYMOLOGY 2

AMBI (both) prefix
ambidextrous skilled with both hands (both right hands)
ambiguous of double meaning
ambivalent possessing conflicting (both) emotions

AN (without) prefix
anarchy lack of government
anemia lack of blood
anesthesia without feeling

ANTE (before) prefix
antecedent preceding event or word
antediluvian ancient (before the flood)
antenuptial before the wedding

ANIM (mind, soul)
animadvert cast criticism upon (turn one's mind)
unanimous of one mind
magnanimity greatness of mind or spirit

ANN (year)
annuity yearly remittance
biennial every two years
perennial flowering yearly; a yearly flowering plant

ANTHROP (man)
anthropology study of man
misanthrope recluse (hater of mankind)
philanthropy love of mankind; charity

TEST—WORD LIST 2 —ANTONYMS

Each of the questions below consists of a word printed in italics, followed by five words or phrases numbered 1 to 5. Choose the numbered word or phrase which is most nearly opposite in meaning to the word in italics and write the number of your choice on your answer paper.

21. *ameliorate* 1) worsen 2) solidify 3) distract 4) undo 5) reverse
22. *apathetic* 1) pitiable 2) ignorant 3) celebrated 4) enthusiastic 5) vicious
23. *aloof* 1) suspicious 2) circumspect 3) gregarious 4) thorough 5) industrious
24. *amble* 1) follow 2) gallop 3) suffice 4) cope 5) deprive
25. *aplomb* 1) scarcity 2) agitation 3) insincerity 4) regret 5) approval
26. *antagonism* 1) clarity 2) seriousness 3) harmony 4) subtlety 5) trepidation
27. *animated* 1) lethargic 2) picturesque 3) momentary 4) brutal 5) vacant
28. *antiseptic* 1) sociable 2) poisonous 3) belligerent 4) placid 5) defensive
29. *apocryphal* 1) proverbial 2) genuine 3) diverse 4) integrated 5) native
30. *anarchy* 1) piety 2) oligarchy 3) division 4) fortune 5) order
31. *altruism* 1) selfishness 2) honesty 3) sadness 4) silliness 5) silence
32. *altercation* 1) agreement 2) magnitude 3) prudence 4) novel plan 5) lack of change
33. *ambulatory* 1) hateful 2) shameful 3) bedridden 4) qualified 5) reticent
34. *amenable* 1) pious 2) humble 3) incapable 4) predictable 5) unruly
35. *anomalous* 1) necessary 2) regular 3) outstanding 4) clear 5) ready
36. *ambivalence* 1) futility 2) certainty 3) quietness 4) severity 5) complexity
37. *animosity* 1) goodwill 2) laxity 3) sincerity 4) lack of spirit 5) false hope
38. *annul* 1) confuse 2) validate 3) intimidate 4) imply 5) announce
39. *append* 1) remove 2) delay 3) appraise 4) squander 5) despair
40. *apprehensive* 1) practical 2) confident 3) reproachful 4) inquisitive 5) valuable

Answers to this test on page 148.

WORD LIST 3 arbiter - bane

arbiter (*ärb'-*) N. a person with power to decide a dispute; judge. As an *arbiter* in labor disputes, he has won the confidence of the workers and the employers.

arbitrary ADJ. fixed or decided; despotic. Any *arbitrary* action on your part will be resented by the members of the board whom you do not consult.

arcade N. a covered passageway, usually lined with shops. The *arcade* was popular with shoppers because it gave them protection from the summer sun and the winter rain.

archipelago (*ärk-*) N. group of closely located islands. When he looked at the map and saw the *archipelagoes* in the South Seas, he longed to visit them.

arduous ADJ. hard; strenuous. His *arduous* efforts had sapped his energy.

aria N. operatic solo. At her Metropolitan Opera audition, Marian Anderson sang an *aria* from Norma.

arid ADJ. dry; barren. The cactus has adapted to survive in an *arid* environment.

aromatic ADJ. fragrant. Medieval sailing vessels brought *aromatic* herbs from China to Europe.

arraign (*-ān'*) V. charge in court; indict. After his indictment by the Grand Jury, the accused man was *arraigned* in the County Criminal Court. arraignment, N.

•**arrogance** N. haughtiness. The *arrogance* of the nobility was resented by the middle class.

articulate ADJ. effective; distinct. Her *articulate* presentation of the advertising campaign impressed her employers. also V.

•**ascendancy** N. controlling influence. I often wonder how leaders of religious cults maintain their *ascendancy* over their followers. ascend, V.

ascetic (*ăs-sĕt'-*) ADJ. practicing self-denial; austere. The cavalier could not understand the *ascetic* life led by the monks.

ascribe (*-krīb'*) V. refer; attribute; assign. I can *ascribe* no motive for her acts.

ashen ADJ. ash-colored; deadly pale. His face was *ashen* with fear.

askew (*-kū'*) ADV. crookedly; obliquely. When he placed his hat *askew* upon his head, his observers laughed.

aspirant N. seeker after position or status. Although I am an *aspirant* for public office, I am not willing to accept the dictates of the party bosses.

aspiration N. noble ambition. Man's *aspirations* should be as lofty as the stars.

assail V. assault. She was *assailed* with questions after her lecture.

assay (*-sā'*) V. analyze; evaluate. When they *assayed* the ore, they found that they had discovered a very rich vein. also N.

assuage V. ease; lessen (pain). Your comforting messages should *assuage* her suffering. assuagement, N.

astral ADJ. relating to the stars. She was amazed at the number of *astral* bodies the new telescope revealed.

astringent ADJ. binding; causing contraction. The *astringent* quality of the unsweetened lemon juice made swallowing difficult.

astute ADJ. wise; shrewd. That was a very *astute* observation. I shall heed it.
atheistic ADJ. denying the existence of God. His *atheistic* remarks shocked the religious worshippers.
attentive ADJ. considerate; thoughtful. Thuy is very *attentive* to her Vietnamese-speaking parents, interpreting for them and helping them deal with an English-speaking world.
attenuate V. make thin; weaken. By withdrawing their forces, the generals hoped to *attenuate* the enemy lines.
attribute (*ăt'*-) N. essential quality. His outstanding *attribute* was his kindness.
attrition N. gradual wearing down. They decided to wage a war of *attrition* rather than to rely on an all-out attack.
augment V. increase. How can we hope to *augment* our forces when our allies are deserting us?
augury N. omen; prophecy. He interpreted the departure of the birds as an *augury* of evil. augur, V.
auspicious ADJ. favoring success. With favorable weather conditions, it was an *auspicious* moment to set sail.
austerity N. sternness; severity. The *austerity* and dignity of the court were maintained by the new justices.
•**authentic** ADJ. genuine. The art expert was able to distinguish the *authentic* Van Gogh painting from the forged copy. authenticate, V.
autocrat N. monarch or other person with supreme power. The nobles tried to limit the powers of the *autocrat* without success. autocracy, N.
autonomous ADJ. self-governing. This island is a colony; however, in most matters, it is *autonomous* and receives no orders from the mother country. autonomy, N.
autopsy (*ôt'-ŏp-sĭ*) N. examination of a dead body; post-mortem. The medical examiner orderd an *autopsy* to determine the cause of death.
averse ADJ. reluctant. He was *averse* to revealing the sources of his information.
aversion N. firm dislike. Their mutual *aversion* was so great that they refused to speak to one another.
avid ADJ. greedy; eager for. She was *avid* for learning and read everything she could get. avidity, N.
avow V. declare openly. I must *avow* that I am innocent.
awe N. solemn wonder. The tourists gazed with *awe* at the tremendous panorama of the Grand Canyon.
babble V. chatter idly. The little girl *babbled* to her doll.
badger V. pester; annoy. The drunkard began to *badger* the bartender.
baffle V. frustrate; perplex. The new code *baffled* the enemy agents.
balk V. foil. He tried to *balk* the escape, but the thieves made their getaway.
bane N. cause of ruin. Lack of public transportation is the *bane* of urban life.

ETYMOLOGY 3

ARCH (chief, first) prefix
archetype original model
archbishop chief bishop
archeology study of antiquities (study of first things)

ARCH (government, ruler, first)
monarch sole ruler
anarchy lack of government
archeology study of first or ancient times

AQUA (water)
aqueduct a passageway for conducting water; a conduit
aquatic living in water
aqua fortis nitric acid (strong water)

ASTER (star)
astronomy study of the stars
asterisk star-like type character (*)
disaster catastrophe (contrary star)

AUD, AUDIT (hear)
audible able to be heard
auditorium place where people may be heard
audience hearers

AUTO (self)
autocracy rule by self (one person)
automobile vehicle that moves by itself
autobiography story of a person's life written by himself

TEST—WORD LIST 3 —SYNONYMS OR ANTONYMS

Each of the questions below consists of a word printed in italics, followed by five words or phrases numbered 1 to 5. Choose the numbered word or phrase which is most nearly the same as or the opposite of the word in italics and write the number of your choice on your answer paper.

41. *arduous* 1) difficult 2) eager 3) emphatic 4) phlegmatic 5) calm
42. *askew* 1) obliquely 2) questioningly 3) painfully 4) charmingly 5) partly
43. *baffle* 1) secure 2) bind 3) pronounce 4) produce 5) frustrate
44. *arid* 1) unknown 2) vacant 3) idle 4) moist 5) tidy
45. *aspiration* 1) breath 2) ambition 3) adaptation 4) cooperation 5) sentiment
46. *atheistic* 1) questionable 2) serious 3) heinous 4) devout 5) deluded
47. *aria* 1) operatic solo 2) orchestral prelude 3) famous singer 4) repertoire 5) stage
48. *assay* 1) endeavor 2) evaluate 3) engage 4) entertain 5) entice
49. *babble* 1) trifle 2) cohere 3) be permanent 4) chafe 5) chatter
50. *averse* 1) eager 2) offended 3) frantic 4) finished 5) greedy
51. *avid* 1) merciful 2) helpful 3) averse 4) immodest 5) gullible
52. *asceticism* 1) indulgence 2) philosophy 3) fulfillment 4) generosity 5) hatred
53. *augment* 1) argue 2) agree 3) enlarge 4) enroll 5) introduce

54. *balk* 1) divide 2) await 3) condemn 4) hinder 5) ignore

55. *badger* 1) nettle 2) spear 3) emulate 4) finish 5) inquire

56. *archipelago* 1) bishop 2) chief actor 3) oligarch 4) group of islands 5) major illness

57. *augury* 1) prediction 2) tearing 3) capsule 4) illness 5) carpenter's tool

58. *autonomous* 1) self-winding 2) self-starting 3) self-governing 4) self-treating 5) self-guiding

59. *auspicious* 1) unfavorable 2) incomplete 3) indecisive 4) unstimulating 5) impartial

60. *arraign* 1) declare innocent 2) rule over 3) dedicate 4) deny 5) abet

Answers to this test on page 148.

WORD LIST 4 barb - cadaverous

barb N. sharp projection from fishhook, etc. The *barb* from the fishhook caught in her finger as she grabbed the fish. barbed, ADJ.

barrage (*-äzh'*) N. barrier laid down by artillery fire. The company was forced to retreat through the *barrage* of heavy cannon.

bedraggle V. wet thoroughly. We must not let the storm *bedraggle* us. bedraggled, ADJ.

beguile (*-gīl'-*) V. delude; cheat; amuse. He *beguiled* himself during the long hours by playing solitaire.

behoove V. be suited to; be incumbent on. In this time of crisis, it *behooves* all of us to remain calm and await the instructions of our superiors.

belated N. delayed. He sent *belated* greetings a week after her birthday.

benediction N. blessing. The appearance of the sun after the many rainy days was like a *benediction*.

benefactor N. gift giver; patron. Scrooge later became Tiny Tim's *benefactor*.

beneficiary N. person entitled to benefits or proceeds of an insurance policy or will. You may change your *beneficiary* as often as you wish.

benevolent (*-nĕv'-*) ADJ. generous; charitable. His *benevolent* nature prevented him from refusing any begger who accosted him.

benign ADJ. kindly; favorable, not malignant. The old man was well liked because of his *benign* attitude toward friend and stranger alike.

benighted ADJ. overcome by darkness. In the *benighted* Middle Ages, intellectual curiosity was discouraged by the authorities.

berate V. scold strongly. He feared she would *berate* him for his forgetfulness.

bestow V. confer. She wished to *bestow* great honors upon the hero.

bicameral (*bī-*) ADJ. two-chambered as a legislative body. The United States Congress is a *bicameral* body.

bizarre (bĭ-zâr') ADJ. fantastic; violently contrasting. The plot of the novel was too *bizarre* to be believed.

blandishment N. flattery. Despite his *blandishments*, the young lady rejected his companionship.

blasphemous (*blăs'-fem-*) ADJ. profane; impious. The people in the room were shocked by her *blasphemous* language.

blatant (*blā'-*) ADJ. loudly offensive. I regard your remarks as *blatant* and ill-mannered. blatancy, N.

bleak ADJ. cold; cheerless. The Aleutian Islands are *bleak* military outposts.

bloated ADJ. swollen or puffed as with water or air. The *bloated* corpse was taken from the river.

bludgeon N. club; heavy-headed weapon. His walking stick served him as a *bludgeon* on many occasions.

bolster V. support; prop up. I do not intend to *bolster* your hopes with false reports of outside assistance; the truth is that we must face the enemy alone.

bountiful ADJ. generous; showing bounty. She distributed gifts in a *bountiful* and gracious manner.

bourgeois (*bo͞or'-zhwä*) N. middle class. The French Revolution was inspired by the *bourgeois*. also ADJ.

bravado (*-vä'-dō*) N. swagger; assumed air of defiance. The *bravado* of the young criminal disappeared when he was confronted by the victims of his brutal attack.

breach N. breaking of contract or duty; fissure; gap. They found a *breach* in the enemy's fortifications and penetrated their lines.

brevity N. conciseness. "*Brevity* is the soul of wit."

broach V. open up. He did not even try to *broach* the subject of poetry.

brocade N. rich, figured fabric. The sofa was covered with expensive *brocade*.

brochure (*brō'-sho͞or'*) N. pamphlet. This *brochure* on farming was issued by the Department of Agriculture.

brooch (*-ō-*) N. ornament fastened with a pin or clasp. She treasured the *brooch* because it was an heirloom.

brusque (*brŭsk'*) ADJ. blunt; abrupt. She was offended by his *brusque* reply.

bullion (*bo͝ol'-yŏn*) N. gold and silver in the form of bars. Much *bullion* is stored in the vaults at Fort Knox.

bulwark (*bo͝ol'-*) N. earthwork or other strong defense; person who defends. The navy is our principal *bulwark* against invasion.

bungle V. spoil by clumsy behavior. I was afraid you would *bungle* this assignment but I had no one else to send.

•**buttress** V. support; prop up. The attorney came up with several far-fetched arguments in a vain attempt to *buttress* his weak case. also N.

cabal (*-băl'*) N. small group of persons secretly united to promote their own interests. The *cabal* was defeated when its scheme was discovered.

cadaverous ADJ. like a corpse; pale. From his *cadaverous* appearance, we saw how the disease had ravaged him.

ETYMOLOGY 4

BELLI (war)
bellicose inclined to fighting
belligerent engaged in war
rebellious warring against authority

BEN, BON (well, good)
benefactor one who does good
benevolence charity (wishing good)
bonus something extra above regular pay

BI (two) prefix
bicameral legislature consisting of two houses
biennial every two years
bicycle two-wheeled vehicle

BIBLIO (book)
bibliography list of books
bibliophile lover of books
Bible The Book

BIO (life)
biology study of living things
biography writing about a person's life
biochemist a study of the chemistry of living things

BREVE (short)
brevity briefness
abbreviate shorten
breve mark placed over vowel to indicate that it is short (ă as in hăt)

CAD, CAS (to fall)
decadent deteriorating
cadence intonation, musical movement
accident unexpected, chance event

TEST—WORD LIST 4 —SYNONYMS

Each of the questions below consists of a word printed in italics, followed by five words or phrases numbered 1 to 5. Choose the numbered word or phrase which is most nearly similar in meaning to the word in italics and write the number of your choice on your answer paper.

61. *cadaverous* 1) corpse-like 2) buxom 3) clear 4) brazen 5) slandered
62. *belated* 1) on time 2) delayed 3) timeless 4) prompt 5) evergreen
63. *buttress* 1) interrupt 2) expedite 3) adorn 4) disclose 5) support
64. *beguile* 1) profane 2) disgust 3) give freely 4) delude 5) bludgeon
65. *bungle* 1) bracket 2) engrave 3) punch 4) order 5) spoil by clumsiness
66. *benediction* 1) pleasure 2) blessing 3) sermon 4) cantor 5) choir
67. *bulwark* 1) sand bags 2) bridge 3) earthwork 4) ditch 5) estuary
68. *berate* 1) scold 2) tense 3) dictate 4) laud 5) hate
69. *brusque* 1) blunt 2) brief 3) keen 4) harsh 5) tough
70. *benign* 1) feeble 2) glamorous 3) courageous 4) kindly 5) insincere
71. *bravado* 1) swagger 2) bravery 3) gallantry 4) criticism 5) ability
72. *bicameral* 1) supreme 2) photogenic 3) two-chambered 4) clannish 5) unorthodox
73. *bizarre* 1) lovely 2) fantastic 3) old-fashioned 4) beautiful 5) modern
74. *bountiful* 1) sordid 2) good-natured 3) stingy 4) superior 5) generous
75. *blandishment* 1) flattery 2) seasoning 3) mildness 4) tolerance 5) sensitivity
76. *bludgeon* 1) volume 2) forecast 3) inferiority 4) oath 5) club
77. *bloated* 1) cursing 2) benign 3) swollen 4) drowned 5) delayed
78. *blatant* 1) flooded 2) bedecked 3) baleful 4) loudly offensive 5) berserk
79. *barb* 1) sharp projection 2) needle 3) advertisement on book 4) razor blade 5) wire
80. *blasphemous* 1) hurried 2) incoherent 3) clever 4) sacrilegious 5) ironical

Answers to this test on page 148.

WORD LIST 5 cajole - chronic

cajole (*-jōl'*) V. coax; wheedle. I will not be *cajoled* into granting you your wish.

callous ADJ. hardened; unfeeling. She had worked in the hospital for so many years that she was *callous* to the suffering in the wards. callus, N.

calumny (*kăl'-*) N. malicious misrepresentation; slander. He could endure his financial failure, but he could not bear the *calumny* that his foes heaped upon him.

•**candor** N. frankness. The *candor* and simplicity of his speech impressed us all; it was clear he held nothing back. candid, ADJ.

canine ADJ. related to dogs; doglike. Some days the canine population of Berkeley seems almost to outnumber the human population.

canny ADJ. shrewd; thrifty. The *canny* Scotsman was more than a match for the swindlers.

cant N. jargon of thieves, pious phraseology. Many listeners were fooled by the *cant* and hypocrisy of his speech.

capitulate V. surrender. The enemy was warned to *capitulate* or face annihilation.

caprice (*-prēs'*) N. whim. Do not act on *caprice*. Study your problem.

caption N. title; chapter heading; text under illustration. I find the *captions* which accompany these cartoons very clever and humorous.

caricature N. distortion; burlesque. The *caricatures* he drew always emphasized a personal weakness of the people he burlesqued.

carping ADJ. finding fault. A *carping* critic disturbs sensitive people.

carrion N. rotting flesh of a dead body. The buzzards ate the *carrion*.

cascade N. small waterfall. We could not appreciate the beauty of the many *cascades* as we were forced to make portages around each of them.

castigate V. punish; scold severely. He decided to *castigate* the culprit personally.

casualty N. serious or fatal accident. The number of *casualties* on this holiday weekend was high.

catapult N. slingshot; a hurling machine. Airplanes are sometimes launched from battleships by *catapults*.

catastrophe N. calamity. The Johnstown flood was a *catastrophe*.

cathartic N. purgative. Some drugs act as laxatives when taken in small doses, but act as *cathartics* when taken in much larger doses.

cauterize (*kôt-*) V. burn with hot iron or caustic. In order to prevent infection, the doctor *cauterized* the wound.

cavalcade N. procession, parade. As described by Chaucer, the *cavalcade* of Canterbury pilgrims was a motley group.

cede (*sēd*) V. transfer, yield title to. I intend to *cede* this property to the city.

celestial ADJ. heavenly. He wrote about the music of "*celestial* spheres."

censor N. overseer of morals; person who reads to eliminate inappropriate remarks. Soldiers dislike having their mail read by a *censor* but understand the need for this precaution.

censure V. blame; critize. He was *censured* for his inappropriate behavior. also N.

cerebral (*sĕ'-*) ADJ. pertaining to the brain. We are just now beginning to make a determined effort to alleviate the suffering caused by *cerebral* palsy.

cerebration N. thought. Mathematics problems sometimes require much *cerebration*.

cessation N. stopping. The workers threatened a *cessation* of all activities if management refused to meet their demands. cease, V.

cession N. yielding to another; ceding. The *cession* of Alaska to the United States is discussed in this chapter.

chafe V. warm by rubbing; make sore by rubbing. The collar *chafed* his neck.

chagrin N. vexation; disappointment. Her refusal to go with us filled us with *chagrin*; we had looked forward to her company.

chalice N. goblet; consecrated cup. In a small room adjoining the cathedral, many ornately decorated *chalices* made by the most famous European goldsmiths were on display.

chameleon (*kă-*) N. lizard that can change the color of its skin. Like a *chameleon*, he assumed the political thinking of every group he met.

chaotic ADJ. in utter disorder. She tried to bring order into the *chaotic* state of affairs.

charlatan (*shär'-*) N. quack; pretender to knowledge. This advertisement is the work of a *charlatan*.

chary (*chăr'-ĭ*) ADJ. cautiously watchful. She was *chary* of her favors.

chasm (*kăzm*) N. abyss. They could not see the bottom of the *chasm*.

chassis (*shăs'-ē*) N. framework and working parts of an automobile. Examining the car after the accident, the owner discovered that the body had been ruined but that the *chassis* was unharmed.

chastise V. punish. I must *chastise* you for this offense.

chauvinist (*shōv'*) N. blindly devoted patriot. A *chauvinist* cannot recognize any faults in his country, no matter how flagrant they may be.

checkered ADJ. marked by changes in fortune. During his *checkered* career he had lived in palatial mansions and in dreary boarding houses.

chicanery (*shĭkā'-*) N. trickery. The lawyer was guilty of *chicanery* in freeing her client.

•**choreography** N. art of dancing. Martha Graham introduced a revolutionary form of *choreography* which seemed awkward and strange to those brought up on classic ballet.

chronic ADJ. long-established, as a disease. His *chronic* headaches worried the doctors.

ETYMOLOGY 5

CAP, CAPT, CEP (to take)
participate to take part
precept a wise saying (originally, a command)
capture seize

CAP, CIP (head)
decapitate remove head
captain chief
capital major

CATA (down) prefix
catastrophe disaster (turning down)
cataract waterfall
catapult hurl (throw down)

CED, CESS (to yield, to go)
recede go back, withdraw
antecedent that which goes before
concede to yield, to agree with

CENT (one hundred)
century one hundred years
centennial hundredth anniversary
Centigrade system of measuring by hundreds

CHRONOS (time)
chronology timetable of events
anachronism a thing out of time sequence as Shakespeare's reference to clocks in *Julius Caesar*
chronicle to register events in order

TEST—WORD LIST 5 —ANTONYMS

Each of the questions below consists of a word printed in italics, followed by five words or phrases numbered 1 to 5. Choose the numbered word or phrase which is most nearly opposite in meaning to the word in italics and write the number of your choice on your answer paper.

81. *callous* 1) hearty 2) formal 3) sympathetic 4) leisurely 5) spry
82. *chaotic* 1) chaste 2) chastened 3) beaten 4) novel 5) orderly
83. *calumny* 1) disappointment 2) illusion 3) turbulence 4) praise 5) avoidance
84. *castigate* 1) commend 2) distribute 3) pursue 4) defer 5) consolidate
85. *cede* 1) move 2) feel 3) hold 4) renew 5) stand
86. *chicanery* 1) drabness 2) certainty 3) promptness 4) honesty 5) futility
87. *chastise* 1) reward 2) pursue 3) direct 4) defy 5) struggle
88. *celestial* 1) windy 2) terrestrial 3) ancestral 4) enormous 5) chronic
89. *chafe* 1) soothe 2) laugh 3) irrigate 4) decry 5) drape
90. *canny* 1) smug 2) dull-witted 3) outspoken 4) coarse 5) snobbish
91. *cajole* 1) convey 2) admire 3) demand 4) mount 5) appoint
92. *chronic* 1) amused 2) established 3) direct 4) misused 5) acute
93. *carping* 1) shrewd 2) leisurely 3) disloyal 4) admiring 5) profound
94. *catastrophe* 1) great height 2) utter confusion 3) dissension 4) success 5) frailty
95. *checkered* 1) uniform 2) defeated 3) hidden 4) tortuous 5) frantic
96. *cessation* 1) negotiation 2) resumption 3) agreement 4) accuracy 5) delay
97. *chagrin* 1) amusement 2) facade 3) jubilation 4) stiffness 5) obsession
98. *candor* 1) inability 2) duplicity 3) hilarity 4) intensity 5) fragility
99. *capitulate* 1) commend 2) perish 3) confirm 4) dismay 5) resist
100. *censure* 1) damage 2) applaud 3) purify 4) waver 5) insist

Answers to this test on page 148.

WORD LIST 6 circlet - concise

circlet N. small ring; band. This tiny *circlet* is very costly because it is set with precious stones.
circumscribe V. limit; confine. Although I do not wish to *circumscribe* your activities, I must insist that you complete this assignment before you start anything else.
circumspect ADJ. prudent; cautious. Investigating before acting, she tried always to be *circumspect*.
circumvent V. outwit; baffle. In order to *circumvent* the enemy, we will make two preliminary attacks in other sections before starting our major campaign.
citadel N. fortress. The *citadel* overlooked the city like a protecting angel.
clairvoyant (*klair-voi'-*) N., ADJ. having foresight; fortuneteller. Cassandra's *clairvoyant* warning was not heeded by the Trojans. clairvoyance, N.
clamber V. climb by crawling. She *clambered* over the wall.
clarion ADJ. shrill trumpet-like sound. We woke to the *clarion* call of the bugle.
clavicle N. collarbone. He broke his *clavicle* in the football game.
cleave V. split asunder. The lightning *cleaved* the tree in two. cleavage, N.
clemency N. disposition to be lenient; mildness, as of the weather. The judge was noted for his *clemency* toward first offenders.
cliché (*klē-shā'*) N. phrase dulled in meaning by repetition. High school compositions are often marred by such *clichés* as "strong as an ox."
climactic ADJ. relating to the highest point. When he reached the *climactic* portions of the book, he could not stop reading.
clique (*klēk*) N. small exclusive group. He charged that a *clique* had assumed control of school affairs.
cloister N. monastery or convent. The nuns lived in the *cloister*.
coalesce V. combine, fuse. The brooks *coalesce* into one large river.
coalition N. association; union. Jesse Jackson's Rainbow *Coalition* brought together people of many different races and creeds.
cog N., ADJ. tooth projecting from a wheel. On steep slopes, *cog* railways are frequently used to prevent slipping.
cogitate V. think over. *Cogitate* over this problem; the solution will come.
collaborate V. work together. Two writers *collaborated* in preparing this book.
collateral N. security given for loan. The sum you wish to borrow is so large that it must be secured by *collateral*.
collusion N. conspiring in a fraudulent scheme. The swindlers were found guilty of *collusion*.
colossal ADJ. huge. Radio City Music Hall has a *colossal* stage.
comely (*kŭm'*) ADJ. attractive; agreeable. I would rather have a *comely* wife than a rich one.
comity N. courtesy; civility. A spirit of *comity* should exist among nations.
commensurate ADJ. equal in extent. Your reward will be *commensurate* with your effort.
commiserate V. feel or express pity or sympathy for. Her friends *commiserated* with the widow.
compact N. agreement; contract. The signers of the Mayflower *Compact* were establishing a form of government.
compatible ADJ. harmonious, in harmony with. They were *compatible* neighbors, never quarreling over unimportant matters.
compilation N. listing of statistical information in tabular or book form. The *compilation* of available scholarships serves a very valuable purpose.
complacent (*-plā'-*) ADJ. self-satisfied. There was a *complacent* look on his face as he examined his paintings. complacency, N.
complaisant (*kŏm-*) ADJ. trying to please; obliging. The courtier obeyed the king's orders in a *complaisant* manner.

complement N. that which completes. A predicate *complement* completes the meaning of the subject.

•**compliance** N. readiness to yield; conformity in fulfilling requirements. When I give an order, I expect *compliance*, not defiance. comply V.

comport V. bear one's self; behave. He *comported* himself with great dignity.

compress V. close; squeeze; contract. She compressed the clothes into a tight bundle.

compunction N. remorse. Have you no *compunctions* when you see the results of your act?

compute V. reckon; calculate. She failed to *compute* the interest.

concatenate V. link as in chain. It is difficult to understand how these events could *concatenate* as they did without outside assistance.

concentric ADJ. having a common center. The target was made of *concentric* circles.

conception N. beginning; forming of an idea. At the first *conception* of the work, she was consulted.

concise ADJ. brief and compact. When you define a new word, be *concise*: the shorter the definition, the easier it is to remember.

ETYMOLOGY 6

CID, CIS (to cut, to kill)
incision a cut (surgical)
homicide killing of a man
fratricide killing of a brother

CIRCUM (around) prefix
circumnavigate sail around the world
circumspect cautious (looking around)
circumscribe place a circle around

CIT, CITAT (to call, to start)
incite to stir up, to start up
excite to stir up
recitation a calling-back again

CIVI (citizen)
civilization society of citizens, culture
civilian a member of community
civil courteous

CLAM, CLAMAT (to cry out)
clamorous loud
declamation a speech
acclamation shouted approval

CLAUD, CLAUS (to close)
claustrophobia fear of close places
enclose to close in
conclude to finish

CLE, CULE (small) noun suffix
molecule small mass
corpuscle blood cell
follicle small sac

COGNOSC, COGNIT (to learn)
agnostic lacking knowledge, skeptical
incognito traveling under assumed name (without knowledge)
cognition knowledge

COM (with, together) prefix
combine merge with
commerce trade with
communicate correspond with
By assimilation
coeditor associate editor
collateral connected
conference meeting
corroborate confirm

COMP, COMPLETE (to fill)
complete filled out
complement that which completes something
comply to fulfil

TEST—WORD LIST 6 —SYNONYMS OR ANTONYMS

Each of the questions below consists of a word printed in italics, followed by five words or phrases numbered 1 to 5. Choose the numbered word or phrase which is most nearly the same as or the opposite of the word in italics and write the number of your choice on your answer paper.

101. *collusion* 1) rust 2) conspiracy 3) consternation 4) ague 5) aggravation
102. *conception* 1) conclusion 2) thoroughness 3) tenacity 4) quality 5) uncertainty
103. *circumscribe* 1) write 2) navigate 3) sail around 4) offend 5) limit
104. *clavicle* 1) organ 2) collar bone 3) hearing aid 4) oracle 5) penance
105. *clemency* 1) downpour 2) futility 3) necessity 4) quietude 5) severity
106. *compatible* 1) dictated 2) discordant 3) disposed 4) delicate 5) solemn
107. *clairvoyant* 1) lacking grace 2) having foresight 3) wandering 4) abstract 5) wry
108. *colossal* 1) striding 2) belligerent 3) wonderful 4) puny 5) loquacious
109. *concise* 1) expurgated 2) expert 3) assiduous 4) desultory 5) verbose
110. *circumspect* 1) roundabout 2) wide-eyed 3) formal 4) rash 5) rueful
111. *citadel* 1) small city 2) hamlet 3) fortress 4) fighting ship 5) shelf
112. *commensurate* 1) unequal 2) attainable 3) uncertain 4) adjusted 5) livid
113. *cleave* 1) fuse 2) depart 3) instigate 4) apply 5) introduce

114. *compliance* 1) simplicity 2) defiance 3) disinterest 4) uselessness 5) isolation
115. *complacent* 1) egotistical 2) comical 3) distorted 4) discontented 5) avid
116. *circumvent* 1) perceive 2) outwit 3) avoid 4) surrender 5) validate
117. *compunction* 1) validity 2) superiority 3) superciliousness 4) dash 5) remorse
118. *compress* 1) expand 2) impress 3) proceed 4) divide 5) weaken
119. *collaborate* 1) work alone 2) depart 3) fashion 4) discard 5) quit
120. *comity* 1) applause 2) disapproval 3) truth 4) discord 5) departure

Answers to this test on page 148.

WORD LIST 7 **concoct - cryptic**

concoct V. prepare by combining; make up in concert. How did you ever *concoct* such a strange dish?

●**concord** N. harmony; agreement. The peace movement dreamed of a world in which nations would live together in *concord*.

concurrent ADJ. happening at the same time. In America, the colonists were resisting the demands of the mother country; at the *concurrent* moment in France, the middle class was sowing the seeds of rebellion.

condescend V. bestow courtesies with a superior air. The king *condescended* to grant an audience to the friends of the condemned man. condescension, N.

condiments N. seasonings; spices. Spanish food is full of *condiments*.

condole V. express sympathetic sorrow. His friends gathered to *condole* with him over his loss.

●**confirm** V. corroborate; verify, support. I have several witnesses who will *confirm* my account of what happened.

●**conformity** N. harmony, agreement. In *conformity* with our rules and regulations, I am calling a meeting of our organization.

confront V. face; challenge. All I ask is the chance to *confront* my accusers face to face.

congeal (*-jēl'*) V. freeze; coagulate. His blood *congealed* in his veins as he saw the dread monster rush toward him.

●**congenial** ADJ. pleasant; friendly. My father loved to go out for a meal with *congenial* companions.

congruence N. correspondence of parts; harmonious relationship. The student demonstrated the *congruence* of the two triangles by using the hypotenuse-arm theorem.

conjugal ADJ. pertaining to marriage. Their dreams of *conjugal* bliss were shattered as soon as their temperaments clashed.

connivance N. pretense of ignorance of something wrong; consent to, or assistance in, wrongdoing. With the *connivance* of her friends, she plotted to embarrass the teacher.

connotation N. suggested or implied meaning of an expression. Foreigners frequently are unaware of the *connotations* of the words they use.

conscientious ADJ. scrupulous; careful. A *conscientious* editor, she checked every definition for its accuracy.

consecrate V. dedicate; sanctify. We shall *consecrate* our lives to this noble purpose.

consistent ADJ. dependable; unchanging; compatible. The witnesses failed to come up with a *consistent* story of what had taken place.

●**consolidation** N. merger; combination. The *consolidation* of the two firms went smoothly; they merged without a hitch.

consort V. associate with. We frequently judge people by the company with whom they *consort*. also N.

constraint N. compulsion; repression of feelings. There was a feeling of *constraint* in the room because no one dared to criticize the speaker.

consummate (*-sŭm'-*) ADJ. complete. You are a *consummate* idiot. also V.

contagion N. infection. Fearing *contagion*, the doctors took great steps to prevent the spread of the disease.

●**contempt** N. scorn; disdain. Brave, but unimaginative, he had nothing but *contempt* for cowards. contemptuous, ADJ.

●**contentious** ADJ. quarrelsome. We heard loud and *contentious* noises in the next room.

context N. writings preceding and following passage quoted. Because these lines are taken out of *context*, they do not convey the message the author intended.

contiguous ADJ. adjacent to; touching upon. The two countries are *contiguous* for a few miles; then they are separated by the gulf.

contingent ADJ. conditional. The continuation of this contract is *contingent* on the quality of your first output. contingency, N.

contortions N. twistings; distortions. As the effects of the opiate wore off, the *contortions* of the patient became more violent and demonstrated how much pain he was enduring.

contumacious ADJ. disobedient; resisting authority. The *contumacious* mob shouted defiantly at the police.

contusion N. bruise. She was treated for *contusions* and abrasions.

convene V. assemble. The assembly will *convene* in January.

conveyance N. vehicle; transfer. During the transit strike, commuters used various kinds of *conveyances*.

convivial ADJ. festive; gay; characterized by joviality. The *convivial* celebrators of the victory sang their college songs.

convoke V. call together. Congress was *convoked* at the outbreak of the emergency.

coquette (*kō-kĕt'*) N. flirt. Because she refused to give him any answer to his proposal of marriage, he called her a *coquette*.

cordiality N. graciousness; warmth. Our hosts greeted us at the airport with great *cordiality*, hugging us heartily.

corporeal (*-pôr' eal*) ADJ. bodily; material. He was not a churchgoer; he was interested only in *corporeal* matters.

corroborate V. confirm. Find a witness to *corroborate* your evidence, or your case will not stand up in court.

corrosion N. destruction by chemical action. The *corrosion* of the girders supporting the bridge took place so gradually that no one suspected any danger until the bridge suddenly collapsed. corrode, V.

cosmic ADJ. pertaining to the universe; vast. *Cosmic* rays derive their name from the fact that they bombard the earth's atmosphere from outer space. cosmos, N.

covenant N. agreement. We must comply with the terms of the *covenant*.

covert (*kŭ'-*) ADJ. secret; hidden; implied. She could understand the *covert* threat in the letter.

covetous ADJ. avaricious; eagerly desirous of. He was *covetous* of fame.

cower V. shrink quivering, as from fear. The frightened child *cowered* in the corner of the room.

crass ADJ. very unrefined; grossly insensible. The philosophers deplored the *crass* commercialism.

●**credibility** N. believability. Because the candidate had made some pretty unbelievable promises, we began to question the *credibility* of everything she said.

credulity (*kre-dūl'-*) N. belief on slight evidence. The witch doctor took advantage of the *credulity* of the superstitious natives. credulous, ADJ.
creed N. system of religious or ethical belief. In any loyal American's *creed*, love of democracy must be emphasized.
crevice N. crack, fissure. The mountain climbers found footholds in the tiny *crevices* in the mountainside.
criterion N. standard used in judging. What *criterion* did you use when you selected this essay as the prize winner? criteria, PL.
crone N. hag. The screeching *crone* frightened us when she smiled.
•**cryptic** ADJ. mysterious; hidden; secret. His *cryptic* remarks could not be interpreted.

ETYMOLOGY 7

CONTRA (against)
contradict disagree
controversy dispute (turning against)
contrary opposed

CORD (heart)
accord agreement (from the heart)
cordial friendly
discord lack of harmony

CORPOR (body)
incorporate to organize into a body
corporeal pertaining to the body, fleshly
corpse a dead body

CRED, CREDIT (to believe)
incredulous not believing, skeptical
credulity gullibility
credence belief

TEST—WORD LIST 7—SYNONYMS

Each of the questions below consists of a word printed in italics, followed by five words or phrases numbered 1 to 5. Choose the numbered word or phrase which is most nearly similar in meaning to the word in italics and write the number of your answer on your answer paper.

121. *cryptic* 1) cheerful 2) obvious 3) hasty 4) lengthy 5) discordant
122. *criteria* 1) halves 2) models 3) capitals 4) edifices 5) standards
123. *conveyance* 1) vehicle 2) despot 3) monarch 4) transition 5) transfer
124. *condole* 1) express sorrow 2) rejoice 3) annoy 4) delight 5) consign
125. *creed* 1) gluttony 2) intermarriage 3) statement of faith 4) church 5) trust
126. *credulity* 1) slovenliness 2) gullibility 3) disbelief 4) pleasure 5) fault
127. *condescend* 1) extort 2) supervise 3) agree 4) deign 5) fortify
128. *corroborate* 1) intend 2) confirm 3) question 4) force 5) contain
129. *convivial* 1) stern 2) sympathetic 3) brief 4) doubtful 5) gay
130. *crevice* 1) crack 2) advice 3) service 4) lava 5) catastrophe
131. *cosmic* 1) annual 2) pearly 3) universal 4) distinguished 5) wanton
132. *condiments* 1) swords 2) seasonings 3) natives 4) troops 5) rates
133. *consecrate* 1) embarrass 2) harass 3) believe 4) dedicate 5) trust
134. *crass* 1) confidential 2) unrefined 3) vivid 4) swift 5) varied
135. *contusion* 1) mix 2) larceny 3) bruise 4) felony 5) riot
136. *conjugal* 1) destined 2) sworn 3) marital 4) jolly 5) well-groomed
137. *covenant* 1) desire 2) condition 3) disagreement 4) condemnation 5) agreement
138. *congeal* 1) melt 2) affect 3) freeze 4) presume 5) dissolve
139. *consummate* 1) complete 2) partial 3) parting 4) composed 5) parallel
140. *covetous* 1) neighborly 2) uxorious 3) avaricious 4) average 5) stingy

Answers to this test on page 149.

WORD LIST 8 culinary - desiccate

culinary (*kūl'-*) ADJ. relating to cooking. Many chefs attribute their *culinary* skill to the wise use of spices.
cull V. pick out; reject. Every month the farmer *culls* his nonlaying hens from his flock and sells them to the local butcher.
culmination N. attainment of highest point. Her inauguration as President of the United States marked the *culmination* of her political career.
culpable ADJ. deserving blame. Corrupt politicians who condone the activities of the gamblers are equally *culpable*.
cumbersome ADJ. heavy, hard to manage. He was burdened down with *cumbersome* parcels.
cursory ADJ. casual; hastily done. A *cursory* glance revealed no trace of the missing book.
•**curtail** V. shorten; reduce. During the coal shortage, we must *curtail* our use of this vital commodity.
•**cynic** N. one who is skeptical or distrustful of human motives. A *cynic* at all times, he was suspicious of all altruistic actions of others. cynical, ADJ.

dally V. trifle with; procrastinate. Laertes told Ophelia that Hamlet could only *dally* with her affections.

●**dawdle** V. loiter; waste time. We have to meet a deadline; do not *dawdle* over this work.

dearth (*dêrth*) N. scarcity. The *dearth* of skilled labor compelled the employers to open trade schools.

debase V. reduce to lower state. Do not *debase* yourself by becoming maudlin.

debilitate V. weaken; enfeeble. Overindulgence *debilitates* character as well as physical stamina.

debutante (*dĕb'-yoo-*) N. young lady during her first year in society. As a *debutante*, she was often mentioned in the society columns of the newspapers.

decadence (*dĕk'-*) N. decay. The moral *decadence* of the people was reflected in the lewd literature of the period.

deciduous ADJ. falling off, as of leaves. The oak is a *deciduous* tree.

decorous ADJ. proper. Her *decorous* behavior was praised by her teachers. decorum, N.

decoy (*-koi'*) N. lure or bait. The wild ducks were not fooled by the *decoy*. also V.

deducible ADJ. derived by reasoning. If we accept your premise, your conclusions are easily *deducible*.

defamation N. harming a person's reputation. Such *defamation* of character may result in a slander suit.

defeatist ADJ. attitude of one who is ready to accept defeat as a natural outcome. If you maintain your *defeatist* attitude, you will never succeed. also N.

deference (*dĕf'-*) N. courteous regard for another's wish. In *deference* to her desires, the employers granted her a holiday.

●**defiance** N. refusal to yield; resistance. When I give an order, I don't expect *defiance*. defy, V.

definitive ADJ. final; complete. Carl Sandburg's *Abraham Lincoln* may be regarded as the *definitive* work on the life of the Great Emancipator.

deflect V. turn aside. His life was saved when his cigarette case *deflected* the bullet.

defunct ADJ. dead; no longer in use or existence. The lawyers sought to examine the books of the *defunct* corporation.

deign (*dān*) V. condescend. Will she *deign* to answer your letter?

delete V. erase; strike out. If you *delete* this unnecessary paragraph, the composition will have more appeal.

delineation N. portrayal. He is a powerful story teller, but he is weakest in his *delineation* of character.

delirium N. mental disorder marked by confusion. The drunkard in his *delirium* saw strange animals.

delusion N. false belief, hallucination. This scheme is a snare and a *delusion*.

demean V. degrade; condescend to do. He could not *demean* himself in this matter.

demeanor N. behavior; bearing. Her sober *demeanor* quieted the noisy revelers.

demise (*mīz'*) N. death. Upon the *demise* of the dictator, a bitter dispute about succession to power developed.

demolition N. destruction. One of the major aims of the air force was the complete *demolition* of all means of transportation by bombing of rail lines and terminals.

demur V. delay; object. Do not *demur* at my request.

demure ADJ. grave; serious; coy. She was *demure* and reserved.

●**denounce** V. condemn; criticize. The reform candidate *denounced* the corrupt city officers for having betrayed the public's trust. denunciation, N.

●**deny** V. contradict; refuse. Do you *deny* his story, or do you support what he says? denial, N.

depict V. portray. In this book, the author *depicts* the slave owners as kind and benevolent masters.

deplete V. reduce; exhaust. We must wait until we *deplete* our present inventory before we order replacements.

deprecate V. disapprove regretfully. I must *deprecate* your attitude and hope that you will change your mind.

deprecatory ADJ. disapproving. Your *deprecatory* criticism has offended the author.

depreciate V. lessen in value. If you neglect this property, it will *depreciate*.

depredation N. plundering. After the *depredations* of the invaders, the people were penniless.

derelict ADJ. abandonded. The *derelict* craft was a menace to navigation. also N.

●**derision** N. ridicule. They greeted his proposal with *derision* and refused to consider it seriously.

●**derivative** ADJ. unoriginal; derived from another source. Although her early poetry was clearly *derivative* in nature, the critics felt she had promise and eventually would find her own voice.

desecrate V. profane; violate the sanctity of. The soldiers *desecrated* the temple, shattering the altar and trampling the holy objects underfoot.

desiccate V. dry up. A tour of this smokehouse will give you an idea of how the pioneers used to *desiccate* food in order to preserve it.

ETYMOLOGY 8

CUR (to care)
curator person in charge
sinecure position without responsibility
secure safe

CURR, CURS (to run)
excursion journey
cursory brief
precursor forerunner

CY (state of being) noun suffix
democracy a democratic state
obstinacy state of being stubborn
accuracy state of being accurate

DA, DAT (to give)
data facts, statistics
mandate command
date given time

DE (down, away) prefix
debase lower in value
decadence deterioration
decant pour off

DEB, DEBIT (to owe)
debt something owed
indebtedness debt
debenture bond

DEMOS (people)
democracy rule of the people
demagogue (false) leader of the people
epidemic widespread disease (among the people)

DERM (skin)
epidermis skin
pachyderm thick-skinned quadruped
dermatology study of skin and its disorders

TEST—WORD LIST 8 —ANTONYMS

Each of the questions below consists of a word printed in italics, followed by five words or phrases numbered 1 to 5. Choose the numbered word or phrase which is most nearly opposite in meaning to the word in italics and write the number of your answer on your answer paper.

141. *derivative* 1) serious 2) outdated 3) fantastic 4) original 5) urgent
142. *defamation* 1) reformation 2) praise 3) publicity 4) proclamation 5) analysis
143. *deplete* 1) shift 2) reward 3) increase 4) remain 5) dawdle
144. *depreciate* 1) estimate 2) defer 3) incur 4) appreciate 5) reciprocate
145. *cull* 1) plant 2) pick out 3) curtail 4) evict 5) accept
146. *demise* 1) decrease 2) crime 3) birth 4) massage 5) reaction
147. *demure* 1) clumsy 2) unappealing 3) remorseful 4) brazen 5) eager
148. *dawdle* 1) decorate 2) hasten 3) fumble 4) mutter 5) topple
149. *culpable* 1) indolent 2) carefree 3) earnest 4) gullible 5) blameless
150. *deprecate* 1) approve 2) improve 3) provide 4) pilfer 5) confer
151. *culmination* 1) promotion 2) permission 3) inception 4) assignment 5) offer
152. *cursory* 1) impetuous 2) costly 3) simulated 4) thorough 5) collecting
153. *deference* 1) support 2) vanity 3) postponement 4) value 5) disrespect
154. *decorous* 1) inured 2) improper 3) courtly 4) noble 5) kindly
155. *delete* 1) erect 2) raze 3) infer 4) insert 5) oppose
156. *desiccate* 1) saturate 2) sate 3) castigate 4) destroy 5) upbuild
157. *dearth* 1) fondness 2) lands 3) abundance 4) hatred 5) loss
158. *demur* 1) smile 2) accept 3) dissemble 4) separate 5) contribute
159. *demolition* 1) freedom 2) denial 3) obedience 4) unfairness 5) construction
160. *deprecatory* 1) tedious 2) dilatory 3) innocent 4) laudatory 5) explanatory

Answers to this test on page 149.

WORD LIST 9 **despotism - diverse**

despotism N. tyranny. The people rebelled against the *despotism* of the king.

desultory (*dĕs'*-) ADJ. aimless; jumping around. The animals' *desultory* behavior indicated that they had no awareness of their predicament.

•**detached** ADJ. emotionally removed; calm and objective; indifferent. A psychoanalyst must maintain a *detached* point of view and stay uninvolved with her patients' personal lives. detachment, N. (secondary meaning)

detergent N. cleansing agent. Many new *detergents* have replaced soap.

•**deterrent** N. something that discourages; hindrance. Does the threat of capital punishment serve as a *deterrent* to potential killers?

detonation N. explosion. The *detonation* could be heard miles away.

detraction N. slandering; aspersion. He is offended by your frequent *detractions* of his ability as a leader.

detriment N. harm; damage. Your acceptance of his support will ultimately prove to be a *detriment* rather than an aid to your cause.

deviate (*dēv'*-) V. turn away from. Do not *deviate* from the truth.

devious ADJ. roundabout; erratic; not straightforward. His plan was so *devious* that it was only with great difficulty we could follow its shifts and dodges.

dexterous ADJ. skillful. The magician was so *dexterous* that we could not follow him as he performed his tricks.

diadem (*dī-á-*) N. crown. The king's *diadem* was on display at the museum.

diaphanous (*dī-af'*-) ADJ. sheer; transparent. They admired her *diaphanous* and colorful dress.

dictum N. authoritative and weighty statement. He repeated the statement as though it were the *dictum* of the most expert worker in the group.

didactic ADJ. teaching; instructional. The *didactic* qualities of his poetry overshadow its literary qualities; the lesson he teaches is more memorable than the lines he writes.

diffusion N. wordiness; spreading in all directions like a gas. Your composition suffers from a *diffusion* of ideas; try to be more compact.

digressive ADJ. wandering away from the subject. Her book was marred by her many *digressive* remarks.

dilapidation N. ruin because of neglect. We felt that the *dilapidation* of the building could be corrected by several coats of paint.

dilemma N. problem; choice of two unsatisfactory alternatives. In this *dilemma*, she knew no one to whom she could turn for advice.

dilettante N. aimless follower of the arts; amateur, dabbler. He was not serious in his painting; he was rather a *dilettante*.

diligence N. steadiness of effort; persistent hard work. Her employers were greatly impressed by her *diligence* and offered her a partnership in the firm.

•**dilute** V. make less concentrated; reduce in strength. She preferred her coffee *diluted* with milk.

dint N. means; effort. By *dint* of much hard work, the volunteers were able to place the raging forest fire under control.

dire ADJ. disastrous. People ignored his *dire* predictions of an approaching depression.

dirge N. lament with music. The funeral *dirge* stirred us to tears.

disavowal N. denial; disclaiming. Her *disavowal* of her part in the conspiracy was not believed by the jury.

discernible ADJ. distinguishable; perceivable. The ships in the harbor were not *discernible* in the fog.

discerning ADJ. mentally quick and observant; having insight. The *discerning* interrogator noticed many discrepancies in his testimony.

disclaim V. disown; renounce claim to. If I grant you this privilege, will you *disclaim* all other rights?

●**disclose** V. reveal. Although competitors offered him bribes, he refused to *disclose* any information about his company's forthcoming product. disclosure, N.

disconcert V. confuse; upset, embarrass. The lawyer was *disconcerted* by the evidence produced by her adversary.

discordant ADJ. unharmonious; conflicting. She tried to unite the *discordant* factions.

discriminating ADJ. able to see differences; prejudiced. They feared he was not sufficiently *discriminating* to judge complex works of modern art. (secondary meaning) discrimination, N.

discursive ADJ. digressing; rambling. They were annoyed and bored by his *discursive* remarks.

disdain V. contempt; treat with scorn. You make enemies of all you *disdain*.

●**disinterested** ADJ. unprejudiced. The only *disinterested* person in the room was the judge.

disparage V. belittle. Do not *disparage* anyone's contribution; these little gifts add up to large sums.

dispatch N. speed; promptness. The efficient editor performed her many tasks with *dispatch*.

●**disperse** V. scatter. The police fired tear gas into the crowd to *disperse* the protesters.

disputatious (*-ta'-*) ADJ. argumentative; fond of argument. People avoided discussing contemporary problems with him because of his *disputatious* manner.

dissemble V. disguise; pretend. Even though you are trying to *dissemble* your motive in joining this group, we can see through your pretense.

●**disseminate** V. scatter (like seeds). The invention of the radio helped propagandists to *disseminate* their favorite doctrines very easily.

●**dissent** V. disagree. In the recent Supreme Court decision, Justice Marshall *dissented* from the majority opinion. also N.

dissertation N. formal essay. In order to earn a graduate degree from many of our universities, a candidate is frequently required to prepare a *dissertation* on some scholarly subject.

dissimulate V. pretend; conceal by feigning. She tried to *dissimulate* her grief by her gay attire.

dissipate V. squander. The young man quickly *dissipated* his inheritance and was soon broke.

dissolute ADJ. loose in morals. The *dissolute* life led by these people is indeed shocking.

●**dissuade** (*dis-wād'-*) V. advise against. He could not *dissuade* his friend from joining the conspirators.

distortion N. twisting out of shape. It is difficult to believe the newspaper accounts of this event because of the *distortions* and exaggerations written by the reporters.

diverge (*dĭ-*) V. vary; go in different directions from the same point. The spokes of the wheel *diverge* from the hub.

●**diverse** ADJ. differing in some characteristics; various. There are *diverse* ways of approaching this problem.

ETYMOLOGY 9

DI, DIURN (day)
diary day book
diurnal pertaining to day time
journey day's travel

DIA (across) prefix
diagonal across a figure
diameter across a circle
diagram (writing across) outline drawing

DIC, DICT (to say)
abdicate renounce
diction speech
verdict statement of jury

DIS, DIF (not) prefix
discord lack of harmony
differ disagree (carry apart)
distrust lack of trust

TEST—WORD LIST 9 —SYNONYMS OR ANTONYMS

Each of the questions below consists of a word printed in italics, followed by five words or phrases numbered 1 to 5. Choose the numbered word or phrase which is most nearly the same as or the opposite of the word in italics and write the number of your choice on your answer paper.

161. *dexterous* 1) sweet 2) sour 3) inept 4) gracious 5) righteous

162. *dilettante* 1) renegade 2) professional 3) lunatic 4) braggart 5) miser

163. *disparage* 1) praise 2) evaluate 3) discourage 4) frustrate 5) function

164. *disclose* 1) conclude 2) convince 3) conceal 4) condone 5) congeal

165. *dire* 1) expensive 2) anecdotal 3) latent 4) insignificant 5) fortunate

166. *disseminate* 1) postulate 2) dry 3) falsify 4) spread 5) eliminate

167. *despotism* 1) tyranny 2) hegemony 3) paradox 4) quotation 5) episode

168. *dissolute* 1) moral 2) lavish 3) magniloquent 4) bombastic 5) resolved

169. *discernible* 1) distinguished 2) shabby 3) intelligent 4) impudent 5) imperceptible

170. *diaphanous* 1) mellifluous 2) abdominal 3) thick 4) scented 5) monotonous

171. *disputatious* 1) argumentative 2) probable 3) plausible 4) reflected 5) cautious

172. *desultory* 1) barren 2) reluctant 3) purposeful 4) complimentary 5) virtuous

173. *discordant* 1) habitual 2) harmless 3) haughty 4) harmonious 5) hampered

174. *dissemble* 1) dismiss 2) convoke 3) muster 4) cluster 5) pretend

175. *disconcert* 1) throw away 2) take over 3) put at ease 4) approach 5) restrain

176. *dilapidation* 1) ruin 2) urbanity 3) mediocrity 4) plausibility 5) niggardliness
177. *dissuade* 1) entice 2) abuse 3) banter 4) convey 5) exhort
178. *detriment* 1) advantage 2) equality 3) item 4) opulence 5) ubiquity
179. *dilemma* 1) maze 2) quandry 3) ruse 4) subterfuge 5) tragedy
180. *devious* 1) erratic 2) sporadic 3) incoherent 4) inchoate 5) episodic

Answers to this test on page 149.

WORD LIST 10 **diversity - enigma**

diversity N. variety; dissimilitude. The *diversity* of colleges in this country indicates that many levels of ability are being cared for.

divest (*dĭ-*) V. strip; deprive. He was *divested* of his power to act.

divulge V. reveal. Not even torture could force him to *divulge* the secret.

●**docile** ADJ. obedient; easily managed. As *docile* as he seems today, that old lion was once a ferocious, snarling beast.

●**dogmatic** ADJ. positive; arbitrary. Do not be so *dogmatic* about that statement; it can be easily refuted.

dolorous (*dŏl'-*) ADJ. sorrowful. She found the *dolorous* lamentations of the bereaved family emotionally disturbing and she left as quickly as she could.

dolt N. stupid person. I thought I was talking to a mature audience; instead, I find myself addressing a pack of *dolts* and idiots.

dormant ADJ. sleeping; lethargic, latent. At fifty her long-*dormant* ambition to write flared up once more; within a year she had completed the first of her great historical novels.

dregs N. sediment; worthless residue. The *dregs* of society may be observed in this slum area of the city.

dross (*drŏss*) N. waste matter; worthless impurities. Many methods have been devised to separate the valuable metal from the *dross*.

drudgery N. menial work. Cinderella's fairy godmother rescued her from a life of *drudgery*.

duplicity N. double-dealing, hypocrisy. People were shocked and dismayed when they learned of his *duplicity* in this affair for he had always seemed honest and straightforward.

earthy ADJ. unrefined; coarse. His *earthy* remarks often embarrassed the ladies in his audience.

ebb V. recede; lessen. His fortunes began to *ebb* during the Recession. also N.

ebullient (*-bŭl'-*) ADJ. showing excitement; overflowing with enthusiasm. Her *ebullient* nature could not be repressed; She was always laughing and gay. ebullience, N.

●**eccentric** ADJ. odd; whimsical; irregular. The comet passed close by the earth in its *eccentric* orbit.

●**eclipse** V. darken; extinguish; surpass. The new stock market high *eclipsed* the previous record set in 1985.

ecstasy N. rapture; joy; any overpowering emotion. The announcement that the war had ended brought on an *ecstasy* of joy that resulted in many uncontrolled celebrations.

eerie (*ē'rĭ*) ADJ. weird. In that *eerie* setting, it was easy to believe in ghosts and other supernatural beings.

effectual ADJ. efficient. If we are to succeed in this endeavor, we must seek *effectual* means of securing our goals.

effervesce (*-vĕs'*) V. bubble over; show excitement. Some of us cannot stand the way she *effervesces* over trifles.

effete (*ĕfēt'*) ADJ. worn out; exhausted; barren. The literature of the age reflected the *effete* condition of the writers; no new ideas were forthcoming.

efficacy N. power to produce desired effect. The *efficacy* of this drug depends on the regularity of the dosage.

effrontery N. shameless boldness. He has the *effrontery* to insult the guest.

effusive ADJ. pouring forth; gushing. Her *effusive* manner of greeting her friends finally began to irritate them.

egoism N. excessive interest in one's self; belief that one should be interested in one's self rather than in others. His *egoism* prevented him from seeing the needs of his colleagues.

egotism N. conceit; vanity. We found his *egotism* unwarranted and irrating.

egregious (*ĕ-grē'-zhos*) ADJ. gross; shocking. He was an *egregious* liar.

ejaculation N. exclamation. He could not repress his *ejaculation* when he heard the surprising news.

elegiacal (*è-lĕ-jī'-*) ADJ. lamenting (a death); mournful. The essay was *elegiacal* in mood. elegy, N.

elicit (*-lĭ'-sĭt*) V. draw out by discussion. The detectives tried to *elicit* where he had hidden his loot.

elucidate V. explain; enlighten. She was called upon to *elucidate* the disputed points in her article.

elusory ADJ. tending to deceive expectations; elusive. He argued that the project was an *elusory* one and would bring disappointment to all.

emanate V. issue forth. A strong odor of sulphur *emanated* from the spring.

emancipate V. set free. At first, the attempts of the Abolitionists to *emancipate* the slaves were unpopular in New England as well as in the South.

embroil V. throw into confusion; involve in strife; entangle. She became *embroiled* in the heated discussion when she tried to arbitrate the dispute.

emolument (*-mŏl'-*) N. salary; compensation. In addition to the *emolument* this position offers, you must consider the social prestige it carries with it.

empirical ADJ. based on experience. He distrusted hunches and intuitive flashes; he placed his reliance entirely on *empirical* data.

emulate (*ĕm'-*) V. rival; imitate. As long as our political leaders *emulate* the virtues of the great leaders of this country, we shall flourish.

encompass V. surround. Although we were *encompassed* by enemy forces, we were cheerful for we were well stocked and could withstand a siege until our allies joined us.

encumber V. burden. Some people *encumber* themselves with too much luggage when they go for short trips.

endearment N. fond statement. Your gifts and *endearments* cannot make me forget your earlier insolence.

●**endorse** V. approve; support. Everyone waited to see which one of the rival candidates for the city council the mayor would *endorse*. endorsement, N. (secondary meaning)

energize V. invigorate; make forceful and active. We shall have to *energize* our activities by getting new members to carry on.

engender V. cause; produce. To receive praise for real accomplishments *engenders* self-confidence in a child.

engross V. occupy fully. The boy was *engrossed* in his studies.

●**enhance** V. advance; improve. Your chances for promotion in this department will be *enhanced* if you take some more courses in evening school.

enigma (*-nĭg'-*) N. puzzle. Despite all attempts to decipher the code, it remained an *enigma*.

ā—ale; ă—add; ä—arm; ȧ—ask; ē—eve; ĕ—end; ẽ—err, her; e—event, allow; ī—ice; i—ill; ō—old; ŏ—odd; ô—orb; o͞o—food; ou—out; th—thin; ū—use; ŭ—up; zh—pleasure

ETYMOLOGY 10

DOC, DOCT (to teach)
docile meek (teachable)
document something that provides evidence
doctor learned man (originally, teacher)

DOMIN (to rule)
dominate having power over
domain land under rule
dominant prevailing

DUC, DUCT (to lead)
viaduct arched roadway
aqueduct artificial waterway
education training (leading out)

DYNAM (power, strength)
dynamic powerful
dynamite powerful explosive
dynamo engine to make electrical power

EGO (I)
egoist person who is self-interested
egotist selfish person
egocentric revolving about self

TEST—WORD LIST 10 —SYNONYMS

Each of the questions below consists of a word printed in italics, followed by five words or phrases numbered 1 to 5. Choose the numbered word or phrase which is most nearly similar in meaning to the word in italics and write the number of your choice on your answer paper.

181. *dross* 1) quiet 2) meekness 3) domain 4) dynamo 5) worthless matter
182. *elucidate* 1) explain 2) flow out 3) magnify 4) elicit 5) erase
183. *engross* 1) enlarge 2) pursue 3) acquit 4) occupy fully 5) exhume
184. *egregious* 1) tiny 2) gross 3) dubious 4) weird 5) wicked
185. *encompass* 1) mislead 2) surround 3) bypass 4) direct 5) convince
186. *duplicity* 1) hypocrisy 2) ambiguity 3) two of a kind 4) energy 5) improvement
187. *endorse* 1) support 2) reconcile 3) distribute 4) negotiate 5) forge
188. *encumber* 1) vegetate 2) burden 3) plant 4) specialize 5) enlighten
189. *effete* 1) gala 2) exhausted 3) triumphant 4) rival 5) improved
190. *effervesce* 1) excite 2) exhaust 3) bubble over 4) understate 5) deny
191. *emancipate* 1) review 2) outlive 3) deny access to 4) set free 5) proclaim
192. *enigma* 1) sphinx 2) reason 3) dummy 4) puzzle 5) question
193. *emulate* 1) sympathize 2) manifest 3) manipulate 4) luxuriate 5) imitate
194. *effrontery* 1) coyness 2) prominence 3) liveliness 4) pallor 5) shameless boldness
195. *emolument* 1) salve 2) law suit 3) salary 4) lyrics 5) marrow
196. *egotism* 1) conceit 2) elation 3) control 4) formula 5) virtuoso
197. *effusive* 1) girlish 2) ghoulish 3) gushing 4) elongated 5) sensitive
198. *dolorous* 1) emotional 2) sorrowful 3) petrifying 4) monetary 5) dominant
199. *dregs* 1) bottom of cup 2) male fowl 3) preserves 4) errors 5) sediment
200. *enhance* 1) survive 2) disembark 3) confuse 4) improve 5) separate

Answers to this test on page 149.

WORD LIST 11 enormity - extort

enormity N. hugeness (in a bad sense). He did not realize the *enormity* of his crime until he saw what suffering he had caused.

enrapture V. please intensely. The audience was *enraptured* by the freshness of the voices and the excellent orchestration.

• **enterprising** ADJ. full of initiative. By coming up with fresh ways to market the company's products, Mike proved himself to be an *enterprising* businessman.

enthrall V. capture; make slave. From the monent he saw her picture, he was *enthralled* by her beauty.

entree (*ŏn'trā*) N. entrance. Because of her wealth and social position, she had *entree* into the most exclusive circles.

entrepreneur N. businessperson; contractor. Opponents of our present tax program argue that it discourages *entrepreneurs* from trying new fields of business activity.

enumerate V. mention one by one; list. It is not necessary for me to *enumerate* all of the advantages of a college education.

epicurean N. person who devotes him- or herself to pleasures of the senses, especially to food. This restaurant is famous for its menu, which can cater to the most exotic whim of the *epicurean*. also ADJ.

epigram N. witty thought or saying, usually short. Poor Richard's *epigrams* made Benjamin Franklin famous.

epilogue N. short speech at conclusion of dramatic work. The audience was so disappointed in the play that many in the theater did not remain to hear the *epilogue*.

epitaph N. inscription on a tomb in memory of a dead person. In his will, he dictated the *epitaph* he wanted placed on his tombstone.

epithet N. descriptive adjective. Homer's writings featured the use of such *epithets* as "rosy-fingered dawn."

epitome (*ĕ-pĭt'ō-mē*) N. summary; concise abstract. This final book is the *epitome* of all her previous books. epitomize, V.

epoch N. period of time. The glacial *epoch* lasted for thousands of years.

equestrian N. rider on horseback. These paths in the park are reserved for *equestrians* and their steeds. also ADJ.

equinox N. the period of equal days and nights; the beginning of spring and autumn. The vernal *equinox* is usually marked by heavy rainstorms.

equity N. fairness; justice. Our courts guarantee *equity* to all.

equivocal ADJ. ambiguous; misleading. The audience saw through his *equivocal* comments and insisted that he come right out and say where he stood on the issue. equivocate, N.

erode V. eat away. The limestone was *eroded* by the dripping water.

errant ADJ. wandering. Many a charming tale has been written about the knights *errant* who helped the weak and punished the guilty during the Age of Chivalry.

•**erratic** ADJ. odd; unpredictable. Investors become anxious when the stock market appears *erratic*.

erroneous ADJ. mistaken; wrong. I thought my answer was correct, but it was *erroneous*.

escapade (*ĕs-ca-pād'*) N. prank; flighty conduct. The headmaster could not regard this latest *escapade* as a boyish joke and expelled the young man.

•**esoteric** (*-tĕr'-*) ADJ. known only to the chosen few. Those students who had access to her *esoteric* discussions were impressed by the scope of her thinking.

espionage (*ĕs'pĭ-*) N. spying. In order to maintain its power, the government developed a system of *espionage* which penetrated every household.

•**espouse** V. adopt; support. She was always ready to *espouse* a worthy cause.

esprit de corps (*ĕs-prē'-de-kôr*) N. comradeship; spirit. West Point cadets are proud of their *esprit de corps*.

estranged ADJ. separated. The *estranged* wife sought a divorce from the husband she had left a year before.

ethereal ADJ. light; heavenly; fine. Visitors were impressed by her *ethereal* beauty, her delicate charm.

eulogy N. praise. All the *eulogies* of his friends could not remove the sting of the calumny heaped upon him by his enemies. eulogize, V.

evanescent ADJ. fleeting; vanishing. In the *evanescent* rays of the sunset, the entire western skyline was bathed in an orange-red hue.

evince V. show clearly. When he tried to answer the questions, he *evinced* his ignorance of the subject matter.

evoke V. call forth. He *evoked* much criticism by his hostile manner.

exemplary (*-ĕm'-*) ADJ. serving as a model; outstanding. Her *exemplary* behavior was praised at commencement.

exhort (*ĭg-zôrt'-*) V. urge. The evangelist will *exhort* all sinners in his audience to reform.

exigency (*ĕx'-ĭj-*) N. urgency. In this *exigency*, we must look for aid from our allies.

exonerate V. acquit; exculpate. I am sure this letter will *exonerate* you of any blame for what occurred.

exotic ADJ. not native; strange. Because of his *exotic* headdress, he was followed in the streets by small children who laughed at his strange appearance.

expatiate (*-pā'-*) V. talk at length. At this time, please give us a brief resumé of your work; we shall permit you to *expatiate* later.

expediency N. that which is advisable or practical. She was guided by *expediency* rather than by ethical considerations.

expeditiously ADV. rapidly and efficiently. Please adjust this matter as *expeditiously* as possible as it is delaying important work.

expiate (*ĕx'-pĭ-āt*) V. make amends for (a sin). He tried to *expiate* his crimes by making a full confession to the authorities.

•**exploit** N. deed or action, particularly a brave deed. Raoul Wallenberg was noted for his *exploits* in rescuing Jews from Hitler's forces.

•**exploit** N. deed or action, particularly a brave deed. Raoul Wallenberg was noted for his *exploits* in rescuing Jews from Hitler's forces.

expunge V. cancel; remove. If you behave, I will *expunge* this notation from your record card.

expurgate V. clean; remove offensive parts of a book. The editors felt that certain passages in the book had to be *expurgated* before it could be used in the class.

extant (*ĕx'-*) ADJ. still in existence. Although the authorities suppressed the book, many copies are *extant* and may be purchased at exorbitant prices.

extirpate V. root up. We must *extirpate* and destroy this monstrous philosophy.

extort V. wring from; get money by threats, etc. The blackmailer *extorted* money from his victim.

ETYMOLOGY 11

ERG (work)
energy power
metallurgy art of working in metal

ERR (to wander)
error mistake
erratic not reliable, wandering
knight-errant wandering knight

EU (good, well, beautiful)
eulogize to praise
euphemism substitution of pleasant way of saying something blunt or unpleasant
eupeptic having good digestion

EX (out) prefix
expel drive out
exit way out
extirpate root out

EXTRA (beyond, outside) prefix
extraordinary exceptional
extracurricular beyond the items in the curriculum
extraterritorial beyond the territory of a nation

TEST—WORD LIST 11—ANTONYMS

Each of the questions below consists of a word printed in italics, followed by five words or phrases numbered 1 to 5. Choose the numbered word or phrase which is most nearly opposite in meaning to the word in italics and write the number of your choice on your answer paper.

201. *esoteric* 1) hard-won 2) well-known 3) sentimental 4) absent 5) civilized

202. *exemplary* 1) contemporary 2) prevalent 3) courteous 4) nefarious 5) immutable

203. *expunge* 1) detract 2) induce 3) append 4) delay 5) admire

ā—ale; ă—add; ä—arm; ȧ—ask; ē—eve; ĕ—end; ê—err, her; e—event, allow; ī—ice; ĭ—ill; ō—old; ŏ—odd; ô—orb; o͞o—food; ou—out; th—thin; ū—use; ŭ—up; zh—pleasure

204. *epilogue* 1) novel 2) prologue 3) poem 4) posterior 5) polemic
205. *exotic* 1) chaotic 2) precarious 3) ordinary 4) inappropriate 5) leisurely
206. *expeditiously* 1) neatly 2) wickedly 3) recklessly 4) doggedly 5) slowly
207. *eulogy* 1) blame 2) funeral 3) lyric 4) song 5) drama
208. *estranged* 1) repulsive 2) reproved 3) admirable 4) reconciled 5) disjointed
209. *equestrian* 1) pedestrian 2) driver 3) bookworm 4) manager 5) equal
210. *exhort* 1) suppose 2) dissuade 3) contend 4) reveal 5) prefer
211. *evince* 1) defeat 2) conquer 3) develop 4) analyze 5) obscure
212. *expatiate* 1) alienate 2) approve 3) demonstrate 4) summarize 5) return
213. *evanescent* 1) lasting 2) abstract 3) radiant 4) exalted 5) accidental
214. *espouse* 1) arouse 2) delude 3) oppose 4) persist 5) abash
215. *erratic* 1) cordial 2) regular 3) momentous 4) unique 5) compact
216. *enormity* 1) insignificance 2) quantity 3) quality 4) stupidity 5) ignorance
217. *expediency* 1) program 2) lack of skill 3) counsel 4) impracticability 5) advice
218. *enrapture* 1) reconcile 2) transform 3) anticipate 4) displease 5) seek
219. *extant* 1) entering 2) nonexistent 3) extended 4) silent 5) deficient
220. *equity* 1) unfairness 2) theatricality 3) sincerity 4) directness 5) unpopularity

Answers to this test on page 149.

WORD LIST 12 **extrude - fluster**

extrude V. force or push out. Much pressure is required to *extrude* these plastics.

exuberant ADJ. abundant; effusive; lavish. His speeches were famous for his *exuberant* language and vivid imagery.

fabricate V. build; lie. If we pre-*fabricate* the buildings in this project, we can reduce the cost considerably.

facetious ADJ. humorous; jocular. Your *facetious* remarks are not appropriate at this serious moment.

facile ADJ. easy; expert. Because he was a *facile* speaker, he never refused a request to address an organization.

facilitate V. make less difficult. He tried to *facilitate* matters at home by getting a part-time job.

faction N. party; clique; dissension. The quarrels and bickering of the two small *factions* within the club disturbed the majority of the members.

fallacious (*-lā'-*) ADJ. misleading. Your reasoning must be *fallacious* because it leads to a ridiculous answer.

fallible ADJ. liable to err. I know I am *fallible*, but I feel confident that I am right this time.

fallow ADJ. plowed but not sowed; uncultivated. Farmers have learned that it is advisable to permit land to lie *fallow* every few years.

fanaticism N. excessive zeal. He could not control the *fanaticism* of his followers.

fancied ADJ. imagined; unreal. You are resenting *fancied* insults. No one has ever said such things about you.

fantastic ADJ. unreal; grotesque; whimsical. Your fears are *fantastic* because no such animal as you have described exists.

fastidious ADJ. difficult to please; squeamish. The waitresses disliked to serve him his dinner because of his very *fastidious* taste.

fawning ADJ. courting favor by cringing and flattering. He was constantly surrounded by a group of *fawning* admirers who hoped to win some favor.

•**feasible** ADJ. practical. This is an entirely *feasible* proposal; I suggest we adopt it.

feint (*fānt*) N. trick, shift, sham blow. The pugilist was fooled by his opponent's *feint* and dropped his guard. also V.

felicitous ADJ. apt; suitably expressed; well-chosen. He was famous for his *felicitous* remarks and was called upon to serve as master of ceremonies at many a banquet.

fervent ADJ. ardent; hot. She laughed at his *fervent* love letters.

fester V. generate pus. The splinter in her finger began to *fester*.

fetid (*fĕt'ĭd*) ADJ. malodorous. The neglected wound became *fetid*.

fetter V. shackle. The prisoner was *fettered* to the wall.

fictitious ADJ. imaginary. Although this book purports to be a biography of George Washington, many of the incidents are *fictitious*.

filial ADJ. pertaining to a son or daughter. Many children forget their *filial* obligations and disregard the wishes of their parents.

finale (*fĭ-nă'-lē*) N. conclusion. It is not until we reach the *finale* of this play that we can understand the author's message.

finesse (*fĭ-nĕs'*) N. delicate skill. The *finesse* and adroitness of the surgeon impressed the observers in the operating room.

finicky ADJ. too particular; fussy. The old lady was *finicky* about her food.

firebrand N. hothead; troublemaker. The police tried to keep track of all the local *firebrands* when the President came to town.

fissure N. crevice. The mountain climbers secured footholds in tiny *fissures* in the rock.

fitful ADJ. spasmodic; intermittent. After several *fitful* attempts, he decided to postpone the start of the project until he felt more energetic.

flaccid (*flăk'sĭd*) ADJ. flabby. His sedentary life had left him with *flaccid* muscles.

flagging ADJ. weak; drooping. The cross-country runners forced their *flagging* bodies up the last hill before the finish line.

flagrant (*flāg'-*) ADJ. conspicuously wicked. We cannot condone such *flagrant* violations of the rules.

flay V. strip off skin; plunder. To my mind, no crime justifies the punishment that the criminal be *flayed* alive.

flick N. light stroke as with a whip. The horse needed no encouragement; one *flick* of the whip was all the jockey had to apply to get the animal to run at top speed. also V.

•**flippant** ADJ. lacking proper seriousness. Your *flippant* comments at this solemn occasion are offensive to me. flippancy, N.

flotilla (*-tĭl'-*) N. small fleet. It is always an exciting and interesting moment when the fishing *flotilla* returns to port.

flout V. reject; mock. The headstrong youth *flouted* all authority; he refused to be curbed.

fluctuation N. wavering. Meteorologists watch the *fluctuations* of the barometer in order to predict the weather.

fluency N. smoothness of speech. She spoke French with *fluency* and ease.

fluster V. confuse; befuddle, as with liquor. The teacher's sudden question *flustered* her and she stammered her reply.

ETYMOLOGY 12

FAC, FIC, FEC, FECT (to make, to do)
factory place where things are made
fiction manufactured story
affect to cause to change

FALL, FALS (to deceive)
fallacious faulty
infallible not prone to error, perfect
falsify to lie

FER, LAT (to bring, to bear)
transfer to bring from one place to another
translate to bring from one language to another
coniferous bearing cones, as pine trees

FIC (making, doing) adjective suffix
terrific making terrible
soporific making sleepy
frantic made excited by pain, grief, etc.

TEST—WORD LIST 12 —SYNONYMS OR ANTONYMS

Each of the questions below consists of a word printed in italics, followed by five words or phrases numbered 1 to 5. Choose the numbered word or phrase which is most nearly the same as or the opposite of the word in italics and write the number of your choice on your answer paper.

221. *fallacious* 1) indifferent 2) contrite 3) correct 4) incorrigible 5) fancy
222. *fawning* 1) arrogant 2) ubiquitous 3) desultory 4) imaginative 5) animal-like
223. *exuberant* 1) sarcastic 2) unruly 3) tardy 4) undulant 5) restrained
224. *facile* 1) short 2) inept 3) vacant 4) fat 5) sick
225. *fallow* 1) criminal 2) silent 3) uncultivated 4) understood 5) sinful
226. *fetter* 1) become infected 2) alter 3) instill 4) shatter 5) shackle
227. *finesse* 1) skill 2) artisan 3) card game 4) analysis 5) destruction
228. *extrude* 1) impede 2) distract 3) enlarge 4) push out 5) run after
229. *fictitious* 1) derivative 2) inhuman 3) imaginary 4) prosaic 5) implausible
230. *feasible* 1) inexact 2) invulnerable 3) unworkable 4) illegal 5) improper
231. *fissure* 1) crevice 2) chaos 3) net 4) labyrinth 5) base of lamp
232. *fabricate* 1) design 2) lie 3) lose 4) conquer 5) insure
233. *fervent* 1) tragic 2) futile 3) fantastic 4) aboveboard 5) indifferent
234. *fastidious* 1) speedy 2) snail-like 3) squeamish 4) sentimental 5) riotous
235. *fitful* 1) frenzied 2) tolerant 3) quaint 4) sentimental 5) constant
236. *felicitous* 1) young 2) sensitive 3) inappropriate 4) vapid 5) tangible
237. *flagrant* 1) aromatic 2) pungent 3) retiring 4) elementary 5) exemplary
238. *finale* 1) introduction 2) interrogation 3) intermission 4) expansion 5) rehearsal
239. *facetious* 1) manufactured 2) solemn 3) grotesque 4) witty 5) incoherent
240. *flout* 1) exile 2) whip 3) mock 4) invite 5) purchase

Answers to this test on page 149.

WORD LIST 13 foible - gloat

foible N. weakness; slight fault. We can overlook the *foibles* of our friends.
forbearance N. patience. We must use *forbearance* in dealing with him because he is still weak from his illness.
foreboding N. premonition of evil. Caesar ridiculed his wife's *forebodings* about the Ides of March.
forte (*fôrt'-ē*) N. strong point or special talent. I am not eager to play this rather serious role, for my *forte* is comedy.
•**forthright** ADJ. outspoken; frank. Never afraid to call a spade a spade, she was perhaps too *forthright* to be a successful party politician.
fortitude N. bravery; courage. He was awarded the medal for his *fortitude* in the battle.
•**fortuitous** ADJ. accidental; by chance. There is no connection between these two events; their timing is entirely *fortuitous*.
•**foster** V. rear; encourage. According to the legend, Romulus and Remus were *fostered* by a she-wolf. also ADJ.
fractious (*frăk'shŭs*) ADJ. unruly. The *fractious* horse unseated its rider.
•**frail** ADJ. weak. The sickly child seemed too *frail* to lift the heavy carton.
frantic ADJ. wild. At the time of the collision, many people became *frantic* with fear.
fraudulent ADJ. cheating; based on fraud. The government seeks to prevent *fraudulent* and misleading advertising.
fraught (*frawt*) ADJ. filled. Since this enterprise is *fraught* with danger, I will ask for volunteers who are willing to assume the risks.
fray N. brawl. The three musketeers were in the thick of the *fray*.
frenzied ADJ. madly excited. As soon as they smelled smoke, the *frenzied* animals milled about in their cages.
friction N. clash in opinion; rubbing against. At this time when harmony is essential, we cannot afford to have any *friction* in our group.

frigid ADJ. intensely cold. Alaska is in the *frigid* zone.
frolicsome ADJ. prankish; gay. The *frolicsome* puppy tried to lick the face of its master.
frowzy ADJ. slovenly; unkempt; dirty. Her *frowzy* appearance and her cheap decorations made her appear ludicrous in this group.
fruition (*froo-ĭ'-*) N. bearing of fruit; fulfillment; realization. This building marks the *fruition* of all our aspirations and years of hard work.
frustrate V. thwart; defeat. We must *frustrate* this dictator's plan to seize control of the government.
fulminate V. thunder; explode. The people against whom he *fulminated* were innocent of any wrongdoing.
fulsome ADJ. disgustingly excessive. His *fulsome* praise of the dictator annoyed his listeners.
funereal (*-nēr'-ē-ăl*) ADJ. sad; solemn. I fail to understand why there is such a *funereal* atmosphere; we have lost a battle, not a war.
fusion N. union; coalition. The opponents of the political party in power organized a *fusion* of labor and farming interests.
●**futile** ADJ. ineffective; fruitless. Why waste your time on *futile* pursuits?
gainsay V. deny. She could not *gainsay* the truth of the report.
gamut (*găm'-*) N. the entire range. In this performance, the leading lady was able to demonstrate the complete *gamut* of her acting ability.
gape (*gāp*) V. open widely. The huge pit *gaped* before her; if she stumbled, she would fall in.
gauntlet N. leather glove; challenge to combat. Now that we have been challenged, we must take up the *gauntlet* and meet our adversary fearlessly.
gazette N. official periodical publication. He read the *gazettes* regularly for the announcement of his promotion.
gelid (*jĕl'-*) ADJ. frozen. Eskimos live in igloos in the *gelid* North.
generality N. vague statement. This report is filled with *generalities*; you must be more specific in your statements.
geniality N. cheerfulness; kindliness; sympathy. This restaurant is famous and popular because of the *geniality* of the proprietor, who tries to make everyone happy.
genteel ADJ. well-bred; elegant. We are looking for a man with a *genteel* appearance who can inspire confidence by his cultivated manner.
gentry N. people of standing; class of people just below nobility. The local *gentry* did not welcome the visits of the summer tourists and tried to ignore their presence in the community.
gesticulation N. motion; gesture. Operatic performers are trained to make exaggerated *gesticulations* because of the large auditoriums in which they appear.
ghastly ADJ. horrible. The murdered man was a *ghastly* sight.
gibber (*jĭb'-*) V. speak foolishly. The demented man *gibbered* incoherently.
gibe (*jīb*) V. mock. As you *gibe* at their superstitious beliefs, do you realize that you, too, are guilty of similarly foolish thoughts?
glaze V. cover with a thin and shiny surface. The freezing rain *glazed* the streets and made driving hazardous.
glean V. gather leavings. After the crops had been harvested by the machines, the peasants were permitted to *glean* the wheat left in the fields.
glimmer V. shine unsteadily or faintly; twinkle. On summer evenings we would watch the fireflies *glimmer* in the dusky garden. also N.
gloat V. express evil satisfaction; view malevolently. As you *gloat* over your ill-gotten wealth, do you think of the many victims you have defrauded?

ETYMOLOGY 13

FY (to make) verb suffix
magnify to make greater
petrify to make into stone
beautify to make beautiful

GAM (marriage)
monogamy marriage to one person
bigamy marriage to two people at the same time
polygamy having many wives or husbands at same time

GEN, GENER (class, race)
genus group of animals with similar characteristics
generic characteristic of a class
gender class organized into sex

TEST—WORD LIST 13 —SYNONYMS

Each of the questions below consists of a word printed in italics, followed by five words or phrases numbered 1 to 5. Choose the numbered word or phrase which is most nearly similar in meaning to the word in italics and write the number of your choice on your answer paper

241. *foreboding* 1) happiness 2) presentiment 3) pretention 4) retreating 5) procedure
242. *fray* 1) skin 2) scare 3) load 4) brawl 5) birth
243. *forthright* 1) frank 2) inaccurate 3) temporary 4) concise 5) impolite
244. *frustrate* 1) disobey 2) thwart 3) deceive 4) deny 5) tend
245. *gelid* 1) stupid 2) direct 3) hurt 4) afraid 5) frozen
246. *gibe* 1) stretch 2) languish 3) mock 4) send 5) note
247. *foible* 1) weakness 2) fall 3) hunger 4) lack 5) nurse
248. *fraught* 1) filled 2) battled 3) vacant 4) varied 5) carried
249. *frowzy* 1) sleepy 2) thrifty 3) slovenly 4) wet 5) empty
250. *fractious* 1) capable 2) whole 3) scrawny 4) ill-timed 5) unruly
251. *gamut* 1) mongrel 2) range 3) canopy 4) score 5) integration
252. *fortitude* 1) quiet 2) coward 3) bravery 4) soldier 5) stronghold
253. *fruition* 1) decay 2) decline 3) realization 4) summer 5) planting
254. *fulminate* 1) explode 2) annoy 3) keep 4) sympathize 5) cure
255. *frail* 1) weak 2) anxious 3) insensitive 4) optimistic 5) absurd

256. *foster* 1) insist 2) encourage 3) compromise 4) transport 5) predict
257. *geniality* 1) heredity 2) environment 3) wealth 4) prodigality 5) cordiality
258. *frigid* 1) dark 2) intensely cold 3) frantic 4) excited 5) pallid
259. *fulsome* 1) domineering 2) devastating 3) disgusting 4) limited 5) hypocritical
260. *frantic* 1) unusual 2) tame 3) quiet 4) niggardly 5) wild

Answers to this test on page 149.

WORD LIST 14 glut - homespun

glut V. overstock; fill to excess. The manufacturers *glutted* the market and could not find purchasers for the many articles they had produced.
gluttonous ADJ. greedy for food. The *gluttonous* boy ate all the cookies.
gnarled (*nărld*) ADJ. twisted. The *gnarled* oak tree had been a landmark for years and was mentioned in several deeds.
goad V. urge on. He was *goaded* by his friends until he yielded to their wishes.
gory ADJ. bloody. The audience shuddered as they listened to the details of the *gory* massacre.
gossamer (*gŏs'*-) ADJ. sheer; like cobwebs. Nylon can be woven into *gossamer* fabrics.
granary (*grăn'*-) N. storehouse for grain. We have reason to be thankful, for our crops were good and our *granaries* are full.
grandiloquent ADJ. pompous; bombastic; using high-sounding language. The politician could never speak simply; she was always *grandiloquent*.
gradiose ADJ. imposing; impressive. His *grandiose* manner impressed those who met him for the first time.
graphic ADJ. pertaining to the art of delineating; vividly described. I was particularly impressed by the *graphic* presentation of the storm.
gratis (*grāt'*-) ADJ. free. The company offered to give one package *gratis* to every purchaser of one of their products.
gratuitous ADJ. given freely; unwarranted. I resent your *gratuitous* remarks; no one asked you to make them.
grueling ADJ. exhausting. The marathon is a *grueling* race.
gruesome ADJ. grisly. People screamed when his *gruesome* countenance was flashed on the screen.
gruff ADJ. rough-mannered. Although he was blunt and *gruff* with most people, he was always gentle with children.
guffaw (*gŭf-faw'*) N. boisterous laughter. The loud *guffaws* that came from the closed room indicated that the members of the committee had not yet settled down to serious business.
guile N. deceit; duplicity. She achieved her high position by *guile* and treachery.
guileless ADJ. without deceit. He is naïve, simple and *guileless*; he cannot be guilty of fraud.
gullible ADJ. easily deceived. He preyed upon *gullible* people who believed his stories of easy wealth.
gustatory ADJ. affecting the sense of taste. This restaurant offers an unusual *gustatory* experience because of the spices the food contains.
guttural ADJ. pertaining to the throat. *Guttural* sounds are produced in the throat or at the back of the tongue and palate.
haggle V. argue about prices. I would rather shop in a store that has fixed prices since I do not like to *haggle* with shopkeepers.
hallowed ADJ. blessed, consecrated. She was laid to rest in *hallowed* ground.
hallucination N. delusion. I think you were frightened by an *hallucination* which you created in your own mind.
•**hamper** V. obstruct. The minority party agreed not to *hamper* the efforts of the leaders who were working to secure a lasting peace.
harangue (*-rāng'*) N. noisy speech. In his lengthy *harangue*, the principal berated the offenders.
harass (*hă'*-) V. annoy by repeated attacks. She used to *harass* her husband by her continual demands for fine attire.
harbinger (*harb'injer*) N. forerunner. The crocus is an early *harbinger* of spring.
harping N. tiresome dwelling on a subject. Her constant *harping* on the good time she had had before her marriage angered her husband.
harry V. raid. The guerilla band *harried* the enemy nightly.
haughtiness N. pride; arrogance. I resent his *haughtiness* because he is no better than we are.
hazardous ADJ. dangerous. Your occupation is too *hazardous* for insurance companies to consider your application.
hazy ADJ. slightly obscure. In *hazy* weather, you cannot see the top of this mountain.
hedonism (*hē'*-) N. belief that pleasure is the sole aim in life. *Hedonism* and asceticism are opposing philosophies of human behavior.
•**heed** V. pay attention to; consider. We hope you will *heed* our advice and get a good night's sleep before the test. also N.
heinous (*hā'*-) ADJ. atrocious; hatefully bad. Hitler's *heinous* crimes will never be forgotten.
heresy N. opinion contrary to popular belief; opinion contrary to accepted religion. Your remarks are pure *heresy*.
hiatus (*hī-āt'*-) N. gap; pause. There was a *hiatus* of twenty years in the life of Rip Van Winkle.
hibernate V. sleep throughout the winter. Bats are one of the many species of animals that *hibernate*.
hierarchy N. body divided into ranks. It was difficult to step out of one's place in this *hierarchy*.
hindmost ADJ. furthest behind. You could always find him in the *hindmost* lines when a battle was being waged.
•**hindrance** N. block; obstacle. Stalled cars along the highway are a *hindrance* to traffic which tow trucks should remove without delay. hinder, V.
histrionic ADJ. theatrical. He was proud of his *histrionic* ability and wanted to play the role of Hamlet.
holocaust N. destruction by fire. Citizens of San Francisco remember that the destruction of the city was caused not by the earthquake but by the *holocaust* that followed.
homespun ADJ. domestic; made at home. *Homespun* wit, like *homespun* cloth, was often coarse and plain.

ETYMOLOGY 14

GRAPH, GRAM (writing)
epigram a pithy statement
telegram an instantaneous message over great distances (tele - far)
stenography shorthand (writing narrowly)

GREG (flock, herd)
gregarious tending to group together as in a herd
aggregate group, total
egregious out of the group; now used in a bad sense as wicked

HELIO (sun)
heliotrope flower that faces the sun
heliograph instrument that uses sun's rays to send signals
helium element abundant in sun's atmosphere

TEST—WORD LIST 14 —ANTONYMS

Each of the questions below consists of a word printed in italics, followed by five words or phrases numbered 1 to 5. Choose the numbered word or phrase which is most nearly opposite in meaning to the word in italics and write the number of your choice on your answer paper.

261. *hamper* 1) abet 2) discard 3) withhold 4) revise 5) deny
262. *goad* 1) begin 2) dissuade 3) deify 4) enter 5) fly
263. *hazy* 1) dangerous 2) clear 3) chilly 4) taut 5) massive
264. *gnarled* 1) straight 2) indirect 3) stern 4) skittish 5) strict
265. *guileless* 1) unresponsive 2) stingy 3) ferocious 4) deceitful 5) curious
266. *grandiloquent* 1) baroque 2) pedantic 3) simple 4) imaginative 5) impossible
267. *haughtiness* 1) lack of humor 2) small stature 3) modesty 4) serenity 5) obedience
268. *heed* 1) disregard 2) worry 3) rue 4) cease 5) squander
269. *gruesome* 1) coarse 2) inept 3) bold 4) witty 5) pleasant
270. *hindrance* 1) instinct 2) support 3) innovation 4) reluctance 5) accuracy
271. *grueling* 1) stern 2) baffling 3) easy 4) hectic 5) ornate
272. *hedonism* 1) deism 2) pragmatism 3) surrealism 4) dogmatism 5) asceticism
273. *hindmost* 1) carefree 2) casual 3) prejudicial 4) foremost 5) hostile
274. *hallowed* 1) desecrated 2) temporary 3) impermeable 4) inflexible 5) solid
275. *gruff* 1) familiar 2) fragrant 3) garish 4) gentle 5) swift
276. *hazardous* 1) rough 2) distressing 3) secure 4) clamorous 5) hostile
277. *gossamer* 1) adhesive 2) iridescent 3) opaque 4) level 5) brief
278. *histrionic* 1) nontheatrical 2) unpopular 3) traditional 4) outdated 5) sedated
279. *guile* 1) bitterness 2) sincerity 3) charm 4) denial 5) readiness
280. *heinous* 1) righteous 2) intuitive 3) outlandish 4) imaginary 5) realistic

Answers to this test on page 149.

WORD LIST 15 homogeneous - incentive

homogeneous (-*jēn'*-) ADJ. of the same kind. Educators try to put pupils of similar abilities into classes because they believe that *homogeneous* groups are advantageous. homogeneity, N.

•**hostility** N. unfriendliness; hatred. Children often feel *hostility* towards the new baby in the family.

humane (-*mān'*) ADJ. kind. Her *humane* and considerate treatment of the unfortunate endeared her to all.

•**humble** ADJ. modest; not proud. He spoke with great feeling of how much he loved his *humble* home, which he would not trade for a palace. humility, N.

humdrum ADJ. dull; monotonous. After her years of adventure, she could not settle down to a *humdrum* existence.

humid ADJ. damp. He could not stand the *humid* climate and moved to a drier area.

hypochondriac (*hī-pō-kŏn'*-) N. person unduly worried about his health; worrier without cause about illness. The doctor prescribed chocolate pills for her patient who was a *hypochrondriac*.

•**hypocritical** ADJ. pretending to be virtuous; deceiving. He is the most *hypocritical* liar I have ever known.

•**hypothetical** ADJ. based on assumptions or hypotheses. Why do we have to consider *hypothetical* cases when we have actual case histories which we may examine? hypothesis, N.

iconoclast N. one who attacks cherished traditions. As a playwright, George Bernard Shaw was an *iconoclast*, overturning traditional notions of morality and proper behavior.

ideology N. ideas of a group of people. That *ideology* is dangerous to this country because it embraces undemocratic philosophies.

idiom N. special usage in language. I could not understand their *idiom* because literal translation made no sense.

idiosyncrasy N. peculiarity; eccentricity. One of his personal *idiosyncrasies* was his habit of rinsing all cutlery given him in a restaurant.

igneous (*ĭg'*-) ADJ. produced by fire; volcanic. Lava, pumice and other *igneous* rocks are found in great abundance around Mount Vesuvius near Naples.

ignoble (*ĭg-nō'*-) ADJ. of lowly origin; unworthy. This plan is inspired by *ignoble* motives and I must, therefore, oppose it.

ignominious (-*mĭn*-) ADJ. disgraceful. The country smarted from the *ignominious* defeat and dreamed of the day when it would be victorious. ignominy, N.

illimitable ADJ. infinite. Having explored the far reaches of the earth, human beings are preparing to reach out into *illimitable* space.

illusory ADJ. deceptive; not real. Unfortunately, the costs of running the lemonade stand were so high that Tom's profits proved *illusory*.

imbecility N. weakness of mind. I am amazed at the *imbecility* of the readers of these trashy magazines.

imbibe V. drink in. The dry soil *imbibed* the rain quickly.

imminent ADJ. impending; near at hand. The *imminent* battle will determine our success or failure in this conflict.

immobility N. state of being immovable. Modern armies cannot afford the luxury of *immobility* as they are vulnerable to attack while standing still.

• **immune** ADJ. exempt. She was fortunately *immune* from the disease and could take care of the sick.

• **impair** V. injure; hurt. Drinking alcohol can *impair* your ability to drive safely; if you're going to drink, don't drive.

• **impartial** ADJ. not biased; fair. As members of the jury, you must be *impartial*, showing no favoritism to either party but judging the case on its merits.

impasse N. predicament from which there is no escape. In this *impasse*, all turned to prayer as their last hope.

impede V. hinder; block; delay. A series of accidents at the rocket plant *impeded* the launching of the space shuttle.

impel V. drive or force onward. A strong feeling of urgency *impelled* her; if she failed to finish the project right then, she knew that she would never get it done.

impending ADJ. nearing; approaching. The entire country was saddened by the news of his *impending* death.

impenitent ADJ. not repentant. We could see by his brazen attitude that he was *impenitent*.

• **imperceptible** ADJ. unnoticeable; undetectable. Fortunately, the stain on the blouse was *imperceptible* after the blouse had gone through the wash.

imperious ADJ.domineering. Her *imperious* manner indicated that she had long been accustomed to assuming command.

impermeable ADJ. impervious; not permitting passage through its substance. This new material is *impermeable* to liquids.

impertinent ADJ. insolent. I regard your remarks as *impertinent* and I resent them.

imperturbability N. calmness. We are impressed by her *imperturbability* in this critical moment and are calmed by it.

impetuous ADJ. violent; hasty; rash. We tried to curb his *impetuous* behavior because we felt that in his haste he might offend some people.

impiety (*-pī'-ĕ-tĭ*) N. irreverence; wickedness. We cannot forgive such an act of *impiety*.

impious (*ĭm'-pĭ-ŭs*) ADJ. irreverent. The congregation was offended by his *impious* remarks.

implacable (*-plā'-*) ADJ. incapable of being pacified. Madame Defarge was the *implacable* enemy of the Evremonde family.

• **implication** N. that which is hinted at or suggested. If I understand the *implications* of your remark, you do not trust our captain.

implicit ADJ. understood but not stated. It is *implicit* that you will come to our aid if we are attacked.

impotent ADJ. weak; ineffective. Although he wished to break the nicotine habit, he found himself *impotent* to resist the craving for a cigarette.

imprecate (*ĭm'-*) V. curse; pray that evil will befall. To *imprecate* Hitler's atrocities is not enough; we must insure against any future practice of genocide.

impregnable (*-prĕg'-na-*) ADJ. invulnerable. Until the development of the airplane as a military weapon, the fort was considered *impregnable*.

impropriety (*-rī-*) N. state of being inappropriate. Because of the *impropriety* of his costume, he was denied entrance into the dining room.

improvident ADJ. thriftless. She was constantly being warned to mend her *improvident* ways and begin to "save for a rainy day."

impugn (*-ūn'*) V. doubt; challenge; gainsay. I cannot *impugn* your honesty without evidence.

inadvertence N. oversight; carelessness. By *inadvertence*, he omitted two questions on the examination.

inanimate ADJ. lifeless. She was asked to identify the still and *inanimate* body.

inarticulate ADJ. speechless; producing indistinct speech. He became *inarticulate* with rage and uttered sounds without meaning.

incapacitate V. disable. During the winter, many people were *incapacitated* by respiratory ailments.

• **incentive** N. spur; motive. Students who dislike school must be given an *incentive* to learn.

ETYMOLOGY 15

IL, ILE (pertaining to, capable of) adjective suffix

puerile pertaining to a child

ductile capable of being led; metal capable of being drawn into wire

civil pertaining to a citizen.

TEST—WORD LIST 15 —SYNONYMS OR ANTONYMS

Each of the questions below consists of a word printed in italics, followed by five words or phrases numbered 1 to 5. Choose the numbered word or phrase which is most nearly the same as or the opposite of the word in italics and write the number of your choice on your answer paper.

281. *idiosyncrasy* 1) speech pattern 2) quirk 3) good deed 4) form of government 5) similarity

282. *imbecility* 1) crime 2) intelligence 3) assurance 4) belligerence 5) culpability

283. *immune* 1) excited 2) incarcerated 3) intolerant 4) exempt 5) fascinated

284. *humane* 1) animal 2) scientific 3) cruel 4) philosophic 5) mortal

285. *imperturbability* 1) irascibility 2) mutability 3) frustration 4) clannishness 5) obduracy

286. *igneous* 1) educated 2) outrageous 3) observant 4) qualified 5) volcanic

287. *impair* 1) divide 2) mend 3) suffer 4) suggest 5) vanish
288. *hypocritical* 1) friendly 2) easily pleased 3) sensitive 4) deceiving 5) sentimental
289. *implicit* 1) faithful 2) innate 3) joint 4) involved 5) stated
290. *homogeneous* 1) mannish 2) instructive 3) dissimilar 4) beneficial 5) disreputable
291. *impenitent* 1) incarcerated 2) offended 3) secure 4) penniless 5) repentant
292. *imprecate* 1) bless 2) impress 3) enlarge 4) jettison 5) depreciate
293. *humdrum* 1) noisy 2) lamentable 3) exciting 4) singing 5) sacred
294. *impregnable* 1) unfit 2) accustomed 3) disappointed 4) just 5) formidable
295. *imminent* 1) famous 2) lamentable 3) remote 4) dramatic 5) gay
296. *humility* 1) scandal 2) arrogance 3) embarrassment 4) conspiracy 5) cupidity
297. *improvident* 1) remorseful 2) affluent 3) astute 4) rehearsed 5) spoiled
298. *ignominious* 1) honorable 2) educated 3) anonymous 4) sentimental 5) pensive
299. *incapacitate* 1) imprison 2) charge 3) endure 4) reassert 5) enable
300. *humid* 1) funny 2) sincere 3) scarce 4) overflowing 5) arid

Answers to this test on page 149.

WORD LIST 16 incessant - integrity

incessant ADJ. uninterrupted. The crickets kept up an *incessant* chirping which disturbed our attempts to fall asleep.

incipient ADJ. beginning; in an early stage. I will go to sleep early for I want to thwart an *incipient* cold.

incisive (-*sīs'*-) ADJ. cutting; sharp. Her *incisive* remarks made us see the fallacy in our plans.

incite V. arouse to action. The demagogue *incited* the mob to take action into its own hands.

inclusive ADJ. tending to include all. This meeting will run from January 10 to February 15 *inclusive*.

incommodious (-*mōd'*-) ADJ. not spacious. In their *incommodious* quarters, they had to improvise for closet space.

•**incongruity** (-*grū'*-) N. lack of harmony; absurdity. The *incongruity* of his wearing sneakers with his formal attire amused the observers.

incredulity (*dūl'*-) N. tendency to disbelief. Your *incredulity* in the face of all the evidence is hard to understand.

increment N. increase. This job has an annual *increment* in salary until you reach the maximum of $18,000 a year.

incumbent N. office holder. The newly elected public official received valuable advice from the present *incumbent*.

incursion N. temporary invasion. The nightly *incursions* and hit and run raids of our neighbors across the border tried the patience of the country to the point where we decided to retaliate in force.

indefatigable (-*făt'*-) ADJ. tireless. She was *indefatigable* in her constant efforts to raise funds for the Red Cross.

•**indict** (-*dīt'*) V. charge. After the grand jury *indicts* the suspect, he will go to trial.

•**indifferent** ADJ. unmoved; lacking concern. Because she felt no desire to marry, she was *indifferent* to his constant proposals.

indigenous (-*dĭ'-jĕn*-) ADJ. native. Tobacco is one of the *indigenous* plants which the early explorers found in this country.

indisputable (-*dĭs'*-) ADJ. too certain to be disputed. In the face of these *indisputable* statements, I withdraw my complaint.

indomitable ADJ. unconquerable. The founders of our country had *indomitable* will power.

•**induce** V. persuade; bring about. Because the baby was overdue, they tried to *induce* labor.

indulge V. humor; treat leniently. A parent who constantly *indulges* a child may thoroughly spoil that child.

industrious ADJ. diligent; hard-working. If you are *industrious* and apply yourself to your assignments, you will do well in college. industry, N.

•**inept** ADJ. unsuited; absurd. She was an *inept* although conscientious student.

•**inevitable** ADJ. unavoidable. Death and taxes are both supposed to be *inevitable*; however, some people avoid taxes for years.

inexorable (-*ĕx'*-) ADJ. relentless; unyielding; implacable. The governor is *inexorable*; he will not suspend the sentence.

infamous (*ĭn'*-) ADJ. notoriously bad. Jesse James was an *infamous* outlaw.

inference N. conclusion drawn from data. I want you to check this *inference* because it may have been based on insufficient data.

infinitesimal ADJ. very small. In the twentieth century, physicists have made their greatest discoveries about the characteristics of *infinitesimal* objects like the atom and its parts.

inflated ADJ. enlarged (with air or gas). He was *inflated* with a sense of his own importance.

influx N. flowing into. The *influx* of refugees into the country has taxed the relief agencies severely.

infraction N. violation. Because of his many *infractions* of school regulations, he was suspended by the dean.

infringe V. violate; encroach. I think your machine *infringes* on my patent.

•**ingenious** ADJ. clever. She came up with an *ingenious* use for styrofoam packing balls. ingenuity, N.

inherent (-*hēr'*-) ADJ. firmly established by nature or habit. Her *inherent* love of justice compelled her to come to their aid.

inhibit V. prohibit; restrain. The child was not *inhibited* in his responses. inhibition, N.

iniquitous ADJ. unjust; wicked. I cannot approve of the *iniquitous* methods you used to gain your present position. iniquity, N.

inkling N. hint. This came as a complete surprise to me as I did not have the slightest *inkling* of your plans.

innate ADJ. inborn. His *innate* love of music was soon recognized by his parents.

innocuous ADJ. harmless. Let her drink it; it is *innocuous*.

•**innovation** N. change; introduction of something new. She loved *innovations* just because they were new.

innuendo (*ĭn-nū-ĕn'*-) N. hint; insinuation. I resent the *innuendoes* in your statement more than the statement itself.

inordinate ADJ. unrestrained; excessive. She had an *inordinate* fondness for candy.

inscrutable ADJ. incomprehensible; not to be discovered. Your motives are *inscrutable*.

insomnia N. wakefulness. He refused to join us in a midnight cup of coffee because he claimed it gave him *insomnia*.

instigate V. urge; start; provoke. I am afraid that this statement will *instigate* a revolt.

insuperable ADJ. insurmountable; invincible. In the face of *insuperable* difficulties they maintained their courage and will to resist.
insurgent ADJ. rebellious. We will not discuss reforms until the *insurgent* troops have returned to their homes.
insurrection N. rebellion; uprising. Given the current state of unrest in South Africa, an *insurrection* seems inevitable.
intangible ADJ. not material; not able to be perceived by touch. Emotions are *intangible*, and yet we know that we feel love and hate, though we cannot grasp them in our hands.
integrity N. wholeness; purity; uprightness. She was a woman of great *integrity*.

ETYMOLOGY 16

IN (in, into, upon, toward) prefix
incursion invasion
insidious treacherous

IN (not, without) prefix
inconsequential not significant
inimical hostile, not friendly
insipid tasteless

TEST—WORD LIST 16 —SYNONYMS

Each of the questions below consists of a word printed in italics, followed by five words or phrases numbered 1 to 5. Choose the numbered word or phrase which is most nearly similar in meaning to the word in italics and write the number of your choice on your answer paper.

301. *incommodious* 1) inconvenient 2) extravagant 3) miserly 4) inclement 5) productive
302. *incredulity* 1) disbelief 2) gullibility 3) uncertainty 4) practicality 5) despair
303. *indict* 1) specify 2) change 3) charge 4) challenge 5) speak
304. *infraction* 1) arithmetic 2) violation 3) likelihood 4) crime 5) improbability
305. *inkling* 1) ball point pen 2) fountain pen 3) goose quill 4) hint 5) iota
306. *incessant* 1) unequal 2) uninterrupted 3) undivided 4) inclined 5) included
307. *innocuous* 1) harmless 2) noisome 3) futile 4) expansive 5) fetid
308. *indulgent* 1) clever 2) intelligent 3) resplendent 4) brilliant 5) humoring
309. *infringe* 1) violate 2) edge 3) remove 4) adjust 5) imprison
310. *innuendo* 1) dogma 2) suggestion 3) subterfuge 4) avowal 5) climax
311. *incipient* 1) finishing 2) awry 3) protective 4) beginning 5) ending
312. *inscrutable* 1) resistant 2) receptive 3) incomprehensible 4) blending 5) countering
313. *iniquitous* 1) unequal 2) limited 3) convenient 4) wicked 5) plastic
314. *indomitable* 1) comparable 2) definite 3) invincible 4) militant 5) gracious
315. *instigate* 1) ferment 2) embellish 3) install 4) appease 5) incite
316. *incisive* 1) cutting 2) specialized 3) proposed 4) secure 5) commuting
317. *indefatigable* 1) slender 2) secure 3) national 4) federal 5) tireless
318. *infamous* 1) notorious 2) renowned 3) inert 4) insane 5) soaring
319. *increment* 1) salary 2) gratuity 3) increase 4) loan 5) advance
320. *inordinate* 1) longitudinal 2) excessive 3) energetic 4) quantitative 5) extraordinary

Answers to this test on page 149.

WORD LIST 17 **interment - lethal**

interment (*-têr'-*) N. burial. *Interment* will take place in the church cemetery at 2 P.M. Wednesday.
interminable ADJ. endless. Her telephone conversation seemed *interminable*.
intimate V. hint. She *intimated* rather than stated her preferences.
intimidation (*-dā'-*) N. fear. The dictator ruled by *intimidation*.
•**intricacy** N. complexity; knottiness. Philip spent many hours designing mazes of such great *intricacy* that none of his classmates could solve them. intricate, ADJ.
introspective ADJ. looking within oneself. We all have our *introspective* moments during which we examine our souls.
intrude V. trespass; enter as an uninvited person. He hesitated to *intrude* on their conversation.
•**intuition** N. power of knowing without reasoning. She claimed to know the truth by *intuition*. intuitive, ADJ.
invective N. abuse. He had expected criticism but not the *invective* which greeted his proposal.
invidious ADJ. designed to create ill-will or envy. We disregarded her *invidious* remarks because we realized how jealous she was.
invulnerable ADJ. incapable of injury. Achilles was *invulnerable* except in his heel.
iota (*ī-ō'-tà*) N. very small quantity. He hadn't an *iota* of common sense.
irascible (*ĭ-răs'-ĭbl*) ADJ. irritable; easily angered. His *irascible* temper frightened me.
ironical (*-rŏn'-*) ADJ. resulting in an unexpected and contrary manner. It is *ironical* that her success came when she least wanted it. irony, N.
irreconcilable ADJ. incompatible. The separated couple were *irreconcilable*.

•**irrelevant** ADJ. not applicable; unrelated. This statement is *irrelevant* and should be disregarded by the jury.
irreparable (-*rĕp'*-) ADJ. not able to be corrected or repaired. Your apology cannot atone for the *irreparable* damage you have done to his reputation.
irrevocable (-*rĕv'*-) ADJ. unalterable. Let us not brood over past mistakes since they are *irrevocable*.
iterate (*ĭt'*-) V. utter a second time; repeat. I will *iterate* the warning I have previously given to you.
itinerant (*ītĭn'*-) ADJ. wandering; traveling. He was an *itinerant* peddler.
jargon N. language used by special group; gibberish. We tried to understand the *jargon* of the peddlers in the market place but could not comprehend.
jeopardy (*jĕp'*-) N. exposure to death or danger. He cannot be placed in double *jeopardy*.
jocose (-*kōs'*) ADJ. given to joking. The salesman was a *jocose* person.
jocular ADJ. said or done in jest. Do not take my *jocular* remarks seriously.
jocund ADJ. merry. Santa Claus is always gay and *jocund*.
jubilation N. rejoicing. There was great *jubilation* when the armistice was announced.
judicious ADJ. wise; determined by sound judgment. I believe that this plan is not *judicious*; it is too risky.
•**justification** N. good or just reason; defense; excuse. The jury found him guilty of the more serious charge because they could see no possible *justification* for his actions.
knavery N. rascality. We cannot condone such *knavery* in public officials.
knell N. tolling of a bell at a funeral; sound of the funeral bell. "The curfew tolls the *knell* of parting day."
labyrinth N. maze. Tom and Betty were lost in the *labyrinth* of secret caves.
lacerate (*lă'-sêr*-) V. mangle; tear. Her body was *lacerated* in the automobile crash.
laconic ADJ. brief and to the point. Will Rogers' *laconic* comments on the news made him world-famous.
laggard ADJ. slow; sluggish. The sailor had been taught not to be *laggard* in carrying out orders.
laity (*lā-ĭ-tĭ*) N. laypersons; persons not connected with the clergy. The *laity* does not always understand the clergy's problems.
languid ADJ. weary; sluggish; listless. Her siege of illness left her *languid* and pallid.
languish V. lose animation; lose strength. In stories, lovelorn damsels used to *languish* and pine away.
lassitude N. languor; weariness. The hot, tropical weather created a feeling of *lassitude* and encouraged drowsiness.
latent (*lāt'*-) ADJ. dormant; hidden. Her *latent* talent was discovered by accident.
latitude N. freedom from narrow limitations. I think you have permitted your son too much *latitude* in this matter.
•**laud** V. praise. We all must *laud* his noble efforts on behalf of such a worthy cause.
lave (*lāv*) V. wash. The running water will *lave* away all stains.
lavish ADJ. liberal; wasteful. The actor's *lavish* gifts pleased her.
lesion N. unhealthy change in structure; injury. Many *lesions* are the result of disease.
lethal ADJ. deadly. It is unwise to leave *lethal* weapons where children may find them.

ETYMOLOGY 17

INTER (between, among) prefix
intervene come between
international between nations
interjection a statement thrown in

IST (one who practices) noun suffix
humorist one who provides humor
specialist one who engages in a specialty
optimist one who is hopeful

IT, ITINER (journey, road)
exit way out
itinerary plan of journey
iterate repeat

ITY (state of being) noun suffix
annuity state of being yearly
credulity state of being gullible
sagacity wisdom

IZE, ISE (to make) verb suffix
victimize to make a victim
rationalize to reason
harmonize to make peaceful

JAC, JACT, JEC (to throw)
projectile missile, something thrown forward
trajectory path taken by thrown object
reject throw back

JUR, JURAT (to swear)
abjure renounce
perjure to testify falsely
jury group of men sworn to seek the truth

LABOR, LABORAT (to work)
laboratory place where work is done
collaborate work together with others
laborious difficult

LEG, LECT (to choose, to read)
election choice
legible able to be read
eligible able to be selected

LEG (law)
legislature law-making body
legitimate lawful
legal lawful

TEST—WORD LIST 17 —ANTONYMS

Each of the questions below consists of a word printed in italics, followed by five words or phrases numbered 1 to 5. Choose the numbered word or phrase which is most nearly opposite in meaning to the word in italics and write the number of your choice on your answer paper.

321. *invulnerable* 1) accidental 2) scolding 3) inhuman 4) prime 5) injury-prone
322. *jeopardy* 1) damage 2) safety 3) loyalty 4) sincerity 5) verdict
323. *laud* 1) aggravate 2) justify 3) predict 4) trespass 5) disparage

324. *introspective* 1) outgoing 2) retrospective 3) revelatory 4) dull-witted 5) conspicuous
325. *intricacy* 1) hostility 2) fragility 3) futility 4) simplicity 5) inaccuracy
326. *lassitude* 1) sleeping 2) undone work 3) width 4) breath 5) liveliness
327. *irascible* 1) hideous 2) vulnerable 3) placid 4) ungrateful 5) noisy
328. *intimate* 1) greet 2) hint 3) insist 4) lurk 5) ransack
329. *judicious* 1) foolish 2) indifferent 3) tentative 4) irritable 5) massive
330. *languid* 1) silent 2) disconsolate 3) extensive 4) energetic 5) colorful
331. *irreconcilable* 1) impatient 2) unusual 3) philosophic 4) agreeable 5) tedious
332. *irrelevant* 1) casual 2) impartial 3) pertinent 4) undecided 5) devious
333. *latitude* 1) clergy 2) boredom 3) restraint 4) wealth 5) cheer
334. *irrevocable* 1) imaginary 2) unrequited 3) satisfied 4) determined 5) cancelable
335. *knavery* 1) integrity 2) trickery 3) knighthood 4) terror 5) temerity
336. *lethal* 1) drowsy 2) respiratory 3) life-giving 4) dormant 5) legal
337. *invidious* 1) noticeable 2) creating good will 3) lacking strength 4) unlikely 5) elusive
338. *irreparable* 1) able to be parted 2) able to be paired 3) able to be corrected 4) repayable 5) tortuous
339. *jocund* 1) round 2) morose 3) inept 4) heavy 5) lively
340. *jubilation* 1) vigor 2) awe 3) woe 4) guile 5) piety

Answers to this test on page 149.

WORD LIST 18 libelous - mendicant

libelous ADJ. defamatory; injurious to the good name of a person. He sued the newspaper because of its *libelous* story.

licentious ADJ. wanton; lewd; dissolute. The *licentious* monarch helped bring about his country's downfall.

linguistic ADJ. pertaining to language. The American tourist will encounter very little *linguistic* difficulty as English has become an almost universal language.

liquidate V. settle accounts; clear up. She was able to *liquidate* all her debts in a short period of time.

●**loathe** V. detest. We *loathed* the wicked villain.

longevity (*-jĕv'-*) N. long life. The old man was proud of his *longevity*.

loquacious ADJ. talkative. She is very *loquacious* and can speak on the telephone for hours.

lout N. clumsy person. The delivery boy is a *lout* who manages to fall over his own feet.

lucent ADJ. shining. The moon's *lucent* rays silvered the river.

lucid ADJ. bright; easily understood. Her explanation was *lucid* and to the point.

lucrative ADJ. profitable. He turned his hobby into a *lucrative* profession.

luminous ADJ. shining; issuing light. The sun is a *luminous* body.

lunar ADJ. pertaining to the moon. *Lunar* craters can be plainly seen with the aid of a small telescope.

luscious ADJ. pleasing to taste or smell. The ripe peach was *luscious*.

lustrous ADJ. shining. Her large and *lustrous* eyes gave a touch of beauty to an otherwise drab face.

luxuriant ADJ. fertile; abundant; ornate. Farming was easy in this *luxuriant* soil.

machinations (*mă-kĭ-nā'-*) N. schemes. I can see through your wily *machinations*.

maelstrom (*māl'-*) N. whirlpool. The canoe was tossed about in the *maelstrom*.

magnanimous ADJ. generous. The philanthropist was most *magnanimous*.

magnate N. person of prominence or influence. The steel *magnate* decided to devote more time to city politics.

maim V. mutilate; injure. The hospital could not take care of all who had been wounded or *maimed* in the railroad accident.

malicious ADJ. dictated by hatred or spite. The *malicious* neighbor spread the gossip.

malignant (*-lĭg'-*) ADJ. having an evil influence; virulent; tending to be fatal. This is a *malignant* disease; we may have to use drastic measures to stop its spread.

mammoth ADJ. gigantic. The *mammoth* corporations of the twentieth century are a mixed blessing.

mandatory ADJ. obligatory. These instructions are *mandatory*; any violation will be severely punished.

manifest ADJ. understandable; clear. His evil intentions were *manifest*, and yet we could not stop him. also V.

manipulate V. operate with the hands; control to one's own advantage. How do you *manipulate* these puppets?

marauder N. raider; intruder. The sounding of the alarm frightened the *marauders*.

maritime ADJ. bordering on the sea; nautical. The *Maritime* Provinces depend on the sea for their wealth.

maudlin ADJ. effusively sentimental. I do not like such *maudlin* pictures. I call them tear-jerkers.

maxim N. proverb; truth pithily stated. Aesop's fables illustrate moral *maxims*.

meager ADJ. scanty; inadequate. His salary was far too *meager* for him to afford to buy a new car.

meander V. wind or turn in its course. It is difficult to sail up this stream because of the way it *meanders* through the countryside.

meddlesome ADJ. interfering. He felt his marriage was suffering because of his *meddlesome* mother-in-law.

mediate V. settle a dispute through the services of an outsider. Let us *mediate* our differences rather than engage in a costly strike.

meditation N. reflection; thought. She reached her decision only after much *meditation*.

medley N. mixture. The band played a *medley* of Gershwin tunes.

●**meek** ADJ. quiet and obedient; spiritless. Can Lois Lane see through Superman's disguise and spot the superhero masquerading as the *meek*, timorous Clark Kent?

melee (*mā-lā'*) N. fight. The captain tried to ascertain the cause of the *melee* which had broken out among the crew members.
mendacious (*-dā'-*) ADJ. lying; false. People soon learned to discount his *mendacious* stories.
mendicant N. beggar. From the moment we left the ship, we were surrounded by *mendicants* and peddlers.

ETYMOLOGY 18

LIBER (book)
library collection of books
libretto the "book" of a musical play
libel slander (originally found in a little book)

LOQU, LOCUT (to talk)
soliloquy speech by one individual
loquacious talkative
elocution speech

LUC (light)
elucidate enlighten
lucid clear
translucent allowing some light to pass through

MAL (bad)
malevolent evil (wishing bad)
malediction curse (state of saying evil)
malefactor evil-doer

MAN (hand)
manufacture create (make by hand)
manuscript writing by hand
emancipate free (to let go from the hand)

MAR (sea)
maritime connected with seafaring
submarine undersea craft
mariner seaman

TEST—WORD LIST 18 —SYNONYMS OR ANTONYMS

Each of the questions below consists of a word printed in italics, followed by five words or phrases numbered 1 to 5. Choose the numbered word or phrase which is most nearly the same as or the opposite of the word in italics and write the number of your choice on your answer paper

341. *malignant* 1) massive 2) evasive 3) benign 4) affluent 5) overt
342. *loquacious* 1) liquid 2) desiccated 3) verbose 4) maudlin 5) solid
343. *maelstrom* 1) whirlpool 2) mountain peak 3) hurricane 4) holocaust 5) gust
344. *meander* 1) wind 2) steer 3) gather 4) select 5) anticipate
345. *libelous* 1) infectious 2) praising 3) full 4) meager 5) untrue
346. *licentious* 1) not permitted 2) unprepared 3) wanton 4) aggressive 5) drinking
347. *maimed* 1) defaced 2) repaired 3) tattooed 4) nominated 5) injured
348. *marauder* 1) eater 2) raider 3) nocturnal animal 4) predator 5) instigator
349. *mammoth* 1) puny 2) cavernous 3) paternal 4) supreme 5) maternal
350. *maudlin* 1) overly sentimental 2) variegated 3) incomprehensible 4) sequestered 5) imaginative
351. *maxim* 1) minimum 2) prolixity 3) mathematical concept 4) proverb 5) latitude
352. *loathe* 1) be eager 2) admire 3) admonish 4) corrupt 5) banish
353. *longevity* 1) latitude 2) effervescence 3) short sightedness 4) long life 5) endurance
354. *mandatory* 1) created 2) manipulated 3) suited 4) compatible 5) optional
355. *lout* 1) club 2) knife 3) clumsy person 4) hero 5) nobleman
356. *lucrative* 1) menial 2) devoted 3) unprofitable 4) massive 5) clerical
357. *melee* 1) menage 2) parley 3) fruit 4) riot 5) station
358. *mendacious* 1) irreparable 2) begging 3) dishonorable 4) quiet 5) truthful
359. *meek* 1) attentive 2) assertive 3) intelligent 4) effective 5) merry
360. *magnanimous* 1) miserly 2) optimistic 3) puny 4) torpid 5) somnolent

Answers to this test on page 149.

WORD LIST 19 mercenary - nadir

mercenary ADJ. interested in money or gain. I am certain that your action was prompted by *mercenary* motives. also N.
mercurial ADJ. fickle; changing. She was of a *mercurial* temperament and therefore unpredictable.
mete (*mēt*) V. measure; distribute. She tried to be impartial in her efforts to *mete* out justice.
meticulous ADJ. excessively careful. He was *meticulous* in checking his accounts and never made mistakes.
metropolis N. large city. Every evening this terminal is filled with the thousands of commuters who are going from this *metropolis* to their homes in the suburbs.
mettle N. courage; spirit. When challenged by the other horses in the race, the thoroughbred proved its *mettle* by its determination to hold the lead.
mien (*mēn*) N. demeanor; bearing. She had the gracious *mien* of a queen.
migratory ADJ. wandering. The return of the *migratory* birds to the northern sections of this country is a harbinger of spring.
militate V. work against. Your record of lateness and absence will *militate* against your chances of promotion.
mincing ADJ. affectedly dainty. Yum-Yum walked across the stage with *mincing* steps.

misadventure N. mischance; ill luck. The young explorer met death by *misadventure*.
misapprehension N. error; misunderstanding. To avoid *misapprehension*, I am going to ask all of you to repeat the instructions I have given.
miscreant N. wretch; villain. His kindness to the *miscreant* amazed all of us who had expected to hear severe punishment pronounced.
misgivings N. doubts. Hamlet described his *misgivings* to Horatio but decided to fence with Laertes despite his foreboding of evil.
mishap N. accident. With a little care you could have avoided this *mishap*.
missile N. object to be thrown. Scientists are experimenting with guided *missiles*.
mite N. very small object or creature; small coin. The criminal was so heartless that he even stole the widow's *mite*.
mitigate V. appease. He did nothing to *mitigate* her wrath.
mobile ADJ. movable; not fixed. The *mobile* blood bank operated by the Red Cross visited our neighborhood today. mobility N.
mode (*mōd*) N. prevailing style. She was not used to their lavish *mode* of living.
modicum N. limited quantity. His story is based on a *modicum* of truth.
molten ADJ. melted. The city of Pompeii was destroyed by volcanic ash rather than by *molten* lava flowing from Mount Vesuvius.
• **momentous** ADJ. very important. On this *momentous* occasion, we must be very solemn.
monotheism N. belief in one God. Abraham was the first to proclaim his belief in *monotheism*.
• **monotony** N. sameness leading to boredom. He took a clerical job, but soon he grew to hate the *monotony* of his daily routine. monotonous, ADJ.
moodiness N. fits of depression or gloom. We could not discover the cause of his recurrent *moodiness*.
morbid ADJ. given to unwholesome thought. These *morbid* speculations are dangerous; we must lighten our thinking by emphasis on more pleasant matters.
morose (*-rōs'*) ADJ. ill-humored; sullen. When we first meet Hamlet, we find him *morose* and depressed.
mortician N. undertaker. The *mortician* prepared the corpse for burial.
mortify V. humiliate; punish the flesh. She was so *mortified* by her blunder that she ran away in tears.
mote N. small speck. The tiniest *mote* in the eye is very painful.
mountebank N. charlatan; boastful pretender. The patent medicine man was a *mountebank*.
muddle V. confuse; mix up. Although you are nervous, try not to *muddle* your words.
multiform ADJ. having many forms. Snowflakes are *multiform* but always hexagonal.
multiplicity N. state of being numerous. He was appalled by the *multiplicity* of details he had to complete before setting out on his mission.
murkiness N. darkness; gloom. The *murkiness* and fog of the waterfront that evening depressed me.
muse V. ponder. He *mused* about the beauty of the statue.
musky ADJ. having the odor of musk. She left a trace of *musky* perfume behind her.
• **mutable** ADJ. changing in form; fickle. His opinions were *mutable* and easily influenced by anyone who had any powers of persuasion. mutability, N.
mutilate V. maim. The torturer threatened to *mutilate* his victim.
mutinous ADJ. unruly; rebellious. The captain had to use force to quiet his *mutinous* crew.
nadir (*nād'-*) N. lowest point. The cold spell reached its *nadir* yesterday.

ETYMOLOGY 19

MITT, MISS (to send)
missile projectile
admit allow in
dismiss send away

MON, MONIT (to warn)
admonish warn
premonition foreboding
monitor watcher (warner)

MORI, MORT (to die)
mortuary funeral parlor
moribund dying
immortal not dying

TEST—WORD LIST 19 —SYNONYMS

Each of the following questions consists of a word printed in italics, followed by five words or phrases numbered 1 to 5. Choose the numbered word or phrase which is most nearly similar in meaning to the word in italics and write the number of your choice on your answer paper.

361. *mercurial* 1) true 2) very hot 3) rainy 4) fickle 5) stern
362. *misgivings* 1) errors 2) doubts 3) gifts 4) quietude 5) accidents
363. *molten* 1) shedded 2) waxen 3) melted 4) baked 5) dampened
364. *mortician* 1) offender 2) applicant 3) aspirant 4) murderer 5) undertaker
365. *migratory* 1) colorful 2) wandering 3) sad 4) impoverished 5) causing headaches
366. *mishap* 1) accident 2) lady driver 3) sadness 4) flower 5) dampness
367. *mountebank* 1) charlatan 2) policeman 3) wanderer 4) talisman 5) ignoramus
368. *mote* 1) ditch 2) shield 3) small speck 4) fly 5) bulbous plant
369. *mutable* 1) changeable 2) quitting 3) unspoken 4) hereditary 5) debatable

370. *mitigate* 1) misunderstand 2) aggravate 3) present 4) appease 5) provoke
371. *morose* 1) certain 2) surly 3) additional 4) adroit 5) pensive
372. *muddle* 1) betray 2) confuse 3) consecrate 4) mix thoroughly 5) undertake
373. *mete* 1) defeat 2) confuse 3) measure 4) sacrifice 5) delay
374. *mobile* 1) unified 2) fixed 3) deficient 4) covering 5) not stationary
375. *mortify* 1) tease 2) fascinate 3) anticipate 4) humiliate 5) deaden
376. *momentous* 1) important 2) restored 3) secure 4) enthralled 5) disliked
377. *mien* 1) unfriendliness 2) countenance 3) performance 4) inactivity 5) sloth
378. *misapprehension* 1) misunderstanding 2) release 3) conviction 4) lack of fear 5) concern
379. *muse* 1) entertain 2) ponder 3) create music 4) imagine 5) bewilder
380. *nadir* 1) zenith 2) potentate 3) dismay 4) magnificence 5) lowest point

Answers to this test on page 149.

WORD LIST 20 naiveté - opprobrious

•**naiveté** (*nah-ēv′-tā*) N. quality of being unsophisticated. I cannot believe that such *naiveté* is unassumed in a person of her age and experience. naive, ADJ.

natal (*nāt′-*) ADJ. pertaining to birth. He refused to celebrate his *natal* day because it reminded him of the few years he could look forward to.

nauseous ADJ. sickened. The foul smells made her *nauseous*.

nemesis N. revenging agent. Captain Bligh vowed to be Christian's *nemesis*.

nepotism N. favoritism (to a relative). John left his position with the company because he felt that advancement was based on *nepotism* rather than ability.

nettle V. annoy; vex. Do not let him *nettle* you with his sarcastic remarks.

nib N. beak; pen point. The *nibs* of post office pens are often clotted and corroded.

nicety (*nī′-se-tĭ*) N. precision; minute distinction. I cannot distinguish between such *niceties* of reasoning.

nomadic ADJ. wandering. Several *nomadic* tribes of Indians would hunt in this area each year.

nonchalance N. indifference; lack of interest. He heard the news of the tragedy with complete *nonchalance*.

noncommittal ADJ. neutral; unpledged; undecided. We were annoyed by his *noncommittal* reply for we had been led to expect definite assurances of his approval.

nonentity N. nonexistence; person of no importance. Of course you are a *nonentity*; you will continue to be one until you prove your value to the community.

non sequitur N. conclusion that does not follow from the facts stated. Your term paper is full of *non sequiturs*; I cannot see how you reached the conclusions you state.

•**nostalgia** N. homesickness, longing for the past. The first settlers found so much work to do that they had little time for *nostalgia*.

novice N. beginner. Even a *novice* can do good work if he follows these simple directions.

noxious ADJ. harmful. We must trace the source of these *noxious* gases.

nugatory ADJ. futile; worthless. This agreement is *nugatory* for no court will enforce it.

numismatist (*-mĭs′-*) N. person who collects coins. The *numismatist* had a splendid collection of antique coins.

nutrient ADJ. providing nourishment. During the convalescent period, the patient must be provided with *nutrient* foods.

oaf N. stupid, awkward person. He called the unfortunate waiter a clumsy *oaf*.

obfuscate V. confuse; muddle. Do not *obfuscate* the issues by dragging in irrelevant arguments.

obliterate V. destroy completely. The tidal wave *obliterated* several island villages.

oblivion N. forgetfulness. Her works had fallen into a state of *oblivion*; no one bothered to read them.

obnoxious ADJ. offensive. I find your behavior *obnoxious*; please amend your ways.

•**obscure** ADJ. dark; vague; unclear. Even after I read the poem a fourth time, its meaning was still *obscure*. obscurity, N.

•**obscure** V. darken; make unclear. At times he seemed purposely to *obscure* his meaning, preferring mystery to clarity.

•**obsessive** ADJ. related to thinking about something constantly; preoccupying. Ballet, which had been a hobby, began to dominate her life; her love of dancing became *obsessive*.

obtrude V. push into prominence. The members of the group object to the manner in which you *obtrude* your opinions into matters of no concern to you.

obtrusive ADJ. pushing forward. I found him a very *obtrusive* person, constantly seeking the center of the stage.

obviate V. make unnecessary; get rid of. I hope this contribution will *obviate* any need for further collections of funds.

occult (*-kŭlt′*) ADJ. mysterious; secret; supernatural. The *occult* rites of the organization were revealed only to members.

odoriferous ADJ. giving off an odor. The *odoriferous* spices stimulated his jaded appetite.

odorous ADJ. fragrant. This variety of hybrid tea rose is more *odorous* than the one you have in your garden.

officious ADJ. meddlesome; excessively trying to please. Browning informs us that the Duke resented the bough of cherries some *officious* fool brought to the Duchess.

olfactory ADJ. concerning the sense of smell. The *olfactory* organ is the nose.

oligarchy N. government by a few. The feudal *oligarchy* was supplanted by an autocracy.

ominous ADJ. threatening. The stranger made an *ominous* gesture to the dog.

omnivorous (*-nĭv′-*) ADJ. eating both plant and animal food; devouring everything. Human beings are *omnivorous* animals.

onerous (*ŏn′-*) ADJ. burdensome. He quit because he found the work too *onerous*. onus, N.

onomatopoeia (*-pē′ȧ*) N. words formed in imitation of natural sounds. Words like "rustle" and "gargle" are illustrations of *onomatopoeia*.

onslaught N. vicious assault. We suffered many casualties during the unexpected *onslaught* of the enemy troops.

•**opaque** ADJ. dark; not transparent. I want something *opaque* placed in this window so that no one will be able to watch me. opacity, N.

opprobrious ADJ. disgraceful. I find your conduct so *opprobrious* that I must exclude you from classes.

ETYMOLOGY 20

NAV (ship)
navigate to sail a ship
circumnavigate sail around the world
naval pertaining to ships

OMNI (all)
omniscient all knowing
omnipotent all powerful
omnivorous eating everything

OPER (to work)
operate to work
cooperation working together
opera musical drama (specialized kind of work)

TEST—WORD LIST 20 —ANTONYMS

Each of the questions below consists of a word printed in italics, followed by five words or phrases numbered 1 to 5. Choose the numbered word or phrase which is most nearly opposite in meaning to the word in italics and write the number of your choice on your answer paper.

381. *obscure* 1) inactive 2) grudging 3) lucid 4) hasty 5) persistent
382. *obliterate* 1) dazzle 2) intrude 3) cleanse 4) conclude 5) construct
383. *occult* 1) superficial 2) permanent 3) violent 4) unconcealed 5) abominable
384. *onerous* 1) unafraid 2) light 3) fragrant 4) generous 5) useless
385. *naiveté* 1) sophistication 2) style 3) birth 4) girlishness 5) simper
386. *opaque* 1) transparent 2) translucent 3) transgressing 4) wealthy 5) prismatic
387. *novice* 1) person of experience 2) new dealer 3) editor 4) journalist 5) pedant
388. *obtrusive* 1) yielding 2) generous 3) inconspicuous 4) indifferent 5) questionable
389. *opprobrious* 1) quiet 2) honorable 3) ancient 4) calamitous 5) disapproving
390. *nettle* 1) vie 2) appease 3) abash 4) disfigure 5) murmur
391. *ominous* 1) burdensome 2) ignorant 3) feigned 4) refreshing 5) unthreatening
392. *noxious* 1) active 2) disarming 3) reticent 4) harmless 5) unfriendly
393. *oblivion* 1) deception 2) selectivity 3) objectivity 4) remembrance 5) frankness
394. *nomadic* 1) rustic 2) stationary 3) convenient 4) repetitive 5) rigid
395. *noncommittal* 1) pledged 2) incoherent 3) irascible 4) chronic 5) detailed
396. *oaf* 1) miser 2) renegade 3) tyrant 4) novice 5) sophisticate
397. *obfuscate* 1) confiscate 2) magnify 3) clarify 4) demonstrate 5) serve
398. *nonchalance* 1) muddle 2) grace 3) interest 4) intensity 5) reaction
399. *nugatory* 1) golden 2) leaden 3) affirmative 4) effective 5) opinionated
400. *obnoxious* 1) gruff 2) solemn 3) helpless 4) valid 5) pleasing

Answers to this test on page 149.

WORD LIST 21 **optimist - perfidious**

•**optimist** N. person who looks on the good side. The pessimist says the glass is half-empty; the *optimist* says it is half-full.

ordinance N. decree. Passing a red light is a violation of a city *ordinance*.

ornate (*nāt'*-) ADJ. excessively decorated; highly decorated. Furniture of this period can be recognized by the *ornate* carvings.

ornithologist N. scientific student of birds. Audubon's drawings of American bird life have been of interest not only to the *ornithologist* but also to the general public.

oscillate (*ŏs'-ĭl-*) V. vibrate pendulum-like; waver. It is interesting to note how public opinion *oscillates* between the extremes of optimism and pessimism.

ostensible ADJ. apparent; professed; pretended. Although the *ostensible* purpose of this expedition is to discover new lands, we are really interested in finding new markets for our products.

ostracize V. exclude from public favor; ban. As soon as the newspapers carried the story of his connection with the criminals, his friends began to *ostracize* him. ostracism, N.

overt (*-vêrt'*) ADJ. open to view. According to the United States Constitution, a person must commit an *overt* act before he may be tried for treason.

pacifist N. one opposed to force; anti-militarist. The *pacifists* urged that we reduce our military budget and recall our troops stationed overseas.

palatable ADJ. agreeable; pleasing to the taste. Paying taxes can never be made *palatable*.

palatial ADJ. magnificent. She proudly showed us through her *palatial* home.

pallid ADJ. pale; wan. Because his occupation required that he work at night and sleep during the day, he had an exceptionally *pallid* complexion.

palpable ADJ. tangible; easily perceptible. I cannot understand how you could overlook such a *palpable* blunder.

paltry (*pawl'*-) ADJ. insignificant; petty. This is a *paltry* sum to pay for such a masterpiece.

panacea (*pa-na-sē'-ă*) N. cure-all; remedy for all diseases. There is no easy *panacea* that will solve our complicated international situation.

pandemonium N. wild tumult. When the ships collided in the harbor, *pandemonium* broke out among the passengers.

panegyric (*-jĭ'*-) N. formal praise. The modest hero blushed as he listened to the *panegyrics* uttered by the speakers about his valorous act.

panorama N. comprehensive view, unobstructed view in all directions. Tourists never forget the impact of their first *panorama* of the Grand Canyon.

pantomime N. acting without dialogue. Because he worked in *pantomime*, the clown could be understood wherever he appeared.

●**paradox** N. statement that looks false but is actually correct; a contradictory statement. Wordsworth's "The child is father to the man" is an example of *paradox*.

paragon N. model of perfection. The class disliked him because the teacher was always pointing to him as a *paragon*.

parley N. conference. The peace *parley* has not produced the anticipated truce.

parody N. humorous imitation; travesty. We enjoyed the clever *parodies* of popular songs which the chorus sang.

paroxysm N. fit or attack of pain, laughter, rage. When he heard of his son's misdeeds, he was seized by a *paroxysm* of rage.

parricide N. person who murders his own father; murder of a father. The jury was shocked by the details of this vicious *parricide*.

partiality N. inclination; bias. As a judge, I must avoid any evidence of *partiality* when I award the prize.

●**passive** ADJ. not active; acted upon. *Passive* resistance proved a very effective weapon. passivity, N.

pastoral ADJ. rural. In these stories of *pastoral* life, we find an understanding of the daily tasks of country folk.

pathetic ADJ. causing sadness, compassion, pity; touching. Everyone in the auditorium was weeping by the time she finished her *pathetic* tale.

pathos N. tender sorrow; pity; quality in art or literature that produces these feelings. A quiet tone of *pathos* ran through the novel.

patriarch (*pāt'*-) N. father and ruler of a family or tribe. In many primitive tribes, the leader and lawmaker was the *patriarch*.

peccadillo N. slight offense. If we examine these escapades carefully, we will realize that they are mere *peccadilloes* rather than major crimes.

peculate V. steal; embezzle. His crime of *peculating* public funds entrusted to his care is especially damnable.

pecuniary ADJ. pertaining to money. I never expected a *pecuniary* reward for my work in this activity.

pedagogue N. teacher; dull and formal teacher. He could never be a stuffy *pedagogue*; his classes were always lively and filled with humor.

pedantic ADJ. showing off learning; bookish. What you say is *pedantic* and reveals an unfamiliarity with the realities of life. pedant, N.

pediatrician N. expert in children's diseases. The family doctor advised the parents to consult a *pediatrician* about their child's ailment.

pell-mell ADV. in confusion; disorderly. The excited students dashed *pell-mell* into the stadium to celebrate the victory.

penance N. self-imposed punishment for sin. The Ancient Mariner said, "I have *penance* done and penance more will do."

penitent ADJ. feeling regret or sorrow for one's offenses; repentant. When he realized the enormity of his crime, he became *penitent*.

pensive ADJ. dreamily thoughtful; thoughtful with a hint of sadness. The *pensive* youth gazed at the painting for a long time and then sighed.

penury (*pĕn'*-) N. extreme poverty. We find much *penury* and suffering in this slum area.

perdition N. damnation; complete ruin. She was damned to eternal *perdition*.

perfidious (*-fid'*-) ADJ. basely false. Your *perfidious* gossip is malicious and dangerous.

ETYMOLOGY 21

PAC (peace)
pacify to make peaceful
pacific peaceful
pacifist person opposed to war

PELL, PULS (to drive)
compulsion a forcing to do
repel drive back
expel drive out, banish

TEST—WORD LIST 21 —SYNONYMS OR ANTONYMS

Each of the following questions consists of a word printed in italics, followed by five words or phrases numbered 1 to 5. Choose the numbered word or phrase which is most nearly the same as or the opposite of the word in italics and write the number of your choice on your answer paper.

401. *ornate* 1) comprehensive 2) plain 3) resolute 4) unfinished 5) planned

402. *pallid* 1) calm 2) embittered 3) wan 4) intelligent 5) indifferent

403. *panegyric* 1) aria 2) epilogue 3) banter 4) repetition 5) denunciation

404. *ordinance* 1) decree 2) gun fire 3) plainness 4) simplicity 5) dexterity

405. *oscillate* 1) embrace 2) instigate 3) waver 4) condemn 5) kiss

406. *overt* 1) ambitious 2) shy 3) timely 4) concealed 5) congealed

407. *paltry* 1) insignificant 2) foul 3) exemplary 4) magniloquent 5) egregious

408. *optimist* 1) killjoy 2) turncoat 3) laggard 4) braggart 5) spendthrift

409. *penury* 1) jail 2) maintenance 3) commissioner 4) affluence 5) falsehood

410. *ostracize* 1) attach 2) ban 3) cancel 4) deface 5) extract
411. *panacea* 1) saturation 2) storm 3) cistern 4) cure-all 5) melody
412. *pacifist* 1) militarist 2) anarchist 3) socialist 4) artist 5) communist
413. *paragon* 1) oil 2) many-sided figure 3) geometric model 4) level 5) model
414. *pastoral* 1) urban 2) sheepish 3) monastic 4) sophisticated 5) poetic
415. *perfidious* 1) exquisite 2) loyal 3) model 4) imperfect 5) destitute
416. *passive* 1) elastic 2) active 3) comatose 4) lethal 5) futuristic
417. *palatable* 1) partial 2) plentiful 3) scarce 4) distasteful 5) harmless
418. *parley* 1) double 2) conference 3) conspiracy 4) debate 5) melange
419. *paroxysm* 1) catastrophe 2) earthquake 3) vexation 4) fit 5) apoplexy
420. *peccadillo* 1) felony 2) peanut 3) tree-climbing animal 4) herb 5) vibration

Answers to this test on page 149.

WORD LIST 22 perjury - precedent

●**perjury** N. false testimony while under oath. When several witnesses appeared to challenge his story, he was indicted for *perjury*.

pernicious ADJ. very destructive. He argued that these books had a *pernicious* effect on young and susceptible minds.

perpetrate V. commit an offense. Only an insane person could *perpetrate* such a horrible crime.

perusal (*o͞oz'*-) N. reading. I am certain that you have missed important details in your rapid *perusal* of this document. peruse, V.

pervade V. spread throughout. As the news of the defeat *pervaded* the country, a feeling of anger directed at the rulers who had been the cause of the disaster grew.

●**pervasive** ADJ. spread throughout; permeating. The *pervasive* odor of mothballs clung to the clothes and did not disappear until they had been thoroughly aired.

perverse ADJ. stubborn; intractable. Because of your *perverse* attitude, I must rate you as deficient in cooperation.

perversity N. stubborn maintenance of a wrong cause. I cannot forgive your *perversity* in repeating such an impossible story.

●**pessimism** N. belief that life is basically bad or evil; gloominess. The good news that we have been receiving lately indicates that there is little reason for your *pessimism*.

pestilential ADJ. causing plague; baneful. People were afraid to explore the *pestilential* swamp. pestilence, N.

●**petulant** ADJ. touchy; peevish. The feverish patient was *petulant* and restless.

●**philanthropist** N. lover of mankind; doer of good. As he grew older, he became famous as a *philanthropist* and benefactor of the needy.

philology N. study of language. The professor of *philology* advocated the use of Esperanto as an international language.

pied (*pīd*) ADJ. variegated; multi-colored. The *pied* antelope may be recognized by its white face.

pious ADJ. devout; religious. The *pious* parents gave their children a religious upbringing. piety, N.

piquant (*pēk'*-) ADJ. pleasantly tart-tasting; stimulating. The *piquant* sauce added to our enjoyment of the meal. piquancy, N.

pithy ADJ. terse; meaty. I enjoy reading his essays because they are always compact and *pithy*.

pittance N. small allowance or wage. She could not live on the *pittance* she received as a pension and had to look for an additional source of revenue.

placid ADJ. peaceful; calm. After his vacation in this *placid* section, he felt soothed and rested.

plagiarism N. theft of another's ideas or writings passed off as original. The editor recognized the *plagiarism* and rebuked the culprit who had presented the manuscript as original.

platitude N. trite remark; commonplace statement. Her *platitudes* impressed the ignorant.

plebeian (*-bē'*-) ADJ. common; pertaining to the common people. His speeches were aimed at the *plebeian* minds and emotions; they disgusted the more refined.

plethora (*plěth'*-) N. excess; overabundance. She offered a *plethora* of reasons for her shortcomings.

podiatrist (*-dī*-) N. doctor who treats ailments of the feet. He consulted a *podiatrist* about his fallen arches.

podium N. pedestal; raised platform. The audience applauded as the conductor made his way to the *podium*.

poignant (*poin'-gånt*) ADJ. keen; piercing; severe. Her *poignant* grief left her pale and weak.

politic ADJ. expedient; prudent; well-devised. Even though he was disappointed, he did not think it *politic* to refuse this offer.

polygamist (*-lĭg'*-) N. one who has more than one wife at a time. He was arrested as a *polygamist* when his two wives filed complaints about him.

polyglot ADJ. speaking several languages. New York City is a *polyglot* community because of the thousands of immigrants who settle there.

ponderous ADJ. weighty; unwieldy. His humor lacked the light touch; his jokes were always *ponderous*.

portend V. foretell; presage. the king did not know what these omens might *portend* and asked his soothsayers to interpret them.

portent N. sign; omen; forewarning. She regarded the black cloud as a *portent* of evil.

portentous (*-těn'*-) ADJ. ominous; serious. I regard our present difficulties and dissatisfactions as *portentous* omens of future disaster.

portly ADJ. stately; stout. The wealthy financier was a *portly* gentleman.

posthumous (*pŏst'*-) ADJ. after death (as of child born after father's death or book published after author's death). The critics acclaimed her after the *posthumous* publication of her novel.

postulate N. self-evident truth. We must accept these statements as *postulates* before pursuing our discussions any further. also V.

potentate (*pōt'*-) N. monarch; sovereign. The *potentate* spent more time at Monte Carlo than he did at home with his people.

potential ADJ. expressing possibility; latent. This juvenile delinquent is a *potential* criminal.

ā—ale; ă—add; ä—arm; ȧ—ask; ē—eve; ĕ—end; ẽ—err, her; e—event, allow; ī—ice; ĭ—ill; ō—old; ŏ—odd; ô—orb; o͞o—food; ou—out; th—thin; ū—use; ŭ—up; zh—pleasure

potion N. dose (of liquid). Tristan and Isolde drink a love *potion* in the first act of the opera.
potpourri (*pō-pōō'-rē*) N. heterogeneous mixture; medley. He offered a *potpourri* of folk songs from many lands.
practical ADJ. based on experience; utilitarian. He was a *practical* man and opposed to theory.
pragmatic ADJ. practical; concerned with practical values. This test should provide us with a *pragmatic* analysis of the value of this course.
prate V. speak foolishly; boast idly. Let us not *prate* about our virtues.
prattle V. babble. The little boy *prattled* endlessly about his toys.
precarious ADJ. uncertain; risky. I think this stock is a *precarious* investment and advise against its purchase.
• **precedent** N. something preceding in time which may be used as an authority or guide for future action. This decision sets a *precedent* for future cases of a similar nature.

ETYMOLOGY 22

PET, PETIT (to seek)
petition request
appetite craving, desire
compete vie with others

PON, POSIT (to place)
postpone place after
preposition that which goes before
positive definite, unquestioned (definitely placed)

PORT, PORTAT (to carry)
portable able to be carried
transport carry across
export carry out (of country)

TEST—WORD LIST 22 —SYNONYMS

Each of the questions below consists of a word printed in italics, followed by five words or phrases numbered 1 to 5. Choose the numbered word or phrase which is most nearly similar in meaning to the word in italics and write the number of your choice on your answer paper.

421. *perjury* 1) destruction 2) false testimony 3) deviltry 4) bailiff's word 5) calm
422. *perusal* 1) mail 2) denial 3) subject 4) peace 5) reading
423. *piquant* 1) teasing 2) tart 3) sweet 4) angry 5) spoiled
424. *potpourri* 1) lack 2) utensil 3) medley 4) display 5) mischief
425. *posthumous* 1) after death 2) immortal 3) fertilized 4) temporary 5) deciduous
426. *pernicious* 1) destructive 2) heated 3) warlike 4) diseased 5) contagious
427. *perverse* 1) overturned 2) modest 3) good-natured 4) curious 5) stubborn
428. *pithy* 1) tall 2) wealthy 3) showy 4) dark 5) terse
429. *plethora* 1) mite 2) excess 3) pride 4) Roman toga 5) cowardice
430. *precarious* 1) preceding 2) cautious 3) dangerous 4) violent 5) postponing
431. *poignant* 1) piercing 2) despondent 3) musical 4) blatant 5) weak
432. *pied* 1) baked 2) voluminous 3) equine 4) variegated 5) lame
433. *pittance* 1) bonus 2) possibility 3) piety 4) potion 5) small wage
434. *polyglot* 1) multi-lingual 2) divorced 3) serene 4) foreign 5) variegated
435. *portend* 1) expand 2) predict 3) demonstrate 4) magnify 5) extol
436. *placid* 1) fecund 2) located 3) serene 4) austere 5) blatant
437. *pestilential* 1) annoying 2) dying 3) upsetting 4) overcast 5) baneful
438. *platitude* 1) repartee 2) trite remark 3) conversation 4) long speech 5) rash
439. *podium* 1) platform 2) apple orchard 3) playground 4) swinging arm 5) community center
440. *philology* 1) psychiatry 2) relativity 3) study of birds 4) study of language 5) study of insects

Answers to this test on page 149.

WORD LIST 23 **precipitate - purveyor**

precipitate (*-cĭp-'itit*) ADJ. headlong; rash. Do not be *precipitate* in this matter; investigate further.
precipitous ADJ. steep. This hill is difficult to climb because it is so *precipitous*.
preclude V. make impossible; eliminate. This contract does not *preclude* my being employed by others at the same time that I am working for you.
precocious ADJ. developed ahead of time. By her rather adult manner of discussing serious topics, the child demonstrated that she was *precocious*.
precursor N. forerunner. Gray and Burns were *precursors* of the Romantic Movement in English literature.
predatory ADJ. plundering. The hawk is a *predatory* bird.
preeminent (*prē-ĕm'-*) ADJ. outstanding; superior. She was *preeminent* in the field of surgery.
premonition N. forewarning. We ignored these *premonitions* of disaster because they appeared to be based on childish fears.
preposterous ADJ. absurd; ridiculous. The excuse he gave was *preposterous*.
• **pretentious** ADJ. ostentatious; pompous; overly ambitious. Your limited resources will not permit you to carry out such a *pretentious* program. pretention, N.

prevaricate V. lie. He was forced to *prevaricate* to save his life.

procrastinate V. postpone; delay. It is wise not to *procrastinate*; otherwise, we find ourselves bogged down in a mass of work which should have been finished long ago.

prodigal ADJ. wasteful; reckless with money. The *prodigal* son squandered his inheritance. also N.

profligate ADJ. dissipated; wasteful; licentious. In this *profligate* company, he lost all sense of decency. also N.

profusion N. lavish expenditure; overabundant condition. Seldom have I seen food and drink served in such *profusion*.

progenitor N. ancestor. We must not forget the teachings of our *progenitors* in our desire to appear modern.

progeny N. children; offspring. He was proud of his *progeny* but regarded George as the most promising of all his children.

prognosticate V. predict. I *prognosticate* disaster unless we change our wasteful ways.

prolific ADJ. abundantly fruitful. He was a *prolific* writer and wrote as many as three books a year.

• **prologue** N. introduction (to a poem or play). In the *prologue* to *Romeo and Juliet*, Shakespeare introduces the audience to the feud between the Montagues and the Capulets.

promiscuous ADJ. mixed indiscriminately; haphazard; irregular. In the opera, "La Boheme," we get a picture of the *promiscuous* life led by the young artists of Paris.

prone ADJ. inclined to; prostrate. She was *prone* to sudden fits of anger.

propagate V. multiply; spread. I am sure disease must *propagate* in such unsanitary and crowded areas.

propensity N. natural inclination. I dislike your *propensity* to belittle every contribution he makes to our organization.

• **prophetic** ADJ. foretelling the future. I have no magical *prophetic* powers; when I predict what will happen, I base my predictions on common sense. prophesy, V.

propitiate V. appease. The natives offered sacrifices to *propitiate* the gods.

propound V. put forth for analysis. In your discussion, you have *propounded* several questions; let us consider each one separately.

propriety N. fitness; correct conduct. I want you to behave at this dinner with *propriety*; don't embarrass me.

propulsive ADJ. driving forward. The jet plane has a greater *propulsive* power than the motor-driven plane.

prostrate V. stretch out full on ground. He *prostrated* himself before the idol.

protégé (*prō'-ĕ-zhā*) N. person under the protection and support of a patron. Cyrano de Bergerac refused to be a *protégé* of Cardinal Richelieu.

protrude V. stick out. She *protruded* her tongue at the audience in derision.

provident ADJ. displaying foresight; thrifty; preparing for emergencies. In her usual *provident* manner, she had insured herself against this type of loss.

• **provocative** ADJ. arousing anger or interest; annoying. In order to prevent a sudden outbreak of hostilities, we must avoid actions that might seem *provocative* to our foe. provoke, V.

proximity N. nearness. The deer sensed the hunter's *proximity* and bounded away.

proxy N. authorized agent. Please act as my *proxy* and vote for this slate of candidates.

prudent ADJ. cautious; careful. A miser hoards money not because he is *prudent* but because he is greedy. prudence, N.

pseudonym N. pen name. Samuel Clemens' *pseudonym* was Mark Twain.

pugnacious ADJ. combative; disposed to fight. As a child he was *pugnacious* and fought with everyone.

pulmonary ADJ. pertaining to the lungs. In his researches on *pulmonary* diseases, he discovered many facts about the lungs of animals and human beings.

pulsate V. throb. We could see the blood vessels in his temple *pulsate* as he became more angry.

pungent (*pŭn'-jent*) ADJ. stinging; caustic. The *pungent* aroma of the smoke made me cough.

puny ADJ. insignificant; tiny; weak. Our *puny* efforts to stop the flood were futile.

purge V. clean by removing impurities; clear of charges. If you are to be *purged* of the charge of contempt of Congress, you must be willing to answer the questions previously asked. also N.

purloin V. steal. You will have to enter illegally in order to *purloin* the documents.

purveyor N. person who supplies foodstuffs; caterer. As a *purveyor* of rare wines and gourmet foods, he traveled through France and Italy every year in search of new products to sell.

ETYMOLOGY 23

PREADO, PREDA (prey)
predacious living by prey
predatory pillaging, plundering

PRE (before) prefix
precocious ahead of time
precursor forerunner

PRO (before, toward) prefix
prognosticate to foretell
propulsive driving forward

TEST—WORD LIST 23 —ANTONYMS

Each of the questions below consists of a word printed in italics, followed by five words or phrases numbered 1 to 5. Choose the numbered word or phrase which is most nearly opposite in meaning to the word in italics and write the number of your choice on your answer paper.

441. *precipitate* 1) incoherent 2) prestigious 3) insincere 4) mature 5) circumspect

442. *preeminent* 1) ephemeral 2) skeptical 3) uninteresting 4) rebellious 5) inferior

443. *prone* 1) unlikely 2) conscious 3) absent 4) arrogant 5) shy

ā—ale; ă—add; ä—arm; ȧ—ask; ē—eve; ĕ—end; ê—err, her; e—event, allow; ī—ice; i—ill; ō—old; ŏ—odd; ô—orb; o͞o—food; ou—out; th—thin; ū—use; ŭ—up; zh—pleasure

444. *precursor* 1) scholar 2) helper 3) follower 4) anticlimax 5) nonentity
445. *procrastinate* 1) tell a falsehood 2) vary 3) dominate 4) hasten 5) renew
446. *prolific* 1) authoritative 2) unproductive 3) controversial 4) distracting 5) furtive
447. *proximity* 1) equivalence 2) caution 3) essence 4) exactness 5) distance
448. *precipitous* 1) upper 2) level 3) gay 4) serious 5) dusty
449. *preposterous* 1) serious 2) disarming 3) brief 4) posthumous 5) praiseworthy
450. *profligate* 1) atomic 2) spurious 3) temperate 4) luxurious 5) averse
451. *promiscuous* 1) needy 2) missing 3) proper 4) haughty 5) leafy
452. *propulsive* 1) repellent 2) agitating 3) deviating 4) additive 5) destroying
453. *pseudonym* 1) true name 2) upper limb 3) alibi 4) confusion 5) homonym
454. *propitiate* 1) irritate 2) remind 3) inhibit 4) involve 5) interrogate
455. *puny* 1) withered 2) gigantic 3) serious 4) obese 5) silent
456. *precocious* 1) cheap 2) tawdry 3) developing slowly 4) mature 5) intelligent
457. *prevaricate* 1) manufacture 2) destroy 3) delay 4) tell the truth 5) belittle
458. *pugnacious* 1) big 2) strong 3) peaceful 4) honest 5) masterful
459. *progenitor* 1) advocate 2) adherent 3) descendant 4) incandescence 5) custodian
460. *provident* 1) courageous 2) immortal 3) precautionary 4) prolific 5) prodigal

Answers to this test on page 149.

WORD LIST 24 **pyromaniac - regime**

pyromaniac N. person with an irresistible desire to set things on fire. The detectives searched the area for the *pyromaniac* who had set these costly fires.

quack N. charlatan; impostor. Do not be misled by the exorbitant claims of this *quack*.

qualms N. misgivings. Her *qualms* of conscience had become so great that she decided to abandon her plans.

quell V. put down; quiet. The police used fire hoses and tear gas to *quell* the rioters.

querulous ADJ. fretful; whining. His classmates were repelled by his *querulous* and complaining statements.

quibble V. equivocate; play on words. Do not *quibble*; I want a straightforward and definite answer. also N.

quip N. taunt. You are unpopular because you are too free with your *quips* and sarcastic comments. also V.

quirk N. startling twist; caprice. By a *quirk* of fate, he found himself working for the man whom he had discharged years before.

quizzical ADJ. bantering; comical; humorously serious. Will Rogers' *quizzical* remarks endeared him to his audiences.

rabid (*răb'*-) ADJ. like a fanatic; furious. She was a *rabid* follower of the Dodgers and watched them play whenever she could go to the ball park.

ramp N. slope; inclined plane. The house was built with *ramps* instead of stairs in order to enable the man in the wheelchair to move easily from floor to floor.

rancid ADJ. having the odor of stale fat. A *rancid* odor filled the ship's galley.

rancor N. bitterness; hatred. Let us forget our *rancor* and cooperate in this new endeavor.

rant V. rave; speak bombastically. As we heard him *rant* on the platform, we could not understand his strange popularity with many people.

rapacious ADJ. excessively grasping; plundering. Hawks and other *rapacious* birds are known as "raptors."

rationalize V. reason; justify an improper act. Do not try to *rationalize* your behavior by blaming your companions.

ravenous (*răv'*-) ADJ. extremely hungry. The *ravenous* dog upset several garbage pails in its search for food.

recalcitrant ADJ. obstinately stubborn. Donkeys are reputed to be the most *recalcitrant* of animals.

recant V. repudiate; withdraw previous statement. Unless you *recant* your confession, you will be punished.

recapitulate V. summarize. Let us *recapitulate* what has been said thus far before going ahead.

recession N. withdrawal; retreat. The *recession* of the troops from the combat area was completed in an orderly manner.

recipient N. receiver. Although he had been the *recipient* of many favors, he was not grateful to his benefactor.

reciprocal ADJ. mutual; exchangeable; interacting. The two nations signed a *reciprocal* trade agreement.

reciprocate V. repay in kind. If they attack us, we shall be compelled to *reciprocate* and bomb their territory.

●**recluse** (*-clōōs*) N. hermit. The *recluse* lived in a hut in the forest. reclusive, ADJ.

reconcile V. make friendly after quarrel; correct inconsistencies. Each month we *reconcile* our check book with the bank statement.

recourse N. resorting to help when in trouble. The boy's only *recourse* was to appeal to his father for aid.

recrimination N. countercharges. Loud and angry *recriminations* were her answer to his accusations.

rectitude N. uprightness. He was renowned for his *rectitude* and integrity.

recumbent ADJ. reclining; lying down completely or in part. The command "AT EASE" does not permit you to take a *recumbent* position.

recurrent ADJ. occurring again and again. These *recurrent* attacks disturbed us and we consulted a physician.

redolent (*rĕd'*-) ADJ. fragrant; odorous; suggestive of an odor. Even though it is February, the air is *redolent* of spring.

redoubtable ADJ. formidable; causing fear. She was a *redoubtable* foe.

redress (*-drĕs'*) N. remedy; compensation. Do you mean to tell me that I can get no *redress* for my injuries? also V.

redundant ADJ. superfluous; excessively wordy; repetitious. Your composition is *redundant*; you can easily reduce its length.

reek V. emit (odor). The room *reeked* of stale tobacco smoke.

●**refute** V. disprove. The defense called several respectable witnesses who were able to *refute* the false testimony of the prosecution's only witness.

regale (*-gāl'*) V. entertain. John *regaled* us with tales of his adventures in Africa.

regeneration N. spiritual rebirth. Modern penologists strive for the *regeneration* of the prisoners.

regime (*rĕ-zhēm'*) N. method or system of government. When a Frenchman mentions the Old *Regime*, he refers to the government existing before the revolution.

ETYMOLOGY 24

PUT, PUTAT (to trim, to calculate)
computation a reckoning
amputate cut off
putative supposed (calculated)

QUAER, QUAESIT (to ask)
inquiry investigation
inquisitive questioning
query question

TEST—WORD LIST 24 —SYNONYMS OR ANTONYMS

Each of the questions below consists of a word printed in italics, followed by five words or phrases numbered 1 to 5. Choose the numbered word or phrase which is most nearly the same as or the opposite of the word in italics and write the number of your choice on your answer paper.

461. *rectitude* 1) latitude 2) integrity 3) stability 4) mobility 5) reluctance
462. *rapacious* 1) sharp 2) plundering 3) slanderous 4) belligerent 5) calm
463. *quack* 1) earthquake 2) charlatan 3) intruder 4) duck 5) deduction
464. *quell* 1) purchase 2) develop 3) destroy 4) incur 5) incite
465. *redolent* 1) ruddy 2) fragrant 3) intolerant 4) intolerable 5) astute
466. *recumbent* 1) occupying 2) burdensome 3) extra 4) dire 5) reclining
467. *recalcitrant* 1) stubborn 2) active 3) alert 4) sending forth 5) final
468. *regale* 1) bore 2) breeze 3) fashion 4) delegate 5) approve
469. *propensity* 1) disinclination 2) advocacy 3) fortune telling 4) rule 5) predecessor
470. *quip* 1) fit out 2) strip 3) torment 4) taunt 5) tolerate
471. *refutation* 1) literacy 2) proof 3) advocacy 4) regulation 5) vituperation
472. *querulous* 1) compassionate 2) contrite 3) complaisant 4) replying 5) dutiful
473. *redundant* 1) bouncing 2) elastic 3) concise 4) pinkish 5) scarce
474. *rabid* 1) indifferent 2) sated 3) scared 4) fantastic 5) futile
475. *ravenous* 1) straightforward 2) untalkative 3) massive 4) timid 5) sated
476. *quizzical* 1) interrogative 2) deliberate 3) bantering 4) candid 5) cynical
477. *rancor* 1) accord 2) disapproval 3) encouragement 4) delay 5) evasion
478. *qualms* 1) charity 2) misgivings 3) prayers 4) donations 5) definition
479. *recipient* 1) parent 2) nominator 3) nominee 4) antagonist 5) donor
480. *recluse* 1) socialite 2) coward 3) savant 4) pacifist 5) martyr

Answers to this test on page 149.

WORD LIST 25 rejuvenate - roseate

rejuvenate V. make young again. The charlatan claimed his elixir would *rejuvenate* the aged and weary.
relegate V. banish; consign to inferior position. If we *relegate* these experienced people to positions of unimportance because of their political persuasions, we shall lose the services of valuably trained personnel.
relevancy N. pertinence; reference to the case in hand. I was impressed by the *relevancy* of your remarks. relevant, ADJ.
relinquish V. abandon. I will *relinquish* my claims to this property if you promise to retain my employees.
relish V. savor; enjoy. I *relish* a good joke as much as anyone else. also N.
remedial ADJ. curative; corrective. Because he was a slow reader, he decided to take a course in *remedial* reading.
reminiscence N. recollection. Her *reminiscences* of her experiences are so fascinating that she ought to write a book.
remnant N. remainder. I suggest that you wait until the store places the *remnants* of these goods on sale.
remunerative ADJ. compensating; rewarding. I find my new work so *remunerative* that I may not return to my previous employment. remuneration, N.
rend V. split; tear apart. In his grief, he tried to *rend* his garments.
render V. deliver; provide; represent. She *rendered* aid to the needy and indigent.
renegade N. deserter; apostate. Because he refused to support his fellow members in their drive, he was shunned as a *renegade*.
renounce V. abandon; discontinue; disown; repudiate. She refused to *renounce* her faith.
renovate V. restore to good condition; renew. They claim that they can *renovate* worn shoes so that they look like new ones.
renunciation N. giving up; renouncing. Do not sign this *renunciation* of your right to sue until you have consulted a lawyer.
reparable (*rěp'-*) ADJ. capable of being repaired. Fortunately, the damages we suffered in the accident were *reparable*.
replete (*-plēt'*) ADJ. filled to capacity; abundantly supplied. This book is *replete* with humorous situations.
reprehensible ADJ. deserving blame. I find your present attitude *reprehensible*.
reprieve N. temporary stay. During the twenty-four hour *reprieve*, the lawyers sought to make the stay of execution permanent.
reprimand V. reprove severely. I am afraid that my parents will *reprimand* me when I show them my report card. also N.
•**reproachful** ADJ. expressing disapproval. He never could do anything wrong without imagining the *reproachful* look in his mother's eye.

ā—ale; ă—add; ä—arm; ȧ—ask; ē—eve; ĕ—end; ê—err, her; e—event, allow; ī—ice; i—ill; ō—old; ŏ—odd; ô—orb; o͞o—food; ou—out; th—thin; ū—use; ŭ—up; zh—pleasure

• **repudiate** V. disown; disavow. She announced that she would *repudiate* all debts incurred by her husband.
requisite N. necessary requirement. Many colleges state that a student must offer three years of a language as a *requisite* for admission.
rescind V. cancel. Because of public resentment, the king had to *rescind* his order.
• **resolution** N. determination. Nothing could shake his *resolution* to succeed despite all difficulties.
resonant (*rĕz'-*) ADJ. echoing; resounding; possessing resonance. His *resonant* voice was particularly pleasing.
respite (*rĕs'-pĭt*) N. delay in punishment; interval of relief; rest. The judge granted the condemned man a *respite* to enable his attorneys to file an appeal.
restitution N. reparation; indemnification. He offered to make *restitution* for the window broken by his son.
• **restraint** N. controlling force. She dreamt of living an independent life, free of all *restraints*.
resuscitate V. revive. The lifeguard tried to *resuscitate* the drowned child by applying artificial respiration.
retaliate V. repay in kind (usually for bad treatment). Fear that we will *retaliate* immediately deters our foe from attacking us.
• **reticence** N. reserve; uncommunicativeness; inclination to be silent. Because of the *reticence* of the key witness, the case against the defendant collapsed.
retraction N. withdrawal. She dropped her libel suit after the newspaper published a *retraction* of its statement.
retribution N. vengeance; compensation; punishment for offenses. The evangelist maintained that an angry deity would exact *retribution* from the sinners.
retrieve V. recover; find and bring in. The dog was intelligent and quickly learned to *retrieve* the game killed by the hunter.
retroactive ADJ. of a law which dates back to a period before its enactment. Because the law was *retroactive* to the first of the year, we found he was eligible for the pension.
revelry N. boisterous merrymaking. New Year's Eve is a night of *revelry*.
• **reverence** N. respect. His attitude of *reverence* was appropriate in a house of worship.
reverberate V. echo; resound. The entire valley *reverberated* with the sound of the church bells.
revile V. slander; vilify. He was avoided by all who feared that he would *revile* and abuse them if they displeased him.
revulsion N. sudden violent change of feeling; reaction. Many people in this country who admired dictatorships underwent a *revulsion* when they realized what Hitler and Mussolini were trying to do.
ribald (*rĭb'-*) ADJ. scurrilous; profane. He sang a *ribald* song which offended many of us.
rift N. opening; break. The plane was lost in the stormy sky until the pilot saw the city through a *rift* in the clouds.
rigor N. severity. Many settlers could not stand the *rigors* of the New England winters.
risible ADJ. inclined to laugh; ludicrous. His remarks were so *risible* that the audience howled with laughter. risibility, N.
risqué (*rĭs'kā*) ADJ. verging upon the improper; off-color. Please do not tell your *risqué* anecdotes at this party.
rococo (*ro-cōc'ō*) ADJ. ornate; highly decorated. At the present time, architects avoid *rococo* designs.
roseate (*rōs'-ē-ăt*) ADJ. rosy; optimistic. I am afraid you will have to alter your *roseate* views in the light of the news that has just arrived.

ETYMOLOGY 25

RID, RIS (to laugh)
derision scorn
risibility inclination to laughter
ridiculous deserving to be laughed at

ROG, ROGAT (to ask)
interrogate to question
prerogative privilege
derogatory disparaging (asking a question to belittle)

TEST—WORD LIST 25 —SYNONYMS

Each of the questions below consists of a word printed in italics, followed by five words or phrases numbered 1 to 5. Choose the numbered word or phrase which is most nearly similar in meaning to the word in italics and write the number of your choice on your answer paper.

481. *remunerative* 1) relating 2) fiscal 3) profitable 4) halcyon 5) expensive
482. *roseate* 1) flowery 2) reddish 3) pink 4) fragrant 5) rosy
483. *ribald* 1) profane 2) hairless 3) brave 4) funny 5) soapy
484. *retribution* 1) vigor 2) return 3) vengeance 4) decor 5) gift
485. *resuscitate* 1) relate 2) re-echo 3) relive 4) revive 5) revamp
486. *reparable* 1) incomparable 2) capable of being repaired 3) payable 4) not payable 5) average
487. *retraction* 1) withdrawal 2) edition 3) deduction 4) elimination 5) extension
488. *reverberate* 1) review 2) echo 3) repay 4) resume 5) recall
489. *rococo* 1) sparse 2) cloudy 3) ornate 4) roseate 5) filmy
490. *retaliate* 1) answer 2) repeat 3) repay in kind 4) summarize 5) cancel
491. *replete* 1) completed 2) vacant 3) vivid 4) filled to capacity 5) covered
492. *revelry* 1) army troop 2) congratulations 3) bugle tune 4) appraisal 5) merrymaking
493. *resonant* 1) echoing 2) accurate 3) robust 4) sticky 5) supreme
494. *relegate* 1) banish 2) award 3) dismiss 4) pray 5) disguise
495. *risqué* 1) taking a chance 2) opportune 3) off-color 4) terse 5) abrupt
496. *reprehensible* 1) prehensile 2) commendable 3) deliberate 4) blameworthy 5) greedy

497. *reprieve* 1) construction 2) remembrance 3) temporary stay 4) recall 5) location

498. *retrieve* 1) try again 2) restore 3) recover 4) fail 5) succeed

499. *relevancy* 1) pertinence 2) belonging 3) memory 4) banquet 5) curtain

500. *risible* 1) smiling 2) ludicrous 3) light 4) scornful 5) watchful

Answers to this test on page 149.

WORD LIST 26 **rote - shrewd**

rote N. repetition. He recited the passage by *rote* and gave no indication that he understood what he was saying.

rueful ADJ. regretful; sorrowful; dejected. The artist has captured the sadness of childhood in his portrait of the boy with the *rueful* countenance. rue, V.

ruminate V. chew the cud; ponder. We cannot afford to wait while you *ruminate* upon these plans.

rummage V. ransack; thoroughly search. When we *rummaged* through the trunks in the attic, we found many souvenirs of our childhood days.

ruse N. trick; stratagem. You will not be able to fool your friends with such an obvious *ruse*.

sacrilegious (*lĕj-*) ADJ. desecrating; profane. His stealing of the alter cloth was a very *sacrilegious* act.

sacrosanct (*săc'-*) ADJ. most sacred; inviolable. The brash insurance salesman invaded the *sacrosanct* privacy of the office of the president of the company.

salient (*sāl'-ĭ-ĕnt*) ADJ. prominent. One of the *salient* features of that newspaper is its excellent editorial page.

saline (*sāl'-īn*) ADJ. salty. The slightly *saline* taste of this mineral water is pleasant.

sallow ADJ. yellowish; sickly in color. We were disturbed by his *sallow* complexion.

salutary ADJ. tending to improve; beneficial; wholesome. The punishment had a *salutary* effect on the boy as he became a model student.

sanction V. approve; ratify. Nothing will convince me to *sanction* the engagement of my daughter to such a worthless young man.

sanguinary ADJ. bloody. The battle of Iwo Jima was unexpectedly *sanguinary*.

sapient (*sāp'-*) ADJ. wise; shrewd. The students enjoyed the professor's *sapient* digressions more than his formal lectures.

●**sarcasm** N. scornful remarks; stinging rebuke. His feelings were hurt by the *sarcasm* of his supposed friends.

sardonic ADJ. disdainful; sarcastic; cynical. I cannot stand her *sardonic* wit.

sate V. satisfy to the full; cloy. The lion *sated* its hunger and dozed.

satiate V. surfeit; satisfy fully. The guests *satiated* themselves and were not likely to pay much attention to the speaker.

satiety (*-tī-ĕ-tĭ*) N. condition of being crammed full; glutted state; repletion. Shelly mentions "Love's sad *satiety*" in his "Ode to a Skylark."

●**satirize** V. mock. Cartoonist Gary Trudeau often *satirizes* contemporary politicians; through the comments of the Doonesbury characters, Trudeau ridicules political corruption and folly. satirical, ADJ.

saturnine (*săt'-ur-nīn*) ADJ. gloomy. The *saturnine* professor had few pupils.

saunter V. stroll slowly. As we *sauntered* through the park, we stopped frequently to admire the spring flowers.

savant (*săv'-ahn*) N. scholar. Our faculty includes many world famous *savants*.

savoir faire (*săv'-wah far'*) N. tact; poise; sophistication. I envy his *savoir faire*; he always knows exactly what to do and say.

scavenger N. collector and disposer of refuse; animal that devours refuse and carrion. The coyote is a *scavenger*.

schism (*sĭzm*) N. division; split. Let us not widen the *schism* by further bickering.

scintilla N. shred; least bit. You have not produced a *scintilla* of evidence to support your argument.

scintillate V. sparkle; flash. I enjoy her dinner parties because the food is excellent and the conversation *scintillates*.

scourge N. lash; whip; severe punishment. They feared the plague and regarded it as a deadly *scourge*.

scrupulous ADJ. conscientious; extremely thorough. I can recommend him for a position of responsibility for I have found him a very *scrupulous* young man.

●**scrutinize** V. examine closely and critically. Searching for flaws, the sergeant *scrutinized* every detail of the private's uniform.

scuttle V. sink. The sailors decided to *scuttle* their vessel rather than surrender it to the enemy.

seclusion N. isolation; solitude. One moment she loved crowds; the next, she sought *seclusion*. secluded, ADJ.

sedate ADJ. composed; grave. The parents were worried because they felt their son was too quiet and *sedate*.

sedulous ADJ. diligent. Stevenson said that he played the "*sedulous* ape" and diligently imitated the great writers of the past.

seethe V. be disturbed; boil. The nation was *seething* with discontent as the noblemen continued their arrogant ways.

seine (*sān*) N. net for catching fish. When the shad run during the spring, you may see fishermen with *seines* along the banks of our coastal rivers.

semblance N. outward appearance; guise. Although this book has a *semblance* of wisdom and scholarship, a careful examination will reveal many errors and omissions.

sensual ADJ. devoted to the pleasures of the senses; carnal, voluptuous. I cannot understand what caused him to drop his *sensual* way of life and become so ascetic.

●**serenity** N. calmness; placidity. The *serenity* of the sleepy town was shattered by a tremendous explosion.

serrated (*sĕ'-rā-tĕd*) ADJ. having a sawtoothed edge. The beech tree is one of many plants that have *serrated* leaves.

●**sever** V. cut; separate. The released prisoner wanted to begin a new life and *sever* his connections with his criminal past.

shackle V. chain; fetter. The criminal's ankles were *shackled* to prevent his escape.

shimmer V. glimmer intermittently. The moonlight *shimmered* on the water as the moon broke through the clouds for a moment. also N.

●**shrewd** ADJ. clever; astute. A *shrewd* investor, he took clever advantage of the fluctuations of the stock market.

ā—ale; ă—add; ä—arm; à—ask; ē—eve; ĕ—end; ê—err, her; e—event, allow; ī—ice; ĭ—ill; ō—old; ŏ—odd; ô—orb; o͞o—food; ou—out; th—thin; ū—use; ŭ—up; zh—pleasure

ETYMOLOGY 26

RUMP, RUPT (to break)
interrupt to break into
bankrupt insolvent
rupture a break

SCRIB, SCRIPT (to write)
transcribe copy
script writing
circumscribe enclose, limit (write around)

SCI (to know)
science knowledge
omniscient knowing all
conscious aware

SED, SESS (to sit)
sedentary inactive (sitting)
session meeting
residence place where one dwells

SENT, SENS (to think, to feel)
resent show indignation
sensitive showing feeling
consent agree

SEQUI, SECUT (to follow)
consecutive following in order
sequence arrangement
sequel that which follows

TEST—WORD LIST 26 —ANTONYMS

Each of the questions below consists of a word printed in italics, followed by five words or phrases numbered 1 to 5. Choose the numbered word or phrase which is most nearly opposite in meaning to the word in italics and write the number of your choice on your answer paper.

501. *sacrilegious* 1) unmarred 2) flagrant 3) sanctifying 4) devoted 5) reflective
502. *sedulous* 1) apish 2) indolent 3) redolent 4) waspish 5) histrionic
503. *sanguinary* 1) pacific 2) polished 3) salubrious 4) conventional 5) imaginary
504. *sallow* 1) edible 2) redundant 3) ruddy 4) finicky 5) abundant
505. *sate* 1) remain standing 2) rise 3) imply 4) refer 5) starve
506. *serenity* 1) exuberance 2) protuberance 3) intolerance 4) knowledge 5) implausibility
507. *sever* 1) soften 2) reduce 3) proceed 4) divert 5) attach
508. *sedate* 1) prompt 2) insensitive 3) boisterous 4) noisome 5) bitter
509. *shrewd* 1) dull-witted 2) even-tempered 3) warm-hearted 4) underhanded 5) ambitious
510. *shackle* 1) emancipate 2) humble 3) reject 4) laud 5) feature
511. *scrutinize* 1) absolve 2) disdain 3) greet warmly 4) clean thoroughly 5) observe inattentively
512. *salutary* 1) nomadic 2) parting 3) military 4) incomplete 5) harmful
513. *sacrosanct* 1) legal 2) unholy 3) repeated 4) secure 5) endless
514. *sapient* 1) wistful 2) foolish 3) wanton 4) humble 5) preeminent
515. *satiate* 1) signify 2) stultify 3) starve 4) explain 5) flood
516. *schism* 1) union 2) undertaking 3) failure 4) plot 5) doctrine
517. *satirical* 1) contemporary 2) unmocking 3) insincere 4) provocative 5) quiet
518. *scrupulous* 1) dishonest 2) flamboyant 3) prosperous 4) persuasive 5) solitary
519. *sardonic* 1) respectful 2) affluent 3) courageous 4) treacherous 5) unruly
520. *savant* 1) spendthrift 2) nomad 3) hermit 4) ignoramus 5) inventor

Answers to this test on page 149.

WORD LIST 27 simian - sunder

simian ADJ. monkey-like. This strange animal has *simian* characteristics.

simile (*sĭm'-ĭ-lē*) N. comparison of one thing with another, using the word *like* or *as*. We are constantly using *similes* and metaphors to convey our thoughts to others.

simulate V. feign. He *simulated* insanity in order to avoid punishment for his crime.

sinuous ADJ. winding; bending in and out; not morally honest. The plane followed the *sinuous* seacoast in its search for the missing sailboat.

•**skeptical** ADJ. doubting; suspending judgment until having examined the evidence supporting a point of view. I am *skeptical* about this project; I want some proof that it can work. skepticism, N.

skimp V. provide scantily; live very economically. They were forced to *skimp* on necessities in order to make their limited supplies last the winter.

skulk V. move furtively and secretly. He *skulked* through the less fashionable sections of the city in order to avoid meeting any of his former friends.

sloth N. laziness. Such *sloth* in a young person is deplorable; get to work!

smolder V. burn without flame; be liable to break out at any moment. The rags *smoldered* for hours before they burst into flame.

solicitous ADJ. worried; concerned. The employer was very *solicitous* about the health of his employees as replacements were difficult to get.

soliloquy N. talking to oneself. The *soliloquy* is a device used by the dramatist to reveal a character's innermost thoughts and emotions.

somnambulist N. sleepwalker. Lady Macbeth became a *somnambulist*.

spasmodic ADJ. fitful, periodic. The *spasmodic* coughing in the auditorium annoyed the performers.

specious (*spē'-*) ADJ. seemingly reasonable but incorrect. Let us not be misled by such *specious* arguments.

spectral ADJ. ghostly. We were frightened by the *spectral* glow that filled the room.

spurious ADJ. false; counterfeit. He tried to pay the bill with a *spurious* banknote.

squalid (*skwŏl'-*) ADJ. dirty; neglected; poor. It is easy to see how crime can breed in such a *squalid* neighborhood.

• **stagnation** N. inactivity; lack of progress or development; staleness. Under Iaccoca's leadership, Chrysler became revitalized after a long period of *stagnation*. stagnate, V.

staid ADJ. sober; sedate. Her conduct during the funeral ceremony was *staid* and solemn.

stamina N. strength; staying power. I doubt that he has the *stamina* to run the full distance of the marathon race.

stentorian ADJ. extremely loud. The town crier had a *stentorian* voice.

stigmatize V. brand; mark as wicked. I do not want to *stigmatize* this young offender for life by sending her to prison.

stint N. supply; allotted amount; assigned portion of work. He perfomed his daily *stint* cheerfully and willingly.

stipend (*stī'-*) N. pay for services. There is a nominal *stipend* attached to this position.

stoic (*stō'ĭc*) N. person who is indifferent to pleasure or pain. She bore the pain like a *stoic*.

stolid ADJ. dull; impassive. I am afraid that this imaginative poetry will not appeal to such a *solid* person.

strident (*strīd'-*) ADJ. loud and harsh. She scolded him in a *strident* voice.

• **subdued** ADJ. less intense; quieter. In the hospital people spoke in a *subdued* tone of voice.

subjugate V. conquer; bring under control. It is not our aim to *subjugate* our foe; we are interested only in establishing peaceful relations.

subsequent ADJ. following; later. In *subsequent* lessons, we shall take up more difficult problems.

subservient ADJ. behaving like a slave; servile; obsequious; truckling. She was proud and dignified; she refused to be *subservient* to anyone.

subsistence N. existence; means of support; livelihood. In these days of inflated prices. my salary provides a mere *subsistence*.

• **substantial** ADJ. ample; solid; in essentials. The scholarship represented a *substantial* sum of money.

substantiate N. verify; support. I intend to *substantiate* my statement by producing witnesses.

subterfuge N. pretense; evasion. As soon as we realized that you had won our support by a *subterfuge*, we withdrew our endorsement of your candidacy.

subtlety (*sŭt'l-tĭ*) N. nicety; cunning; guile; delicacy. The *subtlety* of her remarks was unnoticed by most of her hearers.

subversive ADJ. tending to overthrow or ruin. We must destroy such *subversive* publications.

succinct (*sŭk-sinkt'*) ADJ. brief; terse; compact. Her remarks are always *succint* and pointed.

succulent ADJ. juicy; full of richness. He developed the *succulent* theme fully.

suffuse V. spread over. A blush *suffused* her cheeks when we teased her about her love affair.

sully V. tarnish; soil. He felt that it was beneath his dignity to *sully* his hands in such menial labor.

sultry ADJ. sweltering. He could not adjust himself to the *sultry* climate of the tropics.

sumptuous ADJ. lavish; rich. I cannot recall when I had such a *sumptuous* feast.

sunder V. separate; part. North and South Ireland are politically and religiously *sundered*.

ETYMOLOGY 27

SOLV, SOLUT (to loosen)
absolve free from blame
dissolute morally lax
absolute complete (not loosened)

SPEC, SPECT (to look at)
spectator observer
aspect appearance
circumspect cautious (looking around)

TEST—WORD LIST 27 —SYNONYMS OR ANTONYMS

Each of the questions below consists of a word printed in italics, followed by five words or phrases numbered 1 to 5. Choose the numbered word or phrase which is most nearly the same as or the opposite of the word in italics and write the number of your choice on your answer paper.

521. *stagnation* 1) progress 2) unification 3) tolerance 4) authority 5) remorse

522. *stolid* 1) emotional 2) acute 3) shrewd 4) bright 5) weary

523. *sunder* 1) join 2) meet 3) sanction 4) exclude 5) erupt

524. *substantiate* 1) vacillate 2) ignore 3) condescend 4) surpass 5) verify

525. *spasmodic* 1) chronic 2) fitful 3) organic 4) acute 5) terrific

526. *succulent* 1) sweet 2) swinish 3) lucid 4) dry 5) lurid

527. *staid* 1) inane 2) sober 3) pompous 4) belligerent 5) melancholy

528. *specious* 1) unreasonable 2) true 3) special 4) definite 5) calamitous

529. *simian* 1) ape-like 2) Oriental 3) western 4) duplicated 5) original

ā—ale; ă—add; ä—arm; à—ask; ē—eve; ĕ—end; ê—err, her; e—event, allow; ī—ice; i—ill; ō—old; ŏ—odd; ô—orb; o͞o—food; ou—out; th—thin; ū—use; ŭ—up; zh—pleasure

530. *subterfuge* 1) whim 2) separator 3) pretense 4) device 5) underwater machine
531. *spurious* 1) genuine 2) expensive 3) debatable 4) alleged 5) theoretical
532. *subtlety* 1) oversight 2) custom 3) prediction 4) delicacy 5) fame
533. *subsequent* 1) underground 2) preceding 3) anticipatory 4) causal 5) nonsensical
534. *succinct* 1) sweet 2) juicy 3) wordy 4) outspoken 5) critical
535. *simulate* 1) dramatize 2) promote 3) feign 4) fling 5) sadden
536. *stigmatize* 1) gladden 2) soar 3) organize 4) brand 5) clarify
537. *solicitous* 1) unconcerned 2) suspicious 3) luscious 4) distracted 5) destitute
538. *sumptuous* 1) humble 2) bland 3) original 4) accurate 5) riotous
539. *sultry* 1) cool 2) entrancing 3) blunt 4) soft 5) sweet
540. *subdued* 1) overdue 2) incomplete 3) practical 4) muted 5) absurd

Answers to this test on page 150.

WORD LIST 28 supersede - transcend

supersede V. cause to be set aside; replace. This regulation will *supersede* all previous rules.

supine (*-pīn'*) ADV. lying on back. The defeated pugilist lay *supine* on the canvas.

supplicate V. petition humbly; pray to grant a favor. We humbly *supplicate* your majesty to grant him amnesty.

●**suppress** V. crush; subdue; inhibit. After the armed troops had *suppressed* the rebellion, the city was placed under martial law.

surcease (*-sēs'*) N. cessation. He begged the doctors to grant him *surcease* from his suffering.

surly (*sûrl'-ĭ*) ADJ. rude; cross. Because of his *surly* attitude, many people avoided his company.

surmise (*-mīz'*) V. guess. I *surmise* that he will be late for this meeting.

●**surpass** V. exceed. Her PSAT scores *surpassed* her expectations and raised her hopes for a scholarship.

surveillance (*-vāl'-*) N. watching; guarding. The FBI kept the house under constant *surveillance* in the hope of capturing all the criminals at one time.

sustenance N. means of support, food, nourishment. In the tropics, the natives find *sustenance* easy to obtain.

swelter V. be oppressed by heat. I am going to buy an air-conditioning unit for my apartment as I do not intend to *swelter* through another hot and humid summer.

swindler N. cheat. She was gullible and trusting, an easy victim for the first *swindler* who came along.

sylvan ADJ. pertaining to the woods; rustic. Her paintings of nymphs in *sylvan* backgrounds were criticized as overly sentimental.

●**symmetry** N. arrangement of parts so that balance is obtained; congruity. The addition of a second tower will give this edifice the *symmetry* which it now lacks.

synthesis N. combining parts into a whole. Now that we have succeeded in isolating this drug, our next problem is to plan its *synthesis* in the laboratory.

taciturn ADJ. habitually silent; talking little. New Englanders are reputedly *taciturn* people.

tactile ADJ. pertaining to the organs or sense of touch. His calloused hands had lost their *tactile* sensitivity.

tainted ADJ. contaminated; corrupt. Health authorities are always trying to prevent the sale and use of *tainted* food.

tantalize V. tease; torture with disappointment. Tom loved to *tantalize* his younger brother.

tautological ADJ. needlessly repetitious. In the sentence: "It was visible to the eye," the phrase "to the eye" is *tautological*.

tedious ADJ. boring; tiring. The repetitious nature of work on the assembly line made Martin's job very *tedious*. tedium, N.

tempestuous ADJ. stormy. Quarreling, reconciling, and quarreling again, Tyson and Givens had a *tempestuous* married life.

temporize V. avoid committing oneself; gain time. I cannot permit you to *temporize* any longer; I must have a definite answer today.

tenet N. doctrine; dogma. I cannot accept the *tenets* of your faith.

tenuous ADJ. thin; rare; slim. The allegiance of our allies is held by rather *tenuous* ties.

●**termination** N. end. Because of the unexpected *termination* of his contract, he desperately needed a new job.

terrestrial ADJ. on the earth. We have been able to explore the *terrestrial* regions much more thoroughly than the aquatic or celestial regions.

terse ADJ. concise; abrupt; pithy. I admire his *terse* style of writing.

testy ADJ. irritable; short-tempered. My advice is to avoid discussion with her today as she is rather *testy*.

tether V. tie with a rope. Before we went to sleep, we *tethered* our horses to prevent their wandering off during the night.

therapeutic ADJ. curative. These springs are famous for their *therapeutic* qualities.

thermal ADJ. pertaining to heat. The natives discovered that the hot springs gave excellent *thermal* baths and began to develop their community as a health resort.

throes N. violent or anguished struggle. She was in the *throes* of despair.

throttle V. strangle. The criminal tried to *throttle* the old man.

thwart V. baffle; frustrate. He felt that everyone was trying to *thwart* his plans.

timidity N. lack of self-confidence or courage. If you are to succeed as a salesman, you must first lose your *timidity*.

tirade N. extended scolding; denunciation. Long before he had finished his *tirade*, we were sufficiently aware of the seriousness of our misconduct.

titanic ADJ. gigantic. *Titanic* waves beat against the shore during the hurricane.

toady V. flatter for favors. I hope you see through those who are *toadying* you for special favors.

topography N. physical features of a region. Before the generals gave the order to attack, they ordered a complete study of the *topography* of the region.

torpid ADJ. dormant; dull; lethargic. The *torpid* bear had just come out of his cave after his long hibernation.

tortuous ADJ. winding; full of curves. Because this road is so *tortuous*, it is unwise to go faster than twenty miles an hour.

touchy ADJ. sensitive; irascible. Do not discuss this phase of the problem as he is very *touchy* about it.

toxic ADJ. poisonous. We must seek an antidote for whatever *toxic* substance he has eaten.

tractable ADJ. docile. You will find the children in this school very *tractable* and willing to learn.

tranquillity N. calmness; peace. After the commotion and excitement of the city, I appreciate the *tranquillity* of these fields and forests.

transcend V. exceed; surpass. This accomplishment *transcends* all our previous efforts. transcendental, ADJ.

ETYMOLOGY 28

TANG, TACT (to touch)
tangent touching
contact touching with, meeting
contingent depending upon

TEMPOR (time)
contemporary at same time
extemporaneous impromptu
temporize to delay

TEN, TENT (to hold)
tenable able to be held
tenacity retention
tenure holding of office

TERR (land)
terrestrial pertaining to earth
subterranean underground
Mediterranean Middle Land

TEST—WORD LIST 28 —SYNONYMS

Each of the questions below consists of a word printed in italics, followed by five words or phrases numbered 1 to 5. Choose the numbered word or phrase which is most nearly similar in meaning to the word in italics and write the number of your choice on your answer paper.

541. *tranquillity* 1) calmness 2) hurricane 3) candor 4) storm 5) noise
542. *surveillance* 1) scrutiny 2) testing 3) cartography 4) favoritism 5) convalescence
543. *taciturn* 1) sour 2) garrulous 3) silent 4) long 5) understandable
544. *testy* 1) noisy 2) examining 3) difficult 4) nasty 5) irritable
545. *tactile* 1) irritable 2) enriching 3) sensible 4) hasty 5) pertaining to sense of touch
546. *titanic* 1) disastrous 2) gigantic 3) beautiful 4) magnanimous 5) puny
547. *transcend* 1) interpret 2) ship 3) overcast 4) exceed 5) expel
548. *supersede* 1) work on lawn 2) stretch 3) adjust 4) set aside 5) be superior
549. *tautological* 1) tight 2) repetitious 3) practical 4) coarse 5) pragmatic
550. *tortuous* 1) winding 2) colored 3) coiled 4) painful 5) sadistic
551. *supine* 1) eating a light meal 2) yearning 3) lying on back 4) sitting erect 5) evergreen
552. *temporize* 1) grow angry 2) protect 3) annoy 4) gain time 5) refer
553. *torpid* 1) lukewarm 2) lazy 3) dry 4) muddy 5) dormant
554. *tenet* 1) scholar 2) doctrine 3) medicine 4) cure-all 5) small coin
555. *terrestrial* 1) pertaining to earth 2) astral 3) tiresome 4) fundamental 5) horizontal
556. *therapeutic* 1) medical 2) curative 3) scientific 4) warming 5) zoological
557. *surmise* 1) chance 2) define 3) translate 4) guess 5) conclude
558. *synthesis* 1) building 2) conclusions 3) formal relations 4) antonyms 5) joining
559. *tether* 1) knit 2) embroider 3) combine 4) aid 5) tie with a rope
560. *sylvan* 1) coarse 2) rustic 3) urbane 4) naive 5) crowded

Answers to this test on page 150.

WORD LIST 29 transition - variegated

transition N. going from one state to another. During the period of *transition* from oil heat to gas heat, the furnace will have to be shut off.

translucent ADJ. partly transparent. We could not recognize the people in the next room because of the *translucent* curtains which separated us.

● **transparent** ADJ. permitting light to pass through freely; easily detected. Your scheme is so *transparent* that it will fool no one.

tremor N. trembling; slight quiver. She had a nervous *tremor* in her right hand.

tremulous ADJ. trembling; wavering. She was *tremulous* more from excitement than from fear.

trenchant ADJ. cutting; keen. I am afraid of his *trenchant* wit for it is so often sarcastic.

trepidation N. fear. We must face the enemy without *trepidation* if we are to win this battle.

tribulation N. distress; suffering. After all the trials and *tribulations* we have gone through, we need this rest.

trifling ADJ. trivial; unimportant. Why bother going to see a doctor for a *trifling*, everyday cold?

trite ADJ. hackneyed; commonplace. The plot of this play is *trite*.

truculent (*trŭk'-ū-*) ADJ. aggressive; savage. They are a *truculent* race, ready to fight at any moment.

tumid ADJ. swollen; pompous; bombastic. I especially dislike his *tumid* style.

turbid ADJ. muddy; having the sediment disturbed. The water was *turbid* after the children had waded through it.

turbulence N. state of violent agitation. We were frightened by the *turbulence* of the ocean during the storm.

turgid (*tûr'-jid*) ADJ. swollen; distended. The *turgid* river threatened to overflow the levees and flood the countryside.

turpitude N. depravity. A visitor may be denied admittance to this country if he has been guilty of moral *turpitude*.

ā—ale; ă—add; ä—arm; ȧ—ask; ē—eve; ĕ—end; ê—err, her; e—event, allow; ī—ice; i—ill; ō—old; ŏ—odd; ô—orb; o͞o—food; ou—out; th—thin; ū—use; ŭ—up; zh—pleasure

tyro (*tīr'ō*) N. beginner; novice. For a mere *tyro*, you have produced some marvelous results.
ubiquitous ADJ. being everywhere; omnipresent. You must be *ubiquitous* for I meet you wherever I go.
ulterior ADJ. situated beyond, unstated. You must have an *ulterior* motive for your behavior.
ultimate ADJ. final; not susceptible to further analysis. Scientists are searching for the *ultimate* truths.
ultimatum (*-māt-*) N. last demand; warning. Since they have ignored our *ultimatum*, our only recourse is to declare war.
unassuming ADJ. modest. He is so *unassuming* that some people fail to realize how great a man he really is.
unbridled ADJ. violent. She had a sudden fit of *unbridled* rage.
uncanny ADJ. strange; mysterious. You have the *uncanny* knack of reading my innermost thoughts.
unconscionable ADJ. unscrupulous; excessive. He found the loan shark's demands *unconscionable* and impossible to meet.
uncouth ADJ. outlandish; clumsy; boorish. Most biographers portray Lincoln as an *uncouth* and ungainly young man.
unctuous ADJ. oily; bland, insincerely suave. I am suspicious of his *unctuous* manner.
unearthly ADJ. not earthly; weird. There is an *unearthly* atmosphere in her work which amazes the casual observer.
unequivocal ADJ. clear; obvious. My answer to your proposal is an *unequivocal* and absolute "No."
unfaltering ADJ. steadfast. She approached the guillotine with *unfaltering* steps.
unfeigned ADJ. genuine; real. I am sure her surprise was *unfeigned*.
• **uniformity** N. sameness; monotony. After a while, the *uniformity* of TV situation comedies becomes boring. uniform, ADJ.
unique ADJ. without an equal; single in kind. You have the *unique* distinction of being the first student whom I have had to fail in this course.
unmitigated ADJ. harsh; severe; not lightened. I sympathize with you in your *unmitigated* sorrow.
unprecedented ADJ. novel; unparalleled. For a first novel, Margaret Mitchell's *Gone with the Wind* was an *unprecedented* success.
unwonted ADJ. unaccustomed. He hesitated to assume the *unwonted* role of master of ceremonies at the dinner.
upbraid V. scold; reproach. I must *upbraid* him for his misbehavior.
urbane (*-bān'*) ADJ. suave; refined; elegant. The courtier was *urbane* and sophisticated. urbanity, N.
usurp V. seize another's power or rank. The revolution ended when the victorious rebel general succeeded in *usurping* the throne.
• **vacillation** N. fluctuation; wavering. His *vacillation* when confronted with a problem annoyed everyone who had to wait for him to make his decision.
vacuous ADJ. empty; inane. He was annoyed by her *vacuous* remarks.
vagary (*-gār'-*) N. caprice; whim. She followed every *vagary* of fashion.
validate V. confirm; ratify. I will not publish my findings until I *validate* my results.
vapid (*văp'-*) ADJ. insipid; inane. She delivered an uninspired and *vapid* address.
variegated ADJ. many-colored. He will not like this blue necktie as he is addicted to *variegated* clothing.

ETYMOLOGY 29

URB (city)
urban pertaining to city
urbane polished, sophisticated (pertaining to city dweller)
suburban outside of city

TEST—WORD LIST 29 —ANTONYMS

Each of the questions below consists of a word printed in italics, followed by five words or phrases numbered 1 to 5. Choose the numbered word or phrase which is most nearly opposite in meaning to the word in italics and write the number of your choice on your answer paper.

561. *trepidation* 1) slowness 2) gracefulness 3) courage 4) fascination 5) intuition
562. *unique* 1) plausible 2) equaled 3) original 4) qualitative 5) quantitative
563. *trite* 1) sad 2) proud 3) original 4) emphatic 5) concise
564. *ultimatum* 1) finality 2) plea 3) thunder 4) facility 5) destitution
565. *vacuous* 1) bankrupt 2) loose 3) pompous 4) terse 5) profound
566. *variegated* 1) plain 2) immodest 3) placid 4) particular 5) ambivalent
567. *transparent* 1) dense 2) obvious 3) alternate 4) opaque 5) translucent
568. *turbid* 1) limpid 2) languid 3) swollen 4) nostalgic 5) tumid
569. *unfaltering* 1) wavering 2) stern 3) destitute 4) quivering 5) righteous
570. *turgid* 1) turbid 2) tumid 3) not calm 4) not swollen 5) not clear
571. *unassuming* 1) mysterious 2) boastful 3) ravenous 4) ingenuous 5) profligate
572. *urbane* 1) transient 2) ironic 3) naive 4) cautious 5) negligent
573. *vapid* 1) solid 2) punctual 3) astute 4) hasty 5) candid
574. *trenchant* 1) dull 2) hungry 3) satiated 4) cloudy 5) muddy
575. *upbraid* 1) dishevel 2) adorn 3) alienate 4) praise 5) persuade
576. *ubiquitous* 1) wicked 2) limited 3) omniscient 4) commendable 5) uncouth
577. *unmitigated* 1) gentle 2) distressing 3) aggravated 4) commingling 5) dismayed
578. *tyro* 1) dabbler 2) expert 3) arsonist 4) singer 5) miser
579. *validate* 1) liquidate 2) challenge 3) estimate 4) spend 5) simplify
580. *truculent* 1) authentic 2) notorious 3) vigorous 4) meticulous 5) peaceful

Answers to this test on page 150.

WORD LIST 30 vehement - zenith

vehement ADJ. forceful; impetuous; with marked vigor. She spoke with *vehement* eloquence in defense of her client.

veneer N. thin layer; cover. Casual acquaintances were deceived by his *veneer* of sophistication and failed to recognize his fundamental shallowness.

venerable ADJ. deserving high respect. We do not mean to be disrespectful when we refuse to follow the advice of our *venerable* leader.

vent V. express; utter. He *vented* his wrath on his class.

verbose (*-bōs'*) ADJ. wordy. This article is too *verbose*; we must edit it.

vernal ADJ. pertaining to spring. We may expect *vernal* showers all during the month of April.

• **versatile** ADJ. having many talents; capable of working in many fields. Leonardo da Vinci was a very *versatile* man

vicissitude N. change of fortune. We must accept life's *vicissitudes*.

vie V. contend; compete. When we *vie* with each other for her approval, we are merely weakening ourselves and strengthening her.

• **vigor** N. active strength. Although he was over seventy years old, Jack had the *vigor* of a man in his prime. vigorous, ADJ.

vilify V. slander. Why is she always trying to *vilify* my reputation?

vindicate V. clear of charges. I hope to *vindicate* my client and return him to society as a free man.

vindictive ADJ. revengeful. He was very *vindictive* and never forgave an injury.

virile ADJ. manly. I admire his *virile* strength.

virtuoso N. highly skilled artist. Heifetz is a violin *virtuoso*.

virus (*vīr'-*) N. disease communicator. The doctors are looking for a specific drug to control this *virus*.

viscous (*vĭs'-kus*) ADJ. sticky; gluey. Melted tar is a *viscous* substance.

vituperative ADJ. abusive; scolding. He became more *vituperative* as he realized that we were not going to grant him his wish.

• **vivacious** ADJ. animated; gay. She had always been *vivacious* and sparkling. vivacity, N.

vociferous ADJ. clamorous; noisy. The crowd grew *vociferous* in its anger and threatened to take the law into its own hands.

• **volatile** (*vŏl'-*) ADJ. evaporating rapidly; light-hearted; mercurial. Ethyl chloride is a very *volatile* liquid.

voluble ADJ. fluent; glib. He was a *voluble* speaker, always ready to talk.

voracious (*-rā'-*) ADJ. ravenous. The wolf is a *voracious* animal.

• **vulnerable** ADJ. susceptible to wounds. Achilles was *vulnerable* only in his heel.

vying V. contending. Why are we *vying* with each other for his favors?

waggish ADJ. mischievous; humorous; tricky. He had a *waggish* wit.

waive V. give up temporarily; yield. I will *waive* my rights in this matter in order to expedite our reaching a proper decision.

wan ADJ. having a pale or sickly color; pallid. Suckling asked, "Why so pale and *wan*, fond lover?"

wane V. grow gradually smaller. The moon will *wane* for several days.

wanton ADJ. unruly; unchaste; excessive. Her *wanton* behavior cost her many friends.

wary ADJ. very cautious. The spies grew *wary* as they approached the sentry.

wheedle V. cajole; coax; deceive by flattery. She knows she can *wheedle* almost anything from her father.

whet V. sharpen; stimulate. The odors from the kitchen are *whetting* my appetite; I will be ravenous by the time the meal is served.

wily ADJ. cunning; artful. He is as *wily* as a fox in avoiding trouble.

winsome ADJ. agreeable; gracious; engaging. By her *winsome* manner, she made herself liked by everyone who met her.

• **withhold** V. refuse to give; hold back. The NCAA may *withhold* permission for academically underprepared athletes to participate in intercollegiate sports as freshmen.

witless ADJ. foolish; idiotic. Such *witless* and fatuous statements will create the impression that you are an ignorant individual.

witticism N. witty saying; facetious remark. What you regard as *witticisms* are often offensive to sensitive people.

wizened (*wĭz'-*) ADJ. withered; shriveled. The *wizened* old woman in the home for the aged was still active and energetic.

wont (*wōnt*) N. custom; habitual procedure. As was her *wont*, she jogged two miles every morning before going to work.

worldly ADJ. engrossed in matters of this earth; not spiritual. You must leave your *worldly* goods behind you when you go to meet your Maker.

wrest V. pull away; take by violence. With only ten seconds left to play, our team *wrested* victory from their grasp.

zenith N. point directly overhead in sky; summit. The sun was at its *zenith*.

ETYMOLOGY 30

VENI, VENT (to come)
intervene come between
prevent stop
convention meeting

VIA (way)
deviation departure from way
viaduct roadway (arched)
trivial trifling (small talk at crossroads)

VID, VIS (to see)
vision sight
evidence things seen
vista view

VINCT, VICT (to conquer)
invincible unconquerable
victory winning
vanquish to defeat

VOC, VOCAT (to call)
avocation calling, minor occupation
provocation calling or rousing the anger of
invocation calling in prayer

VOLV, VOLUT (to roll)
revolve roll around
evolve roll out, develop
convolution coiled state

ā—ale; ă—add; ä—arm; à—ask; ē—eve; ĕ—end; ê—err, her; e—event, allow; ī—ice; i—ill; ō—old; ŏ—odd; ô—orb; o͞o—food; ou—out; th—thin; ū—use; ŭ—up; zh—pleasure

TEST—WORD LIST 30 —SYNONYMS OR ANTONYMS

Each of the questions below consists of a word printed in italics, followed by five words or phrases numbered 1 to 5. Choose the numbered word or phrase which is most nearly the same as or the opposite of the word in italics and write the number of your choice on your answer paper.

581. *wanton* 1) moral 2) futile 3) lavish 4) wasted 5) watery
582. *whet* 1) dampen 2) dull 3) grind 4) chisel 5) grain
583. *versatile* 1) poetic 2) conspicuous 3) talented 4) trained 5) childish
584. *veneer* 1) varnish 2) wine 3) bribery 4) cover 5) label
585. *wan* 1) ruddy 2) intelligent 3) ribald 4) dwindling 5) expansive
586. *vindictive* 1) clever 2) venerable 3) lonely 4) hungry 5) forgiving
587. *vilify* 1) concentrate 2) slander 3) steal 4) match 5) negate
588. *wane* 1) be arrogant 2) depart 3) be selfish 4) wax 5) be pallid
589. *vivacious* 1) lethargic 2) hungry 3) impatient 4) inquisitive 5) deadly
590. *vicissitude* 1) proximity 2) change 3) decision 4) conversation 5) dispute
591. *wary* 1) tired 2) circumspect 3) angry 4) feeble 5) weeping
592. *vociferous* 1) ironclad 2) massive 3) nimble 4) oblique 5) quiet
593. *worldly* 1) round 2) naive 3) temperamental 4) celebrated 5) contained
594. *venerable* 1) disreputable 2) antique 3) moderate 4) inexpensive 5) conquerable
595. *vernal* 1) internal 2) solemn 3) grassy 4) spring-like 5) sacred
596. *winsome* 1) victorious 2) repulsive 3) disgraceful 4) sober 5) gigantic
597. *vituperative* 1) operative 2) absent 3) explanatory 4) qualitative 5) abusive
598. *voracious* 1) loud 2) late 3) talented 4) sated 5) truthful
599. *verbose* 1) pithy 2) problematic 3) oral 4) surprised 5) wicked
600. *witless* 1) informed 2) graceful 3) intelligent 4) assured 5) provocative

Answers to this test on page 150.

ANSWER KEY

Word Test 1 *(Page 103)*

1. 1	*6.* 3	*11.* 2	*16.* 2
2. 4	*7.* 2	*12.* 5	*17.* 3
3. 5	*8.* 3	*13.* 5	*18.* 3
4. 2	*9.* 5	*14.* 1	*19.* 5
5. 4	*10.* 1	*15.* 3	*20.* 3

Word Test 2 *(Page 105)*

21. 1	*26.* 3	*31.* 1	*36.* 2
22. 4	*27.* 1	*32.* 1	*37.* 1
23. 3	*28.* 2	*33.* 3	*38.* 2
24. 2	*29.* 2	*34.* 5	*39.* 1
25. 2	*30.* 5	*35.* 2	*40.* 2

Word Test 3 *(Page 106)*

41. 1	*46.* 4	*51.* 3	*56.* 4
42. 1	*47.* 1	*52.* 1	*57.* 1
43. 5	*48.* 2	*53.* 3	*58.* 3
44. 4	*49.* 5	*54.* 4	*59.* 1
45. 2	*50.* 1	*55.* 1	*60.* 1

Word Test 4 *(Page 108)*

61. 1	*66.* 2	*71.* 1	*76.* 5
62. 2	*67.* 3	*72.* 3	*77.* 3
63. 5	*68.* 1	*73.* 2	*78.* 4
64. 4	*69.* 1	*74.* 5	*79.* 1
65. 5	*70.* 4	*75.* 1	*80.* 4

Word Test 5 *(Page 110)*

81. 3	*86.* 4	*91.* 3	*96.* 2
82. 5	*87.* 1	*92.* 5	*97.* 3
83. 4	*88.* 2	*93.* 4	*98.* 2
84. 1	*89.* 1	*94.* 4	*99.* 5
85. 3	*90.* 2	*95.* 1	*100.* 2

Word Test 6 *(Page 111)*

101. 2	*106.* 2	*111.* 3	*116.* 2
102. 1	*107.* 2	*112.* 1	*117.* 5
103. 5	*108.* 4	*113.* 1	*118.* 1
104. 2	*109.* 5	*114.* 2	*119.* 1
105. 5	*110.* 4	*115.* 4	*120.* 4

Word Test 7 *(Page 113)*

121. 2	*126.* 2	*131.* 3	*136.* 3
122. 5	*127.* 4	*132.* 2	*137.* 5
123. 1	*128.* 2	*133.* 4	*138.* 3
124. 1	*129.* 5	*134.* 2	*139.* 1
125. 3	*130.* 1	*135.* 3	*140.* 3

Word Test 8 *(Page 115)*

141. 4	*146.* 3	*151.* 3	*156.* 1
142. 2	*147.* 4	*152.* 4	*157.* 3
143. 3	*148.* 2	*153.* 5	*158.* 2
144. 4	*149.* 5	*154.* 2	*159.* 5
145. 5	*150.* 1	*155.* 4	*160.* 4

Word Test 9 *(Page 116)*

161. 3	*166.* 4	*171.* 1	*176.* 1
162. 2	*167.* 1	*172.* 3	*177.* 5
163. 1	*168.* 1	*173.* 4	*178.* 1
164. 3	*169.* 5	*174.* 5	*179.* 2
165. 5	*170.* 3	*175.* 3	*180.* 1

Word Test 10 *(Page 118)*

181. 5	*186.* 1	*191.* 4	*196.* 1
182. 1	*187.* 1	*192.* 4	*197.* 3
183. 4	*188.* 2	*193.* 5	*198.* 2
184. 2	*189.* 2	*194.* 5	*199.* 5
185. 2	*190.* 3	*195.* 3	*200.* 4

Word Test 11 *(Page 119)*

201. 2	*206.* 5	*211.* 5	*216.* 1
202. 4	*207.* 1	*212.* 4	*217.* 4
203. 3	*208.* 4	*213.* 1	*218.* 4
204. 2	*209.* 1	*214.* 3	*219.* 2
205. 3	*210.* 2	*215.* 2	*220.* 1

Word Test 12 *(Page 121)*

221. 3	*226.* 5	*231.* 1	*236.* 3
222. 1	*227.* 1	*232.* 2	*237.* 5
223. 5	*228.* 4	*233.* 5	*238.* 1
224. 2	*229.* 3	*234.* 3	*239.* 2
225. 3	*230.* 3	*235.* 5	*240.* 3

Word Test 13 *(Page 122)*

241. 2	*246.* 3	*251.* 2	*256.* 2
242. 4	*247.* 1	*252.* 3	*257.* 5
243. 1	*248.* 1	*253.* 3	*258.* 2
244. 2	*249.* 3	*254.* 1	*259.* 3
245. 5	*250.* 5	*255.* 1	*260.* 5

Word Test 14 *(Page 124)*

261. 1	*266.* 3	*271.* 3	*276.* 3
262. 2	*267.* 3	*272.* 5	*277.* 3
263. 2	*268.* 1	*273.* 4	*278.* 1
264. 1	*269.* 5	*274.* 1	*279.* 2
265. 4	*270.* 2	*275.* 4	*280.* 1

Word Test 15 *(Page 125)*

281. 2	*286.* 5	*291.* 5	*296.* 2
282. 2	*287.* 2	*292.* 1	*297.* 2
283. 4	*288.* 4	*293.* 3	*298.* 1
284. 3	*289.* 5	*294.* 5	*299.* 5
285. 1	*290.* 3	*295.* 3	*300.* 5

Word Test 16 *(Page 127)*

301. 1	*306.* 2	*311.* 4	*316.* 1
302. 1	*307.* 1	*312.* 3	*317.* 5
303. 3	*308.* 5	*313.* 4	*318.* 1
304. 2	*309.* 1	*314.* 3	*319.* 3
305. 4	*310.* 2	*315.* 5	*320.* 2

Word Test 17 *(Page 128)*

321. 5	*326.* 5	*331.* 4	*336.* 3
322. 2	*327.* 3	*332.* 3	*337.* 2
323. 5	*328.* 3	*333.* 3	*338.* 3
324. 1	*329.* 1	*334.* 5	*339.* 2
325. 4	*330.* 4	*335.* 1	*340.* 3

Word Test 18 *(Page 130)*

341. 3	*346.* 3	*351.* 4	*356.* 3
342. 3	*347.* 5	*352.* 2	*357.* 4
343. 1	*348.* 2	*353.* 4	*358.* 5
344. 1	*349.* 1	*354.* 5	*359.* 2
345. 2	*350.* 1	*355.* 3	*360.* 1

Word Test 19 *(Page 131)*

361. 4	*366.* 1	*371.* 2	*376.* 1
362. 2	*367.* 1	*372.* 2	*377.* 2
363. 3	*368.* 3	*373.* 3	*378.* 1
364. 5	*369.* 1	*374.* 5	*379.* 2
365. 2	*370.* 4	*375.* 4	*380.* 5

Word Test 20 *(Page 133)*

381. 3	*386.* 1	*391.* 5	*396.* 5
382. 5	*387.* 1	*392.* 4	*397.* 3
383. 4	*388.* 3	*393.* 4	*398.* 3
384. 2	*389.* 2	*394.* 2	*399.* 4
385. 1	*390.* 2	*395.* 1	*400.* 5

Word Test 21 *(Page 134)*

401. 2	*406.* 4	*411.* 4	*416.* 2
402. 3	*407.* 1	*412.* 1	*417.* 4
403. 5	*408.* 1	*413.* 5	*418.* 2
404. 1	*409.* 4	*414.* 1	*419.* 4
405. 3	*410.* 2	*415.* 2	*420.* 1

Word Test 22 *(Page 136)*

421. 2	*426.* 1	*431.* 1	*436.* 3
422. 5	*427.* 5	*432.* 4	*437.* 5
423. 2	*428.* 5	*433.* 5	*438.* 2
424. 3	*429.* 2	*434.* 1	*439.* 1
425. 1	*430.* 3	*435.* 2	*440.* 4

Word Test 23 *(Page 137)*

441. 5	*446.* 2	*451.* 3	*456.* 3
442. 5	*447.* 5	*452.* 1	*457.* 4
443. 1	*448.* 2	*453.* 1	*458.* 3
444. 3	*449.* 1	*454.* 1	*459.* 3
445. 4	*450.* 3	*455.* 2	*460.* 5

Word Test 24 *(Page 139)*

461. 2	*466.* 5	*471.* 2	*476.* 1
462. 2	*467.* 1	*472.* 3	*477.* 1
463. 2	*468.* 1	*473.* 3	*478.* 2
464. 5	*469.* 1	*474.* 1	*479.* 5
465. 2	*470.* 4	*475.* 5	*480.* 1

Word Test 25 *(Page 140)*

481. 3	*486.* 2	*491.* 4	*496.* 4
482. 5	*487.* 1	*492.* 5	*497.* 3
483. 1	*488.* 2	*493.* 1	*498.* 3
484. 3	*489.* 3	*494.* 1	*499.* 1
485. 4	*490.* 3	*495.* 3	*500.* 2

Word Test 26 *(Page 142)*

501. 3	*506.* 1	*511.* 5	*516.* 1
502. 2	*507.* 5	*512.* 5	*517.* 2
503. 1	*508.* 3	*513.* 2	*518.* 1
504. 3	*509.* 1	*514.* 2	*519.* 1
505. 5	*510.* 1	*515.* 3	*520.* 4

Word Test 27 *(Page 143)*

521. 1	*526.* 4	*531.* 1	*536.* 4
522. 1	*527.* 2	*532.* 4	*537.* 1
523. 1	*528.* 2	*533.* 2	*538.* 1
524. 5	*529.* 1	*534.* 3	*539.* 1
525. 2	*530.* 3	*535.* 3	*540.* 4

Word Test 28 *(Page 145)*

541. 1	*546.* 2	*551.* 3	*556.* 2
542. 1	*547.* 4	*552.* 4	*557.* 4
543. 3	*548.* 4	*553.* 5	*558.* 5
544. 5	*549.* 2	*554.* 2	*559.* 5
545. 5	*550.* 1	*555.* 1	*560.* 2

Word Test 29 *(Page 146)*

561. 3	*566.* 1	*571.* 2	*576.* 2
562. 2	*567.* 4	*572.* 3	*577.* 1
563. 3	*568.* 1	*573.* 3	*578.* 2
564. 2	*569.* 1	*574.* 1	*579.* 2
565. 5	*570.* 4	*575.* 4	*580.* 5

Word Test 30 *(Page 148)*

581. 1	*586.* 5	*591.* 2	*596.* 2
582. 2	*587.* 2	*592.* 5	*597.* 5
583. 3	*588.* 4	*593.* 2	*598.* 4
584. 4	*589.* 1	*594.* 1	*599.* 1
585. 1	*590.* 2	*595.* 4	*600.* 3

Mathematics

9

Reviewing Mathematics

This chapter reviews the principles of elementary mathematics through plane geometry, since the PSAT/NMSQT attempts to find out how well these topics have been mastered. The drill is especially important since many students have not had recent experience with some of the ideas such as percents or fractions, and others have never really mastered these topics. However, with a few hints and a bit of practice students should be able to understand the basic concepts involved and put them to use.

Students who have just completed a course in plane geometry may find the exercises in this chapter different from the type they are used to, as these questions do more than check on knowledge. They often attempt to find out whether knowledge can be applied to new situations.

Some mathematics questions are designed to test reasoning and thinking. This chapter furnishes such problems within the framework of familiar topics as well as in special exercises such as evaluating information necessary to solve problems.

Another use of this chapter is to offer drill in a particular topic which may turn up as a weakness when the student attempts to do the sample tests in the latter part of this book.

TIPS FOR HANDLING REGULAR MATHEMATICS QUESTIONS

1. Read each question carefully. Know what the question is asking. Look at the answer choices to direct your attention to the purpose of the question. You may find that some of the answer choices are contrary to fact. As you eliminate those that are obviously wrong, you have fewer items from which to choose. Also, sometimes it is quicker to work back from the answers, but try the easiest choices first. Very often the test makers reward ingenuity.
2. Avoid lengthy computation. Bear in mind that the test is constructed so that the 50 math questions can be completed in 50 minutes. Should you find yourself involved in lengthy computation, you may be misreading the question or missing a shortcut. If you are dealing with a right triangle of the 3-4-5, 5-12-13, or 8-15-17 type, avoid lengthy computations involving the Pythagorean Theorem. Use your time wisely.
3. If you are answering a question that requires you to apply a formula not given to you (for example, the area or circumference of a circle or the sides of a 30°-60°-90° or 45°-45°-90° triangle), write the formula on the question paper to be sure you substitute it correctly.
4. Estimate your answer. Make sure you have chosen a reasonable answer. Give your answer the common-sense test.
5. Don't panic if you encounter a new type of question. It may be nothing more than a combination of familiar topics. If unusual symbols are used, replace them with the definitions that accompany them.
6. Don't expect to be able to answer all questions. Very few students do. Work carefully and accurately on the questions you can answer, and don't waste time worrying about the others.
7. If you skip a question, make sure to skip the corresponding number on the answer sheet.
8. Express your answer in the units required. In solving word problems, convert measurements to the same units. If the problem involves hours, minutes, and seconds and you observe that all the answer choices are in minutes, confine your calculations to minutes.
9. If you find that none of the answer choices resemble the answer you get, the equivalent of your answer may be there. For example,

$$\frac{a+b}{b} = \frac{a}{b} + 1.$$

10. If a geometry problem does not provide a figure, draw one. However, don't waste time making a work of art. No one looks at your scratchwork. If a diagram is furnished, mark it up to help you solve the problem. Also, look for diagrams marked NOT DRAWN TO SCALE. Don't make unwarranted assumptions.

11. Most questions will ask you to choose the one right answer from among five choices. In such questions, if you have spotted a choice you are sure is correct, do not waste time examining the other choices. However, a special type of question sometimes occurs in which several possibilities are presented within the question itself; these possibilities are always identified with Roman numerals I, II, and III. You are then asked to state whether I only is true, II only is true, I and II only are true, and so forth. In this type of question, you must examine *all* the possibilities since several of them (and maybe even all of them) may be correct.

12. Most questions present five possible choices, only one of which fits the requirements stated in the question. However, sometimes a special question is asked in which all *except* one of the choices fit the requirements stated in the question and you are asked to choose the one that is the exception. The examiners warn you of this reverse emphasis by printing the word EXCEPT in bold capital letters. In answering such a question, it is helpful to try to spot some common property that all but one choice share; for example, all but one may be even numbers, or all but one may be positive numbers.

13. Since each regular mathematics question provides five choices, a random guess is likely to be correct only $\frac{1}{5}$ of the time. But $\frac{1}{4}$ of a point is deducted for each wrong answer in the scoring. Therefore, it is unwise to make a random guess. However, if you can definitely rule out one choice, it is not foolhardy to make a guess from the remaining four choices since your odds for picking the right choice now equal the deduction cost for a wrong answer. If you can rule out more than one choce, it is definitely advisable to guess from among the remaining ones since the odds for picking the correct choice are greater than the deduction cost for a wrong answer.

A SUGGESTED STUDY PROGRAM

1. BASIC MATHEMATICS—Review the definitions, important principles, and fundamental operations.
2. ALGEBRA—Review the definitions and basic algebraic operations. Study the hints on solving problems. Do the practice exercises. Study the important facts about inequalities. Do the exercises.
3. GEOMETRY—Review the principles, formulas, and definitions. Study the rules involving coordinate geometry. Do the exercises.
4. FRACTIONS—Review the principles. Study the hints on solving problems. Do the practice exercises. Check your answers.
5. PERCENT—Study the hints on solving problems. Do the practice exercises. Check your answers.
6. AVERAGE—Study the principles. Do the practice exercises. Check your answers.
7. MOTION—Review the formulas. Study the hints on solving problems. Do the exercises. Check your answers.
8. RATIO AND PROPORTION—Study the principles and hints on solving problems. Be able to differentiate between direct and inverse proportions. Study the illustrative examples. Do the practice exercises. Check your answers.
9. WORK—Study the hints on solving problems. Do the practice exercises. Check your answers.
10. DATA INTERPRETATION—Study the explanations given. Do the practice exercises. Check your answers.
11. QUANTITATIVE COMPARISON (Chapter 10)—Study the format of this type of question. Study the hints on solving problems. Do the practice exercises. Check your answers.
12. Take the Sample Tests in Chapter 11. Correct your answers. Analyze the correct answers.

BASIC MATHEMATICS

SYMBOLS USED IN MATHEMATICS

$=$	equals	$\therefore$	therefore
$\neq$	not equal to	$\triangle$	triangle
$>$	more than	$\frown$	arc of circle
$<$	less than	$^\circ$	degree
$\geq$	greater than or equal to	$\angle$	angle
$\leq$	less than or equal to	$m\angle$	measure of the angle (degrees)
$\cong$	congruent	$\perp$	perpendicular
$\sim$	similar	$\parallel$	parallel
$\stackrel{\circ}{=}$	equals in degrees	$\pm$	plus or minus

Whole Numbers

Integers The numbers 0, 1, 2, 3, 4, 5, . . . are called POSITIVE INTEGERS; $7\frac{1}{2}$ is *not* an integer. WHOLE NUMBERS are 1, 2, 3, 4, 5, ...

Divisibility The number 12 divides by 4 evenly. We therefore say that 12 is divisible by 4 or that 4 is a FACTOR of 12. Besides 4, other factors of 12 are: 1, 2, 3, 6, and 12. Any whole number is divisible by itself and 1.

Prime Numbers A whole number greater than 1 which is divisible only by itself and 1 is a PRIME NUMBER; 2, 3, 5, 7, 11, and 13 are all prime. 14 is not prime since it is divisible by 2 and 7.

Odd and Even Numbers A whole number which is divisible by 2 is called an EVEN NUMBER. Other numbers are ODD NUMBERS.

Addition: Even + even = even; odd + odd = even; even + odd = odd.

Subtraction: Even − even = even; odd − odd = even; even − odd or odd − even = odd.

Multiplication: Even × even = even; odd × odd = odd; even × odd = even.

Division (assuming the quotient is an integer): odd ÷ odd = odd; even ÷ odd = even; even ÷ even can be even or odd [if the dividend has more factors of 2 than the divisor, the quotient is even; if the dividend has the same number of factors of 2 as the divisor, the quotient is odd: $36 \div 6 = (9 \times 2 \times 2) \div (3 \times 2) = 6$, but $36 \div 12 = (9 \times 2 \times 2) \div (3 \times 2 \times 2) = 3$].
If an odd number is divided by an even number, the quotient can never be a whole number.

Consecutive Numbers A collection of numbers is CONSECUTIVE if each number is the successor of the number which precedes it. For example, 7, 8, 9, 10 are consecutive, but 7, 8, 10, 13 are not. The following are examples of consecutive even numbers: 4, 6, 8, 10. The following are examples of consecutive primes: 7, 11, 13, 17. However, 7, 13, 19, 23 are not consecutive primes since 11 is a prime between 7 and 13.

Least Common Multiple (L.C.M.) The LEAST COMMON MULTIPLE of two numbers is the smallest number which is a common multiple of both numbers.

Real Numbers

The REAL NUMBERS, also called SIGNED NUMBERS, are *positive numbers*, *negative numbers*, or *zero*. Zero is neither positive nor negative. The following are real numbers: +3, −5, +6.3, −0.2, and $+\frac{2}{3}$. If no sign precedes a number, it may be assumed to be positive. Thus 3 may be considered +3.

Real numbers can be represented on a line. On a horizontal line a point is selected as a starting point (called the *origin*) and is designated by zero. A unit length is selected, and units marked off to the right of the origin are +1, +2, +3, +4, etc.; if this length is marked off to the left of the origin, we obtain points −1, −2, −3, −4, etc. Note the location of $+1\frac{1}{2}$ and $-2\frac{1}{2}$.

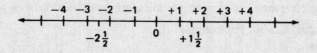

Absolute Value The absolute value of a signed number is the distance of that number from the origin (zero). Thus the value of any nonzero number is *positive*. The absolute value of -3 is 3; the absolute value of $+3$ is also 3.

Fundamental Operations

Addition To add numbers with the *same sign*, add their absolute values and write the result with the common sign.

$14 + 12 = 26$
$-8 + (-9) = -17$

To add numbers with *opposite signs*, find their absolute values, subtract the lesser absolute value from the greater, and then write the result with the same sign as that of the number with the greater absolute value. For example, to add -36 and $+14$, subtract 14 from 36 to get 22 and write the result as -22 since the -36 had the greater absolute value.

$+36 + (-14) = 22$
$-50 + 33 = -17$
$50 + (-33) = 17$
$16 + (-16) = 0$

To add *three or more numbers with different signs* you can, of course, combine them in the order given but it is simpler to add all the positives and all the negatives, and then combine the results. Thus, to add $-22 + 37 + 64 - 18 - 46 + 13 - 85$, we add $37 + 64 + 13 = 114$ and $-22 - 18 - 46 - 85 = -171$. Then we combine the results:

$-171 + 114 = -57$

Subtraction Subtraction is based on the following property:

$a - b = a + (-b)$

This means that subtracting a number is the same as adding its opposite. The number being subtracted is called the *subtrahend*, so to subtract signed numbers, simply change the sign of the subtrahend and add.

$27 - (-18) = 27 + 18 = 45$
$-37 - (-29) = -37 + 29 = -8$
$-26 - 14 = -26 + (-14) = -40$
$42 - (-42) = 84$
$-18 - 15 = -33$

Multiplication Multiply signed numbers by multiplying their absolute values. If the numbers have the same sign, write your answer with a positive sign. If their signs are opposite, write the answer with a negative sign.

$(-4)(-3) = 12$
$(12)(10) = 120$
$(+8)(-7) = -56$
$(-7)(16) = -112$

Division Division follows the same rule: divide absolute values and choose a positive sign for your answer if the original signs were the same, or use a negative sign if they were opposite:

$35 \div 7 = 5$
$-36 \div (-9) = 4$
$16 \div (-4) = -4$
$-27 \div 3 = -9$

Multiplication and Division Involving Fractions

Questions on the PSAT sometimes require knowing the consequences of multiplying or dividing by fractions.

If two positive numbers greater than 1 (they may be whole numbers or fractions such as $\frac{3}{2}$) are multiplied together, the product is greater than either of them. For example:

$2 \times 3 = 6$

If two positive numbers are multiplied together, and one is greater than 1 and the other is a fraction less than 1, the product is greater than one number and less than the other. For example:

$$4 \times \frac{1}{2} = 2$$

If two positive fractions, both less than 1, are multiplied together, the product is less than either of them. For example:

$$\frac{1}{2} \times \frac{1}{3} = \frac{1}{6}$$

If a positive number greater than 1 is divided by a positive fraction less than 1, the quotient is greater than either of them. For example:

$$4 \div \frac{1}{2} = 4 \times \frac{2}{1} = 8$$

If a positive fraction less than 1 is raised to a power, it becomes smaller; the higher the power, the smaller it becomes. For example:

$$\left(\frac{1}{2}\right)^2 = \frac{1}{4} \text{ and } \left(\frac{1}{2}\right)^3 = \frac{1}{8}$$

ALGEBRA

Some Important Facts

1. In algebra we use letters to represent numbers or sets of numbers. Such letters are called *variables*. When two variables, or a numeral and a variable, are written with no sign of operation between them, we mean that the numbers they represent are to be multiplied. Thus $4abc$ means $4 \times a \times b \times c$.
2. The *factors* of a product are two or more numbers or letters which when multiplied yield the product. For example, the factors of 12 are 4 and 3, and the factors of $2xy$ are 2, x, and y. The factors of $x^2 - y^2$ are $(x + y)$ and $(x - y)$.
3. The *coefficient* is any factor of a term. Ordinarily the numerical value that is multiplied by the other terms is called the coefficient. In the term $5xy$, the coefficient is 5.
4. The *exponent*, written as a small number or letter above and to the right of another number or letter, indicates how many times the number or letter is multiplied by itself: $b^4 = b \times b \times b \times b$.
5. An *equation* is an expression of equality between two quantities. Thus $5x = 20$ is an equation because $5x$ is equal to 20 only when $x = 4$.
6. A *root* of an equation is a number which satisfies an equation. In the preceding example, 4 is a root.
7. A *monomial* is an expression consisting of one term, such as $14ab$, $6x$, or xy.
8. A *binomial* is the sum or difference of two monomials, such as $2x + 4y$.
9. A *trinomial* has three terms, such as $9x^2 + 9xy - 4$.

Fundamental Operations

Addition and Subtraction Most algebraic additions and subtractions are carried out with the aid of a simple pattern known as the *distributive law:*

$$ab + ac = a(b + c)$$

or its corollary:

$$ab - ac = a(b - c).$$

When adding polynomials (more than 2 terms), arrange the like terms in vertical columns. For example, to add $3x^2 + 9x - 4$ and $-7x^2 - 4x + 8$, arrange your work as follows:

$$\begin{array}{r} 3x^2 + 9x - 4 \\ \underline{-7x^2 - 4x + 8} \\ -4x^2 + 5x + 4 \end{array}$$

When two polynomials are to be subtracted, arrange them in vertical columns according to like terms and change the sign of every term in the subtrahend. For example, to subtract $9x^2 - 3x - 5$ from $2x^2 + 3x - 8$, change the signs of the first polynomial to $-9x^2 + 3x + 5$, and then add:

$$\begin{array}{r} 2x^2 + 3x - 8 \\ \underline{-9x^2 + 3x + 5} \\ -7x^2 + 6x - 3 \end{array}$$

Multiplication To multiply monomials, multiply the coefficients and add the exponents of variables with the same base. For example:

$$(6x^2)(5x^4) = (6 \cdot 5)(x^2 \cdot x^4) = 30x^6$$

To multiply a polynomial by a monomial, multiply each term of the polynomial by the monomial. For example:

$$3x^2(5x^3 + 2x - 3y) = 15x^5 + 6x^3 - 9x^2y$$

To multiply a polynomial by a polynomial, multiply each term of one polynomial by each term of the other, and combine like terms.

A special case of multiplying polynomials is worth studying separately because of its use in factoring. To multiply a binomial by a binomial, note first how the pairs of terms are named:

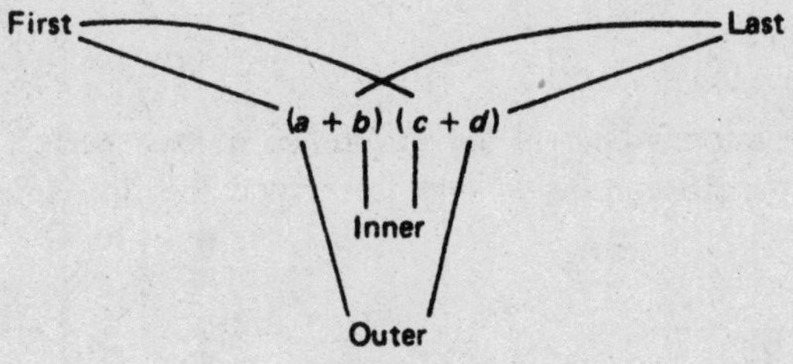

Multiply the binomials term by term in the order F, O, I, L. Frequently, the O and I terms combine to make the product a trinomial or a binomial. For example, to find the product of $3x^2 - 2x - 7$ and $2x - 4$:

$$\begin{array}{rrrrl} 3x^2 & - \; 2x & - \; 7 & & \\ & 2x & - \; 4 & & \\ \hline 6x^3 - & 4x^2 & - \; 14x & & \text{(Partial product when the multiplier is } 2x\text{)} \\ & - \; 12x^2 & + \; 8x & + \; 28 & \text{(Partial product when the multiplier is } -4\text{)} \\ \hline 6x^3 - & 16x^2 & - \; 6x & + \; 28 & \end{array}$$

Removing Parentheses Parentheses are used as grouping symbols and as indicators of multiplication. Often it is necessary to remove the parentheses to simplify expressions which have grouped terms. If the parentheses are preceded by a positive sign they may be removed with no further alteration necessary.

$$(x + y) + (3x - 2y) = x + y + 3x - 2y = x + 3x + y - 2y = 4x - y$$

If the parentheses are preceded by a negative sign, then they may be removed only if the signs of each term inside the parentheses are changed to the opposite sign.

$$(x + y) - (3x - 2y) = x + y - 3x + 2y = x - 3x + y + 2y = -2x + 3y$$
$$(3x^2 + 2x) - (4x^2 - 3x + 5) = 3x^2 + 2x - 4x^2 + 3x - 5 = -x^2 + 5x - 5$$

If the parentheses are preceded by a multiplier, carry out the multiplication first and then use one of the rules just mentioned.

$$(x + y) - 5(x + y) = (x + y) - (5x + 5y) = x + y - 5x - 5y = -4x - 4y$$
$$4(3x^2 + 2x) - 8(x^2 + 3x - 2) = (12x^2 + 8x) - (8x^2 + 24x - 16)$$
$$= 12x^2 + 8x - 8x^2 - 24x + 16 = 4x^2 - 16x + 16$$

When additional grouping symbols are needed, we use brackets, [ ], and braces, { }. If grouping symbols appear within other sets, remove one set at a time starting with the innermost.

$$4x - \{2x - 3[(x + 2) - (3 - x)]\} =$$
$$4x - \{2x - 3[x + 2 - 3 + x]\} =$$
$$4x - \{2x - 3[2x - 1]\} =$$
$$4x - \{2x - 6x + 3\} = 4x - \{-4x + 3\} = 4x + 4x - 3 = 8x - 3$$

Division To divide a monomial by a monomial, divide the coefficients algebraically and subtract exponents of factors which have the same base.

$$x^6 \div x^2 = x^{6-2} = x^4$$
$$-15x^6y^3 \div 3x^2y = \frac{-15}{3}x^{6-2}y^{3-1} + -5x^4y^2$$
$$-18x^3yz^2 \div (-6xyz) = \frac{-18}{-6}x^{3-1}y^{1-1}z^{2-1} = 3x^2z$$

(Note that $y^0 = 1$ as long as y is any number except 0.)

To divide a polynomial by a monomial, divide each term of the dividend by the divisor.

$$(-18x^4 - 6x^3 + 2x^2) \div 2x^2 =$$

$$\frac{-18x^4 - 6x^3 + 2x^2}{2x^2} = \frac{-18x^4}{2x^2} + \frac{-6x^3}{2x^2} + \frac{2x^2}{2x^2} = -9x^2 - 3x + 1$$

Factoring

To factor an expression is to find two or more expressions whose product is the given expression. An expression or a number is *prime* if it does not have any factors except itself and one.

Type 1. To factor a polynomial which has a common monomial factor, find the largest monomial which will divide into each term of the polynomial. This is one factor. Divide the polynomial by this factor to obtain the other factor.

Factor: $4x^3y^3 - 22xy^2$

$2xy^2(2x^2y - 11)$

Type 2. To factor an expression which is the difference of two perfect squares, find the square root of each term. The sum of the two square roots is one factor and the difference of the two square roots is the other factor.

Factor: $x^2 - 64$

$(x + 8)(x - 8)$

Type 3. Trinomials of the form: $ax^2 + bx + c$

The factors are two binomials where (a) the product of the first terms of both binomials equals the first term of the trinomial; (b) the product of the last terms of both binomials equals the last term of the trinomial; and (c) the algebraic sum of the cross products of these terms equals the middle term of the trinomial.

Factor: $x^2 + 8x + 12$

$(x + 6)(x + 2)$

(a)	(b)	(c)
$\begin{array}{r} x + 6 \\ \underline{x + 2} \\ x^2 \end{array}$	$\begin{array}{r} x + 6 \\ \underline{x + 2} \\ + 12 \end{array}$	$\begin{array}{r} x + 6 \\ \underline{x + 2} \\ + 6x \\ \underline{+ 2x} \\ + 8x \end{array}$

Factor: $x^2 - 6x + 8$

$(x - 4)(x - 2)$

(a)	(b)	(c)
$\begin{array}{r} x - 4 \\ \underline{x - 2} \\ x^2 \end{array}$	$\begin{array}{r} x - 4 \\ \underline{x - 2} \\ + 8 \end{array}$	$\begin{array}{r} x - 4 \\ \underline{x - 2} \\ - 4x \\ \underline{- 2x} \\ - 6x \end{array}$

Factor: $x^2 - 3x - 10$

$(x - 5)(x + 2)$

(a)	(b)	(c)
$\begin{array}{r} x - 5 \\ \underline{x + 2} \\ x^2 \end{array}$	$\begin{array}{r} x - 5 \\ \underline{x + 2} \\ - 10 \end{array}$	$\begin{array}{r} x - 5 \\ \underline{x + 2} \\ - 5x \\ \underline{+ 2x} \\ - 3x \end{array}$

Roots of Numbers

Some Important Facts

1. The *square root* of a number is one of its two equal factors. The square root of 100 is +10, since $(+10)(+10) = 100$. Also -10 is the square root of 100, since $(-10)(-10) = 100$. Thus every number has two square roots.
2. The *principal square root* is its positive square root. It is indicated by writing a radical sign ($\sqrt{\ }$) in front of the number. Thus $\sqrt{100} = +10$.

3. A *negative square root* is indicated by a minus sign in front of the radical. Thus $-\sqrt{100}$ means the negative square root of 100.
4. A *radical* is an indicated root of a number or expression. The index of the root is written as a small number above the radical sign. Thus $\sqrt[3]{8}$ where the index is 3, means the cube root of 8, which is 2 since $(2)(2)(2) = 8$. Where no index is written, as in $\sqrt{100}$, the number 2 is understood. Thus $\sqrt{100}$ means $\sqrt[2]{100}$.
5. A *rational* number is a number which can be expressed as the ratio of two integers. Thus, $2\frac{1}{3}$ is a rational number since $2\frac{1}{3} = \frac{7}{3}$.
6. An *irrational* number is a number which cannot be expressed as the RATIO of two integers. Thus, $\sqrt{5}$ is an irrational number.
7. To add or subtract, like radicals are combined. To add or subtract unlike radicals, change them to like radicals. To simplify a radical, separate into two factors, one of which is a perfect square. Thus, to simplify $\sqrt{98}$, write it as $\sqrt{49}\ \sqrt{2}$, which equals $7\sqrt{2}$.

   EXAMPLES:

   $2\sqrt{5} + 5\sqrt{5} = 7\sqrt{5}$

   $6\sqrt{3} - 3\sqrt{3} = 3\sqrt{3}$

   $\sqrt{50} + \sqrt{2}$ can be written as $\sqrt{25}\sqrt{2} + \sqrt{2}$, *or* $5\sqrt{2} + \sqrt{2}$ *or* $6\sqrt{2}$

   $3\sqrt{27} + \sqrt{108}$ can be written as $3\sqrt{9}\sqrt{3} + \sqrt{36}\sqrt{3}$ *or* $(3)(3)\sqrt{3} + 6\sqrt{3}$ *or* $9\sqrt{3} + 6\sqrt{3}$ *or* $15\sqrt{3}$

   $4\sqrt{32} - 6\sqrt{8}$ can be written as $4\sqrt{16}\sqrt{2} - 6\sqrt{4}\sqrt{2}$ *or* $(4)(4)\sqrt{2} - (6)(2)\sqrt{2}$ *or* $16\sqrt{2} - 12\sqrt{2}$ *or* $4\sqrt{2}$
8. To multiply radicals, the product of the square roots of two expressions is equal to the square root of the product of the two expressions. Thus, $(\sqrt{2})(\sqrt{8}) = \sqrt{16} = 4$.

   EXAMPLES:

   $(\sqrt{18})\ (\sqrt{2}) = \sqrt{36} = 6$

   $(2\sqrt{8})\ (3\sqrt{18}) = 6\sqrt{144} = (6)\ (12) = 72$

   $\left(\frac{2}{3}\sqrt{3}\right)(9\sqrt{27}) = \left(\frac{2}{3}\right)\left(\frac{9}{1}\right)(\sqrt{81}) = \left(\frac{2}{3}\right)\left(\frac{9}{1}\right)\left(\frac{9}{1}\right) = 54$

   $\left(\frac{1}{3}\sqrt{8}\right)(3\sqrt{2}) = \left(\frac{1}{3}\right)\left(\frac{3}{1}\right)(\sqrt{16}) = \left(\frac{1}{3}\right)\left(\frac{3}{1}\right)\left(\frac{4}{1}\right) = 4$

   $\left(\frac{1}{25}\sqrt{5}\right)(5\sqrt{5}) = \left(\frac{1}{25}\right)\left(\frac{5}{1}\right)(\sqrt{25}) = \left(\frac{1}{25}\right)\left(\frac{5}{1}\right)\left(\frac{5}{1}\right) = 1$
9. To divide radicals, the quotient of the square roots of two expressions is equal to the square root of the quotient of the two expressions. Thus $\sqrt{32} \div \sqrt{2} = \sqrt{16} = 4$.

   EXAMPLES:

   $\sqrt{75} \div \sqrt{3} = \sqrt{25} = 5$

   $21\sqrt{162} \div 7\sqrt{2} = 3\sqrt{81} = (3)(9) = 27$

   $\frac{25\sqrt{32}}{5\sqrt{2}} = 5\sqrt{16} = (5)(4) = 20$

   $24\sqrt{10} \div 3\sqrt{10} = (8)(1) = 8$

   $\frac{1}{3}\sqrt{27} \div \frac{1}{3}\sqrt{3} = \left(\frac{1}{3}\right)\left(\frac{3}{1}\right)(\sqrt{9}) = 3$

Solving Equations

Some Important Facts

1. An *equation* is an expression of equality between two quantities. Thus $4x = 20$ is an equation because $4x$ is equal to 20 only when $x = 5$.
2. A *root* of an equation is a number which satisfies an equation. In the equation $4x = 20$, the root is 5.
3. Some equations have more than one root. In the equation, $x^2 - 7x + 12 = 0$, the roots are 4 and 3.
4. An equation is not put out of balance if an arithmetic process done to one-half of the equation is also done to the other half of the equation. We may

   add a quantity
   subtract a quantity
   multiply by a quantity

divide by a quantity
raise to a higher power
extract square root, cube root, etc.,

provided the process is applied to both sides of the equation.

EXAMPLES:

Solve for x.
$x - 4 = 12$
Add 4 to both sides of the equation:
$x = 16$

Solve for x.
$4x - 5 = 3x + 2$
Add 5 to both sides of the equation:
$4x = 3x + 7$
Subtract $3x$ from both sides of the equation:
$x = 7$

Solve for x.
$\frac{x}{4} = 12$
Multiply both sides of the equation by 4:
$x = 48$

Solve for x.
$4x = 12$
Divide both sides of the equation by 4:
$x = 3$

Solve for x.
$3\sqrt{x + 2} - 3 = 4$
Add 3 to both sides of the equation:
$3\sqrt{x + 2} = 7$
Square both sides of the equation:
$9(x + 2) = 49$
Remove the parentheses:
$9x + 18 = 49$
Subtract 18 from both sides of the equation:
$9x = 31$
Divide both sides of the equation by 9:
$x = \frac{31}{9} = 3\frac{4}{9}$

Solve for x.
$\sqrt{x^2 - 4} = 4 - x$

Solve for x.
$x + 4 = 12$
Subtract 4 from both sides of the equation:
$x = 8$

Square both sides of the equation:
$(\sqrt{x^2 - 4})^2 = (4 - x)^2$ or
$x^2 - 4 = 16 - 8x + x^2$
Subtract x^2 from both sides of the equation:
$-4 = 16 - 8x$
Add $8x$ to both sides of the equation:
$8x - 4 = 16$
Add 4 to both sides of the equation:
$8x = 20$
Divide both sides of the equation by 8:
$x = \frac{20}{8}$ or $2\frac{1}{2}$

Solve for x.
$\sqrt{3x - 1} = 2$
Square both sides of the equation:
$(\sqrt{3x - 1})^2 = (2)^2$
$3x - 1 = 4$
Add 1 to both sides of the equation:
$3x = 5$
Divide both sides of the equation by 3:
$x = \frac{5}{3}$ or $1\frac{2}{3}$

Solve for x.
$\sqrt{\frac{x}{b}} = a^2$
Square both sides of the equation:
$\left(\sqrt{\frac{x}{b}}\right)^2 = (a^2)^2$
$\frac{x}{b} = a^4$
Multiply both sides of the equation by b:
$x = a^4b$

▶ PRACTICE EXERCISE

1. If $a = \frac{1}{2}$, $b = \frac{2}{3}$ and $c = \frac{3}{4}$, what is the value of $\frac{2a + 3b}{c}$?
   (A) $\frac{1}{4}$ (B) $1\frac{1}{2}$ (C) $2\frac{1}{4}$ (D) 3 (E) 4

2. Which of the following is the equivalent of $\frac{4(O - P) - 8P}{6P - 2O}$?
   (A) −3 (B) −2 (C) 0 (D) 1 (E) 2

3. One-half a number is 17 more than one-third of that number. What is the number?
   (A) 52 (B) 84 (C) 102 (D) 112 (E) 204

4. In which, if any, of the following can the 2's be cancelled out without changing the value of the expression?
   (A) $2x - 2m$ (B) $\frac{\frac{x}{2}}{\frac{2}{m}}$ (C) $\frac{2x - m}{2}$
   (D) $\frac{x^2}{m^2}$ (E) none of these

5. $\frac{1}{y} = \sqrt{.16}$; $y = ?$
(A) .25 (B) .4 (C) 2.5 (D) 4 (E) 10

6. $7x - 5y = 13$
$2x - 7y = 26$
$5x + 2y = ?$
(A) 39 (B) −39 (C) 13 (D) −13 (E) 19.5

7. $-\frac{1}{7}$ and 0 are the roots of which of the following equations?
(A) $7x^2 - 3x = 0$ (B) $7x^2 + 3 = 0$
(C) $7x^2 - 3 = 0$ (D) $7x^2 + x = 0$
(E) $7x + 3 = 0$

8. $3r - 2s = 0$; $\frac{9r^2}{s^2} = ?$
(A) $\frac{1}{4}$ (B) 1 (C) 4 (D) 9 (E) $\frac{81}{4}$

9. $\frac{y}{s-t} = \frac{s+t}{t-s}$; $y = ?$
(A) $-s-t$ (B) $t-s$ (C) $t+s$ (D) $s-t$
(E) $t^2 - s^2$

10. $\frac{a}{b} = c$; $b = c$. Find b in terms of a.
(A) a (B) b (C) $\pm\sqrt{b}$ (D) $\pm\sqrt{a}$
(E) $\pm\sqrt{ac}$

11. $\frac{1}{\frac{1}{N}} \div \frac{1}{N} = ?$
(A) 1 (B) $\frac{1}{N^2}$ (C) $\frac{1}{N}$ (D) N (E) N^2

12. $\frac{a+b}{a-b} \div \frac{b+a}{b-a} = ?$
(A) +1 (B) −1 (C) ±1 (D) $a^2 - b^2$
(E) $b^2 - a^2$

13. $3x + 10 = 9x - 20$
$(x+5)^2 = ?$
(A) 5 (B) 10 (C) 15 (D) 25 (E) 100

14. $a = \frac{ax}{1-x}$
$x = ?$
(A) $\frac{1}{2}$ (B) 1 (C) 2 (D) a (E) $2a$

15. If $x\sqrt{.16} = 2$, then x equals
(A) $\frac{1}{2}$ (B) 4 (C) 5 (D) 10 (E) 50

16. $\sqrt{x^2y^2 - y^2}$ equals
(A) $x - 1$ (B) $y\sqrt{x^2 - 1}$ (C) $y(x^2 - 1)$
(D) $(x^2 - 1)\sqrt{y}$ (E) $xy - y$

17. If $x^2 = 5$, then $6x^6$ equals
(A) 30 (B) 90 (C) 180 (D) 750 (E) 900

18. $17xy + 7 = 19xy$
$4xy = ?$
(A) 2 (B) 3 (C) $3\frac{1}{2}$ (D) 7 (E) 14

19. The expression a^x means that a is to be used as a factor x times. Therefore, if a^x is squared, the result is
(A) $a^{(x2)}$ (B) a^{2x} (C) $2a^{2x}$ (D) $2a^x$ (E) $2ax^n$

20. $2x - 4y = -10$
$5x - 3y = 3$
$3x - 6y = ?$
(A) $\frac{3}{5}$ (B) $\frac{2}{3}$ (C) −7 (D) 15 (E) −15

Solving Problems by Equations

Many types of problems may be solved very easily by using the equation. The following five steps will be very useful.

Hints on Solving Problems

1. Read the problem carefully to determine the unknown quantity. Indicate this quantity by a letter.
2. If more than one unknown quantity is obtained, express each quantity in terms of the *same* letter.
3. From the statement of the problem, determine a relationship which may be written as an equation.
4. Solve this equation.
5. Check your result by applying the answer to the original statement.

EXAMPLES:

If 4 is subtracted from one-fourth of a number, the result is 20. Find the number.

Let x = the number.

$\frac{1}{4}x - 4 = 20$ [equation]

$x - 16 = 80$ [multiplying both sides by 4]

$x = 96$ [adding 16 to both sides]

Check: $\frac{1}{4}$ of 96 = 24; 24 − 4 = 20

Find two consecutive numbers whose sum is 43.

Let x = first number.

$$\begin{aligned} x + 1 &= \text{second number} \\ x + x + 1 &= 43 \quad \text{[equation]} \\ 2x + 1 &= 43 \quad \text{[combining terms]} \\ 2x &= 42 \quad \text{[subtracting 1 from both sides]} \\ x &= 21 \quad \text{[dividing both sides by 2]} \\ x + 1 &= 22 \end{aligned}$$

Check: $21 + 22 = 43$

A rectangular box is to be 4 feet long and 2 feet wide. How high must it be to have a volume of 24 cubic feet?
Use formula: $V = lwh$

Substituting values: $24 = 4 \cdot 2 \cdot h$

$$\begin{aligned} 24 &= 8h \\ h &= 3 \end{aligned}$$

The cost of a new highway was $88,000. The township agreed to pay twice as much as the state, and the county was to pay 4 times as much as the township. How much did each pay?
Let x = amount paid by state.

$$\begin{aligned} 2x &= \text{amount paid by township} \\ 8x &= \text{amount paid by county} \\ x + 2x + 8x &= 88{,}000 \\ 11x &= 88{,}000 \\ x &= \$8{,}000 \quad \text{(state)} \\ 2x &= \$16{,}000 \quad \text{(township)} \\ 8x &= \$64{,}000 \quad \text{(county)} \end{aligned}$$

Mr. Smith, who is 28 years of age, has a son who is 4 years old. In how many years will Mr. Smith be 4 times as old as his son?
Let x equal the time needed to reach the desired age ratio. At that time, the son will be $4 + x$ years old and the father will be $28 + x$ years old.

$$\begin{aligned} 4(4 + x) &= 28 + x \quad \text{[equation]} \\ 16 + 4x &= 28 + x \quad \text{[removing parentheses]} \\ 3x &= 12 \\ x &= 4 \end{aligned}$$

Check: In four years, Mr. Smith will be 32 years old and his son will be 8 years old. The father will be four times as old as his son.

PRACTICE EXERCISE

1. How many cents are there in $2x - 1$ dimes?
(A) $10x$ (B) $20x - 10$ (C) $19x$ (D) $\frac{2x-1}{10}$
(E) $\frac{x}{5} - 1$

2. How many nickels are there in c cents and q quarters?
(A) $\frac{c}{5} + 5q$ (B) $5(c + q)$ (C) $5c + \frac{q}{5}$
(D) $\frac{c+q}{5}$ (E) $c + 25q$

3. How many days are there in w weeks and w days?
(A) $7w^2$ (B) 7 (C) $8w$ (D) $14w$ (E) $7w$

4. How many pupils can be seated in a room with s single seats and d double seats?
(A) sd (B) $2sd$ (C) $2(s + d)$ (D) $2d + s$
(E) $2s + d$

5. A classroom has r rows of desks with d desks in each row. On a particular day when all pupils are present 3 seats are left vacant. The number of pupils in this class is
(A) $dr - 3$ (B) $d + r + 3$ (C) $dr + 3$
(D) $\frac{r}{d} + 3$ (E) $\frac{d}{r} + 3$

6. A storekeeper had n loaves of bread. By noon he had s loaves left. How many loaves did he sell?
(A) $s - n$ (B) $n - s$ (C) $n + s$ (D) $sn - s$
(E) $\frac{n}{s}$

7. A man has d dollars and spends s cents. How many dollars has he left?
(A) $d - s$ (B) $s - d$ (C) $100d - s$
(D) $\frac{100d - s}{100}$ (E) $\frac{d - s}{100}$

8. How much change (in cents) would a woman receive if she purchases p pounds of sugar at c cents per pound after she gives the clerk a one-dollar bill?
(A) $100 - p - c$ (B) $pc - 100$ (C) $100 - pc$
(D) $100 - p + c$ (E) $pc + 100$

9. Sylvia is two years younger than Mary. If Mary is m years old, how old was Sylvia two years ago?
(A) $m + 2$ (B) $m - 2$ (C) $m - 4$
(D) $m + 4$ (E) $2m - 2$

10. A storekeeper sold n articles at $\$D$ each and thereby made a profit of r dollars. The cost to the storekeeper for each article was
(A) $Dn - r$ (B) $D(n - r)$ (C) $\frac{Dn - r}{n}$
(D) $\frac{D(n - r)}{n}$ (E) $\frac{Dn + r}{n}$

Inequalities

Some Important Facts

When one expression is greater than or is less than another expression, we have an inequality. The following symbols are generally used in dealing with inequalities: $>$ for greater than, $<$ for less than, $\neq$ for not equal to, $\geqq$ for greater than or equal to, and $\leqq$ for less than or equal to. Thus, if a number is followed by < 0, we have a negative quantity.

Rules useful in handling problems involving inequalities follow.

1. If equal quantities are added to unequal quantities, the resulting sums are unequal in the same order. If $x > y$ then $x + a > y + a$ and since $9 > 6$ then $11 > 8$.
2. If unequal quantities are added to unequal quantities of the same order, the resulting sums are unequal in the same order. Since $5 > 3$ and $9 > 6$ then $14 > 9$. If $x > y$ and $a > b$ then $x + a > y + b$.
3. If equal quantities are subtracted from unequal quantities, the results are unequal in the same order. Since $25 > 22$, then $20 > 17$. If $x > y$, then $x - a > y - a$.
4. If unequal quantities are subtracted from equal quantities, the remainders are unequal in the opposite order. Since $25 = 25$ and $5 > 3$, then $20 < 22$. If $x = y$ and $a > d$, then $x - a < y - d$.
5. If inequalities are multiplied by *positive* numbers, the order remains the same. If $x > y$ and $z > 0$, then $xz > yz$. However, if inequalities are multiplied by *negative* numbers the order is reversed. If $x > y$ and $z < 0$ then $xz < yz$.
6. If the first of three quantities is greater than the second and the second is greater than the third, then the first is greater than the third. Since $12 > 9$ and $9 > 7$, then $12 > 7$. If $a > b$ and $b > c$, then $a > c$.
7. The whole is greater than any of its parts. If point P lies on line segment AB, then $AB > AP$ and $AB > BP$.
8. A straight line is the shortest distance between two points. In a triangle, the sum of two sides of the triangle is greater than the third side. Also, a perpendicular drawn from a point to a line is the shortest distance from the point to the line.
9. An exterior angle of a triangle is greater than either remote (nonadjacent) interior angle.
10. If two angles of a triangle are unequal, the sides opposite these angles are unequal, and the greater side lies opposite the greater angle.

▶ PRACTICE EXERCISE

1. If $x = y$ and $a < b$, then
(A) $a + x = b + y$ (B) $a + x < b + y$
(C) $a + x > b + y$ (D) $a + x = b$
(E) $a + x = y$

2. If $a < b$ and $c < d$, then
(A) $ac = bd$ (B) $a = d$ (C) $b = c$
(D) $a + c > b + d$ (E) $a + c < b + d$

3. If $k < m$ and $x = y$, then
(A) $k - x > m - y$ (B) $k + x = m + y$
(C) $k - x < m - y$ (D) $k + y = m + x$
(E) $kx = my$

4. If $a = b$ and $x > y$, then
(A) $a - x = b - y$ (B) $a - x > b - y$
(C) $a - x < b - y$ (D) $a + x = b + y$
(E) $a + y = b + x$

5. If $x < y$, $z = \frac{x}{2}$, and $a = \frac{y}{2}$, then
(A) $z > a$ (B) $a > z$ (C) $a = z$ (D) $2a > y$
(E) $2x > 2z$

6. If $K > L$ and $x = K$, then
(A) $x = L$ (B) $x < L$ (C) $K + x < L + x$
(D) $2x < L + x$ (E) $L < x$

7. If $A < B$, $x = 2A$, and $y = 2B$, then
(A) $x = 2B$ (B) $x = A + B$ (C) $x < y$
(D) $x + y > 2A + 2B$ (E) $y = A + B$

8. If $a > b$, $b > c$, and $c > d$, then
(A) $a > d$ (B) $a < d$ (C) $a < c$ (D) $c < d$
(E) $a < b$

9. If $KL > AB$ and $LM > BC$, then

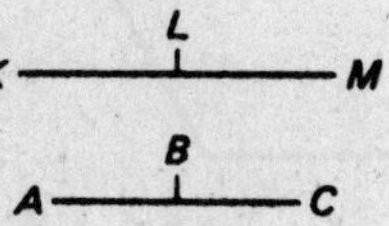

(A) $AC > KM$ (B) $KM > AC$
(C) $KL + LM < AB + BC$
(D) $KL + BC = LM + AB$
(E) $KL + AB = LM + BC$

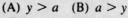

10. If $3x - 4 > 8$, then
(A) $x = 4$ (B) $x = 0$ (C) $x = 4, 0$
(D) $x > 4$ (E) $x < 4$

11. If $x > y > 1$, then
(A) $y + x > 2x$ (B) $x^2 < xy$ (C) $x - y < 0$
(D) $x < y + 1$ (E) $x^2 > y^2$

12. If $2y > 5$, then
(A) $y > 2.5$ (B) $y < 2.5$ (C) $y = 2.5$
(D) $y = 10$ (E) $y = 5$

13. In $\triangle ABC$, K is a point on AB and L is a point on AC, such that $KB = LC$ and $AC > AB$. Which of the following is true?

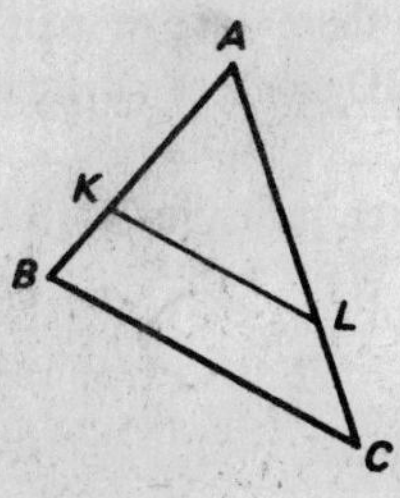

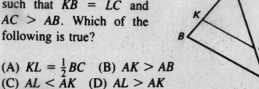

(A) $KL = \frac{1}{2}BC$ (B) $AK > AB$
(C) $AL < AK$ (D) $AL > AK$
(E) $AC < AL$

14. If C is the midpoint of AB, and F is the midpoint of DE, and $AC > FE$, then

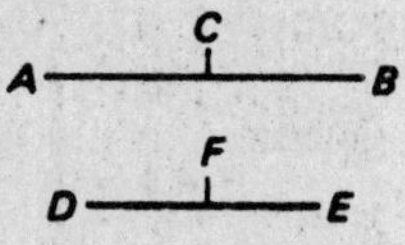

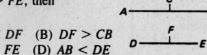

(A) $AC < DF$ (B) $DF > CB$
(C) $AC = FE$ (D) $AB < DE$
(E) $AC + CB > DF + FE$

15. Which of the following true for $\triangle ABC$? (diagram drawn to scale)
(A) $AC < AB$
(B) $BC = AC$
(C) $AC > BC$
(D) $BC > AC$
(E) $AB + BC < AC$

16. LM of $\triangle KLM$ is extended to N. All of the following are true except

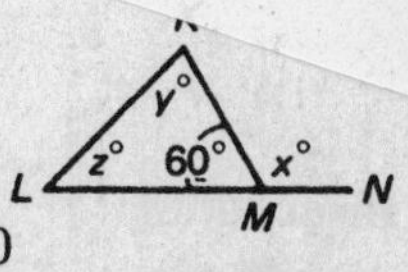

(A) $x = 120$ (B) $y + z = 120$
(C) $x = y + z$ (D) $x < y$
(E) $x > z$

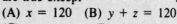

17. In $\triangle ABC$ (not drawn to scale) AD is an angle bisector, and $AC > DC$. Which of the following is true?

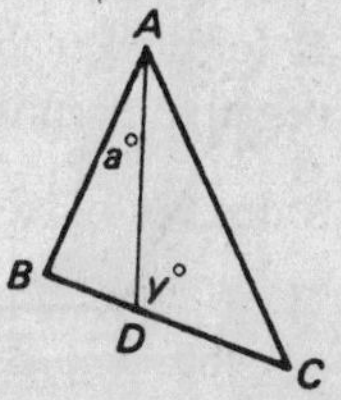

(A) $y > a$ (B) $a > y$
(C) $y + a = 90$
(D) $y = 2a$ (E) $2a = 180 - y$

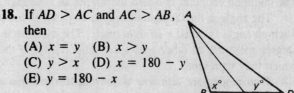

18. If $AD > AC$ and $AC > AB$, then

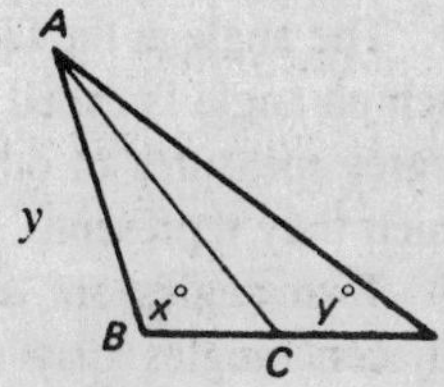

(A) $x = y$ (B) $x > y$
(C) $y > x$ (D) $x = 180 - y$
(E) $y = 180 - x$

19. In the accompanying diagram (not drawn to scale) $AB = AE$ and $BC > ED$, then

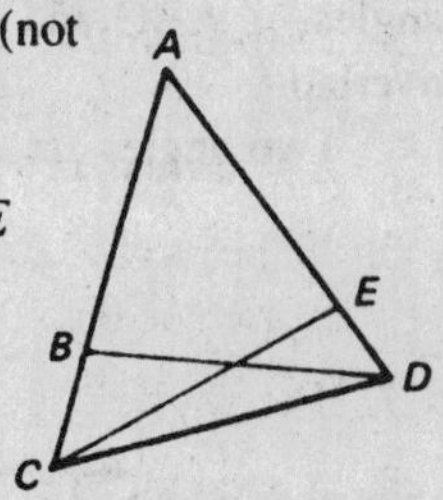

(A) $AC < BC$ (B) $BC > AE$
(C) $AC > AD$
(D) $AE + ED = AB + BC$
(E) $AC < AD$

20. In $\triangle KLM$, $KM > KL$, and MN and LO are angle bisectors, then

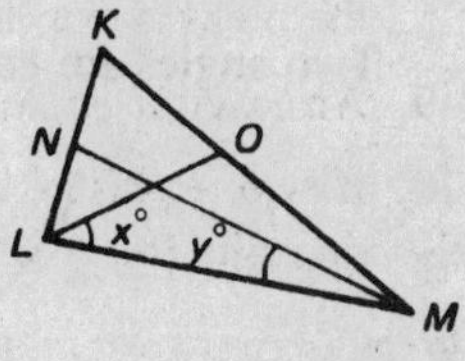

(A) $x + y = 60$
(B) $x = 0$
(C) $x < y$ (D) $x > y$
(E) none of these is correct

GEOMETRY

Some Important Facts

Points, Lines, and Planes

The building blocks of geometry are points, lines, and planes. A point indicates a position and has no length, width, or thickness. A line is a continuous set of points which is straight, infinitely long in two opposite directions, and has no width or thickness. A plane is a flat surface which extends in all directions but has no thickness.

Most geometric figures are formed by joining parts of lines—either line segments or rays. A line segment has two points of a line as endpoints and contains all points of the line which lie between the endpoints. A ray has one point of a line as an endpoint and contains all of the points which lie on a given side of the line.

ings, these figures appear like this:

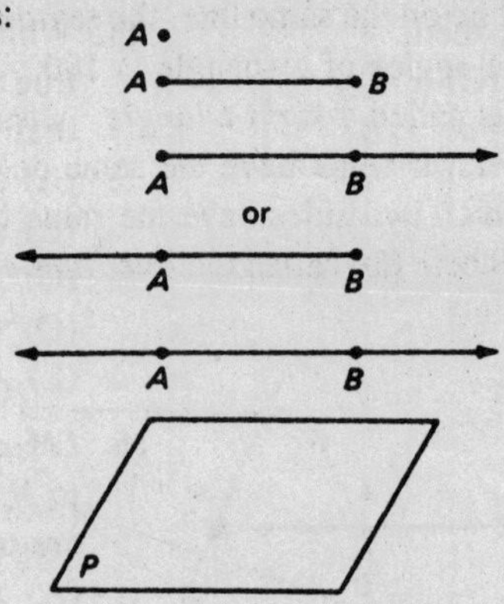

Angles and Triangles

If two different rays have the same endpoint, they form an angle.

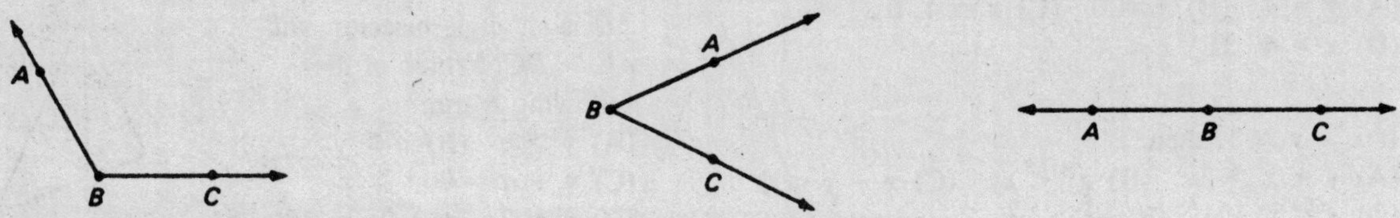

The common endpoint is called the *vertex* and the rays are called the *sides*.

The angle at the far right above has rays which are opposite to each other and is really no different from a line. Such an angle is called a *straight angle*. The measure in degrees of a straight angle is 180. Degree measures of other angles are proportional to the fractional part of a straight angle which they represent.

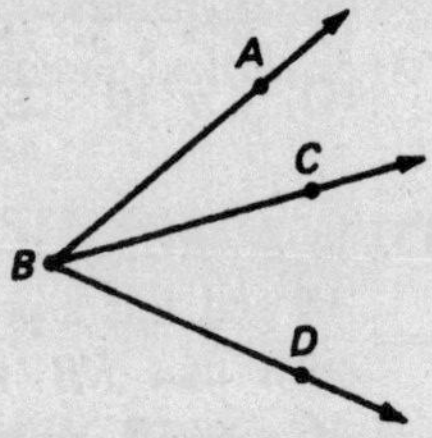

Two angles are *adjacent* if they have the same vertex and share a common side. Adjacent angles may not overlap. In the figure shown, there is one pair of adjacent angles, ∠ ABC and ∠ CBD. Note that ∠ ABC and ∠ ABD are not adjacent since they overlap.

Two angles are *supplementary* if the sum of their degree measures is 180.

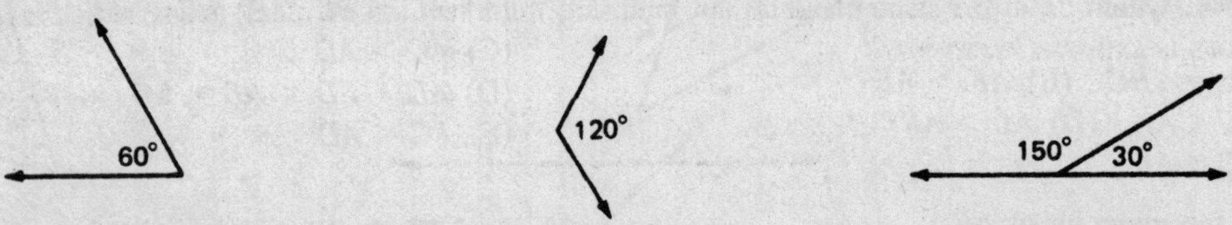

Two angles are *complementary* if the sum of their degree measures is 90.

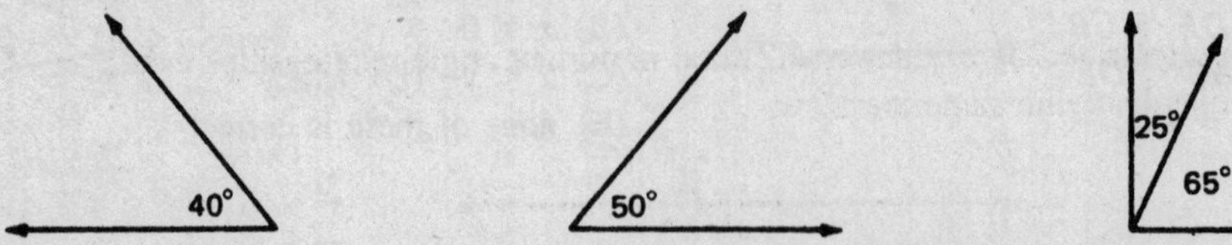

Note that two angles do not have to be adjacent to be supplementary or complementary.

An angle is a right angle if its measure is 90. Note that two adjacent right angles have sides which form a line.

If two lines intersect to form right angles the lines are *perpendicular*.

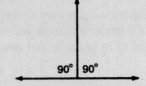

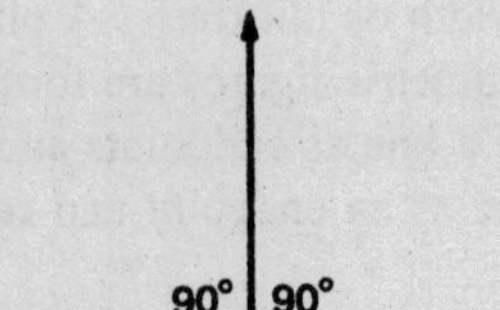

If three points of a plane do not all lie on the same line, the segments which connect these points form a triangle. The sum of the degree measures of the angles of a triangle is 180.

If a triangle has a right angle, it is called a *right triangle*. A triangle is *equilateral* if all sides have the same length. All of the angles of an equilateral triangle have the same degree measure, 60.

An *isosceles triangle* is one in which two sides have the same length. The angles opposite the sides of equal length have the same degree measure. These are called the *base angles*, and the side of the triangle which they share is called the *base* of the isosceles triangle.

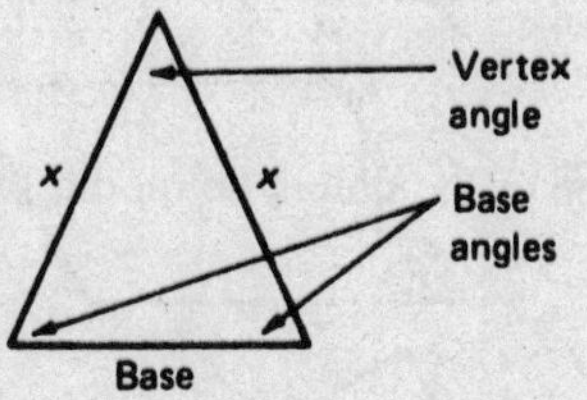

The altitude to the base of an isosceles triangle bisects the base and bisects the vertex angle.

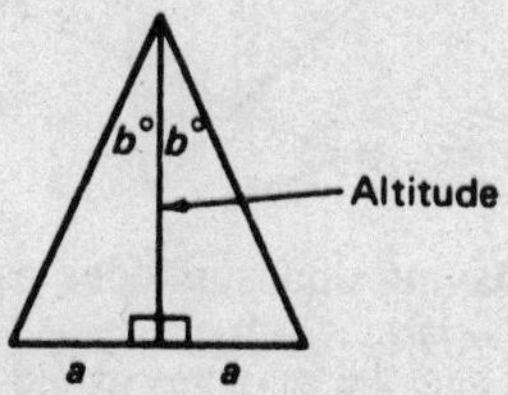

Line-Angle Relationships

Two intersecting lines form two pairs of vertical angles. Note that ∠ 1 and ∠ 2 are vertical angles, and ∠ *a* and ∠ *b* are vertical angles.

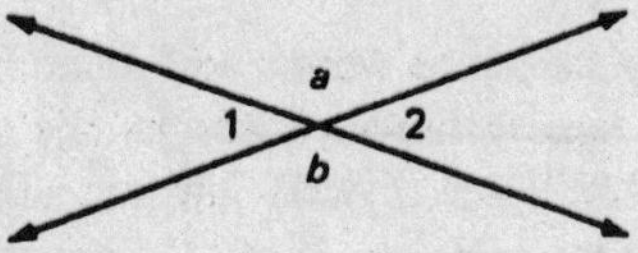

Vertical angles have the same degree measure.

If two lines which lie in the same plane do not intersect, then they are *parallel*. A line which intersects a pair of parallel lines is called a *transversal*.

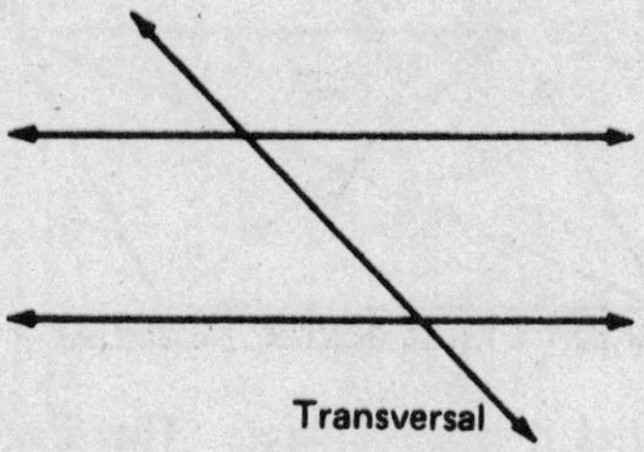

If a pair of parallel lines is intersected by a transversal, three important angle relationships exist:

(1) Alternate interior angles have the same measure:

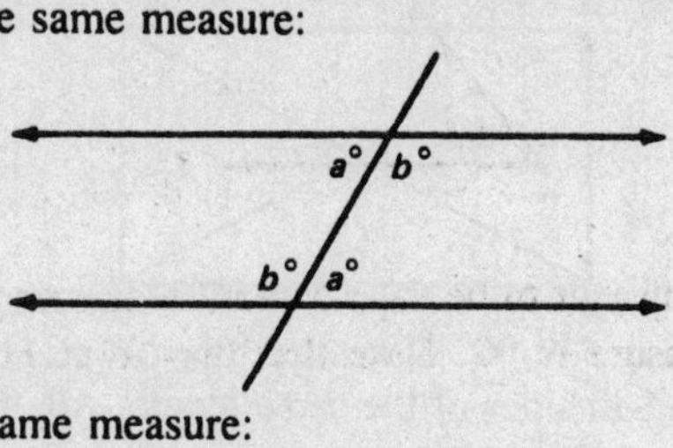

(2) Corresponding angles have the same measure:

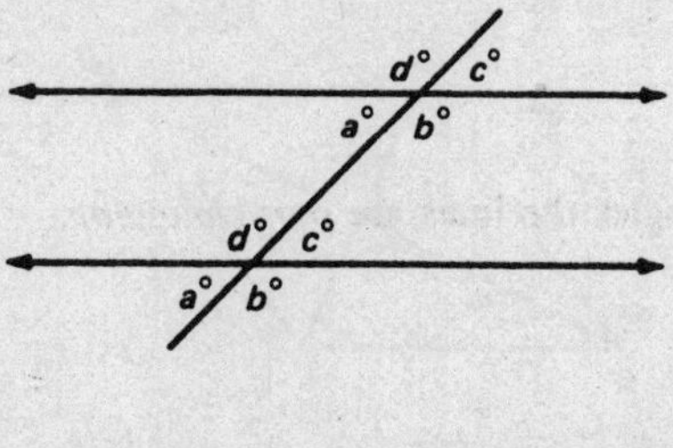

(3) Interior angles on the same side of the transversal are supplementary:

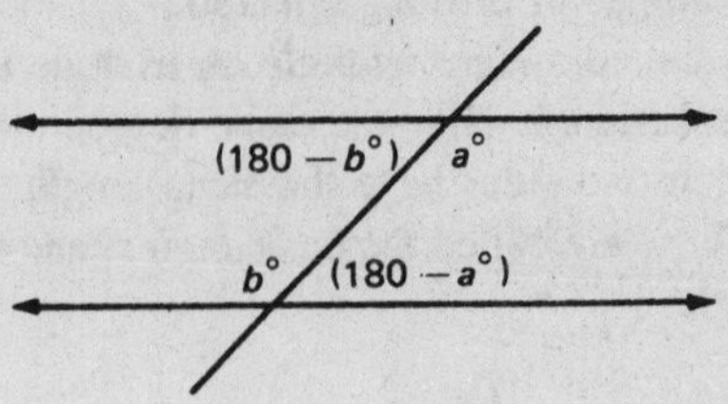

Quadrilaterals

If four points lie in a plane and no three of the points lie on the same line, the segments which connect these points form a quadrilateral.

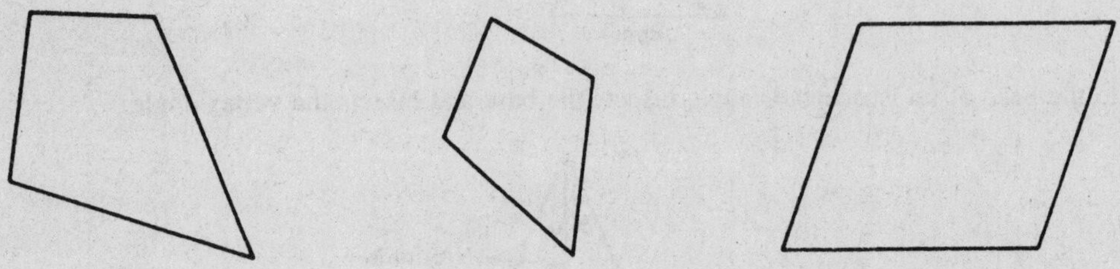

A *parallelogram* is a quadrilateral having opposite sides parallel. The opposite sides of a parallelogram are also equal in length. In the figure below, *AD* is parallel to and equal to *BC*; *AB* is parallel to and equal to *DC*.

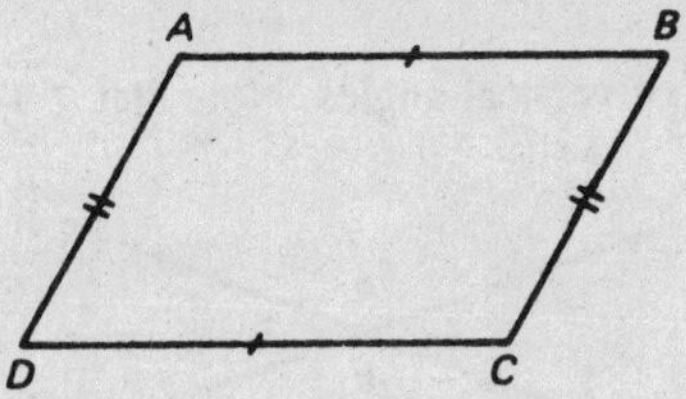

The opposite angles of a parallelogram have the same measure. $\angle A$ has the same measure as $\angle C$; $\angle B$ has the same measure as $\angle D$.

The diagonals of a parallelogram bisect each other. In the following figure; $AE = EC$ and $BE = ED$.

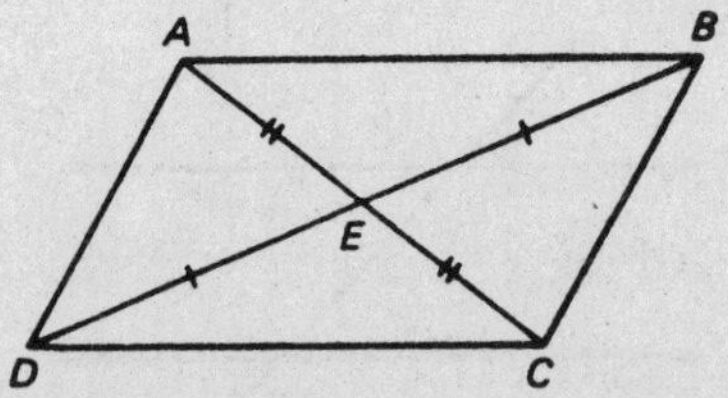

If a parallelogram has four right angles it is a *rectangle*. The diagonals of a rectangle are equal in length. $AC = BD$.

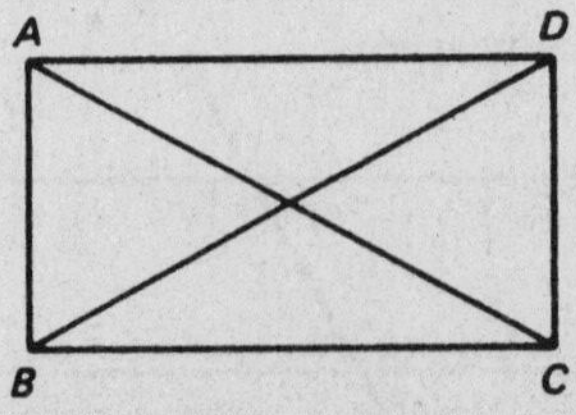

A rhombus is a parallelogram having all sides of the same length. $AB = BC = CD = AD$. The diagonals of a rhombus are perpendicular to each other. $AC \perp BD$.

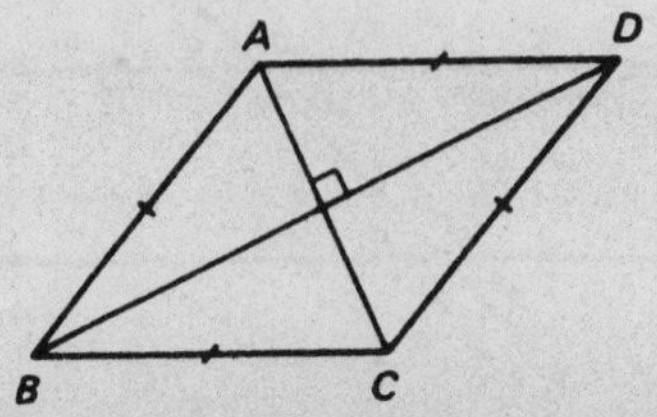

A *square* is a rectangle having all sides of the same length. Thus it has all of the properties of a parallelogram, a rectangle, and a rhombus.

A *trapezoid* is a quadrilateral having one pair of sides parallel (the *bases*) and the other pair nonparallel (the *legs*). *AD* is parallel to *BC*.

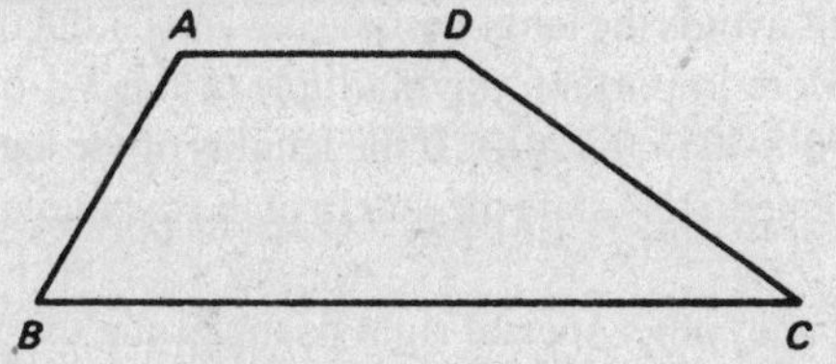

Angle-Circle Relationships

A *circle* is determined by a point and a positive number. The set of all points in a plane which are the given number of units away from the given point is a circle. The given point is its center, the given number its radius.

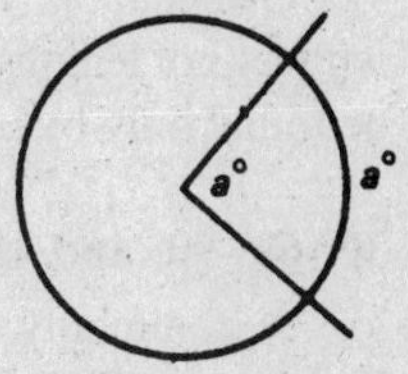

A *central angle* of a circle is an angle whose vertex is the center of the circle. The measure of the arc cut off by the central angle is the same as the measure of the angle.

An *inscribed angle* of a circle is an angle whose vertex is a point of the circle and whose sides intersect two other points of the circle. The measure of an inscribed angle is half the measure of the arc it cuts off. If an angle is inscribed in a semicircle, it must be a right angle.

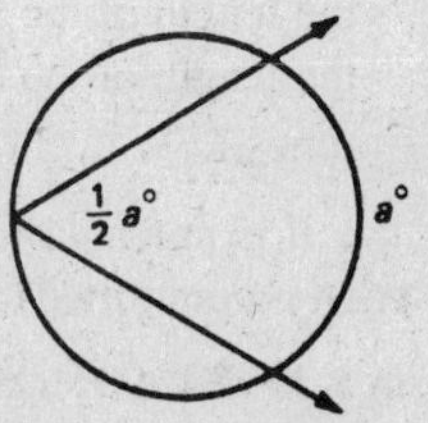

Relationships Among the Sides of Triangles

Two triangles are *similar* if all of their pairs of corresponding angles have the same measure. Roughly speaking, triangles are similar if they have the same shape but not necessarily the same size.

Corresponding sides of similar triangles are proportional.

$$\frac{AB}{A'B'} = \frac{AC}{A'C'} = \frac{BC}{B'C'}$$

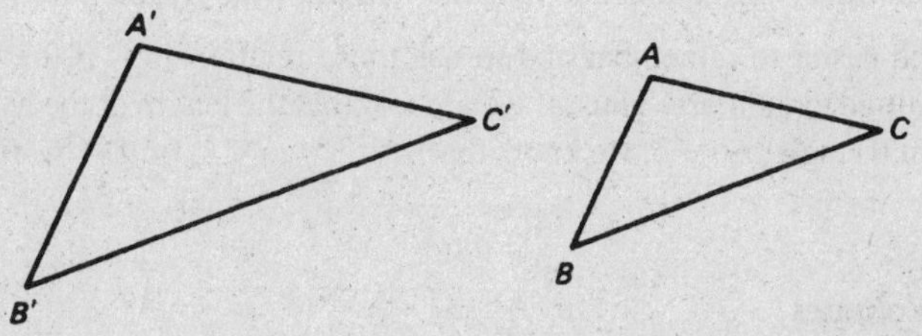

The relationship known as the Pythagorean Theorem states: In a right triangle the square of the length of the hypotenuse is equal to the sum of the squares of the lengths of the legs.

$$(\text{leg})^2 + (\text{leg})^2 = (\text{hypotenuse})^2$$

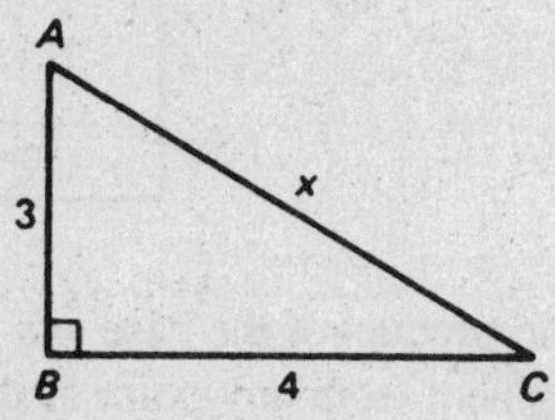

If the triangle shown above is a right triangle, then:

$$(3)^2 + (4)^2 = x^2$$
$$9 + 16 = x^2$$
$$25 = x^2$$
$$5 = x$$

3-4-5, 5-12-13, and 8-15-17 Right Triangles

The calculation above involves a special right triangle with sides of lengths 3, 4, and 5 (5 being the hypotenuse); such triangles occur frequently so that it is worth memorizing the 3-4-5 right triangle combination. Thus, if one leg of a right triangle is known to be of length 3 and the hypotenuse is known to be of length 5, it can immediately be concluded that the remaining leg is of length 4; this avoids the lengthy squaring and taking of a square root that direct application of the Pythagorean Theorem requires. More important, any multiple of the 3-4-5 lengths will also be the lengths of the sides of a right triangle, for example, 6-8-10 or 9-12-15. If the lengths of the legs of a right triangle are known to be 12 and 16, this principle can be used to immediately state the length of the hypotenuse: Since $12 = 4(3)$ and $16 = 4(4)$, the hypotenuse must be 4(5) or 20.

In addition to the 3-4-5 right triangle, other special right triangles are the 5-12-13 and the 8-15-17. They may be used in calculations as illustrated above for the 3-4-5 right tirangle.

One caution: The hypotenuse must always be the longest side in a right triangle. Thus, if a right triangle is given with legs of lengths 5 and 13, it is *not* a 5-12-13 right triangle and the length of its hypotenuse is *not* 12; that length can be found only by using the Pythagorean Theorem: $(5)^2 + (13)^2 = x^2$.

30°-60°-90° and 45°-45°-90° Triangles

A commonly used triangle is one whose angles are 30°, 60°, and 90°. By the use of trigonometry and the Pythagorean Theorem it can be shown that:

the length of the leg opposite the 30° angle equals one-half the length of the hypotenuse;
the length of the leg opposite the 60° angle equals one-half the length of the hypotenuse times $\sqrt{3}$.

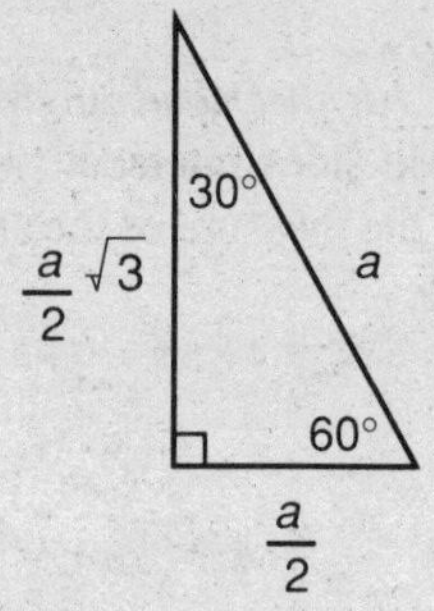

It is much easier to remember and to use these relationships if the diagram at the right is committed to memory. Thus, if we are told that the length of the side opposite 30° in a 30°-60°-90° triangle is 10, we know that $\frac{a}{2} = 10$, or $a = 20$. Therefore, we know immediately that the length of the hypotenuse, a, is 20, and that the length of the side opposite 60°, $\frac{a}{2}\sqrt{3}$, is $10\sqrt{3}$.

Another commonly used triangle is the isosceles right triangle, whose angles are 45°, 45°, and 90°. It can be shown by the use of the Pythagorean Theorem that:

the length of the hypotenuse equals the length of a leg times $\sqrt{2}$;
the length of either leg equals one-half the length of the hypotenuse times $\sqrt{2}$.

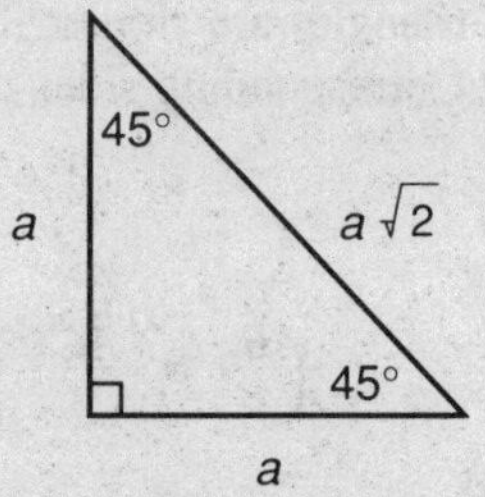

It is much easier to remember and to use these relationships if the diagram at the right is committed to memory. Thus, if we are told that the length of the hypotenuse of an isosceles right triangle is $6\sqrt{2}$, we know that $a\sqrt{2} = 6\sqrt{2}$, or $a = 6$. Hence each leg, a, equals 6.

Areas and Volumes

The area of a rectangle is the product of the length and the width. If the length is 4 and the width is 8, the area is $4 \times 8 = 32$.

$$A = lw = 4 \times 8 = 32$$

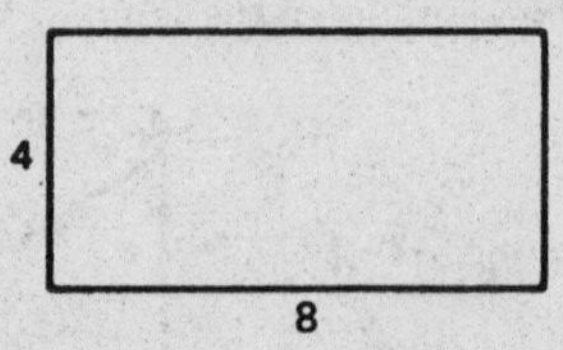

The area of a parallelogram is the product of the base and the altitude to that base. Any side can be used for the base. The altitude to the base is a segment from any point of the opposite side drawn perpendicular to the line containing the base.

$$A = bh = 4 \times 8 = 32$$

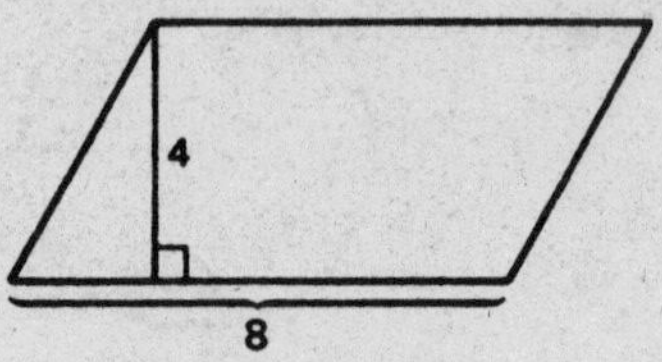

The area of a triangle is equal to one-half the product of a base and the altitude to that base. Any side may be a base. The altitude to the base is the segment from the vertex opposite to the base and perpendicular to the line containing the base.

$A = \frac{1}{2} \times 4 \times 8 = 16$

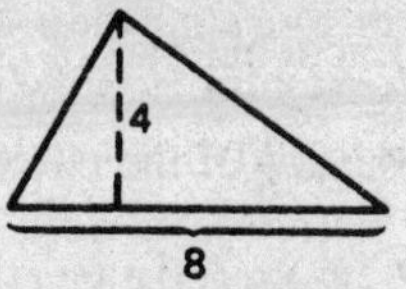

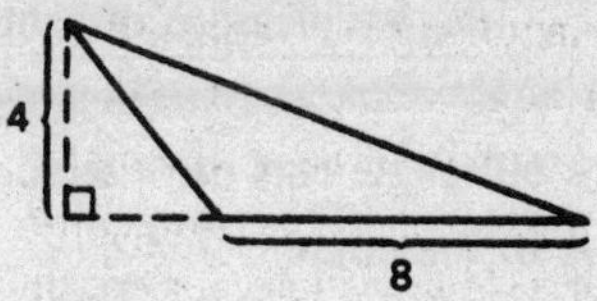

The area of a right triangle is one-half the product of the legs.

$A = \frac{1}{2} \times 4 \times 8 = 16$

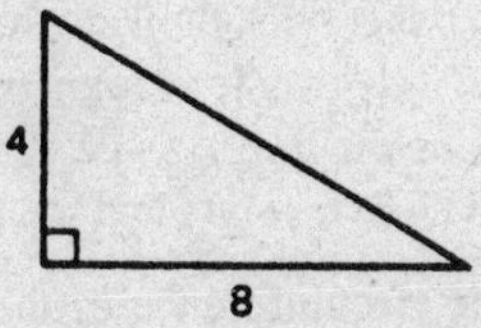

The area of a square is the square of the length of one of its sides.

$A = 4^2 = 16$

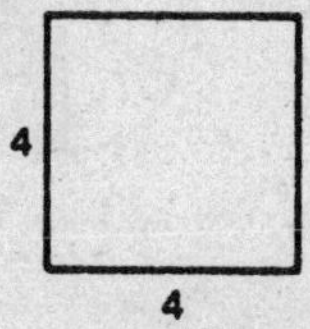

The area of a square is also equal to one-half the square of the length of its diagonal.

$A = \frac{1}{2} \times 8^2 = 32$

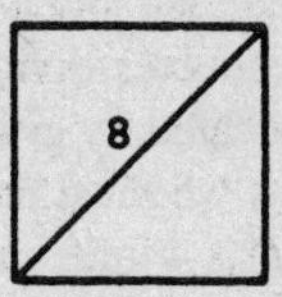

The ratio of the areas of two similar figures is equal to the square of the ratio of any two corresponding linear parts (sides, altitudes, medians, or angle bisectors).

$$\frac{\text{area } \triangle ABC}{\text{area } \triangle A'B'C'} = \left(\frac{5}{10}\right)^2 = \frac{1}{4}$$

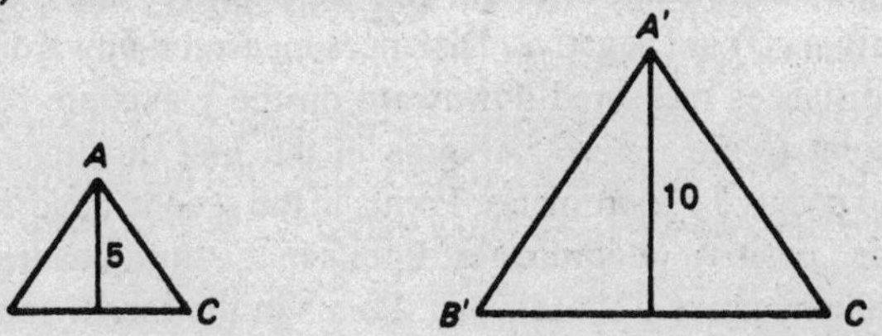

The circumference of (sometimes referred to as the "distance around") a circle is the product of the diameter and π. $C = \pi d$ or $C = 2\pi r$, if r is the radius.

$C = 2 \times \pi \times 5 = 10\pi$

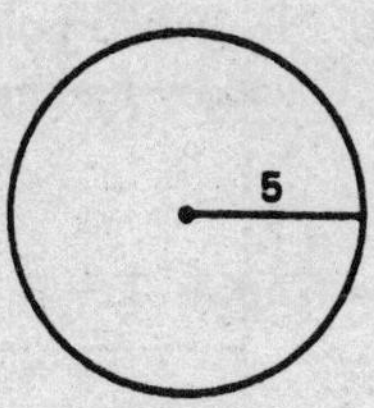

The area of a circle is equal to the product of π and the square of the radius. $A = \pi r^2$.

$A = \pi \times 5^2 = 25\pi$

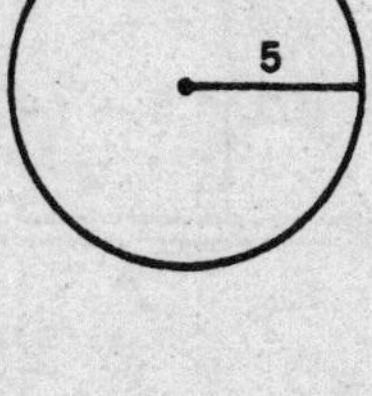

A *sector* of a circle is a pie-shaped region bounded by a central angle and the arc it cuts off. Each sector of a circle represents some fractional part of the circular region. This fractional part can be found by formula.

$$\frac{\text{degree measure of central angle}}{360} = \text{fractional part of circle}$$

Hence a 60° angle cuts off a sector which represents $\frac{1}{6}$ of the circle, and a 150° angle determines a sector which is $\frac{150}{360}$ or $\frac{5}{12}$ of the circle.

To find the area of the sector, find the area of the circle and multiply by the fractional part.

$$A = \frac{1}{4} \times \pi \times 5^2 = \frac{25\pi}{4}$$

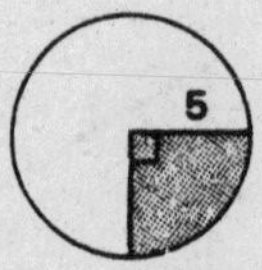

To find the arc length of a sector, find the circumference of the circle and multiply by the fractional part.

$$\text{Arc length} = \frac{1}{4} \times 2\pi \times 5 = \frac{5\pi}{2}$$

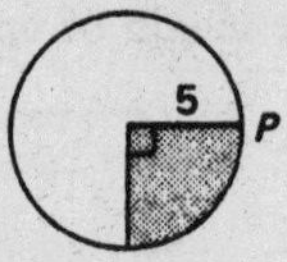

Coordinate Geometry

Coordinate geometry uses principles from algebra to solve geometric problems. In coordinate geometry two lines, called *axes*, are drawn perpendicular to each other (XX' and YY'), and their point of intersection O is called the *origin*. The horizontal line (XX') is called the *abscissa* and is referred to as the x-axis, and the vertical line (YY') is the *ordinate* and is referred to as the y-axis. These axes divide the plane into four quadrants.

Locating Points The position of point P is located by giving the point two coordinates, of which the first is the number of units we must move on the x-axis to come vertically under or above the point. (Point P is 4 units on the x-axis.) The other coordinate indicates how many units we must move up or down on the y-axis to become level with the point. (Point P is 5 units on the y-axis.) Distances measured to the right of the point of origin (O) are positive, and distances measured to the left of origin (O) are negative. Distances measured upward on the y-axis are positive, and distances measured downward on the y-axis are negative. The coordinates of point Q are -4, -5. Points in the first quadrant have positive x coordinates and positive y coordinates. Points in the second quadrant have negative x coordinates and positive y coordinates. Points in the third quadrant have negative x coordinates and negative y coordinates. Points in the fourth quadrant have positive x coordinates and negative y coordinates.

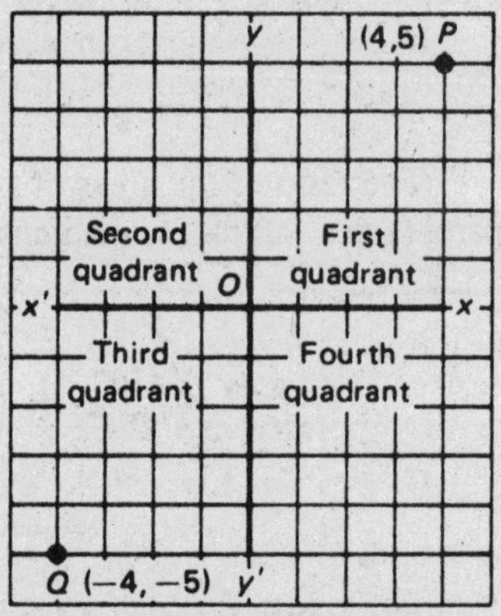

Finding the Distance Between Two Points 1. If two points have their abscissas on a line parallel to the x-axis, the distance is calculated by finding the difference between the abscissas.

$$\text{Length of } AB = 7 - 3 = 4$$

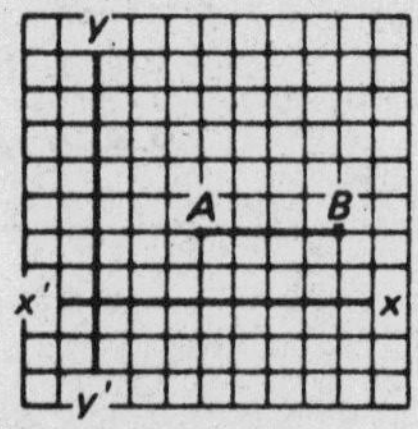

2. If two points have their ordinates on a line parallel to the y-axis, the distance is calculated by finding the difference between the ordinates.

$$\text{Length of } CD = 5 - (-3) = 8$$

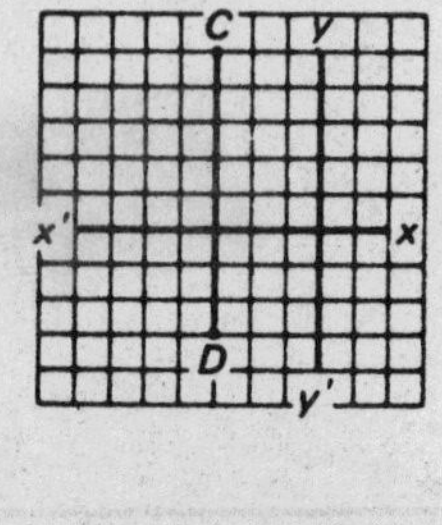

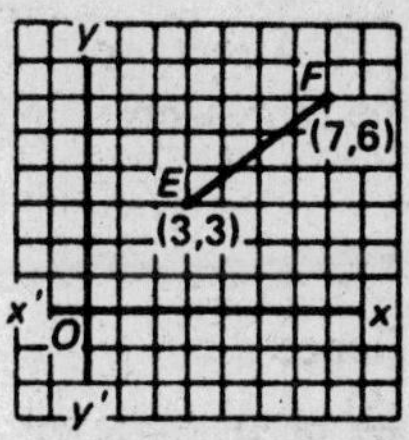

3. In all other cases, apply the formula:

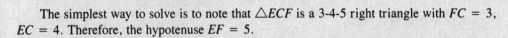

$$\text{distance} = \sqrt{(\text{diff. bet. abscissas})^2 + (\text{diff. bet. ordinates})^2}$$

$$\text{or} \quad \sqrt{(\text{diff. bet. ordinates})^2 + (\text{diff. bet. abscissas})^2}$$

To find the distance of *EF*:

$$EF = \sqrt{(7-3)^2 + (6-3)^2}$$
$$= \sqrt{4^2 + 3^2} \text{ or } \sqrt{25} \text{ or } 5$$
$$\text{or } EF = \sqrt{(6-3)^2 + (7-3)^2}$$
$$= \sqrt{3^2 + 4^2} \text{ or } \sqrt{25} \text{ or } 5$$

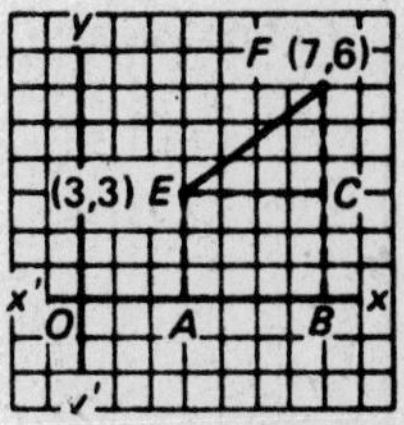

Draw *EA* and *FB* ⊥ *x*-axis. Draw *EC*.
Coordinates of *C* are (7, 3).
Length of *EC* = 4; length of *FC* = 3
∴ by the Pythagorean Theorem, *EF* = 5.

The simplest way to solve is to note that $\triangle ECF$ is a 3-4-5 right triangle with $FC = 3$, $EC = 4$. Therefore, the hypotenuse $EF = 5$.

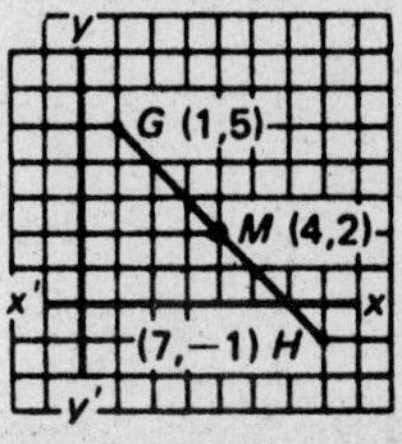

Finding the Midpoint of a Line Segment **The coordinates of the midpoint of a line segment are one-half the sums of the coordinates of the end points. The coordinates of the midpoints of the line segment which joins point $G(1, 5)$ and point $H(7, -1)$ are $\frac{1}{2}(1 + 7)$ *or* 4, and $\frac{1}{2}[5 + (-1)]$ or $\frac{1}{2}(4)$ *or* 2. Therefore $M(4, 2)$ is the midpoint of *GH*.**

Finding the Slope of a Line The slope of a line passing through two points whose coordinates are known is the difference in the *y*-coordinates divided by the difference in the *x*-coordinates.

In the graph above, the slope of the line joining $G(1,5)$ to $H(7,-1)$ is

$$\frac{5-(-1)}{1-7} \text{ or } \frac{5+1}{-6} \text{ or } \frac{6}{-6} \text{ or } -1.$$

A Summary of Important Relationships in Geometry

Right Triangles

In a right triangle, $(\text{leg})^2 + (\text{leg})^2 = (\text{hypotenuse})^2$, or $a^2 + b^2 = c^2$ (Pythagorean Theorem).

Special right triangles have sides in the ratio 3-4-5, or 5-12-13, or 8-15-17, with the longest side in each case representing the hypotenuse.

In a 30°-60°-90° triangle:

the length of the leg opposite the 30° angle equals one-half the length of the hypotenuse;

the length of the leg opposite the 60° angle equals $\frac{1}{2}$ the length of the hypotenuse times $\sqrt{3}$;

the ratio of the shorter leg to the hypotenuse is 1:2.

The relationships can be learned and applied by memorizing the diagram:

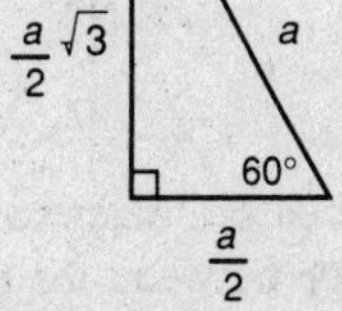

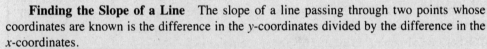

In a 45°-45°-90° triangle:

the length of the hypotenuse equals the length of a leg times $\sqrt{2}$;

the length of the leg equals $\frac{1}{2}$ the length of the hypotenuse times $\sqrt{2}$.

The relationships can be learned and applied by memorizing the diagram:

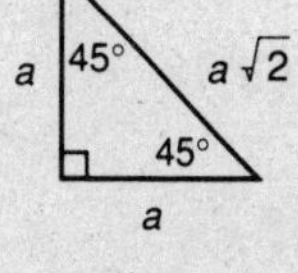

Equilateral Triangles

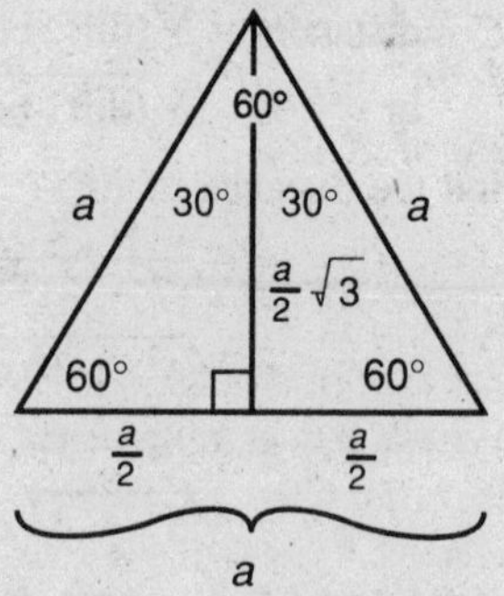

Each angle of an equilateral triangle has a measure of 60°. Each altitude of an equilateral triangle coincides with a median and an angle bisector, and its length equals $\frac{1}{2}$ the side times $\sqrt{3}$.

Areas of Polygons

Area of a rectangle $= bh$.
Area of a square $= s^2$.
Area of a parallelogram $= bh$.
Area of a triangle $= \frac{1}{2}bh$.
Area of a right triangle $= \frac{1}{2}\text{leg} \times \text{leg}$.
Area of a trapezoid $= \frac{1}{2}h(b_1 + b_2)$, where h is the altitude and b_1 and b_2 are the lengths of the bases.
Area of a rhombus $= \frac{1}{2}d_1d_2$, where d_1 and d_2 are the lengths of the diagonals.

Circles

The circumference of a circle $= \pi D$ or $2\pi r$.
Length of an arc $= \frac{n}{360} \times 2\pi r$.
Area of a circle $= \pi r^2$

Coordinate Geometry

Distance between two points $= \sqrt{(x_1 - x_2)^2 + (y_1 - y_2)^2}$
Coordinates of midpoint of line $= \frac{1}{2}(x_1 + x_2), \frac{1}{2}(y_1 + y_2)$
Slope of a line $= \frac{y_2 - y_1}{x_2 - x_1}$

▶ **PRACTICE EXERCISE**

1. The perimeter of a square is p inches. The area of this square is

(A) p^2 (B) $16p^2$ (C) $4p$ (D) $\frac{p^2}{16}$ (E) $4p^2$

2. $\angle 1 = \angle 5 \overset{\circ}{=} 30$
$\angle 3 \overset{\circ}{=}$?
(A) 90 (B) 120
(C) 135 (D) 150
(E) 160

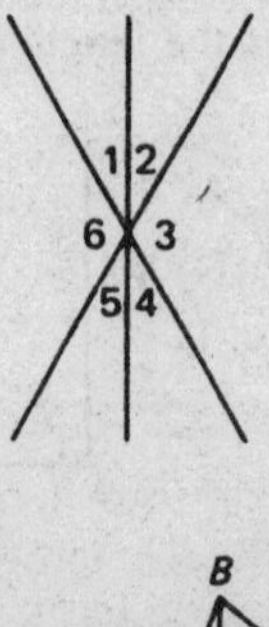

3. In $\triangle ABC$, $BD \perp AC$.
$AB = 13$, $BC = 20$,
$AD = 5$, $DC =$?
(A) 16 (B) 17 (C) 18
(D) 19 (E) 20

4. $AB \perp BC$, $BC \perp CD$.
$AB = 8$, $BC = 5$, $CD = 4$
What is the shortest distance from A to D?
(A) 12 (B) 13 (C) 15
(D) 16 (E) 17

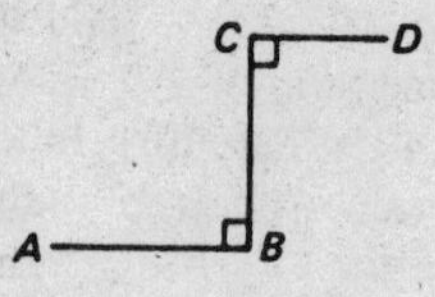

5. One end of a ladder 13 feet long is placed 5 feet from the outer wall of a building that stands on level ground. How far up the building, to the nearest foot, will the ladder reach?
(A) 5 feet (B) 9 feet (C) 12 feet (D) 13 feet
(E) 18 feet

6. AB is a diameter of circle O.
$AC = 10$, $CB = 24$. What is the area of circle O?
(A) 120 (B) 84.5π
(C) 169π (D) 240
(E) $100\pi - 240$

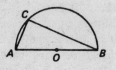

7. $AB = AC$, $DB = DC$, $\angle ABC \overset{\circ}{=} \frac{1}{2} \angle DBC$, $\angle D \overset{\circ}{=} 70$. What is the measure of $\angle A$?
(A) 55° (B) 70°
(C) 105° (D) 110°
(E) 125°

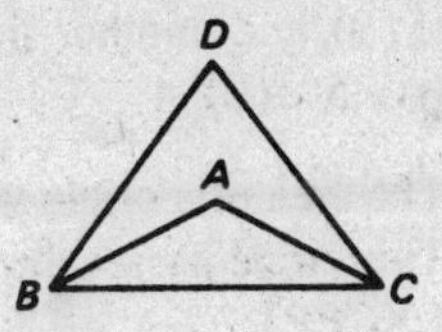

8. The diameter of a hoop is 7. How many revolutions will it make if it is rolled a distance of 182π?
(A) 26 (B) 13π (C) 26π (D) 30π
(E) 52π

9. A cord 200 inches long can go around a square block 10 times. The area of one side of this square is
(A) 20 square inches (B) 25 square inches
(C) 100 square inches (D) 400 square inches
(E) 500 square inches

10. In trapezoid $ABCD$, A and B are right angles and BC is longer than AD. If $AD = 15$ and the diagonals of the trapezoid are 25 and 17, the length of AB is
(A) 8 (B) 12 (C) 15 (D) 17 (E) 20

11. Find the area of a triangle with coordinates $(-16, 0)$, $(-6, 0)$, $(0, 8)$
(A) 32 (B) 40 (C) 48 (D) 64 (E) 80

12. A 15-foot seesaw is balanced at its center on a base which is 3 feet high. How many feet above the ground can an end reach?
(A) 5 (B) 6 (C) 9 (D) 10 (E) 15

13. A rectangular lot 50 feet by 100 feet is surrounded on all sides by a concrete walk 5 feet wide. Find the number of square feet in the surface of the walk.
(A) 775 (B) 1500 (C) 1600 (D) 5000
(E) 6600

14. Straight line MN intersects straight lines AB and CD as shown in figure. If $\angle 2 \overset{\circ}{=} \angle 6$, and $\angle 4 \overset{\circ}{=} 130$, then the measure of $\angle 7 =$
(A) 40° (B) 50°
(C) 60° (D) 90°
(E) 130°

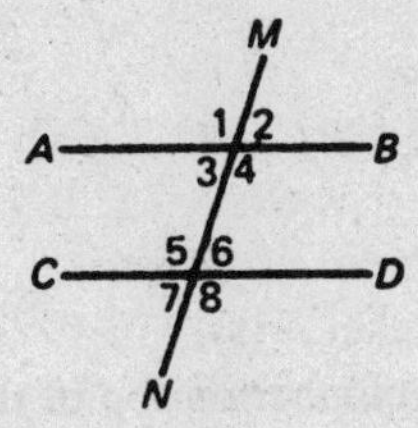

15. JK is perpendicular to KL and MN is perpendicular to JL. If JM is 6, JN is 4, and JL is 18, what is JK?
(A) $\frac{3}{4}$ (B) 12 (C) 18
(D) 27 (E) none of these

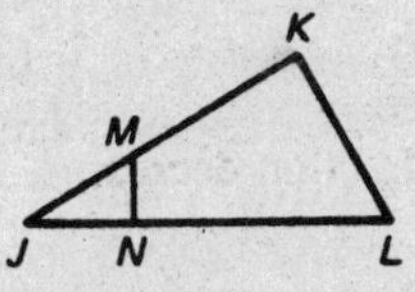

16. Straight line $SROV$ is a diameter of circle O. QRT is a 12-inch chord perpendicular to $SROV$, and RS is 3 inches. How many inches is a radius of circle O?
(A) 4.5 (B) 6 (C) 7.5
(D) 9 (E) 12

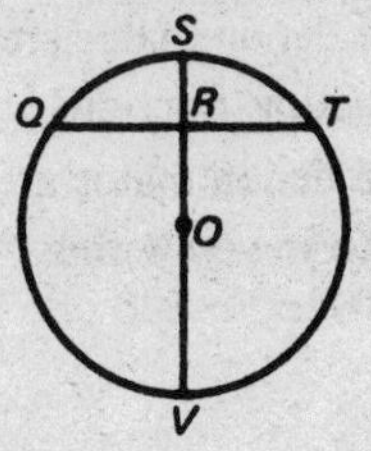

17. If the length of a rectangle is $3u + 2v$ and its perimeter is $10u + 6v$, the width is
(A) $2u + v$ (B) $7u + 4v$ (C) $4u + 2v$
(D) $3.5u + 2v$ (E) $2v + u$

18. In $\triangle ABC$, $AB \perp BC$, $\angle A \overset{\circ}{=} 45$, and $AB = 10$. $(AC)^2$ equals
(A) 10 (B) 20 (C) 100 (D) $2\sqrt{10}$ (E) 200

19. The base of an isosceles triangle is 16 and each of the equal sides is 10. Find the area of the triangle.
(A) 24 (B) 36 (C) 48 (D) 80 (E) 96

20. A rectangular field 100 feet long is twice as long as it is wide. The number of feet of fencing needed is
(A) 150 (B) 300 (C) 400 (D) 500 (E) 600

21. Given right triangles, I, II, III, IV, and V. The following are the lengths of the legs of each triangle: (I) 7 and 4; (II) 12 and 2; (III) 8 and 3; (IV) 6 and 4; (V) 24 and 1. Which of these have the same area?
(A) all of them (B) none of them
(C) only I, II, III, and IV
(D) only II, III, IV, and V
(E) only I, III, IV, and V

22. Four circles each have a radius of $\frac{2}{\pi}$. The sum of the four circumferences is
(A) 4 (B) 8 (C) 16 (D) 24 (E) 32

23. What is the average measure of the angles of $\triangle ABC$?
(A) 30° (B) 60° (C) 90° (D) 180°
(E) cannot be determined from the information furnished

24. Right $\triangle ABE$ shares side BE with rectangle $BCDE$. $AB = BC = 5$ and $CD = 6$. The area of $\triangle ABE$ is
(A) 10 (B) 12.5 (C) 15
(D) 30 (E) 45

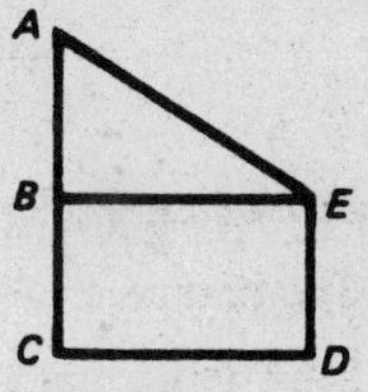

25. KL is the diameter of a circle whose circumference is 10π. If $KM = ML$, then the area of KLM is
(A) 5 (B) $5\sqrt{2}$
(C) $2\sqrt{5}$ (D) 25
(E) 50

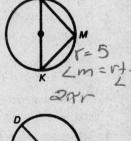

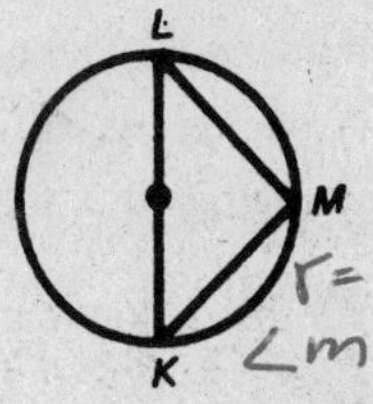

26. Straight line AD intersects circle O at B and C. BC equals radius OD. The measure of the angle formed by drawing radii OB and OC is
(A) 30° (B) 45°
(C) 60° (D) 90°
(E) 180°

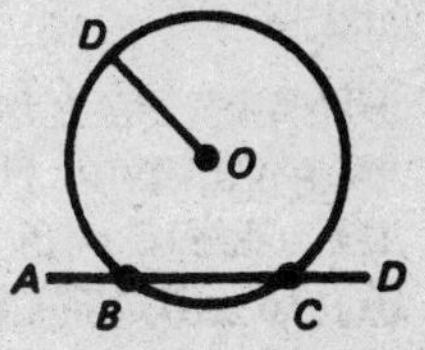

27. Side AB of square $ABCD$ is 10 units. The area of the shaded portion is
(A) $100 - 25\pi$
(B) $25\pi - 100$
(C) $100 - 100\pi$
(D) π
(E) $100 - 10\pi$

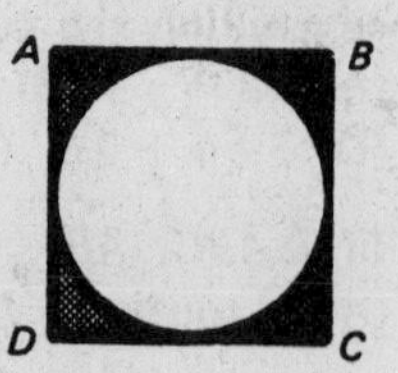

28. Rectangle $ABCD$ is formed by joining the centers of 6 equal circles, each having an area of 4π. The perimeter of $ABCD$ is
(A) 12 (B) 16 (C) 20 (D) 24 (E) 28

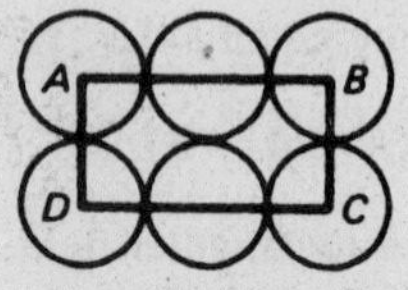

29. Diameter AB = diameter DC = 10. $AB = AD$ and $DC = BC$. The area of the shaded portion is
(A) $100 - 25\pi$
(B) $25\pi - 100$
(C) $100 - 100\pi$
(D) π
(E) $25\pi - 100$

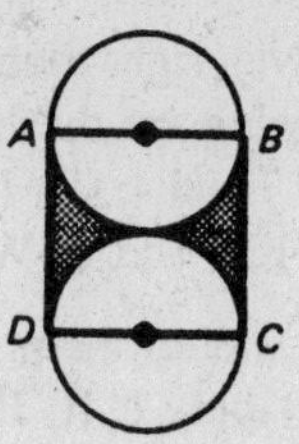

30. In rectangle $ABCD$ several triangles are drawn. All of the following triangles have identical areas EXCEPT
(A) ADC (B) EDC
(C) ACB (D) AED
(E) BCD

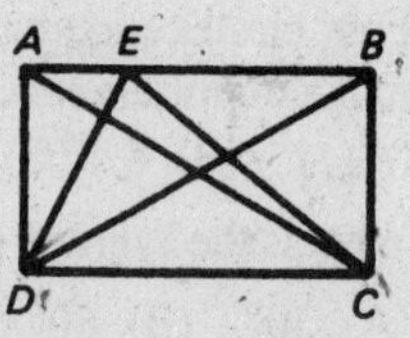

31. The distance between a point with coordinates (5, 9) and another point with coordinates (2, 5) is
(A) 5 (B) 4 (C) 3 (D) 2 (E) 1

32. The area of a circle whose center is at (0, 0) is 25π. This circle passes through all of the following points EXCEPT
(A) (−5, 0) (B) (5, 5) (C) (0, 5) (D) (5, 0) (E) (0, −5)

33. The center of square $ABCD$ is located at point (3, 3) and its sides are along the x and y axes. The area of $ABCD$ is
(A) 6 (B) 9 (C) 24 (D) 36 (E) 81

34. For right $\triangle ABC$ the coordinates of A are (3, 5) and of $C(-2, -2)$; then the coordinates of B are
(A) (−2, 3) (B) (3, −2) (C) (−2, −5) (D) (−2, 8) (E) (5, −2)

35. The vertices of rectangle $ABCD$ are the points A (0, 0), B (8, 0), C (8, k) and D (0, 5); k equals
(A) 2 (B) 3 (C) 4 (D) 5 (E) 6

TYPICAL EXAMINATION PROBLEMS BY TOPICS

Fractions

Some Important Facts

1. A fraction is an indicated division. Thus $\frac{2}{5}$ means $2 \div 5$. The number on top of the fraction sign is called the numerator. The number on bottom is the denominator.
2. A decimal is an indicated fraction in which the denominator is 10, 100, 1000, 10,000 . . . etc. Thus $\frac{3}{10}$ is written as 0.3 and $\frac{3}{100}$ is written as 0.03.
3. As the denominator of a fraction increases, the value of the fraction decreases. $\frac{1}{5}$ is greater than $\frac{1}{50}$. $\frac{1}{5} = 1 \div 5 = 0.2$ and $\frac{1}{50} = 1 \div 50 = 0.02$.
4. As the numerator of a fraction increases, the value of the fraction increases. $\frac{1}{5}$ is less than $\frac{10}{5}$ since $\frac{1}{5} = 0.2$ and $\frac{10}{5} = 2$.
5. The value of a fraction is not changed when the numerator and denominator are multiplied by the same number except zero. Thus $\frac{1}{3} = \frac{3}{9}$. This is useful in adding or subtracting fractions.
6. The value of a fraction is not changed when the numerator and denominator are divided by the same number except zero. Thus $\frac{4}{10} = \frac{2}{5}$. This is called "reducing a fraction to lowest terms."

Hints on Solving Problems

1. To find a number that is a fractional part of a given number, multiply the number by the fraction. The word *of* generally indicates multiplication.

EXAMPLES:

What is $\frac{1}{5}$ of 50? 10 (*answer*)

How much is $\frac{1}{5}$ of $\frac{5}{12}$? $\frac{1}{12}$ (*answer*)

2. To find what fractional part one number is of another, divide the number representing the part by the number representing the whole.

$$\frac{\text{part}}{\text{whole}} = \text{fractional part}$$

Usually the number that follows "part of" is the *whole* and the number that follows "is" is the *part*.

EXAMPLE:

What part of 7 is 2? $\frac{2}{7}$ (*answer*)

3. To find a number when a fractional part of it is known, divide the given part by the fraction.

$$\frac{\text{part}}{\text{fractional part}} = \text{whole}$$

This type of problem can be solved algebraically.

EXAMPLE:

5 is $\frac{1}{4}$ of what number?

Arithmetically: $\frac{5}{\frac{1}{4}} = 5 \div \frac{1}{4}$ *or* 5×4 *or* 20 (*answer*)

Algebraically: Let x = the number.

$$\tfrac{1}{4}x = 5$$

$$x = 20 \text{ (answer)}$$

4. To evaluate or compare fractions, change all fractions to same denominators and inspect numerators, or change all fractions to same numerators and inspect denominators.

EXAMPLES:

Which is the largest fraction: $\frac{1}{6}$, $\frac{1}{4}$, or $\frac{2}{3}$?

$\frac{1}{6} = \frac{2}{12}$, $\frac{1}{4} = \frac{3}{12}$, and $\frac{2}{3} = \frac{8}{12}$. $\frac{2}{3}$ (*answer*)

Which is the smallest: $\frac{4}{28}$, $\frac{2}{3}$, or $\frac{3}{9}$?

$\frac{4}{28} = \frac{1}{7}$, $\frac{2}{3} = \frac{1}{4}$, and $\frac{3}{9} = \frac{1}{3}$. $\frac{4}{28}$ (*answer*)

5. Mixture problems are actually applications of the concept of fractions. The denominator is the sum total of all the components or constituents, and the numerator is the part described.

EXAMPLE:

In a mixture of 3 parts sand and 4 parts gravel, what part of the mixture is composed of sand?

$\frac{3}{3+4}$ *or* $\frac{3}{7}$ (*answer*)

6. Work problems are actually applications of the concept of fractions. The denominator is the total time required to complete a task while the numerator is the time actually worked. This fraction represents the part of the task completed.

EXAMPLE:

Ida has 3 hours of homework to do. What part does she complete in x hours? $\frac{x}{3}$ (*answer*)

▶ PRACTICE EXERCISE

1. What part of 200 is 59?
(A) .295 (B) 2.95 (C) 9.8 (D) 29.5 (E) 98

2. How many thirds are there in $\frac{3}{4}$?
(A) 2 (B) $2\frac{1}{4}$ (C) 3 (D) $3\frac{1}{4}$ (E) 4

3. What part of x is y?
(A) xy (B) $\frac{x}{y}$ (C) $\frac{1}{xy}$ (D) $\frac{y}{x}$ (E) $\frac{x}{100y}$

4. Which of the following has the smallest value?
(A) $\frac{5}{8}$ (B) $\frac{7}{12}$ (C) $\frac{8}{15}$ (D) $\frac{11}{20}$ (E) $\frac{18}{37}$

5. $\frac{1}{3}$ of $\frac{2}{9}$ equals 2 multiplied by
(A) $\frac{1}{27}$ (B) $\frac{2}{27}$ (C) 3 (D) $13\frac{1}{2}$ (E) 27

6. Which of the following has the smallest value?
(A) $\frac{1}{2}$ (B) $\frac{1}{.2}$ (C) $\frac{.1}{.2}$ (D) $\frac{.2}{1}$ (E) $\frac{2}{.1}$

7. A man who owns $\frac{5}{6}$ of a parcel of property sells $\frac{4}{5}$ of his share for $48,000. At that value the entire property is worth
(A) $64,800 (B) $69,200 (C) $72,000
(D) $73,600 (E) $84,000

8. On a two-day hike, 8 campers equally share 4 loaves of bread. If there are 16 slices of bread in each loaf, how many slices of bread does each camper receive daily?
(A) 1 (B) 2 (C) 3 (D) 4 (E) 8

9. When 10 gallons are removed from a tank which is $\frac{5}{8}$ full, the tank is completely emptied. How many gallons are now needed to fill this tank?
(A) 2 (B) 4 (C) 8 (D) 16 (E) 18

10. A group consists of 22 girls and 18 boys. What part of the group is composed of boys?
(A) $\frac{9}{11}$ (B) $\frac{9}{22}$ (C) $\frac{19}{28}$ (D) $\frac{9}{15}$ (E) $\frac{9}{20}$

11. The number which when increased by $\frac{1}{3}$ of itself equals 96 is
(A) 32 (B) 48 (C) 72 (D) 84 (E) 128

12. Joan is three years younger than Martin. How old will Joan be when she is $\frac{4}{5}$ his age?
(A) 4 (B) 8 (C) 9 (D) 10 (E) 12

13. A gasoline gauge registers $\frac{1}{8}$ full. After purchasing 12 gallons of gasoline it registers $\frac{7}{8}$ full. What is the capacity of the tank (in gallons)?
(A) 13 (B) 14 (C) 16 (D) 17 (E) 18

14. In a recent civil service examination, $\frac{1}{8}$ of the candidates failed the first part of the test. Of those eligible to take the second part of the competitive examination, $\frac{2}{7}$ successfully passed. What part of the original candidates were successful in the examination?
(A) $\frac{1}{28}$ (B) $\frac{9}{56}$ (C) $\frac{1}{5}$ (D) $\frac{1}{4}$ (E) $\frac{3}{4}$

15. After 75 gallons of oil are removed from a cylindrical tank, its level is lowered from $\frac{1}{6}$ to $\frac{1}{7}$ of its capacity. How many gallons should now be added to the tank to fill it?
(A) 2625 (B) 2700 (C) 2775 (D) 3075
(E) 3150

16. Jonathan has $\frac{1}{3}$ as many green marbles as he has red marbles and $\frac{1}{6}$ as many red marbles as he has yellow marbles. What part of his collection is made up of yellow marbles?
(A) $\frac{9}{11}$ (B) $\frac{1}{6}$ (C) $\frac{2}{11}$ (D) $\frac{3}{22}$ (E) $\frac{1}{22}$

17. If a 15-gallon gasoline tank is $\frac{3}{8}$ full, how many gallons must be added to completely fill the tank?
(A) 5 (B) $5\frac{5}{8}$ (C) 9 (D) $9\frac{3}{8}$ (E) 10

18. Three chapters of a fraternity voted on a constitutional amendment. In Chapter A it passed with $\frac{3}{4}$ of the members in favor of it. In Chapter B only 2 out of 9 members were against it. Chapter C passed the proposition with 5 of its 36 members voting against it. Arrange the chapters in decreasing order according to the proportion in favor of the amendment.
(A) C,B,A (B) A,B,C (C) A,C,B
(D) B,A,C (E) B,C,A

19. The annual income of a family is budgeted as follows: $\frac{1}{10}$ is for clothing, $\frac{1}{3}$ is for food and $\frac{1}{5}$ is for rent. This leaves $1320 for other expenses and savings. Find the annual income.
(A) $2156 (B) $3600 (C) $23,760
(D) $36,000 (E) $39,600

20. J. C. Nichols department store reports that the average sales on Saturdays is twice that on Thursdays and the average sales on Thursdays is twice that on the other four days. What fraction of the weekly sales are made on Thursdays?
(A) $\frac{1}{7}$ (B) $\frac{1}{5}$ (C) $\frac{2}{7}$ (D) $\frac{1}{3}$ (E) $\frac{2}{5}$

Percent

Some Important Facts

1. Percent means "hundredths."
2. A percent (%) represents a fraction with a denominator of 100. $1\% = \frac{1}{100} = .01$ and $11\% = \frac{11}{100} = .11$ and $1.1\% = \frac{1.1}{100} = .011$.

Hints on Solving Problems

1. Converting a percent to a fraction or decimal involves dropping the percent sign. Dropping the percent sign actually divides a number by 100. Example: 6% changed to 6 actually involves division by 100. Thus 6% does not equal 6 but 6% does equal $\frac{6}{100}$ or .06.

   EXAMPLE:

   Write $\frac{2}{5}$ as a percent.

   $\frac{2}{5} = \frac{?}{100}$ *or* $\frac{40}{100}$ *or* 40% *(answer)*

   What percent of 2 is 4?

   $\left(\frac{?}{100}\right)(2) = 4$ *or* 200% *(answer)*

2. Most problems require a knowledge of the meaning of percent. To find a certain percent of a number, change the percent to a decimal or fraction and multiply.

   EXAMPLE:

   What is 4% of $5?

   (.04)($5) = $.20 *(answer)* *or* $\left(\frac{4}{100}\right)$($5) = $.20 *(answer)*

3. Some problems can best be done algebraically. In one type you are given that one quantity is a certain percent of an unknown quantity and you are asked to find that unknown quantity. Let x = the number and solve, using the definition of percent.

   EXAMPLE:

   9 is 20% of what number?

   If x = the number, then 9 = 20% of x *or* $9 = \left(\frac{20}{100}\right)x$ *or* $9 = \frac{1}{5}x$ *or* $x = 45$. *(answer)*

▶ PRACTICE EXERCISE

1. What percent of 12 is 3?
   (A) $\frac{1}{4}$ (B) 4 (C) 25 (D) 40 (E) 400
2. One-half is $\frac{1}{2}$% of
   (A) $\frac{1}{100}$ (B) $\frac{1}{400}$ (C) 100 (D) 200 (E) 400
3. 104% of 104 equals
   (A) 0 (B) 1 (C) 4.16 (D) 105.04
   (E) 108.16
4. $66\frac{2}{3}$% of 30 is 20% of
   (A) 20 (B) 50 (C) 60 (D) 90 (E) 100
5. In a class composed of x girls and y boys what percent of the class is composed of girls?
   (A) $100xy$ (B) $\frac{x}{x+y}$ (C) $\frac{100x}{x+y}$ (D) $\frac{y}{x+y}$
   (E) $\frac{100y}{x+y}$
6. Seven percent of what number is 14?
   (A) 50 (B) 98 (C) 100 (D) 200 (E) 400
7. A baseball team won W games and lost L games. What percent of its games did it win?
   (A) $\frac{100W}{L}$ (B) $\frac{100W}{L+W}$ (C) $\frac{W}{L}$ (D) $\frac{W}{W+L}$
   (E) $\frac{100W}{100W+L}$
8. If the population of a village was 300 before 1965 and is now 1200, what is the percentage of increase in population?
   (A) 25% (B) 40% (C) 75% (D) 300%
   (E) 400%
9. If a merchant makes a profit of 20% based on the selling price of an article, what percent profit does he make on the cost?
   (A) 20% (B) 25% (C) 30% (D) 40%
   (E) 80%
10. The ABC Company gave each employee an end-of-year bonus to be determined as follows: 15% on that part of a salary which does not exceed $3000, 10% on that part of a salary over $3000 and up to and including $6000, and 5% on that part above $6000. Employee Smith received a bonus of $625. Find his basic salary.
    (A) $3750 (B) $4750 (C) $5750 (D) $6250
    (E) $12,500
11. On the average, 8% of the motorists make a right turn at a particular intersection. At that rate, out of 250 motorists, how many will most probably make this turn?
    (A) 2 (B) 4 (C) 8 (D) 20 (E) 80
12. Thirty prizes were distributed to 5% of the original entrants in a contest. The number of entrants in this contest was
    (A) 15 (B) 60 (C) 150 (D) 300 (E) 600
13. In June a baseball team that played 60 games had won 30% of its games played. After a phenomenal winning streak this team raised its average to 50%. How many games must the team have won in a row to attain this average?
    (A) 12 (B) 20 (C) 24 (D) 30 (E) 45

14. When the price of a pencil eraser rose from four cents to five cents, the percent increase was
(A) 1% (B) 4% (C) 20% (D) 25%
(E) more than 25%

15. A 5-quart solution of sulfuric acid and water is 60% acid. If a gallon of water is added, what percent of the resulting solution is acid?
(A) 3% (B) $33\frac{1}{3}$% (C) 40% (D) 48%
(E) 50%

16. A boy finds that $57\frac{1}{2}$% of his marble collection consists of red marbles, $12\frac{1}{2}$% of his collection consists of blue marbles, and the rest are 24 multi-colored marbles. How many marbles are there in his collection?
(A) 20 (B) 30 (C) 56 (D) 80 (E) 104

17. A man buys 2750 eggs for $100, and loses 350 of these eggs because of breakage. If he sells the remaining eggs at 70¢ a dozen, what percent of his original investment is his profit?
(A) 20% (B) 30% (C) $33\frac{1}{3}$% (D) 40%
(E) 60%

18. A man owns 37.5% of the stock of a corporation, and sells $\frac{2}{3}$ of his stock at a 10% profit. What percent of the stock does he own after this transaction?
(A) 12.5% (B) $33\frac{1}{3}$% (C) $66\frac{2}{3}$% (D) 72.5%
(E) 90%

19. A salesman sold a book at 105% of the marked price instead of discounting the marked price by 5%. If he sold the book for $4.20, what was the price for which he should have sold the book?
(A) $3.00 (B) $3.80 (C) $4.00 (D) $4.18
(E) $4.40

20. Mr. Light can pay for an article in either of two ways. He can pay the list price with a down payment of 20% and the balance in 5 installments of $16 each, or he can pay the cash price of $88. How much does Mr. Light save by paying the cash price?
(A) $8.00 (B) $8.40 (C) $8.80 (D) $9.60
(E) $12.00

Averages

Some Important Facts

1. To find the average of a group of numbers, add the numbers and divide the sum by the quantity of numbers added.

EXAMPLE:

What is the average of 85%, 80%, and 75%? The sum is 240. The average is 240 ÷ 3 *or* 80. (*answer*)

2. When two or more averages are combined into a single average, appropriate weight must be given each average.

EXAMPLE:

A man buys 50 shares of stock at $30 and then buys 100 shares of this stock at $25. What is his average cost per share?
His average is *not* $27.50 but ($30 × 50 plus $25 × 100) ÷ 150 *or* $26.67 per share. (*answer*)

Hints on Solving Problems

1. To find the average, all units must be the same.

EXAMPLE:

What is the average length of three strings of the following lengths: 1 inch, 1 foot, and 1 yard? Change all lengths to inches. Thus, the sum equals 1 inch, 12 inches, and 36 inches *or* 49 inches. The average equals 49 ÷ 3 *or* $16\frac{1}{3}$ inches *or* 1 foot and $4\frac{1}{3}$ inches. (*answer*)

2. The sum is equal to the product of the average and the quantity of numbers.

EXAMPLE:

What number must be added to 5, 7, 0, and 1 to attain an average of 3?
Sum must be 3 × 5 or 15. Sum of four numbers given is 13. To obtain sum of 15, add 2. (*answer*)

▶ PRACTICE EXERCISE

1. A strip of linoleum 13 yards 5 feet 1 inch is to be cut into three equal parts. The length of each part will be
(A) 4 yards 4 feet (B) 4 yards $4\frac{1}{3}$ feet
(C) 4 yards 2 feet $8\frac{1}{3}$ inches (D) 4 yards 1 foot
(E) 4 yards $5\frac{1}{3}$ feet

2. What is the average height of three boys if one boy is x inches and the other boys are each y inches tall?
(A) $\frac{2xy}{3}$ (B) $\frac{x + 2y}{3}$ (C) $\frac{x + y}{3}$ (D) $x + \frac{y}{3}$
(E) $\frac{2}{3}(x + y)$

3. What number must be added to 8, 18, and 26 to attain an average of exactly 18?
(A) 2 (B) 17.5 (C) 18 (D) 20 (E) 34

4. The average of the numbers represented by $z - 8$ and $3z + 2$ is
(A) $11z + 3$ (B) $4z - 6$ (C) $\frac{11z + 3}{2}$
(D) $2z - 3$ (E) $2z - 5$

5. The average of A and another number is B. The other number is
(A) $\frac{AB}{2}$ (B) $2B - A$ (C) $2A - B$ (D) $A - B$
(E) $\frac{A + B}{2}$

6. The average of two numbers is XY. If one number is equal to X, the other number is equal to
(A) Y (B) $2Y$ (C) $XY - X$ (D) $2XY - X$
(E) $XY - 2X$

7. A student who strives to attain an average of 80% has the following grades in a certain subject: 70, 74, 81, and 85. What grade must he get in the next test to achieve his goal?
(A) 85 (B) 87 (C) 89 (D) 90
(E) more than 90

8. The average closing price of the five most active stocks was \$42. The average closing price of the first four stocks on the most active list was \$37. The closing price of the stock that was fifth on the most active list was
(A) \$37 (B) \$42 (C) \$47 (D) \$60 (E) \$62

9. If b boys each have m marbles, and g girls each have n marbles, what is the average number of marbles per child?
(A) $m + n$ (B) $\frac{m + n}{2}$ (C) $\frac{m + n}{b + g}$
(D) $\frac{bm + gn}{m + n}$ (E) $\frac{bm + gn}{b + g}$

10. What was the grade a student received on his first examination, if the grades on his other examinations were 80%, 90%, and 95%, and his average on the four was 75%?
(A) $13\frac{1}{3}$ (B) 33 (C) 34 (D) 35 (E) 36

11. During a closeout sale 30 suits are sold at \$60 each. The price is then reduced to \$50 and 20 suits are sold. At what average price must the remaining 10 suits be sold in order to attain an average of \$55 for the 60 suits?
(A) \$50.00 (B) \$52.50 (C) \$55.00
(D) \$57.50 (E) \$60.00

12. The average of n numbers is a. If x is subtracted from each number, the average will be
(A) $\frac{ax}{n}$ (B) $\frac{an}{x}$ (C) $an - x$ (D) $n - x$
(E) $a - x$

13. If the average of the ages of three men is 44 and no one of them is less than 42 years old, what is the maximum age (in years) of any one man?
(A) 44 (B) 46 (C) 48 (D) 49 (E) 50

14. What fraction must be subtracted from the sum of $\frac{1}{2} + \frac{1}{3}$ in order to have an average of $\frac{1}{6}$?
(A) $-\frac{1}{3}$ (B) $\frac{1}{3}$ (C) $\frac{1}{2}$ (D) $-\frac{1}{2}$ (E) $\frac{2}{3}$

15. Which of the following must be added to the sum of $2d$ and $4d$ in order to have an average of $3d$?
(A) $-3d$ (B) $+3d$ (C) $9d$ (D) $-9d$
(E) none of these

16. The average of three numbers is x. If one number is 5, then the sum of the other two numbers is
(A) $3x$ (B) $\frac{3x}{2}$ (C) $3x - 5$ (D) 5
(E) $\frac{x - 5}{2}$

17. A student attends Central High School for two terms and earns an average of 80%. He then attends Circle High School for five terms and earns an average of 85%. His average for the seven terms would be
(A) 82.5% (B) 82.6% (C) 83.4%
(D) 83.57% (E) 84%

18. If 5 lbs. of nuts worth 60 cents a pound are mixed with 6 lbs. of nuts worth 50 cents a pound, the value (in cents) of each pound of mixture is
(A) 54.5 (B) 55 (C) 55.5 (D) 56 (E) 56.5

19. The average of two numbers is V. If the smaller number is v, then the larger number is
(A) $V - v$ (B) $v - V$ (C) $2v - V$
(D) $2V - v$ (E) $\frac{V - 2v}{2}$

20. Three members of a track team have weights that range from 110 to 135 pounds. Which of the following *cannot* possibly be the average of the three trackmen?
(A) 117 (B) 119 (C) 122 (D) 125 (E) 126

Motion

Some Important Facts

1. distance = rate × time
2. rate = $\frac{\text{distance}}{\text{time}}$
3. time = $\frac{\text{distance}}{\text{rate}}$

Hints on Solving Problems

1. Use the most convenient formula of the three given.
2. Units must be similar.

   distance = rate × time

   miles = $\frac{\text{miles}}{\text{per hour}}$ × hours

   EXAMPLE:

   How far will a car traveling at 30 miles per hour go in 2 minutes?

   $$\text{miles} = \frac{\cancel{30}\text{ miles}}{\cancel{\text{per hour}}} \times \frac{\overset{1}{\cancel{2}}}{\underset{\underset{1}{\cancel{2}}}{\cancel{60}}} \text{ hrs. } \textit{or } 1 \text{ mile } (\textit{answer})$$

3. To calculate the average rate for a trip involving two or more parts, regard the trip as a single trip, using the total distance and the total time to calculate the average rate for the whole trip.

   EXAMPLE:

   A man travels 60 miles at 40 miles per hour and then travels 40 miles at the rate of 60 miles per hour. What is his average rate for the whole trip?

   During the first part he traveled for $\frac{60}{40}$ or $1\frac{1}{2}$ hours. During the second part he traveled for $\frac{40}{60}$ or $\frac{2}{3}$ hour. He spent $1\frac{1}{2}$ plus $\frac{2}{3}$ or $2\frac{1}{6}$ hours on the entire trip. He covered a total of 100 miles. His average rate for the entire trip is $100 \div 2\frac{1}{6}$ or 46.1 miles per hour. (*answer*)

▶ PRACTICE EXERCISE

1. At 40 miles per hour the number of minutes it will take to drive 18 miles is
   (A) $4\frac{1}{2}$ (B) 27 (C) 33 (D) 36 (E) 72
2. How far (in miles) can a car traveling at 30 miles per hour go in an hour and twenty minutes?
   (A) 22.5 (B) 32 (C) 36 (D) 40 (E) 50
3. How far does a car travel when its average rate is 35 miles per hour and it travels for 3 hours and 24 minutes?
   (A) 109 mi. (B) 112 mi. (C) $113\frac{2}{5}$ mi. (D) 119 mi. (E) 129 mi.
4. How many minutes will it take a motorist traveling at 40 miles an hour to reach a point $\frac{2}{5}$ of a mile away?
   (A) $\frac{4}{15}$ (B) $\frac{2}{3}$ (C) 1 (D) 4 (E) $\frac{3}{5}$
5. Twenty minutes after a plane leaves the airport, it is reported to be 80 miles away. The average speed of the plane (in miles per hour) is
   (A) 160 (B) 240 (C) 320 (D) 400 (E) 1600
6. An automobile party leaves at 7:55 A.M. and arrives at its destination 15 miles away at 8:15 A.M. What was the average rate on this trip?
   (A) 5 M.P.H. (B) 15 M.P.H. (C) 30 M.P.H. (D) 45 M.P.H. (E) 50 M.P.H.
7. A man travels for 5 hours at an average rate of 40 M.P.H. He develops some motor trouble and returns to his original starting point in 10 hours. What was his average rate (in miles per hour) on the return trip?
   (A) 20 (B) 25 (C) 26.6 (D) 30 (E) 60
8. Ten minutes after a plane leaves the airport, it is reported that the plane is 40 miles away. What is the average speed of the plane, in miles per hour?
   (A) 80 (B) 120 (C) 160 (D) 200 (E) 240
9. A car travels a distance of 70 miles in $2\frac{1}{2}$ hours. How much faster on the average must it travel to make the trip in $\frac{3}{4}$ hours less time? (M.P.H.)
   (A) 12 (B) 24 (C) 28 (D) 40 (E) 51
10. How many seconds will it take an automobile to cover one mile if it is traveling at 45 miles per hour?
    (A) 27 (B) 45 (C) 60 (D) 80 (E) 90

11. How many feet will an automobile cover in one second when it travels at 45 miles per hour? (1 mile = 5280 feet)
(A) 66 (B) 660 (C) 2138 (D) 3960
(E) 6600

12. A boy rides his bicycle ten miles at an average rate of twelve miles an hour and twelve miles at an average rate of ten miles an hour. What is the average rate for the entire trip?
(A) 10.8 (B) 11 (C) 12 (D) 20.3 (E) 22

13. A man covers d miles in t hours. At that rate how long (in hours) will it take him to cover m miles?
(A) dmt (B) $\frac{md}{t}$ (C) $\frac{mt}{d}$ (D) $\frac{dt}{m}$ (E) $\frac{d}{t}$

14. A motorist travels for 2 hours at 30 miles per hour and then covers the same distance in 3 hours. What was his average rate (in miles per hour) for the entire trip?
(A) 24 (B) 25 (C) 26 (D) 27
(E) none of these

15. Martin traveled m miles at the rate of r miles per hour and arrived at his destination 1 hour late. How much time should he allow himself to make this trip again and arrive on time?
(A) $\frac{m}{r} + 1$ (B) $\frac{m - r}{r}$ (C) $m - r$
(D) $m - r - 1$ (E) $\frac{m + r}{r}$

16. As a motorist approaches the turnpike, he travels at the rate of 20 miles per hour in street traffic. For the first mile on the turnpike he travels at the rate of 30 miles per hour and then covers the next mile in one minute. What is his average rate for the first three miles of this trip?
(A) 25 M.P.H. (B) 30 M.P.H. (C) 33 M.P.H.
(D) $36\frac{2}{3}$ M.P.H. (E) 50 M.P.H.

17. The distance between Chicago and Cleveland is 354 miles. If a person leaves Chicago at 9:50 A.M. Central Time and arrives in Cleveland at 5:30 P.M. the same day Eastern Time, at what average speed does he travel, correct to the nearest mile? (Central Time is one hour earlier than Eastern Time).
(A) 46 M.P.H. (B) 50 M.P.H. (C) 53 M.P.H.
(D) 55 M.P.H. (E) 56 M.P.H.

18. A boy travels on his bicycle at the rate of 6 miles per hour and his sister on hers at the rate of 5 miles per hour. They start at the same time and place and travel over the same road in the same direction. After traveling for 3 hours, the boy turns back. How far from the starting point has his sister traveled when they meet?
(A) 16 miles (B) about 16.4 miles
(C) about 16.9 miles (D) 17 miles
(E) 17.4 miles

19. Mr. B. walks for 4 hours at the rate of y miles an hour. He stops an hour for lunch and then returns to the starting point by a route which is twice as long, but he travels in an auto whose speed is five times that of his walking rate. Find the number of hours spent on the entire trip.
(A) $5\frac{3}{5}$ (B) 6 (C) $6\frac{3}{5}$ (D) 7 (E) 8

20. A train left Albany for Buffalo, a distance of 290 miles, at 10:10 A.M. The train was scheduled to reach Buffalo at 3:45 P.M. If the average rate of the train on this trip was 50 miles per hour, it arrived in Buffalo
(A) about 5 minutes ahead of schedule (B) on time (C) about 5 minutes late (D) about 13 minutes late (E) more than a quarter of an hour late

Ratio and Proportion

Some Important Facts

1. A ratio is an expression that compares two quantities by dividing one by the other.
EXAMPLE:
In a class with 11 girls and 12 boys the ratio of girls to boys is 11 : 12 *or* $\frac{11}{12}$, while the ratio of boys to girls is 12 : 11 *or* $\frac{12}{11}$.

2. A maximum ratio is that ratio that has the largest numerical value. To determine the maximum ratio, write the ratios in the form of fractions and evaluate. If a fraction has a value of more than 1, use the reciprocal. In the illustration above, $\frac{12}{11}$ describes the same ratio expressed as $\frac{11}{12}$.

3. A proportion is a statement of equality that exists between two ratios. For example, $\frac{1}{2} = \frac{5}{10}$ is a proportion. It consists of four terms. The first and last terms are called *extremes* (1 and 10). The second and third terms are called *means* (2 and 5).

4. In a proportion, the product of the means equals the product of the extremes. In the proportion $\frac{1}{2} = \frac{5}{10}$, 5×2 equals 1×10.

Hints on Solving Problems

1. Many verbal problems express a relationship between two variables.

EXAMPLE:

If 3 books cost \$12, what is the cost of b books?

In this problem as you buy more books you pay more money proportionally. Likewise, as you spend more money, you receive more books. When a problem expresses a proportion, it is necessary to determine by logical reasoning whether it is a direct proportion or an inverse proportion.

2. A *direct* proportion is one in which the two variables are so related that if one quantity is multiplied or divided by the same number, the ratio is unchanged. The example given above illustrates this type. Therefore it may be expressed as follows:

$$\frac{3 \text{ books}}{\$12} = \frac{b \text{ books}}{\$\, x}$$
$$3x = 12b$$
$$x = 4b$$
$$(answer) = \$4b$$

3. A direct proportion may be expressed as $\frac{x}{y} = k$ where the value of k remains constant.

4. An *inverse* proportion is one in which an increase by multiplication in one variable results in a corresponding decrease in the other, and a decrease by division in one variable results in a corresponding increase in the other.

EXAMPLE:

If 6 men can do a job in 10 days, how long would it take 3 men to complete this job?

Obviously, since the number of men working has been cut in *half*, the number of days required will be *doubled*.

5. An inverse proportion may be expressed as $xy = k$ where the value of k remains constant. In the example above, (6 men × 10 days) equals (3 men × 20 days) equals 60 man-days. To solve a problem which is an inverse proportion, write one set of conditions as the *extremes:* $\frac{6 \text{ men}}{} = \frac{}{10 \text{ days}}$. Then add the second set of conditions, with an unknown as the *means:* $\frac{6 \text{ men}}{3 \text{ men}} = \frac{x \text{ days}}{10 \text{ days}}$. Solve by cross multiplication, since in a proportion the product of the means equals the product of the extremes.

▶ PRACTICE EXERCISE

1. Snow is accumulating f feet per minute. How much snow will fall in h hours if it continues falling at that rate?
(A) $60fh$ (B) fh (C) $\frac{60f}{h}$ (D) $\frac{60h}{f}$ (E) $\frac{f}{h}$

2. If p pencils cost x cents, how many pencils can be bought for y cents?
(A) $\frac{px}{y}$ (B) $\frac{y}{px}$ (C) $\frac{xy}{p}$ (D) $\frac{x}{py}$ (E) $\frac{py}{x}$

3. If p pencils cost c cents, n pencils at the same rate will cost
(A) $\frac{pc}{n}$ cents (B) npc cents (C) $\frac{cn}{p}$ cents
(D) $\frac{np}{c}$ cents (E) $\frac{1}{npc}$ cents

4. A diagram of a plane is drawn to the scale of 0.5 inches equals 80 feet. If the length of the diagram is 4.5 inches, the actual length of the plane is
(A) 320 feet (B) 360 feet (C) 640 feet
(D) 680 feet (E) 720 feet

5. Joan can wire x radios in $\frac{3}{4}$ minute. At this rate, how many radios can she wire in $\frac{3}{4}$ of an hour?
(A) $\frac{x}{60}$ (B) $\frac{60}{x}$ (C) $60x$ (D) 60 (E) $x + 60$

6. If a light flashes every 6 seconds, how many times will it flash in $\frac{3}{4}$ of an hour?
(A) 225 (B) 250 (C) 360 (D) 450 (E) 480

7. The cost of 7 dozen rulers at \$15.60 per gross is
(A) \$.91 (B) \$1.09 (C) \$1.30 (D) \$2.23
(E) \$9.10

8. How many miles are there in 9.66 kilometers if there are 7 miles in 11.27 kilometers?
(A) 5 (B) 6 (C) 7 (D) 7.5 (E) 7.9

9. The direction for making a certain cereal is to use $1\frac{1}{2}$ cups of cereal with $4\frac{1}{2}$ cups of water. Mrs. Crocker finds that she has $\frac{3}{4}$ cup of cereal left. How much water should she use?
(A) 2 cups (B) $2\frac{1}{3}$ cups (C) $2\frac{1}{4}$ cups
(D) $2\frac{1}{2}$ cups (E) $2\frac{3}{4}$ cups

10. If 15 cans of food are needed for 7 campers for 2 days, the number of cans needed for 4 campers for 7 days is
(A) 15 (B) 20 (C) 25 (D) 30 (E) 35

11. In a summer camp it is found that a quart of milk is consumed by four campers or three counselors. If 16 quarts of milk are brought into the dining room to feed 40 campers and 12 counselors, how many

quarts of milk should be returned after the meal?
(A) 2 (B) $8\frac{4}{7}$ (C) 10 (D) $10\frac{2}{7}$ (E) 14

12. How many 3-cent stamps can be purchased for c cents?
(A) $3c$ (B) $\frac{c}{3}$ (C) $\frac{3}{c}$ (D) $300c$ (E) $\frac{3c}{100}$

13. A box of 12 tablets costs 21 cents. The same brand is packaged in bottles containing 100 tablets and sells for $1.50 per bottle. How much is saved per dozen, by purchasing the larger amount?
(A) $\frac{1}{4}$¢ (B) 1¢ (C) $\frac{1}{2}$¢ (D) $1\frac{3}{4}$¢ (E) 3¢

14. Samuel, Martin, and Leibow invest $5000, $7000, and $12,000 respectively in a business. If the profits are distributed proportionally, what share of a $1111 profit should Leibow receive?
(A) $231.40 (B) $264.00 (C) $333.33
(D) $370.33 (E) $555.50

15. If $5\frac{1}{2}$ yards = 1 rod and 3 feet = 1 yard, how many rods are equivalent to 1 foot?
(A) $\frac{2}{11}$ (B) $\frac{6}{11}$ (C) $\frac{2}{33}$ (D) $\frac{11}{6}$ (E) $\frac{11}{2}$

16. The scale of a certain map is $\frac{3}{4}$ inch = 12 miles. Find in square miles the actual area of a part represented on the map by a square whose side is $\frac{5}{8}$ inch.
(A) $7\frac{1}{2}$ (B) 10 (C) 20 (D) 40 (E) 100

17. There are 27 students in a chemistry class and 22 students in a physics class. Seven of these students take physics and chemistry. What is the ratio of the number of students taking only physics to those taking only chemistry?
(A) 4:3 (B) 34:29 (C) 7:6 (D) 3:4
(E) 22:27

18. Three men enter a business venture. Mr. Merrill invests $40,000 while Mr. Berell invests $50,000 and Mr. Sheryll invests $60,000. When profits are divided proportionately, what part of the profits should Mr. Berell receive?
(A) $\frac{1}{3}$ (B) $\frac{2}{5}$ (C) $\frac{1}{2}$ (D) $\frac{3}{5}$ (E) $\frac{2}{3}$

19. In purchasing food for a party Florence spends $30, Henrietta spends $45, Joan spends half as much as Florence, and Ann spends $\frac{2}{3}$ as much as Joan. The ratio of the amount of money spent by Henrietta and Joan is
(A) 1:3 (B) 2:3 (C) 3:1 (D) 4:1 (E) 3:2

20. A formula for infant feeding requires 13 oz. of evaporated milk and 18 oz. of water. If only 10 oz. of milk are available, how much water, to the nearest ounce, should be used?
(A) 7 oz. (B) 14 oz. (C) 15 oz. (D) 16 oz.
(E) 21 oz.

Work

Some Important Facts

1. Work problems apply principles involving fractions. For example if it takes a man 5 days to complete a job, in one day he does $\frac{1}{5}$ of the job, in two days $\frac{2}{5}$, in x days $\frac{x}{5}$.
2. Work problems involving many men apply the principle of *inverse proportion*. For example, if we increase the number of men on a job (assuming they perform their work at the same rate), the time required to complete the task will be decreased proportionately.

Hints on Solving Problems

1. In problems involving work by one person or by several people working at different rates or time recall:
$$\frac{\text{time actually spent working}}{\text{time required to do the entire task}} = \text{part of task done}$$
2. In problems involving people working at the same rate, apply the principle of inverse proportion and recall: $xy = k$.

▶ PRACTICE EXERCISE

1. It takes h hours to mow a lawn. What part of the lawn is mowed in one hour?
(A) h (B) $\frac{h}{x}$ (C) hx (D) $\frac{1}{h}$ (E) $\frac{x}{h}$

2. A student has three hours of homework. He works from 8:55 P.M. to 9:15 P.M. What part of his work is left uncompleted?
(A) $\frac{1}{3}$ (B) $\frac{2}{3}$ (C) $\frac{5}{6}$ (D) $\frac{4}{5}$ (E) $\frac{8}{9}$

3. Ann can type a manuscript in 10 hours. Florence can type this manuscript in 5 hours. If they both type this manuscript together, it can be completed in
(A) 2 hrs. 30 min. (B) 3 hrs.
(C) 3 hrs. 20 min. (D) 5 hrs.
(E) 7 hrs. 30 min.

4. A man can paint a room in three hours. His son Martin requires four hours to do the same job. If

they both work together, the job could be done in

(A) $1\frac{1}{2}$ hrs. (B) $1\frac{5}{7}$ hrs. (C) 2 hrs. (D) 3 hrs.

(E) $\frac{1}{2}$ hr.

5. Joan and Ann finish the housework in 3 hours. Joan could have done it alone in 5 hours. What part of the work was done by Ann?

(A) $\frac{1}{4}$ (B) $\frac{3}{8}$ (C) $\frac{2}{5}$ (D) $\frac{3}{5}$ (E) $\frac{5}{8}$

6. It was calculated that 75 men could complete a strip on a new highway in 20 days. When work was scheduled to commence, it was found necessary to send 25 men on another road project. How much longer will it take to complete the strip?
(A) 10 days (B) 20 days (C) 30 days
(D) 40 days (E) 60 days

7. If m men take d days to complete a job, how many men will be needed to complete the job in $\frac{2}{3}$ of the time?

(A) $\frac{2}{3}m$ (B) $\frac{1}{3}m$ (C) $1\frac{1}{2}m$ (D) $\frac{2}{3}md$
(E) $1\frac{1}{2}md$

8. A boys' club decides to build a cabin. The job can be done by 3 skilled workmen in 20 days or by 5 of the boys in 30 days. How many days will it take if all work together?

(A) 10 (B) 12 (C) $12\frac{2}{3}$ (D) 13 (e) 14

9. It takes James an hour to do a job that John can do in 40 minutes. One morning they worked together for 12 minutes, then James went away and John finished the job. How long did it take him to finish?
(A) 8 min. (B) 16 min. (C) 20 min.
(D) 22 min. (E) 28 min.

10. In $\frac{1}{3}$ of a working day a crew does $\frac{2}{3}$ of a job. If they work at that rate, what part of a day will be required to complete this job?

(A) $\frac{2}{9}$ (B) $\frac{4}{9}$ (C) $\frac{1}{2}$ (D) $\frac{2}{3}$ (E) $\frac{3}{4}$

11. A can do a piece of work in r days and B, who works faster, can do the same work in s days. Which of the following expressions represents the number of days it would take the two of them to do the work if they worked together?

(A) $\frac{r+s}{2}$ (B) $r-s$ (C) $\frac{1}{r}+\frac{1}{s}$ (D) $\frac{rs}{r+s}$

(E) $\frac{r+s}{rs}$

12. One man can paint a house in 6 days and another man can do the same job in 2 days less. How many days will it take them if they work together?

(A) $1\frac{1}{3}$ (B) $2\frac{2}{5}$ (C) 3 (D) $4\frac{3}{5}$ (E) 5

13. John did a piece of work in 12 hours 13 minutes. A week later he did the same job in 10 hours 5 minutes. Two weeks later he did it in 9 hours 48 minutes. What was the average amount of time spent in doing the job?

(A) 10 hrs. 7 min. (B) 10 hrs. $8\frac{2}{3}$ min.

(C) 10 hrs. 42 min. (D) 10 hrs. 55 min.
(E) 32 hrs. 6 min.

14. In 6 days 4 men, working at uniform speed for 8 hours per day, complete a job. If these men worked at the same pace for 12 hours per day, the job could be completed in
(A) 4 days (B) 8 days (C) 12 days
(D) 16 days (E) 32 days

15. One printing press can print one issue of a newspaper in 4 hours. A second press can do the same job in 2 hours. How many hours would it take to print one issue with both presses working?

(A) $\frac{3}{4}$ (B) $1\frac{1}{3}$ (C) $1\frac{1}{2}$ (D) $2\frac{2}{3}$ (E) 3

16. Florence can do the housework in 6 hours working alone. When Joan helps her, the housework is done in 4 hours. If Joan did it alone, it would take her (?) more hours to do it than Florence can do it alone?
(A) 2 (B) 3 (C) 4 (D) 6 (E) 12

17. If M men can complete a job in H hours, how long will it take 5 men to do this job?

(A) $\frac{5M}{H}$ (B) $\frac{M}{5H}$ (C) $\frac{MH}{5}$ (D) $\frac{5}{MH}$ (E) $\frac{5H}{M}$

18. Melinda has x minutes of homework in each of 5 subjects. What part of her homework does she do each hour?

(A) $\frac{1}{5x}$ (B) $\frac{x}{12}$ (C) $\frac{12}{x}$ (D) $\frac{1}{12x}$ (E) $12x$

19. Marc can seal 50 letters a minute. How many minutes would it take him to seal x letters?

(A) $50x$ (B) $\frac{1}{50x}$ (C) $\frac{50}{x}$ (D) $\frac{x}{50}$ (E) $\frac{1}{x+50}$

20. Five men can paint a house in six days. If two of the men don't work, what will be the increase of time (in days) required to complete the job?

(A) $2\frac{2}{5}$ (B) $3\frac{3}{5}$ (C) 4 (D) 5 (E) 8

Data Interpretation

A graph is a pictorial representation of data which gives an over-all view of the facts, omitting minor details. It is generally used to make comparisons. It is a time saver, in that general conclusions can be drawn without the need for studying a mass of figures.

The line graph depicts continuity. The financial pages of our newspapers and magazines use this type of graph to show trends in business. The bar graph makes comparisons by using varying lengths of bars. In advertising, for example the number of subscriptions to journals, or sales of various products are thus compared pictorially. The circle graph is used to show how various parts make up the whole. The government often releases for publication such graphs to show how the tax dollar is spent.

Graphs and interpretation of data are used for examination purposes because they call for calculations based on interpretations.

PRACTICE EXERCISES

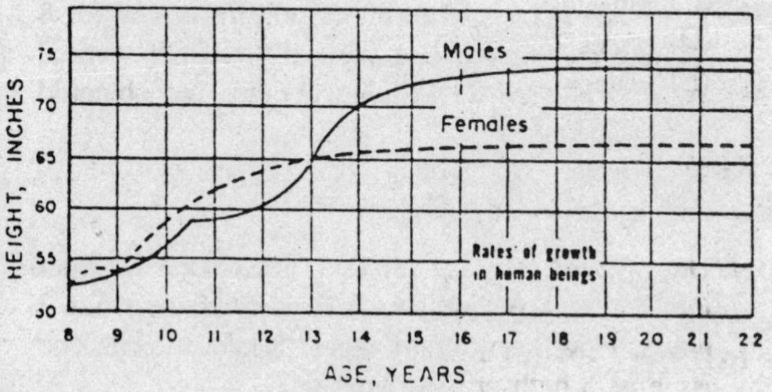

GRAPH 1

Questions 1 - 5 refer to Graph 1

1. How many years old is the male when he reaches the height of an eleven-year-old female?
(A) 10 (B) 11 (C) 12 (D) 12.2 (E) 12.5
2. How many years old is the male when he is one-half foot taller than the female of the same age?
(A) 10.5 (B) 13 (C) 15 (D) 17 (E) 20
3. How many years old is the female when she is 4 ft. 7 in. tall?
(A) 9.2 (B) 9.5 (C) 9.6 (D) 13.3 (E) 21
4. According to this graph, how many years elapse between the occasions when males and females of the same age are also of the same height?
(A) 3.8 (B) 4.1 (C) 8 (D) 9.2 (E) 13
5. How old is the male when he is 20% taller than the female is at the age of 10.5 years?
(A) 10 (B) 10.5 (C) 14 (D) 14.5 (E) 15.2

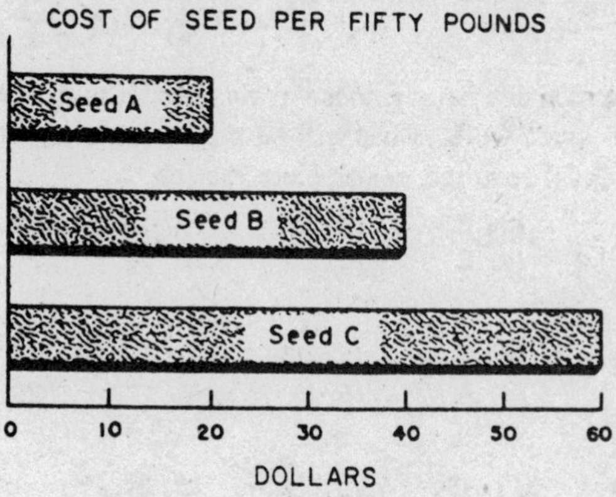

GRAPH 2

Questions 6 - 9 refer to Graph 2

6. What is the cost of $12\frac{1}{2}$ pounds of Seed B?
(A) \$10. (B) \$20. (C) \$40.
(D) \$60 (E) \$75.
7. How many pounds of Seed C would I get for \$30?
(A) $12\frac{1}{2}$ (B) 25 (C) 50 (D) 100 (E) 900
8. The price of one pound of Seed C is what per cent of the price of one pound of Seed B?
(A) 20% (B) $33\frac{1}{3}$% (C) $66\frac{2}{3}$%
(D) 120% (E) 150%
9. What is the ratio of the price of 20 pounds of Seed B to the price of 20 pounds of Seed A?
(A) 1 : 1 (B) 1 : 2 (C) 2 : 1
(D) 2 : 3 (E) 4 : 1

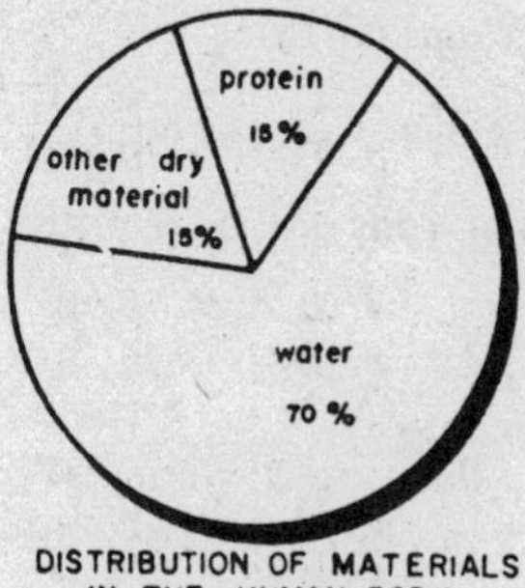

DISTRIBUTION OF MATERIALS IN THE HUMAN BODY

GRAPH 3

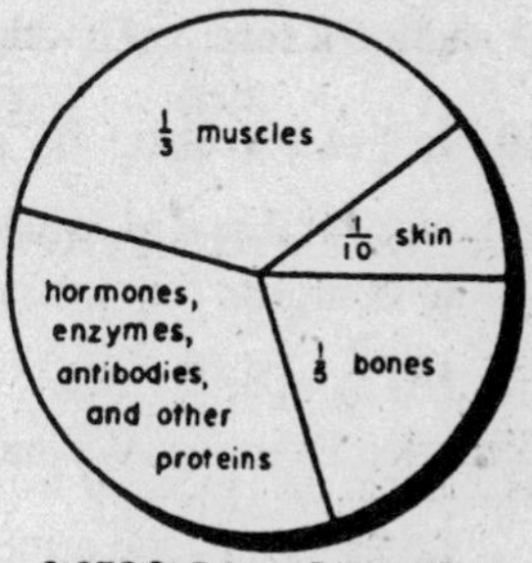

DISTRIBUTION OF PROTEINS IN THE HUMAN BODY

GRAPH 4

Questions 10 - 17 refer to Graphs 3 and 4

10. In terms of the total body weight, the distribution of materials other than water and proteins is equal to
(A) $\frac{1}{15}$ (B) $\frac{85}{100}$ (C) $\frac{1}{20}$ (D) $\frac{3}{20}$ (E) $\frac{1}{5}$
11. A person weighing 170 pounds would, according to these graphs, be composed of water weighing
(A) 17 pounds (B) 70 pounds
(C) 100 pounds (D) 119 pounds
(E) 153 pounds

12. How many degrees of the circle should be used to represent the distribution of protein?
(A) 15 (B) 45 (C) 54 (D) 60 (E) 90

13. What per cent of the entire body weight is made up of skin?
(A) 0.15 (B) 1.0 (C) 1.5 (D) 10. (E) 15.0

14. If the weight of the bones of an individual is represented by x pounds, the weight of the skin of this individual is represented by
(A) $\frac{1}{x+5}$ (B) $\frac{1}{x-5}$ (C) $2x$
(D) $\frac{x}{2}$ (E) $\frac{x}{5}$

15. What part of the proteins in the body is made up of muscles and skin?
(A) $\frac{15}{1300}$ (B) $\frac{1}{130}$ (C) $\frac{1}{13}$ (D) $\frac{13}{30}$ (E) $\frac{1}{30}$

16. The ratio of the distribution of proteins in muscle to the distribution of protein in skin is
(A) 3 : 1 (B) 1 : 3 (C) 3 : 10
(D) $3\frac{1}{3}$: 1 (E) 30 : 1

17. The human body, according to the data furnished by the graphs, is composed mainly of
(A) proteins
(B) hormones, enzymes, antibodies and other proteins
(C) muscles
(D) bones
(E) water

ANSWER KEY

Practice Exercise/Algebra *(Page 161)*

1. E	3. C	5. C	7. D	9. A	11. E	13. E	15. C	17. D	19. B
2. B	4. E	6. D	8. C	10. D	12. B	14. A	16. B	18. E	20. E

Practice Exercise/Solving Problems by Equations *(Page 163)*

1. B	3. C	5. A	7. D	9. C
2. A	4. D	6. B	8. C	10. C

Practice Exercise/Inequalities *(Page 164)*

1. B	3. C	5. B	7. C	9. B	11. E	13. D	15. D	17. A	19. C
2. E	4. C	6. E	8. A	10. D	12. A	14. E	16. D	18. B	20. D

Practice Exercise/Geometry *(Page 174)*

1. D	5. C	9. B	13. C	17. A	21. D	24. C	27. A	30. D	33. D
2. B	6. C	10. A	14. B	18. E	22. C	25. D	28. D	31. A	34. B
3. A	7. E	11. B	15. B	19. C	23. B	26. C	29. A	32. B	35. D
4. B	8. A	12. B	16. C	20. B					

Practice Exercise/Fractions *(Page 178)*

1. A	3. D	5. A	7. C	9. D	11. C	13. C	15. B	17. D	19. B
2. B	4. E	6. A	8. D	10. E	12. E	14. D	16. A	18. A	20. B

Practice Exercise/Percent *(Page 179)*

1. C	3. E	5. C	7. B	9. B	11. D	13. C	15. B	17. D	19. B
2. C	4. E	6. D	8. D	10. B	12. E	14. D	16. D	18. A	20. E

Practice Exercise/Averages *(Page 181)*

1. C	3. D	5. B	7. D	9. E	11. A	13. C	15. B	17. D	19. D
2. B	4. D	6. D	8. E	10. D	12. E	14. B	16. C	18. A	20. A

Practice Exercise/Motion *(Page 182)*

1. B	3. D	5. B	7. A	9. A	11. A	13. C	15. B	17. C	19. C
2. D	4. E	6. D	8. E	10. D	12. A	14. A	16. B	18. B	20. D

Practice Exercise/Ratio and Proportion *(Page 184)*

1. A	3. C	5. C	7. E	9. C	11. A	13. E	15. C	17. D	19. C
2. E	4. E	6. D	8. B	10. D	12. B	14. E	16. E	18. A	20. B

Practice Exercise/Work *(Page 185)*

1. D	3. C	5. C	7. C	9. C	11. D	13. C	15. B	17. C	19. D
2. E	4. B	6. A	8. B	10. C	12. B	14. A	16. D	18. C	20. C

Data Interpretation *(Page 187)*

1. E	3. A	5. E	7. B	9. C	11. D	13. C	15. D	17. E
2. C	4. A	6. A	8. E	10. D	12. C	14. D	16. D	

10

The Quantitative Comparison Question

In the quantitative comparison questions you are given two quantities that are sometimes accompanied by information that concerns either or both quantities. Answering the question properly depends upon your ability to decide which, if either, is the greater quantity. In general, quantitative comparison questions require less time to answer, involve less reading, and require somewhat less computation than the usual multiple-choice questions. This type of question reflects the contemporary emphasis in school mathematics on inequalities; you must use the concepts of "greater than," "less than," and "equal to" to decide which choice is correct. Quantitative comparison questions will appear with the following instructions:

DIRECTIONS: *Each question in this section consists of two quantities, one in Column A and one in Column B. You are to compare the two quantities and on the answer sheet fill in circle*

(A) if the quantity in Column A is greater;

(B) if the quantity in Column B is greater;

(C) if the two quantities are equal;

(D) if the relationship cannot be determined from the information given.

TIPS FOR HANDLING QUANTITATIVE COMPARISON QUESTIONS

1. Learn the format of the Quantitative Comparison questions. Remember that information relating to both columns is centered above the two quantities. Also, since there are only four choices, you do not choose answer **E.**

2. When a problem involves straightforward computation only, eliminate **D,** which cannot possibly be correct since there must be a definite answer. Even if you now have to guess, your chance of guessing correctly has improved.

3. These questions require less time, and many can be answered without lengthy computation. Some questions can be answered correctly in a few seconds.

4. When comparing expressions with variables, don't forget to try negative values, fractions, and zero. For example, $5x$ is greater than $4x$ only if x is positive; $5x$ is less than $4x$ if x is negative, and $5x = 4x$ if x is 0. Also, if $x^2 = 25$, remember that $x = +5$ or $x = -5$. Note, however, that $\sqrt{25} = 5$ only, not -5.

5. Be careful in handling multiplication of negative values. Recall that multiplying a positive number by a negative number gives you a negative, and therefore a smaller, number. If the problem does not specifically tell you that an unknown is not a negative number, it could be negative. Multiplication usually makes a number larger; but when you multiply it by a fraction less than 1 you make the number smaller, and when you divide it by a fraction less than 1 you make the number larger.

6. Eliminate from consideration any quantity that appears in both columns. Confine your thinking to the other terms or expressions.

7. If a question involves several numbers multiplied together, the product will be negative if an odd number of them are negative, but positive if an even number of them are negative; the number that are positive does not affect the product at all. If only a single one of a group of numbers multiplied together can possibly be zero, then the entire product will be zero.

8. If a question involves powers of a variable, and the variable has a negative value, the even powers will be positive but the odd powers will be negative. If the value of a variable can be a positive fraction less than 1, the higher the power of the variable, the smaller its value.

9. If a question involves odd and even numbers, note that, if two even numbers are added, the sum is even, and if two odd numbers are added, the sum is also even. If an odd and an even number are added, the sum is odd.

If either an even or an odd number is multiplied by an even number, the product is even. If two odd numbers are multiplied together, the product is odd.

10. If two fractions have the same numerator, the one with the larger denominator is smaller. If two fractions have the same denominator, the one with the larger numerator is larger.

11. Quantitative Comparison questions provide four choices for answers. If you make a random guess, you are likely to be right only 1 out of 4 times. Since the deduction for a wrong answer on the Quantitative Comparison questions is $\frac{1}{3}$ of a point, it is unwise to make a purely random guess. However, if you can definitely rule out one choice as incorrect, a guess from among the remaining three is not foolhardy since the odds of its being correct equal the deduction cost for a wrong answer. If you can rule out more than one choice, it is certainly advisable to make a guess from among those remaining since the odds of getting the correct choice are better than the deduction cost of a wrong answer.

EXAMPLES:

COLUMN A	COLUMN B
1. $10 - \frac{10}{.1}$	-90

ANALYSIS

$\frac{10}{.1}$ equals $\frac{100}{1}$ or 100

$10 - 100 = -90$

The correct answer is **C**.

COLUMN A	COLUMN B
2. 50%	$\frac{1}{.02}$

ANALYSIS

The value of $\frac{1}{.02} = 50$

50 is greater than 50%

The correct answer is **B**.

In J. J. High School one chemistry class had an average of 70% on a uniform city-wide test and another class had an average of 75% on this test. In K. K. High School the average mark in 2 classes for this same test was 72.5%.

COLUMN A	COLUMN B
3. School average on the chemistry test in J. J. High School	School average on the chemistry test in K. K. High School

ANALYSIS

Since we do not have the number of students involved in these various classes, we may not assign weight to the averages given.

The correct answer is **D**.

In rectangle *ABCD*, $AB = \pi$ and BC = diameter of circle *O*.

COLUMN A	COLUMN B
4. Perimeter of *ABCD*	Circumference of circle *O*

ANALYSIS

Perimeter of $ABCD = \pi + \pi + d + d$ *or* $2(\pi d)$

Circumference of circle $= \pi d$

$2(\pi d) > \pi d$

The correct answer is **A**.

▶PRACTICE EXERCISE

DIRECTIONS: Each of the following questions consists of two quantities, one in Column A and one in Column B. Information concerning both quantities appears centered above both quantities. Diagrams need not be assumed to be drawn to scale. Letters used represent real numbers. After comparing the two quantities, choose

(A) if the quantity in Column A is greater
(B) if the quantity in Column B is greater
(C) if the two quantities are equal
(D) if the relationship between the two quantities cannot be determined from the information given.

COLUMN A	COLUMN B
$x = 0.5$	
1. $\dfrac{\frac{3}{4}}{1 + x}$	x
2. $\dfrac{\frac{1}{4} - \frac{3}{16}}{\frac{1}{8}}$	2
3. 109 inches	3 yards 1 inch
4. $\dfrac{7 + 7 + 7}{7 - 7 - 7}$	3
$x = 7$	
5. x^7	$7x^6$
$0 < k < 32$; k is divisible by 3 and 9.	
6. k	27

$X^2 = 25$

7. X | 5

$\frac{1}{x} < 0$

8. 1 | x

$10x^3 = y$
$x > 1$

9. y | x

$a:b = c:d$

10. bc | ad

---

11. $\sqrt{\frac{1}{.25}}$ | 20%

---

12. $\sqrt{1440}$ | 120

---

13. The average of 90%, $\frac{3}{5}$, and 1.5 | 3

---

14. $\frac{a}{4}$% of 400 | a

---

15. $\frac{a-b}{-c}$ | $\frac{b-a}{c}$

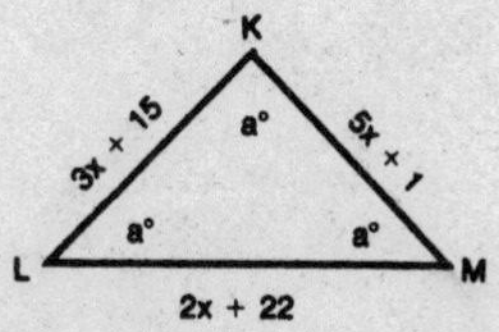

16. x | 7

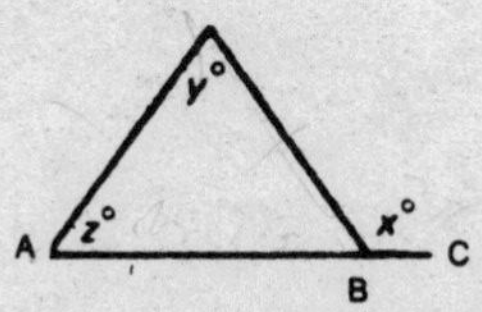

ABC is a straight line.

17. x | z

(This diagram concerns #s 18–20.)

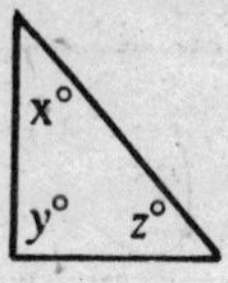

$z = 90$

18. x | y

---

19. $x + y$ | z

---

20. $z - x$ | y

$b \neq -c$

$\frac{a}{-b-c} = \frac{-5}{c+b}$

21. 5 | a

---

22 2 hours, 40 minutes | The elapsed time from 8:55 P.M. to 10:15 the same evening

---

The distance from Mark's house to the Waban school is 3 miles, while the distance from Sara's house to this school is 4 miles.

23. The distance from Mark's house to Sara's house | 5 miles

---

24. $(0.1)(\pi)$ | $\sqrt{.17}$

---

25. $\frac{2+2+2}{2-2-2}$ | $\frac{3+3+3}{3-3-3}$

---

26. $\sqrt{1.44}$ | 0.12

$X^2 = 100$

27. X | 10

$a > 0$, $x > 0$, and $\frac{a}{x} < 1$

28. a | x

$0 < a < b$

29. $\frac{1}{a}$ | $\frac{1}{b}$

	Column A		Column B
30.	105% of 500		50% of 1000
31.	x	$5x = 23 = y$	y
32.	$2X$	$X > Y$ and $Y > Z$	$Y + Z$
33.	$\frac{1}{x + y}$	$x > 0$ and $y > 0$	$\frac{\frac{1}{xy}}{\frac{1}{x} + \frac{1}{y}}$
34.	$\sqrt{\frac{1}{25}}$		$\left(\frac{1}{5}\right)^2$
35.	15%		$\frac{0.3}{2}$
36.	$\frac{z}{y}$	$0 < x < y < z$	$\frac{z}{x}$
37.	The percentage increase from \$5 to \$7		The percentage increase from \$7 to \$9
38.	$a + 1$		$a - 1$
39.	zero	$\frac{1}{a} < 0$	a
40.	1.6 kilometers	1 kilometer = $\frac{5}{8}$ mile	1 mile

ANSWER KEY

1. **C**	*9.* **A**	*17.* **A**	*25.* **C**	*33.* **C**
2. **B**	*10.* **C**	*18.* **D**	*26.* **A**	*34.* **A**
3. **C**	*11.* **A**	*19.* **C**	*27.* **D**	*35.* **C**
4. **B**	*12.* **B**	*20.* **C**	*28.* **B**	*36.* **B**
5. **C**	*13.* **B**	*21.* **C**	*29.* **A**	*37.* **A**
6. **D**	*14.* **C**	*22.* **A**	*30.* **A**	*38.* **A**
7. **D**	*15.* **C**	*23.* **D**	*31.* **B**	*39.* **A**
8. **A**	*16.* **C**	*24.* **B**	*32.* **A**	*40.* **C**

TEST YOURSELF

11

Ten Typical Tests

Many students, after taking the PSAT/NMSQT, report that they found the experience very exhausting. One hour and forty minutes on difficult test material may prove to be very grueling.

To alleviate this situation, the authors wish to offer two suggestions:

1. Become acquainted with the time situation before taking the actual test. The student taking the ten typical tests in this chapter under time conditions will become familiar with the situation before taking the actual test. This familiarity should enable you to find the actual test less rigorous.

2. If students recognize that the 100-minute test may be physically tiring, they should recognize the need for physical fitness. The best advice we can offer is that you stop preparation for the test several days before the scheduled date. Rest and relaxation will enable you to avoid the fatigue of a long hour-plus examination and will prove to be more profitable than last-minute "cramming."

PSAT/NMSQT Answer Sheet

TYPICAL TEST A

Verbal Aptitude Section

1 (A) (B) (C) (D) (E)
2 (A) (B) (C) (D) (E)
3 (A) (B) (C) (D) (E)
4 (A) (B) (C) (D) (E)
5 (A) (B) (C) (D) (E)
6 (A) (B) (C) (D) (E)
7 (A) (B) (C) (D) (E)
8 (A) (B) (C) (D) (E)
9 (A) (B) (C) (D) (E)
10 (A) (B) (C) (D) (E)
11 (A) (B) (C) (D) (E)
12 (A) (B) (C) (D) (E)
13 (A) (B) (C) (D) (E)
14 (A) (B) (C) (D) (E)
15 (A) (B) (C) (D) (E)
16 (A) (B) (C) (D) (E)
17 (A) (B) (C) (D) (E)
18 (A) (B) (C) (D) (E)
19 (A) (B) (C) (D) (E)
20 (A) (B) (C) (D) (E)
21 (A) (B) (C) (D) (E)
22 (A) (B) (C) (D) (E)
23 (A) (B) (C) (D) (E)
24 (A) (B) (C) (D) (E)
25 (A) (B) (C) (D) (E)
26 (A) (B) (C) (D) (E)
27 (A) (B) (C) (D) (E)
28 (A) (B) (C) (D) (E)
29 (A) (B) (C) (D) (E)
30 (A) (B) (C) (D) (E)
31 (A) (B) (C) (D) (E)
32 (A) (B) (C) (D) (E)
33 (A) (B) (C) (D) (E)
34 (A) (B) (C) (D) (E)
35 (A) (B) (C) (D) (E)
36 (A) (B) (C) (D) (E)
37 (A) (B) (C) (D) (E)
38 (A) (B) (C) (D) (E)
39 (A) (B) (C) (D) (E)
40 (A) (B) (C) (D) (E)
41 (A) (B) (C) (D) (E)
42 (A) (B) (C) (D) (E)
43 (A) (B) (C) (D) (E)
44 (A) (B) (C) (D) (E)
45 (A) (B) (C) (D) (E)
46 (A) (B) (C) (D) (E)
47 (A) (B) (C) (D) (E)
48 (A) (B) (C) (D) (E)
49 (A) (B) (C) (D) (E)
50 (A) (B) (C) (D) (E)
51 (A) (B) (C) (D) (E)
52 (A) (B) (C) (D) (E)
53 (A) (B) (C) (D) (E)
54 (A) (B) (C) (D) (E)
55 (A) (B) (C) (D) (E)
56 (A) (B) (C) (D) (E)
57 (A) (B) (C) (D) (E)
58 (A) (B) (C) (D) (E)
59 (A) (B) (C) (D) (E)
60 (A) (B) (C) (D) (E)
61 (A) (B) (C) (D) (E)
62 (A) (B) (C) (D) (E)
63 (A) (B) (C) (D) (E)
64 (A) (B) (C) (D) (E)
65 (A) (B) (C) (D) (E)

Mathematical Aptitude Section*

1 (A) (B) (C) (D) (E)
2 (A) (B) (C) (D) (E)
3 (A) (B) (C) (D) (E)
4 (A) (B) (C) (D) (E)
5 (A) (B) (C) (D) (E)
6 (A) (B) (C) (D) (E)
7 (A) (B) (C) (D) (E)
8 (A) (B) (C) (D) (E)
9 (A) (B) (C) (D) (E)
10 (A) (B) (C) (D) (E)
11 (A) (B) (C) (D) (E)
12 (A) (B) (C) (D) (E)
13 (A) (B) (C) (D) (E)
14 (A) (B) (C) (D) (E)
15 (A) (B) (C) (D) (E)
16 (A) (B) (C) (D) (E)
17 (A) (B) (C) (D) (E)
18 (A) (B) (C) (D) (E)
19 (A) (B) (C) (D) (E)
20 (A) (B) (C) (D) (E)
21 (A) (B) (C) (D) (E)
22 (A) (B) (C) (D) (E)
23 (A) (B) (C) (D) (E)
24 (A) (B) (C) (D) (E)
25 (A) (B) (C) (D) (E)
26 (A) (B) (C) (D) (E)
27 (A) (B) (C) (D) (E)
28 (A) (B) (C) (D) (E)
29 (A) (B) (C) (D) (E)
30 (A) (B) (C) (D) (E)
31 (A) (B) (C) (D) (E)
32 (A) (B) (C) (D) (E)
33 (A) (B) (C) (D) (E)
34 (A) (B) (C) (D) (E)
35 (A) (B) (C) (D) (E)
36 (A) (B) (C) (D) (E)
37 (A) (B) (C) (D) (E)
38 (A) (B) (C) (D) (E)
39 (A) (B) (C) (D) (E)
40 (A) (B) (C) (D) (E)
41 (A) (B) (C) (D) (E)
42 (A) (B) (C) (D) (E)
43 (A) (B) (C) (D) (E)
44 (A) (B) (C) (D) (E)
45 (A) (B) (C) (D) (E)
46 (A) (B) (C) (D) (E)
47 (A) (B) (C) (D) (E)
48 (A) (B) (C) (D) (E)
49 (A) (B) (C) (D) (E)
50 (A) (B) (C) (D) (E)

*If there are more answer spaces than you need, leave them blank.

TYPICAL TEST A

SECTION 1 — **Time—50 minutes 65 Questions** — For each question in this section, choose the best answer and fill in the corresponding circle on the answer sheet.

Each question below consists of a word in capital letters, followed by five lettered words or phrases. Choose the word or phrase that is most nearly opposite in meaning to the word in capital letters. Since some of the questions require you to distinguish fine shades of meaning, consider all the choices before deciding which is best.

Example:

GOOD: (A) sour (B) bad (C) red (D) hot (E) ugly

Ⓐ ● Ⓒ Ⓓ Ⓔ

1. BENEFIT: (A) delay (B) harm (C) uncover (D) collect (E) invest
2. TREMBLE: (A) reduce in number (B) shift in place (C) remain steady (D) weigh carefully (E) stand erect
3. CONTRADICTORY: (A) uninteresting (B) questionable (C) poorly expressed (D) indirectly stated (E) easily reconciled
4. HECTIC: (A) serious (B) chronic (C) serene (D) helpful (E) victorious
5. BLUR: (A) harmony (B) clarity (C) smoothness (D) bulkiness (E) speed
6. SHORT-HANDED: (A) well-established (B) fully staffed (C) even-tempered (D) long-legged (E) broad-minded
7. RUDDY: (A) sallow (B) wholesome (C) immaculate (D) graceful (E) opaque
8. MUTED: (A) unchanged (B) incomplete (C) recognizable (D) similar (E) loud
9. CONSOLIDATION: (A) inception (B) sensitivity (C) fragmentation (D) warranty (E) liability
10. SERVILITY: (A) charm (B) eloquence (C) independence (D) insipidness (E) futility
11. PIETY: (A) doom (B) absence (C) irreverence (D) certainty (E) satiety
12. EXPEDITE: (A) retard (B) implore (C) elevate (D) transmit (E) detach
13. LANGUOR: (A) alertness (B) infallibility (C) mistrust (D) iniquity (E) quietness
14. MALIGNANT: (A) powerful (B) thoughtful (C) belligerent (D) painful (E) beneficial
15. UNDULATE: (A) become pale (B) arrive on time (C) make ready (D) lack keenness (E) remain still
16. SUCCINCT: (A) intolerant (B) verbose (C) awkward (D) futile (E) inappropriate
17. REMISS: (A) necessary (B) loose (C) consequential (D) independent (E) meticulous
18. ASSUAGE: (A) misplace (B) provoke (C) forget about (D) hold in honor (E) feel guilty
19. DESICCATE: (A) renovate (B) magnify (C) drench (D) combine (E) satisfy
20. ABET: (A) regulate (B) wager (C) aver (D) hinder (E) accompany

Each sentence below has one or two blanks, each blank indicating that something has been omitted. Beneath the sentence are five lettered words or sets of words. Choose the word or set of words that, when inserted in the sentence, best fits the meaning of the sentence as a whole.

Example:

Although its publicity has been ----, the film itself is intelligent, well-acted, handsomely produced, and altogether ----.

(A) tasteless . . respectable (B) extensive . . moderate (C) sophisticated . . amateur (D) risque . . crude (E) perfect . . spectacular

● Ⓑ Ⓒ Ⓓ Ⓔ

21. Unhappily, the psychology experiment was ---- by the subjects' awareness of the presence of observers in their midst.
(A) muted (B) mitigated (C) marred (D) clarified (E) concluded

22. Nothing anyone could say was able to alter North's ---- that his attempt to lie to Congress was justified.
(A) demand (B) conviction (C) maxim (D) fear (E) ambivalence

23. Excessive use of coal and oil eventually may ---- the earth's supply of fossil fuels, leaving us in need of a new source of energy.
(A) replenish (B) magnify (C) merge (D) deplete (E) redirect

24. Until James learned to be more ---- about writing down his homework assignments, he seldom knew when any assignment was due.
(A) obstinate (B) contrary (C) opportunistic
(D) methodical (E) literate

25. Despite all the advertisements singing the ---- of the new product, she remained ---- its merits, wanting to see what *Consumer Reports* had to say about its claims.
(A) virtues . . an optimist about
(B) praises . . a skeptic about
(C) joys . . a convert to
(D) defects . . a cynic about
(E) advantages . . a believer in

26. Even though the basic organization of the brain does not change after birth, details of its structure and function remain ---- for some time, particularly in the cerebral cortex.
(A) plastic (B) immutable (C) essential
(D) unknown (E) static

27. In *Gulliver's Travels*, Swift's intent is ----; he exposes the follies of English society by ridiculing the follies of the Lilliputians.
(A) elegiac (B) prophetic (C) satirical
(D) questionable (E) derivative

28. Even the threat of sudden death could not ---- the intrepid pilot and explorer Beryl Markham; a true ----, she risked her life countless times to set records for flying small planes.
(A) intimidate . . patriot
(B) divert . . renegade
(C) interest . . dilettante
(D) daunt . . daredevil
(E) survive . . firebrand

29. The tax investigation became so ---- petty technicalities that the Internal Revenue Service agent could make no progress with the case.
(A) acquainted with (B) unobstructed by
(C) removed from (D) mired in (E) free of

30. As an indefatigable consumer advocate, Ralph Nader is constantly engaged in ---- the claims of unscrupulous merchandisers and cautioning the public to exercise a healthy ----.
(A) asserting . . autonomy
(B) deflating . . prodigality
(C) debunking . . skepticism
(D) affirming . . indifference
(E) exaggerating . . optimism

> Each question below consists of a related pair of words or phrases, followed by five lettered pairs of words or phrases. Select the lettered pair that <u>best</u> expresses a relationship similar to that expressed in the original pair.
>
> Example:
>
> YAWN : BOREDOM : : (A) dream : sleep
> (B) anger : madness (C) smile : amusement
> (D) face : expression (E) impatience : rebellion
>
> Ⓐ Ⓑ ● Ⓓ Ⓔ

31. FOOTBALL : GRIDIRON : : (A) soccer : goal
(B) rugby : arena (C) wrestling : mat
(D) baseball : diamond (E) bowling : pin

32. WILT : WATER : : (A) melt : ice
(B) starve : food (C) breathe : air
(D) blink : light (E) glow : sun

33. GOOSE : GOSLING : : (A) sheep : flock
(B) pig : sty (C) bird : wing
(D) goat : kid (E) rooster : hen

34. CORD : WOOD : : (A) string : kite
(B) bolt : cloth (C) brick : wall
(D) branch : tree (E) ore : metal

35. ORBIT : ECCENTRIC : : (A) habit : instinctive
(B) circle : concentric (C) planet : astronomical
(D) behavior : irregular (E) robot : automatic

36. LOBSTER : CRUSTACEAN : :
(A) ant : insectivore
(B) kangaroo : marsupial
(C) larva : moth (D) bird : aviary
(E) salmon : roe

37. SIMPLE : ELABORATION : :
(A) practical : usefulness (B) foolish : consistency
(C) thrifty : extravagance (D) holy : worship
(E) distant : boundary

38. STORM : SUBSIDE : :
(A) assault : mount (B) riot : incite
(C) spasm : relax (D) turbulence : disturb
(E) attack : escalate

39. DELIRIUM : DISORIENTATION : :
(A) paralysis : immobility (B) anorexia : pain
(C) insomnia : apprehension
(D) rash : vaccination (E) malaria : relapse

40. TENDRIL : VINE : :
(A) trunk : tree (B) pollen : flower
(C) pseudopod : amoeba
(D) trellis : honeysuckle (E) cobra : snake

41. SCURRY : MOVE : : (A) chant : sing
(B) chatter : talk (C) carry : lift
(D) sleep : drowse (E) limp : walk

42. EULOGY : LAUDATORY : :
(A) epigram : lengthy (B) tirade : abusive
(C) elegy : hyperbolic (D) argument : offensive
(E) apology : sincere

43. OBDURATE : FLEXIBILITY : :
(A) accurate : perception (B) turbid : roughness
(C) principled : fallibility
(D) diaphanous : transparency
(E) adamant : submissiveness

44. REPROBATE : BLAMEWORTHY : :
(A) zealot : indifferent (B) charlatan : flagrant
(C) adherent : vociferous (D) braggart : venerable
(E) traducer : slanderous

45. FEUD : ACRIMONY : :
(A) scuffle : confusion (B) crusade : heresy
(C) duel : brevity (D) scrimmage : ceremony
(E) siege : vulnerability

> Each passage below is followed by questions based on its content. Answer the questions following each passage on the basis of what is stated or implied in that passage.

John Greenleaf Whittier was the "Quaker-Puritan" scion of Massachusetts farmers. For this frail young man, however, farm life was too tough an existence. His early interest in books and legends led him toward journalism, with poetry a pleasant sideline. He became a Quaker firebrand and agitator, the politician among abolitionists, and a gadfly to New England congressmen during the original "Great Debate." His impassioned prose and poetry against slavery were often directed at a clergy whose acceptance of it he fought as a Quaker and a Christian.

Only after the Civil War, when emancipation had been at least nominally won, did the aging Whittier emerge as the genial, easygoing "folkbard" remembered today. Until recently the prominence given this last phase of his literary life by scholarly circles has obscured his earlier contributions to American literature and political freedom and tolerance.

46. The primary purpose of this passage is to
(A) denounce a social injustice
(B) evaluate a writer's poetic style
(C) explain a nineteenth-century literary fashion
(D) correct a misconception about an individual
(E) argue against political involvement

47. The author's attitude toward Whittier's early career as a firebrand can best be described as one of
(A) wary skepticism (B) moral censure
(C) reluctant tolerance (D) objective neutrality
(E) open approbation

48. It can be inferred from the passage that New England congressman during the time of the "Great Debate" most likely thought of Whittier as
(A) a cordial teller of tales
(B) an antiabolitionist
(C) an annoying critic
(D) a virtuous Quaker
(E) a literary scholar

49. On the basis of the passage, which of the following attitudes can appropriately be attributed to Whittier?
(A) The aim of literature is to entertain the reading public rather than to advocate a particular cause.
(B) Emancipation can occur only with the full cooperation of the slaveowners, who thus must be won over gently.
(C) A poet must devote himself to his art, forsaking worldly claims in favor of aesthetic values.
(D) It is particularly reprehensible for Christian ministers to tolerate an institution as immoral as slavery.
(E) There is no place in the church for disharmony and strife, for the church is the temple of the Lord.

Perhaps the first point to grasp about natural selection is that a complex creature, or even a complex part of a creature, such as the eye, did not arise in one evolutionary step. Rather it evolved through a series of small steps. Exactly what is meant by small is not necessarily obvious since the growth of an organism is controlled by an elaborate program written in its genes. A small change in a key part of the program can make a large difference. For example, an alteration in one gene in *Drosophila* can produce a fruit fly with legs in place of its antennae.

Each small step is caused by a random alteration in the genetic instructions. Many of these random alterations may do the organism no good (some may even kill it before it is born), but occasionally a particular chance alteration may give that particular organism a selective advantage. This means that in the last analysis the organism will, on average, leave more offspring than it would otherwise. If this advantage persists in its descendants then this beneficial mutant will gradually, over many generations, spread through the population. In favorable cases, every individual will come to possess the improved version of the gene. The older version will have been eliminated. Natural selection is thus a beautiful mechanism for turning rare events (strictly, favorable rare events) into common ones.

50. The author's attitude toward the process of natural selection can best be described as one of
(A) mild skepticism
(B) puzzled fascination
(C) controlled apprehension
(D) appreciative admiration
(E) lofty detachment

51. The author's primary purpose in introducing the reference to *Drosophila* is to
(A) indicate his familiarity with laboratory experiments on fruit flies
(B) describe the process by which a genetic alteration changes the body
(C) provide a vivid illustration of extreme effects of a slight genetic change
(D) give an example of a favorable genetic mutation
(E) demonstrate that it took several evolutionary steps for the fruit fly to reach its present form

52. The passage indicates that the nature of a selective advantage is
(A) immutable (B) reproductive (C) limited
(D) mental (E) inequitable

Tapestries are made on looms. Their distinctive weave is basically simple: the colored weft threads interface regularly with the monochrome warps, as in darning or plain cloth, but as they do so, they form a design by reversing their direction when a change of color is needed. The wefts are beaten down to cover the warps completely. The result is a design or picture that is the fabric itself, not one laid upon a ground like an embroidery, a print, or brocading. The back and front of a tapestry show the same design. The weaver always follows a preexisting model, generally a drawing or painting, known as the cartoon, which in most cases he reproduces as exactly as he can. Long training is needed to become a professional tapestry weaver. It can take as much as a year to produce a yard of very finely woven tapestry.

Tapestry-woven fabrics have been made from China to Peru and from very early times to the present day, but large wall hangings in this technique, mainly of wool, are typically Northern European. Few examples predating the late fourteenth century have survived, but from about 1400 tapestries were an essential part of aristocratic life. The prince or great nobleman sent his plate and his tapestries ahead of him to furnish his castles before his arrival as he traveled through his domains; both had the same function, to display his wealth and social position. It has frequently been suggested that tapestries helped to heat stone-walled rooms, but this is a modern idea; comfort was of minor importance in the Middle Ages. Tapestries were portable grandeur, instant splendor, taking the place, north of the Alps, of painted frescoes further south. They were hung without gaps between them, covering entire walls and often doors as well. Only very occasionally were they made as individual works of art such as altar frontals. They were usually commissioned or bought as sets, or "chambers," and constituted the most important furnishings of any grand room, except for the display of plate, throughout the Middle Ages and the sixteenth century. Later, woven silks, ornamental wood carving, stucco decoration, and painted leather gradually replaced tapestry as expensive wall coverings, until at last wallpaper was introduced in the late eighteenth century and eventually swept away almost everything else.

53. Tapestry weaving may be characterized as which of the following?
I. Time-consuming
II. Spontaneous in concept
III. Faithful to an original
(A) I only
(B) III only
(C) I and II only
(D) I and III only
(E) II and III only

54. Renaissance nobles carried tapestries with them to demonstrate their
(A) piety (B) consequence
(C) aesthetic judgment (D) need for privacy
(E) dislike for cold

55. The primary purpose of the passage is to
(A) explain the process of tapestry-making
(B) contrast Eastern and Western schools of tapestry
(C) analyze the reasons for the decline in popularity of tapestries
(D) introduce tapestry-making in reference to medieval wall-hangings
(E) advocate a return to a more colorful way of life

Rocks which have solidified directly from molten materials are called igneous rocks. Igneous rocks are commonly referred to as primary rocks because they are the original source of material found in sedimentaries and metamorphics. Igneous rocks compose the greater part of the earth's crust, but they are generally covered at the surface by a relatively thin layer of sedimentary or metamorphic rocks. Igenous rocks are distinguished by the following characteristics: (1) they contain no fossils; (2) they have no regular arrangement of layers; and (3) they are nearly always made up of crystals.

Sedimentary rocks are composed largely of minute fragments derived from the disintegration of existing rocks and in some instances from the remains of animals. As sediments are transported, individual fragments are assorted according to size. Distinct layers of such sediments as gravels, sand, and clay build up, as they are deposited by water and occasionally wind. These sediments vary in size with the material and the power of the eroding agent. Sedimentary materials are laid down in layers called strata.

When sediments harden into sedimentary rocks, the names applied to them change to indicate the change in physical state. Thus, small stones and gravel cemented together are known as conglomerates; cemented sand becomes sandstone; and hardened clay becomes shale. In addition to these, other sedimentary rocks such as limestone frequently result from the deposition of dissolved material. The ingredient parts are normally precipitated by organic substances, such as shells of clams or hard skeletons of other marine life.

Both igneous and sedimentary rocks may be changed by pressure, heat, solution, or cementing action. When individual grains from existing rocks tend to deform and interlock, they are called metamorphic rocks. For example, granite, an igneous rock, may be metamorphosed into a gneiss or a schist. Limestone, a sedimentary rock, when subjected to heat and pressure may become marble, a metamorphic rock. Shale under pressure becomes slate.

56. The primary purpose of the passage is to
(A) explain the factors that may cause rocks to change in form
(B) show how the scientific names of rocks reflect the rocks' composition
(C) present a new hypothesis about the nature of rock formation
(D) define and describe several diverse kinds of rocks
(E) explain why rocks are basic parts of the earth's structure

57. The passage would be most likely to appear in a
(A) technical article for practicing geologists
(B) teaching manual for an earth science text
(C) pamphlet about the conservation of natural resources
(D) newspaper feature on the workings of erosion
(E) nonfiction book explaining how oil is found

58. According to the passage, igneous rocks are characterized by
(A) their inability to be changed by heat or pressure
(B) the wealth of fossils they incorporate
(C) their granular composition
(D) their relative rarity
(E) their lack of regular strata

59. The passage contains information that would answer which of the following questions?
I. Which elements form igneous rocks?
II. What produces sufficient pressure to alter a rock?
III. Why is marble called a metamorphic rock?
(A) I only
(B) III only
(C) I and II only
(D) II and III only
(E) I, II, and III

60. Which of the following methods is NOT used by the author?
(A) Concrete examples
(B) Classification and discussion
(C) Specific enumeration
(D) Observation and hypothesis
(E) Cause and effect

There can be no doubt that the emergence of the Negro writer in the post-war period stemmed, in part, from the fact that he was inclined to exploit the opportunity to write about himself. It was more than that, however. The movement that has variously been called the "Harlem Renaissance," the "Black Renaissance," and the "New Negro Movement" was essentially a part of the growing interest of American literary circles in the immediate and pressing social and economic problems. This growing interest coincided with two developments in Negro life that fostered the growth of the New Negro Movement. These two factors, the keener realization of injustice and the improvement of the capacity for expression, produced a crop of Negro writers who constituted the "Harlem Renaissance."

The literature of the Harlem Renaissance was, for the most part, the work of a race-conscious group. Through poetry, prose, and song, the writers cried out against social and economic wrongs. They protested against segregation and lynching. They demanded higher wages, shorter hours, and better conditions of work. They stood for full social equality and first-class citizenship. The new vision of social and economic freedom which they had did not force them to embrace the several foreign ideologies that sought to sink their roots in some American groups during the period.

The writers of the Harlem Renaissance, bitter and cynical as some of them were, gave little attention to the propaganda of the socialists and communists. The editor of the *Messenger* ventured the opinion that the New Negro was the "product of the same world-wide forces that have brought into being the great liberal and radical movements that are now seizing the reins of power in all the civilized countries of the world." Such forces may have produced the New Negro, but the more articulate of the group did not resort to advocating the type of political action that would have subverted American constitutional government. Indeed, the writers of the Harlem Renaissance were not so much revolting against the system as they were protesting its inefficient operation. In this approach they proved as characteristically American as any writers of the period. Like his contemporaries, the Negro writer was merely becoming more aware of America's pressing problems; and like the others, he was willing to use his art, not only to contribute to the great body of American culture but to improve the culture of which he was a part.

It seems possible, moreover, for the historian to assign to the Negro writer a role that he did not assume. There were doubtless many who were not immediately concerned with the injustices heaped on the Negro. Some contrived their poems, novels, and songs merely for the sake of art, while others took up their pens to escape the sordid aspects of their existence. If there is an element of race in their writings, it is because the writings flow out of their individual and group experiences. This is not to say that such writings were not effective as protest literature, but rather that not all the authors were conscious crusaders for a better world. As a matter of fact, it was this detachment, this objectivity, that made it possible for many of the writers of the Harlem Renaissance to achieve a nobility of expression and a poignancy of feeling in their writings that placed them among the masters of recent American literature.

61. The author is primarily concerned with
(A) arguing that the literature of the Harlem Renaissance arose from the willingness of black writers to portray their own lives
(B) depicting the part played by socially conscious black writers in a worldwide ideological and literary crusade
(C) providing examples of the injustices protested by the writers of the Harlem Renaissance
(D) describing the social and political background that led to the blossoming of the Harlem Renaissance
(E) analyzing stages in the development of the New Negro Movement into the Harlem Renaissance

62. In reference to the achievements of the Harlem Renaissance, the passage conveys primarily a sense of
(A) protest (B) betrayal (C) nostalgia
(D) urgency (E) admiration

63. Which of the following is implied by the statement that the writers of the Harlem Renaissance "were not so much revolting against the system as they were protesting its inefficient operation" (paragraph 3)?
(A) Black writers played only a minor part in protesting the injustices of the period.
(B) Left to itself, the system was sure to operate efficiently.
(C) Black writers in general were not opposed to the system as such.
(D) In order for the system to operate efficiently, blacks must seize the reins of power in America.
(E) Black writers were too caught up in aesthetic philosophy to identify the true nature of the conflict.

64. The information in the passage suggests that the author is most likely
(A) a historian concerned with presenting socially conscious black writers of the period as loyal Americans
(B) a literary critic who questions the conclusions of the historians about the Harlem Renaissance
(C) an educator involved in fostering creative writing projects for minority youths
(D) a black writer of fiction interested in discovering new facts about her literary roots
(E) a researcher with questions about the validity of his sources

65. The passage supplies information for answering which of the following questions?
(A) What factors led to the stylistic improvement in the literary works of black writers in the postwar period?
(B) Who were the leading exponents of protest literature during the Harlem Renaissance?
(C) Why were the writers of the Harlem Renaissance in rebellion against foreign ideological systems?
(D) How did black writers in the postwar period define the literary tradition to which they belonged?
(E) With what specific socioeconomic causes did the black writers of the postwar period associate themselves?

SECTION 2 — Time—50 minutes, 50 Questions

In this section solve each problem, using any available space on the page for scratchwork. Then decide which is the best of the choices given and fill in the corresponding circle on the answer sheet.

The following information is for your reference in solving some of the problems.

Circle of radius r: Area $= \pi r^2$ Circumference $= 2\pi r$
The number of degrees of arc in a circle is 360.
The measure in degrees of a straight angle is 180.

Definitions of symbols:

$=$ is equal to	$\leqq$ is less than or equal to
$\neq$ is unequal to	$\geqq$ is greater than or equal to
$<$ is less than	$\parallel$ is parallel to
$>$ is greater than	$\perp$ is perpendicular to

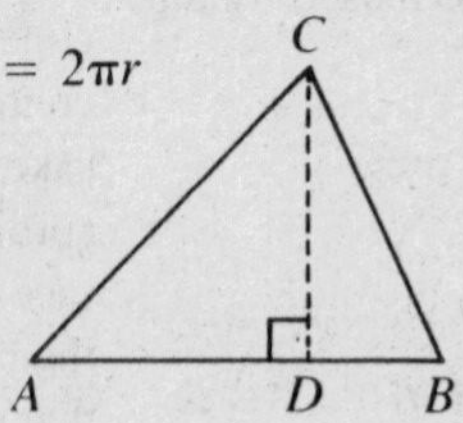

Triangle: The sum of the measures in degrees of the angles of a triangle is 180.

If $\angle CDA$ is a right angle, then

(1) area of $\triangle ABC = \dfrac{AB \times CD}{2}$

(2) $AC^2 = AD^2 + DC^2$

Note: Figures that accompany problems in this test are intended to provide information useful in solving the problems. They are drawn as accurately as possible EXCEPT when it is stated in a specific problem that its figure is not drawn to scale. All figures lie in a plane unless otherwise indicated. All numbers used are real numbers.

1. If $x > 1$, which of the following expressions decrease(s) in value as x increases?

I. $x + \frac{1}{x}$

II. $x^2 - 10x$

III. $\frac{1}{x + 1}$

(A) I only (B) II only (C) III only
(D) I and II only (E) I, II, and III

2. Which of the following has the largest numerical value?
(A) $\frac{1}{5}$ (B) $\left(\frac{1}{5}\right)^2$ (C) 0.3 (D) $\sqrt{0.16}$
(E) 0.01π

3. Which of the following is greater than $\frac{1}{4}$?
(A) $(0.25)^2$ (B) $\sqrt{\frac{1}{4}}$ (C) $\left(\frac{1}{4}\right)^4$ (D) 0.04 (E) $\frac{1}{250}$

4. The equation $x + 3y = 9$ and the equation $2x + 6y = 18$ are plotted on the same graph chart. All of the following points will lie on both graphs EXCEPT
(A) (7,0) (B) (0,3) (C) (6,1)
(D) (12, −1) (E) (3,4)

5. Which of the following has the largest numerical value?
(A) $\sqrt{0.3}$ (B) $\frac{1}{2}$ (C) 0.49 (D) $\left(\frac{1}{7}\right)^2$
(E) $(0.4)^2$

6. What is the thickness (in inches) of a pipe that has an inner diameter of 1.25 inches and an outer diameter of 1.55 inches?
(A) 0.15 (B) 0.2 (C) 0.4 (D) 1.65 (E) 0.3

7. If $x + x + x + x = y + y + y$, then $4x - 3y =$
(A) 0 (B) 1 (C) x (D) y (E) $x - y$

8. The price of a shirt is \$8 more than $\frac{8}{10}$ of its price. What is the price of this shirt?
(A) \$4 (B) \$20 (C) \$40 (D) \$60 (E) \$80

9. If $(x + \frac{1}{2}) + (x - \frac{1}{2}) = 5$, then $2x =$
(A) $\frac{2}{5}$ (B) $\frac{5}{2}$ (C) $2\frac{1}{5}$ (D) 5 (E) 10

10. If two parts of molasses are mixed with three parts of sugar, what part of the mixture is molasses?
(A) $\frac{1}{3}$ (B) $\frac{2}{5}$ (C) $\frac{3}{5}$ (D) $\frac{2}{3}$ (E) $\frac{3}{2}$

11. What percent of 2 is 20% of 20?
(A) 2% (B) 4% (C) 20% (D) 50%
(E) 200%

12. In a school election where 3 candidates sought election the winning candidate received $\frac{3}{5}$ of the votes. One losing candidate received $\frac{1}{4}$ of the remaining votes. What part of the total votes did the candidate with the least number of votes receive?
(A) $\frac{1}{10}$ (B) $\frac{1}{5}$ (C) $\frac{3}{10}$ (D) $\frac{2}{5}$ (E) $\frac{9}{20}$

13. If the complete contents of a fish tank 18 × 6 × 8 inches is poured into a tank with a base of 36 × 18 inches, the height of the water (in inches) will be
(A) $\frac{1}{6}$ (B) $\frac{1}{3}$ (C) $\frac{3}{4}$ (D) $1\frac{1}{3}$ (E) $1\frac{2}{3}$

14. $r = \frac{rs}{1 - s}$
$s^2 + 2s + 1 =$
(A) $\frac{1}{2}$ (B) $1\frac{1}{2}$ (C) $2\frac{1}{4}$ (D) 3 (E) $3\frac{1}{4}$

15. How many dimes must I give the postal clerk for thirty 25¢ postage stamps?
(A) 12 (B) 75 (C) 120 (D) 30 (E) 750

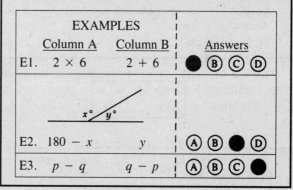

Questions 16-32 each consist of two quantities, one in Column A and one in Column B. You are to compare the two quantities and on the answer sheet fill in circle

A if the quantity in Column A is greater;
B if the quantity in Column B is greater;
C if the two quantities are equal;
D if the relationship cannot be determined from the information given.

Notes:
1. In certain questions, information concerning one or both of the quantities to be compared is centered above the two columns.
2. In a given question, a symbol that appears in both columns represents the same thing in Column A as it does in Column B.
3. Letters such as x, n, and k stand for real numbers.

EXAMPLES

	Column A	Column B	Answers
E1.	2×6	$2 + 6$	● Ⓑ Ⓒ Ⓓ
	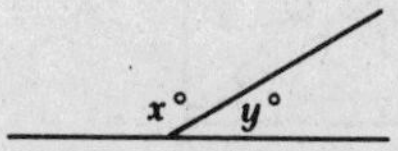		
E2.	$180 - x$	y	Ⓐ Ⓑ ● Ⓓ
E3.	$p - q$	$q - p$	Ⓐ Ⓑ Ⓒ ●

	COLUMN A	COLUMN B
16.	x^3	x^2
	The sum of a, b, and c, three consecutive integers, is 18.	
17.	abc	210
	$x = 1$ and $y = -1$	
18.	$\frac{a(x + y)}{b}$	$\frac{2a(x + y)}{b}$
	$\frac{x}{-y - z} = \frac{-a}{y + z}$	
19.	x	a
	$3x + 5y = 15 + 5y$	
20.	$\frac{x}{5}$	1

	COLUMN A	COLUMN B
21.	The time elapsed from 8:55 A.M. until 10:15 the same morning	2 hours, 40 minutes

Z is 4 miles from *Y*.
X is 3 miles from *Y*.

	COLUMN A	COLUMN B
22.	The distance from *X* to *Z*	5 miles
23.	$(0.1)(\pi)$	Positive value of $\sqrt{0.17}$

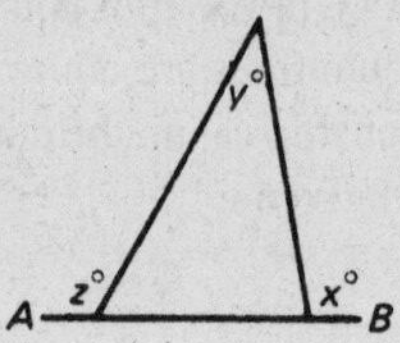

AB is a straight line and $x = 100$, $y = 40$.

	COLUMN A	COLUMN B
24.	z	$x + y$

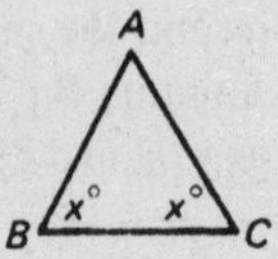

	COLUMN A	COLUMN B
25.	$\frac{BC}{AB} \cdot \frac{AC}{BC}$	1

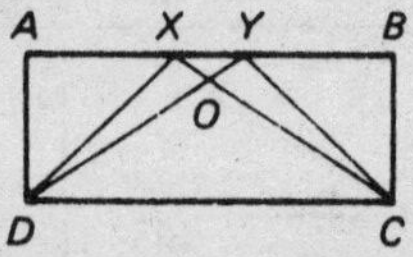

ABCD is a rectangle.

	COLUMN A	COLUMN B
26.	The area of $\triangle XOD$	The area of $\triangle YOC$

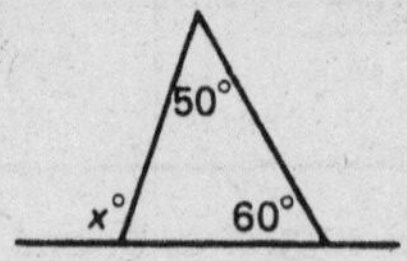

	COLUMN A	COLUMN B
27.	x	70
28.	The product of 2½ and its reciprocal	The product of 3½ and its reciprocal
29.	$3x$	$(-2)x$
30.	The area of a rectangle with length equal to 8 feet	The area of a square with side equal to 8 feet

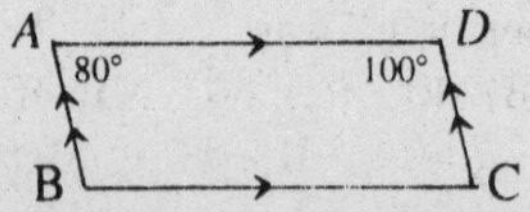

	COLUMN A	COLUMN B
31.	The measure of $\angle B$	The measure of $\angle C$
32.	3^{-2}	2^{-3}

Solve each of the remaining problems in this section using any available space for scratchwork. Then decide which is the best of the choices given and fill in the corresponding circle on the answer sheet.

33. In the town of Toonerville there are two high schools. In one school, $16\frac{2}{3}\%$ of the 300 seniors are planning to go to college. In the other school, 90% of the 500 seniors are not planning to go to college. What percent of the seniors in both schools are planning to go to college?
(A) 12.5% (B) 13.3% (C) 15% (D) 43.3% (E) 87.5%

34. In the accompanying figure, $\angle BAC$ and $\angle DBA$ are right angles. $AC = 9$, $BC = 15$, and $DB = 5$. What is the length of AD?
(A) 17 (B) $\sqrt{74}$
(C) $5\sqrt{2}$ (D) 13
(E) 19

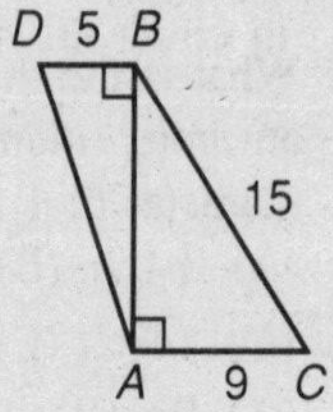

35. How many pounds of baggage are allowed for a plane passenger if the European regulations permit 20 kilograms per passenger?
(1 kg = 2.2 lbs.)
(A) 11 (B) 44 (C) 88 (D) 91 (E) 440

36. The dial of a meter is divided into equal divisions from 0 to 60. When the needle points to 48, the meter registers 80 amperes. What is the maximum number of amperes that the meter will register?
(A) 33.5 (B) 92 (C) 100 (D) 102 (E) 120

37. On a scale drawing *A* is 5 inches and *B* is drawn 11 inches. If the actual size of *B* is 5 meters, then the size (in meters) of *A* is
(A) $2\frac{3}{11}$ (B) $4\frac{6}{11}$ (C) 5 (D) 10 (E) 11

38. $ab = 50$, $a^2 = 100$, $b^2 = 25$; $(a - b)^2 =$
(A) 5 (B) $5\sqrt{3}$ (C) 25 (D) 50 (E) 75

39. Perfume can be purchased in a 0.6-ounce bottle for \$18 or in a 2-ounce bottle for \$50. The difference in price per ounce is
(A) \$1.50 (B) \$2.50 (C) \$5.00 (D) \$10.00
(E) \$25.00

40. Twenty minutes after a car enters a turnpike it is 20 miles from the entrance gate. The average speed (in miles per hour) was
(A) 20 (B) 40 (C) 60 (D) 100 (E) 400

41. How many ice cubes, each $1\frac{1}{2}$ inches on a side, are needed to fill a box which is $9 \times 12 \times 6$ inches? (Assume no space lost in packing the cubes.)
(A) 192 (B) 194.5 (C) 337.5 (D) 436
(E) 648

42. If the diameter of a circle is doubled, then the area will be multiplied by
(A) $\frac{1}{4}$ (B) $\frac{1}{2}$ (C) 2 (D) 4 (E) 16

43. $\angle B$ is formed by secant DCB and tangent AB. If the measure of $\angle B$ is 70° and $\widehat{CA}$ is 70°, how many degrees are in $\widehat{DC}$?
(A) 50 (B) 70 (C) 80
(D) 90 (E) 100

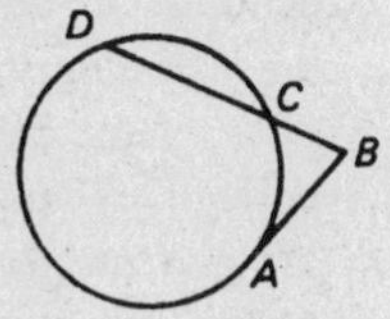

44. In circle O, $AO \perp OB$. The area of $\triangle AOB$ is $\frac{7}{\pi}$. The area of circle O is
(A) 7 (B) 14 (C) 7π
(D) 14π (E) 49π

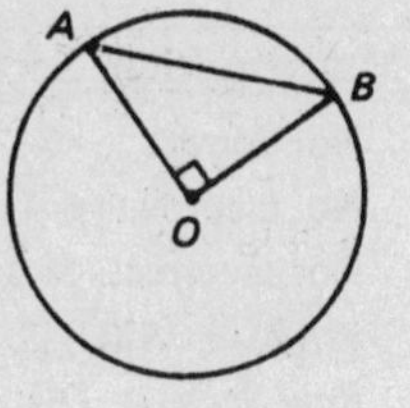

45. If the diagonal of a table with a square top is 6 feet, what is the area of the table top (in square feet)?
(A) $\sqrt{18}$ (B) 9π (C) 18 (D) $18\sqrt{2}$ (E) 36

46. In $\triangle ABC$ the measures of the three angles are represented by $(2x)°$, $(3x - 10)°$, and $(3x + 30)°$. What kind of triangle is ABC?
(A) acute (B) isosceles (C) oblique
(D) obtuse (E) right

47. In the accompanying figure, ACE and BCD are straight lines and B and D are right angles. What is the length of AB if $BC = 12$, $CD = 16$, and $DE = 12$?
(A) 8 (B) 9 (C) $10\frac{2}{3}$
(D) 12 (E) 16

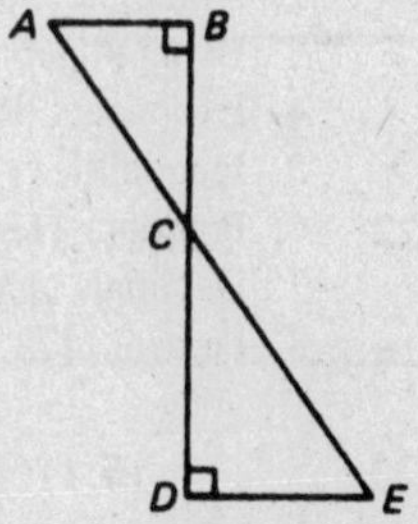

48. The cost of a taxi ride is c cents fo the first $\frac{1}{5}$ mile and x cents for each additional $\frac{1}{5}$ mile. What is the cost (in cents) of a 3-mile taxi ride at these rates?
(A) $14x + c$ (B) $x + 15c$ (C) $15x - c$
(D) $15x + c$ (E) $x + 14c$

49. If $(a + b)^2 - 4 = 5$, then $(a + b) =$
I. $+3$
II. -3
III. $+1$ or -1
(A) I only (B) II only (C) III only
(D) I and II only (E) I, II, and III

50. In the accompanying figure, points A and B are vertices of $\triangle ABC$ (not shown). The area of ABC is 12. Which of the following could be coordinates of vertex C?
(A) $(-4, -4)$
(B) $(-4, 4)$
(C) $(2, 4)$
(D) $(4, -4)$
(E) all of these

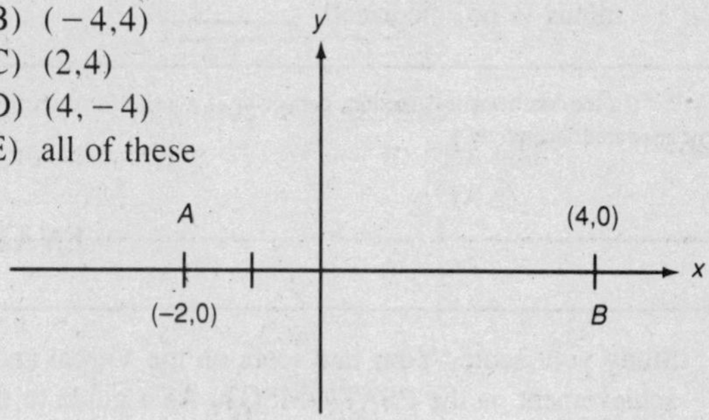

ANSWER KEY

Verbal Aptitude Section

1. B	11. C	21. C	31. D	41. B	51. C	61. D
2. C	12. A	22. B	32. B	42. B	52. B	62. E
3. E	13. A	23. D	33. D	43. E	53. D	63. C
4. C	14. E	24. D	34. B	44. E	54. B	64. A
5. B	15. E	25. B	35. D	45. A	55. D	65. E
6. B	16. B	26. A	36. B	46. D	56. D	
7. A	17. E	27. C	37. C	47. E	57. B	
8. E	18. B	28. D	38. C	48. C	58. E	
9. C	19. C	29. D	39. A	49. D	59. B	
10. C	20. D	30. C	40. C	50. D	60. D	

Mathematical Aptitude Section

Note: Each correct answer to the mathematics questions is keyed by number to the corresponding topic in Chapters 9 and 10. These numerals refer to the topics listed below, with specific page references in parentheses.

1. Basic Fundamental Operations (155–157)
2. Algebraic Operations (157–160)
3. Using Algebra (160–164)
4. Exponents, Roots and Radicals (159–160)
5. Inequalities (164–165)
6. Fractions (176–178)
7. Decimals (176)
8. Percent (178–180)
9. Averages (180–181)
10. Motion (182–183)
11. Ratio and Proportion (183–185)
12. Mixtures and Solutions (177–178)
13. Work (185–186)
14. Coordinate Geometry (172–173)
15. Geometry (165–172, 173–176)
16. Quantitative Comparisons (189–192)

ANSWER KEY

1. **C** (2)	*11.* **E** (3,8)	*21.* **B** (1,16)	*31.* **A** (15,16)	*41.* **A** (15)
2. **D** (1,6,7)	*12.* **A** (6)	*22.* **D** (15,16)	*32.* **B** (4,16)	*42.* **D** (15)
3. **B** (4,6,7)	*13.* **D** (15)	*23.* **B** (1,4,16)	*33.* **A** (8)	*43.* **C** (15)
4. **E** (3,14)	*14.* **C** (2)	*24.* **B** (15,16)	*34.* **D** (15)	*44.* **B** (15)
5. **A** (4,6,7)	*15.* **B** (1)	*25.* **C** (15,16)	*35.* **B** (11)	*45.* **C** (15)
6. **A** (1,7)	*16.* **D** (4,16)	*26.* **C** (15,16)	*36.* **C** (11)	*46.* **E** (15)
7. **A** (2)	*17.* **C** (1,16)	*27.* **A** (15,16)	*37.* **A** (11)	*47.* **B** (15)
8. **C** (1)	*18.* **C** (2,16)	*28.* **C** (6,16)	*38.* **C** (2)	*48.* **A** (1,6)
9. **D** (2)	*19.* **C** (2,16)	*29.* **D** (2,16)	*39.* **C** (1)	*49.* **D** (2)
10. **B** (6)	*20.* **C** (2,16)	*30.* **D** (15,16)	*40.* **C** (10)	*50.* **E** (14,15)

SCORING CHART—TYPICAL TEST A

Verbal Section		**Mathematical Section***		
No. correct	______	No. correct	(A)	______
No. omitted	______	No. incorrect (# 1-15, 33-50)	(B)	______
No. incorrect	______	No. incorrect (# 16-32)	(C)	______
¼ no. incorrect	______	¼ (B) + ⅓ (C)	(D)	______
Raw Score: (no. correct minus ¼ no. incorrect)	______	*Raw Score* = (A) − (D)		______

* **(In the Mathematical section, deduct ¼ of a point for each five-choice question answered incorrectly and ⅓ of a point for each four-choice question answered incorrectly.)**

EVALUATION CHART

Study your score. Your raw score on the Verbal and Mathematical Aptitude Sections is an indication of your probable achievement on the PSAT/NMSQT. As a guide to the amount of work you need or want to do with this book, study the following.

Raw Score		**Self-rating**
Verbal	*Mathematical*	
58–65	41–50	Superior
46–57	25–40	Very good
40–45	20–24	Satisfactory
36–39	16–19	Average
30–35	10–15	Needs further study
20–29	7–9	Needs intensive study
0–19	0–6	Probably inadequate

After you have scored Test A and evaluated your score, use the table on page 383—Test Questions by Topic—to find out which particular math topics are difficult for you and which you should review before going on to the next test.

ANSWER EXPLANATIONS

Verbal Aptitude Section

1. **B** To *benefit* or be helpful to a person is the opposite of to *harm* someone.
"I did it to benefit my country."
2. **C** When you *tremble* or shake, you do not *remain steady* or still.
Think of "trembling like a leaf."
3. **E** Something *contradictory*, or in disagreement, is not *easily reconciled* or made to agree.
Think of being told two "contradictory stories."
4. **C** A situation which is *hectic* or chaotic is not *serene* or calm.
Think of "hectic Christmas shopping."
5. **B** *Clarity* or clearness is the opposite of a *blur* or cloudiness.
"New glasses provide greater clarity."
6. **B** When an office is *short-handed*, there aren't enough workers there, a situation which is the opposite of being *fully staffed*.
Think of being "too short-handed to get the job done."
7. **A** A person whose complexion is *ruddy* has rosy cheeks; someone who is *sallow* is sickly or yellowish.
"The children came in ruddy from playing in the snow."
8. **E** A *muted* noise has been softened or muffled, unlike a *loud* sound.
"Noises from the street were muted, owing to the thick walls."
9. **C** *Consolidation* is uniting things, the opposite of *fragmentation* or breaking things apart.
"She managed the consolidation of several businesses into one huge corporation."
10. **C** *Independence* (freedom of manner) is the opposite of *servility*, the attitude of a servant.
Think of "following one's own plan, with complete independence."
11. **C** *Piety* is a sense of dutifulness in religion, as opposed to *irreverence*, a lack of reverence.
"The priest spoke with great piety."
12. **A** To *expedite* a process is to speed it up; to *retard* a process is to slow it down.
"She paid extra to expedite delivery of the package."
13. **A** *Languor* is a state of lethargy or listlessness. This is the opposite of *alertness*, being lively or watchful.
Think of "lying on the beach in utter languor."
14. **E** Something which is *malignant* is injurious or harmful; something which is *beneficial* is helpful.
Think of "a malignant cancer."
15. **E** To *undulate* means to move in waves, the opposite of to *remain still*.
Think of "octopus tentacles undulating beneath the water."
16. **B** A person who is *succinct* speaks briefly and to the point; someone who is *verbose* is wordy and says everything at great length.
Think of "a succinct telegram."
17. **E** When one is *remiss* and fails to perform a duty, one is not being *meticulous* or careful.
Think of being "remiss in not returning the library books."
18. **B** To *assuage* is to soothe or relieve; to *provoke* is to irritate.
"They tried to assuage his feelings with kind words."
19. **C** To *desiccate* is to dry out, the opposite of to *drench* or soak.
"Raisins are simply desiccated grapes."
20. **D** When you *abet* someone, you encourage her; when you *hinder* anyone, you impede or obstruct her.
Think of "abetting her in her crime."
21. **C** The use of "unhappily" tells us that the experiment was somehow damaged or *marred* by the presence of observers.
22. **B** Remember to think of your own answer before looking at the choices. North clearly had a strong belief, since no one's words could convince him otherwise. This would guide you to choose *conviction*, one meaning of which is belief.
23. **D** If we are likely to be in need of a new source of energy, we must be about to run out of the old source of fuel. This would happen if we *deplete* or exhaust our supply. The phrase "excessive use" is also a clue that we may be running out, through using too much.
24. **D** James didn't know when assignments were due because there was something wrong with the way he wrote them down. He was not orderly or *methodical* about it.
25. **B** The word "despite" signals a contrast. Despite the advertised *praises*, she had doubts—she remained *a skeptic about* the product. Note also that "singing the praises of" is a cliche, a customary phrase.
26. **A** The phrase "even though" tells us that there will be a contrast. This requires a word which is opposite to "does not change." *Plastic* can mean adaptable or pliable when used as an adjective, as it is here.
27. **C** The key word here is "ridiculing," meaning mocking. It complements *satirical* or sarcastic and caustic.
28. **D** Someone who risks his or her life frequently is a *daredevil*. Since the threat of death does not keep this person from such activities, the first missing word must be *daunt*, meaning to lessen one's courage.

29. **D** The agent could make no progress. Look for a word which describes interference with the investigation: it was stuck or *mired in* petty technicalities, minor issues.

30. **C** "Unscrupulous merchandisers" make false claims. *Debunking* means exposing falseness in something. Nader, who is an advocate or protector of the consumer, teaches people to be suspicious and to "exercise *skepticism*." Note that "exercising skepticism" is a cliche, a very commonly used phrase.

31. **D** The playing field in *football* is called the *gridiron*. The playing field in *baseball* is called the *diamond*. (Defining Characteristic)

32. **B** Without *water* plants *wilt*. Without *food* animals *starve*. (Cause and Effect)

33. **D** A *gosling* is a baby *goose*. A *kid* is a baby *goat*. (Age)

34. **B** A measure of *wood* is a *cord*. A measure of *cloth* is a *bolt*. (Defining Characteristic)

35. **D** An *orbit* is a circular path; when something deviates from this circle, it's on an *eccentric orbit*. Someone whose actions are deviating from the norm is engaging in *irregular behavior*. (Manner)

36. **B** A *lobster* is a member of the *crustacean* class. A *kangaroo* is a member of the *marsupial* class. (Class and Member)

37. **C** Something which is *simple* lacks *elaboration* or complex detail. Something which is *thrifty* lacks *extravagance* or excessive expense. (Antonym Variant)

38. **C** When a *storm* ends and the weather becomes calm and quiet—that is, normal—again, the storm is said to *subside*. When a muscle which has tightened in *spasm* goes back to its normal state, it is said to *relax*. (Function)

39. **A** *Delirium* causes *disorientation* or confusion. *Paralysis* causes *immobility* or loss of movement. (Cause and Effect)

40. **C** A *vine* extends a *tendril* or slender coil to grasp its supporting surface. An *amoeba*, a tiny, one-celled creature, puts out a *pseudopod* (a temporary "little foot") to grasp its food. (Part to Whole)

41. **B** To *scurry* is to *move* in a brisk and rapid manner. To *chatter* is to *talk* in a brisk and rapid manner. (Manner)

42. **B** A *eulogy* is a *laudatory* speech, full of praise. A *tirade* is an *abusive* speech, full of condemnation. (Defining Characteristic)

43. **E** Someone who is *obdurate* (unyielding, inflexible) is lacking in *flexibility*. Someone who is *adamant* (unshakable in opposition) is lacking in *submissiveness*. (Antonym Variant)

44. **E** A *reprobate* (corrupt person) is by definition *blameworthy*. A *traducer* (someone who willfully misrepresents another's conduct) is by definition *slanderous* (full of falsehood). (Defining Characteristic)

45. **A** A *feud* or war of revenge is a fight characterized by *acrimony* or bitterness. A *scuffle* or haphazard struggle is a fight characterized by *confusion*. (Defining Characteristic)

46. **D** The passage focuses on an *individual*, John Greenleaf Whittier. The *misconception* the author is correcting is that Whittier was merely a poet, a view which ignores his role as a vigorous opponent of slavery.

47. **E** *Approbation* means approval. The author clearly approves of Whittier's being a political agitator against slavery.

48. **C** Whittier is described in the passage as a "gadfly," an annoying, stinging insect. This word is used for a person who criticizes society's leaders or conventions for their own good.

49. **D** The author notes, in paragraph 1, that Whittier's writing was often directed at the clergy's acceptance of slavery.
Choices **A** and **C** are incorrect. Whittier wrote poetry (literature) against slavery, thus advocating a particular cause and worldly claim. Choices **B** and **E** are incorrect. They have no support within the passage.

50. **D** The author's attitude is most evident in the concluding sentence, in which natural selection is described as "a beautiful mechanism" which increases favorable events.

51. **C** Scanning the passage, you easily find the one sentence which mentions *Drosophila*. The sentence immediately before it tells us the point the author is trying to make with this example: "A small change in a key part of the program can make a large difference."

52. **B** In paragraph 2, we find that an organism with a "selective advantage" will reproduce more, that is, "on average, leave more offspring."

53. **D** Tapestry weaving is time-consuming, taking "as much as a year to produce a yard." In addition, it is faithful to an original ("The weaver always follows a preexisting model.")

54. **B** By using the tapestries "to display his wealth and social position," the nobleman is using them to demonstrate his consequence or importance.

55. **D** Although the passage explains the process of tapestry-making and mentions that large wall-hangings are Western rather than Eastern in origin, Choices **A** and **B** do not reflect the passage's primary purpose. This purpose is to introduce the medieval wall-hanging as a special type of tapestry work.

56. **D** The bulk of the passage defines several different kinds of rocks (igneous, sedimentary, metamorphic) and tells what their characteristics are. Choice **A** is incorrect. Though the passage does mention such factors, it doesn't go into great detail about them. Choice **B** is incorrect. Though the rocks' names do provide information about how they are formed (the root *ign-* means fire, for example; igneous rocks are formed by conditions that involve intense heat), the passage does not

develop this idea. Choice **C** is incorrect. The passage restates widely known facts; it presents no new hypothesis. Choice **E** is incorrect. The passage explains what rocks are made of; it doesn't explain why they are basic parts of the earth.

57. **B** Both the elementary level of the information included and the emphasis on defining and explaining terms suggest the passage would be most likely to be found in a *teaching manual for an earth science* (geology) *text*.

58. **E** This question may be answered by using the process of elimination.
According to the concluding paragraph, igneous rocks *may* be changed by heat or pressure. Therefore, Choice **A** is incorrect.
The final sentence of the opening paragraph states they incorporate *no* fossils, and that they are usually composed of crystals, not grains. Therefore, Choices **B** and **C** are incorrect.
The opening paragraph also states that they are abundant, not rare (they "compose the greater part of the earth's crust"). Therefore, Choice **D** is incorrect.
However, it is true that they lack regular strata: "they have no regular arrangement of layers."
Only Choice **E** is left. It is the correct answer.

59. **B** Again, you can use the process of elimination to answer this question.
Question I cannot be answered on the basis of information in this passage. Therefore, you can eliminate Choices **A, C,** and **E.** Question II cannot be answered on the basis of information in this passage. Therefore, you can eliminate Choice **D.** Question III can be answered on the basis of information in the passage. The final paragraph indicates that marble is called a metamorphic rock because it consists of limestone that has been transformed (metamorphosed) by being "subjected to heat and pressure."
Only Choice **B** is left. It is the correct answer.

60. **D** The author gives concrete examples ("organic substances, such as shells of clams); classifies rock types; lists or enumerates various items; and states cause and effect (being subjected to heat and pressure causes limestone to change into marble, for example). However, he makes no hypotheses and gives no examples of direct observation.

61. **D** The concluding sentence of paragraph 1 mentions factors which produced the crop of black writers who made up the Harlem Renaissance. The next paragraph continues the discussion of these social and political factors.
Choice **A** is incorrect. The opening sentence indicates that the willingness of black writers to portray their own lives was a factor in the Harlem Renaissance. Yet the next sentence makes it clear that this willingness was only *part* of what was going on. Choice **B** is incorrect. The author is concerned with these writers as part of an American literary movement, not a worldwide crusade.
Choice **C** is incorrect. The author cites examples of specific injustices in passing. Choice **E** is incorrect. It is unsupported by the passage.

62. **E** The author's use of such terms as "nobility of expression" and "masters of recent American literature" makes it clear his attitude is one of *admiration*.

63. **C** The writers were more involved with fighting problems in the system than with attacking the system itself. This suggests that fundamentally they *were not opposed to* the democratic system of government.
Choice **A** is incorrect. The fact that the writers did not revolt against the system does not imply that they played only a minor part in fighting abuses of the system. Choices **B, D,** and **E** are incorrect. None is suggested by the statement.

64. **A** The author refers at the beginning of paragraph 4 to historical interpretations of the black writer's role. In addition, the author tries to distinguish black writers from those who "embraced" socialist and communist propaganda (paragraphs 2 and 3). This suggests he is an historian interested in presenting these writers as patriotic.
Choice **B** is incorrect. The author touches on literature only in relationship to historical events. Choices **C, D,** and **E** are incorrect. There is nothing to suggest any of these interpretations in the passage.

65. **E** The passage cites the battles for better working conditions, desegregation, and social and political equality, among others.
Choice **A** is unanswerable on the basis of the passage. The passage mentions an "improvement in the capacity of expression" in the period, but cites no factors leading to this improvement in style. Choice **B** is unanswerable on the basis of the passage, which mentions no specific names. Choice **C** is unanswerable on the basis of the passage. The passage states that the writers did not "embrace the several foreign ideologies that sought to sink their roots" in America. However, it nowhere suggests that the writers were *in rebellion* against these foreign political theories. Choice **D** is unanswerable on the basis of the passage. No such information is supplied.

Mathematical Aptitude Section

1. **C** As x increases in value, the denominator $(x + 1)$ also increases and the value of the fraction $\frac{1}{x+1}$ decreases. The values of expressions I and II will both increase as the value of x increases.

2. **D** (A) $\frac{1}{5} = 0.2$ (B) $\left(\frac{1}{5}\right)^2 = \frac{1}{25} = 0.04$ (C) 0.3
(D) $\sqrt{0.16} = 0.4$
(E) $0.01\pi = 0.01(3.14) = 0.0314$

3. **B** In both (A) $(0.25)^2 = \left(\frac{1}{4}\right)^2$ and (C) $\left(\frac{1}{4}\right)^4$, raising to a power makes the fraction smaller.
(B) $\sqrt{\frac{1}{4}} = \frac{1}{2}$ and $\frac{1}{2} > \frac{1}{4}$. (D) $0.04 = \frac{4}{100}$ and
(E) $\frac{1}{250}$ are both very small.

4. **E** Dividing each term of the second equation by 2 makes it $x + 3y = 9$, and therefore the two equations are equivalent. Any point that lies on one must lie on the other; their graphs are identical. Thus, it is necessary to test each point by substituting in only one of the two equations to see whether it is satisfied. Point (3,4) does not check: $3 + 3(4) \neq 9$.

5. **A** (A) $\sqrt{0.3} = \sqrt{0.30} = 0.5 + \left(\text{more than } \frac{1}{2}\right)$
(B) $\frac{1}{2}$ (C) 0.49 is less than $\frac{1}{2}$ (D) $\left(\frac{1}{7}\right)^2 = \frac{1}{49}$
(E) $(0.04)^2 = 0.0016$

6. **A** Outside radius = 0.775 inch
Inside radius = 0.625 inch
Difference = 0.15

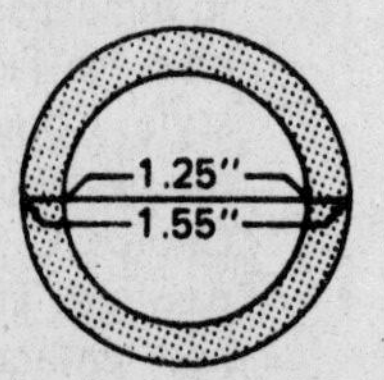

7. **A** $4x = 3y$; subtract $3y$, and then $4x - 3y = 0$.

8. **C** \$8 must equal the remaining $\frac{2}{10}$ of the price. Therefore $\frac{1}{10}$ is \$4, and $\frac{10}{10}$, the whole price, is \$40.

9. **D** $x + \frac{1}{2} + x - \frac{1}{2} = 5$
$2x = 5$

10. **B** $\frac{\text{molasses}}{\text{molasses + sugar}} = \frac{2}{2+3} = \frac{2}{5}$

11. **E** 20% of 20 or $\frac{1}{5} \cdot 20 = 4$
$\% = \frac{?}{100}$
$\frac{?}{100} \cdot 2 = 4$
$\frac{(2)(?)}{100} = 4$; $(2)(?) = 400$; $? = 200$

12. **A** Winning candidate got $\frac{3}{5}$ of the votes.
One loser received $\frac{1}{4}$ of $\frac{2}{5}$ or $\frac{1}{10}$.
Since the other loser received $\frac{3}{4}$ of $\frac{2}{5}$, he must have received more votes than the one who received $\frac{1}{10}$ of the votes.

13. **D** Let x = height of water in tank.
Volume of water in first tank = (18")(6")(8").
This volume is the same for second tank = (36")(18")(x).
$(\overset{3}{\cancel{36''}})(\cancel{18''})(x) = (\cancel{18''})(\cancel{6''})(\overset{4}{\cancel{8''}})$
$3x = 4$
$x = 1\frac{1}{3}$ inches

14. **C** $r = \frac{rs}{1-s}$
$r - rs = rs$
$r = 2rs$
$\frac{r}{2r} = s$
$\frac{1}{2} = s$
Substitute in $s^2 + 2s + 1$:
$\left(\frac{1}{2}\right)^2 + (2)\left(\frac{1}{2}\right) + 1$
$\frac{1}{4} + 1 + 1 = 2\frac{1}{4}$

15. **B** (30)(25¢) = 750 cents or 75 dimes

16. **D** The value of x may be zero, positive, or negative.

17. **C** Since the sum of the consecutive integers $a + b + c = 18$, then $a = 5$, $b = 6$, and $c = 7$.
$\therefore (a)(b)(c) = (5)(6)(7) = 210$.

18. **C** $\frac{a(x+y)}{b} = \frac{a(1-1)}{b} = \frac{a(0)}{b} = 0$
$\frac{2a(x+y)}{b} = \frac{2a(1-1)}{b} = \frac{2a(0)}{b} = 0$

19. **C** Multiply $\frac{-a}{y+z}$ by $\frac{-1}{-1} = \frac{a}{-y-z}$
$\therefore \frac{x}{-y-z} = \frac{a}{-y-z}$
$\therefore x = a$

20. **C** $3x + 5y = 15 + 5y$
$3x = 15$
$x = 5$
$\frac{x}{5} = 1$

21. **B** 1 hour and 20 minutes or $1\frac{1}{3}$ hours elapse from 8:55 A.M. to 10:15 A.M.

22. **D** Z could be anywhere on circumference of circle with radius = 4. X could be anywhere on circumference of circle with radius = 3.

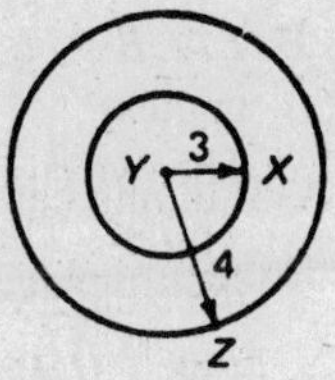

23. **B** $\pi = 3.14+$, $(0.1)(3.14+) = 0.314+$
$\sqrt{0.17} = 0.4+$

24. **B** Since $x = 100$, $m = 180 - 100$ or 80.
$y + m = 40 + 80$ or 120
$z = y + m$ (exterior angle of $\triangle$)
$z = 40 + 80$
$z = 120$
$x + y = 140$

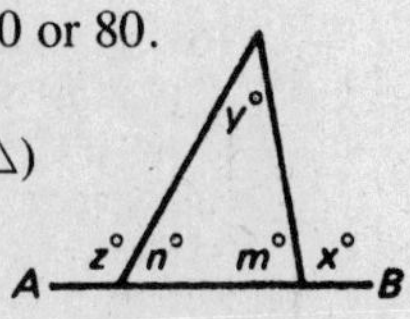

25. **C** Since the base angles are equal, $AB = AC$.
$\therefore \frac{\cancel{BC}}{AB} \cdot \frac{AC}{\cancel{BC}} = 1$

26. **C** $\triangle$s XDC and YDC share the base DC. Since $ABCD$ is a rectangle, XDC and YDC have equal altitudes. Therefore XDC and YDC are equal in area. Subtracting the area of DOC from both XDC and YDC gives YOC equal in area to XOD.

27. **A** $y = 180 - (50 + 60)$ or 70

Or, $x = 50 + 60$, since the exterior angle of a triangle equals the sum of both remote interior (nonadjacent) angles.

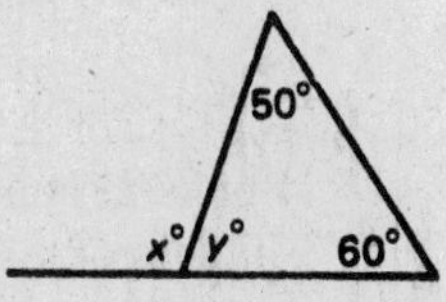

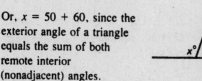

28. **C** The product of any number and its reciprocal is 1. Both products are therefore 1.

29. **D** If $x = 1$, $3x = 1$ and $(-2)x = -2$
If $x = -1$, $3x = -3$ and $(-2)(x) = +2$

30. **D** Since the width of the rectangle is not given, its area cannot be determined.

31. **A** Since opposite angles in a parallelogram have the same measure, angle B has a measure of 100 degrees and angle C has a measure of 80 degrees.

32. **B** $3^{-2} = \frac{1}{3^2} = \frac{1}{9}$

$2^{-3} = \frac{1}{2^3} = \frac{1}{8}$

$\frac{1}{8} > \frac{1}{9}$

33. **A** $16\frac{2}{3}\%$ or $\frac{1}{6}$ of $300 = 50$

10% or $\frac{1}{10}$ of $500 = 50$

Total number going to college = 100

$\frac{100}{800} = \frac{1}{8} = 12\frac{1}{2}\%$ or 12.5%

34. **D** $\triangle BAC$ is a 3-4-5 right triangle with $AC = 3(3)$ and hypotenuse $BC = 3(5)$; therefore $AB = 3(4)$ or 12.
$\triangle ABD$ is a 5-12-13 right triangle; therefore $AD = 13$.

35. **B** If 1 kg = 2.2 lbs., 20 kg = (20)(2.2 lbs.) = 44 pounds.

36. **C** A reading of 48 corresponds to 80 amperes. Let a reading of 60 correspond to x amperes.
$$\frac{48}{80} = \frac{60}{x}$$
$48x = 4800$
$x = 100$

37. **A** $\frac{A}{B} = \frac{5''}{11''} = \frac{x \text{ meters}}{5 \text{ meters}}$
$11x = 25$
$x = 2\frac{3}{11}$

38. **C** $(a - b)^2 = a^2 - 2ab + b^2$
Substitute: $100 - 2(50) + 25$
$100 - 100 + 25 = 25$

39. **C** If 0.6 ounce costs \$18
$\frac{0.6}{1.0} = \frac{\$18}{x}$; $0.6x = 18$; $6x = 180$: $x = \$30$.
Since 1 ounce costs \$30 and the price in the larger bottle is \$25 per ounce, the difference per ounce is \$5.

40. **C** Time = 20 minutes or $\frac{1}{3}$ hour
$\frac{\text{distance}}{\text{time}} = \text{rate}$
$\frac{20}{\frac{1}{3}} = 60$ miles per hour

41. **A** Volume of box = $9'' \times 12'' \times 6'' = 648$ cubic inches
Volume of each ice cube = $\frac{3''}{2} \times \frac{3''}{2} \times \frac{3''}{2} =$
$\frac{27}{8}$ cubic inches
$648 \div \frac{27}{8} = 192$ ice cubes

42. **D** Let diameter = d.
Then radius = $\frac{d}{2}$
Area = $\frac{\pi d^2}{4}$
If diameter is doubled, diameter = $2d$, then radius $= \frac{2d}{2} = d$.
Area = πd^2, which is four times $\frac{\pi d^2}{4}$.

43. **C** $\angle B \stackrel{\circ}{=} \frac{1}{2}(\widehat{DA} - \widehat{CA})$
$70° = \frac{1}{2}(\widehat{DA} - 70°)$
$140° = \widehat{DA} - 70°$
$210° = \widehat{DA}$
$\widehat{DA} + \widehat{CA} + \widehat{DC} = 360°$
$210° + 70° + \widehat{DC} = 360°$
$\widehat{DC} = 360° - 280°$
$\widehat{DC} = 80°$

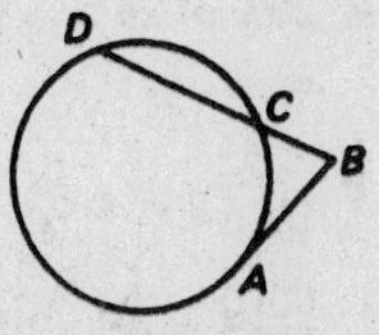

44. **B** Let x = radius of circle.
$OA = OB$ = radius

$\frac{(OA)(OB)}{2}$ = area of triangle $= \frac{7}{\pi}$

$\frac{(x)(x)}{2} = \frac{7}{\pi}$

$\frac{x^2}{2} = \frac{7}{\pi}$

$\pi x^2 = 14$ [area of circle $= (\pi)(\text{radius})^2$]

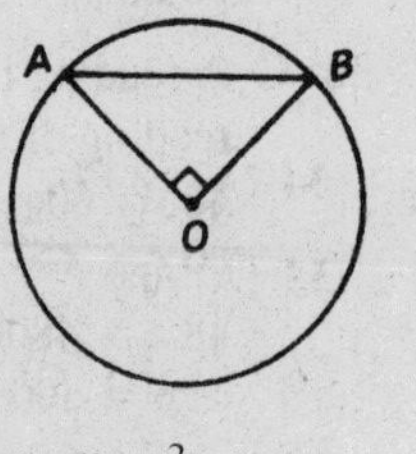

45. **C** Let x = side of square.
$x^2 + x^2 = 36$
[Pythagorean Theorem]
$2x^2 = 36$
$x^2 = 18$
(area of square)

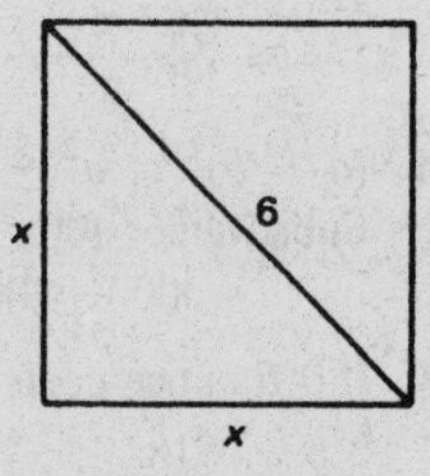

46. **E** $2x + (3x - 10)° + (3x + 30)° = 180°$
$2x + 3x - 10° + 3x + 30° = 180°$
$8x = 160°$
$x = 20°$

Therefore one angle = $2x$ or 40°
A second angle = 60° − 10° or 50°
The third angle is a right angle, since 60° + 30° = 90°.

47. **B** $\angle ACB = \angle DCE$ (vertical angles)
The two right triangles are similar. The corresponding sides are proportional.

$\frac{CD}{BC} = \frac{DE}{AB}$

$\frac{16}{12} = \frac{12}{x}$

$16x = 144$
$x = 9$

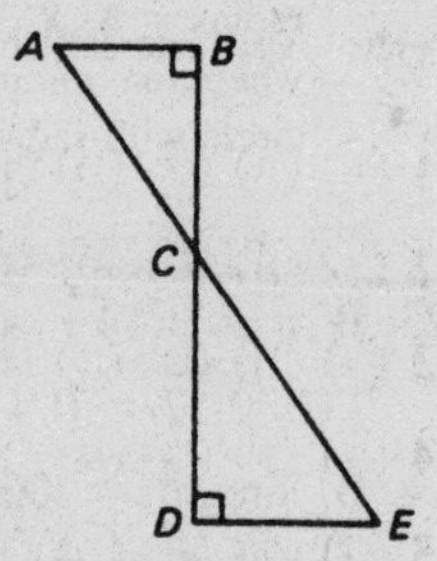

48. **A** The cost of the first mile is c cents + $4x$ cents.
The cost of the second mile is $5x$ cents.
The cost of the third mile is $5x$ cents.
The cost of 3 miles is $c + 14x$ cents.

49. **D** $(a + b)^2 - 4 = 5$
$(a + b)^2 = 9$
$a + b = +3$ or -3

50. **E** The base of $\triangle ABC$ is 6 units. The altitude must be 4 units to attain an area of 12. All choices have altitudes of 4.

PSAT/NMSQT Answer Sheet

TYPICAL TEST B

Verbal Aptitude Section

1 (A) (B) (C) (D) (E)
2 (A) (B) (C) (D) (E)
3 (A) (B) (C) (D) (E)
4 (A) (B) (C) (D) (E)
5 (A) (B) (C) (D) (E)
6 (A) (B) (C) (D) (E)
7 (A) (B) (C) (D) (E)
8 (A) (B) (C) (D) (E)
9 (A) (B) (C) (D) (E)
10 (A) (B) (C) (D) (E)
11 (A) (B) (C) (D) (E)
12 (A) (B) (C) (D) (E)
13 (A) (B) (C) (D) (E)
14 (A) (B) (C) (D) (E)
15 (A) (B) (C) (D) (E)
16 (A) (B) (C) (D) (E)
17 (A) (B) (C) (D) (E)
18 (A) (B) (C) (D) (E)
19 (A) (B) (C) (D) (E)
20 (A) (B) (C) (D) (E)
21 (A) (B) (C) (D) (E)
22 (A) (B) (C) (D) (E)
23 (A) (B) (C) (D) (E)
24 (A) (B) (C) (D) (E)
25 (A) (B) (C) (D) (E)
26 (A) (B) (C) (D) (E)
27 (A) (B) (C) (D) (E)
28 (A) (B) (C) (D) (E)
29 (A) (B) (C) (D) (E)
30 (A) (B) (C) (D) (E)
31 (A) (B) (C) (D) (E)
32 (A) (B) (C) (D) (E)
33 (A) (B) (C) (D) (E)
34 (A) (B) (C) (D) (E)
35 (A) (B) (C) (D) (E)
36 (A) (B) (C) (D) (E)
37 (A) (B) (C) (D) (E)
38 (A) (B) (C) (D) (E)
39 (A) (B) (C) (D) (E)
40 (A) (B) (C) (D) (E)
41 (A) (B) (C) (D) (E)
42 (A) (B) (C) (D) (E)
43 (A) (B) (C) (D) (E)
44 (A) (B) (C) (D) (E)
45 (A) (B) (C) (D) (E)
46 (A) (B) (C) (D) (E)
47 (A) (B) (C) (D) (E)
48 (A) (B) (C) (D) (E)
49 (A) (B) (C) (D) (E)
50 (A) (B) (C) (D) (E)
51 (A) (B) (C) (D) (E)
52 (A) (B) (C) (D) (E)
53 (A) (B) (C) (D) (E)
54 (A) (B) (C) (D) (E)
55 (A) (B) (C) (D) (E)
56 (A) (B) (C) (D) (E)
57 (A) (B) (C) (D) (E)
58 (A) (B) (C) (D) (E)
59 (A) (B) (C) (D) (E)
60 (A) (B) (C) (D) (E)
61 (A) (B) (C) (D) (E)
62 (A) (B) (C) (D) (E)
63 (A) (B) (C) (D) (E)
64 (A) (B) (C) (D) (E)
65 (A) (B) (C) (D) (E)

Mathematical Aptitude Section*

1 (A) (B) (C) (D) (E)
2 (A) (B) (C) (D) (E)
3 (A) (B) (C) (D) (E)
4 (A) (B) (C) (D) (E)
5 (A) (B) (C) (D) (E)
6 (A) (B) (C) (D) (E)
7 (A) (B) (C) (D) (E)
8 (A) (B) (C) (D) (E)
9 (A) (B) (C) (D) (E)
10 (A) (B) (C) (D) (E)
11 (A) (B) (C) (D) (E)
12 (A) (B) (C) (D) (E)
13 (A) (B) (C) (D) (E)
14 (A) (B) (C) (D) (E)
15 (A) (B) (C) (D) (E)
16 (A) (B) (C) (D) (E)
17 (A) (B) (C) (D) (E)
18 (A) (B) (C) (D) (E)
19 (A) (B) (C) (D) (E)
20 (A) (B) (C) (D) (E)
21 (A) (B) (C) (D) (E)
22 (A) (B) (C) (D) (E)
23 (A) (B) (C) (D) (E)
24 (A) (B) (C) (D) (E)
25 (A) (B) (C) (D) (E)
26 (A) (B) (C) (D) (E)
27 (A) (B) (C) (D) (E)
28 (A) (B) (C) (D) (E)
29 (A) (B) (C) (D) (E)
30 (A) (B) (C) (D) (E)
31 (A) (B) (C) (D) (E)
32 (A) (B) (C) (D) (E)
33 (A) (B) (C) (D) (E)
34 (A) (B) (C) (D) (E)
35 (A) (B) (C) (D) (E)
36 (A) (B) (C) (D) (E)
37 (A) (B) (C) (D) (E)
38 (A) (B) (C) (D) (E)
39 (A) (B) (C) (D) (E)
40 (A) (B) (C) (D) (E)
41 (A) (B) (C) (D) (E)
42 (A) (B) (C) (D) (E)
43 (A) (B) (C) (D) (E)
44 (A) (B) (C) (D) (E)
45 (A) (B) (C) (D) (E)
46 (A) (B) (C) (D) (E)
47 (A) (B) (C) (D) (E)
48 (A) (B) (C) (D) (E)
49 (A) (B) (C) (D) (E)
50 (A) (B) (C) (D) (E)

*If there are more answer spaces than you need, leave them blank.

TYPICAL TEST B

SECTION 1	**Time—50 minutes 65 Questions**	For each question in this section, choose the best answer and fill in the corresponding circle on the answer sheet.

Each question below consists of a word in capital letters, followed by five lettered words or phrases. Choose the word or phrase that is most nearly opposite in meaning to the word in capital letters. Since some of the questions require you to distinguish fine shades of meaning, consider all the choices before deciding which is best.

Example:

GOOD: (A) sour (B) bad (C) red (D) hot (E) ugly

Ⓐ ● Ⓒ Ⓓ Ⓔ

1. ACCELERATE: (A) change direction (B) advance steadily (C) reduce speed (D) lose interest (E) become smaller

2. HYPOCRISY: (A) sensitivity (B) flattery (C) competence (D) cheerfulness (E) sincerity

3. LENIENT: (A) erect (B) strict (C) noisy (D) harmonious (E) brief

4. DISREGARD: (A) admit (B) evade (C) heed (D) improve (E) prevent

5. DELETION: (A) injury (B) promptness (C) permission (D) insertion (E) pollution

6. RECTIFY: (A) apologize (B) sanctify (C) make worse (D) rule illegal (E) rebuke

7. IMPETUOUS: (A) circumspect (B) wealthy (C) honest (D) irritable (E) renowned

8. PERTINENCE: (A) lack of interest (B) lack of politeness (C) lack of relevance (D) excessive strength (E) truthful speech

9. IMMUTABLE: (A) reasonable (B) articulate (C) changeable (D) defensible (E) shameless

10. INTER: (A) brighten (B) abandon (C) dissent (D) exhume (E) question

11. BREVITY: (A) strength (B) incompleteness (C) lengthiness (D) stubbornness (E) gravity

12. SUPPLE: (A) slender (B) incisive (C) familiar (D) complex (E) inflexible

13. GAINSAY: (A) donate (B) squander (C) applaud (D) affirm (E) repeat

14. DEARTH: (A) birth (B) laxity (C) abundance (D) clarity (E) hatred

15. BURGEON: (A) hover (B) wither (C) evade (D) jostle (E) pounce

16. PIVOTAL: (A) constant (B) interminable (C) detrimental (D) trivial (E) anticipatory

17. GRATUITOUS: (A) scanty (B) derogatory (C) necessary (D) thankless (E) impartial

18. CONTENTIOUS: (A) agreeable (B) apathetic (C) narrow (D) stern (E) unhappy

19. ICONOCLAST: (A) conventional person (B) wasteful spender (C) publicity seeker (D) dilettante (E) militant

20. MELLIFLUOUS: (A) porous (B) modest (C) devious (D) timorous (E) strident

Each sentence below has one or two blanks, each blank indicating that something has been omitted. Beneath the sentence are five lettered words or sets of words. Choose the word or set of words that, when inserted in the sentence, best fits the meaning of the sentence as a whole.

Example:

Although its publicity has been ----, the film itself is intelligent, well-acted, handsomely produced, and altogether ----.

(A) tasteless . . respectable (B) extensive . . moderate (C) sophisticated . . amateur (D) risque . . crude (E) perfect . . spectacular

● Ⓑ Ⓒ Ⓓ Ⓔ

21. Because of their frequent disarray, confusion, and loss of memory, persons hit by lightning while alone are sometimes ---- victims of assault.
(A) mistaken for (B) attracted to
(C) unaware of (D) avoided by (E) useful to

22. The developing brain can be likened to a highway system that ---- use: less traveled roads may be abandoned, popular roads broadened, and new ones added where they are needed.
(A) suffers from (B) evolves with
(C) detours around (D) atrophies with
(E) buckles under

23. Ms. Sutcliffe's helpful notes on her latest wine discoveries and her no-nonsense warnings to consumers about ---- wines make the present book ---- guide to the numbing array of wines of Burgundy.
(A) excellent . . a useful
(B) overrated . . an inadequate
(C) overpriced . . a trusty
(D) unsatisfactory . . a spotty
(E) vintage . . an unreliable

24. This island is a colony; however, in most matters, it is ---- and receives no orders from the mother country.
(A) submissive (B) amorphous (C) distant
(D) autonomous (E) aloof

25. Like the best ---- fiction, Mark Helprin's *Winter's Tale* is part dream, part mad invention, and all of it hauntingly beautiful.
(A) satiric (B) prosaic (C) naturalistic
(D) documentary (E) fantastic

26. In the face of family and national crises that would have undone a lesser woman, Eleanor Roosevelt ----, maintaining an air of composure and ---- dignity.
(A) fled . . unseemly (B) cowered . . spurious
(C) persevered . . unruffled
(D) triumphed . . false (E) collapsed . . hard-won

27. In Victorian times, countless Egyptian mummies were ground up to produce dried mummy powder, hailed by quacks as a near-magical ---- able to cure a wide variety of ailments.
(A) toxin (B) indisposition
(C) symptom (D) panacea (E) placebo

28. The orator delivered a ---- speech that was ---- by the more sophisticated in the audience who were unswayed by the pompous language.
(A) patriotic . . cheered
(B) bombastic . . ridiculed
(C) sententious . . rejected
(D) eulogistic . . derided
(E) pretentious . . acclaimed

29. During the middle of the eighteenth century, the ---- style in furniture and architecture, marked by scroll work and excessive decoration, flourished.
(A) austere (B) functional (C) rococo
(D) medieval (E) abstract

30. Rather than portraying Joseph II as a radical reformer whose reign was strikingly enlightened, the play *Amadeus* depicts him as ---- thinker, too wedded to orthodox theories of musical composition to appreciate an artist of Mozart's genius.
(A) a revolutionary (B) an idiosyncratic
(C) a politic (D) a doctrinaire (E) a lucid

Each question below consists of a related pair of words or phrases, followed by five lettered pairs of words or phrases. Select the lettered pair that best expresses a relationship similar to that expressed in the original pair.

Example:

YAWN : BOREDOM : : (A) dream : sleep
(B) anger : madness (C) smile : amusement
(D) face : expression (E) impatience : rebellion

(A) (B) ● (D) (E)

31. THERMOMETER : TEMPERATURE : :
(A) calendar : entry (B) barometer : distance
(C) Geiger counter : radiation
(D) pacemaker : heart (E) weather vane : speed

32. FANS : BLEACHERS : :
(A) cheerleaders : pompoms (B) audience : seats
(C) team : goalposts (D) conductor : podium
(E) referee : decision

33. ARCHIPELAGO : ISLAND : :
(A) arbor : bower (B) garden : flower
(C) mountain : valley (D) sand : dune
(E) constellation : star

34. GLOSSARY : WORDS : : (A) catalogue : dates
(B) atlas : maps (C) almanac : synonyms
(D) thesaurus : rhymes (E) lexicon : numbers

35. WOOD : SAND : : (A) coal : burn
(B) brick : lay (C) oil : polish
(D) metal : burnish (E) stone : quarry

36. BUOYANT : SINK : : (A) flammable : burn
(B) waterproof : float (C) adhesive : loosen
(D) volatile : evaporate (E) fragile : fall

37. VINDICTIVE : MERCY : :
(A) avaricious : greed (B) insightful : hope
(C) modest : dignity (D) skeptical : trustfulness
(E) pathetic : sympathy

38. JITTERY : FIDGET : : (A) foolish : weep
(B) touchy : snap (C) drowsy : lull
(D) mulish : roam (E) cranky : excite

39. COMET : TAIL : : (A) star : galaxy
(B) car : headlight (C) river : bank
(D) helicopter : pad (E) vessel : wake

40. DAMPEN : ENTHUSIASM : :
(A) moisten : throat (B) test : commitment
(C) distract : attention (D) reverse : course
(E) mute : sound

41. BOUQUET : WINE : : (A) chaff : wheat
(B) aroma : coffee (C) yeast : bread
(D) octane : gasoline (E) decanter : brandy

42. OFFHAND : PREMEDITATION : :
(A) upright : integrity (B) aboveboard : guile
(C) cutthroat : competition
(D) backward : direction
(E) underlying : foundation

43. SHARD : POTTERY : : (A) handle : pitcher
(B) splinter : bone (C) rift : rock
(D) veneer : wood (E) vessel : clay

44. REFRACTORY : MANAGE : :
(A) redoubtable : impress (B) pedantic : convince
(C) officious : arrange (D) lethargic : stimulate
(E) aggrieved : distress

45. CELERITY : SNAIL : : (A) indolence : sloth
(B) cunning : weasel (C) curiosity : cat
(D) humility : peacock (E) obstinacy : mule

Each passage below is followed by questions based on its content. Answer the questions following each passage on the basis of what is stated or implied in that passage.

With Meredith's *The Egoist* we enter into a critical problem that we have not yet before faced in these studies. That is the problem offered by a writer of recognizably impressive stature, whose work is informed by a muscular intelligence, whose language has splendor, whose "view of life" wins our respect, and yet for whom we are at best able to feel only a passive appreciation which amounts, practically, to indifference. We should be unjust to Meredith and to criticism if we should, giving in to the inertia of indifference, simply avoid dealing with him and thus avoid the problem along with him. He does not "speak to us," we might say; his meaning is not a "meaning for us"; he "leaves us cold." But do not the challenge and the excitement of the critical problem as such lie in that ambivalence of attitude which allows us to recognize the intelligence and even the splendor of Meredith's work, while, at the same time, we experience a lack of sympathy, a failure of any enthusiasm of response?

46. According to the passage, the work of Meredith is noteworthy for its elements of
(A) sensibility and artistic fervor
(B) ambivalence and moral ambiguity
(C) tension and sense of vitality
(D) brilliance and linguistic grandeur
(E) wit and whimsical frivolity

47. It can be inferred from the passage that the author finds the prospect of appraising Meredith's work critically to be
(A) counterproductive (B) highly formidable
(C) somewhat tolerable (D) markedly unpalatable
(E) clearly invigorating

48. It can be inferred from the passage that the author would be most likely to agree with which of the following statements about the role of criticism?
(A) Its chief task should be to make our enjoyment of the things that feed the mind as conscious as possible.
(B) It should be a disinterested attempt to learn and propagate the best that is known and thought in the world.
(C) It should enable us to go beyond personal prejudice to appreciate the virtues of works not to our own tastes.
(D) It should dwell upon virtues rather than imperfections, ignoring such defects as irrelevant.
(E) It should strive both to purify literature and to elevate the literary standards of the reading public.

The classical idea of matter was something with solidity and mass, like wet stone dust pressed in a fist. If matter was composed of atoms, then the atoms too must have solidity and mass. At the beginning of the twentieth century the atom was imagined as a tiny billiard ball or a granite pebble writ small. Then, in the physics of Niels Bohr, the miniature billiard ball become something akin to a musical instrument, a finely tuned Stradivarius 10 billion times smaller than the real thing. With the advent of quantum mechanics, the musical instrument gave way to pure music. On the atomic scale, the solidity and mass of matter dissolved into something light and airy. Suddenly physicists were describing atoms in the vocabulary of the composer—"resonance," "frequency," "harmony," "scale." Atomic electrons sang in choirs like seraphim, cherubim, thrones, and dominions. Classical distinctions between matter and light became muddled. In the new physics, light bounced about like particles, and matter undulated in waves like light.

In recent decades, physicists have uncovered elegant subatomic structures in the music of matter. They use a strange new language to describe the subatomic world: *quark, squark, gluon, gauge, technicolor, flavor, strangeness, charm*. There are *up* quarks and *down* quarks, *top* quarks and *bottom* quarks. There are particles with *truth* and *antitruth*, and there are particles with *naked beauty*. The simplest of the constituents of ordinary matter—the proton, for instance—has taken on the character of a Bach fugue, a four-point counterpoint of matter, energy, space, and time. At matter's heart there are arpeggios, chromatics, syncopation. On the lowest rung of the chain of being, Creation dances.

49. Which of the following would be the most appropriate title for the passage?
(A) Linguistic Implications of Particle Physics
(B) The Influence of Music on Particle Interactions
(C) Matter's Transformation: The Music of Subatomic Physics
(D) Trends in Physics Research: Eliminating the Quark
(E) The Impossible Dream: Obstacles to Proving the Existence of Matter

50. The author refers to quarks, squarks, and charms (paragraph 2) primarily in order to
(A) demonstrate the similarity between these particles and earlier images of the atom
(B) make a distinction between appropriate and inappropriate terms
(C) object to suggestions of similar frivolous names
(D) provide examples of idiosyncratic nomenclature in contemporary physics
(E) cite preliminary experimental evidence supporting the existence of subatomic matter

51. The author's tone in the second paragraph can best be described as one of
(A) scientific detachment
(B) moderate indignation (C) marked derision
(D) admiring wonder (E) qualified skepticism

Given the persistent and intransigent nature of the American race system, which proved quite impervious to black attacks, Du Bois in his speeches and writings moved from one proposed solution to another, and the salience of various parts of his philosophy changed as his perceptions of the needs and strategies of black America shifted over time. Aloof and autonomous in his personality, Du Bois did not hesitate to depart markedly from whatever was the current mainstream of black thinking when he perceived that the conventional wisdom being enunciated by black spokesmen was proving inadequate to the task of advancing the race. His willingness to seek different solutions often placed him well in advance of his contemporaries, and this, combined with a strong-willed, even arrogant personality, made his career as a black leader essentially a series of stormy conflicts.

Thus Du Bois first achieved his role as a major black leader in the controversy that arose over the program of Booker T. Washington, the most prominent and influential black leader at the opening of the twentieth century. Amidst the wave of lynchings, disfranchisement, and segregation laws, Washington, seeking the good will of powerful whites, taught blacks not to protest against discrimination, but to elevate themselves through industrial education, hard work, and property accumulation; then, they would ultimately obtain recognition of their citizenship rights. At first Du Bois agreed with this gradualist strategy, but in 1903 with the publication of his most influential book, *Souls of Black Folk,* he became the chief leader of the onslaught against Washington that polarized the black community into two wings—the "conservative" supporters of Washington and his "radical" critics.

52. The author's primary purpose in the passage is to
(A) explain how Du Bois was influenced by Washington
(B) compare the personalities of Du Bois and Washington
(C) explain why Du Bois gained power in the black community
(D) describe Du Bois's role in early twentieth century black leadership
(E) correct the misconception that Du Bois shunned polarization

53. Which of the following statements about Du Bois does the passage best support?
(A) He sacrificed the proven strategies of earlier black leaders to his craving for political novelty.
(B) Preferring conflict to harmony, he followed a disruptive course that alienated him from the bulk of his followers.
(C) He proved unable to change with the times in mounting fresh attacks against white racism.
(D) He relied on the fundamental benevolence of the white population for the eventual success of his movement.
(E) Once an adherent of Washington's policies, he ultimately lost patience with them for their ineffectiveness.

54. It can be inferred that Booker T. Washington in comparison with Du Bois could be described as all of the following EXCEPT
(A) submissive to the majority
(B) concerned with financial success
(C) versatile in adopting strategies
(D) traditional in preaching industry
(E) respectful of authority

55. The author's attitude towards Du Bois's departure from conventional black policies can best be described as
(A) skeptical (B) derisive (C) shocked
(D) approving (E) resigned

The New World was already an old world to the Indians who were in residence when Europeans took possession of it in the 16th century. But the life story of the human species goes back a million years, and there is no doubt that human beings came only recently to the Western Hemisphere. None of the thousands of sites of aboriginal habitation uncovered in North and South America has antiquity comparable to that of Old World sites. Human occupation of the New World may date back several tens of thousands of years, but no one rationally argues that human life has been here even 100,000 years.

Speculation as to how human beings found their way to America was lively at the outset, and the proposed routes boxed the compass. With one or two notable exceptions, however, students of American anthropology soon settled for the plausible idea that the first immigrants came by way of a land bridge that had connected the northeast corner of Asia to the northwest corner of North America across the Bering Strait. Mariners were able to supply the reassuring information that the strait is not only narrow—it is 56 miles wide—but also shallow; a lowering of the sea level there by 100 feet or so would transform the strait into an isthmus. With little else in the way of evidence to sustain the Bering Strait land bridge, anthropologists embraced the idea that men and women walked dryshod from Asia to America.

Toward the end of the last century, however, it became apparent that the Western Hemisphere was the New World not only for human beings but also for a host of animals and plants. Zoologists and botanists showed that numerous subjects of their respective kingdoms must have originated in Asia and spread to America. (There was evidence also for some movement in the other direction.) These findings were neither astonishing nor wholly unexpected. Such spread of populations is not to be envisioned as an exodus or mass migration, even in the case of animals. It is, rather, a spilling into new territory that accompanies increase in numbers, with movement in the direction of least population pressure and most favorable ecological conditions. But the immense traffic in plant and animal forms placed a heavy burden on the Bering Strait land bridge as the anthropologists had envisioned it. Whereas purposeful human beings could make their way across a narrow bridge (in the absence of a bridge, Eskimos sometimes cross the strait in skin boats), the slow diffusion of plants and animals would require an avenue as broad as a continent and available for ages at a stretch.

56. According to the author, the movement of plants and animals from Asia to America indicates
(A) the role played by zoologists and botanists
(B) they could not have traveled across the Bering Sea
(C) the continents once were connected by a large land mass
(D) the Bering Sea was an isthmus at one time
(E) the migration was in that one direction only

57. The author is refuting the notion that
(A) life arose in America independently of life in Europe
(B) the first settlers in America came during the 16th century
(C) a large continent once existed which has disappeared
(D) American archeological sites antedate European ones
(E) human beings have been in North America for less than 10,000 years

58. By using the words "boxed the compass" (paragraph 2), the author means that according to the proposed routes
(A) the migration of humankind was from West to East
(B) the migration of humankind was from East to West
(C) human beings traveled in all directions
(D) human beings walked from Asia to America
(E) the migration of human, animal, and plant life was limited to one direction

59. The author mentions all of the following reasons for the migration EXCEPT
(A) overcrowding caused by population growth
(B) the attractions of a superior environment
(C) the existence of famine in the land
(D) the existence of a land bridge
(E) a general overflow of population

60. We may assume that in the paragraph that follows this passage the author discusses
(A) the contributions of anthropologists
(B) the contribution of botanists and zoologists
(C) the contribution made by the American Indians
(D) the existence of a large land mass between Asia and North America
(E) the abruptness of the human exodus

Peyton Farquhar was a well-to-do planter, of an old and highly respected Alabama family. Being a slave-owner, and, like other slave-owners, a politician, he was naturally an original secessionist and ardently devoted to the Southern cause. Circumstances had prevented him from taking service with the gallant army which had fought the disastrous campaigns ending with the fall of Corinth, and he chafed under the inglorious restraint, longing for the release of his energies, the larger life of the soldier, the opportunity for distinction. That opportunity, he felt, would come, as it comes to all in war time. Meanwhile, he did what he could. No service was too humble for him to perform in aid of the South, no adventure too perilous for him to undertake if consistent with the character of a civilian who was at heart a soldier, and who in good faith and without too much qualification assented to at least a part of the frankly villainous dictum that all is fair in love and war.

One evening while Farquhar and his wife were sitting near the entrance to his grounds, a grey-clad soldier rode up to the gate and asked for a drink of water. Mrs. Farquhar was only too happy to serve him with her own white hands. While she was gone to fetch the water, her husband approached the dusty horseman and inquired eagerly for news from the front.

"The Yanks are repairing the railroads," said the man, "and are getting ready for another advance. They have reached the Owl Creek bridge, put it in order, and built a stockade on the other bank. The commandant has issued an order, which is posted everywhere, declaring that any civilian caught interfering with the railroad, its bridges, tunnels, or trains, will be summarily hanged. I saw the order."

"How far is it to the Owl Creek bridge?" Farquhar asked.

"About thirty miles."

"Is there no force on this side of the creek?"

"Only a picket post half a mile out, on the railroad, and a single sentinel at this end of the bridge."

"Suppose a man—a civilian and a student of hanging—should elude the picket post and perhaps get the better of the sentinel," said Farquhar, smiling, "what could he accomplish?"

The soldier reflected. "I was there a month ago," he replied. "I observed that the flood of last winter had lodged a great quantity of driftwood against the wooden pier at the end of the bridge. It is now dry and would burn like tow."

The lady had now brought the water, which the soldier drank. He thanked her ceremoniously, bowed to her husband, and rode away. An hour later, after nightfall, he repassed the plantation, going northward in the direction from which he had come. He was a Yankee scout.

61. Peyton Farquhar would most likely consider which of the following a good example of how a citizen should behave in wartime?
(A) He should use even underhanded methods to support his cause.
(B) He should enlist in the army without delay.
(C) He should turn to politics as a means of enforcing his will.
(D) He should avoid involving himself in disastrous campaigns.
(E) He should concentrate on his duties as a planter.

62. It can be inferred from the second paragraph that Mrs. Farquhar is
(A) sympathetic to the Confederate cause
(B) uninterested in news of the war
(C) too proud to perform menial tasks
(D) reluctant to ask her slaves to fetch water
(E) inhospitable by nature

63. As used in the next-to-last paragraph, *tow* is
(A) an act of hauling something
(B) a tugboat
(C) a railroad bridge
(D) a highly combustible substance
(E) a picket post

64. This passage was most likely taken from
(A) a history textbook
(B) Peyton Farquhar's autobiography
(C) a story set in Civil War times
(D) a commentary on the effects of Federal orders on civilians
(E) a treatise on military strategy

65. We may infer from the passage that
(A) the soldier has deserted from the Southern army
(B) the soldier has lost his sense of direction
(C) the scout has been tempting Farquhar into an unwise action
(D) Farquhar knew the soldier was a Yankee scout
(E) the soldier returned to the plantation unwillingly

SECTION 2 Time—50 minutes 50 Questions

In this section solve each problem, using any available space on the page for scratchwork. Then decide which is the best of the choices given and fill in the corresponding circle on the answer sheet.

The following information is for your reference in solving some of the problems.

Circle of radius r: Area $= \pi r^2$ Circumference $= 2\pi r$
The number of degrees of arc in a circle is 360.
The measure in degrees of a straight angle is 180.

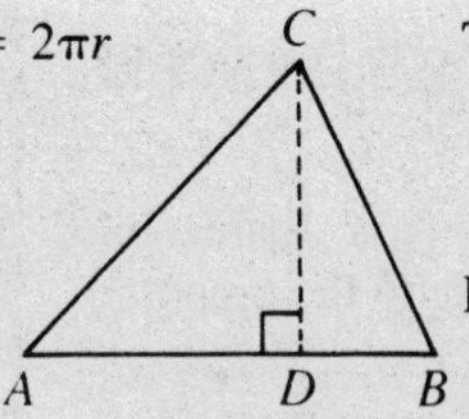

Triangle: The sum of the measures in degrees of the angles of a triangle is 180.

If $\angle CDA$ is a right angle, then

(1) area of $\triangle ABC = \dfrac{AB \times CD}{2}$

(2) $AC^2 = AD^2 + DC^2$

Definitions of symbols:

$=$ is equal to	$\leqq$ is less than or equal to
$\neq$ is unequal to	$\geqq$ is greater than or equal to
$<$ is less than	$\parallel$ is parallel to
$>$ is greater than	$\perp$ is perpendicular to

Note: Figures that accompany problems in this test are intended to provide information useful in solving the problems. They are drawn as accurately as possible EXCEPT when it is stated in a specific problem that its figure is not drawn to scale. All figures lie in a plane unless otherwise indicated. All numbers used are real numbers.

1. $(146 \times 117) + (173 \times 146) + (146 \times 210)$ equals
(A) 69,000 (B) 70,000 (C) 71,000
(D) 72,000 (E) 73,000

2. A certain grade of eggs has a weight of 24 to 26 ounces per dozen. What is the minimum weight (in ounces) of 69 such eggs?
(A) 138 (B) 143 (C) 149 (D) 1656 (E) 1716

3. A boy has 85 cents in 12 coins consisting of nickels and dimes. How many coins are nickels?
(A) 5 (B) 6 (C) 7 (D) 8 (E) 9

4. *L* is east of *M* and west of *N*. *J* is southeast of *N*. *M* is southeast of *F*. Which is farthest west?
(A) *F* (B) *G* (C) *J* (D) *M* (E) *N*

5. How many four-cent baseball cards can I purchase without receiving change for one dollar after buying twenty three-cent cards?
(A) 4 (B) 5 (C) 10 (D) 25 (E) 40

6. How many ounces are there in a cup of shredded coconut if 6 cups weigh one pound?
(A) 0.6 (B) 0.16 (C) 1.6 (D) 2.6 (E) 4.3

7. The cost of sending a telegram to a certain city is 85¢ for the first 15 words and $3\frac{1}{2}$¢ for each additional word, exclusive of tax. How many words did my telegram contain if I paid \$1.97, which included a tax of 70¢?
(A) 12 (B) 27 (C) 36 (D) 47 (E) 147

8. A man who owned $\frac{1}{4}$ share of a business sold $\frac{1}{3}$ of his control last year and sold $\frac{5}{12}$ of his remaining share this year. What part of the business does he now own?
(A) $\frac{1}{5}$ (B) $\frac{5}{144}$ (C) $\frac{7}{72}$ (D) $\frac{65}{72}$ (E) 0

9. What is the value of $\frac{1}{\sqrt{2}}$ correct to the nearest hundredth? ($\sqrt{2} = 1.414$)
(A) 0.67 (B) 0.68 (C) 0.69 (D) 0.70
(E) 0.71

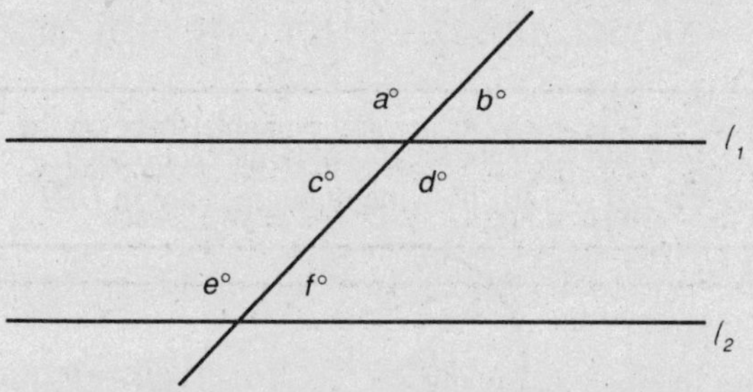

10. If $l_1 \| l_2$, then all of the following are true EXCEPT
(A) $d = a$ (B) $c = f$ (C) $e = a$ (D) $f = b$
(E) $c = d$

11. If $AB = 12$ and $BC = 6$, what is the length of a segment joining the midpoints of AB and BC?
(A) 6 (B) 9 (C) 12 (D) 15 (E) 18

12. A disease killed $\frac{2}{3}$ of the chickens on a farm. The owner then inoculated $\frac{1}{2}$ of the remaining chickens to prevent infection. If 100 were inoculated, how many chickens were lost before the treatment?
(A) 150 (B) 200 (C) 300 (D) 400
(E) 600

13. $\frac{2m}{3} = \frac{b}{a}$, $\frac{2m}{b} =$
(A) $\frac{a}{b}$ (B) $\frac{3}{a}$ (C) $\frac{a}{3}$ (D) a (E) b

14. What is the value of $\frac{3y^2 - x^2}{\frac{1}{2}a^3}$ when $x = -2$, $y = 3$, and $a = -1$?
(A) $2\frac{7}{8}$ (B) -46 (C) 46 (D) -64 (E) 64

15. By selling a television set for \$260 a dealer finds he is making a profit of 30% of cost. At what price must he sell it to make a profit of 40% of cost?
(A) \$196.00 (B) \$254.80 (C) \$280.00
(D) \$282.00 (E) \$322.00

<u>Questions 16-32</u> each consist of two quantities, one in Column A and one in Column B. You are to compare the two quantities and on the answer sheet fill in circle

A if the quantity in Column A is greater;
B if the quantity in Column B is greater;
C if the two quantities are equal;
D if the relationship cannot be determined from the information given.

<u>Notes:</u>
1. In certain questions, information concerning one or both of the quantities to be compared is centered above the two columns.
2. In a given question, a symbol that appears in both columns represents the same thing in Column A as it does in Column B.
3. Letters such as x, n, and k stand for real numbers.

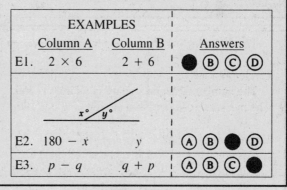

EXAMPLES

	Column A	Column B	Answers
E1.	2×6	$2 + 6$	● Ⓑ Ⓒ Ⓓ
	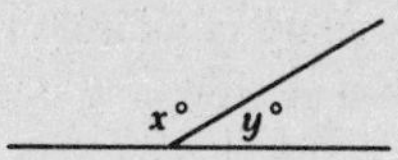		
E2.	$180 - x$	y	Ⓐ Ⓑ ● Ⓓ
E3.	$p - q$	$q + p$	Ⓐ Ⓑ Ⓒ ●

	Column A	Column B
16.	$\frac{6 + 6 + 6}{6 - 6 - 6}$	$\frac{3 + 3 + 3}{3 - 3 - 3}$
17.	0.04	$\frac{1}{25}$
18.	0.12	$\sqrt{1.44}$
	$x^2 = 25$	
19.	x	5

	COLUMN A	COLUMN B
	$0 < p < q$	
20.	$\frac{1}{q}$	$\frac{1}{p}$
	$a = 2, b = 1$, and $c = 0$	
21.	$4a + 2b + 3c^3$	10
22.	105% of 500	50% of 1000
	$2x + y = 16$	
23.	x	y
24.	The average of the measure of the angles of quadrilateral *ABCD*	The average of the measure of the angles of square *KLMN*

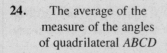

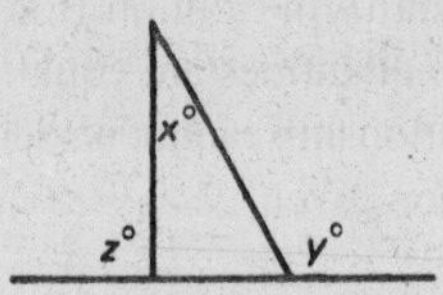

$x = 30$ and $y = 120$

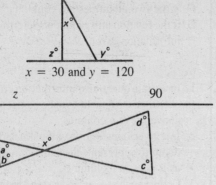

25.	z	90

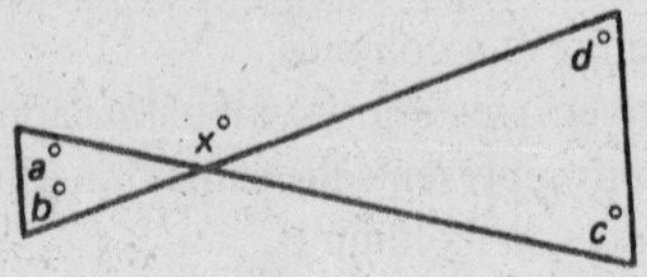

26.	$a + b + c + d$	x

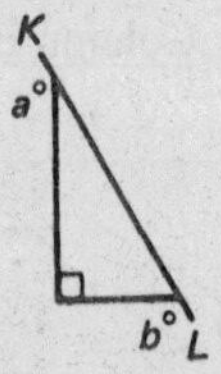

KL is a straight line.

27.	$a + b$	270
	$2^{n+2} = 8$	
28.	n	3
	$x > 1$, $y > 1$	
29.	$xy + 5$	$x(y + 5)$
	AC is the hypotenuse of $\triangle ABC$.	
30.	Measure of $\angle B$	Sum of the measures of $\angle A$ and $\angle C$
31.	$\frac{5x + 6}{5}$	$x + 1$
	$A \neq 0$	
32.	A^{-1}	A

Solve each of the remaining problems in this section using any available space for scratchwork. Then decide which is the best of the choices given and fill in the corresponding circle on the answer sheet.

33. What percent of a foot is a yard?
(A) 3% (B) $\frac{1}{3}$ (C) $33\frac{1}{3}\%$ (D) 300%
(E) $333\frac{1}{3}\%$

34. How long is the shadow of a 35-foot tree, if a 98-foot tree casts a 42-foot shadow at the same time?
(A) 14 (B) 15 ft. (C) 16 ft. (D) 17 ft.
(E) 18 ft.

35. If 4% of motorists on the turnpike leave at a certain exit and 5% of these go to one particular motel for lodging, out of every 10,000 motorists how many motorists may be exptected to go to this motel?
(A) 0.2 (B) 2 (C) 20 (D) 200 (E) 2000

36. During a storewide sale many articles were reduced by 25%. To restore these articles to their original prices they must now increase their price by
(A) 25% (B) 27.5% (C) $33\frac{1}{3}\%$ (D) 40%
(E) 50%

37. *ADB* and *CEB* are secants of circle *O*. If $\angle AOC \overset{\circ}{=} 80$ and $\angle B \overset{\circ}{=} 20$, how many degrees are in $\widehat{DE}$?

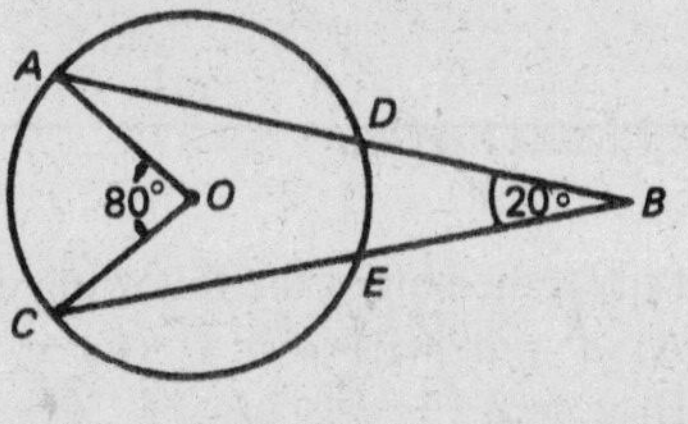

(A) 40 (B) 60 (C) 80 (D) 120 (E) 140

38. Candy which formerly sold for $1.20 per pound is now packaged in two-pound boxes which sell for $3.00. The ratio of the old price to the new price is
(A) 1:5 (B) 2:5 (C) 3:5 (D) 4:5
(E) 5:4

39. In right $\triangle ABC$, leg AB = leg BC. The area of the triangle is 12.5. Hypotenuse AC equals
(A) $\sqrt{5}$ (B) $5\sqrt{2}$ (C) 5 (D) $4\sqrt{5}$ (E) 25

40. A rectangular field 50 meters in width and 120 meters in length is divided into two fields by a diagonal line. What is the length of fence (in meters) required to enclose one of these fields?
(A) 130 (B) 170 (C) 180 (D) 200
(E) 300

41. If there are 5 to 8 eggs in a pound, what is the maximum number of eggs in 40 pounds?
(A) 5 (B) 8 (C) 160 (D) 200 (E) 320

42. A point, X, is 25 feet from the center of a circle. If the diameter of the circle is 14 feet, what is the length (in feet) of a tangent from point X to the circle?
(A) $\sqrt{29}$ (B) 18 (C) $15\sqrt{2}$ (D) 24
(E) $\sqrt{673}$

43. Linda did 24 problems out of 25 correctly. In the next test she did twice as many examples correctly but received a mark only half as good. How many problems were there in the second test?
(A) 25 (B) 48 (C) 50 (D) 75 (E) 100

44. If a garage can wash 5 cars in 25 minutes, how long would it take to wash 25 cars?
(A) 2 hrs. (B) 2 hrs. 5 min. (C) 5 hrs.
(D) 25 hrs. (E) none of these

45. A secondhand car dealer sold a car for Mr. Dee and, after deducting 5% commission, remitted $4750 to Mr. Dee. What was the selling price of the car?
(A) $2375 (B) $4773 (C) $5000
(D) $5500 (E) $50,000

46. If $a - 1$ is an even integer, which of the following must be odd?
I. $3(a - 3)$
II. $2a + 1$
III. $a(a - 1)$
(A) I only (B) II only (C) III only
(D) I and II only (E) I, II, and III

47. If n is a positive integer, which of the following could be a possible value of $\frac{-1^n}{(-1)^n}$?
I. 1
II. -1
III. $\frac{1}{n}$
(A) I only (B) II only (C) III only
(D) I and II only (E) I, II, and III

48. For what values of n and d is $\frac{n}{d} > 1$?
(A) $n = 5, d = 6$ (B) $n = 3, d = 2$
(C) $n = 1, d = 2$ (D) $n = 1, d = 1$
(E) $n = 0, d = 1$

49. In a shipment of 25 stereo components, only 80% of these parts were accepted as satisfactory. How many were not accepted in this shipment?
(A) 5 (B) 6 (C) 10 (D) 15 (E) 20

50. In this figure the lettered points are on the circumference of the circle with center O. Which letter represents the point with coordinates (5,0)?

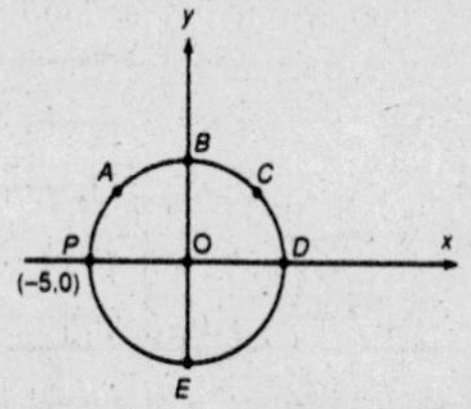

(A) A (B) B (C) C (D) D (E) E

ANSWER KEY

Verbal Aptitude Section

1. C	11. C	21. A	31. C	41. B	51. D	61. A
2. E	12. E	22. B	32. B	42. B	52. D	62. A
3. B	13. D	23. C	33. E	43. B	53. E	63. D
4. C	14. C	24. D	34. B	44. D	54. C	64. C
5. D	15. B	25. E	35. D	45. D	55. D	65. C
6. C	16. D	26. C	36. C	46. D	56. C	
7. A	17. C	27. D	37. D	47. E	57. E	
8. C	18. A	28. B	38. B	48. C	58. C	
9. C	19. A	29. C	39. E	49. C	59. C	
10. D	20. E	30. D	40. E	50. D	60. D	

Mathematical Aptitude Section

Note: Each correct answer to the mathematics questions is keyed by number to the corresponding topic in Chapters 9 and 10. These numerals refer to the topics listed below, with specific page references in parentheses.

1. Basic Fundamental Operations (155–157)
2. Algebraic Operations (157–160)
3. Using Algebra (160–164)
4. Exponents, Roots and Radicals (159–160)
5. Inequalities (164–165)
6. Fractions (176–178)
7. Decimals (176)
8. Percent (178–180)
9. Averages (180–181)
10. Motion (182–183)
11. Ratio and Proportion (183–185)
12. Mixtures and Solutions (177–178)
13. Work (185–186)
14. Coordinate Geometry (172–173)
15. Geometry (165–172, 173–176)
16. Quantitative Comparisons (189–192)

ANSWER KEY

1. **E** (1)	*11.* **B** (15)	*21.* **C** (2,16)	*31.* **A** (2,16)	*41.* **E** (1,11)
2. **A** (1)	*12.* **D** (6)	*22.* **A** (8,16)	*32.* **D** (4,16)	*42.* **D** (15)
3. **C** (3)	*13.* **B** (2,6)	*23.* **D** (2,16)	*33.* **D** (1,8)	*43.* **E** (3)
4. **A** (15)	*14.* **B** (2)	*24.* **C** (15,16)	*34.* **B** (11)	*44.* **B** (11)
5. **C** (1)	*15.* **C** (3,8)	*25.* **C** (15,16)	*35.* **C** (8)	*45.* **C** (3,8)
6. **D** (1)	*16.* **C** (6,16)	*26.* **A** (15,16)	*36.* **C** (8)	*46.* **B** (1)
7. **B** (1)	*17.* **C** (6,7,16)	*27.* **C** (15,16)	*37.* **A** (15)	*47.* **D** (2)
8. **C** (6)	*18.* **B** (4,16)	*28.* **B** (4,16)	*38.* **D** (11)	*48.* **B** (1)
9. **E** (1,4)	*19.* **D** (2,16)	*29.* **B** (2,16)	*39.* **B** (15)	*49.* **A** (8)
10. **E** (15)	*20.* **B** (6,16)	*30.* **C** (15,16)	*40.* **E** (15)	*50.* **D** (14)

SCORING CHART—TYPICAL TEST B

Verbal Section		**Mathematical Section ***		
No. correct	______	No. correct	(A)	______
No. omitted	______	No. incorrect (# 1-15, 33-50)	(B)	______
No. incorrect	______	No. incorrect (# 16-32)	(C)	______
¼ no. incorrect	______	¼ (B) + ⅓ (C)	(D)	______
Raw Score: (no. correct minus ¼ no. incorrect)	______	*Raw Score* = (A) − (D)		______

* (In the Mathematical section, deduct ¼ of a point for each five-choice question answered incorrectly and ⅓ of a point for each four-choice question answered incorrectly).

EVALUATION CHART

Study your score. Your raw score on the Verbal and Mathematical Aptitude Sections is an indication of your probable achievement on the PSAT/NMSQT. As a guide to the amount of work you need or want to do with this book, study the following.

Raw Score		**Self-rating**
Verbal	*Mathematical*	
58–65	41–50	Superior
46–57	25–40	Very good
40–45	20–24	Satisfactory
36–39	16–19	Average
30–35	10–15	Needs further study
20–29	7–9	Needs intensive study
0–19	0–6	Probably inadequate

After completing Test B and scoring it, refer to page 383 to help you determine your weak areas, the areas you should study.

ANSWER EXPLANATIONS

Verbal Aptitude Section

1. **C** To *accelerate* is to go faster, the opposite of to *reduce speed*.
   Think of "the car accelerating."
2. **E** *Hypocrisy* is pretense or fakery, while *sincerity* is honesty.
   "After the facts came out, her hypocrisy was made evident."
3. **B** To be *strict* is to be rigid or harsh, the opposite of to be *lenient* (gentle or merciful).
   Think of "a strict officer, a stickler for rules."
4. **C** The opposite of to *disregard* or ignore is to *heed* or pay attention.
   Think of "disregarding a warning."
5. **D** The opposite of a *deletion* or removal of material is an *insertion* of material.
   Think of "the deletion of objectionable material" from films.
6. **C** The opposite of to *rectify* or correct is to *make worse*. Word Parts Clue: *Rect-* means right; *-ify* means to make. *Rectify* means to make right.
   Think of "rectifying an error."
7. **A** *Impetuous* means foolhardy or acting on impulse; *circumspect* means cautious or careful.
   "The impetuous youth rushed headlong down the mountain."
8. **C** Information which has *pertinence* is meaningful or applicable; facts which have a *lack of relevance* don't have to do with the subject at hand.
   "We ignored his comments because of their lack of pertinence."
9. **C** *Immutable* means fixed and unchanging, the opposite of *changeable*.
   Word Parts Clue: *Im-* means not; *mut-* means change. *Immutable* means not able to change, unchanging.
   "The marble tomb had lasted throughout the centuries and seemed immutable."
10. **D** To *inter* someone is to bury him; to *exhume* a person is to dig him up out of the ground.
    Think of "interring her remains."
11. **C** *Brevity* means briefness or shortness, the opposite of *lengthiness*.
    "Her speech—only 150 words—was notable for its brevity."
12. **E** A pliant, bendable thing is *supple*, whereas an *inflexible* thing is stiff and unbending.
    Think of "soft, supple leather."
13. **D** To *gainsay* is to deny or disagree, the opposite of to *affirm* or assert that something is so.
    "There was no pleasing him: he gainsayed every proposal."
14. **C** A *dearth* of something is a lack thereof; an *abundance* of something means there's plenty of it.
    Think of a "dearth of ready cash."
15. **B** To *burgeon* is to grow rapidly, the opposite of to *wither*, which is to shrink or waste away.
    Think of "plants burgeoning in the spring."
16. **D** A *pivotal* issue is central or crucial, whereas a *trivial* matter is unimportant.
    "This is the pivotal point: we either win now, or lose the entire game."
17. **C** *Gratuitous* means unneeded, the opposite of *necessary*.
    Think of "a stupid, gratuitous remark."
18. **A** *Contentious* means quarrelsome and eager to argue, the opposite of *agreeable*.
    Think of "a contentious fellow, always ready to fight."
19. **A** An *iconoclast* attacks tradition, while a *conventional person* goes along with society's customs.
    "An iconoclast, she fought against the outmoded doctrines of the old regime."
20. **E** A *mellifluous* sound is sweet and smoothly flowing, whereas a *strident* sound is harsh and shrill.
    Think of "mellifluous singing."
21. **A** "Because" signals cause and effect. Because lightning victims are so battered and confused, they seem like assault victims. Remember to make your own guess before looking at the answer choices. *Mistaken for* fits best, when you know you're looking for a phrase which describes the resemblance between the two types of victim.
22. **B** The key word "developing" anticipates the description of the way a highway system changes and grows. The road network is described as similar to the brain, which also *evolves with* use, developing and changing.
23. **C** We look for a negative word such as *overpriced* to describe the wines, because Ms. Sutcliffe gives "warnings" about them. At the same time, we need a positive word such as *trusty* to describe her book, since it contains helpful advice. Note that "trusty guide" is a cliche, a common expression.
24. **D** Since the island generally receives no orders from its mother country, it is *autonomous* or self-governing.
25. **E** Fiction which involves "dream" and "mad invention" is *fantastic:* it presents fantasy.
26. **C** A contrast is implied by the clause "that would have undone a lesser woman." Since Roosevelt was not a lesser woman, she was not undone; she *persevered* or continued striving. Just as she maintained her composure, she also maintained her dignity *unruffled* or undisturbed.
27. **D** A medicine which is said to "cure a wide variety of ailments" is by definition a *panacea*.
28. **B** The speech contained pompous language; therefore it was *bombastic*. The sophisticated people were not impressed by this pretentious wordiness, so they *ridiculed* or mocked it.

29. **C** *Rococo* style, by definition, is characterized by "scroll work and excessive decoration."

30. **D** A man too wedded to "orthodox theories" or doctrines can best be described as *doctrinaire* or dogmatic.

31. **C** A *thermometer* measures *temperature*. A *Geiger counter* measures *radiation*.

(Function)

32. **B** *Fans* or spectators are seated in the *bleachers*. An *audience* is seated in the *seats*.

(Defining Characteristic)

33. **E** An *archipelago* is a group or chain of *islands*. A *constellation* is a group of *stars*. Beware of eye-catchers. A *garden* does not, by definition, consist of *flowers;* a garden may be composed of vegetables instead.

(Part to Whole)

34. **B** A *glossary* or word list is composed of *words*. An *atlas* is composed of *maps*.

(Defining Characteristic)

35. **D** To *sand wood* is to smooth or polish it. To *burnish metal* is to polish it.

(Function)

36. **C** Something which is *buoyant* and tends to float is unlikely to *sink*. Something which is *adhesive* or sticky is unlikely to *loosen*.

(Antonym Variant)

37. **D** Someone who is *vindictive* or vengeful is lacking in *mercy*. Someone who is *skeptical* or suspicious is lacking in *trustfulness*.

(Antonym Variant)

38. **B** Someone *jittery* or nervous tends to *fidget* or move uneasily. Someone *touchy* or irritable tends to *snap* or retort angrily.

(Defining Characteristic)

39. **E** Behind a *comet* stretches its glowing *tail*. Behind a *vessel* (ship) stretches its *wake*, a trail in the water.

(Defining Characteristic)

40. **E** To *dampen enthusiasm* is to diminish it. To *mute* (muffle) *sound* is to diminish it. Note that Choice **C** is incorrect: to *distract attention* is not to diminish it but to divert it in a new direction.

(Defining Characteristic)

41. **B** The *bouquet* of *wine* is its distinctive fragrance. It is analogous to the *aroma* of *coffee*.

(Defining Characteristic)

42. **B** An *offhand* remark is made without forethought or *premeditation*. An *aboveboard* (open) deed is done without trickery or *guile*.

(Antonym Variant)

43. **B** A *shard* is a broken fragment of *pottery*. A *splinter* may be a broken fragment of *bone*.

(Part to Whole)

44. **D** Someone who is *refractory* (stubborn, unmanageable) is, by definition, hard to *manage*. Likewise, someone who is *lethargic* (sluggish, drowsy) is hard to *stimulate*.

(Definition)

45. **D** A *snail* is not noted for *celerity* or speed. A *peacock* is not noted for *humility* or modesty.

(Antonym Variant)

46. **D** The author cites Meredith's intelligence (*brilliance*) and his splendor of language (*linguistic grandeur*).

47. **E** Speaking of the "challenge and excitement of the critical problem as such," the author clearly expects that analyzing Meredith will be stirring and *invigorating*.

48. **C** The author wishes us to recognize the good qualities of Meredith's work even if we find it personally unsympathetic. Thus she would agree that criticism should enable us to appreciate the virtues of works we dislike.
Choices **A, B,** and **E** are unsupported by the passage. Choice **D** is incorrect. While the author wishes the reader to be aware of Meredith's excellences, she does not suggest that the reader should ignore the qualities in Meredith that make his work unsympathetic. Rather, she wishes the reader to appreciate the very ambivalence (simultaneous positive and negative feelings) of critics' responses to him.

49. **C** The opening paragraph discusses changes in the idea of matter, emphasizing the use of musical terminology to describe the concepts of physics. The second paragraph then goes on to develop the theme of the music of matter.
Choice **B** is incorrect. Music does not directly influence the interactions of particles; physicists merely use musical terms to describe these interactions.

50. **D** The author mentions these terms as examples of what he means by the strange new language or *idiosyncratic nomenclature* of modern particle physics.

51. **D** In his references to the elegance of the newly discovered subatomic structures and to the dance of Creation, the author conveys his *admiration* and wonder.

52. **D** The author first discusses Du Bois in relationship to black leaders in general and then provides the specific example of his relationship to Booker T. Washington. Choice **A** is incorrect. The author mentions Du Bois's early support of Washington's gradual approach; then he contrasts it with his later departure from Washington's conservatism. Choice **B** is incorrect. The author discusses

Du Bois's personality only in passing; he discusses Washington's personality not at all. Choice **C** is incorrect. The author's chief concern is to describe Du Bois's position, not to analyze what lay behind his achieving this position. He spends more time showing why Du Bois angered his fellow blacks than he does showing why Du Bois attracted them. Choice **E** is incorrect. It is unsupported by the passage.

53. **E** The last sentence points out that Du Bois originally agreed with Washington's program.
Choice **A** is incorrect. Nothing in the passage suggests that Du Bois sacrificed effective strategies out of a desire to try something new. Choice **B** is incorrect. Du Bois gained in influence, effectively winning away large numbers of blacks from Washington's policies. Choice **C** is incorrect. Du Bois was quick to depart from conventional black wisdom when it proved inadequate to the task of advancing the race. This shows him to be well able to change with the times. Choice **D** is incorrect. Washington, not Du Bois, is described as seeking the good will of whites.

54. **C** The author does *not* portray Washington as versatile. Instead, he portrays Du Bois as versatile. Choice **A** is incorrect. The author portrays Washington as submissive to the majority; he shows him teaching blacks not to protest. Choice **B** is incorrect. The author portrays Washington as concerned with financial success; he shows him advocating property accumulation. Choice **D** is incorrect. The author portrays Washington as traditional in preaching industriousness; he shows him advocating hard work. Choice **E** is incorrect. The author portrays Washington as respectful of authority; he shows him deferring to powerful whites.

55. **D** The author points out that Du Bois's methods led him into conflicts. Yet he describes Du Bois as "often... well in advance of his contemporaries" and stresses that his motives for departing from the mainstream were admirable. Thus his attitude can best be described as *approving*.

56. **C** The concluding sentence of the passage supports this point.

57. **E** The last sentence of paragraph 1 contradicts the idea that human beings have been on the North American continent for less than 10,000 years.

58. **C** Lively speculation about proposed land routes would be likely to come up with many possibilities—many possible routes in many possible directions. In fact, the nautical expression *to box the compass* means to recite in consecutive order the 32 points of the compass. The inference is that the proposed routes suggested that human beings traveled in all the directions of the compass.

59. **C** Famine is not mentioned. The other four choices are mentioned in paragraph 3.

60. **D** Since the passage ends with the idea that plants and animals would have needed a road as wide as a continent in order to spread into North America, we may assume that the author would continue to explore this notion.

61. **A** Farquhar agrees readily with the saying that all is fair in love and war. This implies he is willing to use underhanded or unfair methods to support the Southern cause.

62. **A** Mrs. Farquhar's readiness to fetch water for the gray-clad Confederate soldier suggests some degree of sympathy on her part for the Confederate cause.
Choices **B** and **D** are incorrect. There is nothing in the passage to suggest either of them. Choices **C** and **E** are incorrect. Mrs. Farquhar's action, in hospitably fetching water "with her own white hands," contradicts them.

63. **D** The phrase "burn like tow" and the reference to dry driftwood suggest that tow will catch fire readily. Remember, when asked to give the meaning of an unfamiliar word, to look for nearby context clues.

64. **C** The use of dialogue suggests a work of fiction; so do the descriptive adjectives and the narrative style.

65. **C** The scout is a Yankee soldier disguised as a member of the enemy. By coming to the Farquhar's plantation in Confederate disguise, he is able to learn they are sympathetic to the enemy. By telling Farquhar of the work on the bridge, stressing both the lack of guards and the abundance of fuel, he is tempting Farquhar into an attack on the bridge (and into an ambush). The scout's job is to locate potential enemies and draw them out from cover.

Mathematical Aptitude Section

1. **E** Factor: 146(117 + 173 + 210)
   146(500) = 73,000

2. **A** Minimum weight of 1 dozen eggs = 24 ounces
   Minimum weight of 1 egg = 2 ounces
   Minimum weight of 69 eggs = 138 ounces

3. **C** Let x = number of nickels.
   $12 - x$ = number of dimes
   $5x$ = value (in cents) of nickels
   $10(12 - x)$ or $120 - 10x$ = value (in cents) of dimes
   $5x + 120 - 10x = 85$
   $-5x = -35$
   $x = 7$

4. **A** (see diagram)

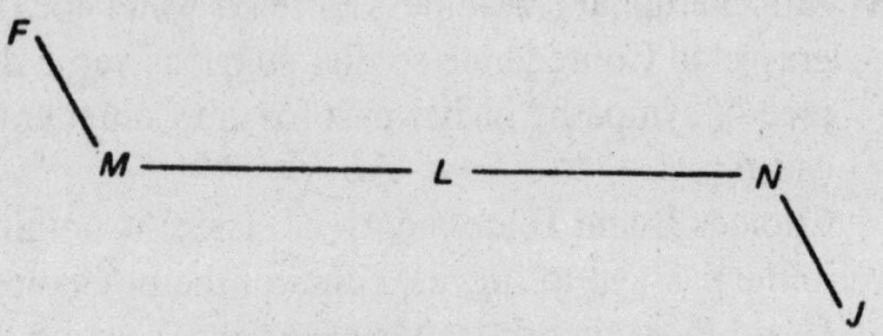

5. **C** Cost of twenty three-cent cards = 60¢
   For 40¢, one can buy 10 four-cent cards.

6. **D** Let x = number of ounces in one cup.
   $$\frac{6 \text{ cups}}{16 \text{ ounces}} = \frac{1 \text{ cup}}{x \text{ ounces}}$$
   $6x = 16$
   $x = 2.6 +$
   Therefore the best answer is 2.6.

7. **B** Cost − tax = \$1.97 − .70 = \$1.27
   Cost of first 15 words = 85¢
   Cost of additional words = 42¢
   At $3\frac{1}{2}$¢ per word, 12 additional words were sent.
   Total number of words = 15 + 12 = 27

8. **C** Since he sold $\frac{1}{3}$ of $\frac{1}{4}$, he still held $\frac{2}{3}$ of $\frac{1}{4}$ or $\frac{1}{6}$. This year he sold $\frac{5}{12}$ of his remaining share, so he held $\frac{7}{12}$ of $\frac{1}{6}$ or he still holds $\frac{7}{72}$ of the business.

9. **E** $\frac{1}{\sqrt{2}} \cdot \frac{\sqrt{2}}{\sqrt{2}} = \frac{1}{2}\sqrt{2}$
   $\frac{1}{2}$ of 1.414 = 0.707 or 0.71

10. **E** Since the lines are parallel, $c = f$ (alternate interior angles) (B); $e = a$ (corresponding angles) (C); and for the same reason $f = b$ (D). For (A), $d = a$ because they are vertical angles. In (E) the angles are supplementary.

11. **B** Let X be the midpoint of AB and Y be the midpoint of BC. $XB = 6$ and $BY = 3$. $XY = 9$.

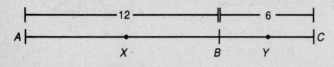

12. **D** 100 chickens = $\frac{1}{2}$ of $\frac{1}{3}$
    100 chickens = $\frac{1}{6}$
    $600 = \frac{6}{6}$.
    600 = number before disease struck
    $\frac{2}{3}$ of 600 = 400 (number of chickens lost before treatment)

13. **B** $\frac{2m}{3} = \frac{b}{a}$
    $\frac{2m}{b} = \frac{3}{a}$ (exchange terms of the means)
    Note that in either case product of means = product of extremes.

14. **B** Substitute:
    $$\frac{3(3)^2 - (-2)^2}{\frac{1}{2}(-1)^3}$$
    $$\frac{3(9) - (4)}{\left(\frac{1}{2}\right)(-1)} = \frac{27 - 4}{-\frac{1}{2}} = \frac{23}{-\frac{1}{2}} = 23 \div -\frac{1}{2}$$
    $$= (23)(-2) = -46$$

15. **C** \$260 = 130% of the cost = 1.3 of the cost
    Let x = cost.
    $1.3x = \$260$
    $13x = \$2600$
    $x = \$200$ (cost)
    40% of \$200 = \$80
    New selling price = \$200 + \$80 = \$280

16. **C** Note that multiplying both numerator and denominator of fraction B by 2 results in fraction A, and thus does not change the fraction's value.

17. **C** 0.04 = 4%
    $\frac{1}{25} = 4\%$

18. **B** $\sqrt{1.44} = 1.2$
    $1.2 > 0.12$

19. **D** $x^2 = 25$
    $x = +5$ and -5

20. **B** The denominator in $\frac{1}{q}$ is larger than the denominator in $\frac{1}{p}$.

21. **C** $4a + 2b - 3c^3 = (4)(2) + (2)(1) - 3(0) = 8 + 2 = 10$

22. **A** 105% of 500 = 525
    50% of 1000 = 500

23. **D** Two different equations are required to find two unknowns.

24. **C** The sum of the angles of any quadrilateral is 360°.
    360° ÷ 4 = 90°
    A square is a quadrilateral with sides equal and each angle = 90°.

25. **C** Since $y = 120$, $a = 60$.
Since the exterior angle of a triangle equals the sum of both remote interior angles, $z = x + a$. Since $x = 30$ [given], $z = 30 + 60$ or 90.

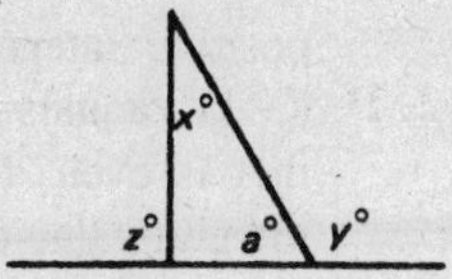

26. **A** $x = a + b$ (see # 25)
$x < a + b + c + d$ or, $a + b + c + d > x$

27. **C** $a + x = 180$
$b + y = 180$
$a + x + b + y = 360$
Since $x + y = 90$, $a + b = 270$.

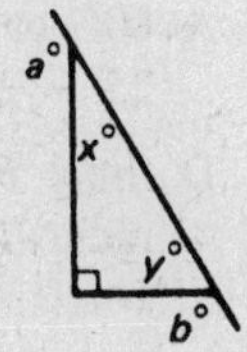

28. **B** Since $2^3 = 8$ and $2^{n+2} = 8$
then $n + 2 = 3$
$n = 1$

29. **B** $x(y + 5) = xy + 5x$
Column A $= xy + 5$
Column B $= xy + 5x$
$5x > 5$ since $x > 1$

30. **C**

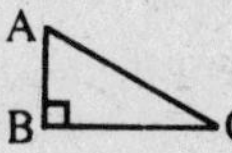

(In a right triangle the right angle is opposite the hypotenuse)

$\angle B \overset{\circ}{=} 90$
$\angle A + \angle C \overset{\circ}{=} 90$

31. **A** $\frac{5x + 6}{5} = \frac{5x}{5} + \frac{6}{5} = x + \frac{6}{5}$

32. **D** Since $A^{-1} = \frac{1}{A}$: if $A = 1$ then $\frac{1}{A} = 1$
if $A = 2$ then $\frac{1}{A} = \frac{1}{2}$

33. **D** $\frac{1 \text{ yard}}{1 \text{ foot}} \times 100 = \%$
$\frac{3 \text{ feet}}{1 \text{ foot}} \times 100 = 300\%$

34. **B** Let x = size of shadow of 35-foot tree.
$\frac{\text{size of tree}}{\text{size of shadow}} = \frac{98'}{42'} = \frac{35'}{x}$
$98x = (42)(35)$
$98x = 1470$
$x = 15$ ft.

35. **C** 5% of 4% $= (.05)(.04) = .0020 = .2\%$ or $\frac{.2}{100}$
$\frac{.2}{100} = \frac{20}{10{,}000}$

36. **C** Price during sale is 75% of normal price.
Change to original is 25%
$\frac{25\%}{75\%} = \frac{1}{3} = 33\frac{1}{3}\%$

37. **A** $\widehat{AC} = 80°$ since central $\angle \overset{\circ}{=} 80$.
Let x = number of degrees in $\widehat{DE}$.
$\angle B \overset{\circ}{=} \frac{1}{2}(\widehat{AC} - \widehat{DE})$
$20° = \frac{1}{2}(80° - x)$
$40° = 80° - x$
$-40° = -x$
$x = 40°$

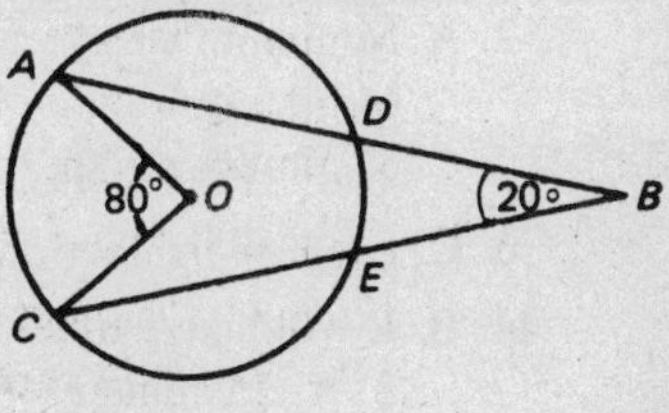

38. **D** Old price for 2 pounds was \$2.40.
Present price for 2 pounds is \$3.00.
Ratio $= \frac{\$2.40}{\$3.00} = \frac{240}{300} = \frac{24}{30} = \frac{4}{5} = 4{:}5$

39. **B** Let x = leg AB or leg BC.
Area $= \frac{1}{2}(x)(x)$
Area $= \frac{x^2}{2}$
Area $= \frac{x^2}{2} = 12.5$ [given]
$x^2 = 25$
$x = 5$ (each leg)
From the 45°-45°-90° triangle, $a = 5$, so $a\sqrt{2} = 5\sqrt{2}$.

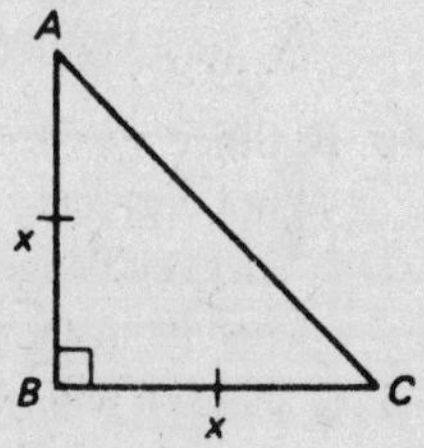

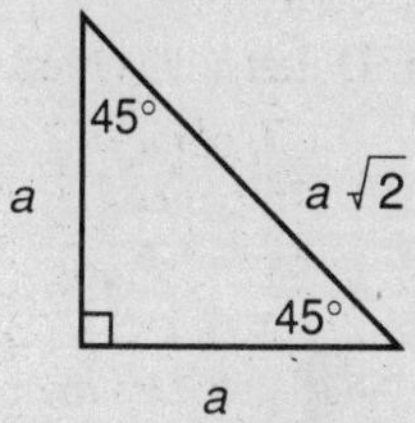

40. **E** Draw AC.
Observe right $\triangle ABC$.
Observe ratio of 5:12.
$\triangle ABD$ is a 5:12:13 $\triangle$ with each dimension multiplied by 10.
$AC = 130$ meters
Perimeter $= 50 + 120 + 130 = 300$ meters

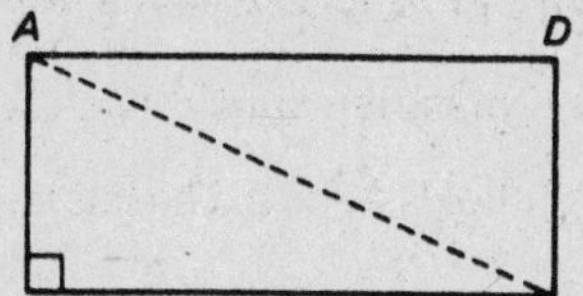

41. **E** Maximum number of eggs in one pound = 8
Maximum number of eggs in 40 pounds = 320

42. **D** Since the diameter is 14, a radius OP is 7.
Since radius $OP \perp$ to tangent PX, OPX is a right $\triangle$.
$\therefore (PX)^2 + 7^2 = 25^2$
$(PX)^2 = 576$
$PX = 24$ feet

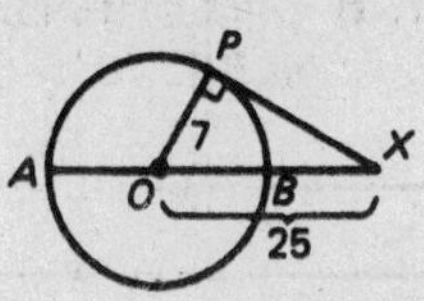

43. **E** First test: $\frac{24}{25} = 96\%$
Second test: 48% and 48 correct
Let x = number of problems in the second test.
$\frac{48}{x} = 48\%$
$\frac{48}{x} = \frac{48}{100}$
$x = 100$

44. **B** It will take 5 times as much time.
5×25 minutes = 125 minutes = 2 hours 5 minutes

45. **C** The dealer remitted 95% of selling price.
Let x = the selling price.
95% (or .95) of x = \$4750
$.95x = 4750$
$95x = 475000$
$x = \$5000$

46. **B** Since $a - 1$ is even, a must be an odd integer. I is not correct: $a - 3$ is even and $3(a - 3)$ results in an even integer. II is correct: $2a$ is even and $2a + 1$ results in an odd integer. III is not correct: $(a - 1)$ is even and $a(a - 1)$ results in an even integer.

47. **D** The numerator, -1^n, has the value -1 for any positive integral value of n. The denominator, $(-1)^n$, equals 1 for any positive integral value of n that is even, but it equals -1 for any positive integral value of n that is odd. Thus, $-1 \div 1 = -1$, but $-1 \div (-1) = 1$.

48. **B** For $\frac{n}{d}$ to be greater than 1, we must have $n > d$. This is true only in choice **B**.

49. **A** 80% or (0.8)(25) or 20 components were accepted. $25 - 20$ or 5 were not accepted.

50. **D** Since PO is a radius and $PO = 5$, OD is also a radius and therefore $OD = 5$. Since D is on the x-axis, OD is (5,0).

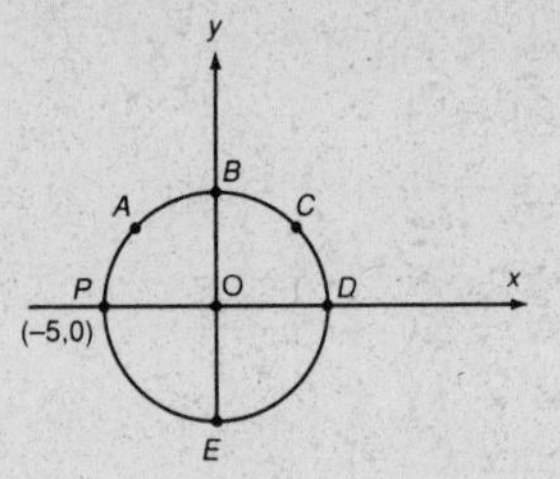

PSAT/NMSQT Answer Sheet

TYPICAL TEST C

Verbal Aptitude Section

1 (A) (B) (C) (D) (E)
2 (A) (B) (C) (D) (E)
3 (A) (B) (C) (D) (E)
4 (A) (B) (C) (D) (E)
5 (A) (B) (C) (D) (E)
6 (A) (B) (C) (D) (E)
7 (A) (B) (C) (D) (E)
8 (A) (B) (C) (D) (E)
9 (A) (B) (C) (D) (E)
10 (A) (B) (C) (D) (E)
11 (A) (B) (C) (D) (E)
12 (A) (B) (C) (D) (E)
13 (A) (B) (C) (D) (E)
14 (A) (B) (C) (D) (E)
15 (A) (B) (C) (D) (E)
16 (A) (B) (C) (D) (E)
17 (A) (B) (C) (D) (E)
18 (A) (B) (C) (D) (E)
19 (A) (B) (C) (D) (E)
20 (A) (B) (C) (D) (E)
21 (A) (B) (C) (D) (E)
22 (A) (B) (C) (D) (E)
23 (A) (B) (C) (D) (E)
24 (A) (B) (C) (D) (E)
25 (A) (B) (C) (D) (E)
26 (A) (B) (C) (D) (E)
27 (A) (B) (C) (D) (E)
28 (A) (B) (C) (D) (E)
29 (A) (B) (C) (D) (E)
30 (A) (B) (C) (D) (E)
31 (A) (B) (C) (D) (E)
32 (A) (B) (C) (D) (E)
33 (A) (B) (C) (D) (E)
34 (A) (B) (C) (D) (E)
35 (A) (B) (C) (D) (E)
36 (A) (B) (C) (D) (E)
37 (A) (B) (C) (D) (E)
38 (A) (B) (C) (D) (E)
39 (A) (B) (C) (D) (E)
40 (A) (B) (C) (D) (E)
41 (A) (B) (C) (D) (E)
42 (A) (B) (C) (D) (E)
43 (A) (B) (C) (D) (E)
44 (A) (B) (C) (D) (E)
45 (A) (B) (C) (D) (E)
46 (A) (B) (C) (D) (E)
47 (A) (B) (C) (D) (E)
48 (A) (B) (C) (D) (E)
49 (A) (B) (C) (D) (E)
50 (A) (B) (C) (D) (E)
51 (A) (B) (C) (D) (E)
52 (A) (B) (C) (D) (E)
53 (A) (B) (C) (D) (E)
54 (A) (B) (C) (D) (E)
55 (A) (B) (C) (D) (E)
56 (A) (B) (C) (D) (E)
57 (A) (B) (C) (D) (E)
58 (A) (B) (C) (D) (E)
59 (A) (B) (C) (D) (E)
60 (A) (B) (C) (D) (E)
61 (A) (B) (C) (D) (E)
62 (A) (B) (C) (D) (E)
63 (A) (B) (C) (D) (E)
64 (A) (B) (C) (D) (E)
65 (A) (B) (C) (D) (E)

Mathematical Aptitude Section*

1 (A) (B) (C) (D) (E)
2 (A) (B) (C) (D) (E)
3 (A) (B) (C) (D) (E)
4 (A) (B) (C) (D) (E)
5 (A) (B) (C) (D) (E)
6 (A) (B) (C) (D) (E)
7 (A) (B) (C) (D) (E)
8 (A) (B) (C) (D) (E)
9 (A) (B) (C) (D) (E)
10 (A) (B) (C) (D) (E)
11 (A) (B) (C) (D) (E)
12 (A) (B) (C) (D) (E)
13 (A) (B) (C) (D) (E)
14 (A) (B) (C) (D) (E)
15 (A) (B) (C) (D) (E)
16 (A) (B) (C) (D) (E)
17 (A) (B) (C) (D) (E)
18 (A) (B) (C) (D) (E)
19 (A) (B) (C) (D) (E)
20 (A) (B) (C) (D) (E)
21 (A) (B) (C) (D) (E)
22 (A) (B) (C) (D) (E)
23 (A) (B) (C) (D) (E)
24 (A) (B) (C) (D) (E)
25 (A) (B) (C) (D) (E)
26 (A) (B) (C) (D) (E)
27 (A) (B) (C) (D) (E)
28 (A) (B) (C) (D) (E)
29 (A) (B) (C) (D) (E)
30 (A) (B) (C) (D) (E)
31 (A) (B) (C) (D) (E)
32 (A) (B) (C) (D) (E)
33 (A) (B) (C) (D) (E)
34 (A) (B) (C) (D) (E)
35 (A) (B) (C) (D) (E)
36 (A) (B) (C) (D) (E)
37 (A) (B) (C) (D) (E)
38 (A) (B) (C) (D) (E)
39 (A) (B) (C) (D) (E)
40 (A) (B) (C) (D) (E)
41 (A) (B) (C) (D) (E)
42 (A) (B) (C) (D) (E)
43 (A) (B) (C) (D) (E)
44 (A) (B) (C) (D) (E)
45 (A) (B) (C) (D) (E)
46 (A) (B) (C) (D) (E)
47 (A) (B) (C) (D) (E)
48 (A) (B) (C) (D) (E)
49 (A) (B) (C) (D) (E)
50 (A) (B) (C) (D) (E)

*If there are more answer spaces than you need, leave them blank.

TYPICAL TEST C

SECTION 1 | **Time—50 minutes** **65 Questions** | For each question in this section, choose the best answer and fill in the corresponding circle on the answer sheet.

Each question below consists of a word in capital letters, followed by five lettered words or phrases. Choose the word or phrase that is most nearly opposite in meaning to the word in capital letters. Since some of the questions require you to distinguish fine shades of meaning, consider all the choices before deciding which is best.

Example:

GOOD: (A) sour (B) bad (C) red (D) hot (E) ugly

Ⓐ ● Ⓒ Ⓓ Ⓔ

1. GRANT: (A) borrow (B) refuse (C) weaken (D) guide (E) divide

2. NEEDY: (A) anxious (B) careless (C) penitent (D) prosperous (E) unnecessary

3. BLEND: (A) confine (B) hold still (C) lack flavor (D) recollect (E) clash

4. INELIGIBLE: (A) readable (B) suitable (C) changeable (D) unrestricted (E) insignificant

5. RANDOM: (A) lengthy (B) automatic (C) equitable (D) inaccurate (E) systematic

6. INVALIDATE: (A) confirm (B) injure (C) evaluate (D) recuperate (E) avoid

7. RECONCILE: (A) dismay (B) marry (C) estrange (D) control (E) disclose

8. PORTLY: (A) swift (B) slim (C) distant (D) healthy (E) rude

9. SEVER: (A) keep moist (B) hold still (C) deviate (D) pursue (E) connect

10. INEQUITY: (A) unity (B) justice (C) clarity (D) intensity (E) dissension

11. LILLIPUTIAN: (A) victorious (B) eternal (C) colossal (D) fanciful (E) conventional

12. WAX: (A) soothe (B) make known (C) grow smaller (D) consider (E) forget

13. DISSEMINATE: (A) gather (B) denounce (C) elucidate (D) fail to adapt (E) refuse to aid

14. CALLOWNESS: (A) maturity (B) rashness (C) softness (D) timidity (E) suspicion

15. NEBULOUS: (A) hypothetical (B) querulous (C) spirited (D) narrow (E) distinct

16. REPUDIATE: (A) respond (B) continue (C) accept (D) reiterate (E) attack

17. TACITURN: (A) immobile (B) energetic (C) disdainful (D) self-satisfied (E) garrulous

18. PETULANCE: (A) obstinacy (B) insincerity (C) amazement (D) composure (E) candor

19. OPPORTUNE: (A) hasty (B) untimely (C) chance (D) justifiable (E) delicate

20. ALOOFNESS: (A) selfishness (B) gregariousness (C) impartiality (D) downheartedness (E) ostentation

Each sentence below has one or two blanks, each blank indicating that something has been omitted. Beneath the sentence are five lettered words or sets of words. Choose the word or set of words that, when inserted in the sentence, best fits the meaning of the sentence as a whole.

Example:

Although its publicity has been ----, the film itself is intelligent, well-acted, handsomely produced, and altogether ----.

(A) tasteless . . respectable (B) extensive . . moderate (C) sophisticated . . amateur (D) risque . . crude (E) perfect . . spectacular

● Ⓑ Ⓒ Ⓓ Ⓔ

21. Criticism that tears down without suggesting areas of improvement is not ---- and should be avoided if possible.
(A) representative (B) constructive (C) mandatory (D) pertinent (E) sagacious

22. Although weeks remain for concessions to be made and for new approaches to be attempted, negotiations have reached such a state that management and union leaders are ---- that their differences can no longer be reconciled.
(A) encouraged (B) bewildered (C) apprehensive (D) relieved (E) skeptical

23. Many educators believe that, far from being a temporary stopgap, useful only as a transitional measure, bilingual education has proved to have definite ---- education in any one tongue.
(A) correlations with
(B) advantages over (C) connotations for
(D) limitations on (E) influence on

24. The columnist was very gentle when she mentioned her friends, but she was bitter and even ---- when she discussed people who ---- her.
(A) laconic . . infuriated (B) acerbic . . irritated
(C) remorseful . . encouraged
(D) militant . . distressed (E) stoical . . alienated

25. Like the theory of evolution, the big-bang model of the universe's formation has undergone modification and ----, but it has ---- all serious challenges.
(A) alteration . . confirmed
(B) refinement . . resisted
(C) transformation . . ignored
(D) evaluation . . acknowledged
(E) refutation . . misdirected

26. There is an essential ---- in human gestures, and when someone raises the palms of his hand together, we do not know whether it is to bury himself in prayer or to throw himself into the sea.
(A) economy (B) dignity (C) insincerity
(D) reverence (E) ambiguity

27. Unable to ---- her wholehearted distaste for media events and unnecessary publicity, Dean Brower continued to make ---- comments throughout the entire ceremony.
(A) control . . garbled (B) maintain . . copious
(C) conceal . . effusive (D) disguise . . caustic
(E) express . . vitriolic

28. The term "rare earths" is in fact a ----, for paradoxically, the rare-earth elements are in actuality ----, being present in low concentration in virtually all minerals.
(A) truism . . essential
(B) misnomer . . ubiquitous
(C) disclaimer . . ephemeral
(D) metaphor . . figurative
(E) mnemonic . . unmemorable

29. The perpetual spinning of particles is much like that of a top, with one significant difference: unlike the top, the particles have no need to be wound up, for ---- is one of their ---- properties.
(A) revolution . . radical (B) motion . . intangible
(C) rotation . . intrinsic (D) acceleration . . lesser
(E) collision . . hypothetical

30. Slander is like counterfeit money: many people who would not coin it ---- it without qualms.
(A) waste (B) denounce (C) circulate
(D) withdraw (E) invest

Each question below consists of a related pair of words or phrases, followed by five lettered pairs of words or phrases. Select the lettered pair that best expresses a relationship similar to that expressed in the original pair.

Example:

YAWN : BOREDOM :: (A) dream : sleep
(B) anger : madness (C) smile : amusement
(D) face : expression (E) impatience : rebellion

Ⓐ Ⓑ ● Ⓓ Ⓔ

31. FURNACE : HEAT :: (A) sponge : moisture
(B) thermometer : temperature
(C) camera : exposure (D) lamp : light
(E) fan : warmth

32. PALOMINO : HORSE :: (A) pecan : nut
(B) mongrel : collie (C) gander : goose
(D) gills : fish (E) leash : dog

33. DROPCLOTH : FURNITURE ::
(A) banner : flagpole (B) towel : rack
(C) pillow : bedding (D) curtain : theatre
(E) apron : clothing

34. YOLK : EGG :: (A) rind : melon
(B) nucleus : cell (C) stalk : corn
(D) duck : fowl (E) web : spider

35. CONFINE : PRISONER ::
(A) impeach : governor (B) trace : fugitive
(C) detain : suspect (D) testify : witness
(E) ambush : sentry

36. SWATCH : FABRIC :: (A) chip : paint
(B) slag : metal (C) mortar : brick
(D) essence : perfume (E) loaf : bread

37. BROWSER : NEWSSTAND :: (A) teller : bank
(B) witness : courtroom (C) investor : factory
(D) window-shopper : store
(E) head waiter : restaurant

38. TEPID : BOILING :: (A) frugal : parsimonious
(B) indifferent : apathetic
(C) contemptuous : disdainful
(D) cold : scorching (E) pleasant : useful

39. CROW : BOASTFUL :: (A) smirk : witty
(B) conceal : sly (C) pout : sulky
(D) blush : coarse (E) bluster : unhappy

40. LIBRETTO : POET :: (A) aria : singer
(B) blueprint : draftsman (C) handwriting : author
(D) scalpel : surgeon (E) somersault : gymnast

41. SKIRMISH : BATTLE :: (A) quiz : examination
(B) injury : scar (C) detour : journey
(D) ambush : retreat (E) recital : concert

42. MEANDER : JOURNEY ::
(A) rehearse : performance (B) soar : flight
(C) observe : phenomenon (D) ramble : speech
(E) clarify : point

43. INDEPENDENT : AUTONOMY ::
(A) courageous : cowardice (B) coy : silence
(C) inventive : resourcefulness
(D) nervous : equanimity (E) prodigal : economy

44. PENITENT : CONTRITION ::
(A) pragmatist : resignation
(B) hedonist : self-indulgence
(C) skeptic : gullibility (D) stoic : arrogance
(E) zealot : trepidation

45. CONTEMPORANEOUS : EVENTS ::
(A) adjacent : objects
(B) modern : times (C) temporary : measures
(D) gradual : degrees (E) repetitive : steps

Each passage below is followed by questions based on its content. Answer the questions following each passage on the basis of what is stated or implied in that passage.

An oft-used, but valuable, analogy compares the immune system with an army. The defending troops are the white blood cells called lymphocytes, born in the bone marrow, billeted in the lymph nodes and spleen, and on exercise in the blood and lymph systems. A body can muster some 200,000,000 cells, making the immune system comparable in mass to the liver or brain.

The lymphocytes are called to action when the enemy makes itself known. They attack anything foreign. Their job is to recognize the enemy for what it is, and then destroy it. One of the key features of the immune system is its specificity. Inoculation with smallpox provokes an attack on any smallpox virus, but on nothing else. This specificity of response depends on the lymphocyte's ability to identify the enemy correctly by the molecules on its surface, called antigens.

An antigen is an enemy uniform. It can be a protein on the surface of a cold virus, or it can be a protein on the surface of a pollen grain, in which case the immune response takes the form of an allergy. An antigen can also be a protein on the surface of a transplanted organ, in which case the immune response "rejects" the transplant. Organs can therefore be transplanted only between closely related people—in whom the antigens are the same—or into people treated with a drug that suppresses the immune system, such as cyclosporin.

46. The author's primary purpose in the passage is to do which of the following?
- (A) Demonstrate the inadequacy of an analogy.
- (B) Advocate a method to strengthen the immune system.
- (C) Compare the immune system to the brain.
- (D) Clarify the workings of the body's defense system.
- (E) Merge two differing views of a bodily process.

47. The author provides information to answer which of the following questions?
- (A) What is the process by which antigens are produced?
- (B) What is the mechanism by which cyclosporin suppresses the immune system?
- (C) What is the process that prevents closely related persons from developing dissimilar antigens?
- (D) How does inoculation with smallpox wear off over a period of years?
- (E) Where do the body's lymphocytes originate?

48. It can be inferred from the passage that treatment with cyclosporin might result in which of the following?
- I. An increased susceptibility to invasion by disease
- II. The rejection of a transplanted organ
- III. An increased effectiveness of antigens
- (A) I only
- (B) II only
- (C) I and II only
- (D) I and III only
- (E) I, II and III

49. In describing the immune system, the author does all of the following EXCEPT
- (A) define a term
- (B) illustrate through a comparison
- (C) refer to an authority
- (D) give an approximation
- (E) develop an extended metaphor

"The emancipation of women," James Joyce told one of his friends, "has caused the greatest revolution in our time in the most important relationship there is—that between men and women." Other modernists agreed: Virginia Woolf, claiming that in about 1910 "human character changed," and, illustrating the new balance between the sexes, urged, "Read the 'Agamemnon,' and see whether...your sympathies are not almost entirely with Clytemnestra." D.H. Lawrence wrote, "Perhaps the deepest fight for 2000 years and more, has been the fight for women's independence."

But if modernist writers considered women's revolt against men's domination one of their "greatest" and "deepest" themes, only recently—in perhaps the past 15 years—has literary criticism begun to catch up with it. Not that the images of sexual antagonism that abound in modern literature have gone unremarked; far from it. But what we are able to see in literary works depends on the perspectives we bring to them, and now that women—enough to make a difference—are reforming canons and interpreting literature, the landscapes of literary history and the features of individual books have begun to change.

50. According to the passage, women are changing the nature of literary criticism by
- (A) noting instances of hostility between men and women
- (B) seeing literature from fresh points of view
- (C) emphasizing the works of early twentieth-century writers
- (D) limiting their criticism to books written by feminists
- (E) resisting masculine authority and control

51. The author quotes James Joyce, Virginia Woolf, and D.H. Lawrence primarily in order to show that
(A) they were too few for their views to make a difference
(B) although well-meaning, they were ineffectual
(C) before the twentieth century, there was little interest in women's literature
(D) modern literature is dependent on the women's movement
(E) the interest in feminist issues is long standing

52. The author's attitude toward women's emancipation can best be described as one of
(A) marked ambivalence (B) qualified approval
(C) scientific detachment (D) open endorsement
(E) warranted skepticism

One simple physical concept lies behind the formation of the stars: gravitational instability. The concept is not new; Newton first perceived it late in the 17th century.

Imagine a uniform, static cloud of gas in space. Imagine then that the gas is somehow disturbed so that one small spherical region becomes a little denser than the gas around it so that the small region's gravitational field becomes slightly stronger. It now attracts more matter to it and its gravity increases further, causing it to begin to contract. As it contracts its density increases, which increases its gravity even more, so that it picks up even more matter and contracts even further. The process continues until the small region of gas finally forms a gravitationally bound object.

53. The primary purpose of the passage is to
(A) demonstrate the evolution of the meaning of a term
(B) depict the successive stages of a phenomenon
(C) establish the pervasiveness of a process
(D) support a theory considered outmoded
(E) describe a static condition

54. It can be inferred from the passage that the author views the information contained within it as
(A) controversial but irrefutable
(B) speculative and unprofitable
(C) uncomplicated and traditional
(D) original but obscure
(E) sadly lacking in elaboration

55. The author provides information that answers which of the following questions?
I. How does the small region's increasing density affect its gravitational field?
II. What causes the disturbance that changes the cloud from its original static state?
III. What is the end result of the gradually increasing concentration of the small region of gas?
(A) I only
(B) II only
(C) I and II only
(D) I and III only
(E) I, II and III

During the 1930's National Association for the Advancement of Colored People (NAACP) attorneys Charles H. Houston, William Hastie, James M. Nabrit, Leon Ransom, and Thurgood Marshall charted a legal strategy designed to end segregation in education. They developed a series of legal cases challenging segregation in graduate and professional schools. Houston believed that the battle against segregation had to begin at the highest academic level in order to mitigate fear of race-mixing that could create even greater hostility and reluctance on the part of white judges. After establishing a series of favorable legal precedents in higher education, NAACP attorneys planned to launch an all-out attack on the separate-but-equal doctrine in primary and secondary schools. The strategy proved successful. In four major United States Supreme Court decisions precedents were established that would enable the NAACP to construct a solid legal foundation upon which the Brown case could rest: *Missouri ex rel. Gaines* v. *Canada,* Registrar of the University of Missouri (1938); *Sipuel* v. *Board of Regents of the University of Oklahoma* (1948); *McLaurin* v. *Oklahoma State Regents for Higher Education* (1950); and *Sweatt* v. *Painter* (1950).

In the Oklahoma case, the Supreme Court held that the plaintiff was entitled to enroll in the University. The Oklahoma Regents responded by separating black and white students in cafeterias and classrooms. The 1950 McLaurin decision ruled that such internal separation was unconstitutional. In the Sweatt ruling, delivered on the same day, the Supreme Court held that the maintenance of separate law schools for whites and blacks was unconstitutional. A year after Herman Sweatt entered the University of Texas law school, desegregation cases were filed in the states of Kansas, South Carolina, Virginia, and Delaware, and in the District of Columbia asking the courts to apply the qualitative test of the Sweatt case to the elementary and secondary schools and to declare the separate-but-equal doctrine invalid in the area of public education.

The 1954 *Brown* v. *Board of Education* decision declared that a classification based solely on race violated the 14th Amendment to the United States Constitution. The decision reversed the 1896 *Plessy* v. *Ferguson* ruling which had established the separate-but-equal doctrine. The *Brown* decision more than any other case launched the "equalitarian revolution" in American jurisprudence and signalled the emerging primacy of equality as a guide to constitutional decisions; nevertheless, the decision did not end state-sanctioned segregation. Indeed, the second *Brown* decision, known as *Brown II* and delivered a year later, played a decisive role in limiting the effectiveness and impact of the 1954 case by providing southern states with the opportunity to delay the implementation of desegregation.

The intervention of the federal government and the deployment of the National Guard in the 1954 Little Rock crisis, and again in 1963 when the enrollment of James Meredith desegregated the University of Mississippi, highlight the role of federal power in promoting social change during this era. While black local and national leaders organized and orchestrated the legal struggles, and students joined in freedom rides and staged sit-ins, another equally important dimension of the rights quest took shape: the battle between federal and state authority and the evolution of the doctrine of federalism. The fact remains that the United States Supreme Court lacked the power to enforce its decisions. President Dwight D. Eisenhower's use of federal troops in Little Rock was a major departure from the reluctance of past presidents to display federal power in the South, especially to protect the lives and rights of black citizens.

56. According to the passage, Houston aimed his legislative challenge at the graduate and professional school level on the basis of the assumption that
(A) the greatest inequities existed at the highest academic and professional levels
(B) the separate-but-equal doctrine applied solely to the highest academic levels
(C) there were clear precedents for reform in existence at the graduate school level
(D) the judiciary would feel less apprehensive about desegregation on the graduate level
(E) the consequences of desegregation would become immediately apparent at the graduate school level

57. The passage suggests that the reaction of the Oklahoma Regents to the 1948 Sipuel decision was one of
(A) resigned tolerance (B) avowed uncertainty
(C) moderate amusement (D) distinct displeasure
(E) unquestioning approbation

58. Which of the following best describes the relationship between the McLaurin decision and the 1954 *Brown v. Board of Education* decision?
(A) The McLaurin decision superseded the Brown decision.
(B) The Brown decision provided a precedent for the McLaurin decision.
(C) The Brown decision reversed the McLaurin decision.
(D) The McLaurin decision limited the application of the Brown decision.
(E) The McLaurin decision provided legal authority for the Brown decision.

59. Which of the following titles best describes the content of the passage?
(A) Executive Intervention in the Fight against Segregated Education
(B) The *Brown* Decision and the Equalitarian Revolution
(C) A Long War: The Struggle to Desegregate American Education
(D) The Emergence of Federalism and the Civil Rights Movement
(E) Education Reform and the Role of the NAACP

60. The aspect of Houston's work most extensively discussed in the passage is its
(A) psychological canniness
(B) judicial complexity
(C) fundamental efficiency
(D) radical intellectualism
(E) exaggerated idealism

The curtain rises; the Cardinal and Daniel de Bosola enter from the right. In appearance, the Cardinal is something between an El Greco cardinal and a Van Dyke noble lord. He has the tall, spare form—the elongated hands and features—of the former; the trim pointed beard, the imperial repose, the commanding authority of the latter. But the El Greco features are not really those of asceticism or inner mystic spirituality. They are the index to a cold, refined but ruthless cruelty in a highly civilized controlled form. Neither is the imperial repose an aloof mood of proud detachment. It is a refined expression of satanic pride of place and talent.

To a degree, the Cardinal's coldness is artificially cultivated. He has defined himself against his younger brother Duke Ferdinand and is the opposite to the overwrought emotionality of the latter. But the Cardinal's aloof mood is not one of bland detachment. It is the deliberate detachment of a methodical man who collects his thoughts and emotions into the most compact and formidable shape—that when he strikes, he may strike with the more efficient and devastating force. His easy movements are those of the slowly circling eagle just before the swift descent with the exposed talons. Above all else, he is a man who never for a moment doubts his destined authority as a governor. He derisively and sharply rebukes his brother the Duke as easily and readily as he mocks his mistress Julia. If he has betrayed his hireling Bosola, he uses his brother as the tool to win back his "familiar." His court dress is a long, brilliant scarlet cardinal's gown with white cuffs and a white collar turned back over the red, both collar and cuffs being elaborately scalloped and embroidered. He wears a small cape, reaching only to the elbows. His cassock is buttoned to the ground, giving a heightened effect to his already tall presence. Richelieu would have adored his neatly trimmed beard. A richly jeweled and ornamented cross lies on his breast, suspended from his neck by a gold chain.

Bosola, for his part, is the Renaissance "familiar" dressed conventionally in somber black with a white collar. He wears a chain about his neck, a suspended ornament, and a sword. Although a "bravo," he must not be thought of as a leather-jacketed, heavy-booted tough, squat and swarthy. Still less is he a sneering, leering, melodramatic villain of the Victorian gaslight tradition. Like his black-and-white clothes, he is a colorful contradiction, a scholar-assassin, a humanist-hangman; introverted and introspective, yet ruthless in action; moody and reluctant, yet violent. He is a man of scholarly taste and subtle intellectual discrimination doing the work of a hired ruffian. In general effect, his impersonator must achieve suppleness and subtlety of nature, a highly complex, compressed, yet well-restrained intensity of temperament. Like Duke Ferdinand, he is inwardly tormented, but not by undiluted passion. His dominant emotion is an intellectualized one: that of disgust at a world filled with knavery and folly, but in which he must play a part and that a lowly, despicable one. He is the kind of rarity that Browning loved to depict in his Renaissance monologues.

61. The primary purpose of the passage appears to be to
(A) provide historical background on the Renaissance church
(B) describe ecclesiastical costuming and pageantry
(C) analyze the appearances and moral natures of two dramatic figures
(D) compare and contrast the subjects of two historical paintings
(E) denounce the corruption of the nobility in Renaissance Italy

62. It can be inferred from the passage that the Cardinal and Bosola
(A) are feuding brothers
(B) are noble lords
(C) together govern the church
(D) are characters in a play
(E) resemble one another in looks

63. In paragraph 2 the author most likely compares the movements of the Cardinal to those of a circling eagle in order to emphasize his
(A) flightiness (B) love of freedom
(C) eminence (D) spirituality
(E) mercilessness

64. As used in paragraph 3, the word *bravo* most nearly means
(A) a courageous man (B) a national hero
(C) a clergyman (D) a humanist
(E) a mercenary killer

65. The author of this passage assumes that the reader is
(A) familiar with the paintings of El Greco and Van Dyke
(B) disgusted with a world filled with cruelty and folly
(C) ignorant of the history of the Roman Catholic Church
(D) uninterested in psychological distinctions
(E) unacquainted with the writing of Browning

SECTION 2 Time—50 minutes 50 Questions

In this section solve each problem, using any available space on the page for scratchwork. Then decide which is the best of the choices given and fill in the corresponding circle on the answer sheet.

The following information is for your reference in solving some of the problems.

Circle of radius r: Area $= \pi r^2$ Circumference $= 2\pi r$
The number of degrees of arc in a circle is 360.
The measure in degrees of a straight angle is 180.

Definitions of symbols:
$=$ is equal to $\leqq$ is less than or equal to
$\neq$ is unequal to $\geqq$ is greater than or equal to
$<$ is less than $\parallel$ is parallel to
$>$ is greater than $\perp$ is perpendicular to

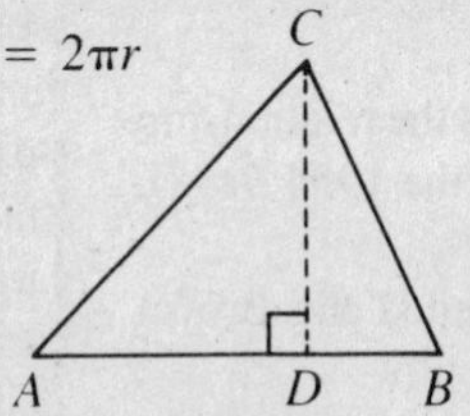

Triangle: The sum of the measures in degrees of the angles of a triangle is 180.

If $\angle CDA$ is a right angle, then

(1) area of $\triangle ABC = \frac{AB \times CD}{2}$

(2) $AC^2 = AD^2 + DC^2$

Note: Figures that accompany problems in this test are intended to provide information useful in solving the problems. They are drawn as accurately as possible EXCEPT when it is stated in a specific problem that its figure is not drawn to scale. All figures lie in a plane unless otherwise indicated. All numbers used are real numbers.

1. How much is $\frac{1}{2}$ of $\frac{x}{2}$?

(A) x (B) $\frac{1}{x}$ (C) $\frac{1}{4}$ (D) $\frac{x}{4}$ (E) $4x$

2. $3 + \frac{3}{0.3}$ equals

(A) 10 (B) 13 (C) 33 (D) 40 (E) 44

3. Which of the following is the closest value of $\frac{42.10 \times 0.0003}{0.002}$?

(A) 0.0063 (B) 0.063 (C) 0.63 (D) 6.3
(E) 63

4. What percent of 7.5 is 0.075?
(A) 0.001% (B) 0.01% (C) 0.1% (D) 1%
(E) 10%

5. How many 5-gallon cans of milk will be needed to fill 120 pint containers?
(A) 3 (B) 6 (C) 9 (D) 15 (E) 40

6. In a graduating class having the same number of boys and girls, the guidance counselor finds that $\frac{1}{2}$ the boys and $\frac{1}{3}$ of the girls are going to college. What percent of the class is going to college?
(A) 33.3% (B) 41.7% (C) 58.3% (D) 66%
(E) 83.3%

7. The first of four afternoon classes begins at 1 P.M. The last class ends at 3:52 P.M. Allowing 4 minutes between classes, how many minutes are there in each class period?
(A) 39 (B) 40 (C) 45 (D) 59 (E) 60

8. All of the following are equal EXCEPT
(A) $1 + \frac{x}{y}$ (B) $\frac{xy + x^2}{x^2}$ (C) $\frac{y^2 + xy}{xy}$
(D) $\frac{y}{x} + 1$ (E) $\frac{x + y}{x}$

9. A group of soldiers forms a solid square with s soldiers on a side. If 56 soldiers are released, the remaining soldiers form a square with $(s - 2)$ soldiers on a side. What is the value of s?
(A) 5 (B) 10 (C) 15 (D) 20 (E) 25

10. $2x + t = 2$
$t =$
(A) x (B) $x - 1$ (C) $2x - 2$ (D) $2 - 2x$
(E) $1 - x$

11. The accompanying figure shows two vertices of square *ABCD*. Which of the following could be the coordinates of vertex *C*?
I. (2, −2)
II. (4, −4)
III. (−2,2)
(A) I only (B) II only (C) I and II only
(D) I and III only (E) II and III only

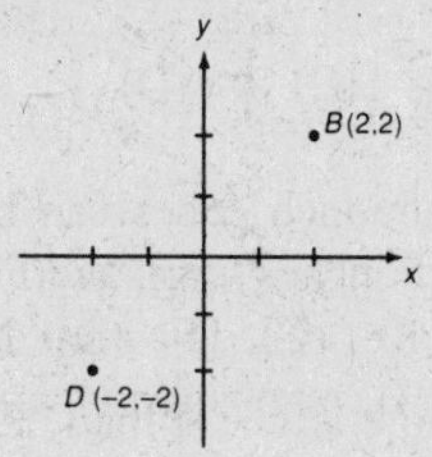

12. The base of a rectangle is 20, which is twice its height. What part of the perimeter is the height?
(A) $\frac{1}{12}$ (B) $\frac{1}{6}$ (C) $\frac{1}{4}$ (D) $\frac{1}{3}$ (E) $\frac{5}{6}$

13. By allowing a discount of 30% on an article formerly selling for $150 a dealer finds he is making a profit of 5% of his cost. His cost was
(A) $52.50 (B) $98.50 (C) $100.00
(D) $105.00 (E) $142.50

14. A grocer paid $2600 for a secondhand delivery truck. At the end of $4\frac{1}{2}$ years he was allowed $440 for it toward the purchase of a new truck. What was the average yearly amount of depreciation?
(A) $220 (B) $450 (C) $480 (D) $550
(E) $2200

15. A diamond ring valued at $7000 was insured at 80% of its value. What was the premium, if the rate was $6 per $1000?
(A) $3.36 (B) $4.20 (C) $33.60
(D) $42.00 (E) $336.00

Questions 16-32 each consist of two quantities, one in Column A and one in Column B. You are to compare the two quantities and on the answer sheet fill in circle

A if the quantity in Column A is greater;
B if the quantity in Column B is greater;
C if the two quantities are equal;
D if the relationship cannot be determined from the information given.

Notes:
1. In certain questions, information concerning one or both of the quantities to be compared is centered above the two columns.
2. In a given question, a symbol that appears in both columns represents the same thing in Column A as it does in Column B.
3. Letters such as x, n, and k stand for real numbers.

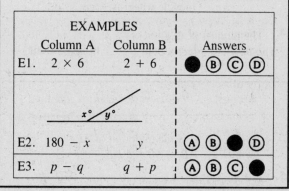

EXAMPLES

	Column A	Column B	Answers
E1.	2×6	$2 + 6$	● Ⓑ Ⓒ Ⓓ
	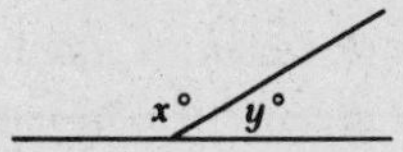		
E2.	$180 - x$	y	Ⓐ Ⓑ ● Ⓓ
E3.	$p - q$	$q + p$	Ⓐ Ⓑ Ⓒ ●

Column A	Column B

In the state lottery 10% of the 2000 tickets sold won prizes ranging from $1.00 to $1000. Florence bought 20 tickets.

	Column A	Column B
16.	Number of winnning tickets held by Florence	One winning ticket

	COLUMN A	COLUMN B

$A > B$
$B > C$

17.	$B + C$	$2A$

$a = 3$ and $b = 2$

18.	$\dfrac{\frac{1}{ab}}{\frac{1}{a} + \frac{1}{b}}$	$\dfrac{1}{a + b}$
19.	30%	$\dfrac{0.9}{2}$
20.	$\dfrac{9x - 13}{8y - 7}$	$\dfrac{13 - 9x}{7 - 8y}$

$0 < a < b < c$

21.	$\dfrac{c}{a}$	$\dfrac{c}{b}$
22.	The percent increase from 50¢ to 70¢	The percent increase from 70¢ to 90¢

Mark, Philip, and Michael have a total of \$35. Mark and Philip have the same amount of money.

23.	The amount of money Michael has.	The amount of money Philip has.

The diameter of the bicycle wheel is $\frac{7}{\pi}$ feet.

24.	The number of revolutions made when going 70 feet	10 revolutions

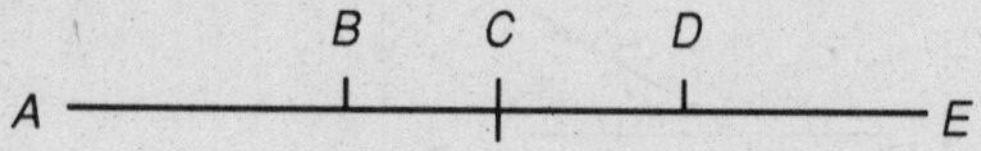

C is the midpoint of AE.
$AB = 90$ and $DE = 85$

25.	BC	CD

$x = 2^2$

26.	x^2	4

In $\triangle ABC$, the measure of $\angle A$ is 86° and the measure of $\angle C$ is 66°.

27.	Length of side AC	Length of side AB

$x > 0$

28.	$\dfrac{x + 6}{8}$	$\dfrac{x + 3}{4}$

	COLUMN A	COLUMN B

In $\triangle ABC$
$AB = 4$ and $BC = 9$

29.	Area of ABC	18

In $\triangle ABC$
$\angle A° = 48°$
$\angle B° = 72°$

30.	Length of side AB	Length of side AC

$\dfrac{x}{28} = \dfrac{2}{14}$
$\dfrac{y}{12} = \dfrac{1}{3}$

31.	x	y
32.	$\dfrac{7}{8}$	$\dfrac{6}{7}$

Solve each of the remaining problems in this section using any available space for scratchwork. Then decide which is the best of the choices given and fill in the corresponding circle on the answer sheet.

33. In distributing milk at a summer camp it is found that a quart of milk will fill either 3 large glass tumblers or 5 small glass tumblers. How many small glass tumblers can be filled with one large glass tumbler?
(A) $\frac{3}{5}$ (B) $1\frac{2}{3}$ (C) $1\frac{2}{5}$ (D) 2 (E) $2\frac{1}{3}$

34. A can of food feeds 3 kittens or 2 dogs. If I have 8 cans of food and I feed 12 kittens, how many dogs can I feed?
(A) 2 (B) 4 (C) 8 (D) 12 (E) 18

35. At 3:55 P.M. a student begins to do her homework which would take three hours to complete. At 4:15 P.M. she is interrupted by a telephone call and does not resume work. What part of her homework is left uncompleted?
(A) $\frac{1}{9}$ (B) $\frac{2}{9}$ (C) $\frac{1}{3}$ (D) $\frac{2}{3}$ (E) $\frac{8}{9}$

36. How many one-inch cubes can be put in a box 5 inches wide, 5 inches long, and 5 inches deep?
(A) 5 (B) 10 (C) 15 (D) 25 (E) 125

37. How much more is $x - 2$ than 2?
(A) $-x$ (B) $x - 4$ (C) x (D) $2 - x$ (E) 0

38. A broad jumper makes an average standing jump of 8 feet. In how many jumps will he cover y yards?
(A) $\frac{3y}{8}$ (B) $\frac{8}{3y}$ (C) $24y$ (D) $\frac{1}{24y}$ (E) $\frac{24}{y}$

39. James is 30 years old and John is 3 years old. James will be five times as old as John in
(A) $3\frac{3}{4}$ years (B) $6\frac{1}{2}$ years (C) $11\frac{1}{4}$ years
(D) 37 years (E) 38 years

40. A solid block $1' \times 2' \times 3'$ weighs 4 pounds. What is the weight (in pounds) of a solid block of the same material $5' \times 6' \times 7'$?
(A) 8 (B) 35 (C) 70 (D) 140 (E) 315

41. Mrs. Lehman finds that her tax bill increased from $2500 to $3000. The percent increase is
(A) 5% (B) 10% (C) $16\frac{2}{3}\%$ (D) 20%
(E) 25%

42. Mr. Liebow received 10 crates of fruit for which he paid $90. He finds that one crate is not suitable for sale because of spoilage. At what price should he sell each of the other crates in order to realize a 20% profit on the total cost?
(A) $1.80 (B) $3.00 (C) $10.80
(D) $12.00 (E) $18.00

43. At 10 A.M. water begins to pour into a cylindrical can 14 inches high and 4 inches in diameter at the rate of 8 cubic inches every 10 minutes. At what time will it begin to overflow? (Use $\pi = \frac{22}{7}$.)
(A) 10:10 A.M. (B) 11:40 A.M. (C) 12:40 A.M.
(D) 1:40 P.M. (E) 2:40 A.M.

44. The width of the ring (shaded portion of the figure) is exactly equal to the radius of the inner circle. What percent of the entire area is the area of the shaded portion?

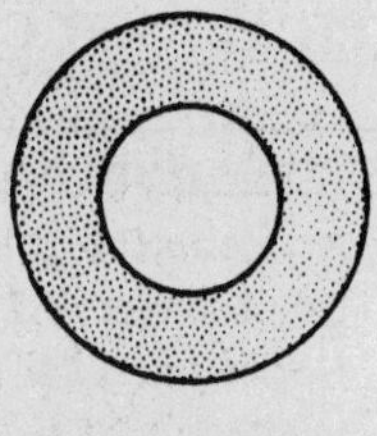

(A) 25% (B) $33\frac{1}{3}\%$
(C) 50% (D) $66\frac{2}{3}\%$ (E) 75%

45. Mr. Adams has a circular flower bed whose diameter is 4 feet. He wishes to increase the size of his bed so that it will have four times as much planting area. What must be the diameter of the new bed?
(A) 6 ft. (B) 8 ft. (C) 10 ft. (D) 12 ft.
(E) 16 ft.

46. In circle O, $OA = 4$, and $\overset{\frown}{AB} = 112°$. What is the measure of $\angle ABO$?
(A) 22° (B) 34° (C) 44°
(D) 45° (E) 68°

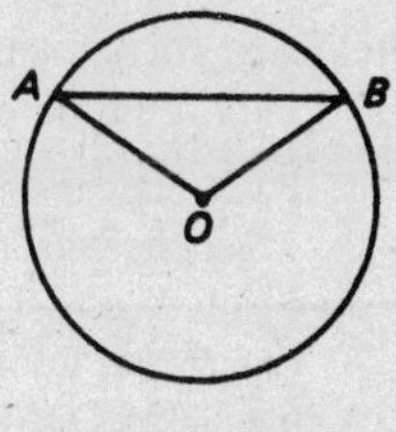

47. The length and width of a rectangle are each $\frac{2}{3}$ of the corresponding parts of $ABCD$. $AEB = 12$, $AGD = 6$. The area of the shaded part is
(A) 24 (B) 32 (C) 36
(D) 40 (E) 48

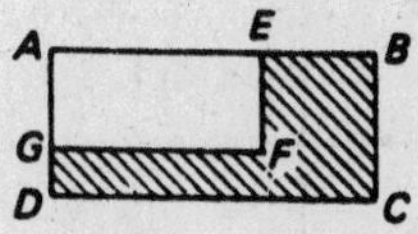

48. An altitude h of a triangle is twice the base to which it is drawn. If the area of the triangle is 225 square inches, then altitude h is
(A) 15 in. (B) 20 in. (C) 25 in. (D) 30 in.
(E) 35 in.

49. John's home is 6.3 miles due north of the community center. Dick's home is 5.5 miles due east of it. Find, to the nearest tenth of a mile, the shortest distance between their homes.
(A) 5.9 (B) 8.3 (C) 8.4 (D) 10.8
(E) 11.8

50. If the perimeter of a square is increased by 80%, by what percent is the area increased?
(A) 4% (B) 20% (C) 64% (D) 80%
(E) 224%

ANSWER KEY

Verbal Aptitude Section

1. B	11. C	21. B	31. D	41. A	51. E	61. C
2. D	12. C	22. C	32. A	42. D	52. D	62. D
3. E	13. A	23. B	33. E	43. C	53. B	63. E
4. B	14. A	24. B	34. B	44. B	54. C	64. E
5. E	15. E	25. B	35. C	45. A	55. D	65. A
6. A	16. C	26. E	36. A	46. D	56. D	
7. C	17. E	27. D	37. D	47. E	57. D	
8. B	18. D	28. B	38. A	48. A	58. E	
9. E	19. B	29. C	39. C	49. C	59. C	
10. B	20. B	30. C	40. B	50. B	60. A	

Mathematical Aptitude Section

Note: Each correct answer to the mathematics questions is keyed by number to the corresponding topic in Chapters 9 and 10. These numerals refer to the topics listed below, with specific page references in parentheses.

1. Basic Fundamental Operations (155–157)
2. Algebraic Operations (157–160)
3. Using Algebra (160–164)
4. Exponents, Roots and Radicals (159–160)
5. Inequalities (164–165)
6. Fractions (176–178)
7. Decimals (176)
8. Percent (178–180)
9. Averages (180–181)
10. Motion (182–183)
11. Ratio and Proportion (183–185)
12. Mixtures and Solutions (177–178)
13. Work (185–186)
14. Coordinate Geometry (172–173)
15. Geometry (165–172, 173–176)
16. Quantitative Comparisons (189–192)

ANSWER KEY

1. **D** (1,6)	*11.* **D** (14)	*21.* **A** (6,16)	*31.* **C** (2,16)	*41.* **D** (8)
2. **B** (1,6,7)	*12.* **B** (15)	22. **A** (8,16)	*32.* **A** (6,16)	*42.* **D** (8)
3. **D** (1,7)	*13.* **C** (3,8)	*23.* **D** (3,16)	*33.* **B** (1)	*43.* **D** (15)
4. **D** (8)	*14.* **C** (1)	*24.* **C** (15,16)	*34.* **C** (1)	*44.* **E** (15)
5. **A** (1)	*15.* **C** (8)	*25.* **B** (15,16)	*35.* **E** (6)	*45.* **B** (3,15)
6. **B** (6,8)	*16.* **D** (16)	*26.* **A** (4,16)	*36.* **E** (15)	*46.* **B** (15)
7. **B** (1)	*17.* **B** (2,16)	*27.* **B** (15,16)	*37.* **B** (2)	*47.* **D** (15)
8. **A** (2)	*18.* **C** (2,16)	*28.* **B** (2,16)	*38.* **A** (2)	*48.* **D** (15)
9. **C** (3,15)	*19.* **B** (6,7,8,16)	*29.* **D** (15,16)	*39.* **A** (3)	*49.* **C** (15)
10. **D** (2)	*20.* **C** (2,16)	*30.* **B** (15,16)	*40.* **D** (15)	*50.* **E** (15)

SCORING CHART TYPICAL TEST C

Verbal Section		**Mathematical Section***		
No. correct	_____	No. correct	(A)	_____
No. omitted	_____	No. incorrect (# 1-15, 33-50)	(B)	_____
No. incorrect	_____	No. incorrect (# 16-32)	(C)	_____
¼ no. incorrect	_____	¼ (B) + ⅓ (C)	(D)	_____
Raw Score: (no. correct minus ¼ no. incorrect)	_____	*Raw Score* = (A) − (D)		_____

* (In the Mathematical section, deduct ¼ of a point for each five-choice question answered incorrectly and ⅓ of a point for each four-choice question answered incorrectly.)

EVALUATION CHART

Study your score. Your raw score on the Verbal and Mathematical Aptitude Sections is an indication of your probable achievement on the PSAT/NMSQT. As a guide to the amount of work you need or want to do with this book, study the following.

Raw Score		**Self-rating**
Verbal	*Mathematical*	
58–65	41–50	Superior
46–57	25–40	Very good
40–45	20–24	Satisfactory
36–39	16–19	Average
30–35	10–15	Needs further study
20–29	7–9	Needs intensive study
0–19	0–6	Probably inadequate

Your scores are most likely improving with each test that you take. To help pinpoint any weak areas you still may have, consult the table on page 383 and plan your remaining review accordingly.

ANSWER EXPLANATIONS

Verbal Aptitude Section

1. **B** To *grant* a request is to permit it, the opposite of to *refuse* it.
Think of "granting a favor."
2. **D** Someone who is *needy* is poor, while a *prosperous* person is wealthy.
Think of "a needy orphan."
3. **E** Things which *blend* harmonize or merge, whereas things which *clash* conflict with one another.
Think of "colors which blend well together."
4. **B** *Ineligible* means inappropriate, the opposite of *suitable* or proper.
Think of "ineligible for service because of poor health."
5. **E** A *random* process is haphazard and guided by chance, the opposite of a *systematic* process, which is orderly and organized.
Think of "a random sample."
6. **A** To *invalidate* is to make valueless or obsolete, whereas to *confirm* is to verify or make firm.
Think of "invalidating a warranty."
7. **C** To *reconcile* means to bring about harmony or friendship again; to *estrange* is to alienate or create hostility.
"After much negotiation, the parties were reconciled."
8. **B** *Portly* means stout or plump, the opposite of *slim*.
Think of "a portly gentleman who appreciates food."
9. **E** To *sever* is to divide or cut through, the opposite of to *connect*.
Think of "severing the cord."
10. **B** *Inequity* is unfairness, the opposite of *justice*.
"There was such inequity at the trial that the decision was overturned."
11. **C** A thing which is extremely small or miniature is *lilliputian;* a huge or enormous thing is *colossal*.
"This tiny dog looks lilliputian next to the St. Bernard."
12. **C** To *wax* is to grow larger, the opposite of to *grow smaller.*
"The waxing moon is almost full."
13. **A** To *disseminate* is to spread or distribute, the opposite of to *gather* in.
Think of "disseminating knowledge freely."
14. **A** *Callowness* is inexperience or immaturity, the opposite of *maturity.*
"The young man's callowness was annoying."
15. **E** A *nebulous* thing is confused or hazy, the opposite of *distinct* or clear and unmistakable.
Think of "a nebulous notion."
16. **C** To *repudiate* something is to cast it off or reject it, the opposite of to agree to it or *accept* it.
Think of "repudiating war in favor of peace."
17. **E** A *garrulous* person is very talkative, whereas a *taciturn* person is usually rather silent.
"The garrulous old woman talked about past events all day long."
18. **D** *Petulance* is grumpiness, particularly over small matters; *composure* is tranquility or calmness.
Think of "sulky petulance."
19. **B** An *opportune* event is fortunate or convenient, the opposite of an *untimely* or premature occurrence.
Think of "the opportune arrival of the money."
20. **B** *Aloofness* is a distant, reserved manner, the opposite of *gregariousness,* the quality of being outgoing and social.
Think of the "aloofness of a judge in court."
21. **B** Criticism that suggests areas of improvement is said to be *constructive*. Remember, before you look at the answer choices, to read the sentence and try to think of a word that makes sense.
22. **C** The leaders would be *apprehensive* in such circumstances that they could not achieve their goal of reconciliation. Note that the phrase "negotiations have reached such a state" generally implies that they have reached a sorry state.
23. **B** If bilingual education is more than a mere stopgap (a somewhat negative description), it must possess certain positive qualities. Thus it has *advantages over* education in a single tongue. Note the use of *far from* to signal the contrast between the negative and positive views on bilingual education.
24. **B** The columnist was *acerbic* (bitingly sarcastic) in writing of those who provoked or *irritated* her. Note the use of *but* to establish the contrast between the two clauses, and the use of *even* to indicate that the missing word is stronger than *bitter.*
25. **B** The writer concedes that the big-bang theory has been changed somewhat: it has undergone *refinement* or polishing. However, he denies that its validity has been threatened seriously by any rival theories: it has *resisted* or defied all challenges.
The use of the support signal *and* indicates that the first missing word is similar to "modification." The use of the contrast signal *but* indicates that the second missing word is contrary in meaning to "undergone modification."
26. **E** The statement that "we do not know" whether a gesture indicates devotion or despair suggests that gestures, by their nature, have *ambiguity* or lack of clarity.

27. **D** Because the dean was not able to *disguise* her distatste for the media barrage, she failed to stifle her *caustic* or sarcastically biting remarks about the event. Note the implicit cause and effect relationship between the opening phrase and the central clause of the sentence.

28. **B** If the rare earths are actually present to some degree in essentially all minerals, then they are not rare after all. Thus the term "rare earths" is a *misnomer* (incorrect designation), for the rare earths are actually *ubiquitous* (omnipresent; found everywhere). Watch out for words that signal the unexpected. Note the use of "paradoxically" here.

29. **C** Particles have no need to be wound up because the property of spinning (*rotation*) is built into their makeup; it is *intrinsic*.

30. **C** Whatever word you choose here must apply equally well both to slander and to counterfeit money. People who would not make up a slanderous statement *circulate* slander by passing it on. Similarly, people who would not coin or make counterfeit money *circulate* counterfeit money by passing it on. Note how the extended metaphor here influences the writer's choice of words.

31. **D** A *furnace* provides *heat* and a *lamp* provides *light*.

(Function)

32. **A** A *palomino* is a type of *horse* and a *pecan* is a type of *nut*.

(Group and Member)

33. **E** A *dropcloth* protectively covers *furniture*. An *apron* protectively covers *clothing*.

(Function)

34. **B** Just as the *yolk* is the center of the *egg*, the *nucleus* is the center of the *cell*.

(Part to Whole)

35. **C** One *confines* a *prisoner* to keep him in prison. One *detains* a *suspect* to keep him in custody.

(Purpose)

36. **A** A *swatch* is a sample patch of *fabric*. A *chip* is a sample of *paint*.

(Function)

37. **D** A *browser* looks at newspapers and magazines at the *newsstand* without necessarily buying anything. A *window-shopper* looks at items in a *store* window without buying anything.

(Defining Characteristic)

38. **A** The relationship involves a matter of degree. *Tepid* (lukewarm) indicates the presence of some heat; *boiling* indicates the presence of a far greater degree of heat. Similarly, *frugal* (economical) indicates the practice of some thrift; *parsimonious* (stingy) indicates the practice of a far greater degree of thrift.

(Degree of Intensity)

39. **C** To *crow* is to express oneself in a *boastful* fashion. To *pout* is to express oneself in a *sulky* fashion.

(Defining Characteristic)

40. **B** A *poet* creates a *libretto*. A *draftsman* creates a *blueprint*.

(Worker and Work Created)

41. **A** A *skirmish* (minor military engagement) is less important than a *battle*. A *quiz* is less important than an *examination*.

(Degree of Intensity)

42. **D** To *meander* is to wander aimlessly during a *journey*. To *ramble* is to wander aimlessly during a *speech*.

(Manner)

43. **C** Someone who is *independent* has *autonomy* or freedom. Someone who is *inventive*, or creative, has *resourcefulness* (cleverness at solving problems).

(Synonym Variant)

44. **B** A *penitent* (person who repents) exhibits *contrition* (remorse). A *hedonist* (person devoted to the pursuit of pleasure as a way of life) exhibits *self-indulgence* (gratification of one's desires).

(Defining Characteristic)

45. **A** *Events* that are *contemporaneous* happen at the same point in time. *Objects* that are *adjacent* are next to each other in space.

(Defining Characteristic)

46. **D** The author is developing the military analogy in order to explain the immune system, the body's system of defense.
Choice **A** is incorrect. The author is not critical of the analogy; he draws on it in order to explain a complex system. Choice **B** is incorrect. The passage is expository, not persuasive: it explains, it doesn't argue. Choice **C** is incorrect. The author compares the mass of the immune system to that of the brain. However, that is only a passing reference. Choice **E** is incorrect. In developing the military analogy, the author offers only one view of the immune system.

47. **E** Sentence 2 states that lymphocytes are "born in the bone marrow." This answers the question as to where the body's lymphocytes *originate*.

48. **A** Cyclosporin is a drug that suppresses the body's immune system. The immune system protects the body from foreign invaders, such as viruses. Suppression or inhibition of the immune system might well make the body more susceptible to disease. It would not, however, make the body more likely to reject a transplanted organ, nor would it be likely to increase the effectiveness of

antigens. Indeed, treatment by cyclosporin makes the body less likely to reject a transplanted organ. Presumably it also makes the immune system less responsive to the presence of antigens.

49. **C** The author never cites or quotes any medical authorities to support his statements about the immune system.
Choice **A** is incorrect. The author identifies *lymphocytes* as white blood cells. He states that *antigens* are protein molecules on a substance's surface that trigger the immune response. Choice **B** is incorrect. The passage is based on the comparison made between the immune system and an army. Choice **D** is incorrect. The author estimates the number of white blood cells available for mustering at approximately 200m. Choice **E** is incorrect. By the use of military terminology ("troops," "billeted," "muster," "uniform") the author develops the central metaphor comparing the immune system to an army.

50. **B** The correct answer, Choice **B,** is a simpler way of expressing the final sentence of the passage. Note the parallel between "points of view" in the answer and "perspectives" in the passage.
Choice **A** is incorrect. In the second to the last sentence, the author states that "images of sexual antagonism" have not been ignored in literary criticism. Choices **C, D** and **E** are incorrect. They are not supported by the passage.

51. **E** Since these three authors were writing over half a century ago, they are mentioned to show that feminist issues are a concern of long standing.
Choices **A** and **B** are incorrect. They are contrary to the very positive tone of the passage. Choice **C** is incorrect. While it is noted that there was little interest in feminism before this century, the writer of the passage quotes modern authors to show the importance of the issue, not its previous lack of attention. Choice **D** is incorrect. It is not supported by the passage.

52. **D** The entire passage is an *endorsement* or support for women's emancipation. Note the first sentence of paragraph 2, in which it is described as one of the "greatest" and "deepest" themes of modern writers.

53. **B** The bulk of the passage records, step by step, what happens in the formation of a star from a small region of interstellar gas. Thus it *depicts the successive stages* of the process.

54. **C** To the author, the concept is both "simple" and "not new," dating as it does from Newton's time.

55. **D** You can answer this question by the process of elimination.
Question I is answerable on the basis of the passage. As the region's density increases, its gravitational field increases in strength. Therefore, you can eliminate Choice **B.**
Question II is not answerable on the basis of the passage, which never states what disturbs the gas. Therefore, you can eliminate Choices **C** and **E.**
Question III is answerable on the basis of the passage. The end result of the process is the formation of a gravitationally bound object. Therefore, you can eliminate Choice **A.**
Only Choice **D** is left. It is the correct answer.

56. **D** Houston believed that the battle had to begin at the graduate level "to mitigate fear" (relieve *apprehension)* of race-mixing or miscegenation. Otherwise, the judges might have ruled against the NAACP-sponsored complaints.

57. **D** The Regents responded to their defeat in *Sipuel* v. *Board of Regents of the University of Oklahoma* by separating black and white students in cafeterias and classrooms (thus undermining the effect of the decision). Hence it seems likely that their reaction to the decision was one of *distinct displeasure.*

58. **E** The 1950 McLaurin decision was one of the decisions which provided legal precedents for the 1954 Brown decision.
Choice **A** is incorrect. *McLaurin* preceded *Brown* (1954). Therefore, it could not have superseded a decision that had yet to be made. Choice **B** is incorrect. *Brown I* followed *McLaurin.* Therefore, it could not have set a precedent for *McLaurin.* Choice **C** is incorrect. *Brown I* reversed *Plessy* v. *Ferguson.* It built on *McLaurin.* Choice **D** is incorrect. *McLaurin* preceded *Brown I.* Therefore, it could not have limited the application of a decision that had yet to be made.

59. **C** Taken as a whole, the passage deals with the entire struggle to desegregate U.S. education, from the NAACP legal maneuvers of the 30's to the executive actions of the 50's and 60's. Only this title is broad enough to cover the passage as a whole.
Choice **A** is incorrect. The passage deals with the long legal maneuvers far more than it deals with executive intervention. Choice **B** is incorrect. The passage deals with much more than *Brown* v. *Board of Education.* Choices **D** and **E** are incorrect. They ignore the central subject of desegregation.

60. **A** In assessing the judges' possible reaction to race-mixing in the lower grades, Houston displayed *psychological canniness.* He was shrewd in seeing potential dangers and in figuring out strategies to avoid these dangers.

61. **C** The author provides the reader both with physical details of dress and bearing and with comments about the motives and emotions of the Cardinal and Bosola.
Choice **A** is incorrect. The passage scarcely mentions the church. Choice **B** is incorrect. The description of ecclesiastical costumes is only one item in the description of the Cardinal. Choice **D** is incorrect. The persons described are characters in a play, not figures in paintings. Choice **E** is incorrect. The author's purpose is description, not accusation.

62. **D** In the opening lines, the curtain rises and the two men "enter from the right" (as a stage direction would say). Later, there are references to gaslit Victorian melodrama. Thus we can infer that Bosola and the Cardinal are characters in a play.
Choice **A** is incorrect. The Cardinal's brother is Duke Ferdinand. Choices **B** and **C** are incorrect. The third paragraph describes Bosola as doing the work of a "hired ruffian" and playing a "lowly, despicable" role. He is a servant, not a noble lord or a lord of the Church. Choice **E** is unsupported by the passage.

63. **E** The eagle is poised to strike "with exposed talons." It, like the Cardinal, gathers itself together to strike with greater force. The imagery emphasizes the Cardinal's *mercilessness*.
Choice **A** is incorrect. The Cardinal is not *flighty* (light-headed and irresponsible); he is cold and calculating. Choice **B** is incorrect. He loves power, not freedom. Choice **C** is incorrect. An eagle poised to strike with bare claws suggests violence, not *eminence* (fame and high position). Choice **D** is incorrect. Nothing in the passage suggests he is spiritual. Beware of eye-catchers. "Eminence" is a title of honor applied to cardinals in the Roman Catholic church. Choice **C** may attract you for this reason.

64. **E** Although Bosola is not a "leather-jacketed" hoodlum, he is a hired "assassin," a "hangman" (despite his scholarly taste and humanist disposition).

65. **A** There are casual references to the elongated hands and features in El Greco's work and to the trim beards and commanding stances in the work of Van Dyke. This implies that the author assumes the reader has seen examples of both painters' art.

Mathematical Aptitude Section

1. **D** $\frac{1}{2} \cdot \frac{x}{2} = \frac{x}{4}$

2. **B** $\frac{3}{0.3} = \frac{30}{3} = 10$
$3 + 10 = 13$

3. **D** $42.10 \times 0.0003 = 0.01263$
$0.01263 \div 0.002 = 6.3+$

4. **D** $\frac{0.075}{7.5} = \frac{75}{7500} = \frac{1}{100} = 1\%$

5. **A** 4 quarts = 1 gallon
2 pints = 1 quart
8 pints = 1 gallon
40 pints = 5 gallons
120 pints = (3)5 gallons

6. **B** $\frac{1}{2}$ of class are boys.
$\frac{1}{2}$ of $\frac{1}{2}$ or $\frac{1}{4}$ of class are boys going to college.
$\frac{1}{2}$ of class are girls.
$\frac{1}{3}$ of $\frac{1}{2}$ or $\frac{1}{6}$ of class are girls going to college.
$\frac{1}{4} + \frac{1}{6} = \frac{5}{12} = 41.7\%$

7. **B** Time from 1 P.M. to 3:52 P.M. = 172 minutes. Time allowed between first and second class, second and third class, and third and last class = 12 minutes. Time for instruction in all four classes = 172 − 12 = 160 minutes.
Time for each class period = 160 ÷ 4 = 40 minutes.

8. **A** (A) $1 + \frac{x}{y} = \frac{y + x}{y}$
(B) $\frac{xy + x^2}{x^2} = \frac{x(y + x)}{x^2} = \frac{y + x}{x}$
(C) $\frac{y^2 + xy}{xy} = \frac{y(y + x)}{xy} = \frac{y + x}{x}$
(D) $\frac{y}{x} + 1 = \frac{y}{x} + \frac{x}{x} = \frac{y + x}{x}$
(E) $\frac{x + y}{x}$

9. **C** $s^2 - 56 = (s - 2)^2$
$s^2 - 56 = s^2 - 4s + 4$
$4s = 60$
$s = 15$

10. **D** $2x + t = 2$
$t = 2 - 2x$

11. **D** See diagram; the square can have vertices lettered either clockwise or counterclockwise.

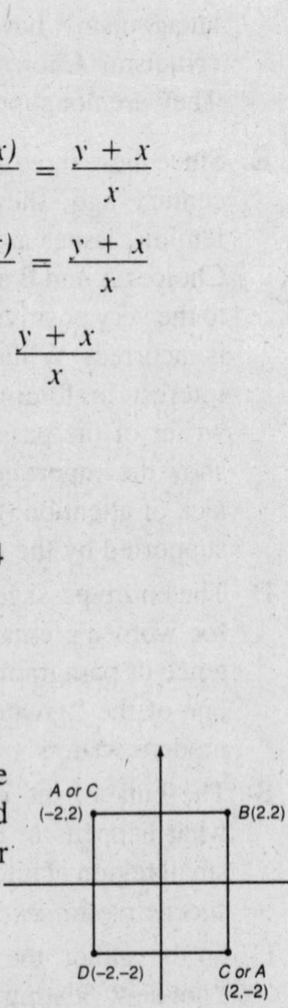

12. **B** Base = 20
Height = 10
Perimeter = 60
$\frac{10}{60} = \frac{1}{6}$

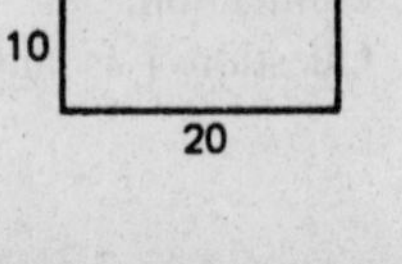

13. **C** A discount of 30% means he is getting 70% of former price.
70% or .7 of \$150 = \$105
Let x = cost.
$1.05x = \$105$
$105x = \$10500$
$x = \$100$

14. **C** \$2600 − \$440 = \$2160 (total depreciation)
\$2160 ÷ $4\frac{1}{2}$ = average yearly depreciation
\$2160 ÷ $\frac{9}{2}$
(\$2160)$\left(\frac{2}{9}\right)$ = \$480

15. **C** (80%) \$7000
(.8) \$7000 = \$5600 (amount of insurance)
\$6 per \$1000 = $\frac{6}{1000} = \frac{.6}{100} = .006$
(\$5600)(.006) = \$33.60 (premium)

16. **D** The 10% winning tickets constitute a statistic true for all 2000 tickets and may not apply to the 20 particular tickets held by Florence.

17. **B** $A > B$
$A > C$
$2A > B + C$

18. **C** $\frac{1}{ab} = \frac{1}{6}$

$\frac{1}{a} + \frac{1}{b} = \frac{1}{3} + \frac{1}{2} = \frac{5}{6}$

[From Column A] $\dfrac{\frac{1}{6}}{\frac{5}{6}} = \frac{1}{6} \cdot \frac{6}{5} = \frac{1}{5}$

[From Column B] $\frac{1}{a + b} = \frac{1}{5}$

19. **B** $\frac{0.9}{2} = 0.45$
$0.45 > 0.30$

20. **C** In Column B multiply by
$\frac{-1}{-1} \cdot \frac{-13 + 9x}{-7 + 8y}$
or $\frac{9x - 13}{8y - 7}$

21. **A** The numerators of both fractions are equal. The denominator of $\frac{c}{a}$ is smaller than the denominator of $\frac{c}{b}$ since $a < b$.
Therefore the value of $\frac{c}{a} > \frac{c}{b}$.

22. **A** Percent increase is calculated by the difference as compared with the original.
In Column A: $\frac{20}{50}$ In Column B: $\frac{20}{70}$
The fraction with the smaller denominator is larger.

23. **D** If x = amount of money Michael has, and
y = amount of money Mark has, then
y = amount Philip has, and
$x + 2y = \$35$.
It is not possible to solve this equation with two unknowns.

24. **C** The circumference of the wheel = (π)(diameter)
or $(\pi)\left(\frac{7}{\pi}\right)$ or 7 feet
The number of revolutions = $\frac{\text{distance}}{\text{circumference}}$ =
$\frac{70 \text{ feet}}{7 \text{ feet}}$ = 10 revolutions

25. **B** $AC = CE$; $90 + BC = CD + 85$: $CD > BC$

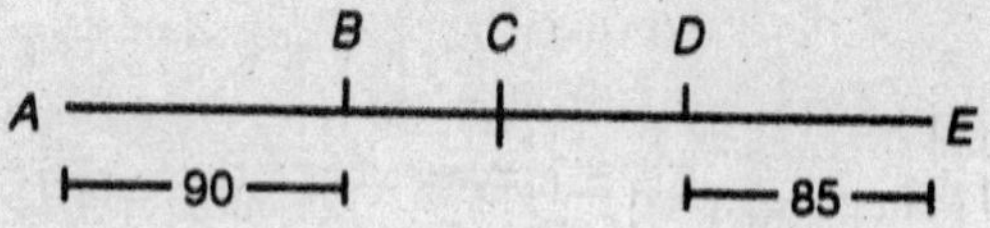

26. **A** $x = 2^2 = 4$
$x^2 = 16$

27. **B** The measure of $\angle B$ = $180° - (86 + 66)$ or $28°$. $AB > AC$ since AB lies opposite the angle with a measure of 66°, and AC lies opposite the angle with a measure of 28°.

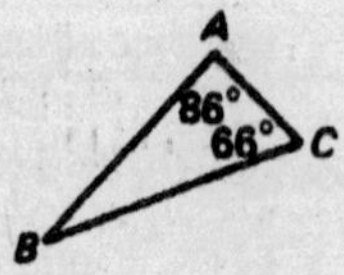

28. **B** $\frac{x + 6}{8} = \frac{x}{8} + \frac{3}{4}$
$\frac{x + 3}{4} = \frac{x}{4} + \frac{3}{4}$
$\frac{x}{4} > \frac{x}{8}$

29. **D** We may not assume that ABC is a right triangle. If it were a right triangle and AB and BC were legs, the area of ABC would be 4×9 divided by 2 or 18.

30. **B** $\angle C \stackrel{\circ}{=} 180 - (48 + 72)$
$\angle C \stackrel{\circ}{=} 180 - 120$ or 60
Therefore
Side AC (opposite $\angle B$) is larger than side AB (opposite $\angle C$).

31. **C** Cross multiply: $14x = 56$ and $x = 4$
$3y = 12$ and $y = 4$

32. **A** To compare fractions change to common denominators
$\frac{7}{8} = \frac{49}{56}$
$\frac{6}{7} = \frac{48}{56}$
$\frac{49}{56} > \frac{48}{56}$

33. **B** $\dfrac{\text{contents of large tumbler}}{\text{contents of small tumbler}} = \dfrac{3}{5}$

Let x = number of small glass tumblers that can be filled with one large glass tumbler.

$\frac{3}{5} = \frac{x}{1}$

$5x = 3$

$x = 1\frac{2}{3}$

34. **C** 12 kittens consume 4 cans.
4 cans are left for the dogs.
4 cans will feed 8 dogs.

35. **E** Twenty minutes (or $\frac{1}{3}$ hour) have elapsed before interruption.
$2\frac{2}{3}$ hours of work was not completed.

$\dfrac{2\frac{2}{3}}{3} = \dfrac{\frac{8}{3}}{3} = \frac{8}{3} \div 3 = \frac{8}{3} \cdot \frac{1}{3} = \frac{8}{9}$

36. **E** Volume = 5″ × 5″ × 5″ = 125 cubic inches
125 ÷ 1 = 125 cubes

37. **B** $(x - 2) - 2 = x - 4$

38. **A** y yards = $3y$ feet

$\dfrac{\text{total distance}}{\text{distance of average jump}}$ = number of jumps

$\frac{3y}{8}$ [substitution]

39. **A** Let x = number of years when James will be five times as old as John will be.
James' age is now 30 years.
James' age at specified time = $30 + x$.
John's age is now 3 years.
John's age at specified time = $3 + x$.

$(30 + x) = 5(3 + x)$

$30 + x = 15 + 5x$

$15 = 4x$

$3\frac{3}{4} = x$

40. **D** (1′)(2′)(3′) = 6 cubic feet = 4 pounds
(5′)((6′)(7′) = 210 cubic feet = 140 pounds

41. **D** Increase = \$3000 − \$2500 = \$500

$\dfrac{\text{increase}}{\text{original}} = \dfrac{\$500}{\$2500} = \dfrac{1}{5} = 20\%$

42. **D** He must realize a profit of 20% or $\frac{1}{5}$ of \$90 or \$18.
He must sell the 9 crates for \$108 or for \$12 each.

43. **D** Volume = $\pi \cdot r^2 \cdot h$
If diameter = 4 inches, radius = 2 inches.

$\left(\frac{22}{7}\right)(2)(2)(14)$ = 176 cubic inches

$\frac{176}{8}$ = 22 ten-minute periods or 220 minutes

220 minutes = 3 hours 40 minutes
3 hours 40 minutes after 10 A.M. is 1:40 P.M.

44. **E** Let r = radius of inner circle.
r = width of shaded portion [given]
$2r$ = radius of large circle

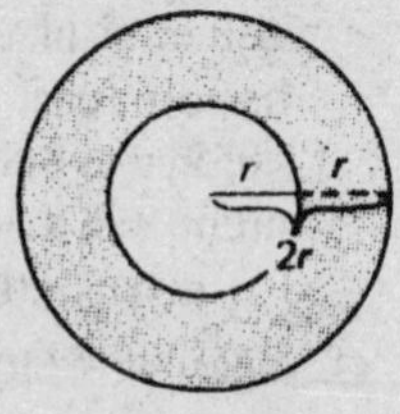

Area of large circle − area of inner circle = area of shaded portion.
Area of circle = πr^2
Area of large circle = $\pi(2r)^2$ or $4\pi r^2$
Area of inner circle = $\pi(r)^2$ or πr^2
Area of shaded portion = $3\pi r^2$

$\dfrac{3\pi r^2}{4\pi r^2} = \dfrac{3}{4} = 75\%$

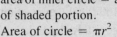

45. **B** Diameter = 4 feet, radius = 2 feet
Area of circle = πr^2 or 4π
Mr. Adams desires area of $4(4\pi)$ or 16π.
Let x = radius.

$\pi x^2 = 16\pi$

$x^2 = 16$

$x = 4$

diameter = 8 ft.

46. **B** $OA = OB$ [radii of same circle]

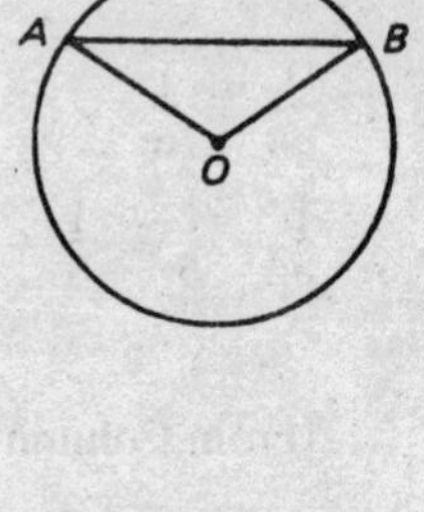

$\angle ABO = \angle BAO$
Since $\widehat{AB}$ = 112°, central $\angle AOB \overset{\circ}{=} 112$.
$\angle ABO + \angle BAO + \angle AOB \overset{\circ}{=} 180$
$\angle ABO + \angle BAO \overset{\circ}{=} 68$
$\angle ABO \overset{\circ}{=} 34$

47. **D** Area of shaded part = area of $ABCD$ − area $AGFE$
Area of $ABCD$ = (12)(6) = 72

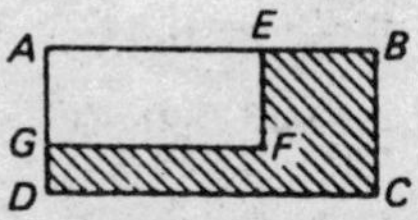

$AE = \left(\frac{2}{3}\right)(12)$ or 8

$AG = \left(\frac{2}{3}\right)(6)$ or 4

Area $AGFE$ = (8)(4) = 32
Area of shaded part = 72 − 32 = 40

48. **D** It is easier to call base x and altitude $2x$.

Area of △ = $\frac{1}{2}(h)(b)$

Area of △ = $\left(\frac{1}{2}\right)(2x)(x)$

Area of △ = x^2

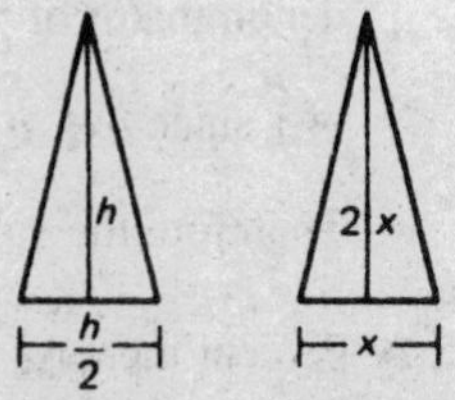

x^2 = 225 square inches [given]
x = 15 inches
$2x$ = 30 inches [altitude]

49. **C** A right triangle is formed, where the required distance is the hypotenuse. Apply the Pythagorean Theorem. Let x = shortest distance between their homes.

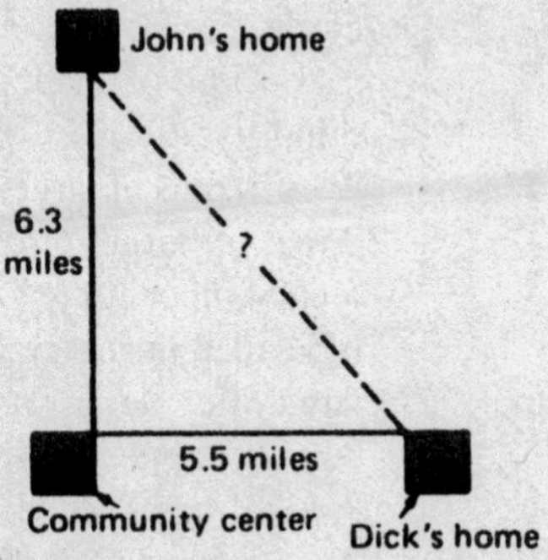

$x^2 = (6.3)^2 + (5.5)^2$
$x^2 = 39.69 + 30.25$
or 69.94
$x = \sqrt{69.94}$
$x = 8.36+ = 8.4$

50. **E** Let s = side of original.
$\therefore$ perimeter = $4s$
$\therefore$ area = s^2
Increase in perimeter of new square = 80% (or 0.8) of $4s = 3.2s$
Perimeter of new square = $3.2s + 4s = 7.2s$
Side of new square = $7.2s \div 4 = 1.8s$
Area of new square = $(1.8s)^2 = 3.24s^2$
Difference in areas of squares = $3.24s^2 - s^2 = 2.24s^2$

$$\frac{\text{difference}}{\text{original}} = \frac{2.24s^2}{1s^2} = 2.24 = 224\%$$

PSAT/NMSQT Answer Sheet

TYPICAL TEST D

Verbal Aptitude Section

1 (A) (B) (C) (D) (E)
2 (A) (B) (C) (D) (E)
3 (A) (B) (C) (D) (E)
4 (A) (B) (C) (D) (E)
5 (A) (B) (C) (D) (E)
6 (A) (B) (C) (D) (E)
7 (A) (B) (C) (D) (E)
8 (A) (B) (C) (D) (E)
9 (A) (B) (C) (D) (E)
10 (A) (B) (C) (D) (E)
11 (A) (B) (C) (D) (E)
12 (A) (B) (C) (D) (E)
13 (A) (B) (C) (D) (E)
14 (A) (B) (C) (D) (E)
15 (A) (B) (C) (D) (E)
16 (A) (B) (C) (D) (E)
17 (A) (B) (C) (D) (E)
18 (A) (B) (C) (D) (E)
19 (A) (B) (C) (D) (E)
20 (A) (B) (C) (D) (E)
21 (A) (B) (C) (D) (E)
22 (A) (B) (C) (D) (E)
23 (A) (B) (C) (D) (E)
24 (A) (B) (C) (D) (E)
25 (A) (B) (C) (D) (E)
26 (A) (B) (C) (D) (E)
27 (A) (B) (C) (D) (E)
28 (A) (B) (C) (D) (E)
29 (A) (B) (C) (D) (E)
30 (A) (B) (C) (D) (E)
31 (A) (B) (C) (D) (E)
32 (A) (B) (C) (D) (E)
33 (A) (B) (C) (D) (E)
34 (A) (B) (C) (D) (E)
35 (A) (B) (C) (D) (E)
36 (A) (B) (C) (D) (E)
37 (A) (B) (C) (D) (E)
38 (A) (B) (C) (D) (E)
39 (A) (B) (C) (D) (E)
40 (A) (B) (C) (D) (E)
41 (A) (B) (C) (D) (E)
42 (A) (B) (C) (D) (E)
43 (A) (B) (C) (D) (E)
44 (A) (B) (C) (D) (E)
45 (A) (B) (C) (D) (E)
46 (A) (B) (C) (D) (E)
47 (A) (B) (C) (D) (E)
48 (A) (B) (C) (D) (E)
49 (A) (B) (C) (D) (E)
50 (A) (B) (C) (D) (E)
51 (A) (B) (C) (D) (E)
52 (A) (B) (C) (D) (E)
53 (A) (B) (C) (D) (E)
54 (A) (B) (C) (D) (E)
55 (A) (B) (C) (D) (E)
56 (A) (B) (C) (D) (E)
57 (A) (B) (C) (D) (E)
58 (A) (B) (C) (D) (E)
59 (A) (B) (C) (D) (E)
60 (A) (B) (C) (D) (E)
61 (A) (B) (C) (D) (E)
62 (A) (B) (C) (D) (E)
63 (A) (B) (C) (D) (E)
64 (A) (B) (C) (D) (E)
65 (A) (B) (C) (D) (E)

Mathematical Aptitude Section*

1 (A) (B) (C) (D) (E)
2 (A) (B) (C) (D) (E)
3 (A) (B) (C) (D) (E)
4 (A) (B) (C) (D) (E)
5 (A) (B) (C) (D) (E)
6 (A) (B) (C) (D) (E)
7 (A) (B) (C) (D) (E)
8 (A) (B) (C) (D) (E)
9 (A) (B) (C) (D) (E)
10 (A) (B) (C) (D) (E)
11 (A) (B) (C) (D) (E)
12 (A) (B) (C) (D) (E)
13 (A) (B) (C) (D) (E)
14 (A) (B) (C) (D) (E)
15 (A) (B) (C) (D) (E)
16 (A) (B) (C) (D) (E)
17 (A) (B) (C) (D) (E)
18 (A) (B) (C) (D) (E)
19 (A) (B) (C) (D) (E)
20 (A) (B) (C) (D) (E)
21 (A) (B) (C) (D) (E)
22 (A) (B) (C) (D) (E)
23 (A) (B) (C) (D) (E)
24 (A) (B) (C) (D) (E)
25 (A) (B) (C) (D) (E)
26 (A) (B) (C) (D) (E)
27 (A) (B) (C) (D) (E)
28 (A) (B) (C) (D) (E)
29 (A) (B) (C) (D) (E)
30 (A) (B) (C) (D) (E)
31 (A) (B) (C) (D) (E)
32 (A) (B) (C) (D) (E)
33 (A) (B) (C) (D) (E)
34 (A) (B) (C) (D) (E)
35 (A) (B) (C) (D) (E)
36 (A) (B) (C) (D) (E)
37 (A) (B) (C) (D) (E)
38 (A) (B) (C) (D) (E)
39 (A) (B) (C) (D) (E)
40 (A) (B) (C) (D) (E)
41 (A) (B) (C) (D) (E)
42 (A) (B) (C) (D) (E)
43 (A) (B) (C) (D) (E)
44 (A) (B) (C) (D) (E)
45 (A) (B) (C) (D) (E)
46 (A) (B) (C) (D) (E)
47 (A) (B) (C) (D) (E)
48 (A) (B) (C) (D) (E)
49 (A) (B) (C) (D) (E)
50 (A) (B) (C) (D) (E)

*If there are more answer spaces than you need, leave them blank.

TYPICAL TEST D

SECTION 1 **Time—50 minutes** **65 Questions** For each question in this section, choose the best answer and fill in the corresponding circle on the answer sheet.

Each question below consists of a word in capital letters, followed by five lettered words or phrases. Choose the word or phrase that is most nearly opposite in meaning to the word in capital letters. Since some of the questions require you to distinguish fine shades of meaning, consider all the choices before deciding which is best.

Example:

GOOD: (A) sour (B) bad (C) red (D) hot (E) ugly

Ⓐ ● Ⓒ Ⓓ Ⓔ

1. ACCUMULATE: (A) weaken (B) scatter (C) endanger (D) permit (E) imitate
2. ROADBLOCK: (A) disorder (B) separation (C) quick reaction (D) need for change (E) aid to progress
3. EXAGGERATE: (A) repeat (B) deny (C) listen (D) persuade (E) understate
4. PROXIMITY: (A) commonness (B) diversity (C) substitution (D) distance (E) complexity
5. GARBLE: (A) express clearly (B) dress neatly (C) eat slowly (D) walk rapidly (E) answer indirectly
6. BLEAK: (A) cheery (B) uniform (C) enigmatic (D) insignificant (E) talkative
7. NAIVETÉ: (A) remoteness (B) competence (C) sophistication (D) inequity (E) intensity
8. CONTRACT: (A) depend (B) expand (C) straighten (D) dismiss (E) contort
9. COMPLIANT: (A) inadequate (B) nondescript (C) irrelevant (D) earnest (E) unyielding
10. AFFLUENCE: (A) extravagance (B) destitution (C) indifference (D) boastfulness (E) hostility
11. INSTIGATE: (A) disclose (B) dissuade (C) dissemble (D) disbelieve (E) discern
12. FLAGRANT: (A) unoriginal (B) inconspicuous (C) indefinite (D) unappealing (E) concise
13. VEHEMENCE: (A) ingenuity (B) proclivity (C) grace in movement (D) lack of intensity (E) incoherence
14. DEFUNCT: (A) indebted (B) erect (C) prone (D) positive (E) extant
15. BADGER: (A) deceive (B) keep clean (C) let alone (D) equip (E) depart
16. INDIGENOUS: (A) alien (B) digestible (C) territorial (D) amenable (E) worthy
17. SALUBRIOUS: (A) valedictory (B) economical (C) indelible (D) impartial (E) unwholesome
18. ABATE: (A) return (B) transmit (C) intensify (D) adjourn (E) oscillate
19. FORTUITOUS: (A) contradictory (B) impassive (C) premeditated (D) fickle (E) illogical
20. FOMENT: (A) suppress (B) emulate (C) condone (D) belittle (E) exacerbate

Each sentence below has one or two blanks, each blank indicating that something has been omitted. Beneath the sentence are five lettered words or sets of words. Choose the word or set of words that, when inserted in the sentence, best fits the meaning of the sentence as a whole.

Example:

Although its publicity has been ----, the film itself is intelligent, well-acted, handsomely produced, and altogether ----.

(A) tasteless . . respectable (B) extensive . . moderate (C) sophisticated . . amateur (D) risque . . crude (E) perfect . . spectacular

● Ⓑ Ⓒ Ⓓ Ⓔ

21. Although the coach was a tyrant who ---- his athletes regularly, the players were ---- as long as they won their games.
(A) pampered . . outspoken
(B) bullied . . dissatisfied
(C) browbeat . . untroubled
(D) oppressed . . rebellious
(E) neglected . . intimidated
22. Allowing women a voice in tribal government did not ---- Cherokee custom, for traditional Cherokee society was matrilineal, granting women the right to own property and to divorce their husbands.
(A) violate (B) emulate (C) retrace (D) preclude (E) fulfill

23. In Renault's portrayal, the philosopher Aristotle, lacking breadth of vision and the ---- to inspire, proves an ---- tutor for the young Alexander of Macedon, whose spirit cried out for a counselor able to speak to his soul.
(A) ability . . illuminating
(B) power . . inadequate (C) will . . illustrious
(D) technique . . acceptable
(E) capacity . . arbitrary

24. According to wildlife specialists, the few remaining pandas are so romantically ---- that their very survival as a species is threatened.
(A) regarded (B) disinclined (C) camouflaged
(D) displayed (E) protected

25. In the course of learning to deal with the world of ideas, the adolescent gradually becomes able to express him or herself in ---- such as courage and philosophy.
(A) abstractions (B) hypotheses (C) proverbs
(D) epigrams (E) alliterations

26. Since the propensity to migrate has persisted in every epoch, its explanation requires a theory ---- any particular period of time.
(A) tailored to (B) unconscious of
(C) inapplicable to (D) independent of
(E) anomalous in

27. In observing the ceremonies and rituals of worship, we must not make a show of our faith: the challenge of religion is to be ---- without becoming ----.
(A) reverent . . relevant
(B) irreverent . . blasphemous
(C) heretical . . caught
(D) pious . . sanctimonious
(E) indulgent . . obvious

28. Relatively few politicans willingly forsake center stage, although a touch of ---- on their parts now and again might well increase their popularity with the voting public.
(A) garrulity (B) misanthropy
(C) self-effacement (D) self-dramatization
(E) self-righteousness

29. Although Mrs. Proudie ---- an interest in the spiritual well-being of the parishioners, in actuality her concern for their welfare was so ---- as to be practically nonexistent.
(A) confessed . . circumstantial
(B) manifested . . exemplary
(C) simulated . . profound
(D) feigned . . negligible
(E) expressed . . moribund

30. The term *baroque*, originally applied to the lavishly ornamented style of architecture that succeeded the Renaissance, is used generally in literary criticism to describe excessive or grandiloquent works that lack ---- of style.
(A) diversity (B) economy (C) prolixity
(D) adornment (E) comprehension

Each question below consists of a related pair of words or phrases, followed by five lettered pairs of words or phrases. Select the lettered pair that best expresses a relationship similar to that expressed in the original pair.

Example:

YAWN : BOREDOM : : (A) dream : sleep
(B) anger : madness (C) smile : amusement
(D) face : expression (E) impatience : rebellion

Ⓐ Ⓑ ● Ⓓ Ⓔ

31. LOAF : BREAD : : (A) icing : cake
(B) wheel : cheese (C) pod : pea
(D) yolk : egg (E) cream : milk

32. BOOK : CHAPTER : : (A) painting : frame
(B) sentence : verb (C) building : story
(D) tree : root (E) movie : scenario

33. CLASP : BRACELET : : (A) hook : coat
(B) buckle : belt (C) diamond : ring
(D) wrist : watch (E) cuff : trousers

34. FLEET : SHIPS : : (A) team : coaches
(B) planet : satellites (C) shelf : books
(D) committee : meetings (E) pack : wolves

35. BANK : MONEY : : (A) cask : wine
(B) ring : diamond (C) chain : link
(D) body : germ (E) transfusion : blood

36. FLIMSY : STRENGTH : : (A) fancy : beauty
(B) hazardous : danger (C) wary : caution
(D) slippery : smoothness (E) clumsy : grace

37. OBSTINATE : MULISH : : (A) gruff : doglike
(B) clever : dull (C) inanimate : beastly
(D) coy : kittenish (E) domestic : fawning

38. REFUGEE : ASYLUM : : (A) patient : illness
(B) hermit : solitude (C) tutor : education
(D) convict : prison (E) judge : courtroom

39. INANE : MEANING : : (A) vacant : space
(B) random : plan (C) affluent : wealth
(D) certain : direction (E) aesthetic : beauty

40. SAP : VITALITY : : (A) sweeten : temperament
(B) divert : traffic (C) invest : income
(D) drain : wound (E) deplete : resources

41. COUNTESS : NOBILITY : : (A) judge : jury
(B) celebrity : fans (C) professor : faculty
(D) miser : parsimony (E) nurse : surgery

42. CIRCUITOUS : ROUTE : :
(A) problematic : solution (B) devious : argument
(C) elliptical : brevity (D) judicious : selection
(E) profound : depth

43. CHAFF : WHEAT : : (A) mote : dust
(B) gold : lead (C) dregs : wine
(D) roll : bread (E) vine : tomato

44. EMPHEMERAL : PERMANENCE : :
(A) erratic : predictability
(B) immaculate : cleanliness
(C) commendable : reputation
(D) spurious : emulation
(E) mandatory : obedience

45. OGLE : OBSERVE : : (A) haggle : outbid
(B) clamor : dispute (C) discern : perceive
(D) flaunt : display (E) glare : glower

> Each passage below is followed by questions based on its content. Answer the questions following each passage on the basis of what is stated or implied in that passage.

Luckily, I am writing a memoir and not a work of fiction, and therefore I do not have to account for my grandmother's unpleasing character and look for the Oedipal fixation or the traumatic experience which would give her that clinical authenticity that is nowadays so desirable in portraiture. I do not know how my grandmother got the way she was; I assume, from family photographs and from the inflexibility of her habits, that she was always the same, and it seems as idle to inquire into her childhood as to ask what was ailing Iago or look for the error in toilet-training that was responsible for Lady Macbeth. My grandmother's sexual history, bristling with infant mortality in the usual style of her period, was robust and decisive: three tall, handsome sons grew up, and one attentive daughter. Her husband treated her kindly. She had money, many grandchildren, and religion to sustain her. White hair, glasses, soft skin, wrinkles, needlework—all the paraphernalia of motherliness were hers; yet it was a cold, grudging, disputatious old woman who sat all day in her sunroom making tapestries from a pattern, scanning religious periodicals, and setting her iron jaw against any infraction of her ways.

46. According to the author, a portrait of a character in a work of modern fiction must have
(A) photographic realism
(B) psychological validity
(C) sympathetic attitudes (D) religious qualities
(E) historical accuracy

47. The author's attitude toward her grandmother is best described as
(A) tolerant (B) appreciative (C) indifferent
(D) nostalgic (E) sardonic

48. The author's primary point in describing her grandmother's physical appearance (last sentence) is best summarized by which of the following axioms?
(A) Familiarity breeds contempt.
(B) You can't judge a book by its cover.
(C) One picture is worth more than ten thousand words.
(D) There's no smoke without fire.
(E) Blood is thicker than water.

When there is no distance between people, the only way that anyone can keep his or her distance is by a code of etiquette that has acceptance in a community. Manners are the antidote to adjustment to the group. They make social intercourse possible without any forfeit of one's personal dignity. They are armor against invasion of privacy; they are the advance patrols that report whether one should withdraw or advance into intimacy. They are the friendly but noncommittal gestures of civilized people. The manners of crowded countries are, I believe, always more formal than those of open countries (as they are, for example, in Europe and Japan), and it may be that we are seeing a rising concern about American manners precisely because we encounter more people in closer quarters than we ever have before. We feel the need to find ways in which to be part of the group without selling out our privacy or our individuality for a mess of adjustment.

49. The title that best expresses the idea of this passage is
(A) The Function of Politeness
(B) Invasions of Privacy
(C) Reasons for Social Relationships
(D) The Need for Complete Privacy
(E) American Manners

50. The author suggests that in Europe good manners are
(A) informal (B) excessive (C) essential
(D) ignored (E) individual

51. According to the author, manners serve to
(A) facilitate relationships among people
(B) preserve certain ceremonies
(C) help people to make friends quickly
(D) reveal character traits
(E) help one to please one's friends

52. Which of the following best describes the style of the fourth sentence?
(A) Hyperbolic (B) Prosaic (C) Paradoxical
(D) Metaphoric (E) Discursive

I walk to the window to watch this extraordinary game that the jackdaws are playing with the wind. A game? Yes, indeed, it is a game, in the most literal sense of the word: practised movements, indulged in and enjoyed for their own sake and not for the achievement of a special object. And rest assured, these are not merely inborn, purely instinctive actions, but movements that have been carefully learned. All these feats that the birds are performing, their wonderful exploitation of the wind, their amazingly exact assessment of distances and, above all, their understanding of local wind conditions, their knowledge of all the up-currents, air pockets and eddies—all this proficiency is no inheritance, but, for each bird, an individually acquired accomplishment.

And look what they do with the wind! At first sight, you, poor human being, think that the storm is playing with the birds, like a cat with a mouse, but soon you see, with astonishment, that it is the fury of the elements that here plays the role of the mouse and that the jackdaws are treating the storm exactly as the cat its unfortunate victim.

Nearly, but only nearly, do they give the storm its head, let it throw them high, high into the heavens, till they seem to fall upwards, then, with a casual flap of a wing, they turn themselves over, open their pinions for a fraction of a second from below against the wind, and dive—with an acceleration far greater than that of a falling stone—into the depths below. Another tiny jerk of the wing and they return to their normal position and, on close-reefed sails, shoot away with breathless speed into the teeth of the gale, hundreds of yards to the west: this all playfully and without effort, just to spite the stupid wind that tries to drive them towards the east. The sightless monster itself must perform the work of propelling the birds through the air at a rate of well over 80 miles an hour; the jackdaws do nothing to help beyond a few lazy adjustments of their black wings. Sovereign control over the power of the elements, intoxicating triumph of the living organism over the pitiless strength of the inorganic!

53. According to the passage, the bird's skill in adapting to wind conditions is
(A) genetically determined (B) limited
(C) undependable (D) dependent on the elements
(E) gained through practice

54. It can be inferred that the "sightless monster" mentioned in the next-to-last sentence is
(A) an unobservant watcher (B) a falling stone
(C) an airplane (D) the powerful windstorm
(E) a blind predator

55. The author does all of the following EXCEPT
(A) use a metaphor (B) argue a cause
(C) clarify a term (D) describe a behavior
(E) dismiss a notion

The lithosphere, or outer shell, of the earth is made up of about a dozen rigid plates that move with respect to one another. New lithosphere is created at mid-ocean ridges by the upwelling and cooling of magma from the earth's interior. Since new lithosphere is continuously being created and the earth is not expanding to any appreciable extent, the question arises: What happens to the "old" lithosphere?

The answer came in the late 1960s as the last major link in the theory of sea-floor spreading and plate tectonics that has revolutionized our understanding of tectonic processes, or structural deformations, in the earth and has provided a unifying theme for many diverse observations of the earth sciences. The old lithosphere is subducted, or pushed down, into the earth's mantle (the thick shell of red-hot rock beneath the earth's thin, cooler crust and above its metallic, partly melted core). As the formerly rigid plate descends it slowly heats up, and over a period of millions of years it is absorbed into the general circulation of the earth's mantle.

The subduction of the lithosphere is perhaps the most significant phenomenon in global tectonics. Subduction not only explains what happens to old lithosphere but also accounts for many of the geologic processes that shape the earth's surface. Most of the world's volcanoes and earthquakes are associated with descending lithospheric plates. The prominent island arcs—chains of islands such as the Aleutians, the Kuriles, the Marianas, and the islands of Japan—are surface expressions of the subduction process. The deepest trenches of the world's oceans, including the Java and Tonga trenches and all others associated with island arcs, mark the seaward boundary of subduction zones. Major mountain belts, such as the Andes and the Himalayas, have resulted from the convergence and subduction of lithospheric plates.

To understand the subduction process it is necessary to look at the thermal regime of the earth. The temperatures within the earth at first increase rapidly with depth, reaching about 1,200 degrees Celsius at a depth of 100 kilometers. Then they increase more gradually, approaching 2,000 degrees C. at about 500 kilometers. The minerals in peridotite, the major constituent of the upper mantle, start to melt at about 1,200 C., or typically at a depth of 100 kilometers. Under the oceans the upper mantle is fairly soft and may contain some molten material at depths as shallow as 80 kilometers. The soft region of the mantle, over which the rigid lithospheric plate normally moves, is the asthenosphere. It appears that in certain areas convection currents in the asthenosphere may drive the plates, and that in other regions the plate motions may drive the convection currents.

56. The primary purpose of the passage is to
(A) refute a current theory (B) describe a process
(C) analyze a technique (D) debate a point
(E) predict a development

57. Each of the following geological phenomena is mentioned in the passage as being relevant to the subduction of the lithosphere EXCEPT
(A) principal archipelagoes
(B) significant rifts in the sea bottom
(C) deserts in process of formation
(D) prominent mountain ranges
(E) volcanic eruptions

58. The style of the passage can best be described as
(A) oratorical (B) argumentative (C) expository
(D) meditative (E) deprecatory

59. According to the passage, which of the following statements is (are) true of the earth's mantle?
I. It is in a state of flux.
II. Its temperature is far greater than that of the lithosphere.
III. It eventually incorporates the subducted lithosphere.
(A) I only (B) II only (C) I and III only
(D) II and III only (E) I, II, and III

60. It can be inferred from the passage that the author regards current knowledge about the relationship between lithospheric plate motions and the convection currents in the asthenosphere as
(A) obsolete (B) unfounded (C) derivative
(D) definitive (E) tentative

Paralleling the growth of interest among professional historians during the early 1960s was a simultaneous groundswell of popular interest in the Afro-American past that was directly stimulated by the drama of the protest movement. Sensing the "Negro Mood," the journalist Lerone Bennett wrote a series of articles on Afro-American history for *Ebony* and soon after brought them together in his popular volume, *Before the Mayflower* (1962). As the nonviolent direct action movement attained its crest in 1963–1964, movement activists introduced black history units into the curricula of the "freedom schools" that accompanied the school integration boycotts. Meanwhile, boards of education began to address themselves to "the racial imbalance and neutralism of pusillanimous textbooks designed to appeal to Southern as well as Northern school adoption committees." In 1964 New York City's school board published *The Negro in American History;* Detroit's social studies teachers produced *The Struggle for Freedom and Rights: Basic Facts about the Negro in American History.* Franklin, surveying the activities among publishers, teachers, and school boards, called these beginnings of curriculum revision "one of the most significant by-products of the current Civil Rights Revolution."

The relationship between these developments at the grass roots level and what was occurring in the scholarly world is of course indirect. Yet given the context of social change in the early 1960s, Negro history was now the object of unprecedented attention among wide segments of the American population, black and white. In academe nothing demonstrated this growing legitimacy of black history better than the way in which certain scholars of both races, who had previously been ambivalent about being identified as specialists in the field, now reversed themselves.

Thus Frenise Logan, returning to an academic career, decided to attempt to publish his doctoral dissertation on blacks in late nineteenth-century North Carolina. A 1960 award encouraged him to do further research, and his expanded *The Negro in North Carolina, 1876–1894* appeared in 1964. It is true that as late as 1963 a white professor advised John W. Blassingame to avoid black history if he wanted to have "a future in the historical profession." Yet more indicative of how things were going was that 1964–65 marked a turning point for two of Kenneth Stampp's former students—Nathan Huggins and Leon Litwack. The changing intellectual milieu seems to have permitted Huggins, whose original intention of specializing in African and Afro-American history had been overruled by practical concerns, to move into what became his long-range commitment to the field. By 1965, when his interest in intellectual history found expression in the idea of doing a book on the Harlem Renaissance, the factors that earlier would have discouraged him from such a study had dissipated. For Litwack the return to Negro history was an especially vivid experience, and he recalls the day he spoke at the University of Rochester, lecturing on Jacksonian democracy. Some students in the audience, sensing that his heart was just not in that topic, urged him to undertake research once again in the field to which he had already contributed so significantly. He settled on the study that became *Been in the Storm So Long* (1979). In short, both Huggins and Litwack now felt able to dismiss the professional considerations that had loomed so large in their earlier decision to work in other specialties and to identify themselves with what had hitherto been a marginal field of inquiry.

61. The author indicates that the growth of scholarly involvement in the study of black history was
(A) unappreciated in academic circles
(B) encouraged by the civil rights movement
(C) systematically organized
(D) unaffected by current events
(E) motivated by purely financial concerns

62. The author cites Logan, Huggins, and Litwack for their
(A) work on curriculum reform in the public schools
(B) participation in the Freedom Summer in Mississippi
(C) return to the field of Afro-American history
(D) research on blacks in nineteenth-century North Carolina
(E) identification with nonviolent direct action

63. Which of the following best describes the purpose of the passage?
(A) To document the sacrifices made by black and white scholars in the field
(B) To defend the validity of black history as a legitimate scholarly pursuit
(C) To investigate the origins of Afro-American studies in American universities
(D) To encourage the return to the study of black history at the grass roots level
(E) To describe black history's coming of age as an academically respectable field

64. The passage suggests that Bennett's work was similar to Logan's work in which of the following ways?
I. Both Bennett's and Logan's books recorded a then relatively unfamiliar aspect of Afro-American history.
II. Both Bennett's and Logan's works were designed to appeal to a primarily academic audience.
III. Both Bennett's and Logan's works were published in a variety of formats.
(A) I only (B) III only (C) I and II only
(D) I and III only (E) II and III only

65. It can be inferred that prior to 1950 for a historian to choose to specialize in black history
(A) was encouraged by the academic establishment
(B) established his academic conventionality
(C) afforded him special opportunities for publication
(D) was detrimental to his professional career
(E) enhanced his contact with his colleagues

SECTION 2	Time—50 minutes 50 Questions	In this section solve each problem, using any available space on the page for scratchwork. Then decide which is the best of the choices given and fill in the corresponding circle on the answer sheet.

The following information is for your reference in solving some of the problems.

Circle of radius r: Area $= \pi r^2$ Circumference $= 2\pi r$
The number of degrees of arc in a circle is 360.
The measure in degrees of a straight angle is 180.

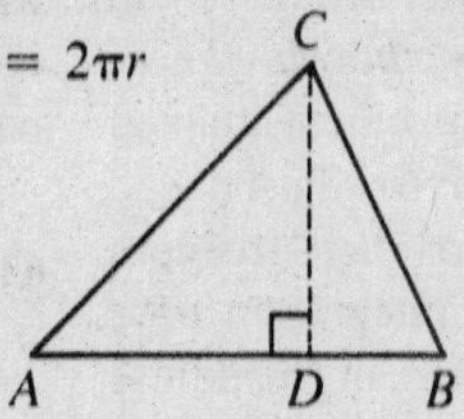

Triangle: The sum of the measures in degrees of the angles of a triangle is 180.

If $\angle CDA$ is a right angle, then

(1) area of $\triangle ABC = \frac{AB \times CD}{2}$

(2) $AC^2 = AD^2 + DC^2$

Definitions of symbols:

- $=$ is equal to
- $\neq$ is unequal to
- $<$ is less than
- $>$ is greater than
- $\leqq$ is less than or equal to
- $\geqq$ is greater than or equal to
- $\parallel$ is parallel to
- $\perp$ is perpendicular to

Note: Figures that accompany problems in this test are intended to provide information useful in solving the problems. They are drawn as accurately as possible EXCEPT when it is stated in a specific problem that its figure is not drawn to scale. All figures lie in a plane unless otherwise indicated. All numbers used are real numbers.

1. $0.9\% =$

(A) $\frac{9}{1000}$ (B) $\frac{9}{100}$ (C) $\frac{9}{10}$ (D) 9 (E) 90

2. In the equation $\frac{3}{x} = \frac{x}{27}$, $x > 0$, what is the value of x?

(A) 3 (B) 6 (C) 9 (D) 18 (E) 81

3. If $\frac{1}{2} + \frac{2}{3} + \frac{3}{y} = \frac{23}{12}$, $y =$

(A) 2 (B) 3 (C) 4 (D) 6 (E) 12

4. If a workman receives time and a half for overtime, 25 hours of overtime would be the equivalent of how many regular working hours?

(A) 6 (B) 12 (C) 18 (D) 30 (E) $37\frac{1}{2}$

5. Which of the following could represent the number of units in the lengths of the three sides of a right triangle?

I. 9, 12, and 15
II. 10, 26, and 24
III. $1\frac{1}{2}$, 2, and $2\frac{1}{2}$

(A) I only (B) II only (C) III only
(D) I and II only (E) I, II, and III

6. Mr. Benedict left half of his estate to his wife, one-fourth to his son, one-fifth to his daughter and the remainder, $5000, to his college. What is the total amount left by Mr. Benedict?

(A) $9250 (B) $10,000 (C) $16,000
(D) $50,000 (E) $100,000

7. An elevator has a capacity of 20 adults or 24 children. How many children can ride with 15 adults?

(A) 4 (B) 6 (C) 7 (D) 9 (E) 18

8. Joan does $\frac{2}{5}$ of her homework in an hour. How many additional hours will she have to work to complete her homework?

(A) 0.5 (B) 1.5 (C) 2.5 (D) 30 (E) 60

9. A sweater marked $60 has a tag stating TAKE 10% OFF PRICE ON TAG. What must I pay for this sweater, taking advantage of this special price and paying the town 10% sales tax?

(A) $48.60 (B) $54. (C) $57.60
(D) $59.40 (E) $60.

10. One season a baseball team played g games and lost a total of l games. What part of their games did they win?

(A) $\frac{l}{g}$ (B) $\frac{g}{l}$ (C) $\frac{g-l}{l}$ (D) $\frac{l-g}{g}$ (E) $\frac{g-l}{g}$

11. What is the ratio of a 10-inch strip to a strip 2 yards long?

(A) 5:1 (B) 1:5 (C) 20:1 (D) 1:7.2
(E) 1:7.5

12. The following is a report of defective parts reported by inspectors in 3 electronic factories:

Brookline	3 per 10,000
Brookville	5 per 100,000
Brooklyn	13 per 1,000,000

Which of the following best expresses the portion of defective parts in the three factories combined?

(A) 5 per 10,000 (B) 66 per 10,000
(C) 66 per 100,000 (D) 93 per 1,000,000
(E) 363 per 1,000,000

13. Ten years ago Lori was y years old. How old will she be x years from now?

(A) $y - x + 10$ (B) $y + x - 10$ (C) $10 + y$
(D) $x + y$ (E) $x + y + 10$

14. An efficiency expert has calculated that about 9.5% of the articles produced in a manufacturing plant are defective. This is equivalent to expressing the defective articles as
(A) 9 out of 15 (B) 9 out of 50 (C) 10 out of 95
(D) 19 out of 100 (E) 19 out of 200

15. $x - 7 = 0$
$y^2 = 25$
$xy =$
(A) $+35$ (B) ± 35 (C) -35 (D) 5 (E) 0

Questions 16-32 each consist of two quantities, one in Column A and one in Column B. You are to compare the two quantities and on the answer sheet fill in circle

A if the quantity in Column A is greater;
B if the quantity in Column B is greater;
C if the two quantities are equal;
D if the relationship cannot be determined from the information given.

Notes:
1. In certain questions, information concerning one or both of the quantities to be compared is centered above the two columns.
2. In a given question, a symbol that appears in both columns represents the same thing in Column A as it does in Column B.
3. Letters such as x, n, and k stand for real numbers.

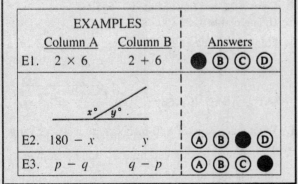

EXAMPLES Column A	Column B	Answers
E1. 2×6	$2 + 6$	● Ⓑ Ⓒ Ⓓ
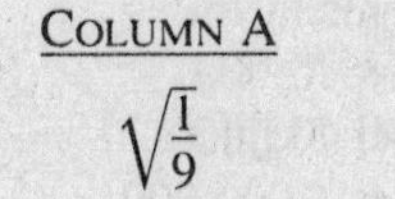		
E2. $180 - x$	y	Ⓐ Ⓑ ● Ⓓ
E3. $p - q$	$q - p$	Ⓐ Ⓑ Ⓒ ●

	COLUMN A	COLUMN B
16.	$\sqrt{\frac{1}{9}}$	$\left(\frac{1}{3}\right)^2$
17.	The number of integers from -5 to 5 inclusive	The number of integers from 5 to 15 inclusive

$1 + x < 0$

18.	x	0

$-10 < a < -1$

19.	$\frac{1}{a^4}$	$\frac{1}{a^5}$

	COLUMN A	COLUMN B
20.	$1 - x$	$1 + x$

$\frac{1}{x} < 0$

21.	x	0

$2x = 24$
$2z = x$

22.	z	12

1 kilometer $= \frac{5}{8}$ mile

23.	5 miles	8 kilometers

Area of circle $= \frac{\pi}{4}$

24.	Radius of circle	0.5

Perimeter of square $ABCD = 4b + 4$

25.	The length of $AB + BC$	$2b$

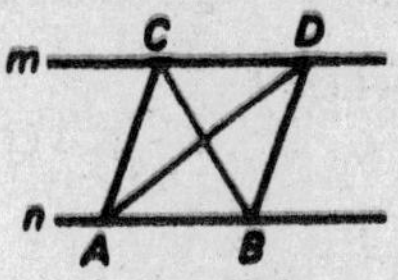

m is parallel to n.

26.	Area of ABC	Area of ABD

In $\triangle ABC$, $BC = 12$, $\angle A \overset{\circ}{=} \angle C$, and the measure of $\angle A \overset{\circ}{=} 45$.

27.	Area of ABC	72
28.	$\frac{t + n}{n}$	$\frac{t}{n} + 1$

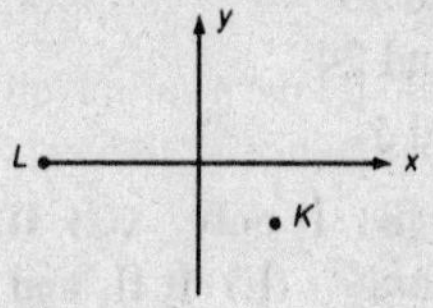

29.	The x-coordinate of point K	The x-coordinate of point L

$x^2 = 144$

30.	x	12

$2a + 3b > 4$

31.	a	b

$x < 0$

32.	Zero	$x^3 - 1$

> Solve each of the remaining problems in this section using any available space for scratchwork. Then decide which is the best of the choices given and fill in the corresponding circle on the answer sheet.

33. If k is the average of 10 and -14, then the average of k and -8 is
(A) -24 (B) -12 (C) -11
(D) -5 (E) $+5$

34. A father can do a job as fast as two sons working together. If one son does the job alone in three hours and the other does it alone in six hours, how many hours does it take the father to do the job alone?
(A) 1 (B) 2 (C) 3 (D) 4 (E) $4\frac{1}{2}$

35. $9x - 12y = -21$
$6x + 4y = 34$
$3x - 4y =$
(A) -54 (B) -13 (C) -7 (D) 7 (E) 13

36. A woman went marketing for sugar for canning. In one store sugar was $35\frac{1}{2}$¢ per pound and she found that she lacked 30¢ of having enough money to buy the number of pounds she needed. She bought the required amount of sugar at another store at 35¢ per pound and had 45¢ left. How much money did she have before making the purchase?
(A) \$52.50 (B) \$52.95 (C) \$53.00
(D) \$53.05 (E) more than \$54.00

37. What is the maximum number of half-pint containers of cream that can be filled with a 4-gallon can of cream? (2 pts. = 1 qt. and 4 qts. = 1 gal.)
(A) 16 (B) 24 (C) 30 (D) 32 (E) 64

38. Which of the following is (are) true of the value of $(152)^3(783)(281) - (29)^5(0)(374)(2)^8$?
I. The last digit in the answer is 4.
II. The answer is an odd number.
III. The answer is a negative number.
(A) I only (B) II only (C) III only
(D) I and II only (E) I, II, and III

39. How long would it take a car traveling at 30 miles per hour to cover a distance of 44 feet? (1 mi. = 5280 ft.)
(A) 1 sec. (B) 2.64 sec. (C) 5.2 sec.
(D) 1 min. (E) 7.7 min.

40. How many students are there in a class if two students remain after four rows of seats are filled, and nine students remain after three rows of seats are filled?
(A) 21 (B) 22 (C) 28 (D) 30 (E) 32

41. $\angle a = \angle b$
$\angle c \stackrel{\circ}{=} 60$
$\angle d \stackrel{\circ}{=}$
(A) 30 (B) 60
(C) 120 (D) 180
(E) none of these

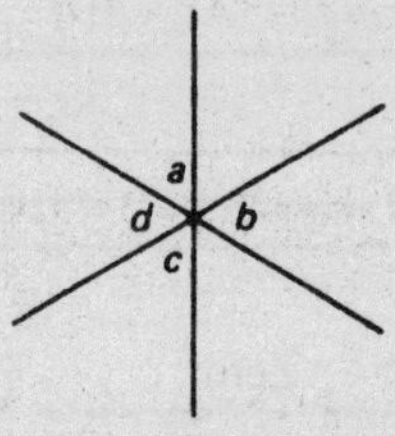

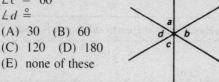

42. How many 2″ squares can be cut from a rectangular paper which is 11″ × 5″?
(A) 10 (B) 11 (C) 12 (D) 13 (E) 14

43. A pulley whose diameter is 9 inches is connected by a belt to another pulley whose diameter is 6 inches. If the larger pulley runs at 1200 revolutions per minute, at how many revolutions per minute does the smaller pulley run?
(A) 800 (B) 1080 (C) 1600 (D) 1800
(E) 2000

44. How many square units are there in the shaded triangle?
(A) 3 (B) 4 (C) 5
(D) 6 (E) 9

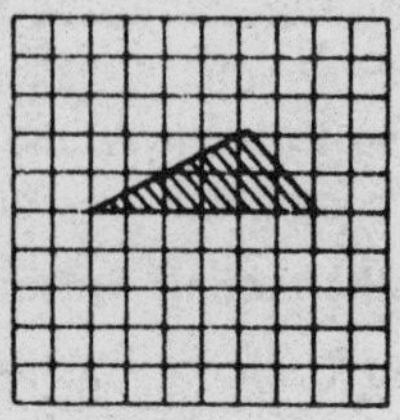

45. $AB = BC$, $\widehat{AB} = 100°$,
$\angle ABC \stackrel{\circ}{=}$
(A) 45 (B) 60 (C) 80
(D) 90 (E) 160

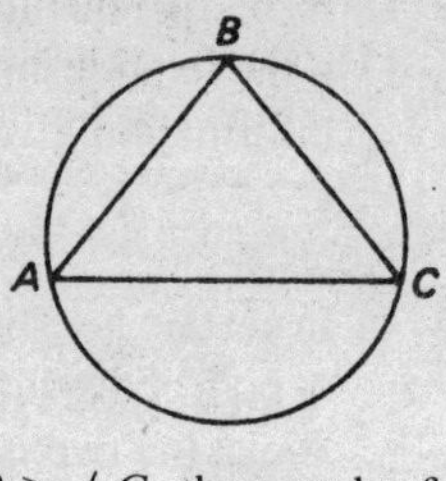

46. In $\angle ABC$, if $\angle A > \angle B$ and $\angle B > \angle C$, then each of the following can be true EXCEPT
(A) $C < 40°$ (B) $A < 170°$ (C) $B > 60°$
(D) $A > 90°$ (E) $C > 60°$

47. Lines ABC and EDC meet at an angle of 40°.
m $\angle CBD = 80°$, m $\angle AED = 60°$, $CD = 2$, $DE = 4$, $BD = 1$. What is the length of AE?
(A) 1.5 (B) 2 (C) 3
(D) 4 (E) 8

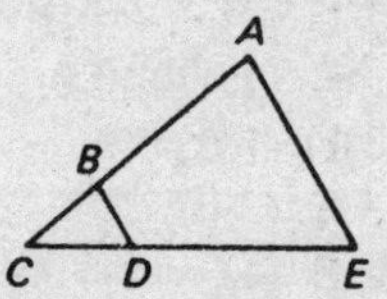

48. A rectangular piece of cardboard 9″ × 12″ is made into an open box by cutting a $2\frac{1}{2}''$ square from each corner and bending up the sides. What is the volume of the box if no allowance is made for overlapping of the edges?
(A) 70 cu. in. (B) $154\frac{3}{8}$ cu. in. (C) 195 cu. in.
(D) 270 cu. in. (E) 700 cu. in.

49. If the length and width of a rectangle are doubled, by what percent is the area increased?
(A) 30% (B) 75% (C) 100% (D) 300%
(E) 400%

50. In pentagon $ABCDE$,
$AB \perp BC$.
$\angle C + \angle D + \angle E + \angle A =$
(A) 450° (B) 540°
(C) 630° (D) 720°
(E) 810°

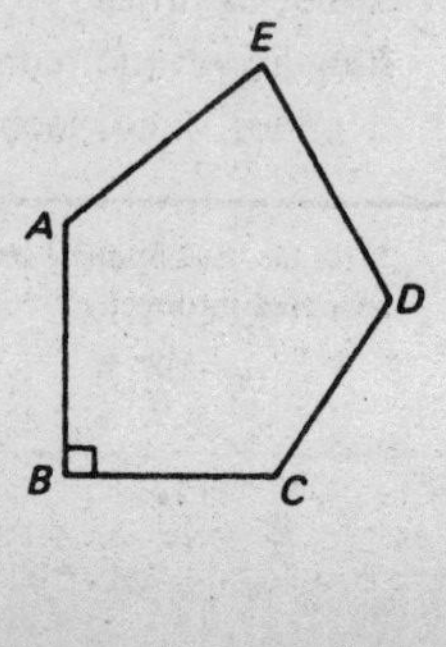

ANSWER KEY

Verbal Aptitude Section

1. **B**	*11.* **B**	*21.* **C**	*31.* **B**	*41.* **C**	*51.* **A**	*61.* **B**
2. **E**	*12.* **B**	*22.* **A**	*32.* **C**	*42.* **B**	*52.* **D**	*62.* **C**
3. **E**	*13.* **D**	*23.* **B**	*33.* **B**	*43.* **C**	*53.* **E**	*63.* **E**
4. **D**	*14.* **E**	*24.* **B**	*34.* **E**	*44.* **A**	*54.* **D**	*64.* **D**
5. **A**	*15.* **C**	*25.* **A**	*35.* **A**	*45.* **D**	*55.* **B**	*65.* **D**
6. **A**	*16.* **A**	*26.* **D**	*36.* **E**	*46.* **B**	*56.* **B**	
7. **C**	*17.* **E**	*27.* **D**	*37.* **D**	*47.* **E**	*57.* **C**	
8. **B**	*18.* **C**	*28.* **C**	*38.* **B**	*48.* **B**	*58.* **C**	
9. **E**	*19.* **C**	*29.* **D**	*39.* **B**	*49.* **A**	*59.* **E**	
10. **B**	*20.* **A**	*30.* **B**	*40.* **E**	*50.* **C**	*60.* **E**	

Mathematical Aptitude Section

Note: Each correct answer to the mathematics questions is keyed by number to the corresponding topic in Chapters 9 and 10. These numerals refer to the topics listed below, with specific page references in parentheses.

1. Basic Fundamental Operations (155–157)
2. Algebraic Operations (157–160)
3. Using Algebra (160–164)
4. Exponents, Roots and Radicals (159–160)
5. Inequalities (164–165)
6. Fractions (176–178)
7. Decimals (176)
8. Percent (178–180)
9. Averages (180–181)
10. Motion (182–183)
11. Ratio and Proportion (183–185)
12. Mixtures and Solutions (177–178)
13. Work (185–186)
14. Coordinate Geometry (172–173)
15. Geometry (165–172, 173–176)
16. Quantitative Comparisons (189–192)

ANSWER KEY

1. **A** (6,8)	*11.* **D** (11)	*21.* **B** (6,16)	*31.* **D** (5,16)	*41.* **B** (15)
2. **C** (2)	*12.* **E** (11)	*22.* **B** (2,16)	*32.* **A** (2,16)	*42.* **A** (15)
3. **C** (2)	*13.* **E** (2)	*23.* **C** (11,16)	*33.* **D** (9)	*43.* **D** (15)
4. **E** (1)	*14.* **E** (8,11)	*24.* **C** (15,16)	*34.* **B** (13)	*44.* **D** (15)
5. **E** (15)	*15.* **B** (2)	*25.* **A** (15,16)	*35.* **C** (2)	*45.* **C** (15)
6. **E** (3,6)	*16.* **A** (4,6,16)	*26.* **C** (15,16)	*36.* **B** (1)	*46.* **E** (15)
7. **B** (1)	*17.* **C** (1,16)	*27.* **C** (15,16)	*37.* **E** (1)	*47.* **C** (15)
8. **B** (6)	*18.* **B** (2,16)	*28.* **C** (2,6,16)	*38.* **A** (1,2)	*48.* **A** (15)
9. **D** (8)	*19.* **A** (6,16)	*29.* **A** (14,16)	*39.* **A** (10)	*49.* **D** (15)
10. **E** (6)	*20.* **D** (2,16)	*30.* **D** (4,16)	*40.* **D** (3)	*50.* **A** (15)

SCORING CHART TYPICAL TEST D

Verbal Section		**Mathematical Section***		
No. correct	______	No. correct	(A)	______
No. omitted	______	No. incorrect (# 1-15, 33-50)	(B)	______
No. incorrect	______	No. incorrect (# 16-32)	(C)	______
¼ no. incorrect	______	¼ (B) + ⅓ (C)	(D)	______
Raw Score: (no. correct minus ¼ no. incorrect)	______	*Raw Score* = (A) − (D)		______

* (In the Mathematical section, deduct ¼ of a point for each five-choice question answered incorrectly and ⅓ of a point for each four-choice question answered incorrectly.)

EVALUATION CHART

Study your score. Your raw score on the Verbal and Mathematical Aptitude Sections is an indication of your probable achievement on the PSAT/NMSQT. As a guide to the amount of work you need or want to do with this book, study the following.

Raw Score: Verbal	Raw Score: Mathematical	Self-rating
58–65	41–50	Superior
46–57	25–40	Very good
40–45	20–24	Satisfactory
36–39	16–19	Average
30–35	10–15	Needs further study
20–29	7–9	Needs intensive study
0–19	0–6	Probably inadequate

Your scores are most likely improving with each test that you take. To help pinpoint any weak areas you still may have, consult the table on page 383 and plan your remaining review accordingly.

ANSWER EXPLANATIONS

Verbal Aptitude Section

1. **B** *Accumulate* or collect is the opposite of *scatter.* Think of "accumulating a vast fortune."
2. **E** A *roadblock* or obstacle to progress is the opposite of an *aid to progress.* "Poor study habits are an educational roadblock."
3. **E** To *exaggerate* is to enlarge upon the truth, while to *understate* is to describe something as less than it actually is. Think of "exaggerating the story 'til it was scarcely believable."
4. **D** *Proximity* or nearness is the opposite of *distance.* "His proximity to the rattlesnake made him nervous."
5. **A** To *garble* is to speak confusedly, the opposite of to *express clearly.* Think of "rumormongers garbling the facts."
6. **A** *Bleak* or dismal and gloomy is the opposite of *cheery.* Think of "a bleak, haunted house."
7. **C** *Naiveté* means innocence or inexperience, in contrast to *sophistication* or worldliness. Think of "the naivete of the average freshman."
8. **B** To *contract* is to draw together or make smaller, while to *expand* is to enlarge. Think of "muscles contracting tightly."
9. **E** Someone who is *compliant* is flexible and agreeable, the opposite of *unyielding.* Word Parts Clue: *Com-* means with; *pliant* means bendable. *Compliant* means to bend with or agree with. Think of "not compliant with the drug-testing program."
10. **B** *Affluence* is wealth, while *destitution* is poverty. Think of "the millionaire's affluence."
11. **B** To *instigate* is to incite or urge forward, the opposite of to *dissuade* or advise against. Think of "instigating a riot."
12. **B** *Flagrant* or shockingly glaring and noticeable is the opposite of *inconspicuous.* Think of "a flagrant violation of the law."
13. **D** *Vehemence* or intensity and force is the opposite of *lack of intensity.* "Raising her voice, she argued with great vehemence."
14. **E** *Defunct* means no longer in existence. Its opposite is *extant,* existing. "This policy is defunct; it no longer applies."
15. **C** To *badger* or pester is the opposite of to *let alone.* "Little brother won't quit badgering me!"
16. **A** An area's native plants and animals are *indigenous,* while those from another place are *alien.* Think of "indigenous to this mountainous region."
17. **E** *Salubrious* means healthful, the opposite of *unwholesome.* Think of "the salubrious effect of quitting smoking."
18. **C** To *abate* is to reduce or put an end to something, while to *intensify* is to heighten or enhance something. Think of "a storm abating."
19. **C** *Fortuitous* or accidental is the opposite of *premeditated* or intended. Think of "a fortuitous discovery."

20. **A** To *foment* or incite and arouse is the opposite of to *suppress*.
Think of "fomenting rebellion."

21. **C** A tyrant or harsh ruler would *browbeat* or bully his subjects, yet if such methods helped players win games, they might remain unworried or *untroubled*. Note the conjunction *although*, which signals a contrast.

22. **A** Since Cherokee society already granted certain rights to women, it did not break with or *violate* Cherokee custom to allow women their rights.

23. **B** Because Aristotle lacked the *power* to inspire, he proved an *inadequate* or unsatisfactory tutor for Alexander, whose spirit longed for an inspiring teacher.

24. **B** Animals that were "romantically *disinclined*" might therefore not be inclined to reproduce.

25. **A** Words like "courage" and "philosophy" are *abstractions* (words representing ideas rather than concrete objects).

26. **D** Because the tendency to migrate exists in all time periods, you cannot fully explain it on the basis of any single time period. Your explanation, like the phenomenon itself, must be *independent of* any particular period of time. The conjunction *since* is used here as a synonym for *because;* it indicates a cause and effect relationship.

27. **D** Someone *sanctimonious* makes a show of religious faith; someone truly *pious* or devout does not.

28. **C** The politicians do not forsake center stage. However, if they did forgo being the center of attention once in a while, the public might like them better for their *self-effacement* (withdrawal from attention).

29. **D** Here the contrast is between reality and pretense. Mrs. Proudie *feigned* or pretended a great interest in the parishioners' welfare. However, her interest was *not* great but actually *negligible* or insignificant, so insignificant as to be almost nonexistent. Note that the conjunction *although* signals the contrast here. Note also that the phrase "so negligible as to be practically nonexistent" is a cliché, a literary commonplace.

30. **B** By definition, an excessive or grandiloquent literary work lacks *economy* or conciseness in verbal expression. Note that you are dealing with a secondary meaning of *economy* here.

31. **B** *Bread* is produced in the shape of a *loaf*. *Cheese* is produced in the shape of a *wheel*.

(Defining Characteristic)

32. **C** A *book* consists of several *chapters*. A *building* consists of several *stories*.

(Part to Whole)

33. **B** A *clasp* is the fastening on a *bracelet*. A *buckle* is the fastening on a *belt*.

(Function)

34. **E** A *fleet* is a group of *ships*. A *pack* is a group of *wolves*.

(Group and Member)

35. **A** One stores *money* in a *bank*. One stores *wine* in a *cask*.

(Function)

36. **E** *Flimsy* means weak and lacking in *strength*. *Clumsy* means awkward and lacking in *grace*.

(Antonym Variant)

37. **D** A person who is *obstinate* or stubborn may be called *mulish* (like a mule). A person who is *coy* or pretends shyness may be called *kittenish* (like a kitten).

(Definition)

38. **B** A *refugee* seeks *asylum* or shelter. A *hermit* seeks *solitude* or isolation.

(Defining Characteristic)

39. **B** Something which is *inane* or senseless lacks *meaning*, by definition. Something which is *random* or haphazard by definition lacks a *plan*.

(Antonym Variant)

40. **E** To *sap vitality* is to weaken or exhaust liveliness. To *deplete resources* is to reduce supplies.

(Defining Characteristic)

41. **C** A *countess* is a member of the *nobility*, the aristocrats. A *professor* is a member of the *faculty*, the teaching staff.

(Group and Member)

42. **B** By definition, a *route* that is *circuitous* follows an indirect course. Similarly, an *argument* that is *devious* follows an indirect course.

(Defining Characteristic)

43. **C** Just as the *wheat* is separated from the worthless straw or *chaff*, the *wine* is separated from the worthless sediment or *dregs*.

(Part to Whole)

44. **A** Something which is *ephemeral* (fleeting, transient) lacks *permanence*. Something which is *erratic* (unpredictable) lacks *predictability*.

(Antonym Variant)

45. **D** To *ogle* is to *observe* or look at someone provocatively (in an attention-getting manner). To *flaunt* is to *display* or show off something provocatively (in an attention-getting manner).

(Manner)

46. **B** The author states (somewhat ironically) that modern fictional characters must have "clinical authenticity." In other words, they must appear to be genuine or valid in psychological terms.

47. **E** In candidly exposing her grandmother's flaws, the author exhibits a *sardonic* or scornful and sarcastic attitude.

48. **B** Although the grandmother's outward appearance was soft and motherly, her essential nature was hard as nails. Clearly, you cannot judge a book (person) by its cover (outward appearance).

49. **A** The passage's central concern is the function of codes of etiquette and good manners; in other words, the function of politeness.

50. **C** The author suggests that in crowded regions such as Europe manners tend to be formal. The writer also suggests that in newly crowded countries, such as the United States, manners become more important because individuals "need" to find ways to deal with large numbers of people in close quarters. This implies that, in a crowded region such as Europe, good manners would be not only important but also *essential*.

51. **A** See sentence 3. In making social intercourse possible, manners facilitate or ease relationships among people.

52. **D** In describing manners as "armor" and "advance patrols," the author is being figurative or *metaphoric*.

53. **E** The author states that the jackdaw's proficiency is not inherited or innate, but "an individually acquired accomplishment." In other words, it has been *gained through practice*.

54. **D** The "sightless monster" is the "stupid wind" that tries to drive the jackdaws toward the east. Note how the author personifies the wind, writing as if the wind had some degree of human intelligence and responsiveness.

55. **B** The author uses several metaphors ("close-reefed sails," "the teeth of the gale," etc.) and clarifies what he means by the term *game*. He describes the jackdaws' behavior in detail and dismisses the notion that their behavior is purely instinctive. However, he never *argues a cause*.

56. **B** The author's purpose is to *describe* the geological process known as the subduction of the lithosphere.
Choice **A** is incorrect. The author is not refuting or disproving a theory. Choice **C** is incorrect. The author is dealing with a process, not a technique. Choice **D** is incorrect. The author is being descriptive and expository, not argumentative. Choice **E** is incorrect. The author makes no predictions about things that may occur in the future; he describes a process that is taking place in the present.

57. **C** Only deserts are not mentioned as related to the subduction of the lithosphere.

58. **C** The author is concerned with explaining what happens in a geological phenomenon. His style is, by definition, expository.

59. **E** All three statements are true. The general circulation or flow of the earth's mantle, mentioned in the second paragraph, is an indication that the mantle is in a state of flux or flow. The second paragraph also indicates that the lithosphere or crust is cooler than the mantle and that the subducted lithosphere is absorbed or incorporated by the mantle.

60. **E** In the last sentence of paragraph 4, the author states that *it appears* that convection currents may in some regions drive the plates, and in other regions be driven by the plates. However, this is merely a hypothesis. Thus, current knowledge of the relationship between the plate motions and the currents is clearly *tentative* or hypothetical. To locate this information in the body of the text, scan the passage for the key words *asthenosphere* and *convection*.

61. **B** The opening sentence maintains that the growth of scholarly activity was stimulated by the protest movement. The protest movement caused an upsurge of popular interest in the Afro-American past. It also created a climate in which professional studies of black history were legitimized.

62. **C** The three men are cited as examples of scholars who were encouraged to resume their earlier researches in black history.
Choices **A, B,** and **E** are incorrect. None of the three men was identified with these concerns in the passage. Choice **D** is incorrect. Only Logan is identified with research on blacks in nineteenth-century North Carolina.

63. **E** The author is describing what occurred during the period to change black history from a marginal or unimportant field to a vital field of specialization.

64. **D** You can arrive at the correct answer by the process of elimination.
Statement I is supported by the passage. At the time Bennett and Logan wrote, both the pre-Mayflower period of black history and the nineteenth-century life of blacks in North Carolina were relatively unexplored. Therefore, you can eliminate Choices **B** and **E.**
Statement II is unsupported by the passage. Bennett's work was a popularization intended for a wide general audience; it was not aimed at academics. Therefore, you can eliminate Choice **C.**
Statement III is supported by the passage. Bennett's work appeared first as a series of magazine articles, then as a book. Logan's work first appeared as a doctoral thesis, then (with revisions) as a book. Therefore, you can eliminate Choice **A.**
Only Choice **D** is left. It is the correct answer.

65. **D** According to the passage, prior to the early 1960s, Negro history was not an object of particularly great renown in academe (the academic environment). In the 1950s, the advice given to Blassingame to avoid black history if he desired "a future in the historical profession" seemed wise—graduate students of the caliber of Huggins and Litwack felt an ambivalence about entering the field because of "practical concerns." What these concerns boiled down to was the sense that to choose black history as one's specialization would be *detrimental* or harmful to one's career.

Mathematical Aptitude Section

1. **A** $0.9\% = \frac{0.9}{100} = \frac{9}{1000}$

2. **C** $\frac{3}{x} = \frac{x}{27}$

$x^2 = 81$

$x = 9$

3. **C** $\frac{1}{2} + \frac{2}{3} + \frac{3}{y} = \frac{23}{12}$

$\frac{6}{12} + \frac{8}{12} + \frac{3}{y} = \frac{23}{12}$

$\frac{14}{12} + \frac{3}{y} = \frac{23}{12}$

$\frac{3}{y} = \frac{9}{12}$

$\frac{3}{y} = \frac{3}{4}$

$y = 4$

4. **E** 25 hours overtime $= 25 + 12\frac{1}{2} = 37\frac{1}{2}$

5. **E** 9, 12, and 15 represent the lengths of the sides of a 3-4-5 right triangle since $9 = 3(3)$, $12 = 3(4)$, and $15 = 3(5)$. Likewise, $1\frac{1}{2}$, 2, and $2\frac{1}{2}$ represent a 3-4-5 triangle since $1\frac{1}{2} = \frac{1}{2}(3)$, $2 = \frac{1}{2}(4)$, and $2\frac{1}{2} = \frac{1}{2}(5)$. 10, 26, and 24 represent the lengths of the sides of a 5-12-13 right triangle since $10 = 2(5)$, $24 = 2(12)$, and $26 = 2(13)$.

6. **E** $\frac{1}{2} + \frac{1}{4} + \frac{1}{5} = \frac{19}{20}$

$\frac{1}{20}$ is left for his college.

Let x = amount left by Mr. Benedict.

$\frac{1}{20}x = \$5000$

$x = \$100{,}000$

7. **B** The elevator carries 5 adults less than capacity when it carries 15 adults. Let x = number of children that can be carried with 15 adults.

$\frac{20 \text{ adults}}{24 \text{ children}} = \frac{5 \text{ adults}}{x \text{ children}}$

$20x = 120$

$x = 6$

8. **B** This is a direct proportion. The more Joan works, the more of her homework she accomplishes. Let x = time required to finish.

$\frac{\text{part of work done}}{\text{time (in hours)}} = \frac{\frac{2}{5}}{1} = \frac{1}{x}$

$\frac{2}{5}x = 1$

$x = \frac{5}{2} = 2\frac{1}{2}$

However, since Joan already worked 1 hour, she must work for $1\frac{1}{2}$ more hours.

9. **D** Note that the sales tax is calculated on the actual selling price, which is \$60 − \$6, or \$54. Since 10% of \$54 = \$5.40, the actual cost of the sweater is \$54. + \$5.40 or \$59.40.

10. **E** $\frac{\text{games won}}{\text{games played}} = \frac{g - l}{g}$

11. **D** $\frac{10 \text{ inches}}{72 \text{ inches}} = \frac{1}{7.2}$ or 1:7.2

12. **E** Brookline 3 per 10,000 or 300 per 1,000,000
Brookville 5 per 100,000 or 50 per 1,000,000
Brooklyn 13 per 1,000,000
Total = 363 per 1,000,000

13. **E** Today Lori is $10 + y$ years old. In x years she will be $10 + y + x$ years old.

14. **E** $9.5\% = \frac{9.5}{100} = \frac{19}{200}$ or 19 out of 200

15. **B** $x - 7 = 0$

$x = 7$

$y^2 = 25$

$y = \pm 5$

$xy = \pm 35$

16. **A** $\sqrt{\frac{1}{9}} = \frac{1}{3}$

$\left(\frac{1}{3}\right)^2 = \frac{1}{9}$

$\frac{1}{3} > \frac{1}{9}$

17. **C** From -5 to zero inclusive there are 6 integers, and from 1 to 5 there are 5 more integers, for a total of 11 integers. From 5 to 15 inclusive there are also 11 integers.

18. **B** $x + 1 < 0$
$\therefore x < -1$

19. **A** Since a is negative, the denominator of $\frac{1}{a^4}$ will be positive for all its values, and the denominator of $\frac{1}{a^5}$ will be negative for all its values.

20. **D** The value of x may be zero, positive, or negative.

21. **B** The value of x must be negative for the value of the fraction $\frac{1}{x}$ to be less than zero (negative.)

22. **B** $2x = 24$
$x = 12$
$2z = 12$
$z = 6$

23. **C** This is a direct proportion. Let x = the number of miles in 8 kilometers.
$$\frac{1 \text{ kilometer}}{\frac{5}{8} \text{ mile}} = \frac{8 \text{ kilometers}}{x \text{ miles}}$$
$x = 5$

24. **C** Area $= \pi r^2 = \frac{\pi}{4}$
$r^2 = \frac{1}{4}$
$r = \frac{1}{2}$ or 0.5

25. **A** Since the perimeter of square $= 4b + 4$, each side $= \frac{1}{4}(4b + 4)$ or $b + 1$, and the length of two sides $= 2b + 2$.
$2b + 2 > 2b$

26. **C** Area of a $\triangle$ = $\frac{1}{2}$(base)(altitude). Both triangles share the same base (AB). Since distances between parallel lines are the same, the two triangles have equal altitudes.

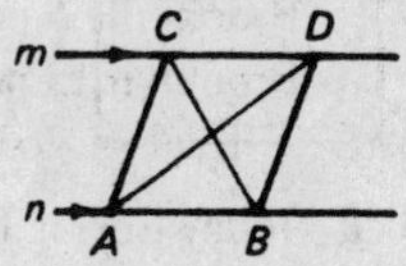

27. **C** Since $\angle A \stackrel{\circ}{=} \angle C$, $BC = AB$, $AB = 12$. Since the measure of $\angle B \stackrel{\circ}{=} 90$, ABC is a right $\triangle$ and the area equals $\frac{1}{2}$(leg)(leg) or $\left(\frac{1}{2}\right)(12)(12)$ or 72.

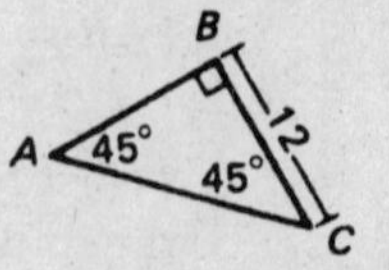

28. **C** $\frac{t + n}{n} = \frac{t}{n} + \frac{n}{n} = \frac{t}{n} + 1$

29. **A** The x-coordinate of K is a positive quantity. The x-coordinate of L is a negative quantity.

30. **D** $X^2 = 144$ and $X = +12$ and -12

31. **D** Various values of a and of b are possible for this inequality.

32. **A** Since X has a negative value and since the cube of any negative value is negative, $X^3 - 1$ is less than zero.

33. **D** The average of 10 and -14 is $-4 \div 2$ or -2 (k).
$$\frac{k + (-8)}{2} = \frac{-2 + (-8)}{2} = -5$$

34. **B** Determine how long it will take the two sons to do it together. That will be time required by father. Let x = time required if both boys work together.
$\frac{x}{3} + \frac{x}{6} = 1$
$2x + x = 6$
$3x = 6$
$x = 2$

35. **C** Note that the required $3x - 4y$ is $\frac{1}{3}$ of first equation. This is easier than solving for x and y and substituting.
$3x = \frac{1}{3}$ of $9x$
$-4y = \frac{1}{3}$ of $-12y$
$\therefore ? = \frac{1}{3}$ of -21 or -7

36. **B** By making the purchase in the second store she saved 30¢ plus 45¢ or 75¢. She saved $\frac{1}{2}$¢ per pound bought. Or she saved 75¢ on 150 pounds. She bought 150 pounds at 35¢ and had 45¢ left. Before the purchase she had 150(.35) + .45 *or* \$52.95

37. **E** 4 gallons = 16 quarts = 32 pints = 64 half-pints

38. **A** The second term contains a factor of 0 and hence that term equals 0; this rules out III as a possibility. Consider only the last digit in each factor in the first term. $2^3 = 8$; when 8 is multiplied by 3 and then by 1, the product is 24 (I). The value is even, thus ruling out II.

39. **A** $\frac{\text{distance (miles)}}{\text{rate (miles per hour)}} = \text{time (hours)}$
44 feet $= \frac{1}{120}$ of a mile
$$\frac{\frac{1}{120} \text{ mile}}{30 \text{ miles per hour}} = \frac{1}{120} \div 30 = \frac{1}{120} \cdot \frac{1}{30}$$
$$= \frac{1}{3600} \text{ hour} = 1 \text{ second}$$

40. **D** Let x = number of pupils in each row.
$4x + 2 = 3x + 9$
$x = 7$ (in one row)
$4x + 2 = 28 + 2 = 30$
or, $3x + 9 = 21 + 9 = 30$

41. **B** $\angle c = \angle x$ [vertical angles]
$\angle c = \angle x \overset{\circ}{=} 60$
$\angle a + \angle x + \angle b \overset{\circ}{=} 180$
$\angle a + \angle b \overset{\circ}{=} 120$
$\angle a = \angle b$ [given]
$\angle b \overset{\circ}{=} 60$
$\angle b = \angle d$ [vertical angles]
$\angle d \overset{\circ}{=} 60$

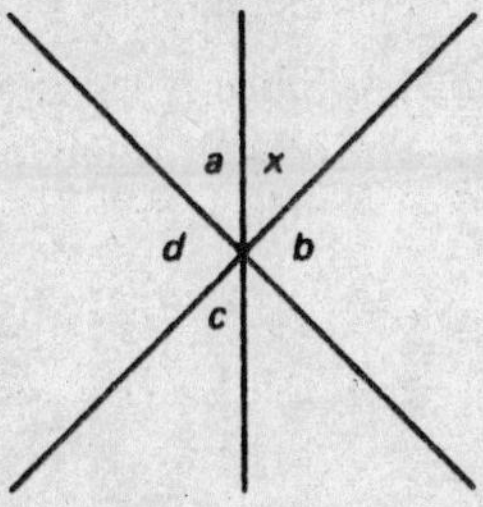

42. **A** See diagram.

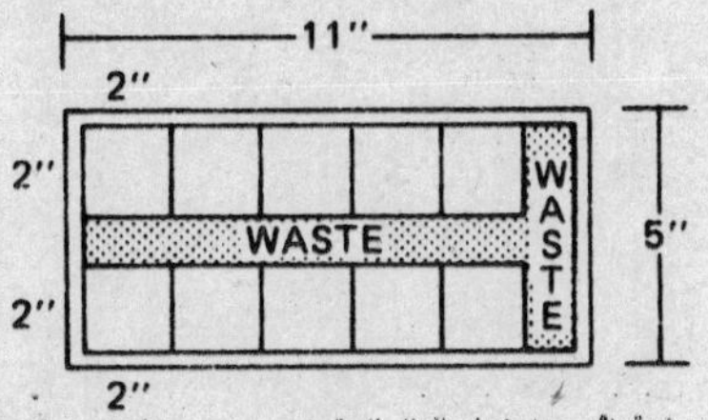

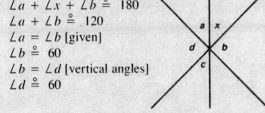

43. **D** Smaller pulleys make more revolutions per minute than larger pulleys. Therefore the number of revolutions per minute is inversely proportional to the circumference of the circle.
Circumference = (π)(diameter)
Circumference of large pulley = 9π
Circumference of small pulley = 6π
Let x = number of revolutions per minute made by the smaller pulley.

$$\frac{6\pi}{9\pi} = \frac{1200}{x}$$
$$\frac{6}{9} = \frac{1200}{x}$$
$$6x = 10800$$
$$x = 1800 \text{ revolutions per minute}$$

44. **D** Base of shaded $\triangle$ = 6 units
Altitude of shaded $\triangle$
= 2 units
Area = $\frac{1}{2}$(base)(altitude)
Area = $\frac{1}{2}(6)(2) = 6$

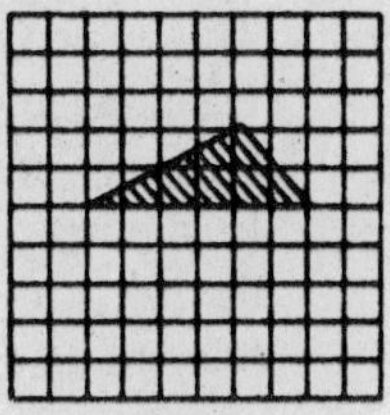

45. **C** $AB = BC$ [given]
$\therefore \widehat{AB} = \widehat{BC} = 100°$
$\therefore \widehat{AC} = 160°$
$\angle ABC \overset{\circ}{=} 80$
[inscribed angle]

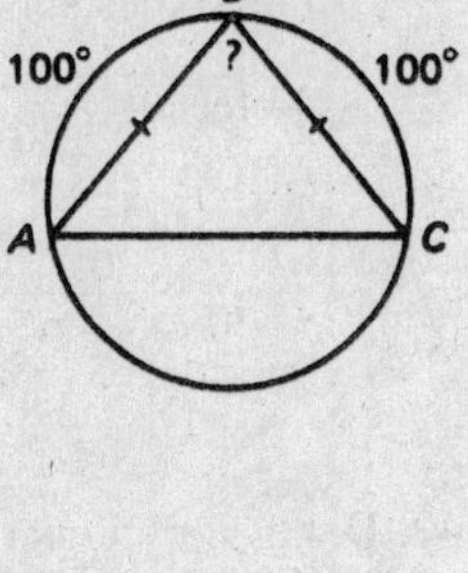

46. **E** Try values satisfying the relationship $A > B > C$ and $A + B + C = 180$.
(A) could be true if $C = 40$, $B = 50$, and $A = 90$.
(B) could be true if $A = 160$, $B = 11$, and $C = 9$.
(C) could be true if $A = 80$, $B = 70$, and $C = 30$.
(D) could be true with the same values as in (B) above.
(E) If $C > 60$, there is less than 120 for A and B together. But each must be > 60 since each is $> C$.

47. **C** Since $\angle C \overset{\circ}{=} 40$ and
$\angle CBD \overset{\circ}{=} 80$,
$\angle BDC$ must $\overset{\circ}{=} 60$.
$\therefore BD \parallel AE$
$\therefore \triangle BCD \sim \triangle ACE$
$\frac{2}{6} = \frac{1}{?}$ [sides are proportional]
$? = 3$

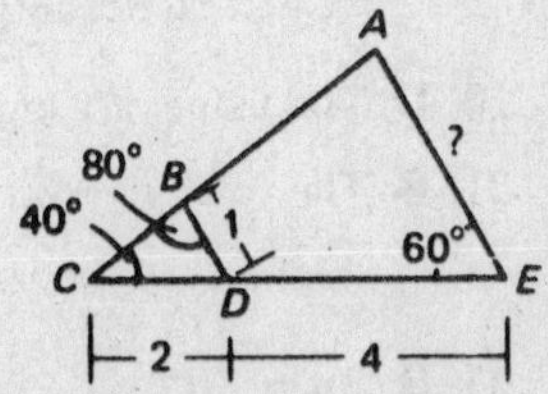

48. **A** Volume of box =
(length)(width)
(height)
Volume of box =
$(7'')(4'')\left(2\frac{1}{2}''\right)$ =
70 cubic inches

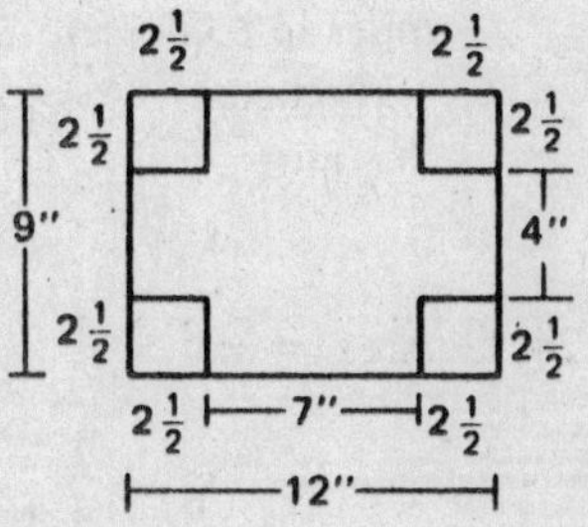

49. **D** Area of original rectangle = lw
Area of enlarged rectangle = $4lw$
Increase = $3lw$
$\frac{\text{increase}}{\text{original}} = \frac{3lw}{lw} = 3 = 300\%$

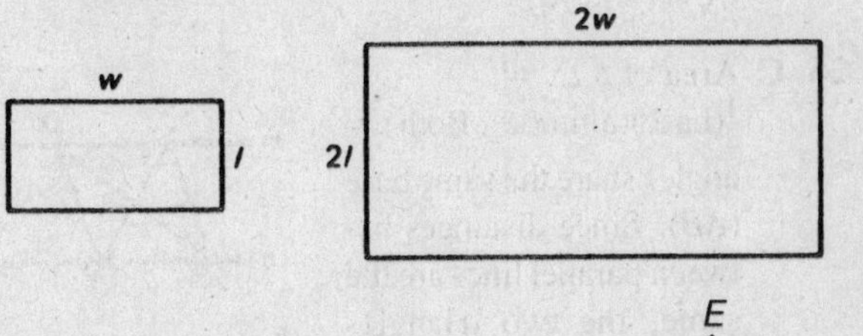

50. **A** $\angle A + \angle B + \angle C + \angle D + \angle E = 3(180°) = 540°$
Since $\angle B \overset{\circ}{=} 90$,
$\angle C + \angle D + \angle E + \angle A \overset{\circ}{=} 450$

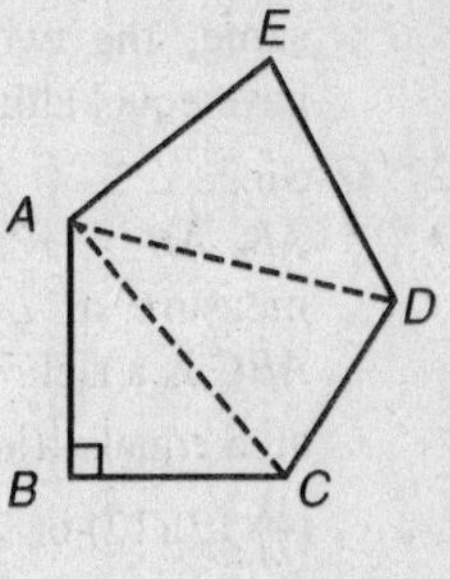

PSAT/NMSQT Answer Sheet

TYPICAL TEST E

Verbal Aptitude Section

1 (A) (B) (C) (D) (E)
2 (A) (B) (C) (D) (E)
3 (A) (B) (C) (D) (E)
4 (A) (B) (C) (D) (E)
5 (A) (B) (C) (D) (E)
6 (A) (B) (C) (D) (E)
7 (A) (B) (C) (D) (E)
8 (A) (B) (C) (D) (E)
9 (A) (B) (C) (D) (E)
10 (A) (B) (C) (D) (E)
11 (A) (B) (C) (D) (E)
12 (A) (B) (C) (D) (E)
13 (A) (B) (C) (D) (E)
14 (A) (B) (C) (D) (E)
15 (A) (B) (C) (D) (E)
16 (A) (B) (C) (D) (E)
17 (A) (B) (C) (D) (E)
18 (A) (B) (C) (D) (E)
19 (A) (B) (C) (D) (E)
20 (A) (B) (C) (D) (E)
21 (A) (B) (C) (D) (E)
22 (A) (B) (C) (D) (E)
23 (A) (B) (C) (D) (E)
24 (A) (B) (C) (D) (E)
25 (A) (B) (C) (D) (E)
26 (A) (B) (C) (D) (E)
27 (A) (B) (C) (D) (E)
28 (A) (B) (C) (D) (E)
29 (A) (B) (C) (D) (E)
30 (A) (B) (C) (D) (E)
31 (A) (B) (C) (D) (E)
32 (A) (B) (C) (D) (E)
33 (A) (B) (C) (D) (E)
34 (A) (B) (C) (D) (E)
35 (A) (B) (C) (D) (E)
36 (A) (B) (C) (D) (E)
37 (A) (B) (C) (D) (E)
38 (A) (B) (C) (D) (E)
39 (A) (B) (C) (D) (E)
40 (A) (B) (C) (D) (E)
41 (A) (B) (C) (D) (E)
42 (A) (B) (C) (D) (E)
43 (A) (B) (C) (D) (E)
44 (A) (B) (C) (D) (E)
45 (A) (B) (C) (D) (E)
46 (A) (B) (C) (D) (E)
47 (A) (B) (C) (D) (E)
48 (A) (B) (C) (D) (E)
49 (A) (B) (C) (D) (E)
50 (A) (B) (C) (D) (E)
51 (A) (B) (C) (D) (E)
52 (A) (B) (C) (D) (E)
53 (A) (B) (C) (D) (E)
54 (A) (B) (C) (D) (E)
55 (A) (B) (C) (D) (E)
56 (A) (B) (C) (D) (E)
57 (A) (B) (C) (D) (E)
58 (A) (B) (C) (D) (E)
59 (A) (B) (C) (D) (E)
60 (A) (B) (C) (D) (E)
61 (A) (B) (C) (D) (E)
62 (A) (B) (C) (D) (E)
63 (A) (B) (C) (D) (E)
64 (A) (B) (C) (D) (E)
65 (A) (B) (C) (D) (E)

Mathematical Aptitude Section*

1 (A) (B) (C) (D) (E)
2 (A) (B) (C) (D) (E)
3 (A) (B) (C) (D) (E)
4 (A) (B) (C) (D) (E)
5 (A) (B) (C) (D) (E)
6 (A) (B) (C) (D) (E)
7 (A) (B) (C) (D) (E)
8 (A) (B) (C) (D) (E)
9 (A) (B) (C) (D) (E)
0 (A) (B) (C) (D) (E)
11 (A) (B) (C) (D) (E)
12 (A) (B) (C) (D) (E)
13 (A) (B) (C) (D) (E)
14 (A) (B) (C) (D) (E)
15 (A) (B) (C) (D) (E)
16 (A) (B) (C) (D) (E)
17 (A) (B) (C) (D) (E)
18 (A) (B) (C) (D) (E)
19 (A) (B) (C) (D) (E)
20 (A) (B) (C) (D) (E)
21 (A) (B) (C) (D) (E)
22 (A) (B) (C) (D) (E)
23 (A) (B) (C) (D) (E)
24 (A) (B) (C) (D) (E)
25 (A) (B) (C) (D) (E)
26 (A) (B) (C) (D) (E)
27 (A) (B) (C) (D) (E)
28 (A) (B) (C) (D) (E)
29 (A) (B) (C) (D) (E)
30 (A) (B) (C) (D) (E)
31 (A) (B) (C) (D) (E)
32 (A) (B) (C) (D) (E)
33 (A) (B) (C) (D) (E)
34 (A) (B) (C) (D) (E)
35 (A) (B) (C) (D) (E)
36 (A) (B) (C) (D) (E)
37 (A) (B) (C) (D) (E)
38 (A) (B) (C) (D) (E)
39 (A) (B) (C) (D) (E)
40 (A) (B) (C) (D) (E)
41 (A) (B) (C) (D) (E)
42 (A) (B) (C) (D) (E)
43 (A) (B) (C) (D) (E)
44 (A) (B) (C) (D) (E)
45 (A) (B) (C) (D) (E)
46 (A) (B) (C) (D) (E)
47 (A) (B) (C) (D) (E)
48 (A) (B) (C) (D) (E)
49 (A) (B) (C) (D) (E)
50 (A) (B) (C) (D) (E)

*If there are more answer spaces than you need, leave them blank.

TYPICAL TEST E

SECTION 1 | **Time—50 minutes** **65 Questions** | For each question in this section, choose the best answer and fill in the corresponding circle on the answer sheet.

Each question below consists of a word in capital letters, followed by five lettered words or phrases. Choose the word or phrase that is most nearly opposite in meaning to the word in capital letters. Since some of the questions require you to distinguish fine shades of meaning, consider all the choices before deciding which is best.

Example:

GOOD: (A) sour (B) bad (C) red (D) hot (E) ugly

Ⓐ ● Ⓒ Ⓓ Ⓔ

1. FLUSTER: (A) soothe (B) diminish (C) strengthen (D) divert (E) allow
2. DETERIORATE: (A) withdraw (B) release (C) initiate (D) improve (E) elevate
3. SCRAWNY: (A) sensible (B) shallow (C) plump (D) boring (E) incompetent
4. OVERRULE: (A) undertake (B) eliminate (C) decide in favor (D) make an offer (E) fail to state
5. WILY: (A) straightforward (B) tactful (C) young (D) aimless (E) obedient
6. FLIPPANCY: (A) coherence (B) seriousness (C) rivalry (D) fidelity (E) charity
7. DIFFIDENCE: (A) boldness (B) fame (C) acerbity (D) monotony (E) indifference
8. TURBULENT: (A) absurd (B) placid (C) candid (D) significant (E) fortunate
9. HAMPER: (A) unwrap (B) animate (C) facilitate (D) treat lightly (E) caution tactfully
10. ADULTERATED: (A) solid (B) immature (C) exalted (D) pure (E) virtuous
11. DISTEND: (A) deflate (B) prolong (C) commence (D) forecast (E) prevent
12. TRANSIENT: (A) permanent (B) diligent (C) spontaneous (D) buoyant (E) puny
13. ELATED: (A) downcast (B) inebriated (C) punctual (D) insulted (E) lamented
14. PROSAIC: (A) imaginative (B) contradictory (C) hesitant (D) redundant (E) disorderly
15. DISSONANCE: (A) amalgamation (B) harmony (C) neutrality (D) resolution (E) proximity
16. DISPARAGE: (A) resemble (B) eulogize (C) vacillate (D) annoy (E) appear
17. FELICITOUS: (A) inappropriate (B) ineffable (C) irrational (D) atypical (E) uncertain
18. DOLTISH: (A) immature (B) coarse (C) clever (D) stable (E) genial
19. CHAGRIN: (A) frown (B) disguise (C) make indifferent (D) make aware (E) please
20. ACRIMONY: (A) irrelevance (B) ambiguity (C) affability (D) false witness (E) qualified statement

Each sentence below has one or two blanks, each blank indicating that something has been omitted. Beneath the sentence are five lettered words or sets of words. Choose the word or set of words that, when inserted in the sentence, best fits the meaning of the sentence as a whole.

Example:

Although its publicity has been ----, the film itself is intelligent, well-acted, handsomely produced, and altogether ----.

(A) tasteless . . respectable (B) extensive . . moderate (C) sophisticated . . amateur (D) risque . . crude (E) perfect . . spectacular

● Ⓑ Ⓒ Ⓓ Ⓔ

21. Impressed by the extraordinary potential of the new superconductor, scientists predict that its use will ---- the computer industry, creating new products overnight.
(A) justify (B) alienate (C) nullify (D) revolutionize (E) overestimate
22. In order that they may be able to discriminate wisely among the many conflicting arguments put before them, legislators must be trained to ---- the truth.
(A) confuse (B) condemn (C) disturb (D) condone (E) discern
23. In their new collections of lighthearted, provocative dresses, French fashion designers are gambling that even ---- professional women are ready for a bit of ---- in style.
(A) strict . . reticence
(B) serious . . frivolity
(C) elegant . . tradition
(D) modern . . harmony
(E) unsentimental . . propriety

24. Irony can, after a fashion, become a mode of escape: to laugh at the terrors of life is in some sense to ---- them.
(A) exaggerate (B) revitalize (C) corroborate
(D) evade (E) license

25. No matter how ---- the revelations of the coming year may be, they will be hard put to match those of the past decade, which have ---- transformed our view of the emergence of Mayan civilization.
(A) minor . . dramatically
(B) profound . . negligibly
(C) striking . . radically
(D) bizarre . . nominally
(E) questionable . . possibly

26. Few other plants can grow beneath the canopy of the sycamore tree, whose leaves and pods produce a natural herbicide that leaches into the soil, ---- other plants that might compete for water and nutrients.
(A) inhibiting (B) distinguishing
(C) nourishing (D) encouraging (E) refreshing

27. Black women authors such as Zora Neale Hurston, originally ---- by both white and black literary establishments to obscurity as minor novelists, are being rediscovered by black feminist critics today.
(A) inclined (B) relegated
(C) subjected (D) diminished (E) characterized

28. Even when a judge does not say anything ----, his or her tone of voice can signal a point of view to jurors and thus ---- the jury in a criminal trial.
(A) coherent . . circumvent
(B) questionable . . perjure
(C) prejudicial . . influence
(D) material . . convene
(E) constructive . . corrupt

29. So intense was her ambition to attain the pinnacle of worldly success that not even the opulence and lavishness of her material possessions seemed ---- the ---- of that ambition.
(A) necessary for . . fulfillment
(B) adequate to . . fervor
(C) appropriate to . . ebullience
(D) relevant to . . languor
(E) consonant with . . insignificance

30. Critics of the movie version of *The Color Purple* ---- its saccharine, overoptimistic mood as out of keeping with the novel's more ---- tone.
(A) applauded . . somber
(B) condemned . . hopeful
(C) acclaimed . . positive
(D) denounced . . sanguine
(E) decried . . acerbic

Each question below consists of a related pair of words or phrases, followed by five lettered pairs of words or phrases. Select the lettered pair that <u>best</u> expresses a relationship similar to that expressed in the original pair.

Example:

YAWN : BOREDOM : : (A) dream : sleep
(B) anger : madness (C) smile : amusement
(D) face : expression (E) impatience : rebellion

Ⓐ Ⓑ ● Ⓓ Ⓔ

31. PEBBLE : SLINGSHOT : : (A) arrow : quiver
(B) ball : cannon (C) missile : target
(D) hilt : dagger (E) barrel : rifle

32. DOOR : LATCH : : (A) window : pane
(B) necklace : clasp (C) lock : key
(D) wall : plaster (E) house : foundation

33. DRIZZLE : POUR : : (A) rumple : fold
(B) moisten : waterproof (C) tingle : chill
(D) dam : flood (E) smolder : blaze

34. CAPTION : PHOTOGRAPH : :
(A) frame : painting (B) subject : portrait
(C) signature : letter (D) title : article
(E) stanza : poem

35. ERADICATE : ERROR : :
(A) acknowledge : fault (B) arbitrate : dispute
(C) penalize : foul (D) uproot : weed
(E) erase : blackboard

36. TYRANNOSAUR : DINOSAUR : :
(A) lizard : crocodile (B) whale : fish
(C) condor : bird (D) frog : tadpole
(E) tiger : leopard

37. GANDER : GOOSE : : (A) fawn : deer
(B) porpoise : whale (C) mare : horse
(D) panda : bear (E) ram : sheep

38. ESTABLISH : TEMPO : :
(A) maintain : equilibrium (B) divide : forces
(C) set : pace (D) invest : funds
(E) perform : combo

39. PROLIFIC : AUTHOR : : (A) melodious : singer
(B) veracious : witness (C) dynamic : actor
(D) loquacious : speaker (E) agile : acrobat

40. LOCOMOTION : FEET : :
(A) perspiration : sweat (B) amnesia : brain
(C) sensation : hands (D) digestion : stomach
(E) sound : ears

41. MENTOR : PROTÉGÉ : : (A) competitor : rival
(B) writer : plagiarist (C) doctor : surgeon
(D) sponsor : candidate (E) truant : dawdler

42. GARBLED : COMPREHEND : :
(A) controversial : dispute
(B) negligible : disregard (C) mangled : believe
(D) methodical : organize
(E) camouflaged : discern

43. TRAVELER : ITINERARY : :
(A) lecturer : outline (B) tourist : vacation
(C) pedestrian : routine (D) explorer : safari
(E) soldier : furlough

44. PURIST : CORRECTNESS : :
(A) miser : generosity (B) saint : elevation
(C) nomad : refuge (D) judge : accuracy
(E) martinet : discipline

45. BROWSE : PERUSE : : (A) weight : balance
(B) scale : descend (C) jostle : arrange
(D) stroll : march (E) observe : reject

Each passage below is followed by questions based on its content. Answer the questions following each passage on the basis of what is stated or implied in that passage.

Among the men and women who have contributed to human happiness, advancement and welfare, must be included philosophers as well as statesmen, inventors, scientists and captains of industry. A philosopher helps people to seek truth and to inquire what are the most worthwhile things that life affords. This is the way in which Ralph Waldo Emerson contributed to the greatness of America. Though he lived in an intellectual aristocracy, he had respect for the common man and his rights. He believed in democracy, in the dignity of human life, in the right and duty of each man to be independent and self-reliant and to follow the dictates of his conscience. He condemned slavery and sang the praises of those who had the courage to oppose it. He raised his voice in protest against the coming industrialism, which threatened to stifle the individual and to keep men and women from developing their various powers and capacities. His appeals for freedom of thought and action have as much ringing force today as they did a century ago.

46. According to the passage, Emerson was noted for his support of
I. individual self-sufficiency
II. the glories of industrialization
III. the emancipation of slaves
(A) I only
(B) III only
(C) I and II only
(D) I and III only
(E) I, II, and III

47. Which of the following statements about Emerson's beliefs can be inferred from the passage?
(A) Specialization enables human beings to develop their capacities to the fullest.
(B) Freedom of thought and action can lead to anarchy.
(C) America's strength resides in her intellectual aristocracy.
(D) A true philosopher is worth more to society than a captain of industry.
(E) It is better to be a nonconformist than to sacrifice one's convictions.

48. The author regards Emerson's pleas on behalf of freedom of thought as
(A) outdated because of changing circumstances
(B) limited by his intellectually aristocratic outlook
(C) more important than his denunciation of slavery
(D) relevant to contemporary conditions
(E) contrary to the dictates of conscience

It was absolutely necessary to interrupt him now.

"You are too hasty, Sir," she cried. "You forget that I have made no answer. Let me do it without further loss of time. Accept my thanks for the compliment you are paying me. I am very sensible of the honour of your proposals, but it is impossible for me to do otherwise than decline them."

"I am not now to learn," replied Mr. Collins with a formal wave of the hand, "that it is usual with young ladies to reject the addresses of the man whom they secretly mean to accept, when he first applies for their favour; and that sometimes the refusal is repeated a second or even a third time. I am therefore by no means discouraged by what you have just said, and shall hope to lead you to the altar ere long."

"Upon my word, Sir," cried Elizabeth, "your hope is rather an extraordinary one after my declaration. I do assure you that I am not one of those young ladies (if such young ladies there are) who are so daring as to risk their happiness on the chance of being asked a second time. I am perfectly serious in my refusal. You could not make *me* happy, and I am convinced that I am the last woman in the world who would make *you* so. Nay, were your friend Lady Catherine to know me, I am persuaded she would find me in every respect ill qualified for the situation."

"Were it certain that Lady Catherine would think so," said Mr. Collins very gravely—"but I cannot imagine that her ladyship would at all disapprove of you. And you may be certain that when I have the honour of seeing her again I shall speak in the highest terms of your modesty, economy, and other amiable qualifications."

49. It can be inferred that in the paragraphs immediately preceding this passage
(A) Elizabeth and Mr. Collins quarreled
(B) Elizabeth met Mr. Collins for the first time
(C) Mr. Collins asked Elizabeth to marry him
(D) Mr. Collins gravely insulted Elizabeth
(E) Elizabeth discovered that Mr. Collins was a fraud

50. On the basis of his behavior in this passage, Mr. Collins may best be described as
(A) malicious in intent
(B) both obtuse and obstinate
(C) unsure of his acceptance
(D) kindly and understanding
(E) sensitive to Elizabeth's wishes

51. It can be inferred from the last paragraph that Mr. Collins
    (A) will take Elizabeth's words seriously
    (B) admires Elizabeth's independence
    (C) is very disappointed by her decision
    (D) would accept Lady Catherine's opinion
    (E) means his remarks as a joke

In "Pseudoscience and Society in Nineteenth-Century America," Arthur Wrobel remarks that belief in phrenology, homeopathy, and hydropathy was not confined to the poor and the ignorant, but pervaded much of 19th-century literature. Such credulity is not as extensive in contemporary literature, but astrology is one pseudoscience that does seem to engage a big segment of the reading public. Literary allusions to it abound, appearing in everything from Shakespeare to Don DeLillo's "Libra." A 1986 Gallup poll showed that 52 percent of American teenagers subscribe to it, as does at least 50 percent of the nation's departing First Couple.

Given these figures, it may not be entirely inappropriate to note here that no mechanism through which the alleged zodiacal influences exert themselves has ever been specified by astrologers. Gravity certainly cannot account for these natal influences, since even the gravitational pull of the attending obstetrician is orders of magnitude greater than that of the relevant planet or planets. Nor is there any empirical evidence; top astrologers (as determined by their peers) have failed repeatedly to associate personality profiles with astrological data at a rate higher than that of chance. Neither of these fatal objections to astrology, of course, is likely to carry much weight with literate but innumerate people who don't estimate magnitudes or probabilities, or who are overimpressed by vague coincidences yet unmoved by overwhelming statistical evidence.

52. The author regards the lack of empirical evidence for astrology as
    (A) an oversight on the part of the astrologers
    (B) a strong argument against its validity
    (C) a flaw that will be corrected in time
    (D) the unfortunate result of too small a sampling
    (E) a major reason to keep searching for fresh data
53. The author's attitude toward astrology can best be described as one of
    (A) grudging respect (B) amused tolerance
    (C) open disdain (D) disguised hostility
    (E) puzzled fascination
54. The term "innumerate" (last sentence) is best interpreted to mean which of the following?
    (A) various in kind
    (B) too numerous to count
    (C) scientifically sophisticated
    (D) unable to use mathematics
    (E) indifferent to astrology
55. The author cites the abundance of literary allusions to astrology primarily in order to
    (A) argue for its acceptance
    (B) refute its scientific validity
    (C) establish its pervasiveness
    (D) contrast it with the pseudosciences
    (E) explain the mechanisms by which it works

During the decade of 1880–1890 it was becoming increasingly evident that the factors which had brought about the existence of two separate suffrage institutions were steadily diminishing in importance.

The National Woman Suffrage Association had been launched by the intellectually irrepressible Elizabeth Cady Stanton and the ever catholic Susan B. Anthony. Both were ready to work with anyone, whatever their views on other matters, as long as they wholeheartedly espoused woman suffrage. Consequently in its earlier years the National was both aggressive and unorthodox. It damned both Republicans and Democrats who brushed the suffrage question aside. It was willing to take up the cudgels for distressed women whatever their circumstances, be they "fallen women," divorce cases, or underpaid seamstresses.

The American Woman Suffrage Association, by contrast, took its tone and outlook from a New England which had turned its back on those fiery days when abolitionists, men and women alike, had stood up to angry mobs. Its advocacy of worthy causes was highly selective. Lucy Stone was not interested in trade unionism and wished to keep the suffrage cause untarnished by concern with divorce or "the social evil." The very epitome of the American's attitude was its most distinguished convert and leader, Julia Ward Howe—erudite, honored lay preacher, the revered author of "The Battle Hymn of the Republic," who cast a highly desirable aura of prestige and propriety over the women's cause.

It was not that Mrs. Howe in herself made suffrage respectable; she was a symbol of the forces that were drawing the suffrage movement into the camp of decorum. American society was becoming rapidly polarized. The middle class was learning to identify organized labor with social turmoil. A succession of strikes during the depression of 1873–1878, in textiles, mining, and railroads, culminated in the Great Railroad Strike of 1877 involving nearly 100,000 workers from the Atlantic coast to the Mississippi valley; they did not help to reassure women taught by press and pulpit to identify any type of militancy with radicalism. Nor was this trend allayed by the hysteria whipped up over the Molly Maguire trials for secret conspiracy among Pennsylvania coal miners, or the alleged communistic influences at work in such growing organizations as the Knights of Labor and the A.F. of L. The existence of a small number of socialists was used to smear all organized labor with the taint of "anarchism." The crowning touch took place during the widespread agitation for an eight-hour day in 1886 when a bomb, thrown by a hand unknown to this day into a radical meeting in Chicago's Haymarket Square, touched off a nation-wide wave of panic.

The steady trend of the suffrage movement toward the conservative and the conventional during the last twenty years of the nineteenth century must be viewed in this setting, in order to avoid the misconception that a few conservative women took it over, through their own superior ability and the passivity of the former militants. Even the latter were changing their views, judging by their actions. It was one thing to challenge the proprieties at the Centennial of 1876; ten years later it would have been inconceivable even to the women who took part in the demonstration. Susan Anthony herself would have thought twice about flouting Federal election laws and going to jail in an era which witnessed the Haymarket hysteria.

56. The author's primary purpose in the passage is to
(A) contrast Susan B. Anthony with Julia Ward Howe
(B) recount the advances in the suffrage movement from 1880 to 1890
(C) account for the changes occurring in the suffrage movement from 1880 to 1890
(D) explain the growing divisions within the women's movement
(E) point out aspects of the suffrage movement which exist in contemporary feminism

57. The passage singles out Julia Ward Howe as an example of
(A) a venerated figurehead
(B) an overzealous advocate
(C) a heterodox thinker (D) an ordained cleric
(E) a militant activist

58. The author's attitude toward the public reaction to the Molly Maguire trials is that the reaction was
(A) appropriate (B) disorganized
(C) overwrought (D) necessary (E) understated

59. The author stresses the growing antiradical bias of the American middle class during the decade 1880–1890 in order to
(A) question a trend that proved destructive to the suffrage movement
(B) explain the unexpected emergence of an able body of radical leaders
(C) refute the contention that Anthony was unchanged by her experiences
(D) correct a misapprehension about changes in the suffrage movement
(E) excuse the growing lack of militancy on the part of the National

60. The passage suggests that, by 1890, attempts to effect woman suffrage by violating the proprieties and defying Federal laws would probably have been viewed even by movement members with
(A) indifference (B) defiance
(C) disapprobation (D) respect (E) optimism

The African elephant—mythic symbol of a continent, keystone of its ecology and the largest land animal remaining on earth—has become the object of one of the biggest, broadest international efforts yet mounted to turn a threatened species off the road to extinction. But it is not only the elephant's survival that is at stake, conservationists say. Unlike the endangered tiger, unlike even the great whales, the African elephant is in great measure the architect of its environment. As a voracious eater of vegetation, it largely shapes the forest-and-savanna surroundings in which it lives, thereby setting the terms of existence for millions of other storied animals—from zebras to gazelles to giraffes and wildebeests—that share its habitat. And as the elephant disappears, scientists and conservationists say, many other species will also disappear from vast stretches of forest and savanna, drastically altering and impoverishing whole ecosystems.

It is the elephant's metabolism and appetite that make it a disturber of the environment and therefore an important creator of habitat. In a constant search for the 300 pounds of vegetation it must have every day, it kills small trees and underbrush and pulls branches off big trees as high as its trunk will reach. This creates innumerable open spaces in both deep tropical forests and in the woodlands that cover part of the African savannas. The resulting patchwork, a mosaic of vegetation in various stages of regeneration, in turn creates a greater variety of forage that attracts a greater variety of other vegetation-eaters than would otherwise be the case.

In studies over the last 20 years in southern Kenya near Mount Kilimanjaro, Dr. David Western has found that when elephants are allowed to roam the savannas naturally and normally, they spread out at "intermediate densities." Their foraging creates a mixture of savanna woodlands (what the Africans call bush) and grassland. The result is a highly diverse array of other plant-eating species: those like the zebra, wildebeest and gazelle, that graze; those like the giraffe, bushbuck and lesser kudu, that browse on tender shoots, buds, twigs and leaves; and plant-eating primates like the baboon and vervet monkey. These herbivores attract carnivores like the lion and cheetah.

When the elephant population thins out, Dr. Western said, the woodlands become denser and the grazers are squeezed out. When pressure from poachers forces elephants to crowd more densely onto reservations, the woodlands there are knocked out and the browsers and primates disappear.

Something similar appears to happen in dense tropical rain forests. In their natural state, because the overhead forest canopy shuts out sunlight and prevents growth on the forest floor, rain forests provide slim pickings for large, hoofed plant-eaters. By pulling down trees and eating new growth, elephants enlarge natural openings in the canopy, allowing plants to regenerate on the forest floor and bringing down vegetation from the canopy so that smaller species can get at it.

In such situations, the rain forest becomes hospitable to large plant-eating mammals such as bongos, bush pigs, duikers, forest hogs, swamp antelopes, forest buffaloes, okapis, sometimes gorillas and always a host of smaller animals that thrive on secondary growth. When elephants disappear and the forest reverts, the larger animals give way to smaller, nimbler animals like monkeys, squirrels and rodents.

61. The passage is primarily concerned with

(A) explaining why elephants are facing the threat of extinction
(B) explaining difficulties in providing sufficient forage for plant-eaters
(C) explaining how the elephant's impact on its surroundings affects other species
(D) distinguishing between savannas and rain forests as habitats for elephants
(E) contrasting elephants with members of other endangered species

62. A necessary component of the elephant's ability to transform the landscape is its

(A) massive intelligence (B) threatened extinction
(C) ravenous hunger (D) lack of grace
(E) ability to regenerate

63. It can be inferred from the passage that

(A) the lion and the cheetah commonly prey upon elephants
(B) the elephant is dependent upon the existence of smaller plant-eating mammals for its survival
(C) elephants have an indirect effect on the hunting patterns of certain carnivores
(D) the floor of the tropical rain forest is too overgrown to accommodate larger plant-eating species
(E) the natural tendency of elephants is to crowd together in packs

64. The passage contains information that would answer which of the following questions?

I. How does the elephant's foraging affect its surroundings?
II. How do the feeding patterns of gazelles and giraffes differ?
III. What occurs in the rain forest when the elephant population dwindles?

(A) I only
(B) II only
(C) I and II only
(D) II and III only
(E) I, II, and III

65. Which of the following statements best expresses the author's attitude toward the damage to vegetation caused by foraging elephants?

(A) It is a regrettable by-product of the feeding process.
(B) It is a necessary but undesirable aspect of elephant population growth.
(C) It fortuitously results in creating environments suited to diverse species.
(D) It has the unexpected advantage that it allows scientists access to the rain forest.
(E) It reinforces the impression that elephants are a disruptive force.

SECTION **2** **Time—50 minutes 50 Questions**

In this section solve each problem, using any available space on the page for scratchwork. Then decide which is the best of the choices given and fill in the corresponding circle on the answer sheet.

The following information is for your reference in solving some of the problems.

Circle of radius r: Area $= \pi r^2$ Circumference $= 2\pi r$
The number of degrees of arc in a circle is 360.
The measure in degrees of a straight angle is 180.

Definitions of symbols:
- $=$ is equal to
- $\neq$ is unequal to
- $<$ is less than
- $>$ is greater than
- $\leqq$ is less than or equal to
- $\geqq$ is greater than or equal to
- $\parallel$ is parallel to
- $\perp$ is perpendicular to

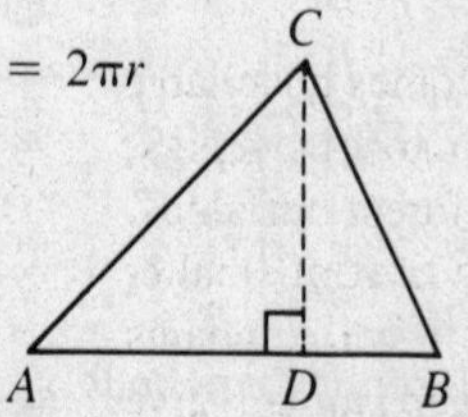

Triangle: The sum of the measures in degrees of the angles of a triangle is 180.

If $\angle CDA$ is a right angle, then

(1) area of $\triangle ABC = \dfrac{AB \times CD}{2}$

(2) $AC^2 = AD^2 + DC^2$

Note: Figures that accompany problems in this test are intended to provide information useful in solving the problems. They are drawn as accurately as possible EXCEPT when it is stated in a specific problem that its figure is not drawn to scale. All figures lie in a plane unless otherwise indicated. All numbers used are real numbers.

1. $\left(\frac{4}{5} \div \frac{4}{5}\right) - \left(\frac{5}{6} \div \frac{5}{6}\right) =$
(A) -2 (B) -1 (C) 0 (D) 1 (E) 2

2. For which of the following value(s) of x is it possible to obtain a value for $\dfrac{x}{3x-5}$?

I. $\frac{1}{2}$
II. 0
III. $-\frac{5}{3}$

(A) I only (B) II only (C) III only
(D) I and II only (E) I, II, and III

3. How many square units are there in the area of square $ABCD$ with coordinates as follows: $A(-4,4)$ $B(4,4)$ $C(4,-4)$ $D(-4,-4)$?
(A) 12 (B) 16 (C) 32 (D) 64 (E) 100

4. If $\textcircled{x}$ is defined by the equation $\textcircled{x} = \dfrac{\sqrt{x}}{2}$ then $\textcircled{100}$ equals
(A) 5 (B) 10 (C) 20 (D) 25 (E) 50

5. Which of the following has the largest numerical value?
(A) $\frac{8}{0.8}$ (B) $\frac{0.8}{8}$ (C) $(0.8)^2$ (D) $\sqrt{0.8}$
(E) 0.8π

6. The number of washers $\frac{3}{32}$ inch thick that can be cut from a piece of stock $25\frac{1}{2}$ inches long, allowing $\frac{1}{16}$ inch for waste for each cut is
(A) 160 (B) 163 (C) 260 (D) 272
(E) 408

7. Mr. Grey left $\frac{1}{3}$ of his property to his wife and the remainder to be divided equally between his two children. If each child received \$10,000, then the wife received
(A) \$3333.33 (B) \$5000.00 (C) \$6666.67
(D) \$10,000.00 (E) \$20,000.00

8. Each of the following sets of three numbers could represent the lengths of the sides of a triangle EXCEPT
(A) 9, 11, 14 (B) 5, 5, 8 (C) 8, 17, 8
(D) 3, 4, 6 (E) 3, 2, 2

9. There are 216 couples competing in a dance contest. After each half hour one-third of the contestants are eliminated. How many couples will remain eligible for the prize after the first hour?
(A) 24 (B) 46 (C) 48 (D) 96 (E) 98

10. B equals 30% of
(A) $30B$ (B) $\dfrac{B}{30}$ (C) $\dfrac{30}{B}$ (D) $\dfrac{3B}{10}$ (E) $\dfrac{10B}{3}$

11. By how much is $\frac{3}{4}$ larger than 20% of 2?
(A) $\frac{1}{35}$ (B) $\frac{1}{7}$ (C) $\frac{4}{7}$ (D) $3\frac{3}{7}$ (E) $3\frac{4}{7}$

12. The drawing below represents 3 stacks of playing cards, each with 6 cards. What is the least number of cards that must be moved in order to have a ratio of 1:2:3 for the distribution of these cards in the stacks?
(A) 2 (B) 3 (C) 4 (D) 5 (E) 6

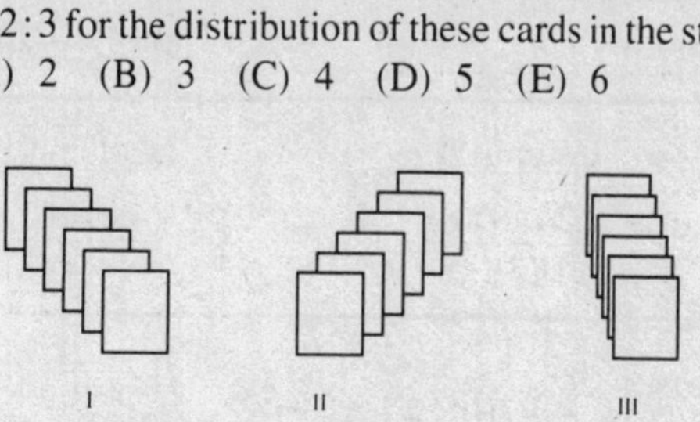

13. If 8 men can do a job in 12 days, what is the percentage increase in number of days required to do the job when 2 men are released?
(A) $16\frac{2}{3}\%$ (B) 25% (C) $33\frac{1}{3}\%$ (D) 40%
(E) 48%

14. In a class of c pupils there are b boys. The ratio of girls to boys is:
(A) $c:b$ (B) $b:c$ (C) $\frac{c-b}{b}$ (D) $\frac{b-c}{b}$
(E) $\frac{b-c}{c}$

15. If in the number 4315 the digits representing tens and thousands were interchanged, the value of the new number formed in relation to the original number would be
(A) unchanged (B) 280 more (C) 280 less
(D) 2970 more (E) 2970 less

<u>Questions 16-32</u> each consist of two quantities, one in Column A and one in Column B. You are to compare the two quantities and on the answer sheet fill in circle

A if the quantity in Column A is greater;
B if the quantity in Column B is greater;
C if the two quantities are equal;
D if the relationship cannot be determined from the information given.

Notes:
1. In certain questions, information concerning one or both of the quantities to be compared is centered above the two columns.
2. In a given question, a symbol that appears in both columns represents the same thing in Column A as it does in Column B.
3. Letters such as x, n, and k stand for real numbers.

EXAMPLES

	Column A	Column B	Answers
E1.	2×6	$2 + 6$	● Ⓑ Ⓒ Ⓓ
	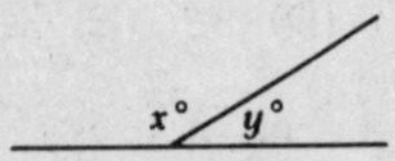		
E2.	$180 - x$	y	Ⓐ Ⓑ ● Ⓓ
E3.	$p - q$	$q - p$	Ⓐ Ⓑ Ⓒ ●

	Column A	Column B
16.	$\frac{(624)(9)(8)}{(4)(3)(2)}$	$\frac{(4)(9)(624)}{(5)(4)(3)}$
17.	$\frac{1}{\sqrt{81}}$	$\frac{1}{0.9}$
18.	$6R^6$	R^7

$x^2 + y^2 = 61$

19.	x	y

$2x + y = 1$

20.	y	$1 - 2x$

$x \neq 0$

21.	$\frac{\frac{x}{2}}{\frac{2}{x}}$	$\frac{x^2}{2}$

$25 < \sqrt{x} < 36$

22.	x	5
23.	$(x + y)(x - y)$	$x^2 - y^2$

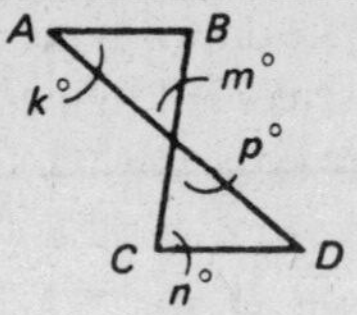

AB is parallel to CD and $p = 60$, $k = 40$.

24.	n	m

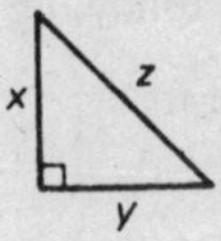

25.	x^2	$2^2 - y^2$

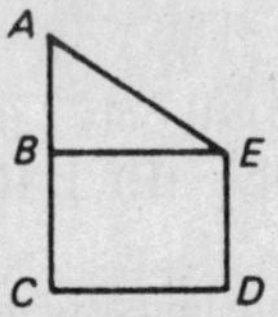

perimeter of square $BCDE = 40$
$AB = BC$

26.	Area of ABE	50

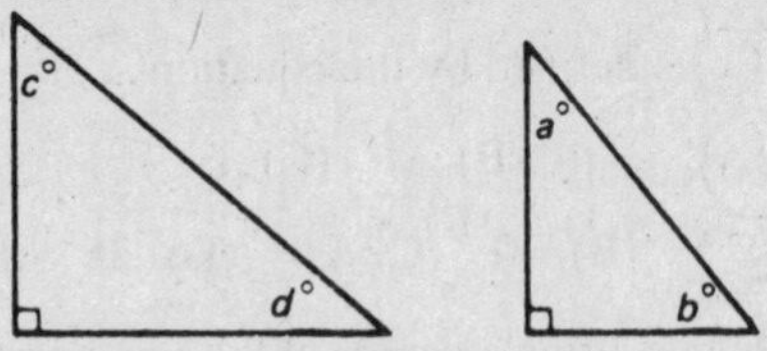

$a = 40$ and $c = 50$

27.	b	d

$ab = 5$
$a^2 + b^2 = 7$

28.	$(a + b)^2$	12

$z = 0$

29.	$\frac{(2x)(xz)}{x + y}$	zero

$x = \sqrt{9} + \sqrt{16}$

	Column A	Column B
30.	x	5

$60 + x = y - 40$

31.	The value of $x - y$	20
32.	The area of a square with a perimeter of 16 meters	The area of a rectangle with a perimeter of 16 meters

Solve each of the remaining problems in this section using any available space for scratchwork. Then decide which is the best of the choices given and fill in the corresponding circle on the answer sheet.

33. A certain ore, when refined, yields an average of $1\frac{1}{4}$ pounds of metal to the ton. The number of tons of ore that will be needed to yield 200 pounds of metal is
(A) 40 (B) 80 (C) 160 (D) 200 (E) 250

34. $x + 2y = 1\frac{1}{3}$
$+x - y = +\frac{1}{3}$
$3y =$
(A) 0 (B) $-\frac{1}{3}$ (C) $\frac{1}{3}$ (D) 1 (E) $1\frac{2}{3}$

35. The fraction $\frac{5Y3X}{2Y8}$, in which X and Y stand for two unknown digits, represents a division which results in a quotient that is a whole number. Which of the follwing is (are) true?
I. X may equal 2.
II. X may equal 6 or 0.
III. X may equal 4.
(A) I only (B) II only (C) III only
(D) I and II only (E) I, II, and III

36. $a - x = 1$
$b + 1 = x$
$ab =$
(A) $x^2 - 1$ (B) x^2 (C) $(x + 1)^2$
(D) $(x - 1)^2$ (E) $x^2 + 1$

37. To obtain a final average of 80% in a certain subject, what grade must a student earn in a test after having an average of 77.5% in four examinations?
(A) 85 (B) 87 (C) 89 (D) 90
(E) more than 90

38. When the radius of a circle is doubled, the area is multiplied by
(A) 2 (B) 2π (C) $2\pi r$ (D) 3.14 (E) 4

39. How many tiles (each one foot square) are necessary to form a one-foot border around the inside of a room which is 24 feet by 14 feet?
(A) 36 (B) 37 (C) 72 (D) 74 (E) 76

40. The area of a triangle whose legs are in the ratio of 2:3 is 48. The length of the hypotenuse is
(A) $\sqrt{13}$ (B) 8 (C) $4\sqrt{13}$ (D) 12
(E) 208

41. If the perimeter of a square is 16, then its area is
(A) 4 (B) 8 (C) 16 (D) 64 (E) 256

42. A picture frame is 1 foot long and 9 inches wide. How long will a larger picture frame of the same proportions be if it is 3 feet wide?
(A) 4 in. (B) 4 ft. (C) 12 ft. (D) 36 in.
(E) 36 ft.

43. A cow is attached to a rope in a pasture bordered by two fences (each 60 feet long) which meet at an angle of 24°. If the rope attached to the cow is 15 feet long, over how many square feet can the cow graze?

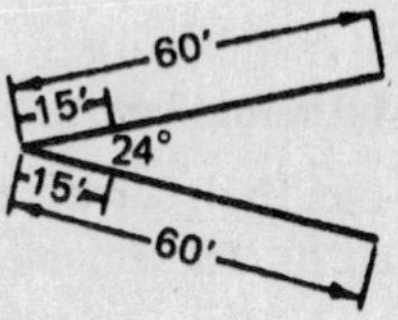

(A) 2π (B) 15π (C) 30π (D) 45π
(E) 240π

44. The area of a circle is 154. What is the diameter of the circle? $\left(\text{Use } \pi = \frac{22}{7}.\right)$
(A) 3.14 (B) 7 (C) 14 (D) 21 (E) 49

45. AOC is a diameter of circle O. Line $AB = 12$, $OA = 10$. Find the length of line BC.

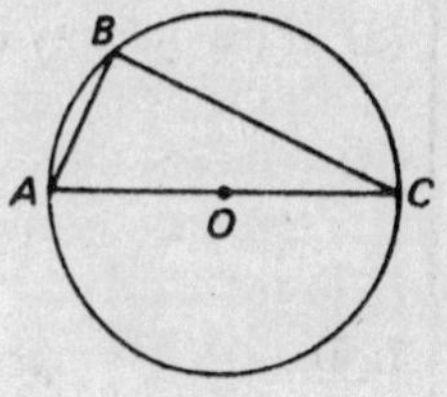

(A) 12 (B) 16 (C) 18
(D) 20 (E) 22

46. In $\triangle ABC$, $AD = DB = 2$, $BE = EC = 3$, $DE = 4$, $AC =$

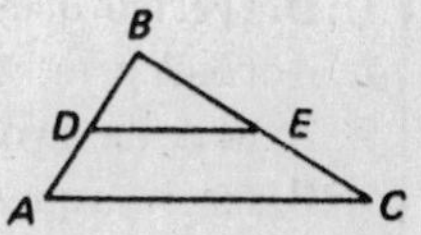

(A) 6 (B) 7 (C) 8
(D) 9 (E) 12

47. Find the vertex angle of an isosceles triangle if it exceeds each base angle by 30°.
(A) 50° (B) 70° (C) 75° (D) 80° (E) 105°

48. AB is parallel to CD. $EFGH$ is a straight line. If $\angle AFE$ is 4 times $\angle CGH$, what is the measure of $\angle HGD$?

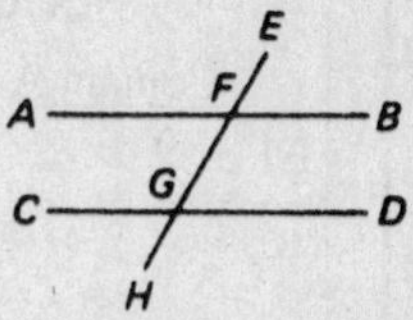

(A) 36 (B) 120 (C) 135
(D) 144 (E) 160

49. $AB \parallel CD$. $AB = 32$, $BC = 10$, $CD = 20$, $AD = 10$. The area of $ABCD$ is

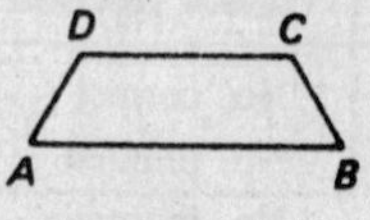

(A) 72 (B) 112 (C) 128
(D) 208 (E) 256

50. Lines ABC and EDC meet at an angle of 30°. $BF = DF$, $AF = FE$. $\angle EDF \overset{\circ}{=} 80$. What is the measure of $\angle BFD$?

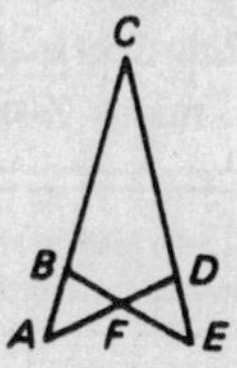

(A) 80° (B) 100°
(C) 130° (D) 150°
(E) 160°

ANSWER KEY

Verbal Aptitude Section

1. **A**	11. **A**	21. **D**	31. **B**	41. **D**	51. **D**	61. **C**
2. **D**	12. **A**	22. **E**	32. **B**	42. **E**	52. **B**	62. **C**
3. **C**	13. **A**	23. **B**	33. **E**	43. **A**	53. **C**	63. **C**
4. **C**	14. **A**	24. **D**	34. **D**	44. **E**	54. **D**	64. **E**
5. **A**	15. **B**	25. **C**	35. **D**	45. **D**	55. **C**	65. **C**
6. **B**	16. **B**	26. **A**	36. **C**	46. **D**	56. **C**	
7. **A**	17. **A**	27. **B**	37. **E**	47. **E**	57. **A**	
8. **B**	18. **C**	28. **C**	38. **C**	48. **D**	58. **C**	
9. **C**	19. **E**	29. **B**	39. **D**	49. **C**	59. **D**	
10. **D**	20. **C**	30. **E**	40. **D**	50. **B**	60. **C**	

Mathematical Aptitude Section

Note: Each correct answer to the mathematics questions is keyed by number to the corresponding topic in Chapters 9 and 10. These numerals refer to the topics listed below, with specific page references in parentheses.

1. Basic Fundamental Operations (155–157)
2. Algebraic Operations (157–160)
3. Using Algebra (160–164)
4. Exponents, Roots and Radicals (159–160)
5. Inequalities (164–165)
6. Fractions (176–178)
7. Decimals (176)
8. Percent (178–180)
9. Averages (180–181)
10. Motion (182–183)
11. Ratio and Proportion (183–185)
12. Mixtures and Solutions (177–178)
13. Work (185–186)
14. Coordinate Geometry (172–173)
15. Geometry (165–172, 173–176)
16. Quantitative Comparisons (189–192)

ANSWER KEY

1. **C** (6)	11. **A** (6,8)	21. **B** (2,6,16)	31. **B** (2,16)	41. **C** (15)
2. **D** (2)	12. **B** (11)	22. **A** (4,16)	32. **D** (15,16)	42. **B** (15)
3. **D** (14,15)	13. **C** (8,11,13)	23. **C** (2,16)	33. **C** (11)	43. **B** (15)
4. **A** (2,4)	14. **C** (11)	24. **A** (15,16)	34. **D** (2)	44. **C** (15)
5. **A** (4,6,7)	15. **E** (1)	25. **C** (15,16)	35. **E** (1)	45. **B** (15)
6. **B** (1)	16. **A** (1,16)	26. **C** (15,16)	36. **A** (2)	46. **C** (15)
7. **D** (6)	17. **B** (4,6,7,16)	27. **A** (15,16)	37. **D** (8)	47. **D** (15)
8. **C** (15)	18. **D** (4,16)	28. **A** (2,16)	38. **E** (15)	48. **D** (15)
9. **D** (6)	19. **D** (2,16)	29. **C** (2,16)	39. **C** (15)	49. **D** (15)
10. **E** (3,8)	20. **C** (2,16)	30. **A** (4,16)	40. **C** (15)	50. **C** (15)

SCORING CHART TYPICAL TEST E

Verbal Section		**Mathematical Section***		
No. correct	_____	No. correct	(A)	_____
No. omitted	_____	No. incorrect (# 1-15, 33-50)	(B)	_____
No. incorrect	_____	No. incorrect (# 16-32)	(C)	_____
¼ no. incorrect	_____	¼ (B) + 1/3 (C)	(D)	_____
Raw Score: (no. correct minus ¼ no. incorrect)	_____	*Raw Score* = (A) − (D)		_____

* (In the Mathematical section, deduct ¼ of a point for each five-choice question answered incorrectly and 1/3 of a point for each four-choice question answered incorrectly.)

EVALUATION CHART

Study your score. Your raw score on the Verbal and Mathematical Aptitude Sections is an indication of your probable achievement on the PSAT/NMSQT. As a guide to the amount of work you need or want to do, study the following.

Raw Score: *Verbal*	Raw Score: *Mathematical*	Self-rating
58-65	41-50	Superior
46-57	25-40	Very good
40-45	20-24	Satisfactory
36-39	16-19	Average
30-35	10-15	Needs further study
20-29	7-9	Needs intensive study
0-19	0-6	Probably inadequate

Your scores are most likely improving with each test that you take. To help pinpoint any weak areas you still may have, consult the table on page 383 and plan your remaining review accordingly.

ANSWER EXPLANATIONS

Verbal Aptitude Section

1. **A** The opposite of to *fluster* or discompose is to *soothe*.
Think of "being flustered by reporters' questions."
2. **D** The opposite of to *deteriorate* or become worse is to *improve*.
Think of "deteriorating highways crumbling."
3. **C** The opposite of *scrawny* or skinny is *plump*.
Think of "scrawny, undernourished children."
4. **C** The opposite of to *overrule* or rule against is to *decide in favor*.
Think of "Objection overruled!"
5. **A** The opposite of *wily* (deceitful, tricky) is *straightforward*.
Think of "Wily Coyote."
6. **B** The opposite of *flippancy* or lightness of manner is *seriousness*.
Think of "inappropriate flippancy."
7. **A** The opposite of *diffidence* (shyness, timidity) is *boldness*.
Think of "the diffidence of a new student in school."
8. **B** The opposite of *turbulent* or stormy is *placid* or calm.
Think of "turbulent weather."
9. **C** The opposite of to *hamper* (impede or hinder) is to *facilitate* (make easy).
Think of "hampering progress."
10. **D** *Adulterated* (made impure) is the opposite of *pure*.
Think of "adulterated food."
11. **A** To *distend* (enlarge, as by swelling) is the opposite of to *deflate*.
Word Parts Clue: *Tend-* means stretch; *dis-* means apart. Something distended is enlarged by being stretched apart.
Think of "a distended stomach."
12. **A** *Transient* (fleeting, temporary) is the opposite of *permanent*.
Think of "transient youth."
13. **A** The opposite of *elated* (overjoyed) is *downcast* or gloomy.
Think of "elated by success."
14. **A** The opposite of *prosaic* (dull, matter-of-fact) is *imaginative*.
Think of "being bored by a commonplace, prosaic job."
15. **B** The opposite of *dissonance* or discord is *harmony*.
Word Parts Clue: *Dis-* means apart; *son-* means sound. *Dissonance* is the state of sounding apart, that is, not in harmony.
Think of "jarring dissonance."
16. **B** The opposite of to *disparage* or belittle is to *eulogize* or praise.
Think of "rival candidates disparaging each other."
17. **A** The opposite of *felicitous* (happily suited to a situation; appropriate) is *inappropriate*.
Think of a "felicitous remark."
18. **C** The opposite of *doltish* or stupid is *clever*.
Think of a "doltish blockhead."

19. **E** The opposite of to *chagrin* (vex; disappoint) is to *please*. Beware of eye-catchers: Choice **A** is incorrect. *Chagrin* is unrelated to *grin*.
Think of "being chagrined by a defeat."

20. **C** The opposite of *acrimony* or bitterness is *affability* or agreeableness.
Think of "bitter acrimony."

21. **D** Such an extraordinarily useful material would *revolutionize* or make radical changes in an industry.

22. **E** To make the correct decisions, the lawmakers must be able to *discern* or recognize the truth.

23. **B** There is a chance that *serious* women may not be attracted by an inappropriate *frivolity* or lightheartedness in style—hence the gamble.

24. **D** If irony is a mode of escape, then the ironic person is *evading* or escaping life's terrors.

25. **C** A contrast is set up here by the expression "no matter how." It tells us that, although future "revelations" (surprising news) may be *striking*, they will not equal past ones. These past revelations *radically* transformed or thoroughly changed our view.

26. **A** Since "few other plants can grow beneath the canopy of the sycamore," it must be *inhibiting* or restraining the other plants.

27. **B** Certain authors have been *relegated* or sent off to "obscurity," a state of being hidden or forgotten. Therefore they must be "rediscovered."

28. **C** Judges are not supposed to *influence* juries. The phrase "even when" signals a contrast: even when judges don't actually say injurious or *prejudicial* things, they may still affect the jury through their tone of voice.

29. **B** The phrase "not even" signals the contrast between the subject's "opulence" or wealth and her dissatisfaction with what she owned, her "material possessions." Not even all these possessions seemed *adequate to* the *fervor* (great intensity of feeling) of her ambition, her great desire to own even more.

30. **E** Critics sometimes praise, but more often *decry* or condemn things. Here the critics see the "saccharine" (too sweet) mood of the movie as inconsistent with the *acerbic* (sour, bitter) tone of the book.

31. **B** A *pebble* is shot from a *slingshot;* a *ball* is shot from a *cannon*.

(Function)

32. **B** A *latch* is the part of the *door* that closes it; a *clasp* is the part of the *necklace* that closes it.

(Function)

33. **E** To *drizzle* or rain lightly is less intense than to *pour;* to *smolder* or barely burn is less intense than to *blaze*.

(Degree of Intensity)

34. **D** A *caption* is a heading for a *photograph;* a *title* is a heading for an *article*.

(Function)

35. **D** To *eradicate* an *error* is to wipe it out or eliminate it; to *uproot* a *weed* is to pull it out or eliminate it.

(Purpose)

36. **C** A *tyrannosaur* is a kind of *dinosaur;* a *condor* is a kind of *bird*.

(Class and Member)

37. **E** A *gander* is a male *goose;* a *ram* is a male *sheep*.

(Sex)

38. **C** One *establishes* a *tempo* to arrange the speed at which music is played. One *sets* a *pace* to arrange the speed at which a race is run.

(Purpose)

39. **D** An *author* who is *prolific* (highly productive) by definition writes a lot; a *speaker* who is *loquacious* (talkative) by definition talks a lot.

(Defining Characteristic)

40. **D** *Locomotion* is a function of the *feet; digestion* is a function of the *stomach*.

(Function)

41. **D** A *mentor*, by definition, aims to assist a *protégé;* a *sponsor*, by definition, aims to assist a *candidate*.

(Function)

42. **E** Something *garbled* or confused is difficult to *comprehend;* something *camouflaged* or hidden is difficult to *discern* or perceive.

(Antonym Variant)

43. **A** A *traveler* follows an *itinerary* or plan of his journey; a *lecturer* follows an *outline* or plan of his lecture.

(Worker and Tool)

44. **E** A *purist* is concerned with strict *correctness;* a *martinet* is concerned with strict *discipline*.

(Defining Characteristic)

45. **D** To *browse* or read in a leisurely manner is less intense than to *peruse* or read carefully; to *stroll* or walk in a leisurely manner is less intense than to *march*.

(Degree of Intensity)

46. **D** This question may be answered by elimination.
Statement I is supported by the passage. Emerson believed in "the right and duty of each man to be self-sufficient." Therefore Choice **B** may be eliminated.
Statement II is not supported by the passage. Emerson "raised his voice in protest *against* the coming industrialism." Therefore Choices **C** and **E** may be eliminated.
Statement III is supported by the passage. Emerson "condemned slavery," so he supported the emancipation of the slaves. Therefore we may eliminate Choice **A**.
This leaves Choice **D**. It is the correct answer.

47. E Emerson believed that a person should "follow the dictates of his conscience," and be "independent" or nonconformist.
Choice **A** is incorrect. According to the passage, specialization, a by-product of industrialization, prevents human beings from developing their capacities. Choice **B** is incorrect. Emerson believed that freedom of thought and action is essential to individual independence and dignity. Choice **C** is incorrect. Emerson "had respect for the common man," rather than the intellectual aristocracy. Choice **D** is incorrect. The author of the passage, not Emerson, says that philosophers are of value to society, along with captains of industry. It's not clear from the passage how Emerson himself felt about the matter.

48. D The author states that Emerson's pleas for freedom of thought "have as much ringing force today as they did a century ago."

49. C Among other clues, Mr. Collins states that he hopes to lead Elizabeth "to the altar ere long."

50. B *Obtuse* means thick-headed and *obstinate* means stubborn. Both apply to Mr. Collins, who can't seem to understand that Elizabeth is telling him "no."

51. D Mr. Collins breaks off in the middle of a sentence which begins: "Were it certain that Lady Catherine would think so —." He then finishes it awkwardly by saying, "but I cannot imagine that her ladyship would at all disapprove of you." By implication, his unspoken thought was that, if Lady Catherine *didn't* approve of Elizabeth, then Mr. Collins wouldn't want to marry her after all.

52. B The final sentence characterizes these absences of empirical evidence as "fatal objections to astrology." In general, the author sees it as invalid, a "pseudoscience," not a real science.

53. C The author's tone is frequently sarcastic. He states that people who believe in astrology are "overimpressed by vague coincidences." Therefore, his attitude is one of *disdain* or contempt.

54. D The author contrasts the word "innumerate" with the word "literate." Since *illiterate* means unable to read, *innumerate* must mean unable to use mathematics.
Word Parts Clue: *In-* means not; *numer-* means number. *Innumerate* means not having numbers, unable to use numbers. *Innumerable*, on the other hand, means uncountable, too many to be counted.

55. C The author comments that belief in pseudosciences was more pervasive last century than it is in this one; however, "astrology is one pseudoscience that does seem to engage a big segment of the reading public." In support of this, he continues: "Literary allusions to it abound."

56. C The passage points out that in this period the differences between the two branches of the suffrage movement were diminishing in importance. Thus, it is *accounting for changes* occurring in the movement.
Choice **A** is incorrect. Both women are mentioned (along with other suffragist leaders) in the context of the movements they led; but while the movements are directly contrasted, Anthony and Howe are not. Choice **B** is incorrect. The movement did not advance in this period. Choice **D** is incorrect. The divisions were becoming less important, not more so, as the two branches became increasingly alike in nature. Choice **E** is incorrect. It is unsupported by the passage.

57. A The reverend Mrs. Howe stood for the forces of propriety that were engulfing the suffragist movement. The embodiment of decorum, she was a *venerated figurehead* to be admired and respected, not a revolutionary firebrand to be followed into battle.
Choice **B** is incorrect. Nothing in the passage suggests Mrs. Howe was overzealous. Choice **C** is incorrect. Mrs. Howe was orthodox (conventional in opinions) in her thinking, not heterodox (unconventional in opinions). Choice **D** is incorrect. A lay preacher is by definition not a member of the clergy. Therefore, Mrs. Howe was not an ordained cleric. Choice **E** is incorrect. Mrs. Howe was characterized by a lack of militancy.

58. C The author refers to the public's reaction to the Molly Maguire trials as "hysteria" that was "whipped up" or deliberately incited. Clearly, her attitude toward it is that it was *overwrought* or overexcited. Note how the use of words that convey emotion ("hysteria") helps you to determine the author's attitude to the subject.

59. D The first sentence of the final paragraph indicates that the author's concern is to avoid a misconception or *correct a misapprehension* about what caused the trend toward conservatism in the suffrage movement.

60. C If even the radical Susan B. Anthony would have had second thoughts about flouting or disregarding Federal election laws, we may logically infer that the ordinary, not quite so militant movement member would have viewed such actions with disapproval or *disapprobation*.

61. C The author's emphasis is on the elephant as an important "creator of habitat" for other creatures.

62. C The author states that it is the elephant's metabolism and appetite—in other words, its voracity or *ravenous hunger*—that leads to its creating open spaces in the woodland and transforming the landscape.

63. **C** Since the foraging of elephants creates a varied landscape that attracts a diverse group of plant-eating animals, and since the presence of these plant-eaters in turn attracts carnivores, it follows that elephants *have an indirect effect on the hunting patterns of carnivores*.

64. **E** You can arrive at the correct choice through the process of elimination.
Question I is answerable on the basis of the passage. The elephant's foraging opens up its surroundings by knocking down trees and stripping off branches. Therefore, you can eliminate Choices **B** and **D.**
Question II is answerable on the basis of the passage. Gazelles are grazers; giraffes are browsers. Therefore, you can eliminate Choice **A.**
Question III is answerable on the basis of the passage. The concluding sentence states that when elephants disappear the forest reverts. Therefore, you can eliminate Choice **C.**
Only Choice **E** is left. It is the correct answer.

65. **C** The author believes that elephants have a fortuitously favorable effect on the environment in that their foraging allows a greater variety of creatures to exist in mixed-growth habitats.

Mathematical Aptitude Section

1. **C** $\left(\frac{4}{5} \div \frac{4}{5}\right) = \left(\frac{\cancel{4}}{\cancel{5}} \cdot \frac{\cancel{5}}{\cancel{4}}\right) = 1$

$\frac{5}{6} \div \frac{5}{6} = 1$

$1 - 1 = 0$

2. **D** Since division by 0 is undefined, no value can be obtained if the denominator of the fraction is 0. This occurs if $x = -\frac{5}{3}$. Therefore III cannot be used for x. I and II can; notice that, when $x = 0$, the fraction has a value: 0.

3. **D** Observe the diagram. Each side equals 8 units. The area equals 64 square units.

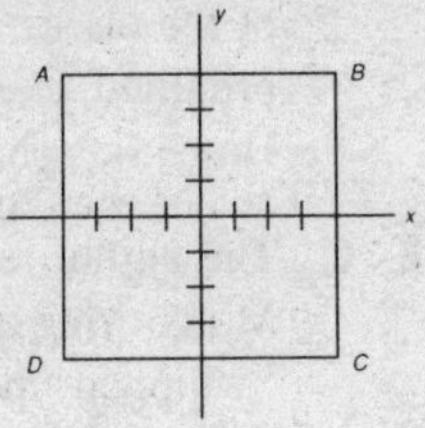

4. **A** $\textcircled{100} = \frac{\sqrt{100}}{2} = \frac{10}{2} = 5$

5. **A** $\frac{8}{0.8} = \frac{80}{8} = 10$

$\frac{0.8}{8} = \frac{8}{80} = \frac{1}{10}$

$(0.8)^2 = .64$

$\sqrt{0.8} = 0.89$

$0.8\pi = (0.8)(3.14) = 2.5+$

6. **B** Each washer consumes $\left(\frac{3}{32} + \frac{1}{16}\right)$ inch or $\frac{5}{32}$.

$25\frac{1}{2}$ inches $\div \frac{5}{32} =$ number of washers that can be cut

$\frac{51}{2} \div \frac{5}{32}$

$\frac{51}{\cancel{2}} \cdot \frac{\cancel{32}^{16}}{5} = \frac{816}{5} = 163\frac{1}{5} = 163$ washers

7. **D** Since $\frac{2}{3}$ was left for the two children and each received $\frac{1}{2}$ of $\frac{2}{3}$, each child received $\frac{1}{3}$. If $\frac{1}{3} =$ \$10,000, the wife also received \$10,000.

8. **C** The sum of two sides of a triangle must be greater than the third side. In **(C)**, $8 + 8 < 17$.

9. **D** At the end of the first half-hour, $\frac{1}{3}$ of 216 or 72 were eliminated, leaving 144 couples. During the second half-hour, $\frac{1}{3}$ of 144 or 48 were eliminated, leaving 96 couples.

10. **E** Let $x =$ quantity desired.

$B = (30\%)(x)$

$B = \frac{30}{100}x$ or $\frac{3}{10}x$

$\left(\frac{10}{3}\right)B = \frac{\cancel{3}}{\cancel{10}}x\left(\frac{\cancel{10}}{\cancel{3}}\right)$

$\frac{10B}{3} = x$

11. **A** 20% or $\left(\frac{1}{5}\right)$ of $2 = \frac{2}{5}$

$\frac{3}{7} - \frac{2}{5}$

$\frac{15}{35} - \frac{14}{35} = \frac{1}{35}$

12. **B** A distribution of 3 cards in I, 6 in II, and 9 in III will give a 1:2:3 ratio. Therefore, move 3 cards from stack I to stack III.

13. **C** This is an inverse proportion. Let $x =$ time required when 2 of 8 men are released.

$\frac{8 \text{ men}}{6 \text{ men}} = \frac{x}{12 \text{ days}}$

$6x = 96$

$x = 16$ days

Increase in time = 4 days

$\frac{\text{increase}}{\text{original}} = \frac{4}{12} = \frac{1}{3} = 33\frac{1}{3}\%$

14. **C** Number of girls $= c - b$

Ratio of girls to boys $= \frac{c - b}{b}$

15. **E** The new number would be 1345.
$4315 - 1345 = 2970$

16. **A** $\frac{(624)(9)(8)}{(4)(3)(2)}$ (cancelled; 2 written above the 8) $\frac{(4)(9)(642)}{(5)(4)(2)}$
$1 > \frac{1}{5}$

17. **B** $\frac{1}{\sqrt{81}} = \frac{1}{9}$
$\frac{1}{9} < \frac{1}{0.9}$ since the fraction with the greater denominator is smaller if the numerators are the same.

18. **D** If $R = 6$, $6R^6 = R^7$ but if R is negative, R^7 is negative and $6R^6$ is positive.

19. **D** $x^2 + y^2 = 61$
x and/or y may be negative, positive, or equal to zero.

20. **C** If $2x + y = 1$, then
$y = 1 - 2x$.

21. **B** $\frac{x}{2} \div \frac{2}{x}$ or $\frac{x}{2} \cdot \frac{x}{2} = \frac{x^2}{4}$
$\frac{x^2}{2} > \frac{x^2}{4}$ since x^2 must be positive.

22. **A** $\sqrt{x} > 25$; therefore $x > 5$.

23. **C** Factor $x^2 - y^2$: $(x + y)(x - y)$.

24. **A** Since AB is parallel to CD and $p = m$ [vertical angles] and $p = 60$, $m = 60$. Since $k = 40$, $x = 80$. Since $x = n$ [alternate interior angles of parallel lines], $n = 80$ and $n > m$.

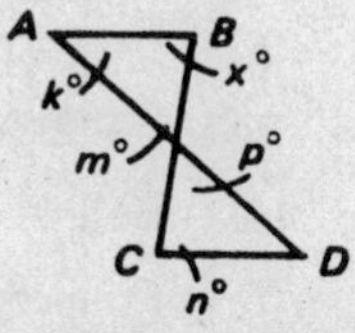

25. **C** Applying the Pythagorean Theorem, $x^2 + y^2 = z^2$
By subtraction,
$x^2 = z^2 - y^2$.

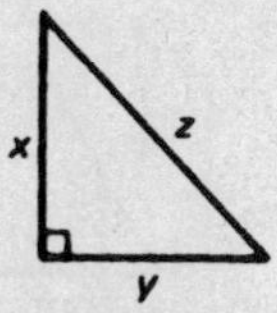

26. **C** Since the perimeter of the square = 40, each side = 10. ∴ $AB = BE = 10$
Area of $\triangle ABE$ = $\frac{1}{2}(10)(10)$ or 50

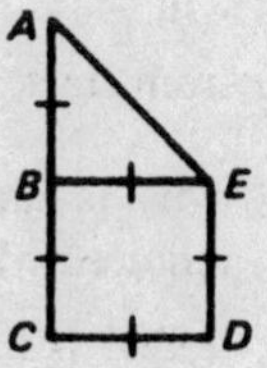

27. **A** Since $a = 40$, $b = 50$.
Since $c = 50$, $d = 40$.
∴ $b > d$

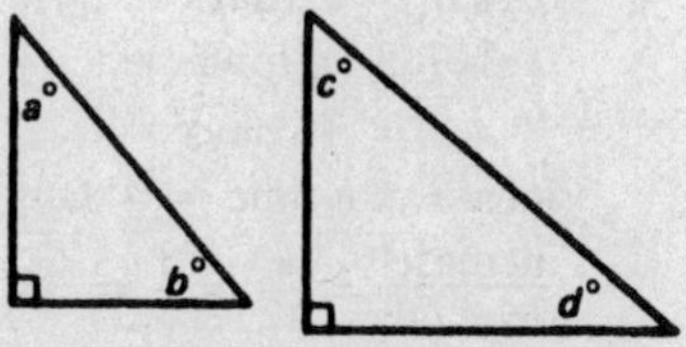

28. **A** $(a + b)^2 = a^2 + 2ab + b^2 = 17$

29. **C** Since $z = 0$, the numerator of the fraction in Column A = 0, and therefore the value of the fraction is zero.

30. **A** $\sqrt{9} = 3$ and $\sqrt{16} = 4$
The sum is 7. This is not to be confused with $\sqrt{9 + 16}$

31. **B** $60 + x = y - 40$ (given)
$x = y - 100$
$x - y = -100$
$20 > -100$

32. **D** The side of the square = 4 and the area = 16 square meters. The rectangle with a perimeter of 16 meters may possibly have sides of 5 and 3, 6 and 2, etc. The areas would then vary accordingly.

33. **C** This is a direct proportion.
Let x = number of tons of ore required to yield 200 pounds of metal.

$\frac{\text{lbs. of metal}}{\text{tons of ore.}} = \frac{1\frac{1}{4}}{1} = \frac{200}{x}$

$1\frac{1}{4}x = 200$

$\frac{5}{4}x = 200$

$x = 160$

34. **D** $x + 2y = 1\frac{1}{3}$ (1)
$+x - y = +\frac{1}{3}$ (2)
$-x + y = -\frac{1}{3}$ [divide (2) by -1] (3)
$x + 2y = 1\frac{1}{3}$ (1)
$3y = 1$ [add (1) and (3)]

35. **E** The last digit of the quotient must multiply by 8 to give a product whose last digit is X. $4 \times 8 = 3\underline{2}$ (I); $2 \times 8 = 1\underline{6}$ and $5 \times 8 = 4\underline{0}$ (II); $3 \times 8 = 2\underline{4}$ (III).

36. **A** $a - x = 1$
$a = x + 1$ (1)
$b + 1 = x$
$b = (x - 1)$ (2)
$ab = (x + 1)(x - 1)$ [multiply (1) by (2)]
$ab = x^2 - 1$

37. **D** Sum of four examinations = (77.5)(4) = 310
Sum required for average of 80% after five examinations = (80)(5) = 400
Difference (or grade required on fifth test) = 90

38. **E** Let x = radius of original circle.
Then $2x$ = radius of enlarged circle.
Area of original circle = πx^2
Area of enlarged circle = $\pi(2x)^2$ or $4\pi x^2$
Area of enlarged circle is four times that of the original circle.

39. **C** See diagram:

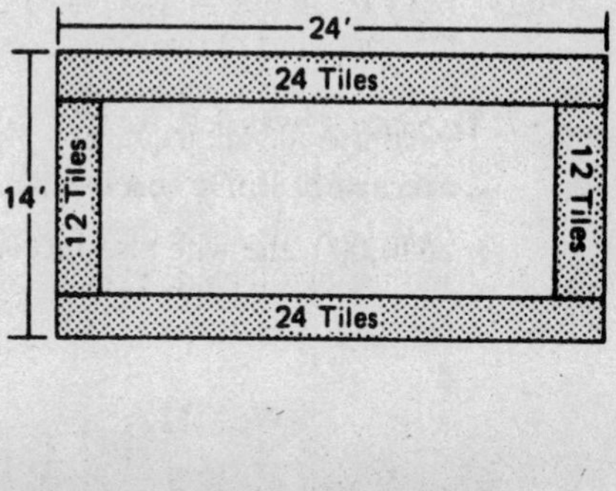

40. **C** Let legs = $2x$ and $3x$.

$\text{Area} = \frac{(2x)(3x)}{2} = 48$

$\frac{6x^2}{2} = 48$

$3x^2 = 48$

$x^2 = 16$

$x = 4$

Legs = 8 and 12

Apply the Pythagorean Theorem.

$h^2 = (8)^2 + (12)^2$

$h^2 = 64 + 144 = 208$

$h = \sqrt{208} = \sqrt{16}\sqrt{13} = 4\sqrt{13}$

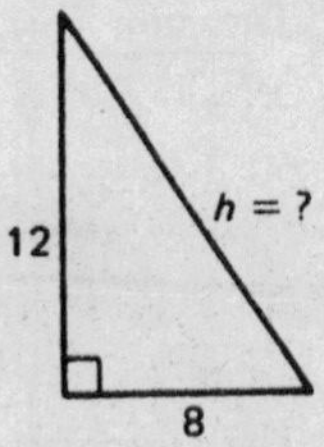

41. **C** Perimeter = 16
Each side = 4
Area = $(\text{side})^2 = 16$

42. **B** The width of the larger frame is 3 feet (36 inches) wide, as compared with 9 inches of the smaller frame. The length must also be four times as much as the 1 foot of the smaller frame, or 4 feet.

43. **B** The area of the sector over which the cow may graze is $\frac{24}{360}$ or $\frac{1}{15}$ of the area of the circle with the radius of 15. Since area of circle is $\pi(15)^2$ or 225π, the cow can graze over $\frac{1}{15}$ of 225π or 15π square feet.

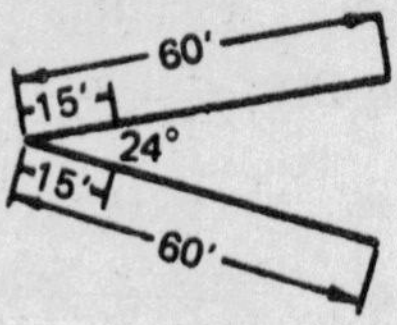

44. **C** Area of circle = πr^2

$\pi r^2 = 154$

$\frac{22}{7}r^2 = 154$

$r^2 = (154)\left(\frac{7}{22}\right)$

$r^2 = 49$

$r = 7$

Diameter = 14

45. **B** ∠B is inscribed in a semicircle. Therefore ∠B is a right ∠ and △ABC is a right △.
Radius OA = 10; diameter (hypotenuse) = 20
Line AB = 12 [given]
△ABC is a 3-4-5 right △ with AB = 4(3) and AC = 4(5).
∴ BC = 4(4) = 16.

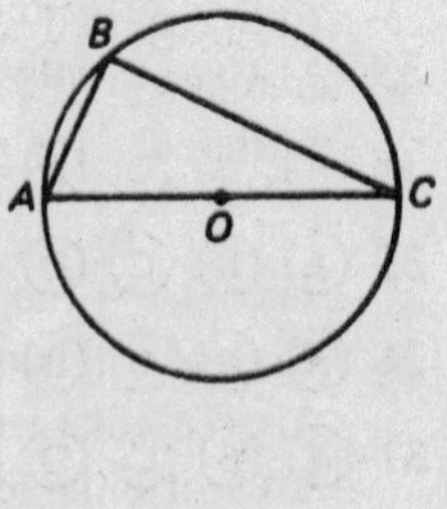

46. **C** Recall: The line that joins the midpoints of two sides of a triangle is parallel to the third side and equal to one-half of it. Or observe $BDE \sim BAC$, since they have a common angle (B) and the two included sides are proportional.

$\frac{DE}{AC} = \frac{1}{2}$

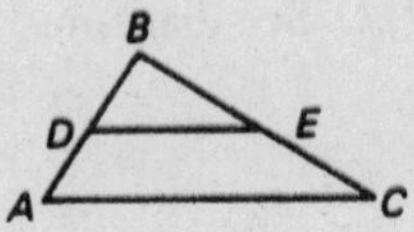

47. **D** Let x = each base angle. Then the vertex angle = x + 30°. Since the sum of the angles of a triangle equals a straight angle.

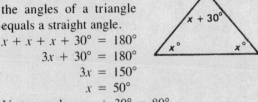

$x + x + x + 30° = 180°$

$3x + 30° = 180°$

$3x = 150°$

$x = 50°$

Vertex angle = x + 30° = 80°

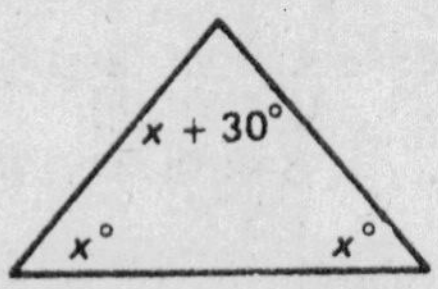

48. **D** Let $x \overset{\circ}{=}$ ∠CGH. Then $4x \overset{\circ}{=}$ ∠AFE.
∠AFE = ∠CGF [corresponding angles]
∠CFG = ∠HGD [vertical angles]
∴ ∠HGD = $4x$
∠HGD + ∠CGH $\overset{\circ}{=}$ 180 [supplementary angles]
or $4x + x \overset{\circ}{=} 180$
$5x \overset{\circ}{=} 180$
$x \overset{\circ}{=} 36$
Then $4x$ (∠HGD) $\overset{\circ}{=}$ 144.

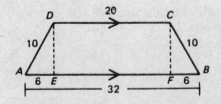

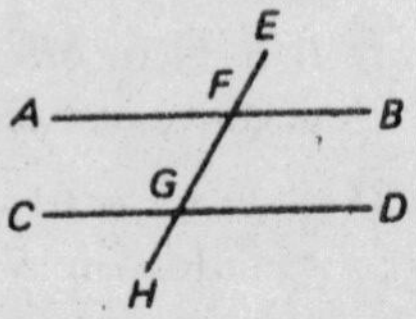

49. **D** Draw $DE \perp AB$.
Draw $CF \perp AB$.
DC = 20; AE = FB = 6
△AED is a 3-4-5 right triangle with AE = 2(3) and AD = 2(5).
∴ DE = 2(4) = 8.

Area of trapezoid = $\frac{1}{2}h(DC + AB)$

Area of trapezoid = $\frac{1}{2}(8)(52)$

Area of trapezoid = 208

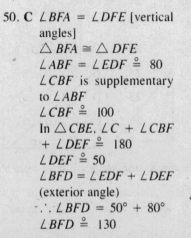

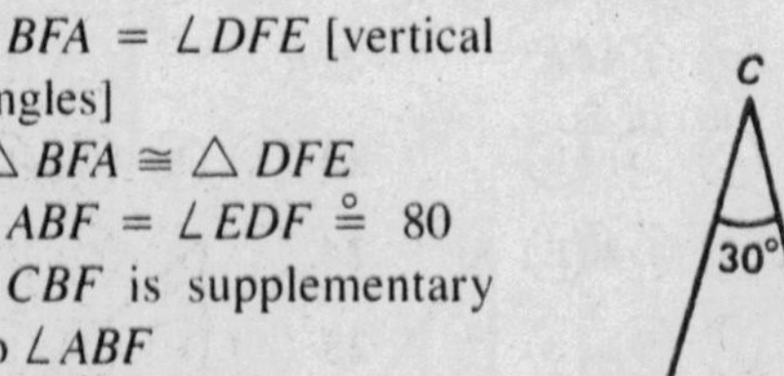

50. **C** ∠BFA = ∠DFE [vertical angles]
△BFA ≅ △DFE
∠ABF = ∠EDF $\overset{\circ}{=}$ 80
∠CBF is supplementary to ∠ABF
∠CBF $\overset{\circ}{=}$ 100
In △CBE, ∠C + ∠CBF + ∠DEF $\overset{\circ}{=}$ 180
∠DEF $\overset{\circ}{=}$ 50
∠BFD = ∠EDF + ∠DEF (exterior angle)
∴ ∠BFD = 50° + 80°
∠BFD $\overset{\circ}{=}$ 130

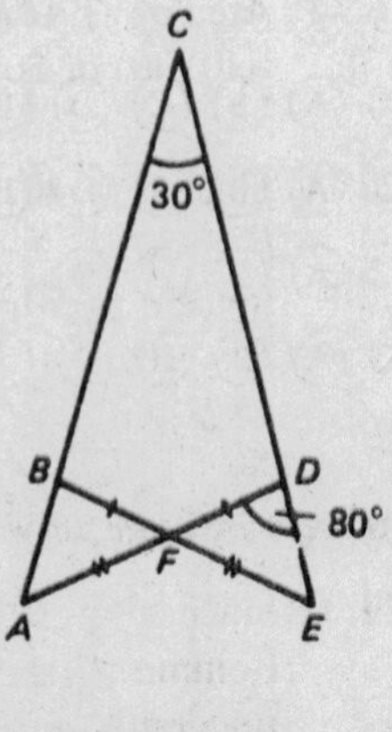

PSAT/NMSQT Answer Sheet

TYPICAL TEST F

Verbal Aptitude Section

1 (A) (B) (C) (D) (E)
2 (A) (B) (C) (D) (E)
3 (A) (B) (C) (D) (E)
4 (A) (B) (C) (D) (E)
5 (A) (B) (C) (D) (E)
6 (A) (B) (C) (D) (E)
7 (A) (B) (C) (D) (E)
8 (A) (B) (C) (D) (E)
9 (A) (B) (C) (D) (E)
10 (A) (B) (C) (D) (E)
11 (A) (B) (C) (D) (E)
12 (A) (B) (C) (D) (E)
13 (A) (B) (C) (D) (E)
14 (A) (B) (C) (D) (E)
15 (A) (B) (C) (D) (E)
16 (A) (B) (C) (D) (E)
17 (A) (B) (C) (D) (E)
18 (A) (B) (C) (D) (E)
19 (A) (B) (C) (D) (E)
20 (A) (B) (C) (D) (E)
21 (A) (B) (C) (D) (E)
22 (A) (B) (C) (D) (E)
23 (A) (B) (C) (D) (E)
24 (A) (B) (C) (D) (E)
25 (A) (B) (C) (D) (E)
26 (A) (B) (C) (D) (E)
27 (A) (B) (C) (D) (E)
28 (A) (B) (C) (D) (E)
29 (A) (B) (C) (D) (E)
30 (A) (B) (C) (D) (E)
31 (A) (B) (C) (D) (E)
32 (A) (B) (C) (D) (E)
33 (A) (B) (C) (D) (E)
34 (A) (B) (C) (D) (E)
35 (A) (B) (C) (D) (E)
36 (A) (B) (C) (D) (E)
37 (A) (B) (C) (D) (E)
38 (A) (B) (C) (D) (E)
39 (A) (B) (C) (D) (E)
40 (A) (B) (C) (D) (E)
41 (A) (B) (C) (D) (E)
42 (A) (B) (C) (D) (E)
43 (A) (B) (C) (D) (E)
44 (A) (B) (C) (D) (E)
45 (A) (B) (C) (D) (E)
46 (A) (B) (C) (D) (E)
47 (A) (B) (C) (D) (E)
48 (A) (B) (C) (D) (E)
49 (A) (B) (C) (D) (E)
50 (A) (B) (C) (D) (E)
51 (A) (B) (C) (D) (E)
52 (A) (B) (C) (D) (E)
53 (A) (B) (C) (D) (E)
54 (A) (B) (C) (D) (E)
55 (A) (B) (C) (D) (E)
56 (A) (B) (C) (D) (E)
57 (A) (B) (C) (D) (E)
58 (A) (B) (C) (D) (E)
59 (A) (B) (C) (D) (E)
60 (A) (B) (C) (D) (E)
61 (A) (B) (C) (D) (E)
62 (A) (B) (C) (D) (E)
63 (A) (B) (C) (D) (E)
64 (A) (B) (C) (D) (E)
65 (A) (B) (C) (D) (E)

Mathematical Aptitude Section*

1 (A) (B) (C) (D) (E)
2 (A) (B) (C) (D) (E)
3 (A) (B) (C) (D) (E)
4 (A) (B) (C) (D) (E)
5 (A) (B) (C) (D) (E)
6 (A) (B) (C) (D) (E)
7 (A) (B) (C) (D) (E)
8 (A) (B) (C) (D) (E)
9 (A) (B) (C) (D) (E)
10 (A) (B) (C) (D) (E)
11 (A) (B) (C) (D) (E)
12 (A) (B) (C) (D) (E)
13 (A) (B) (C) (D) (E)
14 (A) (B) (C) (D) (E)
15 (A) (B) (C) (D) (E)
16 (A) (B) (C) (D) (E)
17 (A) (B) (C) (D) (E)
18 (A) (B) (C) (D) (E)
19 (A) (B) (C) (D) (E)
20 (A) (B) (C) (D) (E)
21 (A) (B) (C) (D) (E)
22 (A) (B) (C) (D) (E)
23 (A) (B) (C) (D) (E)
24 (A) (B) (C) (D) (E)
25 (A) (B) (C) (D) (E)
26 (A) (B) (C) (D) (E)
27 (A) (B) (C) (D) (E)
28 (A) (B) (C) (D) (E)
29 (A) (B) (C) (D) (E)
30 (A) (B) (C) (D) (E)
31 (A) (B) (C) (D) (E)
32 (A) (B) (C) (D) (E)
33 (A) (B) (C) (D) (E)
34 (A) (B) (C) (D) (E)
35 (A) (B) (C) (D) (E)
36 (A) (B) (C) (D) (E)
37 (A) (B) (C) (D) (E)
38 (A) (B) (C) (D) (E)
39 (A) (B) (C) (D) (E)
40 (A) (B) (C) (D) (E)
41 (A) (B) (C) (D) (E)
42 (A) (B) (C) (D) (E)
43 (A) (B) (C) (D) (E)
44 (A) (B) (C) (D) (E)
45 (A) (B) (C) (D) (E)
46 (A) (B) (C) (D) (E)
47 (A) (B) (C) (D) (E)
48 (A) (B) (C) (D) (E)
49 (A) (B) (C) (D) (E)
50 (A) (B) (C) (D) (E)

*If there are more answer spaces than you need, leave them blank.

TYPICAL TEST F

SECTION 1	**Time—50 minutes** **65 Questions**	For each question in this section, choose the best answer and fill in the corresponding circle on the answer sheet.

Each question below consists of a word in capital letters, followed by five lettered words or phrases. Choose the word or phrase that is most nearly opposite in meaning to the word in capital letters. Since some of the questions require you to distinguish fine shades of meaning, consider all the choices before deciding which is best.

Example:

GOOD: (A) sour (B) bad (C) red (D) hot (E) ugly

Ⓐ ● Ⓒ Ⓓ Ⓔ

1. WITHER: (A) praise (B) plant (C) bloom (D) blunder (E) prefer
2. INVIGORATE: (A) dismiss (B) deny (C) gaze (D) return (E) tire
3. GRASP: (A) lack of comprehension (B) lack of sincerity (C) fear (D) kindness (E) lack of relevance
4. EXTRICATE: (A) interfere (B) ignore (C) save (D) entangle (E) solace
5. AMPLE: (A) complex (B) hidden (C) immature (D) inadequate (E) unwarranted
6. FLUENCY: (A) hesitancy (B) imitation (C) rejection (D) concord (E) dissipation
7. STAGNATION: (A) progress (B) acceptance (C) steadiness (D) indifference (E) inconvenience
8. ALTRUISTIC: (A) impartial (B) petulant (C) selfish (D) quizzical (E) alluring
9. DISPARITY: (A) cheerfulness (B) proximity (C) isolation (D) likeness (E) distraction
10. OSCILLATE: (A) be accurate (B) allow to deteriorate (C) remain steady (D) become hard (E) thrust in deeper
11. OMNISCIENT: (A) powerful (B) scientific (C) wasteful (D) magnanimous (E) ignorant
12. VERBOSITY: (A) illiteracy (B) terseness (C) enlargement (D) serenity (E) resignation
13. AMENABLE: (A) intractable (B) likable (C) irreverent (D) magnificent (E) hectic
14. COALESCE: (A) separate (B) arrange in rows (C) become transparent (D) respond quickly (E) downgrade
15. DAUNT: (A) believe in (B) wonder about (C) embolden (D) disapprove (E) obliterate
16. HERMETIC: (A) incurable (B) transient (C) sluggish (D) cumbersome (E) penetrable
17. DISTASTE: (A) unawareness (B) endurance (C) relish (D) earnestness (E) indecision
18. BANAL: (A) tumultuous (B) dry (C) original (D) enthusiastic (E) noisy
19. DECORUM: (A) plainness (B) unseemliness (C) futility (D) reluctance (E) quaintness
20. APOSTATE: (A) patient sufferer (B) inspiring teacher (C) expert artist (D) loyal follower (E) hasty thinker

Each sentence below has one or two blanks, each blank indicating that something has been omitted. Beneath the sentence are five lettered words or sets of words. Choose the word or set of words that, when inserted in the sentence, best fits the meaning of the sentence as a whole.

Example:

Although its publicity has been ----, the film itself is intelligent, well-acted, handsomely produced, and altogether ----.

(A) tasteless . . respectable (B) extensive . . moderate (C) sophisticated . . amateur (D) risque . . crude (E) perfect . . spectacular

● Ⓑ Ⓒ Ⓓ Ⓔ

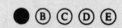

21. Even though previous reporters had lampooned the candidate throughout the campaign, he ---- further interviews.
(A) resisted (B) halted (C) sidestepped (D) welcomed (E) dreaded
22. The distinctive qualities of African music were not appreciated or even ---- by Westerners until fairly recently.
(A) deplored (B) revered (C) ignored (D) neglected (E) perceived
23. Geologists recognize that tiny ---- in the course of time become mighty chasms.
(A) grievances (B) molecules (C) fissures (D) rivulets (E) pebbles
24. To the cynic, there are no wholly altruistic, unselfish acts; every human deed is ---- an ulterior selfish motive.
(A) independent of (B) emulated by (C) disguised as (D) founded upon (E) similar to
25. Edison's remark that genius is "one percent inspiration and ninety-nine percent perspiration" implies the value of ----.
(A) eagerness (B) thoughtfulness (C) eccentricity (D) diligence (E) intuition

26. She had taken the shocking news quietly, neither ---- fate nor uttering any word of bitterness.
(A) conspiring with (B) submitting to
(C) railing against (D) dissenting from
(E) mulling over

27. You may wonder how the expert on fossil remains is able to trace descent through teeth, which seem ---- pegs upon which to hang whole ancestries.
(A) novel (B) reliable
(C) specious (D) inadequate (E) academic

28. Whereas off-Broadway theater over the past several seasons has clearly ---- a talent for experimentation and improvisation, one deficiency in the commercial stage of late has been its marked incapacity for ----.
(A) manifested . . spontaneity
(B) lampooned . . theatricality
(C) cultivated . . orthodoxy
(D) disavowed . . histrionics
(E) betrayed . . burlesque

29. Unlike the gregarious Capote, who was never happier than when he was in the center of a crowd of celebrities, Faulkner in later years grew somewhat ---- and shunned company.
(A) congenial (B) imperious
(C) dispassionate (D) reclusive (E) ambivalent

30. In the tradition of scholarly ----, the poet and scholar A.E. Housman once assailed a German rival for relying on manuscripts "as a drunkard relies on lampposts, for ---- rather than illumination."
(A) animosity . . current
(B) discourse . . stability
(C) erudition . . shadow
(D) invective . . support
(E) competition . . assistance

Each question below consists of a related pair of words or phrases, followed by five lettered pairs of words or phrases. Select the lettered pair that <u>best</u> expresses a relationship similar to that expressed in the original pair.

Example:

YAWN : BOREDOM :: (A) dream : sleep
(B) anger : madness (C) smile : amusement
(D) face : expression (E) impatience : rebellion

Ⓐ Ⓑ ● Ⓓ Ⓔ

31. LAWN : MOWER :: (A) forest : timber
(B) flower : petal (C) garden : weed
(D) nail : clipper (E) corral : fence

32. AUDIT : BOOKS :: (A) hear : records
(B) inspect : buildings (C) publish : texts
(D) perform : plays (E) distribute : films

33. BOBBIN : THREAD :: (A) swatch : fabric
(B) sweater : yarn (C) shoe : lace
(D) bow : string (E) reel : tape

34. BRUSH : SHOVE :: (A) comb : trim
(B) prick : stab (C) edit : write
(D) remove : replace (E) wash : bathe

35. BUNGALOW : BUILDING ::
(A) cathedral : chapel (B) engine : automobile
(C) dinghy : boat (D) index : book
(E) flap : tent

36. LAIR : BEAR :: (A) fang : rattlesnake
(B) viper : reptile (C) vixen : fox
(D) pack : wolf (E) burrow : rabbit

37. HEFTY : WEIGHT :: (A) lofty : height
(B) narrow : distance (C) thin : texture
(D) olfactory : smell (E) agile : bulk

38. DEPOSE : MONARCH :: (A) propose : suitor
(B) dismiss : employee (C) defend : claim
(D) support : candidate (E) deride : heckler

39. ARSONIST : CONFLAGRATION ::
(A) kleptomaniac : arrest (B) thug : assault
(C) felon : collusion (D) pyromaniac : burial
(E) orator : mob

40. PENSIVE : REFLECT :: (A) retiring : exhaust
(B) melancholy : gladden (C) unruly : disobey
(D) irate : pacify (E) tactful : offend

41. SPECTACLES : SEEING ::
(A) dictaphone : speaking (B) paper : writing
(C) hurdles : running (D) flippers : swimming
(E) manacles : freeing

42. ENIGMATIC : TEXT :: (A) reckless : conduct
(B) wordy : prose (C) brusque : manner
(D) obscure : remark (E) cursory : investigation

43. IMPASSABLE : TRAVERSE ::
(A) implausible : express (B) inevitable : recover
(C) interminable : commence
(D) impalpable : touch (E) insuperable : disdain

44. APLOMB : NONCHALANT ::
(A) composure : indefatigable
(B) wariness : petulant (C) disdain : unworthy
(D) affability : cordial (E) ardor : indifferent

45. JUGGERNAUT : UNSTOPPABLE ::
(A) catastrophe : unnatural
(B) turncoat : treacherous
(C) charlatan : knowledgeable
(D) killjoy : insufferable (E) astronaut : robust

Each passage below is followed by questions based on its content. Answer the questions following each passage on the basis of what is stated or implied in that passage.

To keep clear of concealment, to keep clear of the need of concealment, to do nothing which he or she might not do out on the middle of Boston Common at noonday—I cannot say how more and more it seems to me the glory of a young person's life. It is an awful hour when the first necessity of hiding anything comes. The whole life is different thenceforth. When there are questions to be feared and eyes to be avoided and subjects which must not be touched, then the bloom of life is gone. Put off that day as long as possible. Put it off forever if you can.

46. The author regards the occasion when one first must conceal something as
(A) anticlimactic (B) insignificant (C) fleeting
(D) momentous (E) enviable

47. The author's tone throughout the passage can best be described as
(A) hostile (B) condescending (C) playful
(D) serious (E) impersonal

48. Which of the following does the author recommend to his audience?
I. To deny the necessity of aging
II. To act in an aboveboard manner
III. To rationalize one's misconduct
(A) I only
(B) II only
(C) I and II only
(D) II and III only
(E) I, II, and III

Most people want to know how things are made. They frankly admit, however, that they feel completely at sea when it comes to understanding how a piece of music is made. Where a composer begins, how he manages to keep going—in fact, how and where he learns his trade—all are shrouded in impenetrable darkness. The composer, in short, is a person of mystery, and the composer's workshop an unapproachable ivory tower.

One of the first things laypersons want to hear about is the part inspiration plays in composing. They find it difficult to believe that composers are not much preoccupied with that question, that composing is as natural for the composer as eating or sleeping. Composing is something that the composer happens to have been born to do; and because of that, it loses the character of a special virtue in the composer's eyes.

The composer, therefore, does not say to himself: "Do I feel inspired?" He says to himself: "Do I feel like composing today?" And if he feels like composing, he does. It is more or less like saying to himself: "Do I feel sleepy?" If you feel sleepy, you go to sleep. If you don't feel sleepy, you stay up. If the composer doesn't feel like composing, he doesn't compose. It's as simple as that.

49. The author of the passage indicates that creating music is an activity that is
(A) difficult (B) rewarding (C) inspirational
(D) fraught with anxiety (E) instinctive

50. When considering the work involved in composing music, the layperson often
(A) exaggerates the difficulties of the composer in commencing work
(B) minimizes the mental turmoil that the composer undergoes
(C) is unaware that a creative process is involved
(D) loses the ability to enjoy the composition
(E) loses the ability to judge the work apart from the composer

51. The author's approach toward the subject is
(A) highly emotional (B) casually informative
(C) negative in tone
(D) deeply philosophical
(E) consciously prejudiced

The average citizen today is knowledgeable about "landmark" court decisions concerning such questions as racial segregation, legislative apportionment, prayers in the public schools, or the right of a defendant to counsel in a criminal prosecution. Too often, however, he or she thinks that these decisions settle matters once and for all. Actually, of course, these well-publicized court decisions are merely guideposts pointing toward a virtually endless series of vexing legal questions. It is often more difficult to determine how far the courts should travel along a road than to decide what road should be taken.

Illustrations of this difficulty exist in all areas of the law, and especially in those most familiar to the lay public. For example, this nation could hardly have failed to agree that state-compelled racial segregation in the public schools was a denial of the equal protection of the laws guaranteed by the 14th Amendment. The real difficulty lay in determining how desegregation should be accomplished and how to solve the problem of *de facto* school segregation, perpetuated by the practical if unfortunate realities of residential patterns.

Similarly, there was substantial editorial approval of the Supreme Court's initial decision that grossly inequitable legislative apportionment was a proper matter for judicial scrutiny. The traditional democratic ideal of majority rule, it was argued, could not be subverted by apportionment schemes which at times appeared to give rural voters twice the electoral strength of their urban counterparts. But when this principle was extended to render unlawful the composition of virtually every state legislature in the nation, the reaction to such an extension received as much attention as the apportionment decision itself.

52. According to the author, the effect of many decisions in the courts has been to
(A) make startling headlines
(B) lead to more legal complications
(C) contradict the Constitution
(D) deny states' rights
(E) provide final solutions to many problems

53. The author implies that, insofar as important court decisions are concerned, the general public's understanding is
(A) undisputed (B) absolute (C) unfounded
(D) limited (E) prejudiced

54. According to the author, the Supreme Court's initial decision on legislative apportionment was based on the principle of
(A) majority rule (B) rural jurisdiction
(C) equal protection under the law
(D) judicial scrutiny (E) editorial approval

55. As used in the passage, the word "landmark" most nearly means
(A) exciting (B) equitable (C) significant
(D) publicized (E) legal

Most of the intelligent land animals have prehensile, grasping organs for exploring their environment—hands in human beings and their anthropoid relatives, the sensitive inquiring trunk in the elephant. One of the surprising things about the porpoise is that his superior brain is unaccompanied by any type of manipulative organ. He has, however, a remarkable range-finding ability involving some sort of echo-sounding. Perhaps this acute sense—far more accurate than any that human ingenuity has been able to devise artificially—brings him greater knowledge of his watery surroundings than might at first seem possible. Human beings think of intelligence as geared to things. The hand and the tool are to us the unconscious symbols of our intellectual attainment. It is difficult for us to visualize another kind of lonely, almost disembodied intelligence floating in the wavering green fairyland of the sea—an intelligence possibly near or comparable to our own but without hands to build, to transmit knowledge by writing, or to alter by one hairsbreadth the planet's surface. Yet at the same time there are indications that this is a warm, friendly, and eager intelligence quite capable of coming to the assistance of injured companions and striving to rescue them from drowning. Porpoises left the land when mammalian brains were still small and primitive. Without the stimulus provided by agile exploring fingers, these great sea mammals have yet taken a divergent road toward intelligence of a high order. Hidden in their sleek bodies is an impressively elaborated instrument, the reason for whose appearance is a complete enigma. It is as though both the human being and the porpoise were each part of some great eye which yearned to look both outward on eternity and inward to the sea's heart—that fertile entity like the mind in its swarming and grotesque life.

56. According to the passage, which of the following statements about porpoises is true?
(A) They have always been water-dwelling creatures.
(B) They at one time possessed prehensile organs.
(C) They lived on land in prehistoric times.
(D) Their brains are no longer mammalian in nature.
(E) They developed brains to compensate for the lack of a prehensile organ.

57. The author suggests that human failure to understand the intelligence of the porpoise is due to
(A) the inadequacy of human range-finding equipment
(B) a lack of knowledge about the sea
(C) the want of a common language
(D) the primitive origins of the human brain
(E) human inclination to judge other life by our own

58. The author's primary purpose is apparently to
(A) examine the porpoise's potential for surpassing humankind
(B) question the need for prehensile organs in human development
(C) refute the theory that porpoises are unable to alter their physical environment
(D) explore two different but complementary types of mammalian intelligence
(E) indicate the superiority of human intelligence over that of the porpoise

59. The "impressively elaborated instrument" referred to in the next-to-last sentence is best interpreted to mean which of the following?
(A) A concealed manipulative organ
(B) An artificial range-finding device
(C) A complex, intelligent brain
(D) The porpoise's hidden eye
(E) An apparatus for producing musical sounds

60. Which of the following best characterizes the tone of the passage?
(A) Restrained skepticism (B) Pedantic assertion
(C) Wondering admiration
(D) Amused condescension (E) Ironic speculation

The explosion of a star is an awesome event. The most violent of these cataclysms, which produce supernovae, probably destroys a star completely. Within our galaxy of roughly 100 billion stars the last supernova was observed in 1604. Much smaller explosions, however, occur quite frequently, giving rise to what astronomers call novae and dwarf novae. On the order of 25 novae occur in our galaxy every year, but only two or three are near enough to be observed. About 100 dwarf novae are known altogether. If the exploding star is in a nearby part of the galaxy, it may create a "new star" that was not previously visible to the naked eye. The last new star of this sort that could be observed clearly from the Northern Hemisphere appeared in 1946. In these smaller explosions the star loses only a minute fraction of its mass and survives to explode again.

Astrophysicists are fairly well satisfied that they can account for the explosions of supernovae. The novae and dwarf novae have presented more of a puzzle. From recent investigations that have provided important new information about these two classes of exploding star, the picture that emerges is quite astonishing. It appears that every dwarf nova—and perhaps every nova—is a member of a pair of stars. The two stars are so close together that they revolve around a point that lies barely outside the surface of the larger star. As a result the period of rotation is usually only a few hours, and their velocities range upward to within a two-hundredth of the speed of light.

Astronomers use the term "cataclysmic variable" to embrace the three general classes of exploding star: dwarf novae, novae and supernovae. A cataclysmic variable is defined as a star that suddenly and unpredictably increases in brightness by a factor of at least 10. Dwarf novae are stars that increase in brightness by a factor of 10 to 100 within a period of several hours and decline to their former brightness in two or three days. In this period they emit some 10.38 to 10.39 ergs of energy. At maximum brilliance a dwarf nova shines about as intensely as our sun; previously it had been only about a hundredth as bright. The number of outbursts ranges anywhere from three to 30 a year, but for any one star the intervals have a fairly constant value. Moreover, the maximum brightness from outburst to outburst is the same within a factor of two for a given star. The dwarf novae are often referred to, after their prototypes, as U Geminorum or SS Cygni stars. (The stars of each constellation are designated by letters or numbers.) A subgroup of dwarf novae, called Z Camelopardalis stars, do not always descend to minimum brightness between outbursts but may stay at some intermediate level for several months.

61. The author's primary purpose in the passage is to
(A) compare the characteristics of novae with those of other stars
(B) explain why supernovae are so much less frequent than novae and dwarf novae
(C) account for the unpredictability of cataclysmic variables as a class
(D) describe the nature and range in scale of cataclysmic variables
(E) explain what happens during the stages of a star's destruction

62. According to the passage, our observations of novae are hampered by their
(A) extreme brightness (B) loss of mass
(C) speed of rotation (D) distance from earth
(E) tremendous violence

63. Dwarf novae differ from supernovae in which of the following aspects?
I. Magnitude of outburst
II. Frequency of observation
III. Periodicity of flare-ups
(A) I only
(B) II only
(C) I and II only
(D) I and III only
(E) I, II, and III

64. By the term "new star" (paragraph 1) the author means one that has
(A) recently gained in mass
(B) moved from a distant galaxy
(C) become bright enough to strike the eye
(D) not previously risen above the horizon
(E) become visible by rotating in its orbit

65. The passage provides information that would answer which of the following questions?
I. In which century were astronomers last able to observe the explosion of a supernova?
I. Why do the Z Camelopardalis stars remain at intermediate levels of brightness after some outbursts?
III. How rapidly after outburst do dwarf novae achieve their maximum level of brilliance?
(A) I only
(B) III only
(C) I and II only
(D) I and III only
(E) II and III only

SECTION 2 **Time—50 minutes** **50 Questions**

In this section solve each problem, using any available space on the page for scratchwork. Then decide which is the best of the choices given and fill in the corresponding circle on the answer sheet.

The following information is for your reference in solving some of the problems.

Circle of radius r: Area $= \pi r^2$ Circumference $= 2\pi r$
The number of degrees of arc in a circle is 360.
The measure in degrees of a straight angle is 180.

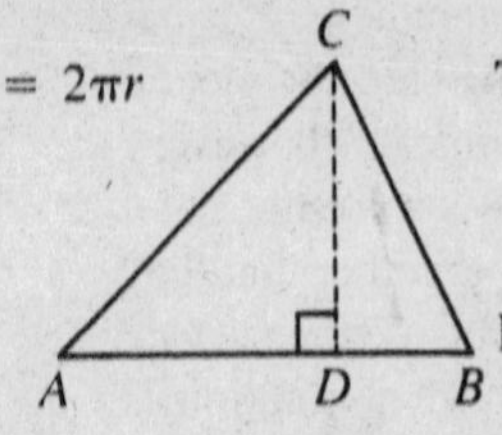

Triangle: The sum of the measures in degrees of the angles of a triangle is 180.

If $\angle CDA$ is a right angle, then

(1) area of $\triangle ABC = \frac{AB \times CD}{2}$

(2) $AC^2 = AD^2 + DC^2$

Definitions of symbols:
- $=$ is equal to
- $\neq$ is unequal to
- $<$ is less than
- $>$ is greater than
- $\leqq$ is less than or equal to
- $\geqq$ is greater than or equal to
- $\parallel$ is parallel to
- $\perp$ is perpendicular to

Note: Figures that accompany problems in this test are intended to provide information useful in solving the problems. They are drawn as accurately as possible EXCEPT when it is stated in a specific problem that its figure is not drawn to scale. All figures lie in a plane unless otherwise indicated. All numbers used are real numbers.

1. How much more is $\frac{1}{3}$ of $\frac{1}{4}$ than $\frac{1}{4}$ of $\frac{1}{12}$?
(A) $\frac{1}{4}$ (B) $\frac{1}{16}$ (C) $1\frac{2}{3}$ (D) 3 (E) 4

2. $100 - \frac{100}{0.2}$ equals
(A) -400 (B) -50 (C) 50 (D) 99.8 (E) 400

3. $\dfrac{5 + \frac{3}{4}}{1 - \frac{13}{36}}$ equals the square of what number?
(A) $\sqrt{3}$ (B) $2\frac{1}{4}$ (C) 3 (D) 9 (E) 81

4. What is the largest integer that is a factor of all three of the following numbers: 2160, 1344, 1440?
(A) 6 (B) 8 (C) 12 (D) 16 (E) 48

5. $\frac{1}{4}\%$ of $2 =$
(A) $\frac{1}{200}$ (B) $\frac{1}{100}$ (C) $\frac{1}{80}$ (D) $\frac{1}{8}$ (E) $\frac{4}{5}$

6. $2^x = \dfrac{\sqrt[4]{81}}{\sqrt{18}}$; $x =$
(A) -1 (B) $-\frac{1}{2}$ (C) 0 (D) $\frac{1}{2}$ (E) 1

7. A man earns d dollars each week and spends s dollars a week. In how many weeks will he have Q dollars?
(A) $\frac{ds}{Q}$ (B) $\frac{Q}{ds}$ (C) $\frac{Q}{s-d}$ (D) $\frac{Q}{d-s}$
(E) $\frac{d-s}{Q}$

8. What part of \$3.00 is a dime?
(A) $\frac{1}{300}$ (B) $\frac{1}{30}$ (C) $\frac{1}{3}$ (D) $33\frac{1}{3}$ (E) $3\frac{1}{3}$

9. What percent of k is 10?
(A) $10k$ (B) $\frac{k}{10}$ (C) $\frac{10}{k}$ (D) $\frac{1000}{k}$ (E) $\frac{k}{1000}$

10. A school now has a registration of \$50, which represents a $6\frac{1}{4}\%$ increase over the previous year. The registration in the previous year was
(A) 644 (B) 722 (C) 797 (D) 800
(E) 903

11. If 2 erasers cost 6¢, how many erasers can be bought for 36¢?
(A) 6 (B) 12 (C) 18 (D) 36 (E) 72

12. During the drama society's performance in a school auditorium, with 750 seats in the orchestra and 400 seats in the balcony, $\frac{2}{3}$ of the seats in the orchestra and $\frac{3}{8}$ of the seats in the balcony are sold. What part of all the seats are left unsold?
(A) $\frac{10}{23}$ (B) $\frac{13}{23}$ (C) $\frac{23}{24}$ (D) $\frac{24}{25}$ (E) $\frac{13}{25}$

13. Three boys have marbles in the ratio of 19:5:3. If the boy with the least number has 9 marbles, how many marbles does the boy with the greatest number have?
(A) 27 (B) 33 (C) 57 (D) 81 (E) 171

14. A bowler has an average of 150 points a game for 12 games. If he bowls 6 more games, how high an average must he make in these games to raise his average for the 18 games to 160?
(A) 170 (B) 175 (C) 180 (D) 210
(E) 225

15. On a certain map the scale is given as 1 inch = 1 mile. A boy copies the map, making each dimension three times as large as the given dimensions. On his map how many miles will 6 inches represent?
(A) 2 (B) 3 (C) 6 (D) 18 (E) 20

Questions 16-32 each consist of two quantities, one in Column A and one in Column B. You are to compare the two quantities and on the answer sheet fill in circle

A if the quantity in Column A is greater;
B if the quantity in Column B is greater;
C if the two quantities are equal;
D if the relationship cannot be determined from the information given.

Notes:

1. In certain questions, information concerning one or both of the quantities to be compared is centered above the two columns.
2. In a given question, a symbol that appears in both columns represents the same thing in Column A as it does in Column B.
3. Letters such as x, n, and k stand for real numbers.

EXAMPLES

	Column A	Column B	Answers
E1.	2×6	$2 + 6$	● Ⓑ Ⓒ Ⓓ
	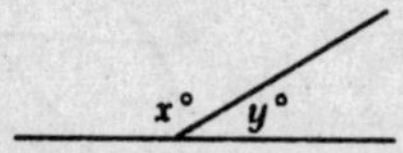		
E2.	$180 - x$	y	Ⓐ Ⓑ ● Ⓓ
E3.	$p - q$	$q - p$	Ⓐ Ⓑ Ⓒ ●

	Column A	Column B
	$\frac{(7)(7)(21)}{x} = (7)(3)$	
16.	21	x
17.	$\sqrt{\frac{1}{4}}$	$(0.25)^2$
	$2^{n+1} = 32$	
18.	n	5
	$xy = 0$	
19.	y	x
	$x^2 - y^2 = 0$	
20.	$x + y$	0
21.	$\frac{a + b}{b}$	$\frac{a}{b} + 1$
	$a + 3 = 5$, $b + 3 = 7$	
22.	$b - a$	a

	Column A	Column B
	City A is 10 miles from City B and City C is 5 miles from City B.	
23.	Distance from City A to City C	15 miles

24.	The average of a, b, and c	x
	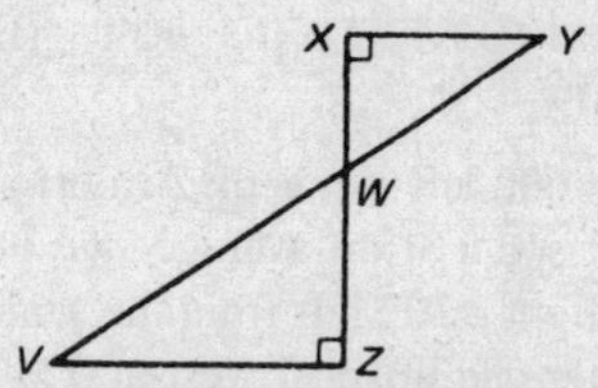	
	$XY = 8$, $WY = 10$, $VZ = 16$; $ZX \perp XY$ and $XZ \perp VZ$	
25.	Length of XWZ	$XY + WY$
	$abc = 0$ and $a = 1$	
26.	1	bc
	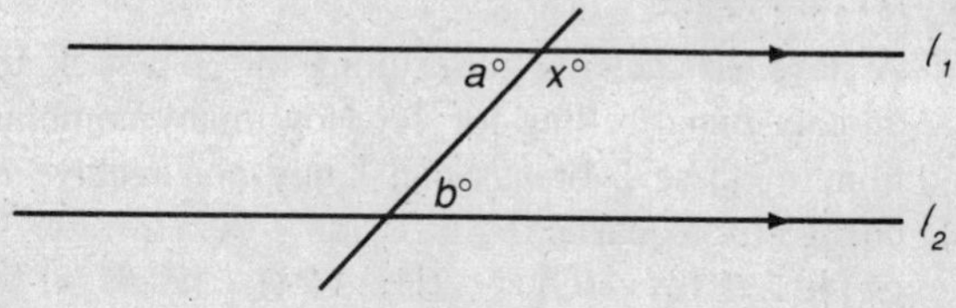	
	$a + b = 110°$	
27.	x	110
	$4x > 3y$	
28.	x	y
29.	$(1)^{27}$	$(3)^9$
	x is an integer.	
30.	The maximum value of $10 - x^2$	11
	$x = \frac{y}{7}$	
31.	$7x$	y
	$a^2 - 11a + 30 = 0$	
32.	a	7

> Solve each of the remaining problems in this section using any available space for scratchwork. Then decide which is the best of the choices given and fill in the corresponding circle on the answer sheet.

33. History of First-Class Letter Rates

1885–1917	2 cents	March 2, 1974	10 cents
1917–1919 (war years)	3 cents	December 31, 1975	13 cents
1919	2 cents	May 29, 1978	15 cents
July 6, 1932	3 cents	March 22, 1981	18 cents
August 1, 1958	4 cents	November 1, 1981	20 cents
January 7, 1963	5 cents	February 17, 1985	22 cents
January 7, 1968	6 cents	April 3, 1988	25 cents
May 16, 1971	8 cents		

The percentage increase of letter rates by 1978 as compared with the rate in 1932 was
(A) 8% (B) 12% (C) 40% (D) 80%
(E) 400%

34. Flight #602 left Kennedy Airport at 1:00 P.M. and traveled south at an average rate of 200 miles per hour. Flight #302 left from the same point one-half hour later and traveled west at 320 miles per hour. How far apart are these planes at 4:00 P.M.?
(A) 1000 miles (B) 1200 miles (C) 1400 miles
(D) 1600 miles (E) 2800 miles

35. Three men own a business establishment in the ratio of 19:5:3. What part of the total business does the man with the smallest interest control?
(A) 3% (B) 9% (C) 11.1% (D) 16.6%
(E) 88.8%

36. A store has chewing gum selling for 3¢ a stick and another brand selling for 4¢. How many combinations of these 2 brands can I buy and receive no change for a quarter?
(A) 0 (B) 1 (C) 2 (D) 3 (E) 4

37. If $x + y = 16$, what does $x - z$ equal?
(A) $z + 16$ (B) 8 (C) $16 - y$ (D) $z(16 - y)$
(E) $16 - y - z$

38. If a and b are positive integers and $\frac{a - b}{3.5} = \frac{4}{7}$, then which of the following is (are) correct?
I. $b < a$
II. $b \geq a$
III. $b \leq a$
(A) I only (B) II only (C) III only
(D) I and II only (E) I, II, and III

39. 10^x means that 10 is to be used as a factor x times, and 10^{-x} means $\frac{1}{10^x}$. Very large and very small numbers, therefore, are frequently written as decimals multiplied by 10^x, where x is a positive or a negative integer. All of the following are correct EXCEPT
(A) $470{,}000 = 4.7 \times 10^5$
(B) 450 billion $= 4.5 \times 10^{11}$
(C) $0.00000000075 = 7.5 \times 10^{-10}$
(D) 86 hundred-thousandths $= 8.6 \times 10^{-2}$
(E) 26 million $= 2.6 \times 10^7$

40. The graduating class of a certain school desires to leave as a memorial two prizes of $50 each to be awarded annually for the two best essays. What is the minimum amount of money that must be invested in 10% bonds to insure the necessary income?
(A) $1000 (B) $10,000 (C) $4000
(D) $5000 (E) more than $10,000

41. A farmer has enough feed to take care of 60 chickens for 8 days. How long will this feed last if he purchases 20 additional chickens?
(A) 2 days (B) 5 days (C) 6 days
(D) $10\frac{2}{3}$ days (E) 24 days

42. A rectangular fish tank 25″ by 9″ has water in it to a level of 2″. This water is carefully poured into a cylindrical container with a diameter of 10″. How high (in terms of π) will the water reach in the cylindrical container?
(A) 18π (B) $\frac{\pi}{18}$ (C) $\frac{18}{\pi}$ (D) $\frac{9}{2\pi}$ (E) $\frac{9\pi}{2}$

43. AB and CD are chords of a circle intersecting at E. If $\overset{\frown}{AD} = 60°$ and $\angle AED \overset{\circ}{=} 45$, what is the measure of $\angle EDB$?
(A) 15° (B) 20°
(C) 30° (D) 45°
(E) 60°

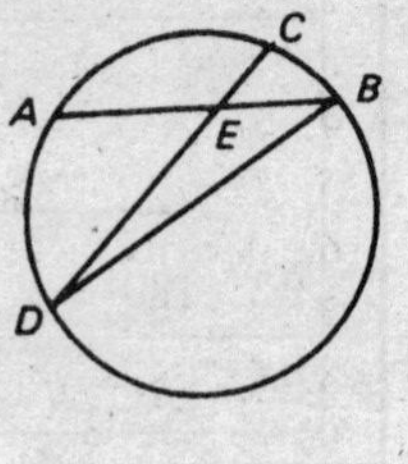

44. AOC is a diameter of circle O. $\angle BAC \overset{\circ}{=} 30$. $\overset{\frown}{BC} = \overset{\frown}{CD}$. How many degrees are there in the measure of $\overset{\frown}{AD}$?
(A) 60 (B) 120
(C) 150 (D) 165
(E) 180

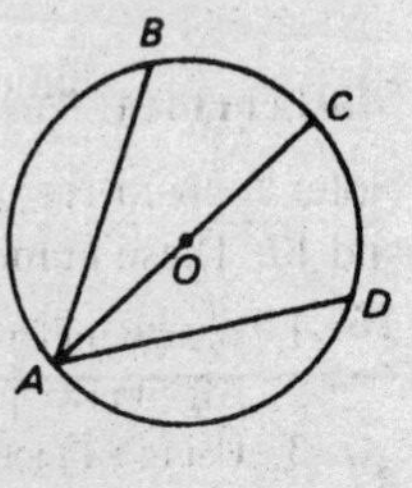

45. If ☒ is defined by the equation x ☒ $y = x + xy + y$ for all numbers x and y, what is the value of a if 8 ☒ $a = 3$?
(A) -5 (B) $-\frac{5}{9}$ (C) $\frac{3}{8}$ (D) $\frac{5}{9}$ (E) 5

46. $AD = 10$, $AE = 8$, $\angle B = \angle C \overset{\circ}{=} 45$; $BC =$
(A) 16 (B) 18 (C) 26
(D) 36 (E) none of these

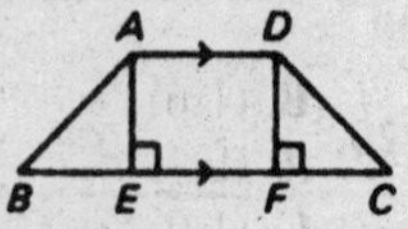

47. $\angle BAD = \angle CAD$, $BA = BC$, $DA = DC$, and $\angle B \overset{\circ}{=} 120$. $\angle ADC$ has a measure of
(A) 60° (B) 120°
(C) 150° (D) 160°
(E) 165°

48. The base of a 39-foot ladder is placed 15 feet from a building which is 200 feet tall. How many feet up the building will the ladder extend?

(A) 36 (B) 54 (C) 146 (D) 161 (E) 185

49. A box was made in the form of a cube. If a second cubical box has inside dimensions three times those of the first box, how many times as much does it contain?

(A) 3 (B) 6 (C) 9 (D) 12 (E) 27

50. *ABCD* is a square of side 10. *AFC* is an arc of a circle with the center at *D*. *AGC* is an arc of a circle with the center at *B*. Which of the following correctly express(es) the area of the shaded portion?

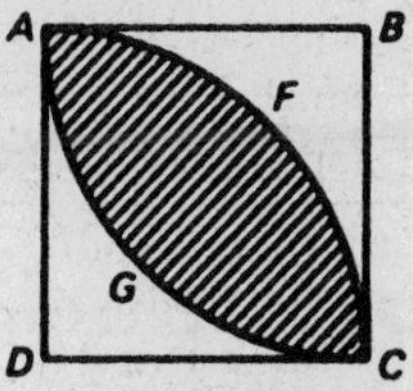

I. $50\pi - 100$
II. $100 - 50\pi$
III. $100\pi - 100$

(A) I only (B) II only (C) III only
(D) I and II only (E) I, II, and III

ANSWER KEY

Verbal Aptitude Section

1. **C**	*11.* **E**	*21.* **D**	*31.* **D**	*41.* **D**	*51.* **B**	*61.* **D**
2. **E**	*12.* **B**	22. **E**	*32.* **B**	42. **D**	52. **B**	62. **D**
3. **A**	*13.* **A**	23. **C**	*33.* **E**	*43.* **D**	*53.* **D**	*63.* **E**
4. **D**	*14.* **A**	24. **D**	*34.* **B**	*44.* **D**	*54.* **A**	*64.* **C**
5. **D**	*15.* **C**	25. **D**	*35.* **C**	*45.* **B**	*55.* **C**	*65.* **D**
6. **A**	*16.* **E**	26. **C**	*36.* **E**	*46.* **D**	*56.* **C**	
7. **A**	*17.* **C**	27. **D**	*37.* **A**	*47.* **D**	*57.* **E**	
8. **C**	*18.* **C**	28. **A**	*38.* **B**	*48.* **B**	*58.* **D**	
9. **D**	*19.* **B**	29. **D**	*39.* **B**	*49.* **E**	*59.* **C**	
10. **C**	*20.* **D**	*30.* **D**	*40.* **C**	*50.* **A**	*60.* **C**	

Mathematical Aptitude Section

Note: Each correct answer to the mathematics questions is keyed by number to the corresponding topic in Chapters 9 and 10. These numerals refer to the topics listed below, with specific page references in parentheses.

1. Basic Fundamental Operations (155–157)
2. Algebraic Operations (157–160)
3. Using Algebra (160–164)
4. Exponents, Roots and Radicals (159–160)
5. Inequalities (164–165)
6. Fractions (176–178)
7. Decimals (176)
8. Percent (178–180)
9. Averages (180–181)
10. Motion (182–183)
11. Ratio and Proportion (183–185)
12. Mixtures and Solutions (177–178)
13. Work (185–186)
14. Coordinate Geometry (172–173)
15. Geometry (165–172, 173–176)
16. Quantitative Comparisons (189–192)

ANSWER KEY

1. **B** (1,6)	*11.* **B** (11)	*21.* **C** (2,16)	*31.* **C** (16,2)	*41.* **C** (11)
2. **A** (6,7)	*12.* **A** (6)	*22.* **C** (2,16)	*32.* **B** (16,2)	*42.* **C** (15)
3. **C** (1,6)	*13.* **C** (11)	*23.* **D** (15,16)	*33.* **E** (8)	*43.* **A** (15)
4. **E** (1)	*14.* **C** (9)	*24.* **C** (15,16)	*34.* **A** (10)	*44.* **B** (15)
5. **A** (8)	*15.* **A** (11)	*25.* **C** (15,16)	*35.* **C** (11)	*45.* **B** (2)
6. **B** (4)	*16.* **B** (6,16)	*26.* **A** (2,16)	*36.* **C** (1)	*46.* **C** (15)
7. **D** (2)	*17.* **A** (4,6,7,16)	*27.* **A** (15,16)	*37.* **E** (2)	*47.* **C** (15)
8. **B** (6)	*18.* **B** (4,16)	*28.* **D** (16,5)	*38.* **A** (5)	*48.* **A** (15)
9. **D** (8)	*19.* **D** (2,16)	*29.* **B** (16,4)	*39.* **D** (4,7)	*49.* **E** (15)
10. **D** (8)	*20.* **D** (2,16)	*30.* **B** (16,4)	*40.* **A** (2)	*50.* **A** (2,15)

SCORING CHART TYPICAL TEST F

Verbal Section		Mathematical Section*		
No. correct	____	No. correct	(A)	____
No. omitted	____	No. incorrect (# 1-15, 33-50)	(B)	____
No. incorrect	____	No. incorrect (# 16-32)	(C)	____
¼ no. incorrect	____	¼ (B) + 1/3 (C)	(D)	____
Raw Score: (no. correct minus ¼ no. incorrect)	____	*Raw Score* = (A) − (D)		____

* (In the Mathematical section, deduct ¼ of a point for each five-choice question answered incorrectly and 1/3 of a point for each four-choice question answered incorrectly.)

EVALUATION CHART

Study your score. Your raw score on the Verbal and Mathematical Aptitude Sections is an indication of your probable achievement on the PSAT/NMSQT. As a guide to the amount of work you need or want to do, study the following.

Raw Score *Verbal*	Raw Score *Mathematical*	Self-rating
58-65	41-50	Superior
46-57	25-40	Very good
40-45	20-24	Satisfactory
36-39	16-19	Average
30-35	10-15	Needs further study
20-29	7-9	Needs intensive study
0-19	0-6	Probably inadequate

Your scores are most likely improving with each test that you take. To help pinpoint any weak areas you still may have, consult the table on page 384 and plan your remaining review accordingly.

ANSWER EXPLANATIONS

Verbal Aptitude Section

1. **C** To *wither* is to shrivel or to waste away; to *bloom* is to flourish.
Think of a "plant withering from lack of water."

2. **E** To *invigorate* is to give energy to something; to *tire* is to exhaust something, to make it weary.
Think of "an invigorating shower."

3. **A** One's *grasp* is one's understanding; one's *lack of comprehension* is one's inability to understand.
Think of "having a grasp of the problem."

4. **D** To *extricate* is to free something or someone; to *entangle* is to catch or to snarl.
Think of "extricating the quarterback from beneath the pileup."

5. **D** *Ample* means more than enough, abundant; *inadequate* means lacking or insufficient.
Think of "an ample meal."

6. **A** *Fluency* is a smooth, effortless flowing; *hesitancy* is a pausing, a doubt or delay.
Think of "fluency in a foreign language."

7. **A** *Stagnation* is sluggishness or standing still; *progress* is moving forward.
Think of "the stagnation of the stinking swamp."

8. **C** An *altruistic* person is devoted to the welfare of others; a *selfish* person is concerned only with herself.
Think of "an altruistic social worker."

9. **D** *Disparity* is difference; *likeness* is similarity.
Think of a "disparity in their stories."

10. **C** To *oscillate* is to waver or to go through a series of changes; to *remain steady* is to stay still.
Think of "oscillating between two points."

11. **E** An *omniscient* person knows everything; an *ignorant* person lacks knowledge, is uneducated.
Word Parts Clue: *Omni-* means all; *scien-* means knowing. *Omniscient* means all-knowing.
Think of an "omniscient guide."

12. **B** *Verbosity* is wordiness; *terseness* is brevity or conciseness.
Think of the "politician's boring verbosity."

13. **A** An *amenable* person is agreeable or easily managed; an *intractable* person is obstinate and not easily controlled.
Think of being "amenable to their suggestion."

14. **A** To *coalesce* is to grow together or merge; to *separate* is to go apart.
Think of "flour and milk coalescing into batter."

15. **C** To *embolden* is to make someone brave; to *daunt* is to lessen someone's courage.
Think of "trying to embolden frightened troops."

16. **E** *Hermetic* means airtight; *penetrable* means able to be entered or permeable.
Think of a "jar with a hermetic seal."

17. **C** *Distaste* is a dislike for something; *relish* is a liking or particular enjoyment of something.
Think of "her distaste for boring relatives."

18. **C** *Banal* means commonplace or trite; *original* means fresh, not copied.
Think of "his banal, overused jokes."

19. **B** *Decorum* is orderliness or abiding by customs of politeness; *unseemliness* is behaving outside the bounds of good taste.
"Her grace and decorum demanded respect."

20. **D** An *apostate* has renounced or abandoned some former loyalty; a *loyal follower* remains faithful to a cause.
Think of "faithless apostate."

21. **D** In contrast to what might have been expected, the candidate *welcomed* further interviews. Note how the use of "even though" indicates a contrast between one idea and another, setting up a reversal of thought.

22. **E** The phrase "or even" indicates that the missing word is less intense than "appreciated," yet not negative, because the speaker's attitude is favorable toward African music. *Perceived* fits the sentence, while Choice **B,** *revered,* would be too positive and the other choices too negative.

23. **C** *Fissures* are small cracks. "Chasms," which some fissures turn into, are gorges or ravines.

24. **D** To the cynic (a person who expects nothing but the worst of human actions and motives), human actions are *founded* or based upon selfish motives.

25. **D** *Diligence* is steady effort or energy: when you work with diligence you tend to produce perspiration.

26. **C** To *rail against* fate would be to complain angrily about it or utter words of bitterness about it. Note how the use of parallel structure *(neither...nor)* indicates that the two principal phrases linked together are similar in meaning.

27. **D** If "you may wonder" how the expert reaches his or her conclusions, it appears that it is questionable to rely on teeth for guidance in interpreting fossils. Choice **D,** *inadequate,* creates the element of doubt that the clause tries to develop. Choice **C,** *specious,* also creates an element of doubt; however, nothing in the context justifies the idea that the reasoning is specious or false. Note that here you are dealing with an extended metaphor. Picture yourself hanging a heavy winter coat on a slim wooden peg. Wouldn't you worry that the peg might prove inadequate or flimsy?

28. **A** The off-Broadway and Broadway theaters are contrasted here. The former has *manifested* or shown a talent for improvisation, extemporaneous or spontaneous performance. The latter has manifested no such talent for *spontaneity.* Note the use of "whereas" to establish the contrast.

29. **D** Capote was *gregarious* or social and companionable; since Faulkner is contrasted with him, Faulkner must have been *reclusive,* preferring to lead a solitary life.

30. **D** The key word here is *assailed.* Housman is attacking his rival. Thus he is in the tradition of scholarly *invective* (vehement verbal attack). He criticizes his foe for turning to manuscripts merely for confirmation or *support* of old theories and not for enlightenment or illumination. Note the use of figurative language, in this case the simile of the drunkard.

31. **D** A *mower* cuts *lawns;* a *clipper* cuts *nails.*
(Function)

32. **B** One *audits* or examines *books* (financial records) to find errors: one *inspects buildings* to find flaws.
(Purpose)

33. **E** A *bobbin* is a spool on which *thread* is wound; a *reel* is a spool on which *tape* is wound.
(Definition)

34. **B** To *brush* or lightly touch something is less extreme than to *shove* it; to *prick* or lightly cut something is less extreme than to *stab* it.
(Degree of Intensity)

35. **C** A *bungalow* is a small *building;* a *dinghy* is a small *boat.*
Beware eye-catchers. Though cathedrals and chapels are buildings, a cathedral is not a kind of chapel.
(Class and Member)

36. **E** A *bear's* home is a *lair;* a *rabbit's* home is a *burrow.*
(Function)

37. **A** A thing which is *hefty* has a lot of *weight;* a thing which is *lofty* has a lot of *height*.

(Synonym Variant)

38. **B** To *depose* a *monarch* is to get rid of him; to *dismiss* an *employee* is to get rid of or fire him.

(Function)

39. **B** An *arsonist* is a criminal who makes a fire or *conflagration;* a *thug* is a criminal who makes an *assault* or attack on someone.

(Definition)

40. **C** Someone who is *pensive* or thoughtful will *reflect* on things or ponder them; someone who is *unruly* or undisciplined will *disobey* or refuse to follow orders.

(Synonym Variant)

41. **D** People use *spectacles* for *seeing* better; people use *flippers* for *swimming* better.

(Function)

42. **D** An *enigmatic text* is a piece of writing which is mysterious and hard to understand; an *obscure remark* is an utterance which is vague and hard to understand.

(Manner)

43. **D** An obstacle which is *impassable* is impossible to *traverse* or get across; an object which is *impalpable* is impossible to *touch*—it has no material substance.

(Definition)

44. **D** Someone with *aplomb* (self-confidence, poise) is *nonchalant* (casual, without concern); someone with *affability* (friendliness) is *cordial* (friendly, warm).

(Synonym Variant)

45. **B** A *juggernaut* is a dangerous force or object which is *unstoppable* and crushes everything in its path; a *turncoat* is a dangerous person who is *treacherous,* who turns against her friends.

(Definition)

46. **D** *Momentous* means extremely important. Since the author states that "The whole life is different" after the point at which one first conceals something, that point is clearly momentous.

47. **D** The author does not make jokes or use sarcasm. There is no anger or condescension in the passage, nor is the speaker impersonal (the message is urgent and strongly worded). In general, the author's tone is *serious*.

48. **B** The correct answer may be found by elimination. Statement I is not supported by the passage. The author does not deny the necessity of aging, but rather the necessity of hiding things. Therefore Choices **A, C,** and **E** may be eliminated.
Statement III is not supported by the passage. The author does not suggest that people rationalize their misconduct. Therefore Choice **D** may be eliminated.
That leaves Choice **B.** It is the correct answer.

49. **E** Composing is described here as an entirely natural and *instinctive* activity, like eating and sleeping.

50. **A** The author states (paragraph 2) that the layperson "finds it difficult to believe that composers are not much preoccupied" or concerned with the question of inspiration (the stimulus needed to create a piece). Thus the layperson may mistakenly imagine it's very hard for the composer to begin work, while the author maintains that it's really very easy.

51. **B** The tone of this passage is not at all negative, nor is it consciously prejudiced (though there may be some overgeneralization about laypersons). The author is somewhat philosophical, but not *deeply* philosophical, and does not become highly emotional. Both eliminating the other choices, and the passage's *casual,* conversational tone and *informative* content lead us to Choice **B.**

52. **B** The passage states that "court decisions are merely guideposts pointing toward a virtually endless series of vexing legal questions." In other words, once a decision is made, it still has to be interpreted and put into practice; and this generates more decisions. This flatly contradicts Choice **E,** the provision of final solutions.
Choice **A** is true, but the main concern of the passage is not the publicity which follows major court decisions. Choices **C** and **D** are not supported by the passage.

53. **D** In the first two sentences, the author explains that while the average citizen is knowledgeable about major Supreme Court decisions, he or she frequently "thinks that these decisions settle matters once and for all." This notion is incorrect, and therefore the public's understanding is *limited.*

54. **A** Apportionment here means distributing representatives' votes on the basis of population density, so that city and country voters each have their fair share of votes. The author describes the Court as trying to protect the "traditional democratic ideal of *majority rule*" from being "subverted" (ruined, corrupted) by apportionment schemes.

55. **C** For tourists, a landmark is an important structure or natural wonder, to which they will want to give attention. Used figuratively, the word means a turning point in history or politics, such as a *significant* Supreme Court decision.

56. **C** The author states: "Porpoises left the land when mammalian brains were still small and primitive." This indicates that porpoises were once land animals, mammals like ourselves, whose evolutionary development took them back into the sea.

57. **E** The passage indicates that human beings think of intelligence in terms of our own ability to manipulate our environment—the many things we can build and do with our hands. Since porpoises have no hands, we have trouble appreciating their high level of intelligence.

58. **D** The concluding sentence compares human intelligence and the porpoise's intelligence as *complementary* (balanced) abilities: the porpoise can look inward and the human being can look outward.

59. **C** The entire passage has concentrated on the porpoise's brain, so it is safe to assume that this is what is meant by the "impressively elaborated instrument." The items mentioned in the other answer choices have not been mentioned at all. Note that Choice **B**, an artificial range-finding device, is incorrect because the porpoise's range-finder is entirely natural, not artificial.

60. **C** The author's tone is distinctly admiring. The passage speaks of porpoises' "remarkable range-finding ability," mentions their care for each other, and repeatedly praises the porpoise's intelligence.

61. **D** The author states what cataclysmic variables are and describes how the three general classes of exploding stars range in magnitude and other characteristics. Choice **A** is incorrect. The author gives far more emphasis to dwarf novae than to novae. Choice **B** is incorrect. The author offers no such explanation. Choice **C** is incorrect. The author states their unpredictability; he does not explain or account for it. Choice **E** is incorrect. The author offers no such explanation.

62. **D** Paragraph 1 tells us that "25 novae occur in our galaxy every year, but only two or three are *near enough* to be observed." Thus our observations of novae are hampered by their distance.

63. **E** You can arrive at the correct answer by the process of elimination.
Statement I is accurate. Dwarf novae explosions are less violent than are those of supernovae. Therefore, you can eliminate Choice **B.**
Statement II is accurate. Dwarf novae are observed more frequently than are supernovae. Therefore, you can eliminate Choices **A** and **D.**
Statement III is accurate. Dwarf novae, unlike supernovae, flare up periodically rather than flaring up once and being totally consumed. Therefore, you can eliminate Choice **C.**
Only Choice **E** is left. It is the correct answer.

64. **C** Paragraph 1 states: "If the exploding star is in a nearby part of the galaxy, it may create a 'new star' that was not previously visible to the naked eye." Thus a new star is one that has become bright enough to strike the eye.

65. **D** You can arrive at the correct answer by the process of elimination.
Question I is answerable on the basis of the passage. Paragraph 1 states that the last supernova was observed in 1604. Therefore, you can eliminate Choices **B** and **E.**
Question II is unanswerable on the basis of the passage. No reason for the phenomenon is given in the passage. Therefore, you can eliminate Choice **C.**
Question III is answerable on the basis of the passage. Paragraph 3 states that dwarf novae increase in brightness "within a period of several hours" and decline from this maximum level of brilliance over a period of two to three days. Therefore, you can eliminate Choice **A.**
Only Choice **D** is left. It is the correct answer.

Mathematical Aptitude Section

1. **B** $\frac{1}{3}$ of $\frac{1}{4} = \frac{1}{12} = \frac{4}{48}$

$\frac{1}{4}$ of $\frac{1}{12} = \frac{1}{48}$

$\frac{4}{48} - \frac{1}{48} = \frac{3}{48} = \frac{1}{16}$

2. **A** $\frac{100}{0.2} = \frac{1000}{2} = 500$

$100 - 500 = -400$

3. **C** $\dfrac{5\frac{3}{4}}{1 - \frac{13}{36}} = \dfrac{5\frac{3}{4}}{\frac{23}{36}} = \dfrac{\frac{23}{4}}{\frac{23}{36}} = \frac{23}{4} \div \frac{23}{36} = \frac{\cancel{23}}{\cancel{4}} \cdot \frac{\overset{9}{\cancel{36}}}{\cancel{23}} = 9$

$(?)^2 = 9$

$? = 3$

4. **E** Since 2160, 1344, and 1440 are divisible by the largest number (48), the correct answer is (**E**). It may be easier to discover that all are divisible by both 6 and 8, and hence by 48, without actually dividing by 48.

5. **A** $\frac{1}{4}\% = \frac{1}{400}$

$\frac{1}{400} \cdot 2 = \frac{1}{200}$

6. **B** $\sqrt[4]{81} = 3$

$\sqrt{18} = \sqrt{9}\sqrt{2} = 3\sqrt{2}$

$2^x = \frac{3}{3\sqrt{2}} = \frac{1}{\sqrt{2}} = 2^{-\frac{1}{2}}$

$2^x = 2^{-\frac{1}{2}}$

$x = -\frac{1}{2}$

7. **D** He saves $d - s$ dollars per week.

In $\frac{Q}{d - s}$ weeks he will have Q dollars.

8. **B** $\frac{1 \text{ dime}}{\$3.00} = \frac{10¢}{300¢} = \frac{10}{300} = \frac{1}{30}$

9. **D** $\frac{?}{100} \cdot k = 10$

$\frac{?}{100} = \frac{10}{k}$

$? = \frac{1000}{k}$

10. **D** Let x = registration of previous year.

$\left(6\frac{1}{4}\%\right)$ of x = increase over previous year.

$\left(6\frac{1}{4}\%\right)$ of $x + x$ = present registration.

$0.0625x + x = 850$

$1.0625x = 850$

$10625x = 8500000$

$x = 800$

11. **B** This is a direct proportion. Let x = the number of erasers that can be bought for 36¢.

$\frac{\text{number of erasers}}{\text{cost in ¢}} = \frac{2}{6} = \frac{x}{36}$

$6x = 72$

$x = 12$

12. **A** $\frac{1}{3}$ of 750 = 250 unsold seats in orchestra

$\frac{5}{8}$ of 400 = 250 unsold seats in balcony

500 = total unsold seats

$\frac{500}{1150} = \frac{10}{23}$

13. **C** Basic ratio = $19x:5x:3x$

If $3x = 9$, then $19x = (19)(3) = 57$.

14. **C** To have average of 160 for 18 games, sum = 2880.

He has average of 150 for 12 games, sum = 1800.

Required additional points = 1080

Average for 6 more games = 1080 ÷ 6 = 180

15. **A** 6 inches on the boy's map = 2 inches on original map

2 inches = 2 miles on original scale

16. **B** $\frac{(7)(7)(21)}{x} = (7)(3)$

$(7)(7)(21) = (7)(3)(x)$

$49 = x$

17. **A** $\sqrt{\frac{1}{4}} = \frac{1}{2}$

$(.25)^2 = \left(\frac{1}{4}\right)^2 = \frac{1}{16}$

$\frac{1}{2} > \frac{1}{16}$

18. **B** $2^{n+1} = 32$

$2^5 = 32$

$n + 1 = 5$

$n = 4$

19. **D** Either, or both x and $y = 0$.

20. **D** $x^2 - y^2 = 0$

$(x + y)(x - y) = 0$

$x + y = 0$ or $x - y = 0$

Therefore we cannot tell if Column A = Column B or is greater or less than it.

21. **C** $\frac{a + b}{b} = \frac{a}{b} + \frac{b}{b} = \frac{a}{b} + 1$

22. **C** $a + 3 = 5$ $\qquad b + 3 = 7$

$a = 2$ $\qquad b = 4$

$b - a = 4 - 2 = 2$

23. **D** City C could be at any point on the circumference of the circle with radius 5 miles. City A could be at any point on the circumference of the circle with radius 10 miles.

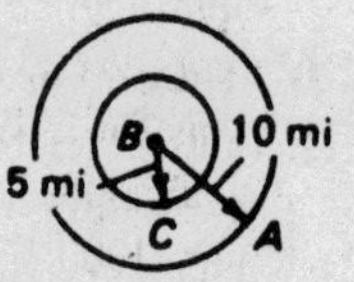

24. **C** $a + b + c = 180°$, with average of 60°. Since triangle ABC is equilateral, $x = 60°$.

25. **C** △s XWY and WVZ are right triangles. $a = b$ [vertical angles]. △$XWY \sim WVZ$.

$\frac{XY}{VZ} = \frac{8}{16} = \frac{1}{2} = \frac{WY}{VW} = \frac{10}{20}$

Right △ WXY is a 3-4-5 triangle with all dimensions multiplied by 2, so $WX = 6$.

Right △ WVZ is a 3-4-5 triangle with all dimensions multiplied by 4, so $WZ = 12$

$XWZ = 18$

$XY + WY = 8 + 10 = 18$

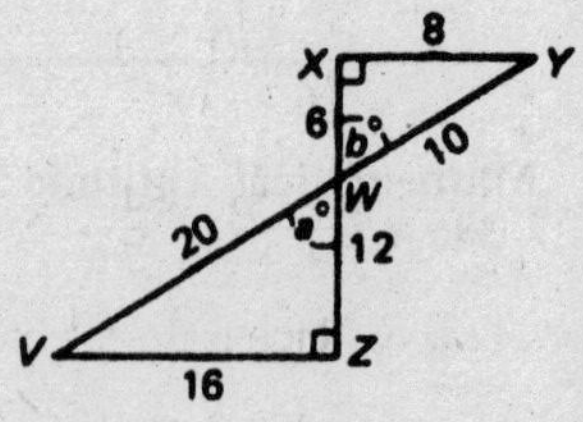

26. **A** Either b or c must equal zero.

Therefore $bc = 0$.

27. **A** Alternate interior angles a and b are equal.

$a = b = \frac{1}{2}(110°) = 55°$

$x + 55° = 180°$

$x = 125$

28. **D** Many different values may be substituted for x and for y in the inequality, producing different values and relationships. We know only that $x > \frac{3}{4}y$.

29. **B** $(1)^{27} = 1$, while $(3)^9$ or $(3)(3)(3)(3)(3)(3)(3)(3)(3)$ is much greater in value than 1.

30. **B** Since x is squared, x^2 has a positive value. Ten minus any positive value is less than 11.

31. **C** Cross multiply: $7x = y$

32. **B** Solve by factoring:

$a^2 - 11a + 30 = 0$

$(a - 6)(a - 5) = 0$

$a = 6$ and 5

33. **E** The change is 15¢ − 3¢ or 12¢.

Change ÷ original × 100 = percentage change.

$\frac{12}{3} = 4 = 400\%$

34. **A** Time in flight for #602 = 3 hours.

$200 \times 3 = 600$ miles covered by #602.

Time in flight for #302 = $2\frac{1}{2}$ hours.

$320 \times 2\frac{1}{2} = 800$ miles covered by #302.

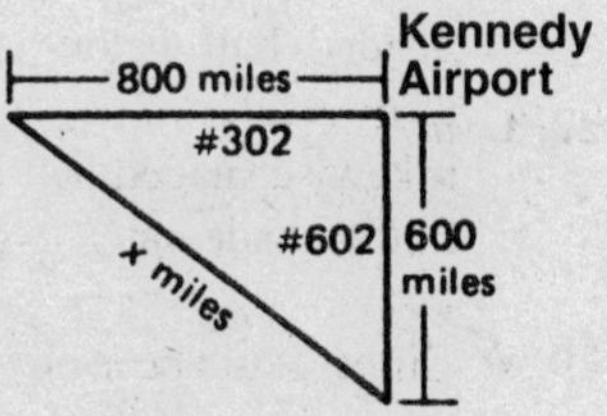

This forms a right triangle. Observe 3, 4, 5 ratio, with each dimension multiplied by 200.

$x = 1000$. ∴ Distance = 1000 miles

35. **C** Total = 27

$\frac{3}{27} = \frac{1}{9} = 11.1\%$

36. **C** Possibilities are

three 3¢ + four 4¢ = 25

seven 3¢ + one 4¢ = 25

37. **E** $x + y = 16$

$x = 16 - y$

$(16 - y) - z = 16 - y - z$

38. **A** $\frac{a - b}{3.5} = \frac{4}{7}$

Since $3.5 = \frac{1}{2}$ of 7, $a - b = \frac{1}{2}$ of $4 = 2$.

Since $a - b = 2$, $b < a$.

39. **D** $10^x = \underbrace{(10)(10)(10)\ \ldots\ldots\ldots\ 10}_{x \text{ times}}$

$$10^{-x} = \frac{1}{\underbrace{(10)(10)(10)\ \ldots\ldots\ldots\ (10)}_{x \text{ times}}}$$

(A) is true.

$470{,}000 = (4.7)(10)(10)(10)(10)(10) = 4.7 \times 10^5$

(B) is true. 450 billion $= 4.5 \times 10^{11}$

(C) is true. $0.00000000075 = 7.5 \times 10^{-10}$

(D) is not true. $\frac{86}{100{,}000} = \frac{8.6}{10{,}000} = 8.6 \times 10^{-4}$

(E) is true. 26 million $= 2.6 \times 10^7$

40. **A** Necessary money = 2 × \$50 = \$100.

Let x = amount of money to be invested to yield \$100 per year.

10% or (.10) of $x = 100$

$.10x = 100$

$x = \$1000$

41. **C** This is an inverse proportion, since the more chickens you feed the less time it will last.

Let x = number of days food will last for 80 chickens.

$\frac{60 \text{ chickens}}{80 \text{ chickens}} = \frac{x}{8 \text{ days}}$

$80x = 480$

$x = 6$ days

42. **C** Volume of water in rectangular tank $= (25'')(9'')(2'')$

Let x = height of this volume of water in cylindrical container.

Volume in cylindrical container = $(\pi)(\text{radius})^2(\text{height})$ or $(\pi)(5)^2(x)$ or $(25)(x)(\pi)$

Since volumes are equal,

$(25'')(9'')(2'') = (25)(x)(\pi)$

$18 = \pi x$

$\frac{18}{\pi} = x$.

43. **A** $\angle EDB \overset{\circ}{=} \frac{1}{2}\widehat{CB}$

$\angle AED \overset{\circ}{=} \frac{1}{2}(\widehat{AD} + \widehat{CB})$.

Let $x \overset{\circ}{=} \widehat{CB}$.

$45° = \frac{1}{2}(60 + x)$

$90 = 60 + x$

$30° = x$

Since $\widehat{CB} = 30°$, then

$\angle EDB \overset{\circ}{=} 15$.

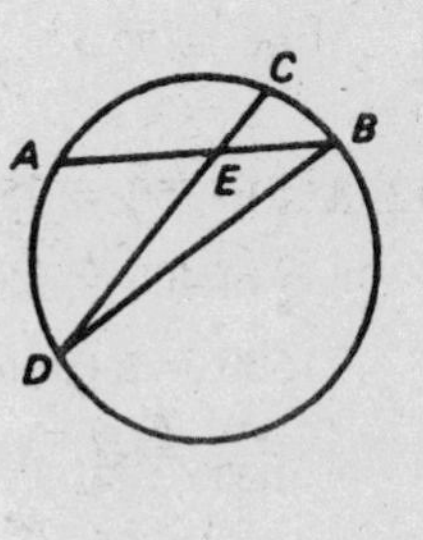

44. **B** If $\angle BAC \overset{\circ}{=} 30$, then

$\widehat{BC} = 60°$.

If $\widehat{BC} = \widehat{CD}$,

$\widehat{CD} = 60°$.

Since AOC is the diameter,

$\widehat{ADC} = 180°$.

Since $\widehat{CD} = 60°$.

$\widehat{AD} = 120°$.

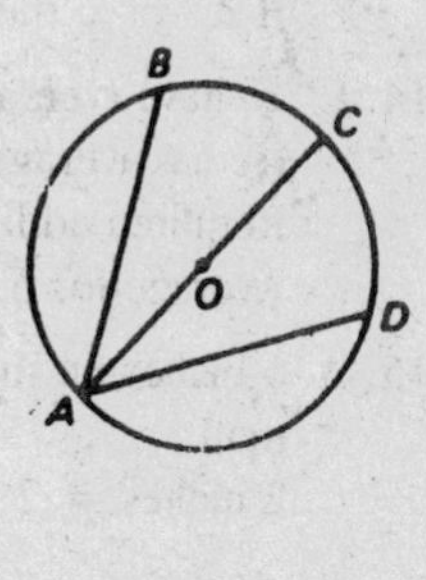

45. **B** $8 + 8a + a = 3$

$$9a = -5$$

$$a = -\frac{5}{9}$$

46. **C** $\angle BAE \overset{\circ}{=} 45$, since $\angle AEB$ is a right angle and $\angle ABE \overset{\circ}{=} 45$.

$\therefore AE = EB = 8$

Likewise $FC = 8$

$EF = AD = 10$

$BC = 8 + 10 + 8 = 26$

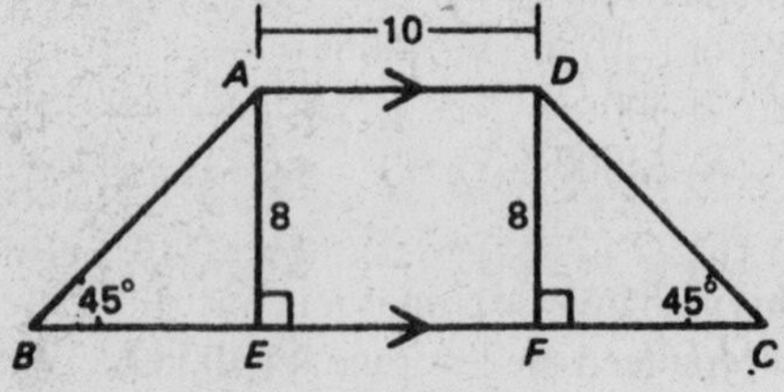

47. **C** $\angle BAC + \angle BCA =$
$180° - 120° = 60°$

Since $BA = BC$,

$\angle BAC = \angle BCA \overset{\circ}{=} 30.$

DA bisects $\angle BAC$ [given].

$\angle DAC \overset{\circ}{=} 15$

Since $DA = DC$, $\angle DCA \overset{\circ}{=} 15$.

$\angle ADC = 180° - (\angle DCA + \angle DAC)$

$\angle ADC \overset{\circ}{=} 180 - 30 = 150$

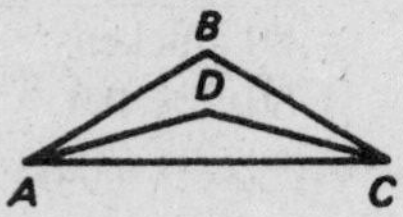

48. **A** Let x = number of feet ladder will extend up the building. The right triangle formed is a 5-12-13 triangle with all dimensions multiplied by 3. $39 = 3(13)$, $15 = 3(5)$, so $x = 3(12) = 36$.

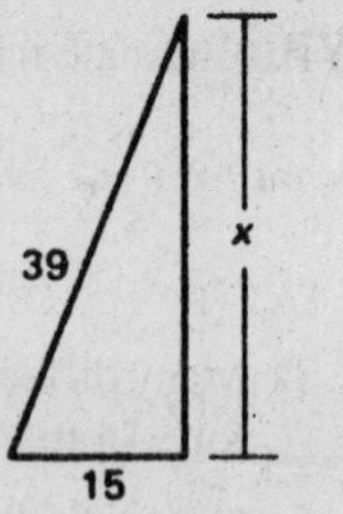

49. **E** Assume x, x, x are, respectively, the sides of the original cube.

Then $3x$, $3x$, $3x$ will be the sides of the enlarged box.

Volume of original box $= x^3$

Volume of enlarged box $= (3x)(3x)(3x)$ or $27x^3$

50. **A** Draw AC.

Area of $\triangle ADC$

$$= \frac{10 \times 10}{2} = 50$$

$AFCD = \frac{1}{4}$ of circle

Area of this $\frac{1}{4}$ of circle

$$= \frac{\pi(10)^2}{4} = 25\pi$$

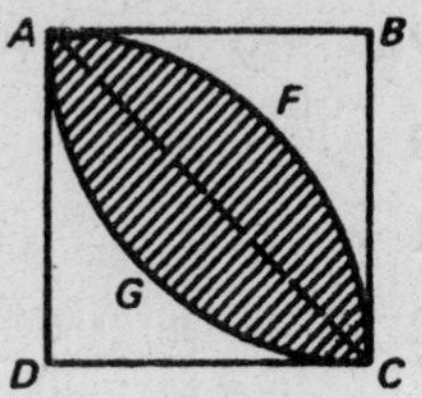

Shaded half below $AC = 25\pi - \triangle ADC$ or $25\pi - 50$

Likewise shaded half above $AC = 25\pi - 50$

Entire shaded area $= 50\pi - 100$

PSAT/NMSQT Answer Sheet

TYPICAL TEST G

Verbal Aptitude Section

1 Ⓐ Ⓑ Ⓒ Ⓓ Ⓔ
2 Ⓐ Ⓑ Ⓒ Ⓓ Ⓔ
3 Ⓐ Ⓑ Ⓒ Ⓓ Ⓔ
4 Ⓐ Ⓑ Ⓒ Ⓓ Ⓔ
5 Ⓐ Ⓑ Ⓒ Ⓓ Ⓔ
6 Ⓐ Ⓑ Ⓒ Ⓓ Ⓔ
7 Ⓐ Ⓑ Ⓒ Ⓓ Ⓔ
8 Ⓐ Ⓑ Ⓒ Ⓓ Ⓔ
9 Ⓐ Ⓑ Ⓒ Ⓓ Ⓔ
10 Ⓐ Ⓑ Ⓒ Ⓓ Ⓔ
11 Ⓐ Ⓑ Ⓒ Ⓓ Ⓔ
12 Ⓐ Ⓑ Ⓒ Ⓓ Ⓔ
13 Ⓐ Ⓑ Ⓒ Ⓓ Ⓔ
14 Ⓐ Ⓑ Ⓒ Ⓓ Ⓔ
15 Ⓐ Ⓑ Ⓒ Ⓓ Ⓔ
16 Ⓐ Ⓑ Ⓒ Ⓓ Ⓔ
17 Ⓐ Ⓑ Ⓒ Ⓓ Ⓔ
18 Ⓐ Ⓑ Ⓒ Ⓓ Ⓔ
19 Ⓐ Ⓑ Ⓒ Ⓓ Ⓔ
20 Ⓐ Ⓑ Ⓒ Ⓓ Ⓔ
21 Ⓐ Ⓑ Ⓒ Ⓓ Ⓔ
22 Ⓐ Ⓑ Ⓒ Ⓓ Ⓔ
23 Ⓐ Ⓑ Ⓒ Ⓓ Ⓔ
24 Ⓐ Ⓑ Ⓒ Ⓓ Ⓔ
25 Ⓐ Ⓑ Ⓒ Ⓓ Ⓔ
26 Ⓐ Ⓑ Ⓒ Ⓓ Ⓔ
27 Ⓐ Ⓑ Ⓒ Ⓓ Ⓔ
28 Ⓐ Ⓑ Ⓒ Ⓓ Ⓔ
29 Ⓐ Ⓑ Ⓒ Ⓓ Ⓔ
30 Ⓐ Ⓑ Ⓒ Ⓓ Ⓔ
31 Ⓐ Ⓑ Ⓒ Ⓓ Ⓔ
32 Ⓐ Ⓑ Ⓒ Ⓓ Ⓔ
33 Ⓐ Ⓑ Ⓒ Ⓓ Ⓔ
34 Ⓐ Ⓑ Ⓒ Ⓓ Ⓔ
35 Ⓐ Ⓑ Ⓒ Ⓓ Ⓔ
36 Ⓐ Ⓑ Ⓒ Ⓓ Ⓔ
37 Ⓐ Ⓑ Ⓒ Ⓓ Ⓔ
38 Ⓐ Ⓑ Ⓒ Ⓓ Ⓔ
39 Ⓐ Ⓑ Ⓒ Ⓓ Ⓔ
40 Ⓐ Ⓑ Ⓒ Ⓓ Ⓔ
41 Ⓐ Ⓑ Ⓒ Ⓓ Ⓔ
42 Ⓐ Ⓑ Ⓒ Ⓓ Ⓔ
43 Ⓐ Ⓑ Ⓒ Ⓓ Ⓔ
44 Ⓐ Ⓑ Ⓒ Ⓓ Ⓔ
45 Ⓐ Ⓑ Ⓒ Ⓓ Ⓔ
46 Ⓐ Ⓑ Ⓒ Ⓓ Ⓔ
47 Ⓐ Ⓑ Ⓒ Ⓓ Ⓔ
48 Ⓐ Ⓑ Ⓒ Ⓓ Ⓔ
49 Ⓐ Ⓑ Ⓒ Ⓓ Ⓔ
50 Ⓐ Ⓑ Ⓒ Ⓓ Ⓔ
51 Ⓐ Ⓑ Ⓒ Ⓓ Ⓔ
52 Ⓐ Ⓑ Ⓒ Ⓓ Ⓔ
53 Ⓐ Ⓑ Ⓒ Ⓓ Ⓔ
54 Ⓐ Ⓑ Ⓒ Ⓓ Ⓔ
55 Ⓐ Ⓑ Ⓒ Ⓓ Ⓔ
56 Ⓐ Ⓑ Ⓒ Ⓓ Ⓔ
57 Ⓐ Ⓑ Ⓒ Ⓓ Ⓔ
58 Ⓐ Ⓑ Ⓒ Ⓓ Ⓔ
59 Ⓐ Ⓑ Ⓒ Ⓓ Ⓔ
60 Ⓐ Ⓑ Ⓒ Ⓓ Ⓔ
61 Ⓐ Ⓑ Ⓒ Ⓓ Ⓔ
62 Ⓐ Ⓑ Ⓒ Ⓓ Ⓔ
63 Ⓐ Ⓑ Ⓒ Ⓓ Ⓔ
64 Ⓐ Ⓑ Ⓒ Ⓓ Ⓔ
65 Ⓐ Ⓑ Ⓒ Ⓓ Ⓔ

Mathematical Aptitude Section*

1 Ⓐ Ⓑ Ⓒ Ⓓ Ⓔ
2 Ⓐ Ⓑ Ⓒ Ⓓ Ⓔ
3 Ⓐ Ⓑ Ⓒ Ⓓ Ⓔ
4 Ⓐ Ⓑ Ⓒ Ⓓ Ⓔ
5 Ⓐ Ⓑ Ⓒ Ⓓ Ⓔ
6 Ⓐ Ⓑ Ⓒ Ⓓ Ⓔ
7 Ⓐ Ⓑ Ⓒ Ⓓ Ⓔ
8 Ⓐ Ⓑ Ⓒ Ⓓ Ⓔ
9 Ⓐ Ⓑ Ⓒ Ⓓ Ⓔ
10 Ⓐ Ⓑ Ⓒ Ⓓ Ⓔ
11 Ⓐ Ⓑ Ⓒ Ⓓ Ⓔ
12 Ⓐ Ⓑ Ⓒ Ⓓ Ⓔ
13 Ⓐ Ⓑ Ⓒ Ⓓ Ⓔ
14 Ⓐ Ⓑ Ⓒ Ⓓ Ⓔ
15 Ⓐ Ⓑ Ⓒ Ⓓ Ⓔ
16 Ⓐ Ⓑ Ⓒ Ⓓ Ⓔ
17 Ⓐ Ⓑ Ⓒ Ⓓ Ⓔ
18 Ⓐ Ⓑ Ⓒ Ⓓ Ⓔ
19 Ⓐ Ⓑ Ⓒ Ⓓ Ⓔ
20 Ⓐ Ⓑ Ⓒ Ⓓ Ⓔ
21 Ⓐ Ⓑ Ⓒ Ⓓ Ⓔ
22 Ⓐ Ⓑ Ⓒ Ⓓ Ⓔ
23 Ⓐ Ⓑ Ⓒ Ⓓ Ⓔ
24 Ⓐ Ⓑ Ⓒ Ⓓ Ⓔ
25 Ⓐ Ⓑ Ⓒ Ⓓ Ⓔ
26 Ⓐ Ⓑ Ⓒ Ⓓ Ⓔ
27 Ⓐ Ⓑ Ⓒ Ⓓ Ⓔ
28 Ⓐ Ⓑ Ⓒ Ⓓ Ⓔ
29 Ⓐ Ⓑ Ⓒ Ⓓ Ⓔ
30 Ⓐ Ⓑ Ⓒ Ⓓ Ⓔ
31 Ⓐ Ⓑ Ⓒ Ⓓ Ⓔ
32 Ⓐ Ⓑ Ⓒ Ⓓ Ⓔ
33 Ⓐ Ⓑ Ⓒ Ⓓ Ⓔ
34 Ⓐ Ⓑ Ⓒ Ⓓ Ⓔ
35 Ⓐ Ⓑ Ⓒ Ⓓ Ⓔ
36 Ⓐ Ⓑ Ⓒ Ⓓ Ⓔ
37 Ⓐ Ⓑ Ⓒ Ⓓ Ⓔ
38 Ⓐ Ⓑ Ⓒ Ⓓ Ⓔ
39 Ⓐ Ⓑ Ⓒ Ⓓ Ⓔ
40 Ⓐ Ⓑ Ⓒ Ⓓ Ⓔ
41 Ⓐ Ⓑ Ⓒ Ⓓ Ⓔ
42 Ⓐ Ⓑ Ⓒ Ⓓ Ⓔ
43 Ⓐ Ⓑ Ⓒ Ⓓ Ⓔ
44 Ⓐ Ⓑ Ⓒ Ⓓ Ⓔ
45 Ⓐ Ⓑ Ⓒ Ⓓ Ⓔ
46 Ⓐ Ⓑ Ⓒ Ⓓ Ⓔ
47 Ⓐ Ⓑ Ⓒ Ⓓ Ⓔ
48 Ⓐ Ⓑ Ⓒ Ⓓ Ⓔ
49 Ⓐ Ⓑ Ⓒ Ⓓ Ⓔ
50 Ⓐ Ⓑ Ⓒ Ⓓ Ⓔ

*If there are more answer spaces than you need, leave them blank.

TYPICAL TEST G

SECTION 1	Time—50 minutes 65 Questions	For each question in this section, choose the best answer and fill in the corresponding circle on the answer sheet.

Each question below consists of a word in capital letters, followed by five lettered words or phrases. Choose the word or phrase that is most nearly opposite in meaning to the word in capital letters. Since some of the questions require you to distinguish fine shades of meaning, consider all the choices before deciding which is best.

Example:

GOOD: (A) sour (B) bad (C) red (D) hot (E) ugly

Ⓐ ● Ⓒ Ⓓ Ⓔ

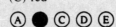

1. MONOTONOUS: (A) varied (B) brave (C) solemn (D) violent (E) timely

2. DECLINE: (A) accept (B) displease (C) summarize (D) show concern (E) use frequently

3. BUSTLE: (A) inactivity (B) frustration (C) efficiency (D) consternation (E) sophistication

4. DILIGENT: (A) early (B) lazy (C) weary (D) sly (E) aged

5. MIGRATE: (A) avoid labor (B) divide equally (C) trade places (D) squander freely (E) refrain from moving

6. REVERE: (A) advance (B) wake (C) clothe (D) dishonor (E) mistake

7. OBSTINATE: (A) yielding (B) fleeting (C) finite (D) fascinating (E) permanent

8. PROTRACT: (A) make circular (B) set loose (C) retrace (D) involve (E) shorten

9. NOVICE: (A) veteran (B) genius (C) flatterer (D) rebel (E) villain

10. FLAMBOYANT: (A) fireproof (B) hideous (C) conservative (D) authentic (E) insistent

11. CONCENTRATE: (A) scatter (B) reveal (C) impress (D) incline (E) forget

12. ABOMINATE: (A) suppress (B) appreciate (C) discern (D) evaluate (E) modify

13. VIVACIOUS: (A) unkind (B) dramatic (C) versatile (D) phlegmatic (E) vigilant

14. IMPLACABILITY: (A) compassion (B) gullibility (C) prodigality (D) coherence (E) adulation

15. FANATICAL: (A) celebrated (B) merciful (C) apathetic (D) devious (E) unpersuasive

16. REVILE: (A) compose (B) awake (C) deaden (D) praise (E) secrete

17. PROBITY: (A) fallacy (B) improbability (C) conviction (D) depravity (E) avidity

18. SOPORIFIC: (A) stimulating (B) pessimistic (C) hallucinatory (D) sentimental (E) realistic

19. BELIE: (A) perjure oneself (B) represent accurately (C) answer unwillingly (D) investigate thoroughly (E) grant immunity

20. TANTAMOUNT: (A) not negotiable (B) not equivalent (C) not ambitious (D) not evident (E) not relevant

Each sentence below has one or two blanks, each blank indicating that something has been omitted. Beneath the sentence are five lettered words or sets of words. Choose the word or set of words that, when inserted in the sentence, best fits the meaning of the sentence as a whole.

Example:

Although its publicity has been ----, the film itself is intelligent, well-acted, handsomely produced, and altogether ----.

(A) tasteless . . respectable
(B) extensive . . moderate
(C) sophisticated . . amateur (D) risque . . crude
(E) perfect . . spectacular

● Ⓑ Ⓒ Ⓓ Ⓔ

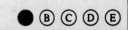

21. Advances in health care have lengthened life spans, lowered infant mortality rates, and, thus, ---- the overpopulation problem.
(A) eliminated (B) aggravated (C) minimized (D) distorted (E) discouraged

22. They greeted his proposal with ---- and refused to give it serious study.
(A) acclaim (B) detachment (C) fervor (D) derision (E) approbation

23. While some scientists point to the vast uncertainties about global warming as reason to delay action in confronting the greenhouse effect, many experts argue that the possibility of ---- damage ---- strong measures now to reduce the human impact on global systems that remain beyond scientists' understanding.
(A) excessive . . precludes
(B) aggravated . . sidetracks
(C) accelerated . . warrants
(D) illusory . . justifies
(E) ambiguous . . demands

24. Holroyd manages to make each successive phase of Shaw's life seem significant of itself, rather than simply as ---- of what was to come or as raw material for Shaw's plays.
(A) an application (B) a foretoken
(C) a predilection (D) a plagiarism
(E) a recollection

25. The renovation of historic Union Station is salutary not just as an example of ---- restoration but also as a reminder that in this age of retrenchment and diminished dreams, ambitious federal public works programs can still ----.
(A) impeccable . . succeed
(B) inadequate . . inspire
(C) flawless . . terminate
(D) archaic . . flourish
(E) partial . . impede

26. The epiphyte plants of the rain forest use trees for physical support but do not, like ----, sap nutrients from their hosts.
(A) fauna (B) predators (C) parasites
(D) insectivores (E) stumps

27. For centuries, physicists have had good reason to believe in the principle of equivalence propounded by Galileo: it has ---- many rigorous tests that ---- its accuracy to extraordinary precision.
(A) endured . . compromised
(B) passed . . presupposed
(C) borne . . postulated
(D) survived . . proved
(E) inspired . . equated

28. To the embittered ex-philanthropist, all the former recipients of her charity were ----, as stingy with their thanks as they were wasteful of her largesse.
(A) louts (B) misers (C) ingrates
(D) prigs (E) renegades

29. Among contemporary writers of fiction, Mrs. Woolf is ---- figure, in some ways as radical as James Joyce, in others no more modern than Jane Austen.
(A) a doctrinaire (B) an introspective
(C) a peripheral (D) a disinterested
(E) an anomalous

30. Physicists dream of a unified theory of matter that could replace the current ---- of mutually inconsistent theories that clutter the field.
(A) bonanza (B) concord (C) dearth
(D) integration (E) welter

Each question below consists of a related pair of words or phrases, followed by five lettered pairs of words or phrases. Select the lettered pair that best expresses a relationship similar to that expressed in the original pair.

Example:

YAWN : BOREDOM : : (A) dream : sleep
(B) anger : madness (C) smile : amusement
(D) face : expression (E) impatience : rebellion

Ⓐ Ⓑ ● Ⓓ Ⓔ

31. SCHOOL : TRUANT : : (A) university : teacher
(B) hospital : patient (C) courtroom : defendant
(D) jail : convict (E) army : deserter

32. STROLLER : BABY : : (A) moving van : mover
(B) ambulance : driver (C) bus : passenger
(D) shopping cart : cashier (E) carriage : horse

33. FLURRY : BLIZZARD : : (A) mud : slide
(B) mist : snow (C) geyser : steam
(D) breeze : gale (E) avalanche : waterfall

34. CARPET : FLOOR : : (A) mosaic : tile
(B) tapestry : wall (C) beam : ceiling
(D) rug : fringe (E) knob : door

35. TREATY : NATIONS : : (A) map : mountains
(B) contract : individuals
(C) reconciliation : ideas (D) agreement : terms
(E) boundary : states

36. KANGAROO : MARSUPIAL : :
(A) rose : hybrid (B) mushroom : fungus
(C) antelope : gazelle (D) alligator : swamp
(E) dog : flea

37. SNICKER : DISRESPECT : : (A) chortle : grief
(B) coax : petulance (C) swagger : movement
(D) moan : suffering (E) bellow : disgust

38. CHOREOGRAPHER : DANCE : :
(A) astrologer : stars (B) calligrapher : pen
(C) director : film (D) driver : automobile
(E) photographer : camera

39. TASTE : GUSTATORY : : (A) touch : furtive
(B) eyes : visionary (C) hearing : impaired
(D) smell : olfactory (E) remark : derogatory

40. EMBARK : YACHT : : (A) import : car
(B) enhance : performance
(C) repair : motorcycle (D) mount : steed
(E) moor : boat

41. POVERTY : PAUPER : : (A) hunger : gourmet
(B) modesty : braggart (C) ignorance : tutor
(D) slowness : sluggard (E) army : deserter

42. SERMON : SPEECH : : (A) stanza : poetry
(B) minister : congregation
(C) pilgrimage : journey (D) lectern : lecture
(E) repentance : prayer

43. EMBRACE : POSITION : :
(A) disentangle : knot (B) espouse : cause
(C) propose : ceremony (D) reverse : decision
(E) enforce : law

44. MERCURIAL : MOOD : : (A) jovial : wrath
(B) hypocritical : conduct (C) ominous : weather
(D) frugal : economy (E) erratic : course

45. COMMUTE : SENTENCE : :
(A) travel : journal (B) reduce : fine
(C) convict : crime (D) refurbish : house
(E) transcribe : copy

> Each passage below is followed by questions based on its content. Answer the questions following each passage on the basis of what is stated or implied in that passage.

For all of E.E. Cummings's typographical innovations, he was an old-fashioned poet. He wrote about death and love, the graces of nature and the disgraces of civilization. He implored beautiful ladies for their favors and wittily thanked them afterwards. He distrusted power and satirized people in power. He adored Paris and said so in random lines as taking as any in English about that lovely city. He valued childhood and described its innocence with wide-open-eyed clarity. He adored puns and practiced them like an Elizabethan.

In all this he was an old-fashioned poet. Even his typography, which seemed so modern, was ancient in intention. Cummings revered Latin and Greek verse and understood that English, for all its excellences, had never achieved the concision and special effects available to the interlocking syntaxes of those inflected languages. In his poems he wanted to make many things happen simultaneously. He wanted to catch action in words and yet keep it shivering. He wanted words to merge as impressions in the mind do. He wanted to reach backward and forward, pulling past and future into a present instant. To do this he used punctuation like a second language. This was not an innovation so much as a thorough realization of a lost art.

46. Throughout the passage, the author's primary purpose is to
(A) emphasize Cummings's revolutionary technique
(B) account for Cummings's choice of subject matter
(C) contrast Cummings with foreign poets
(D) provide specific examples of Cummings's verse
(E) stress Cummings's traditional poetic roots

47. As used in paragraph 1, "taking" most nearly means
(A) grasping (B) pleasing (C) selective
(D) resounding (E) ironic

48. It can be inferred from the passage that the Elizabethans
(A) believed in the value of practice
(B) were contemporaries of Cummings
(C) employed modern typography
(D) enjoyed playing with words
(E) lacked childlike vision

When school was out, I hurried to find my sister and get out of the schoolyard before seeing anybody in my class. But Barbara and her friends had beaten us to the playground entrance and they seemed to be waiting for us. Barbara said, "So now you're in the A class." She sounded impressed.

"What's the A class?" I asked.

Everybody made superior yet faintly envious giggling sounds. "Well, why did you think the teacher moved you to the front of the room, dopey? Didn't you know you were in the C class before, way in the back of the room?"

Of course I hadn't known. The Wenatchee fifth grade was bigger than my whole school had been in North Dakota, and the idea of subdivisions within a grade had never occurred to me. The subdividing for the first marking period had been done before I came to the school, and I had never, in the six weeks I'd been there, talked to anyone long enough to find out about the A, B, and C classes.

I still could not understand why that had made such a difference to Barbara and her friends. I didn't yet know that it was disgraceful and dirty to be a transient laborer and ridiculous to be from North Dakota. I thought living in a tent was more fun than living in a house. I didn't know that we were gypsies, really (how that thought would have thrilled me then!), and that we were regarded with the suspicion felt by those who plant toward those who do not plant. It didn't occur to me that we were all looked upon as one more of the untrustworthy natural phenomena, drifting here and there like mists or winds, that farmers of certain crops are resentfully forced to rely on. I didn't know that I was the only child who had camped on the Baumanns' land ever to get out of the C class. I did not know that school administrators and civic leaders held conferences to talk about the problem of transient laborers.

I only knew that for two happy days I walked to school with Barbara and her friends, played hopscotch and jump rope with them at recess, and was even invited into the house for some ginger ale—an exotic drink I had never tasted before.

49. The tone of this passage as a whole is
(A) reflective (B) joyful (C) impersonal
(D) pessimistic (E) suspicious

50. This passage as a whole is presented from the point of view of
(A) an understanding teacher (B) a younger sister
(C) a mature adult (D) a helpful parent
(E) an envious pupil

51. The narrator had most probably been placed in the C class because
(A) she was a poor reader
(B) she had come from a small school
(C) the marking system confused her
(D) all migrant children were placed in the C class
(E) all migrant children lived in tents

52. The basic reason the people in the community distrusted the transient workers was that the transient workers
(A) tended to be lawbreakers
(B) had little schooling
(C) were from North Dakota
(D) were afraid of strangers
(E) were temporary residents

53. After the narrator was moved to the A class, what was the attitude of Barbara and Barbara's friends toward her?
(A) Dislike (B) Acceptance (C) Dismay
(D) Apology (E) Jealousy

Market prices are determined in a free economy in the following ways: In such an economy there is a constant interplay between two factors—"supply" and "demand." The producers of goods control the supply, while the consumers control the demand. Market prices are determined at a point where supply and demand are equal.

Each producer, acting individually, determines his marginal cost of production and the rate of profit he desires, and fixes his selling price accordingly. However, he must reckon with a number of factors. He has competitors who also produce the same article and who are seeking the same consumers. These may be more or less efficient than he is, and their cost of production may be lower or higher than his. Perhaps they are content with a lower rate of profit. There may be similar or comparable products to which the consumer might shift were the producer to make the price of his article too high. He has to consider the purchasing power as well as the tastes and interests of the consumer. Finally, he must also consider the factor of elasticity of demand. Will it pay him to produce more and thus sell more products at a lower price or to restrict production and raise prices? The producer, weighing all these factors, will fix a price and produce an amount which will bring him the greatest net return.

The demand on the part of buyers is also governed by a variety of factors. The price a manufacturer is willing to pay for raw materials is determined by what he expects to get from his finished product. Such a buyer must also consider the general prosperity of the community to be expected in the near future. He must gauge what the future supply of materials will be. Consumer demand, too, is determined by the factor of general business conditions. When income of workers and farmers is high, demand for goods is high. Prices will then tend to rise. If there is a slump or depression, demand will fall and prices will decline.

54. The title that best expresses the ideas of this passage is
(A) The Law of Supply and Demand
(B) Determining Value
(C) Factors Controlling Demand
(D) A Free Economy
(E) Determining Prices

55. A factor that may control demand NOT mentioned by the author is
(A) the changing taste of the consumer
(B) lower prices (C) competing products
(D) increased taxation (E) the cost of production

56. The passage suggests that, to compete effectively in the marketplace with more efficient competitors producing the same article at a lower cost of production, an individual producer would most likely have to
(A) reassess local consumer preferences
(B) reduce prices and accept a lower profit rate
(C) restrict production and raise prices
(D) stockpile necessary raw materials for production
(E) anticipate a depression in the business community

A few species demonstrate conditions which are neither complete hibernation nor aestivation. Instead of going into a long 'sleep' during the most adverse season, they become torpid for a few hours each day. This kind of behavior is known in other animals—bats become torpid during daytime, and hummingbirds at night. The first time I appreciated this phenomenon was while working with fat mice (*Steatomys*) in Africa. These mice, incidentally, have a most appropriate name, for their bodies are so full of fat they resemble little furry balls. Fat storage as a method of survival has rebounded to some extent as far as the fat mice are concerned. They are regarded as a succulent delicacy by many African tribes who hunt them with great tenacity; when captured, the mice are skewered and fried in their own fat. A captive fat mouse was once kept without food or water for thirty-six days; at the end of that time it had lost a third of its weight but appeared quite healthy. During the dry season, some captives spent the day in such a deep state of torpor that they could be roughly handled without waking. The body temperature was a couple of degrees above room temperature and the respiration was most irregular, several short pants being followed by a pause of up to three minutes. Just before dusk the mice woke up of their own accord and respired normally. In this case the torpid state was not induced by shortage of food or abnormal temperatures. The forest dormouse of southern Asia and Europe also undergoes periods of torpidity during the day; this species has been recorded as having pauses of up to seventeen minutes between breaths. There is also a record of a leaf-eared mouse of the Peruvian desert which became torpid under severe conditions.

57. The primary focus of the passage is on
(A) the inhumane treatment of laboratory specimens
(B) irregularities of respiration in mammals
(C) conditions that induce rodents to hibernate
(D) rodent species that exhibit brief periods of dormancy
(E) the similarities among rodent species

58. The tone of the passage can best be described as
(A) apologetic (B) facetious (C) exhortatory
(D) authoritative (E) ironic

59. This passage would most likely appear in which of the following types of publications?
(A) A geographical atlas
(B) A history of African exploration
(C) A textbook on rodent biology
(D) A guide to the care of laboratory animals
(E) A general-interest periodical

60. It can be inferred that in the paragraph preceding this passage the author most likely discussed
(A) his initial journey to Africa
(B) the problems caused by sleep deprivation
(C) other types of dormant states
(D) the physical appearance of rodents
(E) methods for measuring rodent respiration

The process that makes new stars out of clouds of dust and gas seems to yield single stars and double stars in roughly equal numbers. Stars born in pairs circle each other in gravitationally bound orbits throughout their evolution. If the distance between them is large, their interaction may be negligible. The closer the two stars get to each other, however, the greater the effect on their evolution is and the more likely it is that the radiation they emit will exhibit features setting them apart from the common run of stars.

Among the several hundred million binary systems estimated to lie within 3,000 light-years of the solar system, and thus to be theoretically detectable on sky-survey photographs, a tiny fraction, no more than a few hundred, belong to a curious subclass whose radiation has a wavelength distribution so peculiar that it long defied explanation. Such systems radiate strongly in the visible region of the spectrum, but some of them do so even more strongly at both shorter and longer wavelengths: in the ultraviolet region and in the infrared and radio regions.

This odd distribution of radiation is best explained by the pairing of a cool red-giant star and an intensely hot small star that is virtually in contact with its larger companion as the two travel around a common center. Such objects have become known as symbiotic stars. On photographic plates only the giant star can be discerned, but evidence for the existence of the hot companion has now been supplied by satellite-borne instruments capable of detecting ultraviolet radiation at wavelengths that are absorbed by the earth's atmosphere (and therefore cannot be detected by instruments on the ground). Recently two symbiotic-star systems, the first to be detected outside our galaxy, have been observed in the Large Cloud of Magellan, one of the satellite galaxies associated with ours.

The spectra of symbiotic stars indicate that the cool red giant is surrounded by a very hot ionized gas. The existence of the ionized gas marked such objects as being peculiar several decades before satellite observations finally identified the ionizing source as the radiation from an invisible hot companion. Symbiotic stars also flared up in outbursts indicating the ejection of material in the form of a shell or a ring, reminiscent of the recurrent outbursts of a nova. Symbiotic stars may therefore represent a transitory phase in the evolution of certain types of binary systems in which there is a substantial transfer of matter from the larger partner to the smaller. It seems likely that in the course of the transfer the material often forms a disk around the smaller partner. In at least one instance, however, a symbiotic star has evidently expelled matter in the form of a highly directional jet, resembling the much larger jets associated with active galaxies and quasars.

61. The author's primary purpose in this passage is to
(A) argue the special importance of paired symbiotic stars
(B) illustrate the complexity of identifying types of stars
(C) interpret the mechanics of wavelength distribution
(D) explain the nature and characteristics of companion stars
(E) list the recorded observations of paired symbiotic stars

62. The author finds new evidence for the existence of symbiotic-star systems outside our galaxy in
(A) sky-survey photographs
(B) astronomers' charts of the constellations
(C) disturbances in the longer radio wavelengths
(D) satellite measurements of ultraviolet radiation
(E) radiation in the visible region of the spectrum

63. According to the passage, the presence of extremely hot ionized gas paired with a cool red-giant star was regarded by astronomers as
(A) propitious (B) insignificant (C) singular
(D) permanent (E) negligible

64. The author, in discussing the ejection of matter when symbiotic stars flare up, assumes an attitude of
(A) bewilderment (B) supposition
(C) confidence (D) dissension (E) astonishment

65. In the concluding two sentences of the passage, the author
(A) defines a process and gives examples of that process
(B) states a theory and refutes it conclusively
(C) presents a hypothesis and mentions one exception to it
(D) considers a possibility and tentatively rejects it
(E) verifies a conclusion and provides supporting evidence

SECTION 2 **Time—50 minutes 50 Questions**

In this section solve each problem, using any available space on the page for scratchwork. Then decide which is the best of the choices given and fill in the corresponding circle on the answer sheet.

The following information is for your reference in solving some of the problems.

Circle of radius r: Area $= \pi r^2$ Circumference $= 2\pi r$
The number of degrees of arc in a circle is 360.
The measure in degrees of a straight angle is 180.

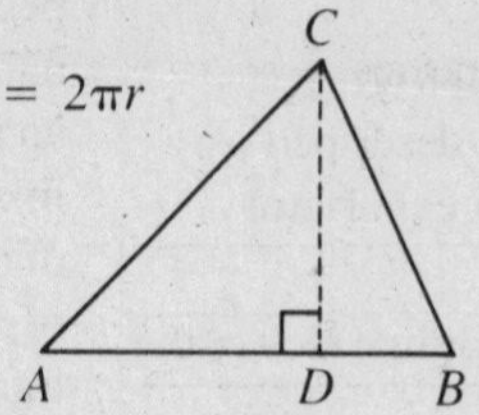

Triangle: The sum of the measures in degrees of the angles of a triangle is 180.

If $\angle CDA$ is a right angle, then

(1) area of $\triangle ABC = \dfrac{AB \times CD}{2}$

(2) $AC^2 = AD^2 + DC^2$

Definitions of symbols:

$=$ is equal to	$\leqq$ is less than or equal to
$\neq$ is unequal to	$\geqq$ is greater than or equal to
$<$ is less than	$\parallel$ is parallel to
$>$ is greater than	$\perp$ is perpendicular to

Note: Figures that accompany problems in this test are intended to provide information useful in solving the problems. They are drawn as accurately as possible EXCEPT when it is stated in a specific problem that its figure is not drawn to scale. All figures lie in a plane unless otherwise indicated. All numbers used are real numbers.

1. $\dfrac{\frac{2}{3} + \frac{1}{4}}{\frac{1}{6} + \frac{2}{3} + \frac{1}{12}} =$

(A) 0 (B) $\frac{1}{16}$ (C) -1 (D) 1 (E) 3

2. $z + \frac{1}{z} = 2$; $z =$

(A) $\sqrt{3}$ (B) $\frac{1}{2}$ (C) 1 (D) $1\frac{1}{2}$ (E) 2

3. $2x = 3(a + b)$; $\dfrac{3}{2x} =$

(A) $\dfrac{1}{a + b}$ (B) $a + b$ (C) $2(a + b)$
(D) $3(a + b)$ (E) $2x(a + b)$

4. $13 = \dfrac{13w}{1 - w}$; $(2w)^2 =$

(A) $\frac{1}{4}$ (B) $\frac{1}{2}$ (C) 1 (D) 2 (E) 4

5. If $r = \sqrt{\dfrac{3V}{\pi h}}$, by what number must we multiply V in order to multiply r by 9?

(A) 3 (B) $\frac{9}{2}$ (C) 9 (D) 18 (E) 81

6. A tailor cuts a 2-yard piece of ribbon into three equal parts. How can the length of each part be expressed?

I. 24 inches
II. $\frac{2}{3}$ yard
III. 1.5 feet

(A) I only (B) II only (C) III only
(D) I and II only (E) I, II, and III

7. A part-time shoe salesman receives a salary of \$50 for working 3 evenings and a commission of 4% on all sales. What must be the amount of his sales in order that his salary for 3 evenings may be \$200?

(A) \$375 (B) \$600 (C) \$650 (D) \$850
(E) \$3750

8. One-half of the students in a city school plan to enter liberal arts colleges and one-third of the students plan to go to junior college. The remaining 300 pupils expect to seek permanent employment after graduation. How many students are there in this school?

(A) 360 (B) 350 (C) 900 (D) 1350
(E) 1800

9. A typist has a task which she normally completes in three hours. What part of this task can she complete from 8:55 A.M. to 9:15 A.M.?

(A) $\frac{1}{6}$ (B) $\frac{1}{3}$ (C) $\frac{2}{3}$ (D) $\frac{1}{5}$ (E) $\frac{1}{9}$

10. A motorist paid \$9.24 for six gallons of gasoline. This included a tax of 4¢ per gallon. The basic price (per gallon) of the gasoline before inclusion of the tax is

(A) \$1.50 (B) \$1.54 (C) \$1.56 (D) \$1.60
(E) more than \$1.60

11. If x is an odd integer, which of the following is (are) always true?

I. $(x + 1)(x - 1)$ is even.
II. $x + 483$ is even.
III. $x^2 + 2$ is even.

(A) I only (B) II only (C) III only
(D) I and II only (E) I, II, and III

12. How many posts are needed for a 50-foot fence if each post is 5 feet from the next post?

(A) 8 (B) 9 (C) 10 (D) 11 (E) 12

13. A salesman operates a car which averaged 15 miles to a gallon of gasoline. By installing a new carburetor, he improved the mileage by $\frac{1}{5}$. How much will he save on gasoline during a year in which he covers 5400 miles, if the average cost of gasoline is \$1.35 per gallon?
(A) \$25.92 (B) \$64.80 (C) \$81.00
(D) \$108.00 (E) \$810.00

14.

x	-7	-3	1	?
y	0	1	2	3

The table shows values of x and y that satisfy a first-degree equation. What is the missing value of x?
(A) -3 (B) -2 (C) 2 (D) 4 (E) 5

15. A fish tank $1' \times 1\frac{1}{2}' \times \frac{1}{2}'$ is carefully used to fill a large tank which has a capacity of 15 cubic feet. How many times will the contents of the smaller tank be required to be emptied into the larger tank to completely fill the tank?
(A) 8 (B) 10 (C) 11 (D) 20
(E) more than 20

<u>Questions 16-32</u> each consist of two quantities, one in Column A and one in Column B. You are to compare the two quantities and on the answer sheet fill in circle

A if the quantity in Column A is greater;
B if the quantity in Column B is greater;
C if the two quantities are equal;
D if the relationship cannot be determined from the information given.

<u>Notes:</u>
1. In certain questions, information concerning one or both of the quantities to be compared is centered above the two columns.
2. In a given question, a symbol that appears in both columns represents the same thing in Column A as it does in Column B.
3. Letters such as x, n, and k stand for real numbers.

EXAMPLES

	Column A	Column B	Answers
E1.	2×6	$2 + 6$	● Ⓑ Ⓒ Ⓓ

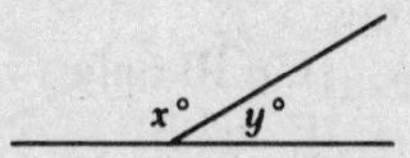

	Column A	Column B	Answers
E2.	$180 - x$	y	Ⓐ Ⓑ ● Ⓓ
E3.	$p - q$	$q - p$	Ⓐ Ⓑ Ⓒ ●

	Column A	Column B
16.	$\frac{1}{8}$	$\left(\frac{1}{0.08}\right)^2$
17.	$x + y$	$x - y$

$x^2 = xy$

18.	x	y

$\frac{1}{x} < 1$

19.	x	0

$xyz = 0$

20.	x	y
21.	$(0.25)^2$	$\left(\frac{1}{4}\right)^4$
22.	$20\%x$	10% of $\frac{x}{2}$

$x = 2$ and $y = 3$

23.	$x + y$	$\dfrac{\frac{1}{xy}}{\frac{1}{x} + \frac{1}{y}}$
24.	The time required to travel a mile and a half at 20 miles per hour	The time required to travel $\frac{3}{4}$ mile at 10 miles per hour

The sum of the sides of a square $= s$.
The length of a rectangle is $\frac{s}{2}$, which is 4 times its width.

25.	The area of the square	The area of the rectangle

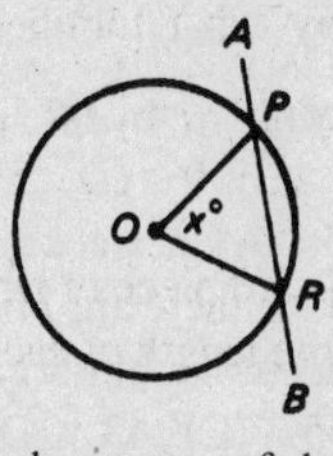

O is the center of the circle.
$PR = OP$

26.	x	$60°$

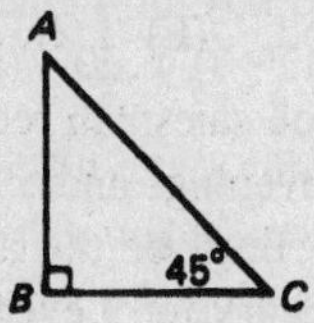

27.	AB	BC

	COLUMN A	COLUMN B
	$x > 0$	
28.	$24x\%$	$\frac{6x}{25}$
	$x > 0 > y$	
29.	$x + y$	y
30.	$\frac{6a - 5}{2}$	$3a - 3$
	$X^2 = 144$, $Y^2 = 100$	
31.	X	Y
	$-3a - 2 < 1$	
32.	a	-1

Solve each of the remaining problems in this section using any available space for scratchwork. Then decide which is the best of the choices given and fill in the corresponding circle on the answer sheet.

33. After a 40% reduction is allowed, a painting is sold for \$48. The original marked price was
(A) \$67.50 (B) \$80.00 (C) \$120.00
(D) \$128.00 (E) \$192.00

34. If 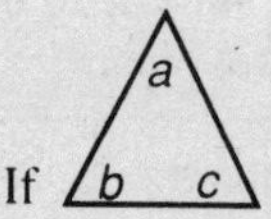

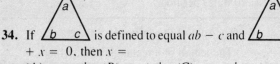

is defined to equal $ab - c$ and 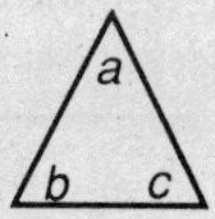

$+ x = 0$, then $x =$
(A) $ac - b$ (B) $ac + b$ (C) $c - ab$
(D) $ab - c$ (E) $ab + c$

35. $X = 66\frac{2}{3}\%\ Y$
$Y = 33\frac{1}{3}\%\ Z$
What percent of X is Z?
(A) $16\frac{2}{3}$ (B) $22\frac{2}{9}$ (C) 45 (D) 300 (E) 450

36. A man works 5 days a week and binds 35 sets of books each week. If there are 7 books in a set, what is the number of books he binds each day?
(A) 25 (B) 35 (C) 43 (D) 49 (E) 81

37. If a farmer has enough food to take care of 10 chickens for 8 days, how many days would this quantity of food last for 4 chickens?
(A) $3\frac{1}{5}$ (B) 12 (C) 20 (D) 32 (E) 35

38. A map measuring 8″ × 10″ and drawn to the scale 1″ = 50 miles is pasted on a sheet of paper of the same size. Find the least number of sheets of this paper that would have to be taped together to hold this same map if it were drawn to the scale 2″ = 25 miles.
(A) 2 (B) 3 (C) 4 (D) 8 (E) 16

39. How many degrees are there in an angle formed by the hands of a clock at 2:30?
(A) 100° (B) 105° (C) 110° (D) 115°
(E) 120°

40. AB is parallel to DC, $\overset{\frown}{AD}$ equals 110° and $\overset{\frown}{AB}$ equals 30°. The measure of $\angle CED$ equals
(A) 40° (B) 70°
(C) 80° (D) 110°
(E) 140°

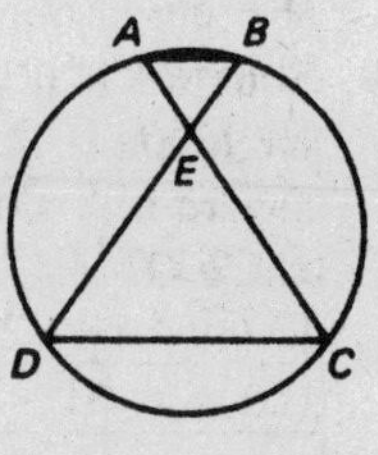

41. CB and AB are tangent to circle O. If $\angle COA \overset{\circ}{=} 140$, what is the measure of $\angle B$?
(A) 30° (B) 40°
(C) 70° (D) 110°
(E) 140°

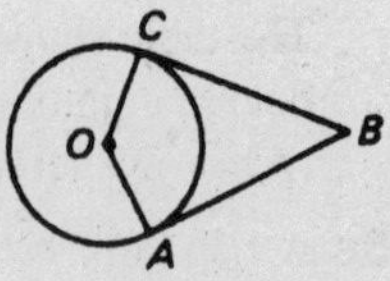

42. $\overset{\frown}{AB}$ of circle O contains 72° and is 6π long. Find the area of circle O.
(A) 9 (B) 36 (C) 30π (D) 225π (E) 900

43. In $\triangle ABC$, $\angle B = 3\angle A$, and $\angle C = 8\angle A$. What is the measure of $\angle B$?
(A) 15° (B) 30° (C) 45° (D) 60° (E) 120°

44. In $\triangle ABC$, AF and CE meet in D. If $AE = EB$, $BF = FC$, then $\frac{AD \times CD}{FD \times ED}$ equals
(A) 1 (B) 2 (C) 4
(D) 6 (E) 8

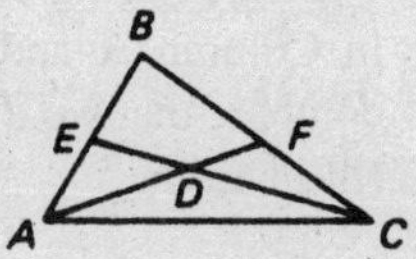

45. The graphs of $x + 3y = 4$ and $2x + 6y = 8$ are drawn on the same axes. Which of the following will be true?
I. If the coordinates of any point on the graph of the first equation are doubled, the result will be the coordinates of a point on the graph of the second equation.
II. The two graphs will intersect in only one point.
III. The two graphs have the same y-intercept.
(A) I only (B) II only (C) III only
(D) I and II only (E) I, II, and III

46. $ABCDEF$ is a regular hexagon. If the perimeter = 12, find the area of $ABCDEF$.
(A) $6\sqrt{3}$ (B) $12\sqrt{3}$ (C) 12 (D) 24
(E) 36

47. A radian is an angle of such size that, when its vertex is placed at the center of any circle, its sides will cut off an arc equal in length to the radius of the circle. One radian is exactly equal to
(A) 57° (B) 60°
(C) 90° (D) $\frac{180°}{\pi}$
(E) $\frac{360°}{\pi}$

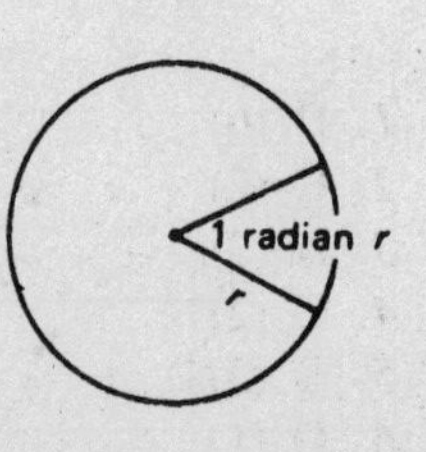

48. If the hypotenuse of a right triangle is 10 and one leg is $5\sqrt{3}$, then the area of the triangle is
(A) 5 (B) $25\sqrt{3}$ (C) 25 (D) $50\sqrt{3}$
(E) $12.5\sqrt{3}$

49. Square *ABCD* is inscribed in circle *O*. If the side of the square is 2, find the area of circle *O*.

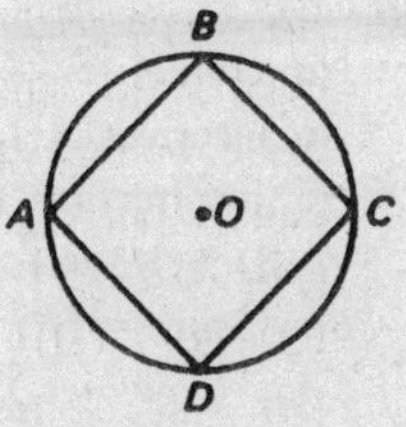

(A) π (B) 2π (C) 4π
(D) 8π (E) 16π

50. The length of a rectangle is represented by the numerical value of $5V^3$. If the rectangle is equal in area to a square with a side represented by $4V$, what is the width of the rectangle in terms of V?

(A) $\frac{1}{80V^5}$ (B) $\frac{4}{5V}$ (C) $\frac{16}{5V}$ (D) $\frac{16}{5V^2}$
(E) $\frac{5V}{16}$

ANSWER KEY

Verbal Aptitude Section

1. **A**	*11.* **A**	*21.* **B**	*31.* **E**	*41.* **D**	*51.* **D**	*61.* **D**
2. **A**	*12.* **B**	*22.* **D**	*32.* **C**	*42.* **C**	*52.* **E**	*62.* **D**
3. **A**	*13.* **D**	*23.* **C**	*33.* **D**	*43.* **B**	*53.* **B**	*63.* **C**
4. **B**	*14.* **A**	*24.* **B**	*34.* **B**	*44.* **E**	*54.* **E**	*64.* **B**
5. **E**	*15.* **C**	*25.* **A**	*35.* **B**	*45.* **B**	*55.* **D**	*65.* **C**
6. **D**	*16.* **D**	*26.* **C**	*36.* **B**	*46.* **E**	*56.* **B**	
7. **A**	*17.* **D**	*27.* **D**	*37.* **D**	*47.* **B**	*57.* **D**	
8. **E**	*18.* **A**	*28.* **C**	*38.* **C**	*48.* **D**	*58.* **D**	
9. **A**	*19.* **B**	*29.* **E**	*39.* **D**	*49.* **A**	*59.* **C**	
10. **C**	*20.* **B**	*30.* **E**	*40.* **D**	*50.* **C**	*60.* **C**	

Mathematical Aptitude Section

Note: Each correct answer to the mathematics questions is keyed by number to the corresponding topic in Chapters 9 and 10. These numerals refer to the topics listed below, with specific page references in parentheses.

1. Basic Fundamental Operations (155–157)
2. Algebraic Operations (157–160)
3. Using Algebra (160–164)
4. Exponents, Roots and Radicals (159–160)
5. Inequalities (164–165)
6. Fractions (176–178)
7. Decimals (176)
8. Percent (178–180)
9. Averages (180–181)
10. Motion (182–183)
11. Ratio and Proportion (183–185)
12. Mixtures and Solutions (177–178)
13. Work (185–186)
14. Coordinate Geometry (172–173)
15. Geometry (165–172, 173–176)
16. Quantitative Comparisons (189–192)

ANSWER KEY

1. **D** (6)	*11.* **D** (1,2)	*21.* **A** (4,6,7,16)	*31.* **D** (4,16)	*41.* **B** (15)
2. **C** (2)	*12.* **D** (1)	*22.* **D** (8,16)	*32.* **A** (5,16)	*42.* **D** (15)
3. **A** (2)	*13.* **C** (6)	*23.* **A** (2,6,16)	*33.* **B** (8)	*43.* **C** (15)
4. **C** (2)	*14.* **E** (3)	*24.* **C** (10,16)	*34.* **C** (2)	*44.* **C** (15)
5. **E** (2,4)	*15.* **D** (15)	*25.* **C** (15,16)	*35.* **E** (3,8)	*45.* **C** (14)
6. **D** (1)	*16.* **B** (4,6,7,16)	*26.* **C** (15,16)	*36.* **D** (1)	*46.* **A** (15)
7. **E** (8)	*17.* **D** (2,16)	*27.* **C** (15,16)	*37.* **C** (11)	*47.* **D** (15)
8. **E** (3,6)	*18.* **D** (2,16)	*28.* **C** (6,8,16)	*38.* **E** (11,15)	*48.* **E** (4,15)
9. **E** (6)	*19.* **D** (6,16)	*29.* **B** (5,16)	*39.* **B** (15)	*49.* **B** (15)
10. **A** (1)	*20.* **D** (1,16)	*30.* **A** (2,6,16)	*40.* **B** (15)	*50.* **C** (15)

SCORING CHART TYPICAL TEST G

Verbal Section		Mathematical Section*		
No. correct	_____	No. correct	(A)	_____
No. omitted	_____	No. incorrect (# 1-15, 33-50)	(B)	_____
No. incorrect	_____	No. incorrect (# 16-32)	(C)	_____
¼ no. incorrect	_____	¼ (B) + 1/3 (C)	(D)	_____
Raw Score: (no. correct minus ¼ no. incorrect)	_____	*Raw Score* = (A) − (D)		_____

*** (In the Mathematical section, deduct ¼ of a point for each five-choice question answered incorrectly and 1/3 of a point for each four-choice question answered incorrectly.)**

EVALUATION CHART

Study your score. Your raw score on the Verbal and Mathematical Aptitude Sections is an indication of your probable achievement on the PSAT/NMSQT. As a guide to the amount of work you need or want to do, study the following.

Raw Score *Verbal*	Raw Score *Mathematical*	Self-rating
58-65	41-50	Superior
46-57	25-40	Very good
40-45	20-24	Satisfactory
36-39	16-19	Average
30-35	10-15	Needs further study
20-29	7-9	Needs intensive study
0-19	0-6	Probably inadequate

Your scores are most likely improving with each test that you take. To help pinpoint any weak areas you still may have, consult the table on page 384 and plan your remaining review accordingly.

ANSWER EXPLANATIONS

Verbal Aptitude Section

1. **A** The opposite of *monotonous* (dull; unchanging) is *varied*.
Think of "monotonous routine."
2. **A** The opposite of to *decline* or refuse is to *accept*.
Think of "declining an invitation."
3. **A** The opposite of *bustle* (commotion; activity) is *inactivity*.
Think of "the bustle of Christmas shopping."
4. **B** The opposite of *diligent* (hard-working) is *lazy*.
Think of "a diligent student."
5. **E** The opposite of to *migrate* or move from one location to another is to *refrain from moving*.
Think of "migrating to a new land."
6. **D** The opposite of to *revere* or honor is to *dishonor*.
Think of "revering one's ancestors."
7. **A** The opposite of *obstinate* or stubborn is *yielding*.
Think of "obstinate as a mule."
8. **E** The opposite of to *protract* (draw out or lengthen) is to *shorten*.
Think of "protracting a meeting."
9. **A** The opposite of a *novice* or beginner is a *veteran*.
Word Parts Clue: *Nov-* means new. A novice is someone new at an activity.
Think of "starting out as a novice."
10. **C** The opposite of *flamboyant* (flashy; ostentatious) is *conservative* or restrained.
Beware of eye-catchers. Choice A is incorrect. Don't be misled by *flam-* in *flamboyant*. It doesn't mean flammable or likely to go up in flames.
Think of "Madonna's flamboyant costumes."

11. **A** The opposite of to *concentrate* or bring together is to *scatter.* Choice **E** is incorrect. If you do not concentrate or focus your attention on something, you may forget it. However, that is the result of your failure to concentrate; forgetting is not the opposite of concentrating.
Think of "concentrating your forces in one spot."

12. **B** The opposite of to *abominate* or loathe is to *appreciate*.
Think of "abominating vile acts."

13. **D** The opposite of *vivacious* or lively is *phlegmatic* (dull; sluggish).
Word Parts Clue: *Viv-* means life. Someone vivacious is full of life.
Think of "bubbly, vivacious Oprah Winfrey."

14. **A** The opposite of *implacability* (the inability to be assuaged or pacified; mercilessness) is *compassion* or mercy.
Think of "merciless implacability."

15. **C** The opposite of *fanatical* (excessively enthusiastic) is *apathetic* or indifferent.
Think of "fanatical religious maniacs."

16. **D** To *revile* (verbally abuse) something is the opposite of *praising* it.
Think of "reviled as a traitor."

17. **D** The opposite of *probity* (uprightness; integrity) is *depravity* (debasement; corruption).
Think of "unimpeachable probity."

18. **A** The opposite of *soporific* (causing sleepiness) is *stimulating*.
Think of being put to sleep by "a soporific lecturer."

19. **B** The opposite of to *belie* or misrepresent is to *represent accurately.*
Context Clue: "Arnold Schwarzenegger's macho appearance belies his actual sensitivity."

20. **B** The opposite of *tantamount* or equivalent in value is *not equivalent*.
Context Clue: "Failure to publish is tantamount to suppression."

21. **B** To *aggravate* a problem is to make it worse. When people live longer and fewer babies die, overpopulation is made worse.

22. **D** *Derision* is making fun of something. Since they did not take his proposal seriously, they treated it with derision. Choice **B** is a less appropriate answer because *detachment* or indifference is not so nearly opposite to "serious study."

23. **C** This sentence contrasts the opinion of "some scientists" with that of "many experts." The first group thinks that action should be delayed. Therefore, the second group must want action soon: because damage is *accelerated*, it "*warrants* strong measures now." Choice **D** is incorrect because *illusory* means not real; if the damage were not real, then there would be no reason to take action.

24. **B** A *foretoken* is an advance indication. Earlier phases of one's life may be foretokens of later stages.

25. **A** Both missing words must be positive. The speaker is praising the installation as *impeccable* (without fault) and saying that, despite recent drawbacks, such programs can still *succeed*.

26. **C** By definition, *parasites* sap or drain nutrients from their hosts.

27. **D** The physicists have had good reason to believe in the principle because it has *survived* rigorous or strict tests. These tests have *proved* that the principle is accurate. Note how the second clause supports the first, explaining why the physicists have had reason to be confident in the principle.

28. **C** The embittered benefactor thinks of the former recipients as *ingrates* (ungrateful persons) because they did not thank her sufficiently for her generosity. She does not think of them as *misers* (hoarders of wealth); although they are stingy in expressing thanks, they are extravagant in spending money. She certainly does not think of them as *louts* (clumsy oafs), *prigs* (self-righteous fussbudgets), or *renegades* (traitors): what she specifically resents in them is ingratitude, not cloddishness, self-satisfaction, or treachery.

29. **E** If Mrs. Woolf combines both modern radical and old-fashioned nonradical elements in her fictions, then she presents *an anomalous* or contradictory image.

30. **E** The field is cluttered by a *welter* or chaotic jumble of contradictory theories. Choice **A** is incorrect. While *bonanza* means abundance, it is an abundance of good things, a desired abundance. Here the abundance of theories is undesired; it is a confusion, not a blessing.

31. **E** A *truant* runs away from *school;* a *deserter* runs away from the *army.*
(Definition)

32. **C** A *stroller* carries a baby; a bus *carries* a passenger.
(Function)

33. **D** A *flurry* is a short, light snowfall, while a *blizzard* is a very heavy fall of snow; a *breeze* is a light gust of wind, while a *gale* is an extremely strong wind.
(Degree of Intensity)

34. **B** A *carpet* is a rug which lies on the *floor;* a *tapestry* is a rug which hangs on the *wall*.
(Function)

35. **B** A formal agreement between *nations* is a *treaty;* a formal agreement between *individuals* is a *contract*.
(Defining Characteristic)

36. **B** A *kangaroo* is a kind of *marsupial;* a *mushroom* is a kind of *fungus*.
(Class and Member)

37. **D** A *snicker* is a noise people make which shows *disrespect;* a *moan* is a noise people make which indicates *suffering*.
(Action and Its Significance)

38. **C** A *choreographer* designs a *dance;* a *director* designs a *film.*

(Worker and Work Created)

39. **D** *Gustatory* means of or relating to the sense of *taste; olfactory* means of or relating to the sense of *smell.* Choice **B** is incorrect. *Visionary* means seeing visions; it does not mean relating to the sense of sight.

(Defining Characteristic)

40. **D** To *embark* on a *yacht* is to get on a boat; to *mount* a *steed* is to get on a horse.

(Function)

41. **D** A *pauper* is a poor person, someone characterized by *poverty;* a *sluggard* is a sluggish person, someone characterized by *slowness.*

(Defining Characteristic)

42. **C** A *sermon* is a religious *speech;* a *pilgrimage* is a religious *journey.*

(Class and Member)

43. **B** To *embrace* a *position* is to choose a particular point of view; to *espouse* a *cause* is to support a particular movement.

(Function)

44. **E** Frequently shifting emotions indicate a *mercurial mood;* frequently shifting directions indicate an *erratic course.*

(Manner)

45. **B** A judge may *commute* a prisoner's *sentence,* making it shorter; a judge may *reduce* a convicted person's *fine,* making it smaller.

(Function)

46. **E** Again and again, the author repeats the idea that Cummings, the supposedly radical poet, actually was markedly conventional in his choice of subject matter and in his use of classical poetic effects. Clearly, his intent is to *stress Cummings's traditional poetic roots.*

47. **B** Since Cummings truly loved Paris and wanted to communicate his feeling, he tried to describe the city in a *pleasing* manner. He wanted people to "take to" Paris, as he had.

48. **D** According to the passage, Cummings "practiced puns like an Elizabethan." This suggests that the Elizabethans enjoyed puns, that is, *enjoyed playing with words.* (Puns are a form of humorous word play—think of the joker who offers to tell you a fish story "just for the halibut...").

49. **A** The author is *reflecting on* or considering her childhood. She is remembering and analyzing past events.

50. **C** The speaker is an *adult,* looking back in time. Her description implies that she did not understand the prejudice of the other children, because she was young and innocent. As an adult, she is clear about the attitude of the other pupils; as a child, it made no sense to her.

51. **D** Paragraph 5 states: "I was the only child who had camped on the Baumanns' land ever to get out of the C class." This suggests that the school administrators dealt with the "problem of transient laborers" by *placing all migrant children in the C class.*

52. **E** The primary reason the community did not like transient laborers was that they were always *temporary residents.* The people of the community could never really get to know or trust them.

53. **B** Barbara and her friends began to play with the narrator and invite her to one of their homes because of her transfer to the A class. This upward change in her academic status led to a similar change in her social status: the other children began to treat her with *acceptance.*

54. **E** The passage discusses supply and demand as they relate to *prices.* It primarily examines which factors go into the producer's decision about the best price to set for a product.
Choices **A** and **D** are incorrect. They are too general. Choice **C** is incorrect. The passage concentrates on prices and supply more than on demand. Choice **B** is incorrect. The value (cost to produce) is not the same as the price (cost to buy). Price is emphasized more than value.

55. **D** Taxes are not mentioned anywhere in the passage.

56. **B** The producer will have to *reduce prices and accept a lower profit rate:* he cannot maintain the same profit margin as his competitors, because they produce the product more cheaply.
Choice **A** is incorrect. Consumers clearly favor the product as it is, because it is being successfully sold by several producers: the price must change, not the product. Choice **C** is incorrect. The competitors are already underselling this producer or are capable of doing so. By raising prices, the producer would drive all his customers to buy from his competitors. Choice **D** is incorrect. It will not help the producer to stockpile materials unless he can find a way to make a reasonable profit on the product. Choice **E** is incorrect. A depression in the business community is both hard to anticipate and generally damaging for everyone.

57. **D** The author is discussing the behavior of various rodents that become *dormant* or inactive for brief periods of time.

58. **D** The author presents factual information in an *authoritative*, scholarly manner.

59. **C** This detailed account of a particular aspect of rodent behavior clearly belongs in a *textbook on rodent biology.*

60. **C** In the opening sentence the author refers to hibernation and aestivation, two other types of dormant states. This suggests he has just been discussing these dormant states in some detail.

61. **D** The passage discusses the nature and *characteristics of paired stars*.
Choice **A** is incorrect. The author describes paired stars and comments on their rarity, not their special importance. Choice **B** is incorrect. The author describes some of the complexities of determining star types, but that is not the focus of the passage. Choice **C** is incorrect. The passage mentions wavelength distribution, but that is not the main issue in the reading. Choice **E** is incorrect. The passage does not list the "few hundred" observable symbiotic stars.

62. **D** Paragraph 3 states that "evidence for the existence of the hot companion has now been supplied by *satellite-borne* instruments capable of detecting *ultraviolet radiation* at wavelengths that are absorbed by the earth's atmosphere."

63. **C** The author writes, in paragraph 4: "The existence of the ionized gas marked such objects as being *peculiar* several decades before satellite observations finally identified the ionizing source as the radiation from an invisible hot companion." Note that *singular* means unusual, not single (one alone).

64. **B** In the final sentence, the key word "evidently" suggests that the author is not absolutely certain. His tone is one of *supposition* or consideration—the reader can sense that an assumption is being made.

65. **C** The *hypothesis* (proposed explanation) is that matter "forms a disk around the smaller partner." The *exception* is the one observed instance of matter being "expelled in the form of a highly directional jet."

Mathematical Aptitude Section

1. **D** $\dfrac{\frac{2}{3}+\frac{1}{4}}{\frac{1}{6}+\frac{2}{3}+\frac{1}{12}}$ Multiply all terms in numerator and denominator by 12 to clear fractions:

$$\frac{8+3}{2+8+1} = \frac{\cancel{11}}{\cancel{11}} = 1$$

2. **C** $z + \frac{1}{z} = 2$

$$\frac{z^2+1}{z} = 2$$
$$z^2 + 1 = 2z$$
$$z^2 - 2z + 1 = 0$$
$$(z-1)(z-1) = 0 \text{ [factoring]}$$
$$z = 1$$

3. **A** $2x = 3(a+b)$

$$\frac{2x}{(a+b)} = \frac{3(a+b)}{(a+b)} \text{ [divide by } (a+b)\text{]}$$
$$\frac{2x}{(a+b)} = 3$$
$$\frac{\cancel{2x}}{(a+b)(\cancel{2x})} = \frac{3}{2x} \text{ [divide by } 2x\text{]}$$
$$\frac{1}{a+b} = \frac{3}{2x}$$

4. **C** $13 = \dfrac{13w}{1-w}$

$$13(1-w) = 13w$$
$$13 - 13w = 13w$$
$$13 = 26w$$
$$\frac{1}{2} = w$$
$$(2w)^2 = \left(2\cdot\frac{1}{2}\right)^2 = (1)^2 = 1$$

5. **E** If r is multiplied by 9, V must be multiplied by 81, since $\sqrt{81} = 9$. Recall: If equals be multiplied by equals, the results are equal.

6. **D** 2 yards = 72 inches
$72 \div 3 = 24$ inches $= \frac{24}{36}$ or $\frac{2}{3}$ yard.

7. **E** Total salary = \$200
Income from commission = \$150
Let x = amount of sales.
4% or (.04) of x = \$150
$.04x = 150$
$4x = 15000$
$x = \$3750$

8. **E** $\frac{1}{2} + \frac{1}{3} = \frac{5}{6}$ accounts for part of students going on for further education. Therefore $\frac{1}{6}$ expect to seek permanent employment.
Let x = number of students in this school.

$$\frac{1}{6}x = 300.$$
$$x = 1800.$$

9. **E** Time elapsed from 8:55 to 9:15 = 20 minutes $\left(\frac{1}{3}\text{ hour}\right)$

$$\frac{\text{time actually put in on task}}{\text{time required to complete task}} = \text{part of task completed}$$

$$\frac{\frac{1}{3}\,\cancel{\text{hour}}}{3\,\cancel{\text{hours}}} = \frac{1}{3} \div 3 = \left(\frac{1}{3}\right)\left(\frac{1}{3}\right) = \frac{1}{9}$$

10. **A** Total cost = \$9.24
Cost of tax = \$.24
Basic price = \$9.00
Basic price per gallon = \$9.00 ÷ 6 gallons = 1.50 per gallon

11. **D** If x is odd, $x + 1$ and $x - 1$ are both even; their product, $(x + 1)(x - 1)$, will also be even (I). $x + 483$ is the sum of two odd numbers, and is therefore even (II). If x is odd, x^2, the product of two odd numbers, is also odd; when 2 is added to it, the sum is odd (III).

12. **D** $\frac{\text{50-foot fence}}{\text{5-foot spaces}} = 10$ spaces
This will require 11 posts. Observe that there will be a post at the point where the fence begins.

13. **C** Improvement = 3 miles to the gallon for a total of 18 miles per gallon
Consumption for 5400 miles with old carburetor = 360 gallons
Consumption for 5400 miles with new carburetor = 300 gallons
Saving = 60 gallons at \$1.35 per gallon = \$81.00

14. **E** Observe the values of y: $0 + 1 = 1$; $1 + 1 = 2$. $2 + 1 = 3$.
Observe the values of x: $-7 + 4 = -3$; $-3 + 4 = 1$.
$\therefore 1 + 4 = 5$

15. **D** Volume of small fish tank $= (1')\left(1\frac{1}{2}'\right)\left(\frac{1}{2}'\right)$
$= (1')\left(\frac{3'}{2}\right)\left(\frac{1'}{2}\right) = \frac{3}{4}$ cubic foot
15 cubic feet ÷ $\frac{3}{4}$ cubic foot
$15 \cdot \frac{4}{3}$
$\overset{5}{\cancel{15}} \cdot \frac{4}{\cancel{3}} = 20$ times

16. **B** $\left(\frac{1}{0.08}\right)^2 = \frac{1}{0.0064}$
If two fractions have the same numerator, the one with the smaller denominator is larger.

17. **D** x and/or y may be negative, or equal to zero

18. **D** $x^2 = xy$. Dividing by x gives $x = y$, but this is possible only if x does not equal 0. If $x = 0$, y can have any value.

19. **D** Since $\frac{1}{x} < 1$, x can have any value greater than 1 or any negative value, but may not have a value between 0 and 1 inclusive.

20. **D** At least one of the factors (x, y, or z) must be equal to zero, regardless of the value of the other factor(s), which are then completely unrestricted.

21. **A** $(0.25)^2 = \left(\frac{1}{4}\right)^2 = \left(\frac{1}{4}\right)\left(\frac{1}{4}\right) = \frac{1}{16}$
$\left(\frac{1}{4}\right)^4 = \left(\frac{1}{4}\right)\left(\frac{1}{4}\right)\left(\frac{1}{4}\right)\left(\frac{1}{4}\right) = \frac{1}{256}$
$\frac{1}{16} > \frac{1}{256}$

22. **D** 20% of $x = \left(\frac{1}{5}\right)(x) = \frac{x}{5}$
10% of $\frac{x}{2} = \left(\frac{1}{10}\right)\left(\frac{x}{2}\right) = \frac{x}{20}$
Since x can have any value, $\frac{x}{5} > \frac{x}{20}$ if x is positive, $\frac{x}{5} = \frac{x}{20}$ if $x = 0$, and $\frac{x}{5} < \frac{x}{20}$ if x is negative.

23. **A** $x + y = 5$ [Column A]
$\frac{1}{xy} = \frac{1}{6}$ [Column B]
$\frac{1}{x} + \frac{1}{y} = \frac{1}{2} + \frac{1}{3} = \frac{5}{6}$
$\frac{\frac{1}{6}}{\frac{5}{6}} = \frac{1}{6} \cdot \frac{6}{5} = \frac{1}{5}$
$5 > \frac{1}{5}$

24. **C** The time required for each would be the same since one is traveling twice as fast but is also covering twice as much distance.

25. **C** Since the perimeter of the square = s, each side equals $\frac{s}{4}$; the area $= \frac{s^2}{16}$. The length of the rectangle $= \frac{s}{2}$ and its width is $\frac{1}{4}$ of $\frac{s}{2}$ or $\frac{s}{8}$; its area $= \left(\frac{s}{2}\right)\left(\frac{s}{8}\right)$ or $\frac{s^2}{16}$.

26. **C** Since $OP = OR$, $PR = OP = OR$. $\therefore \triangle OPR$ is equilateral. $\therefore \angle C \overset{\circ}{=} 60$.

27. **C** If one acute angle of a right triangle has a measure of 45°, then the other acute angle has a measure of 45°. $\therefore ABC$ is an isosceles right $\triangle$.

28. **C** $24x\% = \frac{24x}{100} = \frac{6x}{25}$

29. **B** Subtract y from both columns
$x > 0$

30. **A** $\frac{6a - 5}{2} = 3a - \frac{5}{2}$ or $3a - 2\frac{1}{2}$
$3a - 2\frac{1}{2}$ is greater than $3a - 3$

31. **D** $X^2 = 144$ and $X = +12, -12$
$Y^2 = 100$ and $Y = +10, -10$

32. **A** Add 2 to both sides of the inequality
$-3a < 3$ and $-a < 1$ (divide by 3) or $a > -1$.

33. **B** The painting was sold for 60% of the original marked price.
Let x = original marked price.
60% of x or $.6x = \$48$.
$6x = 480$
$x = \$80$

34. **C** $ab - c + x = 0$
$x = c - ab$

35. **E** $X = 66\frac{2}{3}\%\ Y$ *or* $X = \frac{2}{3}Y$ (1)

$Y = 33\frac{1}{3}\%\ Z$ *or* $Y = \frac{1}{3}Z$ (2)

$\frac{3}{2}X = Y$ $\left[\text{multiply (1) by } \frac{3}{2}\right]$

$\frac{1}{3}Z = Y$ (2)

$\frac{1}{3}Z = \frac{3}{2}X$ [both are equal to Y]

$Z = \frac{9}{2}X$ [multiply by 3]

$Z = 4\frac{1}{2}X$ *or* $Z = 450\%X$

36. **D** 5 days = 35 sets
1 day = 7 sets
7 books = 1 set
49 books = 7 sets

37. **C** This is an inverse proportion.
Let x = number of days food will last for 4 chickens.

$\frac{10 \text{ chickens}}{4 \text{ chickens}} = \frac{x}{8 \text{ days}}$

$4x = 80$

$x = 20$ days

38. **E** Original scale = 1″ = 50 miles
Since new scale 2″ = 25 miles
Then 4″ = 50 miles
Since the new linear scale is four times the old, four times as much paper is needed in the width and four times as much in the length. Therefore 4×4 or 16 sheets would have to be taped together to hold the map.

39. **B** The angle between two minute units on a clock = $\frac{360°}{60} = 6°$.
At half past 2 the hour hand is midway between 2 and 3.
The distance from this point to the 6 on the clock is 17.5 minutes $(17.5)(6°) = 105°$.

40. **B** Recall: parallel chords intercept equal arcs.

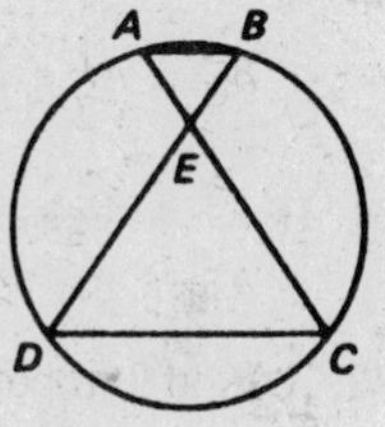

$\widehat{AD} = \widehat{BC} = 110°$

$\widehat{CD} = 360° - (\widehat{AD} + \widehat{AB} + \widehat{BC})$

or $360° - (110° + 30° + 110°) = 110°$

$\angle CED \overset{\circ}{=} \frac{1}{2}(\widehat{CD} + \widehat{AB})$ or

$\frac{1}{2}(30° + 110°) = 70°$

41. **B** Draw OB. $\angle OCB$ is a right angle (radius drawn to tangent at point of contact of tangent). OB bisects angle COA. $\angle COB \overset{\circ}{=} 70$.

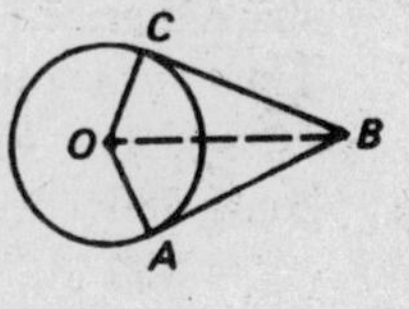

$\therefore \angle CBO \overset{\circ}{=} 20$. Likewise, $\angle OBA \overset{\circ}{=} 20$. $\angle B \overset{\circ}{=} 40$.

42. **D** $\widehat{AB} = 72° = \frac{1}{5}$ of 360° (circumference)

$5(6\pi) = 30\pi$ = circumference.

Let d = diameter and r = radius.

$\pi d = 30\pi$

$d = 30$

$r = 15$

Area $= \pi r^2$

Area $= \pi(15)^2 = 225\pi$

43. **C** Let x = number of degrees in $\angle A$ (the smallest of the angles).
Then $3x$ = number of degrees in $\angle B$ (the desired quantity).
Then $8x$ = number of degrees in $\angle C$ (necessary to find the sum of the angles of the triangle).
Since the sum of the angles of a triangle equals a straight angle,

$x + 3x + 8x \overset{\circ}{=} 180$.

$12x \overset{\circ}{=} 180$

$x \overset{\circ}{=} 15$

$3x \overset{\circ}{=} 45$ ($\angle B$)

44. **C** Draw EF.

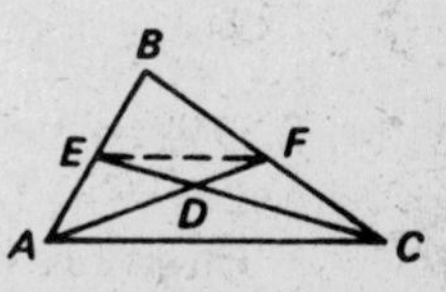

$EF \parallel AC$, $EF = \frac{1}{2}AC$ [line joining the midpoints of 2 sides of a triangle is parallel to the third and equal to $\frac{1}{2}$ of it]

$\angle FED = \angle DCA$ [alternate interior angles of parallel lines]

Also, $\angle EFD = \angle DAC$

$\triangle EDF \sim \triangle ADC$

Since $EF = \frac{1}{2}AC$, $ED = \frac{1}{2}DC$ and $DF = \frac{1}{2}AD$ [corresponding sides of similar triangles]

Let $DE = a$.

Then $DC = 2a$.

Let $DF = b$.

Then $AD = 2b$.

Substitute: $\frac{(2b)(2a)}{(b)(a)} = \frac{4\cancel{ab}}{\cancel{ab}} = 4$

45. **C** Multiplying each term of the first equation by 2 shows that it is equivalent to the second equation. The graphs of the two equations are identical, so only III is true.

46. **A** Draw OC, OD.

$\triangle OCD = \frac{1}{6}$ of $ABCDEF$

Since perimeter = 12,

$CD = 2$.

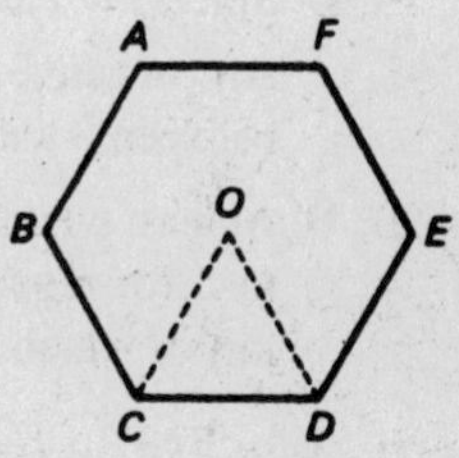

O is center of circumscribed circle.

$OC = OD$ (radii)

$\angle COD = \frac{1}{6}(360°) = 60°$

$\therefore \triangle OCD$ is equilateral.

Area of equilateral $\triangle = \frac{s^2}{4}\sqrt{3}$

Area $= \frac{2^2}{4}\sqrt{3} = \sqrt{3}$

Area of hexagon $= 6(\sqrt{3}) = 6\sqrt{3}$

47. **D** Let x = central angle of a radian.
Length of arc of one radian $= r$
Radius $= r$
Circumference $= 2\pi r$

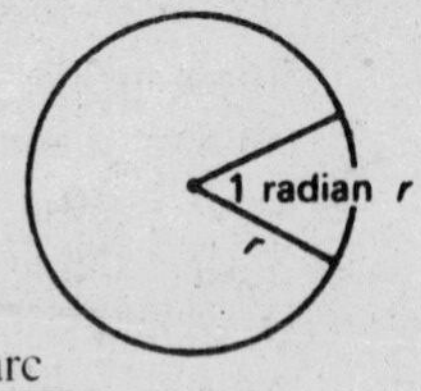

$$\frac{\text{central angle}}{360^\circ} = \frac{\text{length of arc}}{\text{circumference}}$$

$$\text{or } \frac{x}{360^\circ} = \frac{r}{2\pi r}$$

$$2\pi x = 360^\circ$$

$$x = \frac{360^\circ}{2\pi}$$

$$x = \frac{180^\circ}{\pi}$$

48. **E** Let the hypotenuse be a; $a = 10$ and one leg, $5\sqrt{3}$, is $\frac{a}{2}\sqrt{3}$. Thus, the triangle is a 30°-60°-90° triangle. The other leg is the one opposite 30°, or $\frac{a}{2}$.

$$\frac{a}{2} = \frac{10}{2} = 5$$

$$\text{Area of } \triangle = \frac{(5\sqrt{3})(5)}{2} = 12.5\sqrt{3}$$

49. **B** Draw OD and OC, radii of circle.
$\triangle DOC$ is a right isosceles triangle.
$DC = 2$ [given]
Let r = radii, OD, OC.
Using the Pythagorean Theorem,

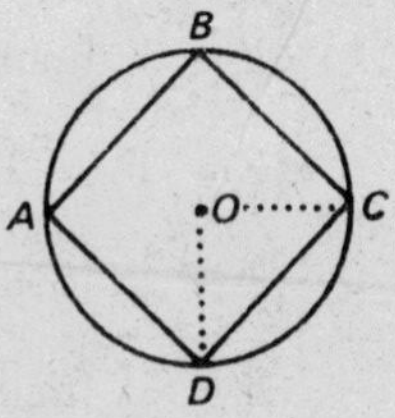

$$r^2 + r^2 = 2r^2$$
$$2r^2 = 4$$
$$r^2 = 2.$$

Area of circle $(\pi r^2) = 2\pi$

50. **C** Area of square $= (4V)^2 = 16V^2$
Length of rectangle $= 5V^3$ [given]
Let w = width of rectangle
Area of rectangle = (length)(width)

$$16V^2 = 5V^3 w$$

$$\frac{16V^2}{5V^3} = w \quad \text{or} \quad w = \frac{16}{5V}$$

PSAT/NMSQT Answer Sheet

TYPICAL TEST H

Verbal Aptitude Section

1 (A) (B) (C) (D) (E)	18 (A) (B) (C) (D) (E)	34 (A) (B) (C) (D) (E)	50 (A) (B) (C) (D) (E)
2 (A) (B) (C) (D) (E)	19 (A) (B) (C) (D) (E)	35 (A) (B) (C) (D) (E)	51 (A) (B) (C) (D) (E)
3 (A) (B) (C) (D) (E)	20 (A) (B) (C) (D) (E)	36 (A) (B) (C) (D) (E)	52 (A) (B) (C) (D) (E)
4 (A) (B) (C) (D) (E)	21 (A) (B) (C) (D) (E)	37 (A) (B) (C) (D) (E)	53 (A) (B) (C) (D) (E)
5 (A) (B) (C) (D) (E)	22 (A) (B) (C) (D) (E)	38 (A) (B) (C) (D) (E)	54 (A) (B) (C) (D) (E)
6 (A) (B) (C) (D) (E)	23 (A) (B) (C) (D) (E)	39 (A) (B) (C) (D) (E)	55 (A) (B) (C) (D) (E)
7 (A) (B) (C) (D) (E)	24 (A) (B) (C) (D) (E)	40 (A) (B) (C) (D) (E)	56 (A) (B) (C) (D) (E)
8 (A) (B) (C) (D) (E)	25 (A) (B) (C) (D) (E)	41 (A) (B) (C) (D) (E)	57 (A) (B) (C) (D) (E)
9 (A) (B) (C) (D) (E)	26 (A) (B) (C) (D) (E)	42 (A) (B) (C) (D) (E)	58 (A) (B) (C) (D) (E)
10 (A) (B) (C) (D) (E)	27 (A) (B) (C) (D) (E)	43 (A) (B) (C) (D) (E)	59 (A) (B) (C) (D) (E)
11 (A) (B) (C) (D) (E)	28 (A) (B) (C) (D) (E)	44 (A) (B) (C) (D) (E)	60 (A) (B) (C) (D) (E)
12 (A) (B) (C) (D) (E)	29 (A) (B) (C) (D) (E)	45 (A) (B) (C) (D) (E)	61 (A) (B) (C) (D) (E)
13 (A) (B) (C) (D) (E)	30 (A) (B) (C) (D) (E)	46 (A) (B) (C) (D) (E)	62 (A) (B) (C) (D) (E)
14 (A) (B) (C) (D) (E)	31 (A) (B) (C) (D) (E)	47 (A) (B) (C) (D) (E)	63 (A) (B) (C) (D) (E)
15 (A) (B) (C) (D) (E)	32 (A) (B) (C) (D) (E)	48 (A) (B) (C) (D) (E)	64 (A) (B) (C) (D) (E)
16 (A) (B) (C) (D) (E)	33 (A) (B) (C) (D) (E)	49 (A) (B) (C) (D) (E)	65 (A) (B) (C) (D) (E)
17 (A) (B) (C) (D) (E)			

Mathematical Aptitude Section*

1 (A) (B) (C) (D) (E)	14 (A) (B) (C) (D) (E)	27 (A) (B) (C) (D) (E)	39 (A) (B) (C) (D) (E)
2 (A) (B) (C) (D) (E)	15 (A) (B) (C) (D) (E)	28 (A) (B) (C) (D) (E)	40 (A) (B) (C) (D) (E)
3 (A) (B) (C) (D) (E)	16 (A) (B) (C) (D) (E)	29 (A) (B) (C) (D) (E)	41 (A) (B) (C) (D) (E)
4 (A) (B) (C) (D) (E)	17 (A) (B) (C) (D) (E)	30 (A) (B) (C) (D) (E)	42 (A) (B) (C) (D) (E)
5 (A) (B) (C) (D) (E)	18 (A) (B) (C) (D) (E)	31 (A) (B) (C) (D) (E)	43 (A) (B) (C) (D) (E)
6 (A) (B) (C) (D) (E)	19 (A) (B) (C) (D) (E)	32 (A) (B) (C) (D) (E)	44 (A) (B) (C) (D) (E)
7 (A) (B) (C) (D) (E)	20 (A) (B) (C) (D) (E)	33 (A) (B) (C) (D) (E)	45 (A) (B) (C) (D) (E)
8 (A) (B) (C) (D) (E)	21 (A) (B) (C) (D) (E)	34 (A) (B) (C) (D) (E)	46 (A) (B) (C) (D) (E)
9 (A) (B) (C) (D) (E)	22 (A) (B) (C) (D) (E)	35 (A) (B) (C) (D) (E)	47 (A) (B) (C) (D) (E)
10 (A) (B) (C) (D) (E)	23 (A) (B) (C) (D) (E)	36 (A) (B) (C) (D) (E)	48 (A) (B) (C) (D) (E)
11 (A) (B) (C) (D) (E)	24 (A) (B) (C) (D) (E)	37 (A) (B) (C) (D) (E)	49 (A) (B) (C) (D) (E)
12 (A) (B) (C) (D) (E)	25 (A) (B) (C) (D) (E)	38 (A) (B) (C) (D) (E)	50 (A) (B) (C) (D) (E)
13 (A) (B) (C) (D) (E)	26 (A) (B) (C) (D) (E)		

*If there are more answer spaces than you need, leave them blank.

TYPICAL TEST H

SECTION 1 **Time—50 minutes 65 Questions** For each question in this section, choose the best answer and fill in the corresponding circle on the answer sheet.

Each question below consists of a word in capital letters, followed by five lettered words or phrases. Choose the word or phrase that is most nearly opposite in meaning to the word in capital letters. Since some of the questions require you to distinguish fine shades of meaning, consider all the choices before deciding which is best.

Example:

GOOD: (A) sour (B) bad (C) red (D) hot (E) ugly

Ⓐ ● Ⓒ Ⓓ Ⓔ

1. AFFIRM: (A) manage (B) deny (C) hire (D) respect (E) announce

2. DIMINISH: (A) increase (B) brighten (C) unite (D) await (E) enforce

3. SPENDTHRIFT: (A) economical person (B) insecure person (C) liar (D) debtor (E) truant

4. LEISURELY: (A) tailored (B) compact (C) hectic (D) mature (E) unathletic

5. MAR: (A) restore (B) divorce (C) begin (D) verify (E) distract

6. GRANDIOSE: (A) unwanted (B) eloquent (C) silent (D) simple (E) functional

7. DISCLOSE: (A) conceal (B) perceive (C) set free (D) give back (E) locate

8. DISCORDANT: (A) harmonious (B) unthreatening (C) tentative (D) relevant (E) clear

9. PERTAIN: (A) hinder (B) divide (C) be rude (D) be irrelevant (E) refresh

10. PROVIDENT: (A) diffident (B) prodigal (C) insensitive (D) commonplace (E) certain

11. EQUIVOCATE: (A) be clear (B) make welcome (C) remain aloof (D) deprecate (E) mistake

12. CIRCUITOUS: (A) direct (B) detached (C) unremarkable (D) labyrinthine (E) radial

13. FIASCO: (A) cameo (B) mansion (C) pollution (D) success (E) gamble

14. GREGARIOUS: (A) antisocial (B) anticipatory (C) glorious (D) egregious (E) similar

15. PLACATE: (A) nettle (B) identify (C) remove (D) reply (E) retaliate

16. SPORADIC: (A) overdue (B) latent (C) vivid (D) inconsequential (E) frequent

17. IOTA: (A) waste of money (B) new phenomenon (C) large amount (D) indebtedness (E) stratagem

18. PROMULGATE: (A) expedite (B) stifle (C) reproduce (D) vacillate (E) consolidate

19. PERTINACIOUS: (A) courteous (B) expeditious (C) irresolute (D) inaccurate (E) gullible

20. REPINE: (A) endure grudgingly (B) maintain composure (C) express satisfaction (D) arouse hostility (E) attract attention

Each sentence below has one or two blanks, each blank indicating that something has been omitted. Beneath the sentence are five lettered words or sets of words. Choose the word or set of words that, when inserted in the sentence, best fits the meaning of the sentence as a whole.

Example:

Although its publicity has been ----, the film itself is intelligent, well-acted, handsomely produced, and altogether ----.

(A) tasteless . . respectable (B) extensive . . moderate (C) sophisticated . . amateur (D) risque . . crude (E) perfect . . spectacular

● Ⓑ Ⓒ Ⓓ Ⓔ

21. Though he was theoretically a skilled craftsman, the judging committee found his work ---- and lacking in polish.
(A) crude (B) accomplished (C) distinguished (D) adequate (E) conceptual

22. The dean tried to retain control of the situation on campus, but her attempt was ---- by the board of trustees.
(A) endorsed (B) frustrated (C) disclosed (D) witnessed (E) justified

23. Mark's silence was interpreted as a sign of ----, and he was accepted as a loyal member of the group.
(A) reluctance (B) acquiescence (C) pugnacity (D) inarticulateness (E) wisdom

24. Although I am not an ardent admirer of the work of George Eliot, simple justice demands a prefatory ---- her many admirable qualities.
(A) skepticism regarding (B) effusion over (C) denial of (D) tribute to (E) dismissal of

25. Bernard Shaw's goal as an anchorman is ----; when he covered the attempted assassination of President Reagan in 1981, his eyes were not enlarged and his voice was not high-pitched.
(A) accuracy (B) eloquence (C) dispassion
(D) credibility (E) sensitivity

26. Upon realizing that their position was ----, the general ---- the troops to retreat to a neighboring hill.
(A) valuable . . remonstrated
(B) untenable . . ordered
(C) evident . . urged
(D) exposed . . neglected
(E) salubrious . . commanded

27. Because he could not support the cures he obtained with scientific data, he was accused by some skeptics of being ----.
(A) a zealot (B) an artist (C) a mendicant
(D) a charlatan (E) a dilettante

28 The doctor warned her patient that his ---- nature made him susceptible to a stroke, and urged him to curb his temper.
(A) chronic (B) chimerical (C) choleric
(D) capricious (E) candid

29. Critics have been misled by Williams's obvious ---- exaggerated theatrical gestures into ---- his plays as mere melodramas, "full of sound and fury, signifying nothing."
(A) disinclination for . . disparaging
(B) repudiation of . . misrepresenting
(C) indulgence in . . acclaiming
(D) propensity for . . denigrating
(E) indifference to . . lauding

30. Mr. Southern is a historian who has entered so thoroughly into the spirit of the age that even its paradoxes leave him ----.
(A) nonplussed (B) indifferent (C) undaunted
(D) ambivalent (E) intransigent

Each question below consists of a related pair of words or phrases, followed by five lettered pairs of words or phrases. Select the lettered pair that best expresses a relationship similar to that expressed in the original pair.

Example:

YAWN : BOREDOM :: (A) dream : sleep
(B) anger : madness (C) smile : amusement
(D) face : expression (E) impatience : rebellion

Ⓐ Ⓑ ● Ⓓ Ⓔ

31. MUFFLER : NECK :: (A) lace : collar
(B) elbow : arm (C) sash : waist
(D) cuticle : finger (E) skirt : hem

32. BARGE : VESSEL :: (A) cargo : hold
(B) brake : automobile (C) shovel : implement
(D) squadron : plane (E) link : chain

33. LAUREL WREATH : VICTORY ::
(A) rosebud : charity (B) maple leaf : sweetness
(C) blindfold : visibility (D) palm tree : idleness
(E) olive branch : peace

34. DANDELION : WEED :: (A) marigold : petal
(B) plant : lawn (C) corsage : flower
(D) turnip : vegetable (E) peanut : tree

35. GRATING : EAR :: (A) warm : touch
(B) smooth : skin (C) garish : eye
(D) beating : heart (E) peeling : nose

36. INVENTOR : PATENT ::
(A) architect : blueprint (B) librarian : catalog
(C) author : copyright (D) editor : manuscript
(E) engineer : bridge

37. LEOPARD : CARNIVOROUS ::
(A) tiger : striped (B) quadruped : omnivorous
(C) cow : herbivorous (D) cat : feline
(E) seal : trained

38. BREEZE : CYCLONE :: (A) ripple : tidal wave
(B) gust : wind (C) dune : sandstorm
(D) warning : forecast (E) weather : phenomenon

39. RAMSHACKLE : SOUNDNESS ::
(A) garbled : clarity (B) decrepit : demolition
(C) humdrum : monotony
(D) flimsy : transparency (E) steadfast : speed

40. BURST : SOUND :: (A) ebb : tide
(B) tinder : fire (C) blast : wind
(D) glimmer : light (E) shard : pottery

41. AGITATOR : FIREBRAND ::
(A) miser : spendthrift (B) renegade : turncoat
(C) anarchist : backslider
(D) maverick : scapegoat (E) reprobate : hothead

42. CALLOW : MATURITY ::
(A) incipient : fruition (B) eager : anxiety
(C) youthful : senility (D) apathetic : disinterest
(E) pallid : purity

43. TIRADE : ABUSIVE :: (A) diatribe : political
(B) satire : pungent (C) panegyric : laudatory
(D) eulogy : lamentable (E) elegy : religious

44. SKULDUGGERY : SWINDLER ::
(A) surgery : quack (B) quandary : craven
(C) chicanery : trickster (D) forgery : speculator
(E) cutlery : butcher

45. SELF-RESPECTING : VAINGLORIOUS ::
(A) loyal : perfidious (B) healthful : salubrious
(C) querulous : cantankerous
(D) modest : lascivious (E) careful : punctilious

Each passage below is followed by questions based on its content. Answer the questions following each passage on the basis of what is stated or implied in that passage.

There is controversy and misunderstanding about the proper functions of juvenile courts and their probation departments. There are cries that the whole process produces delinquents rather than rehabilitates them. There are speeches by the score about "getting tough" with the kids. Another large group thinks we should be more understanding and gentle with delinquents. This distrust of the services offered can be attributed in large part to the confusion in the use of these services throughout the country.

On the one hand, the juvenile courts are tied to the criminal court system, with an obligation to decide guilt and innocence for offenses specifically stated and formally charged. On the other, they have the obligation to provide treatment, supervision and guidance to youngsters in trouble, without respect to the crimes of which they are accused. These two conflicting assignments must be carried out—quite properly—in an informal, private way, which will not stigmatize a youngster during his or her formative years.

And, as the courts' preoccupation with the latter task has increased, the former (that of dispensing justice) has retreated, with the result that grave injustices are bound to occur.

46. The title below that best expresses the ideas of this passage is
(A) Grave Injustices
(B) A Problem for Today's Teenagers
(C) Rehabilitating Youthful Criminals
(D) Fitting the Punishment to the Crime
(E) Justice for Juvenile Offenders

47. The author contends that public distrust of juvenile courts is primarily the result of
(A) the resentment of those convicted by them
(B) the dual function of these courts
(C) lack of sufficient probation officers
(D) injustices done by the courts
(E) the cost of keeping the courts

48. It can be inferred from the passage that the author
(A) is familiar with the scope of the problem
(B) is impatient with the juvenile justice system
(C) sides with those who favor leniency for juvenile offenders
(D) regards all offenses as equal in importance
(E) favors maximum sentences at all times

49. The tone of the passage can best be described as
(A) cynical (B) reverent (C) optimistic
(D) objective (E) sarcastic

In the field of language an Americanism is generally regarded by the English as ipso facto obnoxious, and when a new one of any pungency begins to force its way into British usage the guardians of the national linguistic chastity belabor it with great vehemence and predict calamitous consequences if it is not put down. If it makes progress despite these alarms, they often switch to the doctrine that it is really old English and search the *Oxford Dictionary* for examples of its use in Chaucer's time; but while it is coming in they give it no quarter. Here the unparalleled English talent for discovering moral obliquity comes into play, and what begins as an uproar over a word sometimes ends as a holy war to keep the knavish Yankee from undermining and ruining the English Kulture and overthrowing the British Empire.

50. According to the passage, if an Americanism finds acceptance in British usage, the English
(A) refuse to allow the word to be included in the dictionaries
(B) deny that it really is an Americanism
(C) feel that their cultural level is lowered
(D) will not admit that it is accepted
(E) claim that it is not American slang but good American usage

51. With which one of the following statements about British English would the author be most likely to agree?
(A) British English contains less slang than American English.
(B) British English is lacking in humor.
(C) British English is no longer a growing language.
(D) The alertness of literary critics has preserved the purity of British English.
(E) The absorption of Americanisms into British English is inevitable.

52. The author regards the British assumption of American linguistic inferiority with
(A) wholehearted approval
(B) grudging acceptance (C) bitter resentment
(D) sardonic humor (E) watchful concern

The great trees furnish support for much of the other plant life of the forest. Climbers are abundant, much more so than elsewhere. Greedy for light, they have various adaptations for hoisting themselves to the upper canopy—some are twiners, others are equipped with tendrils, hooks or suckers. An entire group of plants is unfitted to start low and climb high to reach the light. These are epiphytes, plants that grow on trees without parasitizing them or deriving any advantage except a platform near the sun. They are extraordinarily common. However, in order to grow close to the sunlight, they have had to pay a price—they have lost their root connection with the forest floor and its abundant moisture. For soil, they must often make do with the small amounts of debris that lodge in crannies in the trees, with dust from the atmosphere and organic matter and seeds deposited by ants that often nest in the roots of epiphytes—a small but vital source of humus and minerals. So well have these plants managed to create their own environment that the spoonfuls of soil in which they grow do not differ significantly from normal soil in microbiological processes.

Some of the epiphytes have developed remarkable adaptations for conserving water. Many are encased in a waxy layer that retards evaporation. The roots of some orchids have a spongy tissue that not only soaks up water but also carries on photosynthesis. The staghorn fern accumulates water-holding humus in a sort of bucket structure at the base of its leaves. The large group of tropical plants known as bromeliads are living cisterns—their long branching leaves spring from the same place around the stem, and overlap so tightly at their bases that they can hold water, as much as four-and-a-half quarts in a large plant. These bromeliad tanks become a center of life, holding breeding frogs, snails and aquatic insects, all of which add to the supply of nutrients in the water. Hairs at the base of the leaves line the tank and perform the job of absorbing water and nutrients, making the bromeliad independent of a root connection with the soil.

53. According to the passage, epiphytes are particularly adapted to
(A) the floor of the tropical rain forest
(B) a sunless environment
(C) the dissipation of rainwater
(D) drawing sustenance from a host
(E) the retention of liquid

54. It can be inferred from the passage that which of the following is true of epiphytes?
(A) They lack root systems.
(B) They do not require large amounts of soil for growth.
(C) They are incapable of photosynthesis.
(D) They are hard to perceive in the dense rain forest canopy.
(E) They need different nutrients than other plants do.

55. The passage can best be described as
(A) enthusiastic exhortation
(B) sophisticated analysis
(C) straightforward description
(D) indirect exposition
(E) forceful argument

The atmosphere is a mixture of several gases. There are about ten chemical elements which remain permanently in gaseous form in the atmosphere under all natural conditions. Of these permanent gases, oxygen makes up about 21 percent and nitrogen about 78 percent. Several other gases, such as argon, carbon dioxide, hydrogen, neon, krypton, and xenon, comprise the remaining one percent of the volume of dry air. The amount of water vapor and its variations in amount and distribution are of extraordinary importance in weather changes. Atmospheric gases hold in suspension great quantities of dust, pollen, smoke, and other impurities which are always present in considerable, but variable, amounts.

The atmosphere has no definite upper limits but gradually thins until it becomes imperceptible. Until recently it was assumed that the air above the first few miles gradually grew thinner and colder at a constant rate. It was also assumed that upper air had little influence on weather changes. Recent studies of the upper atmosphere, currently being conducted by earth satellites and missile probings, have shown these assumptions to be incorrect. The atmosphere has three well-defined strata.

The layer of the air next to the earth, which extends upward for about ten miles, is known as the *troposphere*. On the whole, it makes up about 75 percent of all the weight of the atmosphere. It is the warmest part of the atmosphere because most of the solar radiation is absorbed by the earth's surface, which warms the air immediately surrounding it. A steady decrease of temperature with increasing elevation is a most striking characteristic. The upper layers are colder because of their greater distance from the earth's surface and rapid radiation of heat into space. The temperatures within the troposphere decrease about 3.5 degrees per 1,000-foot increase in altitude. Within the troposphere, winds and air currents distribute heat and moisture. Strong winds, called jet streams, are located at the upper levels of the troposphere. These jet streams are both complex and widespread in occurrence. They normally show a wave-shaped pattern and move from west to east at velocities of 150 mph, but velocities as high as 400 mph have been noted. The influences of changing locations and strengths of jet streams upon weather conditions and patterns are no doubt considerable. Current intensive research may eventually reveal their true significance.

Above the troposphere to a height of about 50 miles is a zone called the *stratosphere*. The stratosphere is separated from the troposphere by a zone of uniform temperatures called the tropopause. Within the lower portions of the stratosphere is a layer of ozone gases which filters out most of the ultraviolet rays from the sun. The ozone layer varies with air pressure. If this zone were not there, the full blast of the sun's ultraviolet light would burn our skins, blind our eyes, and eventually result in our destruction. Within the stratosphere, the temperature and atmospheric composition are relatively uniform.

The layer upward of about 50 miles is the most fascinating but the least known of the three strata. It is called the *ionosphere* because it consists of electrically charged particles called ions, thrown from the sun. The northern lights (aurora borealis) originate within this highly charged portion of the atmosphere. Their effect upon weather conditions if any is, as yet, unknown.

56. According to the passage, studies in the stratosphere have been made possible by
(A) weather balloons (B) meteorologists
(C) jet planes (D) earth satellites
(E) photographs of jet streams

57. The passage indicates that life as we know it exists on the earth because the atmosphere
(A) contains a layer of ozone gases
(B) contains electrically charged particles
(C) is warmest at the bottom
(D) carries the ultraviolet rays of the sun
(E) provides the changes in weather

58. The title that best expresses the ideas of this passage is
(A) The Makeup of the Atmosphere
(B) Studying the Atmosphere
(C) Atmosphere and Weather
(D) Temperature in the Stratosphere
(E) The Sun's Rays

59. The troposphere is the warmest part of the atmosphere because it
(A) is nearest the sun
(B) contains electrically charged particles
(C) radiates heat into space
(D) has winds and air currents which distribute the heat
(E) is warmed by the earth's heat

60. This passage is most probably an excerpt from
(A) a specialized scientific journal
(B) a general-interest magazine
(C) a basic meteorology textbook
(D) the script for a weather report
(E) a book on the history of space explorations

As the works of dozens of women writers have been rescued from what E.P. Thompson calls "the enormous condescension of posterity," and considered in relation to each other, the lost continent of the female tradition has risen like Atlantis from the sea of English literature. It is now becoming clear that, contrary to Mill's theory, women have had a literature of their own all along. The woman novelist, according to Vineta Colby, was "really neither single nor anomalous," but she was also more than a "register and spokesman for her age." She was part of a tradition that had its origins before her age, and has carried on through our own.

Many literary historians have begun to reinterpret and revise the study of women writers. Ellen Moers sees women's literature as an international movement, "apart from, but hardly subordinate to the mainstream: an undercurrent, rapid and powerful. This 'movement' began in the late eighteenth century, was multinational, and produced some of the greatest literary works of two centuries, as well as most of the lucrative potboilers." Patricia Meyer Spacks, in *The Female Imagination*, finds that "for readily discernible historical reasons women have characteristically concerned themselves with matters more or less peripheral to male concerns, or at least slightly skewed from them. The differences between traditional female preoccupations and roles and male ones make a difference in female writing." Many other critics are beginning to agree that when we look at women writers collectively we can see an imaginative continuum, the recurrence of certain patterns, themes, problems, and images from generation to generation.

This book is an effort to describe the female literary tradition in the English novel from the generation of the Brontes to the present day, and to show how the development of this tradition is similar to the development of any literary subculture. Women have generally been regarded as "sociological chameleons," taking on the class, lifestyle, and culture of their male relatives. It can, however, be argued that women themselves have constituted a subculture within the framework of a larger society, and have been unified by values, conventions, experiences, and behaviors impinging on each individual. It is important to see the female literary tradition in these broad terms, in relation to the wider evolution of women's self-awareness and to the ways any minority group finds its direction of self-expression relative to a dominant society, because we cannot show a pattern of deliberate progress and accumulation. It is true, as Ellen Moers writes, that "women studied with a special closeness the works written by their own sex;" in terms of influences, borrowings, and affinities, the tradition is strongly marked. But it is also full of holes and hiatuses, because of what Germaine Greer calls the "phenomenon of the transience of female literary fame"; "almost uninterruptedly since the Interregnum, a small group of women have enjoyed dazzling literary prestige during their own lifetimes, only to vanish without trace from the records of posterity." Thus each generation of women writers has found itself, in a sense, without a history, forced to rediscover the past anew, forging again and again the consciousness of their sex. Given this perpetual disruption, and also the self-hatred that has alienated women writers from a sense of collective identity, it does not seem possible to speak of a movement.

61. Which of the following would be the most appropriate title for the passage?
(A) A Unique Phenomenon: Nineteenth and Twentieth Century Feminine Literary Movements
(B) A Literature of Their Own: The Female Literary Tradition
(C) Adaptive Coloration: Feminine Adoption of Masculine Cultural Criteria
(D) The Emergence of the Contemporary Women's Novel
(E) Fame Versus Fortune: The Dilemma of the Woman Writer

62. In the first paragraph, the author makes use of all the following techniques EXCEPT
(A) extended metaphor
(B) enumeration and classification
(C) classical allusion
(D) direct quotation
(E) comparison and contrast

63. In the second paragraph of the passage the author's attitude toward the literary critics cited can best be described as one of
(A) irony
(B) ambivalence
(C) disparagement
(D) receptiveness
(E) awe

64. Which of the following words could best be substituted for "forging" (next-to-last sentence) without substantially changing the author's meaning?
(A) counterfeiting (B) creating (C) exploring
(D) diverting (E) straining

65. It can be inferred from the passage that the author considers Moers's work to be
(A) fallacious and misleading
(B) scholarly and definitive
(C) admirable, but inaccurate in certain of its conclusions
(D) popular, but irrelevant to mainstream female literary criticism
(E) idiosyncratic, but of importance historically

SECTION **2** **Time—50 minutes** **50 Questions**

In this section solve each problem, using any available space on the page for scratchwork. Then decide which is the best of the choices given and fill in the corresponding circle on the answer sheet.

The following information is for your reference in solving some of the problems.

Circle of radius r: Area $= \pi r^2$ Circumference $= 2\pi r$
The number of degrees of arc in a circle is 360.
The measure in degrees of a straight angle is 180.

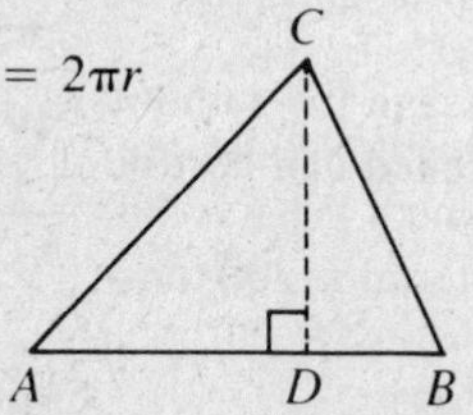

Triangle: The sum of the measures in degrees of the angles of a triangle is 180.

If $\angle CDA$ is a right angle, then

(1) area of $\triangle ABC = \frac{AB \times CD}{2}$

(2) $AC^2 = AD^2 + DC^2$

Definitions of symbols:

$=$ is equal to	$\leqq$ is less than or equal to
$\neq$ is unequal to	$\geqq$ is greater than or equal to
$<$ is less than	$\parallel$ is parallel to
$>$ is greater than	$\perp$ is perpendicular to

Note: Figures that accompany problems in this test are intended to provide information useful in solving the problems. They are drawn as accurately as possible EXCEPT when it is stated in a specific problem that its figure is not drawn to scale. All figures lie in a plane unless otherwise indicated. All numbers used are real numbers.

1. $\frac{1}{2} + \frac{3}{4} \div \left(\frac{5}{6} \times \frac{7}{8}\right) - \frac{9}{10} =$
(A) $\frac{18}{35}$ (B) $\frac{22}{35}$ (C) $\frac{57}{70}$ (D) $\frac{7}{12}$ (E) $1\frac{5}{7}$

2. $\frac{1}{2}\%$ equals
(A) 0.005% (B) $\frac{1}{200}$ (C) 0.5 (D) 50%
(E) 5%

3. How many thirds are there in 75% of an apple pie?
(A) $\frac{1}{4}$ (B) 1 (C) 2 (D) $2\frac{1}{4}$ (E) 3

4. 0.3% of what number = 2163?
(A) 72.1 (B) 721 (C) 7210
(D) 72,100 (E) 721,000

5. What number put in the parentheses will make the following statement true? $\frac{(\quad)}{5}$ cubic feet $= \frac{1}{3}$ cubic yard
(A) $1\frac{2}{3}$ (B) 5 (C) 15 (D) 20 (E) 45

6. A farmer sold $\frac{3}{8}$ of his strawberries for \$60. At that rate what would he receive for the remainder of his crop?
(A) \$20 (B) \$60 (C) \$100 (D) \$120
(E) \$160

7. A man left his estate to his three children to be distributed in the ratio of 1:2:1. If the value of the estate was \$40,000, how much did the child with the greatest share receive?
(A) \$2000 (B) \$13,333.33 (C) \$13,334
(D) \$20,000 (E) \$30,000

8. A merchant paid \$60 for a chair. He wishes to put a price tag on it so that he could offer his customers a discount of 10% of the price marked on the tag and still make a profit of 20% of the cost. What price should he mark on the tag?
(A) \$72.00 (B) \$78.00 (C) \$79.20
(D) \$80.00 (E) \$85.00

9. If, after successive discounts of 15% and 10% have been allowed on the marked price, the net price of a certain article is \$306, the marked price is
(A) \$230.00 (B) \$234.09 (C) \$382.50
(D) \$400.00 (E) \$408.00

10. How much can be saved by purchasing a radio for cash at \$72 instead of paying \$15 down and five monthly payments of \$13 each?
(A) \$7 (B) \$8 (C) \$9 (D) 10
(E) none of these

11. Point M is the midpoint of line KL, and point C is the midpoint of line AB. If $KM > AC$, then which of the following is (are) true?
I. $KL < AB$
II. $KL > AB$
III. $KM < AC$
(A) I only (B) II only (C) III only
(D) I and II only (E) I, II, and III

12. Which of the following statements is (are) true of the length of segments on line l?

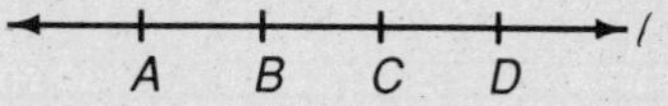

I. $AB + BC = AD - CD$
II. $AD - BC = AB + CD$
III. $AB + CD = AD$
(A) I only (B) II only (C) III only
(D) I and II only (E) I, II, and III

13. The length of a rectangle is 3 inches greater than its width and its area is 88 square inches. An equation that may be used to find the width w of the rectangle is

(A) $3w^2 = 88$ (B) $\frac{w^2}{3} = 88$
(C) $w^2 + 3w - 88 = 0$ (D) $w^2 - 3w = 88$
(E) $w = 29.3$

14. On the average, 800 pounds of valuable oxides are obtained from every 2 tons of ore mined. What is the ratio of valuable oxides to other material in 100 tons of ore? (1 ton = 2000 pounds)
(A) 1:400 (B) 1:5 (C) 1:4 (D) 2:1
(E) 4:1

15. How many pints of flour should be used with 3 pints of milk in a recipe which calls for 2 parts of milk and 3 parts of flour?
(A) 2 (B) 3 (C) $4\frac{1}{2}$ (D) 5. (E) 6

Questions 16-32 each consist of two quantities, one in Column A and one in Column B. You are to compare the two quantities and on the answer sheet fill in circle

A if the quantity in Column A is greater;
B if the quantity in Column B is greater;
C if the two quantities are equal;
D if the relationship cannot be determined from the information given.

Notes:
1. In certain questions, information concerning one or both of the quantities to be compared is centered above the two columns.
2. In a given question, a symbol that appears in both columns represents the same thing in Column A as it does in Column B.
3. Letters such as x, n, and k stand for real numbers.

EXAMPLES

	Column A	Column B	Answers
E1.	2×6	$2 + 6$	● Ⓑ Ⓒ Ⓓ
	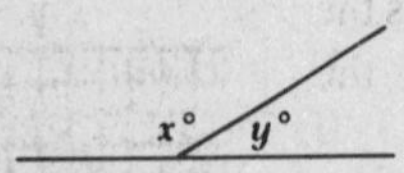		
E2.	$180 - x$	y	Ⓐ Ⓑ ● Ⓓ
E3.	$p - q$	$q - p$	Ⓐ Ⓑ Ⓒ ●

	Column A	Column B
16.	$10 - \frac{10}{0.1}$	-9
17.	$\sqrt{4}$	$\frac{1}{0.5}$
18.	0.6%	$\frac{6}{1000}$
19.	$\frac{2548}{14}$ inches	5 yards 2 inches

$x = y = 5$

20.	$\frac{1}{x} \div \frac{1}{\frac{1}{x}}$	$\frac{1}{y}$
21.	$(y + 160) - (120 - y)$	$(x + 10) - (x - 2y - 30)$

$a = b^2 - 1$

22.	a	b

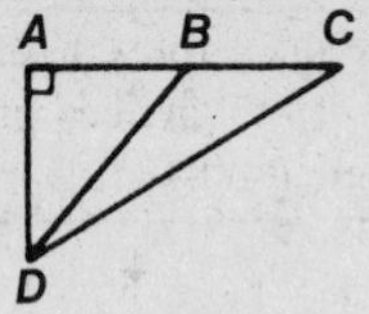

$AB = BC$
$AD \perp AC$

23.	Area of ABD	Area of BCD

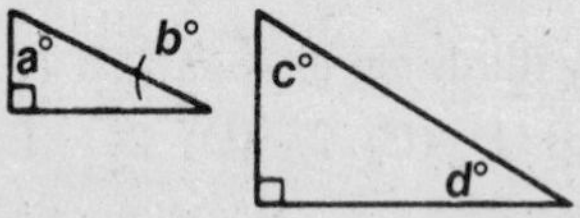

24.	$\frac{a + b}{2}$	$\frac{1}{2}(c + d)$

$x > 0$ and $y > 0$
$x = \frac{y}{2}$

25.	$y + 2$	$2x + 2$
26.	$\frac{1}{2}$	$\sqrt{\frac{1}{4}}$

$7x = 35 + 7y$

27.	y	$x - 7$
28.	0.08	$\sqrt{0.64}$
29.	The original price of a TV set, including delivery charge.	The reduced price of the same set during a sale at a 10% reduction but a 10% delivery charge.

	Column A	Column B
30.	Lori's rate driving to school was 30 miles per hour. Going home her average speed was 40 miles per hour.	Average rate of 35 miles per hour.
	$xy = k$	
31.	x	y
	It takes m men to complete a task in 12 days. D days is the time required by $m - 12$ men.	
32.	12	D

Solve each of the remaining problems in this section using any available space for scratchwork. Then decide which is the best of the choices given and fill in the corresponding circle on the answer sheet.

33. $\sqrt{\frac{2 + x^2}{2}} = 3$

What is the value of x?
(A) ± 2 (B) ± 3 (C) ± 4 (D) ± 5
(E) ± 6

34. $5x - 3y = 3$
$2x - 4y = -10$
$3x + y =$
(A) -30 (B) -13 (C) -7 (D) 7 (E) 13

35. Five candidates run for office in a club that has a membership of 356. What is the least number of votes the successful candidate must receive to be victorious?
(A) 69 (B) 70 (C) 71 (D) 72 (E) 178

36. A motorist travels D miles in T hours and then travels d miles at t hours. His average rate for the entire trip is
(A) $\frac{1}{2}\left(\frac{D}{T} + \frac{d}{t}\right)$ (B) $\frac{2Dd}{Tt}$ (C) $\frac{D + d}{T + t}$
(D) $\frac{Dt + dT}{2Tt}$ (E) $\frac{d}{t} + \frac{D}{T}$

37. A bus has a capacity of 20 adults or 24 children. How many children can ride with 15 adults?
(A) 4 (B) 6 (C) 7 (D) 9 (E) 18

38. 1500 is greater than 1200 by
(A) 2.5% (B) 3% (C) 11.9% (D) 20%
(E) 25%

39. How many squares 2″ × 2″ can be cut from a piece of cardboard 8″ × 4″?
(A) 2 (B) 4 (C) 8 (D) 12 (E) 16

40. Melinda has 10 problems to do before watching a television program scheduled for 9 P.M. She takes 10 minutes on the average to do a problem. What is the latest time she could begin to do her homework and have her work done by the time the television program begins?
(A) 7:10 P.M. (B) 7:20 P.M. (C) 7:30 P.M.
(D) 7:45P.M. (E) 8:00 P.M.

41. If $3x - 6 = 1$, what is the value of $x - 2$?
(A) $\frac{1}{3}$ (B) $\frac{1}{2}$ (C) 1 (D) 2 (E) 3

42. For $X \neq 0$, let X be defined by $\textcircled{X} = X^2 + \frac{1}{X^2}$
Then $\textcircled{2} =$
(A) 1 (B) 2 (C) 4 (D) $4\frac{1}{4}$ (E) $4\frac{1}{2}$

43. In a right triangle, sides x, y, z have values such that $x < y < z$. Which of the following expresses the value of z^2?
(A) $x^2 + y^2$ (B) $x^2 - y^2$ (C) $x - y$
(D) $x + y$ (E) $y^2 - x^2$

44. AB is a diameter.
If $OC = BC$, then $\frac{x}{2}$ equals
(A) 20 (B) 30 (C) 60
(D) 90 (E) 120

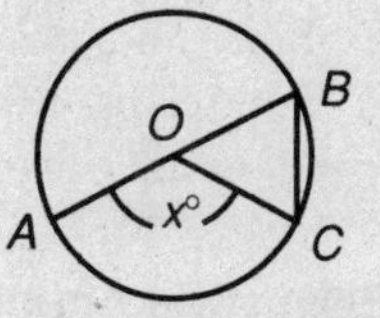

45. If a square with an area 144 is equal in perimeter to an equilateral triangle, what is a side of the triangle?
(A) 4 (B) 9 (C) 12 (D) 16 (E) 18

46. A pond 100 feet in diameter is surrounded by a circular grass walk which is 2 feet wide. The number of square feet of grass on the walk is
(A) 4π (B) 20π (C) 196π (D) 204π
(E) 270π

47. Which of the following is the equation of line RS in the figure?
(A) $y = x$
(B) $y = -x$
(C) $y = 4 - x$
(D) $y = x - 4$
(E) $y = x + 4$

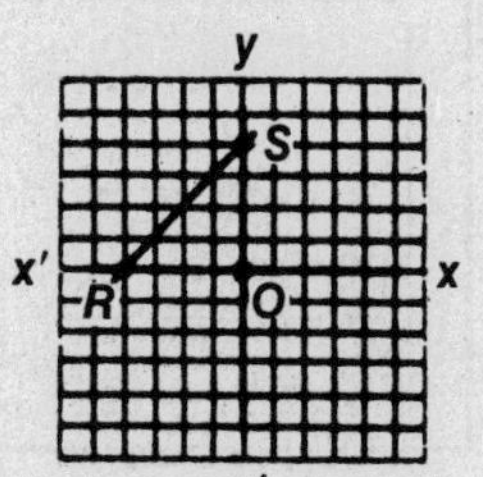

48. Quadrilateral $ABCD$ is inscribed in circle O.
$\angle DAB \overset{\circ}{=} 80$, $\angle ABC \overset{\circ}{=} 120$, $\angle ADC \overset{\circ}{=}$
(A) 60 (B) 80 (C) 100 (D) 120 (E) 160

49. RS and RT are tangent to circle O. $\angle SRT \stackrel{\circ}{=} 30$. $\angle SOT \stackrel{\circ}{=}$

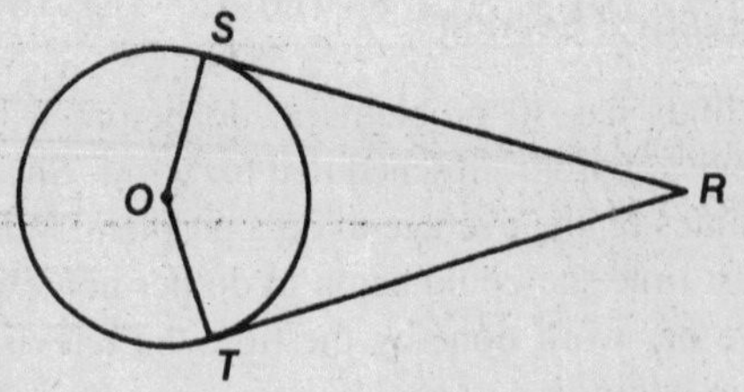

(A) 110 (B) 120 (C) 150 (D) 250
(E) 300

50. In $\triangle ABC$, AP is drawn so that $\angle 1 = \angle 2$. All of the following are true EXCEPT

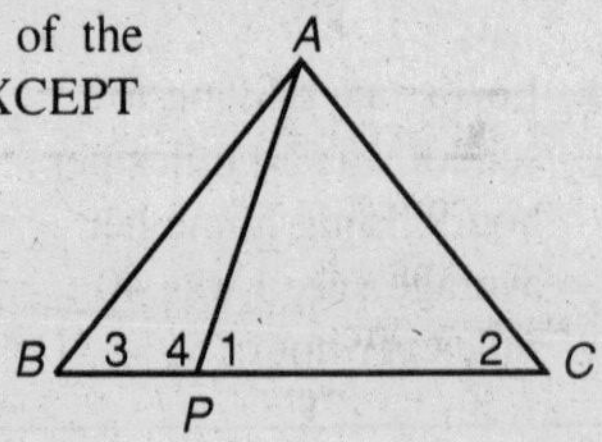

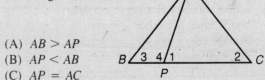

(A) $AB > AP$
(B) $AP < AB$
(C) $AP = AC$
(D) The measure of $\angle 2$ is greater than the measure of $\angle 3$.
(E) $AP > AB$

ANSWER KEY

Verbal Aptitude Section

1. **B**	*11.* **A**	*21.* **A**	*31.* **C**	*41.* **B**	*51.* **E**	*61.* **B**
2. **A**	*12.* **A**	*22.* **B**	*32.* **C**	*42.* **A**	*52.* **D**	*62.* **B**
3. **A**	*13.* **D**	*23.* **B**	*33.* **E**	*43.* **C**	*53.* **E**	*63.* **D**
4. **C**	*14.* **A**	*24.* **D**	*34.* **D**	*44.* **C**	*54.* **B**	*64.* **B**
5. **A**	*15.* **A**	*25.* **C**	*35.* **C**	*45.* **E**	*55.* **C**	*65.* **C**
6. **D**	*16.* **E**	*26.* **B**	*36.* **C**	*46.* **E**	*56.* **D**	
7. **A**	*17.* **C**	*27.* **D**	*37.* **C**	*47.* **B**	*57.* **A**	
8. **A**	*18.* **B**	*28.* **C**	*38.* **A**	*48.* **A**	*58.* **C**	
9. **D**	*19.* **C**	*29.* **D**	*39.* **A**	*49.* **D**	*59.* **E**	
10. **B**	*20.* **C**	*30.* **C**	*40.* **C**	*50.* **B**	*60.* **C**	

Mathematical Aptitude Section

Note: Each correct answer to the mathematics questions is keyed by number to the corresponding topic in Chapters 9 and 10. These numerals refer to the topics listed below, with specific page references in parentheses.

1. Basic Fundamental Operations (155–157)
2. Algebraic Operations (157–160)
3. Using Algebra (160–164)
4. Exponents, Roots and Radicals (159–160)
5. Inequalities (164–165)
6. Fractions (176–178)
7. Decimals (176)
8. Percent (178–180)
9. Averages (180–181)
10. Motion (182–183)
11. Ratio and Proportion (183–185)
12. Mixtures and Solutions (177–178)
13. Work (185–186)
14. Coordinate Geometry (172–173)
15. Geometry (165–172, 173–176)
16. Quantitative Comparisons (189–192)

ANSWER KEY

1. **B** (1,6)	*11.* **B** (5,15)	*21.* **C** (2,16)	*31.* **D** (2,16)	*41.* **A** (2)
2. **B** (6,8)	*12.* **D** (15)	*22.* **D** (2,16)	*32.* **B** (11,16)	*42.* **D** (2)
3. **D** (8)	*13.* **C** (3)	*23.* **C** (15,16)	*33.* **C** (4)	*43.* **A** (15)
4. **E** (8)	*14.* **C** (11)	*24.* **C** (15,16)	*34.* **E** (2)	*44.* **C** (15)
5. **E** (1)	*15.* **C** (11)	*25.* **C** (2,16)	*35.* **D** (1)	*45.* **D** (15)
6. **C** (6,11)	*16.* **B** (6,7,16)	*26.* **C** (4,16)	*36.* **C** (10)	*46.* **D** (15)
7. **D** (11)	*17.* **C** (4,6,7,16)	*27.* **A** (2,16)	*37.* **B** (1)	*47.* **E** (14)
8. **D** (3,8)	*18.* **C** (6,8,16)	*28.* **B** (4,16)	*38.* **E** (8)	*48.* **A** (15)
9. **D** (3,8)	*19.* **C** (11,16)	*29.* **A** (8,16)	*39.* **C** (15)	*49.* **C** (15)
10. **B** (8)	*20.* **B** (2,16)	*30.* **D** (10,16)	*40.* **B** (1)	*50.* **E** (5,15)

SCORING CHART TYPICAL TEST H

Verbal Section		Mathematical Section*		
No. correct	_____	No. correct	(A)	_____
No. omitted	_____	No. incorrect (# 1-15, 33-50)	(B)	_____
No. incorrect	_____	No. incorrect (# 16-32)	(C)	_____
¼ no. incorrect	_____	¼ (B) + ⅓ (C)	(D)	_____
Raw Score: (no. correct minus ¼ no. incorrect)	_____	*Raw Score* = (A) − (D)		_____

* (In the Mathematical section, deduct ¼ of a point for each five-choice question answered incorrectly and ⅓ of a point for each four-choice question answered incorrectly.)

EVALUATION CHART

Study your score. Your raw score on the Verbal and Mathematical Aptitude Sections is an indication of your probable achievement on the PSAT/NMSQT. As a guide to the amount of work you need or want to do with this book, study the following.

Raw Score		Self-rating
Verbal	*Mathematical*	
58–65	41–50	Superior
46–57	25–40	Very good
40–45	20–24	Satisfactory
36–39	16–19	Average
30–35	10–15	Needs further study
20–29	7–9	Needs intensive study
0–19	0–6	Probably inadequate

Your scores are most likely improving with each test that you take. To help pinpoint any weak areas you still may have, consult the table on page 384 and plan your remaining review accordingly.

ANSWER EXPLANATIONS

Verbal Aptitude Section

1. **B** The opposite of to *affirm* or state to be true is to *deny*.
Think of "helping the defendant by affirming his testimony."

2. **A** The opposite of to *diminish* (lessen or reduce) is to *increase*.
Think of "feeling one's strength diminish."

3. **A** The opposite of a *spendthrift* or wasteful person is an *economical person*.
Think of "spendthrifts on a buying spree."

4. **C** The opposite of *leisurely* or unhurried is *hectic* (frantic; rapid-paced; chaotic).
Think of "enjoying a leisurely dinner."

5. **A** The opposite of to *mar* or spoil is to *restore* or mend.
Think of a scratch "marring the finish" of a tabletop.

6. **D** The opposite of *grandiose* (showy; overelaborate; pompous) is *simple*.
Think of "having grandiose plans."

7. **A** The opposite of to *disclose* or reveal is to *conceal* or hide.
Think of unintentionally "disclosing a secret."

8. **A** The opposite of *discordant* (harsh-sounding) is *harmonious*.
Think of "harsh, discordant tones."

9. **D** The opposite of to *pertain* or relate to something is to *be irrelevant* to it.
Think of "evidence pertaining to a lawsuit."

10. **B** The opposite of *provident* (careful or thrifty) is *prodigal* (extravagant).
Think of "provident management of one's resources."

11. **A** The opposite of to *equivocate* (speak ambiguously in order to mislead) is to *be clear*.
Think of political candidates "equivocating and not taking a stand."

12. **A** The opposite of *circuitous* (roundabout) is *direct*.
Think of losing time following "a circuitous route."

13. **D** The opposite of a *fiasco* or complete failure is a *success.*
"The show was a flop—a total fiasco!"

14. **A** The opposite of *gregarious* or sociable is *antisocial.*
Word Parts Clue: *Greg-* means crowd. Someone gregarious loves a crowd.

15. **A** The opposite of to *placate* or soothe is to *nettle* or annoy.
Think of "placating someone before she explodes."

16. **E** The opposite of *sporadic* (occasional; scattered; infrequent) is *frequent.*
Think of "occasional sporadic showers."

17. **C** The opposite of an *iota* (very small amount; jot) is a *large amount.*
"You'll get nothing! Not one iota!"

18. **B** The opposite of to *promulgate* (proclaim; declare; promote) is to *stifle* or suppress.
Think of "openly promulgating a law."

19. **C** The opposite of *pertinacious* (persevering; stubborn; dogged) is *irresolute.*
Think of "a pertinacious encyclopedia salesman."

20. **C** To *repine* is to complain or express discontent. Its opposite is to *express satisfaction.*
Think of "repining the pains of old age."

21. **A** *Though* calls for a contrast. From a skilled craftsman we expect fine work; instead, the work here is not polished but *crude.*

22. **B** The use of *but* indicates that the dean's attempt to keep control failed. It did so because it was *frustrated* by the board of trustees. None of the other possible actions of the board of trustees would necessarily have caused the dean's attempt to fail.

23. **B** *And* here is a support signal. The fact that Mark was accepted as a loyal member of the group supports the idea that the members thought he agreed with them, even though he said nothing. Thus, they assumed his silence was a sign of *acquiescence* or agreement.

24. **D** *Although* the writer does not personally enjoy Eliot's novels, before he criticizes her he feels he should, to be fair, pay *tribute* or give due recognition to her literary virtues.

25. **C** While all the answer choices are plausible goals for an anchorman, only one is acceptable in light of the second clause: *dispassion* or calm. Shaw's maintenance of his composure is illustrated by his ability to maintain the normal pitch of his voice.

26. **B** If the general realized that he could not maintain his position because it was *untenable* (indefensible), he would *order* his troops to retreat.

27. **D** A person who could not support his claims for alleged cures with hard scientific data might as a consequence be called a *charlatan* (a faker or quack) by skeptics or disbelievers in his powers.

28. **C** It would be reasonable to urge a *choleric* (hot-tempered; easily angered) person to curb or restrain his temper.

29. **D** It is Williams's *propensity* or liking for theatricality that causes critics to *denigrate* or belittle his plays as mere melodrama. Note how the use of *mere* and the sense of the Shakespearean quotation convey the idea that Williams's plays have been sullied or belittled.

30. **C** Because Mr. Southern so understands the spirit of the age, he is unafraid of or *undaunted by* its paradoxes. To say that a historian has entered thoroughly into the spirit of an age is a compliment. Thus, the missing word must be complimentary in meaning.

31. **C** One wears a *muffler* around one's *neck;* one wears a *sash* around one's *waist.*
(Defining Characteristic)

32. **C** A *barge* is a kind of *vessel* or ship; a *shovel* is a kind of *implement* or tool.
(Class and Member)

33. **E** A *laurel wreath* is the symbol of *victory.* An *olive branch* is the symbol of *peace.*
Beware eye-catchers. We may associate *idleness* with the notion of lying under a *palm tree;* however, this is not an essential or necessary relationship.
(Symbol and Abstraction It Represents)

34. **D** A *dandelion* is a kind of *weed;* a *turnip* is a kind of *vegetable.*
(Class and Member)

35. **C** A *grating* sound by definition offends the *ear;* a *garish* appearance offends the *eye.*
(Defining Characteristic)

36. **C** An *inventor* protects his or her invention by obtaining a *patent;* an *author* protects his or her literary work by obtaining a *copyright.*
(Function)

37. **C** A *leopard* is by definition a *carnivorous* (meat-eating) animal; a *cow* is by definition a *herbivorous* (grass-eating) animal.
(Defining Characteristic)

38. **A** A *breeze* is less forceful than a *cyclone;* a *ripple* is less forceful than a *tidal wave.*
(Degree of Intensity)

39. **A** Something *ramshackle* or rickety lacks *soundness* or solidity. Something *garbled* or jumbled lacks *clarity.*
(Antonym Variant)

40. **C** A *burst* is a sudden, violent outbreak of *sound.* A *blast* is a sudden, violent outbreak (heavy gust) of *wind.*
Beware eye-catchers. Choice **D** is incorrect. A *glimmer* is a feeble or intermittent *light,* not a sudden, violent flare or blast of light.
(Degree of Intensity)

41. **B** *Agitator* (trouble-maker) is a synonym for *firebrand*. *Renegade* (traitor) is a synonym for *turncoat*.

(Synonym)

42. **A** Someone *callow* is immature and will not reach full development till *maturity*. Something *incipient* is beginning to become apparent and will not reach full development till *fruition*.

(Antonym Variant)

43. **C** A *tirade* (scolding, denunciatory speech) is by definition *abusive; a panegyric* (eulogy) is by definition *laudatory* (full of praise).

(Defining Characteristic)

44. **C** *Skulduggery* or dishonest, unscrupulous behavior is the mark of the *swindler. Chicanery* or trickery is the mark of the *trickster*.

(Defining Characteristic)

45. **E** *Self-respecting* is less extreme than *vainglorious* or excessively proud. *Careful* is less extreme than *punctilious* or excessively attentive to fine points.

(Degree of Intensity)

46. **E** The author discusses the two aspects of providing justice for juvenile offenders.

47. **B** The last sentence of paragraph 1 indicates that the confusion of the dual functions creates the distrust.

48. **A** The author's explanation of the two sides of the problem indicates that he is familiar with the subject.

49. **D** The passage is written in an objective, analytical manner.

50. **B** Sentence 2 indicates that those Americanisms that make progress with the British public (that is, find acceptance and are popularly used) are co-opted by the British, who say such terms are really old English and therefore not really Americanisms at all.

51. **E** Since the British, according to this passage, justify their adoption of Americanisms by maintaining they are actually British terms whose use dates back to ancient days ("Chaucer's time"), it is clear that these terms are being incorporated into British English and that this absorption of Americanisms is inevitable.

52. **D** Obviously, the author does not take the British attitude of superiority seriously. He exaggerates this position, talking about a "holy war," and poking fun at British purists with such terms as "guardians of the national linguistic chastity." He looks on their assumption of American linguistic inferiority with humor, but there is an edge to his amusement: he is *sardonic* (mocking) in ridiculing them.

53. **E** The second paragraph discusses the various methods epiphytes adopt in order to retain or conserve moisture.

Choice **A** is incorrect. Epiphytes have lost their root connection with the forest floor. Choice **B** is incorrect. Epiphytes seek the sun; they are not adapted to a sunless environment. Choice **C** is incorrect. Epiphytes have developed ways to conserve rainwater, not to dissipate or squander it. Choice **D** is incorrect. Epiphytes are not parasites; they do not derive nourishment ("sustenance") from the tree trunks to which they attach themselves.

54. **B** The first paragraph states that epiphytes grow in "spoonfuls" of soil. We can infer from this that they do not need particularly large amounts of soil for growth.

Choice **A** is incorrect. Although epiphytes have lost their root connection with the forest floor, they do possess root systems. Choice **C** is incorrect. The passage states that the roots of some orchids carry on photosynthesis; epiphytes clearly are not incapable of photosynthesis. Choice **D** is incorrect. Nothing in the passage suggests epiphytes are hard to spot. Choice **E** is incorrect. Epiphytes have "managed to create their own environment" so well that the soil in which they grow does not differ significantly from normal soil in microbiological processes. This does not suggest that their need for nutrients differs from that of plants that grow in normal soil.

55. **C** Epiphytes are described in a straightforward, direct manner.

Choice **A** is incorrect. The author is not exhorting or urging anyone to do anything. Choice **B** is incorrect. The author is not analyzing epiphytes, that is, thoroughly studying each of the individual features that comprise these plants in order to understand their structure. He is simply saying what they are like. Choice **D** is incorrect. The author is being direct rather than indirect in presenting what he knows about epiphytes. Choice **E** is incorrect. The author is not being particularly forceful in his presentation; neither is he presenting an argument.

56. **D** In paragraph 2, we are informed that studies of the upper atmosphere are being conducted by earth satellites and missile probings.

57. **A** Paragraph 4 discusses the ozone layers in the stratosphere. We learn the importance of these layers in reducing the destructive effects of ultraviolet radiation, which, if unchecked, would result in the annihilation of life on earth as we know it.

58. **C** Throughout the five paragraphs of this passage, the atmosphere is discussed in terms of its relationship to our weather.

59. **E** The third sentence of paragraph 3 states that the earth absorbs solar radiation or heat. This in turn warms the layer of air nearest the earth, that is, the troposphere.

60. **C** Meteorology is the study of atmospheric conditions, with an emphasis on forecasting the weather. (Television stations sometimes call their weather announcers "meteorologists.") This general introduction to the relationship between the atmosphere and weather most likely comes from *a basic meteorology textbook*.
Choice **A** is incorrect. The passage is too elementary to be appropriate to a specialized scientific journal. Choice **B** is incorrect. The passage is too technical and too dully presented to be appropriate to a general-interest magazine. Choice **D** is incorrect. The passage is far too lengthy and technical to be appropriate to a concise script. Choice **E** is incorrect. The passage barely touches on space explorations.

61. **B** Both the author's use of the phrase "a literature of their own" in the opening paragraph and her ongoing exploration of what she means by the female literary tradition in the English novel support this choice.
Choice **A** is incorrect. It is not the uniqueness of the phenomenon but the traditional nature of the phenomenon that interests the author. Choice **C** is incorrect. The passage deals specifically with women's *literary* tradition. Choice **D** is incorrect. The passage is concerned with the roots of female writing, not with its present-day manifestations. Choice **E** is incorrect. The author presents no such choice.

62. **B** The writer neither lists (*enumerates*) nor sorts (*classifies*) anything in the opening paragraph.
Choice **A** is incorrect. The writer likens the female tradition to a lost continent and develops the metaphor by describing the continent "rising...from the sea of English literature." Choice **C** is incorrect. The author refers or *alludes* to the classical legend of Atlantis. Choice **D** is incorrect. The author quotes Colby and Thompson. Choice **E** is incorrect. The author contrasts the revised view of women's literature with Mills's view.

63. **D** The author opens the paragraph by stating that many literary critics have begun reinterpreting the study of women's literature. She then goes on to cite individual comments that support her assertion. Clearly, she is *receptive* or open to the ideas of these writers, for they and she share a common sense of the need to reinterpret their common field.
Choices **A** and **B** are incorrect. The author cites the literary critics straightforwardly, presenting their statements as evidence supporting her thesis. Choice **C** is incorrect. The author does not *disparage* or belittle these critics. By quoting them respectfully, she implicitly acknowledges their competence. Choice **E** is incorrect. The author quotes the critics as acknowledged experts in the field. However, she is quite ready to disagree with their conclusions (as she disagrees with Moers's view of women's literature as an international movement). Clearly, she does not look on these critics with *awe*.

64. **B** If women writers have no history, they have to rediscover the past. In the process, they *create* or forge their consciousness of what their sex has achieved. Here *forge* is used with its meaning of *fashion* or *make*, as blacksmiths forge metal by hammering it into shape. It is in this sense that James Joyce used *forge* in *A Portrait of the Artist as a Young Man*, whose hero goes forth to "forge in the smithy of (his) soul the uncreated conscience of (his) race."

65. **C** The author both cites Moers's work in support of her own assertions and argues against the validity of Moers's conclusion that women's literature is an international movement. Thus, while she finds Moers's work basically *admirable* and worthy of respect, she considers it *inaccurate* in some of the conclusions it draws.
Choice **A** is incorrect. The author would not cite Moers as she does in the second paragraph if she believed Moers to be wholly *misleading*. Choice **B** is incorrect. Since the author disagrees with at least one of Moers's conclusions, she obviously does not find Moers's work the *definitive* or final word. Choices **D** and **E** are incorrect. Neither is supported by the author's mentions of Moers.

Mathematical Aptitude Section

1. **B** $\frac{1}{2} + \frac{3}{4} \div \left(\frac{5}{6} \times \frac{7}{8}\right) - \frac{9}{10}$

$\frac{1}{2} + \frac{3}{4} \div \left(\frac{35}{48}\right) - \frac{9}{10}$

$\frac{1}{2} + \frac{3}{\not{4}} \cdot \frac{\overset{12}{\not{48}}}{35} - \frac{9}{10}$

$\frac{1}{2} + \frac{36}{35} - \frac{9}{10}$

$\frac{35}{70} + \frac{72}{70} - \frac{63}{70} = \frac{44}{70} = \frac{22}{35}$

2. **B** $\frac{1}{2}\% = \frac{\frac{1}{2}}{100} = \frac{1}{2} \div 100 = \frac{1}{2} \cdot \frac{1}{100} = \frac{1}{200}$

3. **D** Let x = number of thirds in 75%.

$\frac{x}{3} = 75\%$

$\frac{x}{3} = \frac{3}{4}$

$4x = 9$

$x = \frac{9}{4} = 2\frac{1}{4}$

4. **E** $(0.3\%)(x) = 2163$

$0.003x = 2163$

$3x = 2{,}163{,}000$

$x = 721{,}000$

5. **E** 27 cubic feet = 1 cubic yard

9 cubic feet = $\frac{1}{3}$ cubic yard

or $\frac{45}{5}$ cubic feet = $\frac{1}{3}$ cubic yard

6. **C** $\frac{3}{8} = \$60$

$\frac{1}{8} = \$20$

Remainder of crop $\left(\frac{5}{8}\right) = \$100$

7. **D** The child with the greatest share would receive $\frac{2}{4}$ or $\frac{1}{2}$ of \$40,000 = \$20,000.

8. **D** Cost = \$60

Profit = \$12

Actual selling price = \$72

Actual selling price (\$72) = 90% of marked price

Let x = marked price.

90% of x or $.9x = \$72$

$9x = \$720$

$x = \$80$

9. **D** Let x = marked price.

$0.85x$ = price after first discount of 15%

$0.9(0.85x)$ = price after second discount of 10%

$0.765x = \$306$

$765x = 306000$

$x = \$400$

10. **B** 5 payments of \$13 each = \$65 + \$15 (down payment) = \$80

\$80 − \$72 = \$8 saving

11. **B** $KM = \frac{1}{2}KL$ and $AC = \frac{1}{2}AB$. Since $KM > AC$, $KL > AB$ since doubles, triples, etc. of unequal quantities are unequal in the same order.

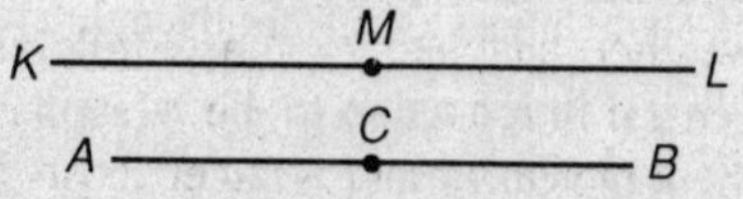

12. **D** I. $AD - CD = AC$, and $AB + BC = AC$

II. $AD - BC = AB + CD$

III. This is not true because $AB + CD = AD - BC$.

13. **C** Let w = width.

Then $w + 3$ = length [given].

$(w)(w + 3)$ = area

$w^2 + 3w = 88$ [given]

$w^2 + 3w - 88 = 0$ [subtraction]

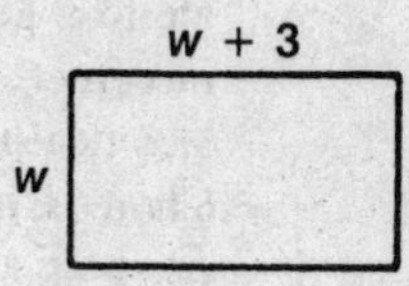

14. **C** 800 pounds of valuable oxide + 3200 pounds of other material = 4000 pounds of ore

Ratio $= \frac{800}{3200} = \frac{8}{32} = \frac{1}{4}$ or 1:4. The ratio is the same for any number of tons.

15. **C** Let x = number of pints of flour to be used with 3 pints of milk.

$\frac{\text{milk}}{\text{flour}} = \frac{2 \text{ parts}}{3 \text{ parts}} = \frac{3 \text{ pints}}{x}$

$2x = 9$; $x = 4\frac{1}{2}$ pints of flour

16. **B** $\frac{10}{0.1} = \frac{100}{1} = 100$

$10 - 100 = -90$

$-9 > -90$

17. **C** $\sqrt{4} = 2$

$\frac{1}{0.5} = \frac{10}{5} = 2$

18. **C** $0.6\$ = \frac{0.6}{100} = \frac{6}{1000}$

19. **C** $\frac{2548}{14}$ inches = 182 inches

5 yards 2 inches = 182 inches

20. **B** $\frac{1}{5} \div \frac{1}{\frac{1}{5}}$ [Column A] $\quad \frac{1}{y} = \frac{1}{5}$ [Column B]

$\frac{1}{5} \div \frac{5}{1}$

$\frac{1}{5} \cdot \frac{1}{5} = \frac{1}{25}$

21. **C** $(y + 160) - (120 - y) =$

$y + 160 - 120 + y = 2y + 40$

$(x + 10) - (x - 2y - 30) =$

$x + 10 - x + 2y + 30 = 2y + 40$

22. **D** To solve for a and b we need 2 equations involving a and b.

23. **C** The two triangles have the same altitude (AD) and have equal bases ($AB = BC$).

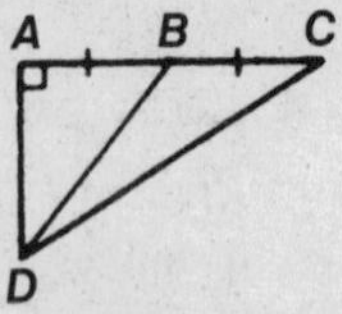

24. **C** The acute angles of a right triangle are complementary.

25. **C** $x = \frac{y}{2}$
$y = 2x$ (cross multiplication)
$y + 2 = 2x + 2$ (addition of 2)

26. **C** $\sqrt{\frac{1}{4}} = \frac{1}{2}$

27. **A** $7x = 35 + 7y$
$7x - 35 = 7y$
$x - 5 = y$ (division by 7)
Since $x - 5 > x - 7$, then $y > x - 7$.

28. **B** $\sqrt{0.64} = 0.8$
$0.8 > 0.08$

29. **A** Experiment with convenient values. If the original price was \$100, then the reduced price is \$100 − \$10 or \$90 plus 10% of \$90 or \$9. for a total of \$99.

30. **D** We may not assume that Lori used the same route (with the exact same distance) on both trips.

31. **D** Various combinations may provide the same product—(6)(6) = (3)(12) = (2)(18).

32. **B** This is an inverse proportion. As one decreases the size of the working crew the time to complete the task is increased.

33. **C** $\left(\sqrt{\frac{2 + x^2}{2}}\right)^2 = (3)^2$
$\frac{2 + x^2}{2} = 9$
$2 + x^2 = 18$
$x^2 = 16$
$x = \pm 4$

34. **E** $5x - 3y = 3$ (1)
$2x - 4y = -10$ (2)
Subtract equation (2) from equation (1):
$3x + y = 13$

35. **D** $\frac{356}{5} = 71+$.
If one candidate gets 72 votes he can be a winner, because we then have 356 − = 284 votes to be divided among four other candidates and it is possible for each of these four to receive 71 votes. If a candidate gets 71 votes, it is not possible to be the winner, since 356 − 71 = 285 votes remaining to be divided among the other four candidates. One of these four must receive more than 71 and would thus be the winner.

36. **C** Total Distance = $(D + d)$ miles
Total Time = $(T + t)$ hours
Average rate for entire trip = $\frac{D + d}{T + t}$

37. **B** When 15 adults ride the bus, they are using $\frac{15}{20}$ or $\frac{3}{4}$ of capacity, leaving $\frac{1}{4}$ of capacity unused. We therefore can add $\frac{1}{4}$ capacity of bus when children ride, or $\frac{1}{4}$ of 24 = 6.

38. **E** Difference = 300
$\frac{\text{difference}}{\text{original}} = \frac{300}{1200} = \frac{1}{4} = 25\%$

39. **C** Four of the 2″ squares can fit along the 8″ side, and two along the 4″ side.
$4 \times 2 = 8$ squares.

40. **B** Time required for homework = (10)(10 minutes) = 100 minutes = 1 hour and 40 minutes.
She must begin to work 1 hour and 40 minutes before 9 P.M. or at 7:20 P.M.

41. **A** $3x - 6 = 1$
$x - 2 = \frac{1}{3}$ [divide by 3]

42. **D** Substitute: ② $= 2^2 + \frac{1}{2^2} = 4 + \frac{1}{4}$ or $4\frac{1}{4}$

43. **A** Side z is the longest side and must be the hypotenuse—the Pythagorean Theorem

44. **C** Radii OC and OB are equal. Since $OC = BC$, OBC is an equilateral triangle; $\angle BOC$ has a measure of 60° and x, its supplement, has a measure of 120°.
$\frac{x}{2} = 60$

45. **D** Area of square = $s^2 = 144$
Side = 12 and perimeter of square = 48
Perimeter of equilateral triangle = 48 [given]
Side of triangle = $48 \div 3 = 16$

46. **D** Diameter of outer circle = 104 feet
Radius of outer circle = 52 feet
Area of outer circle = $\pi r^2 = (52)^2\pi = 2704\pi$
Radius of inner circle = 50 feet
Area of inner circle = $\pi r^2 = (50)^2\pi = 2500\pi$
Difference = area of circular grass walk = $2704\pi - 2500\pi = 204\pi$

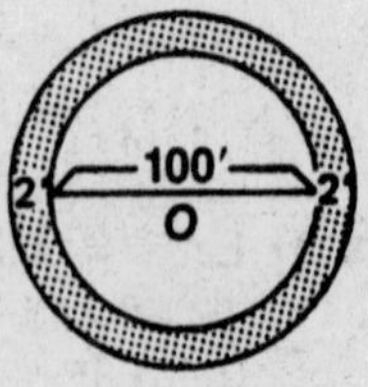

47. **E** From the graph we observe:
AT S, $x = 0$, $y = +4$.
At R, $x = -4$, $y = 0$.
$\therefore y = x + 4$.
Or apply formula
$y = mx + b$.
Since $x = 0$ when $y =$ 4 (at 0,4)
$4 = m(0) + b$
$b = 4$, and since $x = -4$ when $y = 0$
(at -4,0) $0 = m(-4) + 4$
$m = 1$.
Substituting values of m and b: $y = x + 4$.

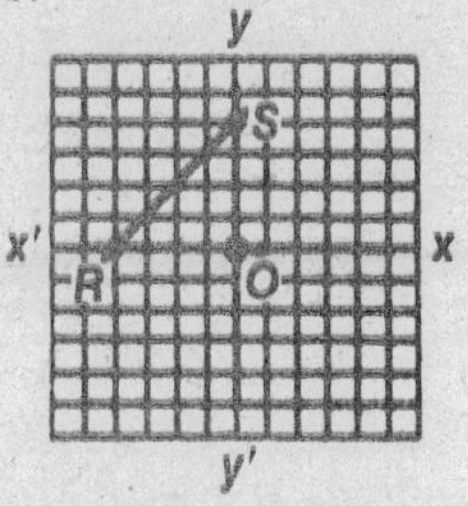

48. **A** Since $\angle ABC \stackrel{\circ}{=} 120$, then
$\widehat{ADC} = 240°$.
$\angle ADC \stackrel{\circ}{=} \frac{1}{2}\widehat{ABC} = 360° - \widehat{ADC}(240°) = 120°$
$\angle ADC \stackrel{\circ}{=} \frac{1}{2}\widehat{ABC}$
$\angle ADC \stackrel{\circ}{=} 60$.
Recall: An inscribed angle is measured by one-half of its intercepted arc.

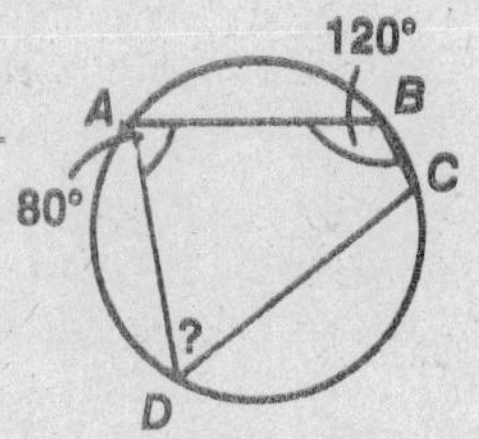

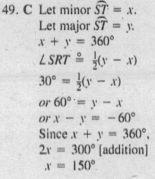

49. **C** Let minor $\widehat{ST} = x$.
Let major $\widehat{ST} = y$.
$x + y = 360°$
$\angle SRT \stackrel{\circ}{=} \frac{1}{2}(y - x)$
$30° = \frac{1}{2}(y - x)$
or $60° = y - x$
or $x - y = -60°$
Since $x + y = 360°$,
$2x = 300°$ [addition]
$x = 150°$

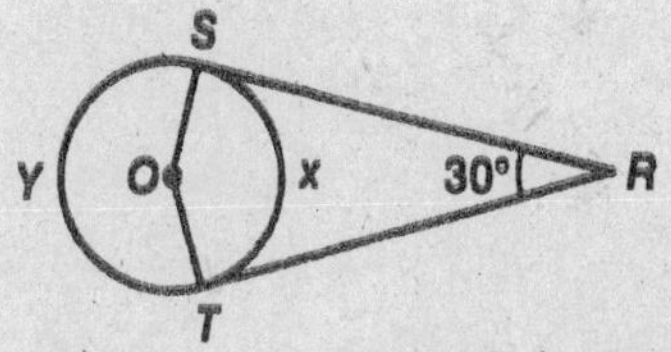

50. **E** $AP = AC$ since $\angle 1 = \angle 2$ (C). $\angle 1 > \angle 3$ (exterior $\angle$). Therefore, $\angle 2 > \angle 3$ (D), and in $\triangle BAC$, $AB > AC$. If $AB > AC$, then also $AB > AP$ (or $AP < AB$)(B) and (A). (E) contradicts (A) and (B) and is therefore incorrect.

PSAT/NMSQT Answer Sheet

TYPICAL TEST I

Verbal Aptitude Section

1 Ⓐ Ⓑ Ⓒ Ⓓ Ⓔ
2 Ⓐ Ⓑ Ⓒ Ⓓ Ⓔ
3 Ⓐ Ⓑ Ⓒ Ⓓ Ⓔ
4 Ⓐ Ⓑ Ⓒ Ⓓ Ⓔ
5 Ⓐ Ⓑ Ⓒ Ⓓ Ⓔ
6 Ⓐ Ⓑ Ⓒ Ⓓ Ⓔ
7 Ⓐ Ⓑ Ⓒ Ⓓ Ⓔ
8 Ⓐ Ⓑ Ⓒ Ⓓ Ⓔ
9 Ⓐ Ⓑ Ⓒ Ⓓ Ⓔ
10 Ⓐ Ⓑ Ⓒ Ⓓ Ⓔ
11 Ⓐ Ⓑ Ⓒ Ⓓ Ⓔ
12 Ⓐ Ⓑ Ⓒ Ⓓ Ⓔ
13 Ⓐ Ⓑ Ⓒ Ⓓ Ⓔ
14 Ⓐ Ⓑ Ⓒ Ⓓ Ⓔ
15 Ⓐ Ⓑ Ⓒ Ⓓ Ⓔ
16 Ⓐ Ⓑ Ⓒ Ⓓ Ⓔ
17 Ⓐ Ⓑ Ⓒ Ⓓ Ⓔ
18 Ⓐ Ⓑ Ⓒ Ⓓ Ⓔ
19 Ⓐ Ⓑ Ⓒ Ⓓ Ⓔ
20 Ⓐ Ⓑ Ⓒ Ⓓ Ⓔ
21 Ⓐ Ⓑ Ⓒ Ⓓ Ⓔ
22 Ⓐ Ⓑ Ⓒ Ⓓ Ⓔ
23 Ⓐ Ⓑ Ⓒ Ⓓ Ⓔ
24 Ⓐ Ⓑ Ⓒ Ⓓ Ⓔ
25 Ⓐ Ⓑ Ⓒ Ⓓ Ⓔ
26 Ⓐ Ⓑ Ⓒ Ⓓ Ⓔ
27 Ⓐ Ⓑ Ⓒ Ⓓ Ⓔ
28 Ⓐ Ⓑ Ⓒ Ⓓ Ⓔ
29 Ⓐ Ⓑ Ⓒ Ⓓ Ⓔ
30 Ⓐ Ⓑ Ⓒ Ⓓ Ⓔ
31 Ⓐ Ⓑ Ⓒ Ⓓ Ⓔ
32 Ⓐ Ⓑ Ⓒ Ⓓ Ⓔ
33 Ⓐ Ⓑ Ⓒ Ⓓ Ⓔ
34 Ⓐ Ⓑ Ⓒ Ⓓ Ⓔ
35 Ⓐ Ⓑ Ⓒ Ⓓ Ⓔ
36 Ⓐ Ⓑ Ⓒ Ⓓ Ⓔ
37 Ⓐ Ⓑ Ⓒ Ⓓ Ⓔ
38 Ⓐ Ⓑ Ⓒ Ⓓ Ⓔ
39 Ⓐ Ⓑ Ⓒ Ⓓ Ⓔ
40 Ⓐ Ⓑ Ⓒ Ⓓ Ⓔ
41 Ⓐ Ⓑ Ⓒ Ⓓ Ⓔ
42 Ⓐ Ⓑ Ⓒ Ⓓ Ⓔ
43 Ⓐ Ⓑ Ⓒ Ⓓ Ⓔ
44 Ⓐ Ⓑ Ⓒ Ⓓ Ⓔ
45 Ⓐ Ⓑ Ⓒ Ⓓ Ⓔ
46 Ⓐ Ⓑ Ⓒ Ⓓ Ⓔ
47 Ⓐ Ⓑ Ⓒ Ⓓ Ⓔ
48 Ⓐ Ⓑ Ⓒ Ⓓ Ⓔ
49 Ⓐ Ⓑ Ⓒ Ⓓ Ⓔ
50 Ⓐ Ⓑ Ⓒ Ⓓ Ⓔ
51 Ⓐ Ⓑ Ⓒ Ⓓ Ⓔ
52 Ⓐ Ⓑ Ⓒ Ⓓ Ⓔ
53 Ⓐ Ⓑ Ⓒ Ⓓ Ⓔ
54 Ⓐ Ⓑ Ⓒ Ⓓ Ⓔ
55 Ⓐ Ⓑ Ⓒ Ⓓ Ⓔ
56 Ⓐ Ⓑ Ⓒ Ⓓ Ⓔ
57 Ⓐ Ⓑ Ⓒ Ⓓ Ⓔ
58 Ⓐ Ⓑ Ⓒ Ⓓ Ⓔ
59 Ⓐ Ⓑ Ⓒ Ⓓ Ⓔ
60 Ⓐ Ⓑ Ⓒ Ⓓ Ⓔ
61 Ⓐ Ⓑ Ⓒ Ⓓ Ⓔ
62 Ⓐ Ⓑ Ⓒ Ⓓ Ⓔ
63 Ⓐ Ⓑ Ⓒ Ⓓ Ⓔ
64 Ⓐ Ⓑ Ⓒ Ⓓ Ⓔ
65 Ⓐ Ⓑ Ⓒ Ⓓ Ⓔ

Mathematical Aptitude Section*

1 Ⓐ Ⓑ Ⓒ Ⓓ Ⓔ
2 Ⓐ Ⓑ Ⓒ Ⓓ Ⓔ
3 Ⓐ Ⓑ Ⓒ Ⓓ Ⓔ
4 Ⓐ Ⓑ Ⓒ Ⓓ Ⓔ
5 Ⓐ Ⓑ Ⓒ Ⓓ Ⓔ
6 Ⓐ Ⓑ Ⓒ Ⓓ Ⓔ
7 Ⓐ Ⓑ Ⓒ Ⓓ Ⓔ
8 Ⓐ Ⓑ Ⓒ Ⓓ Ⓔ
9 Ⓐ Ⓑ Ⓒ Ⓓ Ⓔ
10 Ⓐ Ⓑ Ⓒ Ⓓ Ⓔ
11 Ⓐ Ⓑ Ⓒ Ⓓ Ⓔ
12 Ⓐ Ⓑ Ⓒ Ⓓ Ⓔ
13 Ⓐ Ⓑ Ⓒ Ⓓ Ⓔ
14 Ⓐ Ⓑ Ⓒ Ⓓ Ⓔ
15 Ⓐ Ⓑ Ⓒ Ⓓ Ⓔ
16 Ⓐ Ⓑ Ⓒ Ⓓ Ⓔ
17 Ⓐ Ⓑ Ⓒ Ⓓ Ⓔ
18 Ⓐ Ⓑ Ⓒ Ⓓ Ⓔ
19 Ⓐ Ⓑ Ⓒ Ⓓ Ⓔ
20 Ⓐ Ⓑ Ⓒ Ⓓ Ⓔ
21 Ⓐ Ⓑ Ⓒ Ⓓ Ⓔ
22 Ⓐ Ⓑ Ⓒ Ⓓ Ⓔ
23 Ⓐ Ⓑ Ⓒ Ⓓ Ⓔ
24 Ⓐ Ⓑ Ⓒ Ⓓ Ⓔ
25 Ⓐ Ⓑ Ⓒ Ⓓ Ⓔ
26 Ⓐ Ⓑ Ⓒ Ⓓ Ⓔ
27 Ⓐ Ⓑ Ⓒ Ⓓ Ⓔ
28 Ⓐ Ⓑ Ⓒ Ⓓ Ⓔ
29 Ⓐ Ⓑ Ⓒ Ⓓ Ⓔ
30 Ⓐ Ⓑ Ⓒ Ⓓ Ⓔ
31 Ⓐ Ⓑ Ⓒ Ⓓ Ⓔ
32 Ⓐ Ⓑ Ⓒ Ⓓ Ⓔ
33 Ⓐ Ⓑ Ⓒ Ⓓ Ⓔ
34 Ⓐ Ⓑ Ⓒ Ⓓ Ⓔ
35 Ⓐ Ⓑ Ⓒ Ⓓ Ⓔ
36 Ⓐ Ⓑ Ⓒ Ⓓ Ⓔ
37 Ⓐ Ⓑ Ⓒ Ⓓ Ⓔ
38 Ⓐ Ⓑ Ⓒ Ⓓ Ⓔ
39 Ⓐ Ⓑ Ⓒ Ⓓ Ⓔ
40 Ⓐ Ⓑ Ⓒ Ⓓ Ⓔ
41 Ⓐ Ⓑ Ⓒ Ⓓ Ⓔ
42 Ⓐ Ⓑ Ⓒ Ⓓ Ⓔ
43 Ⓐ Ⓑ Ⓒ Ⓓ Ⓔ
44 Ⓐ Ⓑ Ⓒ Ⓓ Ⓔ
45 Ⓐ Ⓑ Ⓒ Ⓓ Ⓔ
46 Ⓐ Ⓑ Ⓒ Ⓓ Ⓔ
47 Ⓐ Ⓑ Ⓒ Ⓓ Ⓔ
48 Ⓐ Ⓑ Ⓒ Ⓓ Ⓔ
49 Ⓐ Ⓑ Ⓒ Ⓓ Ⓔ
50 Ⓐ Ⓑ Ⓒ Ⓓ Ⓔ

*If there are more answer spaces than you need, leave them blank.

TYPICAL TEST I

SECTION 1	Time—50 minutes 65 Questions	For each question in this section, choose the best answer and fill in the corresponding circle on the answer sheet.

Each question below consists of a word in capital letters, followed by five lettered words or phrases. Choose the word or phrase that is most nearly opposite in meaning to the word in capital letters. Since some of the questions require you to distinguish fine shades of meaning, consider all the choices before deciding which is best.

Example:

GOOD: (A) sour (B) bad (C) red (D) hot (E) ugly

Ⓐ ● Ⓒ Ⓓ Ⓔ

1. INFLUENCE: (A) lack of concern (B) lack of trust (C) lack of power (D) lack of shame (E) lack of vitality

2. ADORN: (A) hate (B) warn (C) repair (D) cause grief (E) remove decoration

3. PRUDENT: (A) rash (B) ugly (C) childish (D) afraid (E) active

4. BRAGGART: (A) critic (B) hypocrite (C) happy individual (D) modest person (E) tyrant

5. PUNITIVE: (A) enormous (B) undamaged (C) rewarding (D) restive (E) languishing

6. HILARITY: (A) gloom (B) heartiness (C) weakness (D) casualty (E) paucity

7. DOCILE: (A) unhealthy (B) rapid (C) unmanageable (D) ignorant (E) recognizable

8. SYMMETRY: (A) irregularity of form (B) lack of clarity (C) lack of depth (D) proximity (E) artificiality

9. OMINOUS: (A) unthreatening (B) inconclusive (C) sweet-smelling (D) self-imposed (E) lonely

10. CHIDE: (A) unite (B) fear (C) record (D) acclaim (E) mature

11. DESPICABLE: (A) self-centered (B) worthy of esteem (C) inevitable (D) featureless (E) trite

12. PROTRUSION: (A) order (B) deviation (C) scarcity (D) weakness (E) recess

13. UNWITTING: (A) clever (B) intense (C) sensitive (D) redundant (E) intentional

14. UNSEEMLY: (A) effortless (B) proper (C) conducive (D) apparent (E) informative

15. FACILITY: (A) impermanence (B) frugality (C) indifference (D) inability (E) tranquility

16. MUSHROOM: (A) shrivel (B) cling (C) drift (D) bustle (E) evade

17. PERIPHERAL: (A) pivotal (B) dependable (C) natural (D) automatic (E) inflexible

18. RUE: (A) relinquish (B) reconsider (C) act cautious (D) behave pleasantly (E) rejoice over

19. DISABUSE: (A) maltreat (B) violate (C) cancel (D) deceive (E) involve

20. TYRO: (A) expert (B) dilettante (C) planner (D) victim (E) potentate

Each sentence below has one or two blanks, each blank indicating that something has been omitted. Beneath the sentence are five lettered words or sets of words. Choose the word or set of words that, when inserted in the sentence, best fits the meaning of the sentence as a whole.

Example:

Although its publicity has been ----, the film itself is intelligent, well-acted, handsomely produced, and altogether ----.

(A) tasteless . . respectable (B) extensive . . moderate (C) sophisticated . . amateur (D) risque . . crude (E) perfect . . spectacular

● Ⓑ Ⓒ Ⓓ Ⓔ

21. Her audacious approach won her an interview when a less ---- method would have been sure to fail.
(A) daring (B) ingratiating (C) conventional (D) intelligent (E) arrogant

22. The plot of the motion picture *Hoosiers* is ----; we have all seen this story, the tale of an underdog team going on to win a championship, in one form or another countless times.
(A) inept (B) absorbing (C) intricate (D) controversial (E) trite

23. Knowing that the results of future experiments might well cause her to rethink her hypothesis, she voiced ---- opinion which she insisted was subject to change.
(A) an unqualified (B) a definitive (C) a dogmatic (D) a blunt (E) a tentative

24. Although he was ---- by nature, he ---- contact with others during the period of his trial.
(A) gracious . . sought
(B) magnanimous . . attempted
(C) altruistic . . evaded
(D) gregarious . . shunned
(E) prodigal . . avoided

25. Language, culture, and personality may be considered independently of each other in thought, but they are ---- in fact.
(A) autonomous (B) pervasive
(C) equivocal (D) inseparable (E) immutable

26. Since depression seems to result when certain cells in the brain receive too little of two key chemicals, the neurotransmitters norepinephrine and serotonin, one goal of treatment is to make more of the chemicals ---- the nerve cells that need them.
(A) analogous to (B) dependent on
(C) available to (D) regardless of
(E) interchangeable with

27. The sudden shift from ---- to ---- in Hugo's novels can startle readers, especially when he abruptly juxtaposes a scene of chaste and holy love with one of coarse and profane licentiousness.
(A) devotion . . frivolity
(B) piety . . ribaldry
(C) vulgarity . . adultery
(D) decorum . . salubrity
(E) purity . . maturity

28. In the end, the Normandie lacked even the dignity of being sunk by the enemy at sea; she burned and went down ---- at her Manhattan pier in 1942, while incompetents were transforming her into a troop ship.
(A) majestically (B) ignominiously
(C) militantly (D) negligently
(E) auspiciously

29 This psychological biography presents a picture of a deeply ---- individual, unable to ---- anyone else's success, whose ruthless pursuit of recognition and fame has been marked by hypocritical gestures of openness and affection.
(A) altruistic . . comprehend
(B) egotistical . . tolerate
(C) modest . . admit
(D) apathetic . . match
(E) indolent . . vilify

30. She conducted the interrogation not only with dispatch but also with ----, being a person who is ---- in manner yet subtle in discrimination.
(A) elan . . enthusiastic
(B) equanimity . . abrupt
(C) finesse . . expeditious
(D) zeal . . doctrinaire
(E) trepidation . . cursory

Each question below consists of a related pair of words or phrases, followed by five lettered pairs of words or phrases. Select the lettered pair that best expresses a relationship similar to that expressed in the original pair.

Example:

YAWN : BOREDOM : : (A) dream : sleep
(B) anger : madness (C) smile : amusement
(D) face : expression (E) impatience : rebellion

Ⓐ Ⓑ ● Ⓓ Ⓔ

31. PRY : CROWBAR : : (A) peek : curtain
(B) skate : rink (C) leap : frog
(D) perch : rooster (E) dig : shovel

32. TROUGH : PIGS : : (A) carton : eggs
(B) den : bears (C) manger : cattle
(D) flock : sheep (E) corral : horses

33. SIDEWALK : PEDESTRIAN : :
(A) hangar : plane (B) sidecar : motorcycle
(C) highway : robber (D) boardwalk : shore
(E) waterway : boat

34. STUDIO : SCULPTOR : : (A) gallery : painting
(B) smithy : blacksmith (C) gymnasium : spectator
(D) park : monument (E) apartment : renter

35. INTIMIDATE : FEAR : : (A) mitigate : pain
(B) commiserate : sorrow (C) exasperate : irritation
(D) exonerate : guilt (E) remunerate : poverty

36. INSIPID : FOOD : : (A) savory : potions
(B) musky : aroma (C) vapid : remarks
(D) horrendous : noise (E) spectacular : views

37. HAWK : TALONS : : (A) monkey : tail
(B) eagle : wings (C) lion : claws
(D) tiger : stripes (E) rhinoceros : horn

38. FIRE : PYROMANIAC : :
(A) destruction : saboteur (B) hay : farmer
(C) holocaust : earthquake (D) maelstrom : ship
(E) ransom : arsonist

39. ARIA : DIVA : : (A) opera : librettist
(B) soliloquy : actor (C) compound : chemist
(D) air : melody (E) duet : conductor

40. OPHTHALMOLOGIST : EYES : :
(A) entomologist : ears (B) apologist : tongue
(C) dermatologist : skin (D) philatelist : coins
(E) geologist : genes

41. IRKSOME : CHAFE : : (A) awesome : distress
(B) tiresome : endure (C) fulsome : praise
(D) lurid : shock (E) pallid : allure

42. SLAG : METAL : : (A) veneer : wood
(B) dregs : wine (C) lawn : grass
(D) chapter : book (E) pedestal : statue

43. DAPPER : APPEARANCE : :
(A) childish : manner (B) precise : speech
(C) humble : demeanor (D) worn : countenance
(E) shambling : gait

44. MALINGERER : WORK : :
(A) recluse : company (B) thief : plunder
(C) arbitrator : negotiation
(D) benefactor : philanthropy
(E) counselor : client

45. OGLE : FLIRTATIOUSNESS : :
(A) observe : nonchalance (B) mute : intensity
(C) gape : astonishment (D) squint : diffidence
(E) peer : effrontery

Each passage below is followed by questions based on its content. Answer the questions following each passage on the basis of what is stated or implied in that passage.

That one citizen is as good as another is a favorite American axiom, supposed to express the very essence of our Constitution and way of life. But just what do we mean when we utter that platitude? One surgeon is not as good as another. We soon become aware of this when we require the attention of either. Yet in political and economic matters we appear to have reached a point where knowledge and specialized training count for very little. A newspaper reporter is sent out on the street to collect the views of various passers-by on such a question as "Should the United States defend Grenada?" The answer of the barfly who doesn't even know where the island is located, or that it is an island, is quoted in the next edition just as solemnly as that of the college teacher of history. With the basic tenets of democracy—that all men are born free and equal and are entitled to life, liberty, and the pursuit of happiness—no decent American can possibly take issue. But that the opinion of one citizen on a technical subject is just as authoritative as that of another is manifestly absurd. And to accept the opinions of all comers as having the same value is surely to encourage a cult of mediocrity.

46. Which phrase best expresses the main idea of this passage?
(A) The myth of equality
(B) A distinction about equality
(C) The essence of the Constitution
(D) Technical competence
(E) Knowledge and specialized training

47. The author most probably included the example of the question on Grenada in order to
(A) move the reader to resentment
(B) show that he is opposed to opinion sampling
(C) show that he has thoroughly researched his subject
(D) illustrate the kind of opinion sampling he objects to
(E) provide a humorous but temporary diversion from his main point

48. The author's attitude toward the American tendency to give equal credence to all citizens' opinions on technical matters can best be described as
(A) ambivalent (B) respectful (C) defensive
(D) deprecatory (E) remorseful

We were about a quarter mile away when quiet swept over the colony. A thousand or more heads periscoped. Two thousand eyes glared. Save for our wading, the world's business had stopped. A thousand avian personalities were concentrated on us, and the psychological force of this was terrific. Contingents of homecoming feeders, suddenly aware of four strange specks moving across the lake, would bank violently and speed away. Then the chain reaction began. Every throat in that rookery let go with a concatenation of wild, raspy, terrorized trumpet bursts. With all wings now fully spread and churning, and quadrupling the color mass, the birds began to move as one, and the sky was filled with the sound of judgment day.

49. The title that best expresses the ideas of this passage is
(A) Our Shore Birds (B) A Quiet Colony
(C) Judgment Day (D) Waiting
(E) An Unwelcome Intrusion

50. According to the passage, when they first noticed the visitors, the birds of the colony
(A) flew away (B) churned their wings
(C) became very still (D) set up a series of cries
(E) glared at the homecoming birds

51. The reaction of the visitors to the episode described in this passage was probably one of
(A) impatience (B) fear (C) anger
(D) sadness (E) awe

52. The author's primary purpose in this passage is to
(A) explain a natural catastrophe
(B) issue a challenge (C) denounce an expedition
(D) evoke an experience (E) demonstrate a thesis

It was not until modern scholarship uncovered the secret of reading Middle English that we could understand that Chaucer, far from being a rude versifier, was a perfectly accomplished technician, and that his verse is rich in music and elegant to the highest degree. Chaucer's own urbane personality is a delight to encounter in his books. He is avowedly a bookworm, yet few poets observe nature with more freshness and delight. He is a master of genial satire, but can sympathize with true piety and goodness with as much pleasure as he attacks the hypocritical.

It is not an uncommon estimate of Chaucer that he must be counted among the few greatest of English poets. In range of interest he is surpassed only by Shakespeare. He was recognized already in the Renaissance, when it came to England, as the Father of English Poetry. He was a man of wide learning, and wrote with ease on religion, philosophy, ethics, science, rhetoric. No one has more completely summed up an age than Chaucer has his, yet the people of his great poems are revealed as men and women are in all times.

Master of verse, as Chaucer was, he introduced into English poetry many verse forms: the heroic couplet (in which form most of *The Canterbury Tales* is written); verse written in iambic pentameter, rhyming ababbcc, (*Troilus and Criseyde*); the terza rima, three-line stanzas, rhyming aba, bcb, cdc, etc. (which he imitated from Dante, in some of his minor poems); and the eight-line iambic pentameter stanza, rhyming ababbcbc (the Monk's Tale).

53. According to this passage, Chaucer wrote on all of the following topics EXCEPT
(A) matters of faith
(B) the application of moral standards
(C) principles of literary composition
(D) the study of natural phenomena
(E) the nature of music

54. The passage suggests that Chaucer was underrated for a time because
(A) he had been surpassed in popularity by Shakespeare
(B) he used foreign poetic forms such as the heroic couplet
(C) people lacked the knowledge to appreciate his poetic technique
(D) readers were not drawn to the works of a bookworm
(E) his satire proved too gentle to suit the taste of the average reader

55. The title below that best expresses the ideas of this passage is
(A) Chaucer as Satirist
(B) Chaucer—Shakespeare's Peer
(C) The Crudities of Chaucer's Poetry
(D) A Great English Poet
(E) Inventor of the Terza Rima

Five main weather elements act upon rock. Frost and ice fracture rock. It can be gradually eroded by airborne dust. The action of the seas, whether through the constant movement of tides or the pounding of heavy storm waves, remorselessly wears away the coastlines. Rivers are immensely powerful destructive agencies—one has but to look at the Grand Canyon to appreciate their enormous power. And such rocks as escape all these influences are worn away over the eons by the effect of rain.

Whatever the cause of erosion, the net result is the same. The rock is reduced to its tiniest possible constituents—rock particles or, simply, dust. Rain and melting snow carry this dust down to the tiniest rivulets and the mightiest rivers, which, in turn, transport it to lakes, inland seas and the coastal regions of the oceans. Dust, however fine and powdery, is still heavier than water, and whenever the water becomes sufficiently still, it will gradually sink to the bottom, not only in lakes and seas but also in the sluggish lower reaches of rivers and where flood conditions exist, in the form of silt.

And so, over unimaginably long reaches of time, whole mountain ranges are carried down to the seas, and in the process, through the effects of gravity, new rock is born as layer after layer of dust accumulates on the bottom, building up to a depth of ten, a hundred, perhaps even a thousand feet, the lowermost layers being gradually compacted by the immense and steadily increasing pressures from above, until the particles fuse together and reform as a new rock.

It is in the intermediate and final processes of the new rock formation that oil comes into being. Those lakes and seas of hundreds of millions of years ago were almost choked by water plants and the most primitive forms of aquatic life. On dying, they sank to the bottom of the lakes and seas along with the settling dust particles and were gradually buried deep under the endless layers of more dust and more aquatic and plant life that slowly accumulated above them. The passing of millions of years and the steadily increasing pressures from above gradually changed the decayed vegetation and dead aquatic life into oil.

Described this simply and quickly, the process sounds reasonable enough. But this is where the gray and disputatious area arises. The conditions necessary for the formation of oil are known; the cause of the metamorphosis is not. It seems probable that some form of chemical catalyst is involved, but this catalyst has not been isolated. The first purely synthetic oil, as distinct from secondary synthetic oils such as those derived from coal, has yet to be produced. We just have to accept that oil is oil, that it is there, bound up in rock strata in fairly well-defined areas throughout the world but always on the sites of ancient seas and lakes, some of which are now continental land, some buried deep under the encroachment of new oceans.

56. According to the author, which of the following statements is (are) true?
I. The action of the seas is the most important factor in erosion of the earth's surface.
II. Scientists have not been able to produce a purely synthetic oil in the laboratory.
III. Gravity plays an important role in the formation of new rock.
(A) I only (B) II only (C) III only
(D) I and III only (E) II and III only

57. The Grand Canyon is mentioned in the first paragraph to illustrate
(A) the urgent need for dams
(B) the devastating impact of rivers
(C) the effect of rain
(D) a site where oil may be found
(E) the magnificence of nature

58. According to the author, our understanding of the process by which oil is created is
(A) biased (B) systematic (C) erroneous
(D) deficient (E) adequate

59. We can infer that prospectors should search for oil deposits
(A) wherever former seas existed
(B) in mountain streambeds
(C) where coal deposits are found
(D) in the Grand Canyon
(E) in new rock formations

60. The author does all of the following EXCEPT
(A) describe a process (B) state a possibility
(C) cite an example (D) propose a solution
(E) mention a limitation

The Captain's Dinner was strange. We were off the coast of Lower California. The water was so calm that we could hear flying fish slap against it. We ate at a long table out on deck, under an awning between us and the enormous stars.

The Captain looked well in his white uniform, and smiled almost warmly at us all, probably thanking God that most of us would leave him in a few days. The waiters were excited, the way the Filipino boys used to be at boarding school when there was a Christmas party, and the table looked like something from a Renaissance painting.

There were galantines and aspics down the center, with ripe grapes brought from Italy and stranger fruits from all the ports we'd touched, and crowning everything two stuffed pheasants in their dulled but still dashing feathers. There were wineglasses on stems, and little printed menus, proof that this masterpiece of a meal was known about in Rome, long since.

We ate and drank and heard our own suddenly friendly voices over the dark waters. The waiters glided deftly, perhaps dreaming that they served at Maxim's instead of on this fifth-rate freighter, and we drank Asti Spumanti, undated but delightful.

And finally, while we clapped, the chef stood before us, bowing in the light from the narrow stairs. He wore his high bonnet and whites, and a long-tailed morning coat, and looked like a drawing by Ludwig Bemelmans, with oblique sadness in his pasty outlines.

There was a silence after our applause. He turned nervously toward the light, and breathed not at all. We heard shuffling and bumps. Then, up through the twisting white closeness of the stairway, borne on the backs and arms of three awestruck kitchen boys, rose something almost too strange to talk about.

The chef stood back, bowing, discreetly wiping the sweat from his white face. The Captain applauded. We all clapped, and even cheered. The three boys set the thing on a special table.

It was a replica, about as long as a man's coffin, of the cathedral at Milano. It was made in white and pink sugar. There was a light inside, of course, and it glowed there on the deck of the little ship, trembling in every flying buttress with the Mexican ground swell, pure and ridiculous; and something about it shamed me.

It was a little dusty. It had undoubtedly been mended, after mighty storms, in the dim galleys of a hundred ships, better but never worse than this. It was like a flag flying for the chef, a bulwark all in spun sugar against the breath of corruption. It was his masterpiece, made years ago in some famous kitchen, and he showed it to us now with dignity.

61. It can be inferred from the passage that the author is most likely
(A) a student at a boarding school
(B) an officer of a vessel at anchor
(C) an enemy of the ship's captain
(D) a passenger near the end of a voyage
(E) a newcomer on board the vessel

62. The author's general attitude toward the freighter in the third and fourth paragraphs is best described as
(A) condescending (B) suspicious (C) bitter
(D) apathetic (E) admiring

63. It can be inferred from the passage that Maxim's (paragraph 4) was most likely which of the following?
I. A renowned restaurant
II. An eminent cargo vessel
III. A desirable place to work
(A) I only (B) II only (C) I and III only
(D) II and III only (E) I, II, and III

64. The evidence in the passage suggests that the chef most likely sweats
(A) from his labors in transporting the replica
(B) from the heat of the kitchen
(C) because he is afflicted with shortness of breath
(D) out of fear for his irreplaceable creation
(E) from his exertions in constructing the cathedral

65. Which of the following statements best expresses the author's impression of the chef?
(A) Reduced to working on cargo vessels, he is ashamed of his loss of professional prestige.
(B) Although he has come down in the world, he retains the memory of his youthful achievements.
(C) He applies himself with diligence to new creations, hoping to gain renown.
(D) He prefers heading his own kitchen to working as an underling in a more famous establishment.
(E) Despite his early promise, he is unable to create an original work of art.

SECTION 2	Time—50 minutes 50 Questions	In this section solve each problem, using any available space on the page for scratchwork. Then decide which is the best of the choices given and fill in the corresponding circle on the answer sheet.

The following information is for your reference in solving some of the problems.

Circle of radius r: Area $= \pi r^2$ Circumference $= 2\pi r$
The number of degrees of arc in a circle is 360.
The measure in degrees of a straight angle is 180.

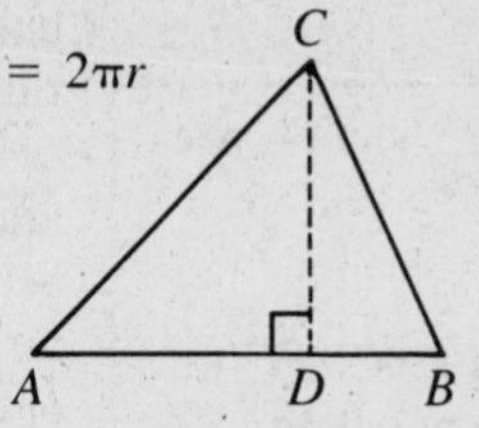

Triangle: The sum of the measures in degrees of the angles of a triangle is 180.

If $\angle CDA$ is a right angle, then

(1) area of $\triangle ABC = \frac{AB \times CD}{2}$

(2) $AC^2 = AD^2 + DC^2$

Definitions of symbols:

$=$ is equal to	$\leqq$ is less than or equal to
$\neq$ is unequal to	$\geqq$ is greater than or equal to
$<$ is less than	$\parallel$ is parallel to
$>$ is greater than	$\perp$ is perpendicular to

Note: Figures that accompany problems in this test are intended to provide information useful in solving the problems. They are drawn as accurately as possible EXCEPT when it is stated in a specific problem that its figure is not drawn to scale. All figures lie in a plane unless otherwise indicated. All numbers used are real numbers.

1. 32 is $\frac{2}{7}$ of what number?
(A) $9\frac{1}{7}$ (B) 14 (C) 64 (D) 112 (E) 224

2. How much less is $\frac{1}{2}$ of $\frac{4}{7}$ than $\frac{5}{7}$ of $\frac{1}{2}$?
(A) $\frac{1}{7}$ (B) $\frac{2}{7}$ (C) $\frac{3}{7}$ (D) $\frac{1}{14}$ (E) $\frac{3}{14}$

3. $\sqrt{\frac{16}{36} + \frac{1}{4}} =$
(A) $\frac{3}{5}$ (B) $\frac{6}{7}$ (C) $\frac{25}{36}$ (D) $\frac{5}{6}$ (E) $\frac{7}{6}$

4. The equivalent of 0.2% is
(A) 0.002 (B) 0.02 (C) 0.2 (D) 2 (E) 20

5. If $\boxed{K}$ is defined by the equation
$\boxed{K} = \frac{\sqrt{K}}{2}$ for all numbers K, which of the following equals 5?
(A) $\boxed{10}$ (B) $\boxed{20}$ (C) $\boxed{25}$
(D) $\boxed{50}$ (E) $\boxed{100}$

6. The number of pupils in a school increased from 2500 to 3000. The percent of increase is
(A) 0.05% (B) 0.5% (C) 5% (D) 20%
(E) 25%

7. A round-trip ticket cost $54.50 while a one-way ticket cost $29.00. How much will be saved by buying 3 round-trip tickets instead of buying one-way tickets?
(A) $10.50 (B) $10.65 (C) $11.50
(D) $31.00 (E) $35.50

8. Half of the members of a graduating class are going to college. One-fourth of these are going to the local municipal college. What part of the graduating class is going to the municipal college?
(A) $\frac{1}{8}$ (B) $\frac{1}{4}$ (C) $\frac{3}{8}$ (D) $\frac{1}{5}$ (E) $\frac{7}{8}$

9. If books bought at prices ranging from $2.00 to $3.50 are sold at prices ranging from $3.00 to $4.25, what is the greatest possible profit that might be made by selling 8 books?
(A) $6 (B) $8 (C) $12 (D) $14 (E) $18

10. There are 10 automobiles waiting to enter a tollgate. If the average length of each car is 16 feet and the average space between each car is 6 inches, what is the length (in feet) of the distance between the front of the first car and the rear of the last vehicle?
(A) 164 (B) $164\frac{1}{2}$ (C) 165 (D) 166 (E) 220

11. If y represents the tens digit and x the units digit of a two-digit number, then the number is represented by
(A) $y + x$ (B) yx (C) $10x + y$
(D) $10y + x$ (E) $10yx$

12. The expression $\sqrt{4 - 3x}$ has a real value for each of the following values of x EXCEPT
(A) -4 (B) 0 (C) $\frac{2}{3}$ (D) 1 (E) 2

13. If $\frac{1}{x} = \frac{a}{b}$ then x equals the
(A) sum of a and b (B) product of a and b
(C) difference of a and b (D) quotient of b and a
(E) quotient of a and b

14. Find the area of $ABCD$.
(A) 13.5
(B) 15
(C) 18
(D) 27
(E) 36

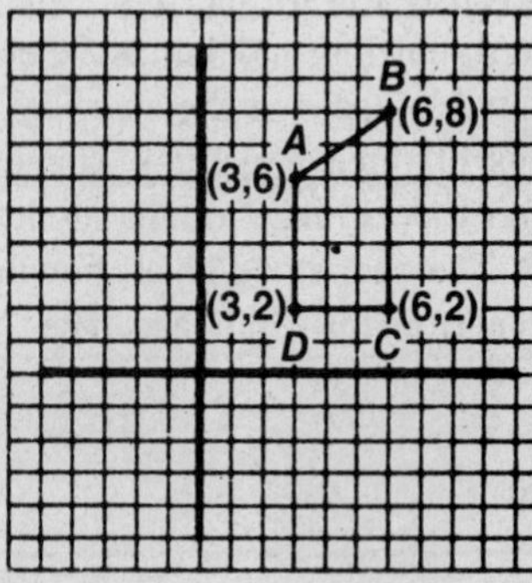

15. A circular pond 40 feet in diameter is surrounded by a patch of grass 2 feet wide. What is the area of the grass?
(A) 4π sq. ft. (B) 84π sq. ft. (C) 164π sq. ft. (D) 336π sq. ft. (E) 400π sq. ft.

Questions 16-32 each consist of two quantities, one in Column A and one in Column B. You are to compare the two quantities and on the answer sheet fill in circle

A if the quantity in Column A is greater;
B if the quantity in Column B is greater;
C if the two quantities are equal;
D if the relationship cannot be determined from the information given.

Notes:
1. In certain questions, information concerning one or both of the quantities to be compared is centered above the two columns.
2. In a given question, a symbol that appears in both columns represents the same thing in Column A as it does in Column B.
3. Letters such as x, n, and k stand for real numbers.

EXAMPLES

	Column A	Column B	Answers
E1.	2×6	$2 + 6$	● Ⓑ Ⓒ Ⓓ

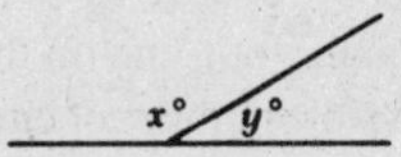

	Column A	Column B	Answers
E2.	$180 - x$	y	Ⓐ Ⓑ ● Ⓓ
E3.	$p - q$	$q - p$	Ⓐ Ⓑ Ⓒ ●

	Column A	Column B
16.	(2)(4)(6)(8)(10)(12)	(24)(40)(8)(6)

$x^2 - 25 = 0$

17.	x	5

$5y + 15 = 3x + 5y$

18.	y	0
19.	$\sqrt{\frac{1}{9}} + \sqrt{\frac{1}{16}}$	$\sqrt{\frac{1}{16} + \frac{1}{9}}$

$x = 0$, $y > 1$, and $z > 1$

20.	$2x(y + z)$	$y(x + z)$

	Column A	Column B
21.	The largest integer less than $\frac{15}{7}$	The largest integer less than $\frac{41}{14}$

$a = 5, 10$
$b = 2, 3$

22.	a^2	b^3

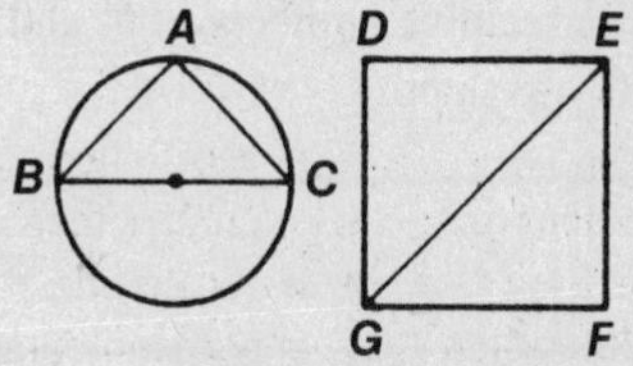

Diameter $BC = 10$
$AB = AC$
Perimeter of square $DEFG = 20$

23.	Area of ABC	Area of $DEFG$

In $\triangle KML$, the measure of $\angle L$ equals the measure of $\angle M$.

24.	Measure of $\angle K$	60°

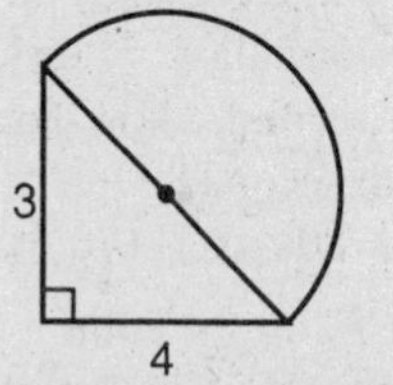

25.	The perimeter of this semicircle	$5 + 2.5\pi$

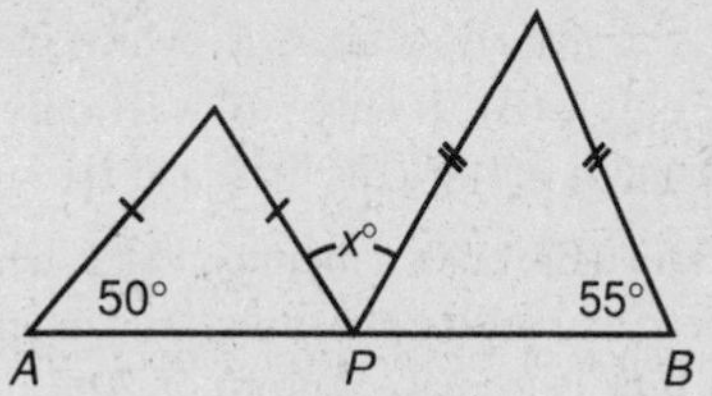

P is a point on line segment AB.

26.	Value of x	75°

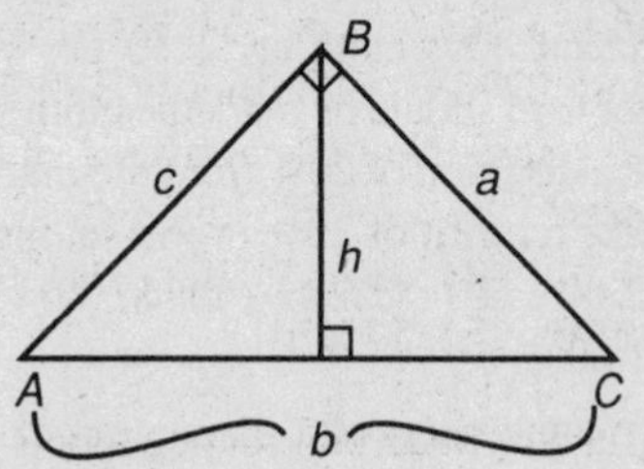

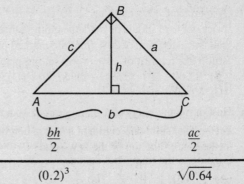

27.	$\frac{bh}{2}$	$\frac{ac}{2}$
28.	$(0.2)^3$	$\sqrt{0.64}$

	Column A	Column B
	$x^2 + y^2 = 100$	
29.	x	y
	1 kilometer = $\frac{5}{8}$ mile	
30.	1 mile	$\frac{5}{8}$ kilometer
	The average of the three consecutive numbers a, b, and c is V.	
31.	$a + c$	$2b$
32.	1.2	$\sqrt{14.4}$

> Solve each of the remaining problems in this section using any available space for scratchwork. Then decide which is the best of the choices given and fill in the corresponding circle on the answer sheet.

33. $\dfrac{9K^3 - 9m^2K}{3K^2 - 3mK}$ is equivalent to $3K +$
(A) m (B) $3m$ (C) 1 (D) 2 (E) 3

34. The distance s in feet that a body falls in t seconds is given by the formula $s = 16t^2$. If a body has been falling for 5 seconds, how far (in feet) will it fall during the 6th second?
(A) 16 (B) 80 (C) 176 (D) 400 (E) 576

35. In $\triangle CDE$, $CE > CD$. Point A bisects side CD, and point B bisects side CE. Which of the following is (are) true?
I. $CB = AD$
II. $AC = BC$
III. $CB > CA$
(A) I only (B) II only (C) III only
(D) I and II only (E) I, II, and III

36. A certain radio costs a merchant \$72, which includes overhead and selling expenses. At what price must he sell it if he is to make a profit of 20% on the selling price?
(A) \$86.40 (B) \$90.00 (C) \$92.00
(D) \$100.00 (E) \$144.00

37. A merchant buys cloth at \$1.60 per yard. At what price per yard should he mark the cloth so that he may sell it at a discount of 20% from the marked price and still make a profit of 20% of the selling price?
(A) \$2.00 (B) \$2.24 (C) \$2.40 (D) \$2.50
(E) \$2.60

38. A metal cube with an edge of one foot is melted into a rectangular solid one-eighth of a foot in height. What is the area of the top of the new solid?
(A) $\frac{1}{64}$ sq. ft. (B) $\frac{1}{8}$ sq. ft. (C) $\frac{1}{4}$ sq. ft.
(D) 4 sq. ft. (E) 8 sq. ft.

39. In the accompanying diagram (not drawn to scale), which of the following is (are) always true?
I. $d > b$
II. $a > d$
III. $d > c$

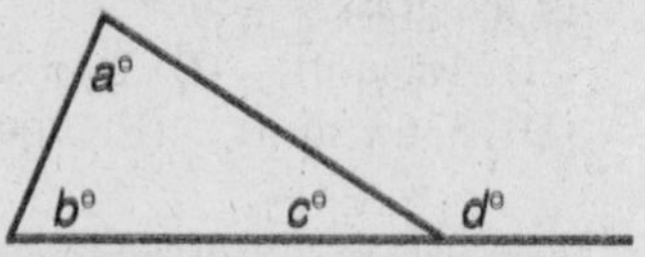

(A) I only (B) II only (C) III only
(D) I and II only (E) I, II, and III

40. How long is the shadow of a 30-foot tree when a 20-foot pole casts a 14-foot shadow?
(A) 4.7 feet (B) 8.4 feet (C) 9.3 feet
(D) 21 feet (E) 24 feet

41. A cup of oatmeal weighs 3 ounces. A cup of pancake mix weighs 5 ounces. How many cups of oatmeal will have the same weight as 3 cups of pancake mix?
(A) $\frac{3}{5}$ (B) $1\frac{2}{3}$ (C) 3 (D) 5 (E) 15

42. The ratio of boys to girls in a senior class is 5:3. If $\frac{9}{10}$ of the boys may graduate and all the girls may or may not graduate, what is the maximum part of the senior class that may graduate?
(A) $\frac{3}{5}$ (B) $\frac{7}{8}$ (C) $\frac{15}{16}$ (D) $\frac{2}{3}$ (E) $\frac{27}{50}$

43. Abe can mow the lawn in 15 minutes. Ben can mow the lawn in 20 minutes. Carl can mow the lawn in 30 minutes. They work together for 5 minutes. What part of the lawn was mowed?
(A) $\frac{1}{4}$ (B) $\frac{2}{3}$ (C) $\frac{3}{4}$ (D) $\frac{4}{5}$ (E) all of it

44. Given a circle A whose diameter is 2 feet and a rectangular piece of tin B, 10 feet by 4 feet, find, correct to the nearest square foot, the tin that will be left after the greatest possible number of circles of the size of A have been cut from B.

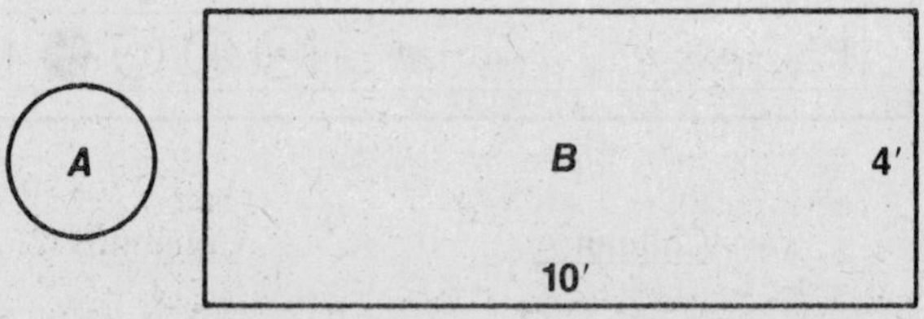

(A) zero (B) 1 sq. ft. (C) 2 sq. ft.
(D) 9 sq. ft. (E) 20 sq. ft.

45. The sum of the base angles of an isosceles triangle is one-half the vertex angle. How many degrees are there in the vertex angle?
(A) 80 (B) 90 (C) 110 (D) 120 (E) 140

46. In $\triangle ABC$, $AB = 2\sqrt{2}$, $BC = 8$, $\angle ABC \stackrel{\circ}{=} 45$. Find area ABC.
(A) $4\sqrt{2}$ (B) 8 (C) $8\sqrt{2}$ (D) 16
(E) $16\sqrt{2}$

47. The sum of three sides of a square equals x. The area of this square, in terms of x, equals
(A) $3x$ (B) $\frac{x}{3}$ (C) $\frac{3}{x}$ (D) $\frac{x^2}{3}$ (E) $\frac{x^2}{9}$

48. The distance between point P (3,0) and point Q is 5. The coordinates of point Q could be any of the following EXCEPT
(A) $(-8,0)$ (B) $(3,-5)$ (C) $(3,5)$ (D) $(8,0)$
(E) $(-2,0)$

49. What part of the large circle is shaded?
(A) $\frac{1}{5}$ (B) $\frac{1}{4}$ (C) $\frac{1}{3}$
(D) $\frac{1}{2}$ (E) none of these

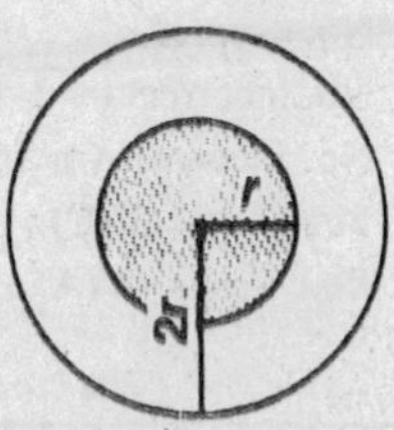

50. A rectangle is revolved through 360° about its longer side as an axis. If the longer side is a units and the shorter side is b units, the volume of the resulting solid in cubic units is
(A) πab^2 (B) πa^2b
(C) $2\pi ab$ (D) $2\pi ab^2$
(E) πab

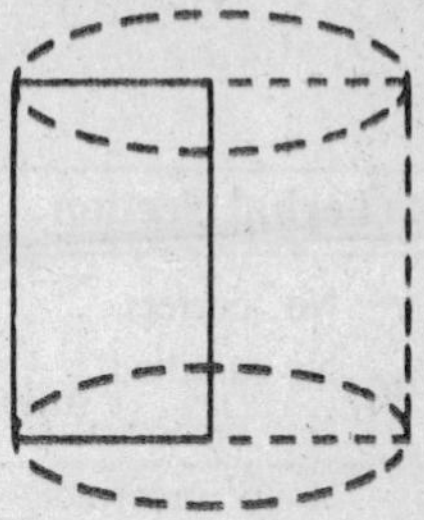

ANSWER KEY

Verbal Aptitude Section

1. C	*11.* B	*21.* A	*31.* E	*41.* D	*51.* E	*61.* D
2. E	*12.* E	*22.* E	*32.* C	*42.* B	*52.* D	*62.* A
3. A	*13.* E	*23.* E	*33.* E	*43.* B	*53.* E	*63.* C
4. D	*14.* B	*24.* D	*34.* B	*44.* A	*54.* C	*64.* D
5. C	*15.* D	*25.* D	*35.* C	*45.* C	*55.* D	*65.* B
6. A	*16.* A	*26.* C	*36.* C	*46.* B	*56.* E	
7. C	*17.* A	*27.* B	*37.* C	*47.* D	*57.* B	
8. A	*18.* E	*28.* B	*38.* A	*48.* D	*58.* D	
9. A	*19.* D	*29.* B	*39.* B	*49.* E	*59.* A	
10. D	*20.* A	*30.* C	*40.* C	*50.* C	*60.* D	

Mathematical Aptitude Section

Note: Each correct answer to the mathematics questions is keyed by number to the corresponding topic in Chapters 9 and 10. These numerals refer to the topics listed below, with specific page references in parentheses.

1. Basic Fundamental Operations (155–157)
2. Algebraic Operations (157–160)
3. Using Algebra (160–164)
4. Exponents, Roots and Radicals (159–160)
5. Inequalities (164–165)
6. Fractions (176–178)
7. Decimals (176)
8. Percent (178–180)
9. Averages (180–181)
10. Motion (182–183)
11. Ratio and Proportion (183–185)
12. Mixtures and Solutions (177–178)
13. Work (185–186)
14. Coordinate Geometry (172–173)
15. Geometry (165–172, 173–176)
16. Quantitative Comparisons (189–192)

ANSWER KEY

1. **D** (6)	*11.* **D** (3)	*21.* **C** (1,16)	*31.* **C** (9,16)	*41.* **D** (1)
2. **D** (1,6)	*12.* **E** (4)	*22.* **D** (2,16)	*32.* **B** (4,16)	*42.* **C** (11)
3. **D** (4,6)	*13.* **D** (2)	*23.* **C** (15,16)	*33.* **B** (2)	*43.* **C** (13)
4. **A** (8)	*14.* **B** (14)	*24.* **D** (15,16)	*34.* **C** (2)	*44.* **D** (15)
5. **E** (2)	*15.* **B** (15)	*25.* **C** (15,16)	*35.* **C** (5,15)	*45.* **D** (15)
6. **D** (8)	*16.* **C** (1,16)	*26.* **C** (15,16)	*36.* **B** (3,8)	*46.* **B** (15)
7. **A** (1)	*17.* **D** (2,16)	*27.* **C** (15,16)	*37.* **D** (3,8)	*47.* **E** (15)
8. **A** (6)	*18.* **D** (2,16)	*28.* **B** (4,16)	*38.* **E** (15)	*48.* **A** (14)
9. **E** (1)	*19.* **A** (4,6,16)	*29.* **D** (2,16)	*39.* **A** (5,15)	*49.* **B** (15)
10. **B** (1)	*20.* **B** (2,16)	*30.* **A** (11,16)	*40.* **D** (11,15)	*50.* **A** (15)

SCORING CHART TYPICAL TEST I

Verbal Section		Mathematical Section*		
No. correct	_____	No. correct	(A)	_____
No. omitted	_____	No. incorrect (# 1-15, 33-50)	(B)	_____
No. incorrect	_____	No. incorrect (# 16-32)	(C)	_____
¼ no. incorrect	_____	¼ (B) + 1/3 (C)	(D)	_____
Raw Score: (no. correct minus ¼ no. incorrect)	_____	*Raw Score* = (A) − (D)		_____

* (In the Mathematical section, deduct ¼ of a point for each five-choice question answered incorrectly and 1/3 of a point for each four-choice question answered incorrectly.)

EVALUATION CHART

Study your score. Your raw score on the Verbal and Mathematical Aptitude Sections is an indication of your probable achievement on the PSAT/NMSQT. As a guide to the amount of work you need or want to do, study the following.

Raw Score: *Verbal*	Raw Score: *Mathematical*	Self-rating
58-65	41-50	Superior
46-57	25-40	Very good
40-45	20-24	Satisfactory
36-39	16-19	Average
30-35	10-15	Needs further study
20-29	7-9	Needs intensive study
0-19	0-6	Probably inadequate

Before you take the final test in this book, review any topics you still feel unsure about. (Use the table on page 384 to help you identify these topics.)

ANSWER EXPLANATIONS

Verbal Aptitude Section

1. **C** The opposite of *influence* (the power to have a strong effect on others) is *lack of power.*
Think of "big shots with influence."

2. **E** The opposite of to *adorn* (beautify or decorate) is to *remove decoration.*
Think of "adorning your hair with flowers."

3. **A** The opposite of *prudent* or cautious is *rash* (heedless; impetuous).
Think of "a prudent investment policy."

4. **D** The opposite of a *braggart* or boaster is a *modest person.*
Think of "a boastful braggart."

5. **C** The opposite of *punitive* or punishing is *rewarding.*
Think of having to pay "a punitive fine."

6. **A** The opposite of *hilarity* (merriment; cheerfulness) is *gloom* (cheerlessness).
Think of "noisy, mirthful hilarity."

7. **C** The opposite of *docile* (easily managed or taught) is *unmanageable.*
Think of "docile, obedient children."

8. **A** The opposite of *symmetry* (balance of proportion; regularity of form) is *irregularity of form.*
Think of "symmetry along a central axis."

9. **A** The opposite of *ominous* (menacing; forbidding) is *unthreatening.*
Think of "an ominous warning."

10. **D** The opposite of to *chide* or scold is to *acclaim* or applaud.
Think of "being chided for misbehaving."

11. **B** The opposite of *despicable* (disgraceful; contemptible) is *worthy of esteem*.
Think of "a mean, despicable deed."

12. **E** The opposite of a *protrusion* (something that protrudes or juts out) is a *recess* or indentation. Note that *recess* here has an unfamiliar secondary meaning.
Beware of eye-catchers. Choice **C** is incorrect. The capitalized word is *protrusion*, not *profusion* (abundance).
Think of "the protrusion of a tongue."

13. **E** The opposite of *unwitting* (unaware; accidental) is *intentional* (deliberate; purposeful).
Think of "an unwitting insult."

14. **B** The opposite of *unseemly* (not suitable or appropriate) is *proper*.
Think of being criticized for "unseemly behavior."

15. **D** The opposite of *facility* (aptitude; ease; skill) is *inability*. Note that *facility* here has a less common secondary meaning.
Think of "an enviable facility with words."

16. **A** The opposite of to *mushroom* (grow rapidly; flourish) is to *shrivel* or shrink. Note that *mushroom* here is a verb.
Think of our "numbers mushrooming—a population explosion!"

17. **A** The opposite of *peripheral* (marginal; minor; outlying) is *pivotal* or central.
Think of "peripheral vision."

18. **E** The opposite of to *rue* or regret something is to *rejoice over* it.
Think of having to "rue one's mistakes."

19. **D** The opposite of to *disabuse* (undeceive) is to *deceive*.
Beware of eye-catchers. Choice **A** is incorrect. *Disabuse* is unrelated to physical *maltreatment* or abuse.
Think of "disabusing someone of a misapprehension."

20. **A** The opposite of a *tyro* or beginner is an *expert*. Don't confuse *tyro* with *tyrant;* they're very different in meaning.
Think of "an inexperienced tyro."

21. **A** An audacious or *daring* approach succeeded; a less daring approach would have failed.

22. **E** A plot that people have seen over and over again is by definition *trite* (stale; overdone). Note that the second clause gives you the information you need to fill in the word missing in the first clause.

23. **E** The scientist is aware that future data may cause her to change her opinion. Therefore, she is willing to express only a *tentative* (temporary; provisional) opinion.

24. **D** A *gregarious* or sociable person normally seeks the company of others. However, because of his legal problems, this usually sociable individual is *shunning* or avoiding others. Note how the signal word *although* sets up a contrast.

25. **D** The statement asserts that the three are not in fact independent or separate but are instead *inseparable*. Again, the signal word (in this case, *but)* sets up a contrast that lets you know you are looking for an antonym or near-antonym of *independent*.

26. **C** If depression occurs when nerve cells get too little of certain chemicals, it makes sense to have these cells get more of the chemicals. This can be done by making more of the chemicals *available to* the cells.

27. **B** The contrast in Hugo's novels is between *piety* or devotion ("a scene of chaste and holy love") and *ribaldry* or indecency (a scene of "coarse and profane licentiousness"). Note that the sentence's parallelism demands that the two missing words be antonyms or near-antonyms.

28. **B** To sink *ignominiously* is to do so shamefully or disgracefully. Such an end lacks dignity or honor. Note again how the clue to the missing word in one clause can be found in the clause without the blank. In this case, the key phrase is "lacked ...even the dignity of being sunk."

29. **B** An *egotistical* or self-centered and conceited person would find it difficult to *tolerate* or bear someone else's success.

30. **C** That the interrogator is subtle in discrimination or judgment shows she can conduct matters with *finesse* (tact; delicacy); that she is *expeditious* (efficient and prompt) in manner shows she can conduct matters with *dispatch* (speed). Note the use of parallel structure in this sentence.

31. **E** A *crowbar* is a tool used for *prying;* a *shovel* is a tool used for *digging*.
(Definition)

32. **C** A *trough* is a feeding bin for *pigs;* a *manger* is a feeding bin for *cattle*.
(Function)

33. **E** A *pedestrian* travels along a *sidewalk;* a *boat* travels along a *waterway*.
(Function)

34. **B** A *sculptor* works in a *studio;* a *blacksmith* works in a *smithy*.
(Worker and Workplace)

35. **C** To *intimidate* someone is to cause that person *fear;* to *exasperate* someone is to cause that person *irritation*.
(Cause and Effect)

36. **C** By definition, *food* that is *insipid* (dull; tasteless) lacks flavor; *remarks* that are *vapid* (inane; empty) lack sense.
(Defining Characteristic)

37. **C** A *hawk* seizes its prey with its *talons;* a *lion*, with its *claws*.
(Part to Whole)

38. **A** A *pyromaniac* seeks to set *fires;* a *saboteur* seeks to create *destruction.*

(Purpose)

39. **B** A *diva* (singer) performs an *aria;* an *actor* performs a *soliloquy.*

(Defining Characteristic)

40. **C** An *ophthalmologist* is a physician who specializes in the treatment of disorders of the *eyes;* a *dermatologist* is a physician who specializes in the treatment of disorders of the *skin.*

(Defining Characteristic)

41. **D** Something *irksome* (annoying; vexing) by definition *chafes;* something *lurid* (revolting; horrifying) by definition *shocks.*

(Definition)

42. **B** *Slag* is the waste matter or residue left over when *metal* is made; the *dregs* are the waste matter or residue left over when *wine* is made.

(Part to Whole)

43. **B** *Dapper* (trim) is a term for being correct in *appearance; precise* (carefully distinct) is a term for being correct in *speech.*

(Defining Characteristic)

44. **A** A *malingerer* (someone who goofs off) shuns *work;* a *recluse* (hermit) shuns *company.*

(Defining Characteristic)

45. **C** To *ogle* (look at someone coquettishly) indicates *flirtatiousness;* to *gape* (stare at in wonder) indicates *astonishment.*

(Action and Its Significance)

46. **B** In both the opening sentences and the concluding two sentences of the passage, the author makes a distinction about the nature of equality that is central to his argument.
Choice **A** is incorrect. The author does not disagree with the belief that all men and women are created equal; equality is not a myth to him. However, he believes the notion of equality can be carried too far.
Choices **C, D,** and **E** are also incorrect. Although these ideas are touched on in the passage, they are not central to the author's point.

47. **D** The author is pointing out the foolishness that exists when a question is asked of an uninformed or unqualified person. He does so by giving an example of the kind of opinion sampling he dislikes.
Choice **A** is incorrect. Resentment or bitterness would be an unlikely response on the reader's part. Choice **B** is incorrect. The example doesn't show that the author objects to all opinion sampling. Instead, it shows that he objects to opinion sampling that fails to take into account the qualifications of those asked to give their opinions. Choice **C** is incorrect. The casual mention of Grenada shows no sign of being the result of heavy research. Choice **E** is incorrect. The example the author gives does not divert or draw away attention from what he's trying to say.

48. **D** The author says it's absurd to treat all opinions as equally valid. His attitude is clearly *deprecatory* or disapproving.

49. **E** The passage describes the birds' reaction to the approach of the four human intruders ("the four strange specks moving across the lake").

50. **C** The opening sentence indicates that, before anything else happened, "quiet swept over the colony." In other words, the birds *became very still.*

51. **E** The author writes of the intense psychological force of the birds' concentration on the visitors and of the birds' cries filling the sky "with the sound of judgment day." Clearly, the experience has impressed him greatly, and his reaction is best characterized as one of *awe* (an overwhelming feeling of wonder mixed with fear).
Choice **A** is incorrect. Nothing in the visitors' approach suggests that they are impatient or hasty. Choice **B** is incorrect. While the birds are afraid ("terrorized"), the visitors' reaction is not simply one of fear. They are more overwhelmed by the experience than frightened by it. Choice **C** is incorrect. While the birds may have been angered by the visitors' intrusion, the visitors are not angry. Choice **D** is incorrect. Sadness is an unlikely response to such an overwhelming, sudden display.

52. **D** By describing what happened at the rookery in great detail, the author is trying to *evoke* or produce a vivid impression of *an experience* he wishes to share.

53. **E** The passage indicates Chaucer wrote on religion, ethics, rhetoric, and science. It does not indicate he wrote on *music.*

54. **C** The opening sentence states that Chaucer was considered a "rude versifier" until scholars learned to understand his technique. This suggests that people's failure to understand just what Chaucer was doing caused them to undervalue his poetic skill.

55. **D** The passage as a whole develops the idea of Chaucer's greatness as a poet.
Choice **A** is incorrect. The passage mentions Chaucer's skills as a satirist but does not dwell on them. Choice **B** is incorrect. Though great, Chaucer is not considered Shakespeare's peer or equal: he is "surpassed by Shakespeare." Choice **C** is incorrect. The passage stresses Chaucer's technical expertise, not the supposed "crudities" of his verse. Choice **E** is incorrect. It is too narrow in scope to be a good title for the passage as a whole.

56. **E** You can arrive at the correct choice by the process of elimination.
Statement I is false. While sea action plays a part in erosion, the author does not say it is the most important factor in erosion. Therefore, you can eliminate Choices **A** and **D.**
Statement II is true. The first purely synthetic oil "has yet to be produced." Therefore, you can eliminate Choice **C.**
Statement III is true. New rock is born or created "through the effects of gravity." Therefore, you can eliminate Choice **B.**
Only Choice **E** is left. It is the correct answer.

57. **B** The author mentions the Grand Canyon in the context of speaking of rivers as "immensely powerful destructive agencies." The dramatic canyon illustrates the *devastating impact* a river can have.

58. **D** In the last paragraph the author states that "the cause of the metamorphosis" of decayed vegetation and dead aquatic life into oil is not known. We lack full understanding of the process by which oil is created; therefore, our understanding is *deficient*.
Choice **C** is incorrect. Our knowledge is not *erroneous* or false; it is simply incomplete.

59. **A** The last sentence states that oil is always found "on the sites of ancient seas and lakes."

60. **D** The author describes several processes (erosion, rock formation, oil formation): He states the possibility that a chemical catalyst is involved in oil formation. He cites the Grand Canyon as an example of what a river can do to the land. He mentions the limitation of our ability to produce oil synthetically. However, he never proposes a solution to any problem.

61. **D** The author is a passenger who was aboard while the boat touched at several ports (paragraph 3).

62. **A** The author is condescending in commenting on "dulled...feathers" and a "fifth-rate freighter."

63. **C** Since the waiters are said to be dreaming they served at Maxim's, it is most likely that Maxim's is both a famous restaurant and a desirable place to work.

64. **D** The chef sweats because he is nervous while his delicate sugar cathedral is being carried up the stairs.

65. **B** The last sentence states that the chef originally made the sugar cathedral in a famous kitchen. He has come down in the world, but retains his self-esteem.

Mathematical Aptitude Section

1. **D** Let x = the number.
$\frac{2}{7}x = 32$
$x = 112$

2. **D** $\frac{1}{2} \cdot \frac{4}{7} = \frac{2}{7}$ or $\frac{4}{14}$
$\frac{5}{7} \cdot \frac{1}{2} = \frac{5}{14}$
Difference $= \frac{1}{14}$

3. **D** $\sqrt{\frac{16}{36} + \frac{1}{4}}$
$\sqrt{\frac{16}{36} + \frac{9}{36}}$
$\sqrt{\frac{25}{36}} = \frac{5}{6}$

4. **A** $0.2\% = \frac{0.2}{100}$ or 0.002

5. **E** $100 \;=\; \frac{\sqrt{100}}{2} = \frac{10}{2} = 5$

6. **D** Increase = 500
$\frac{\text{increase}}{\text{original}} = \frac{500}{2500} = \frac{1}{5} = 20\%$

7. **A** Saving on one round-trip = \$58.00 − \$54.50 = \$3.50
Savings on 3 round-trips = \$10.50

8. **A** $\frac{1}{4}$ of $\frac{1}{2} = \frac{1}{8}$

9. **E** Greatest profit will be made when they are purchased at lowest price (\$2.00) and sold for the maximum price (\$4.25). Maximum profit for each book is \$2.25. Therefore for 8 books, maximum profit = \$18.00.

10. **B** Length of all cars $= 10 \times 16$ feet = 160 feet. Observe that there are nine spaces between 10 automobiles. Distance of these nine spaces = 6 inches $\times 9 = 54$ inches or $4\frac{1}{2}$ feet. Distance from front of first car to rear of last vehicle $= 160 + 4\frac{1}{2}$ $= 164\frac{1}{2}$ feet.

11. **D** Any two-digit number = ten times the tens digit plus the units digit.
y = tens digit [given]
x = units digit [given]
$10y + x$ = the number

12. **E** $\sqrt{4 - 3x}$ will have a real value unless $4 - 3x$ is negative. This will occur if $3x > 4$. Of the choices given, only $x = 2$ makes $3x > 4$.

13. **D** $\frac{1}{x} = \frac{a}{b}$
$ax = b$ [product of means = product of extremes]
$x = \frac{b}{a}$

14. **B** Draw $AE \perp BC$.
Area of rectangle formed equals base (3) $\times$ altitude (4) = 12.
Area of triangle AEB equals $\frac{1}{2}$ (base 2 $\times$ altitude 3) = 3.
Area of $ABCD = 12 + 3 = 15$.

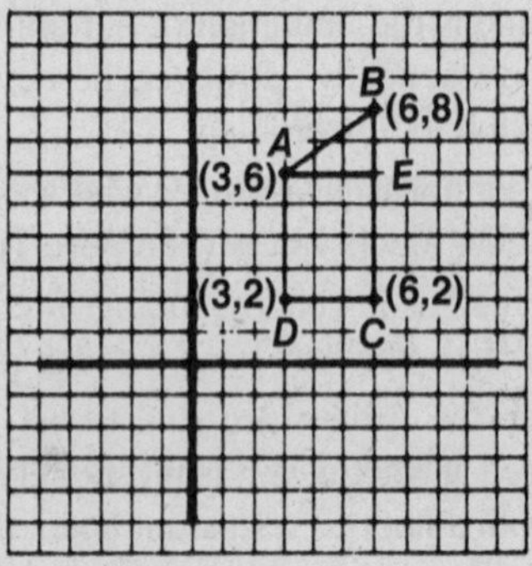

15. **B** Diameter of outer circle = 44 feet
Radius = 22 feet
Area of outer circle = $\pi r^2 = \pi(22)^2 = 484\pi$ square feet
Diameter of inner circle = 40 feet
Radius = 20 feet
Area of inner circle = $\pi r^2 = \pi(20)^2 = 400\pi$ square feet
Area of patch (difference of two circles) = $484\pi - 400\pi = 84\pi$ square feet

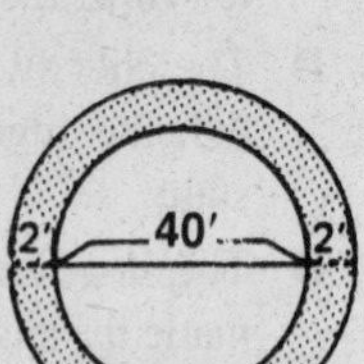

16. **C** Note both columns have the factors (8) and (6). Consider the other factors. (4)(10) in Column A cancel (40) in Column B. Also the factors (2)(12) in Column A cancel (24) in Column B.

17. **D** $x^2 - 25 = 0$
$x^2 = 25$
$x = +5$ *and* -5

18. **D** In this equation $x = 5$. Any value of y will satisfy this equation.

19. **A** $\sqrt{\frac{1}{9}} + \sqrt{\frac{1}{16}} = \frac{1}{3} + \frac{1}{4} = \frac{7}{12}$

$\sqrt{\frac{1}{16} + \frac{1}{9}} = \sqrt{\frac{25}{144}} = \frac{5}{12}$

$\frac{7}{12} > \frac{5}{12}$

20. **B** If $x = 0$, $2x(y + z) = 0$.
For Column B, $y(x + z) = y(0 + z)$.
Since y and z are positive, the value of $y(x + z)$ is positive.

21. **C** Since $\frac{15}{7} = 2\frac{1}{7}$ and $\frac{41}{14} = 2\frac{13}{14}$, the largest integer less than $\frac{15}{7}$ is 2 and the largest integer less than $\frac{41}{14}$ is also 2.

22. **D** If $a = 5$, $a^2 = 25$.
If $a = 10$, $a^2 = 100$.
If $b = 2$, $b^3 = 8$.
If $b = 3$, $b^3 = 27$.

23. **C** $\triangle ABC$ is inscribed in a semicircle. $\therefore$ ABC is a right triangle. Since $AB = AC$, ABC is an isosceles right triangle. Since $BC = 10$, $AC = AB = 5\sqrt{2}$. The area of $ABC = \frac{1}{2}(AC)(AB)$ or $\frac{1}{2}(5\sqrt{2})(5\sqrt{2})$ or 25. The perimeter of the square equals 20. Therefore each side equals 5 and the area of the square is 5^2 or 25.

24. **D** Only if $\triangle KML$ is equilateral would the vertex angle K be equal to the measures of angles L and M. If $\triangle KLM$ is isosceles, then K could be more than or less than 60°.

25. **C** The perimeter of the semicircle equals the diameter plus half the circumference of the circle. The diameter, the hypotenuse of a 3:4:5 triangle, equals 5. The circumference equals 5π. One-half the circumference (2.5π) plus 5 equals the perimeter of the semicircle.

26. **C** The value of
$x = 180 - (55 + 50)$
$= 180 - 105$
$= 75°$

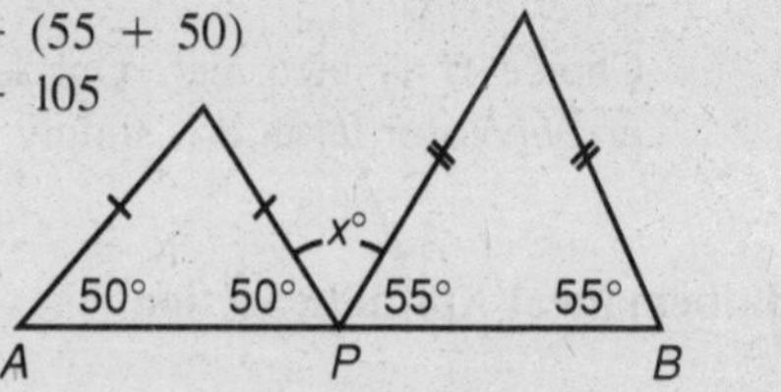

27. **C** Since $AB \perp BC$, the area of $ABC = \frac{1}{2}(AB)(BC)$ or $\frac{1}{2}ac$ or $\frac{ac}{2}$ or $\frac{bh}{2}$.

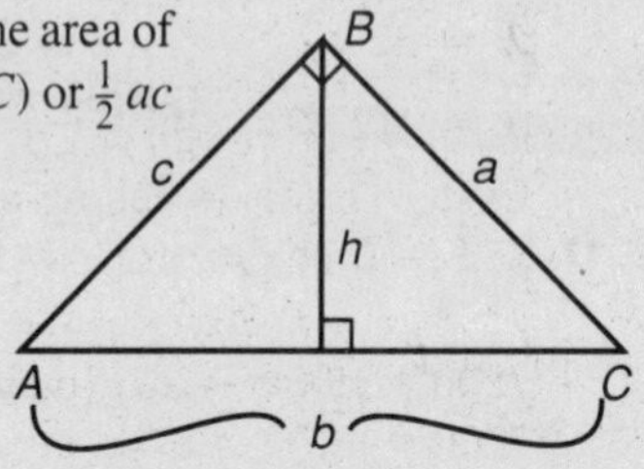

28. **B** $(0.2)^3 = (0.2)(0.2)(0.2) = (0.008)$
$\sqrt{0.64} = 0.8$
$0.8 > 0.008$

29. **D** With negative values as well as positive values for x and for y the sum of their squares would equal 10.

30. **A** If 1 kilometer = $\frac{5}{8}$ mile, then
$\frac{5}{8}$ of a kilometer = $\left(\frac{5}{8}\right)\left(\frac{5}{8}\right)$ mile or $\frac{25}{64}$ mile, which is less than 1 mile.

31. **C** Let $x = a$, then $x + 1 = b$ and $x + 2 = c$
$a + c = x + x + 2$ or $2x + 2$
$2b = x + 1 + x + 1$ or $2x + 2$

32. **B** Estimate the value of $\sqrt{14.4}$. 14 is less than 16 but more than 9. The value of $\sqrt{14.4}$ is more than 3 but less than 4.

33. **B** Factor and cancel:

$$\frac{9K^3 - 9m^2K}{3K^2 - 3mK}$$

$$\frac{9K(K^2 - m^2)}{3K(K - m)}$$

$$\frac{\overset{3}{\cancel{9}}K(K + m)\cancel{(K - m)}}{\cancel{3}K\cancel{(K - m)}} = 3K + 3m$$

34. **C** $s = 16t^2$ [given]
$s = 16(5)^2$ [substitution]
$s = 16(25) = 400$ feet covered in 5 seconds
For 6 seconds, $t = 6$
$s = 16t^2$
$s = 16(6)^2$
$s = 16(36) = 576$ feet
$576 - 400 = 176$ feet

35. **C** $CB = \frac{1}{2}CE$ and $AD = \frac{1}{2}CD$, but since $CE > CD$, CB cannot equal AD. For the same reason II is not correct. However, consider the following: CB is one half of CE, and CA is one half of CD. Since $CE > CD$, one half of CE (or CB) $>$ one half of CD (or CA). Doubles, triples, halves, thirds, etc., of unequal quantities are unequal in the same order.

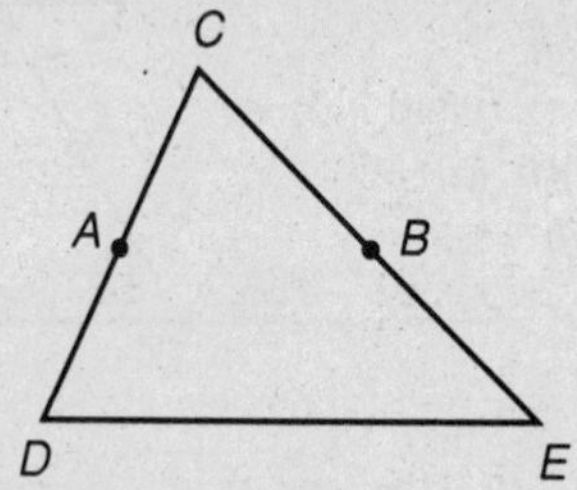

36. **B** Let x = selling price.
$0.20x$ = profit [given]
Cost + profit = selling price
$\$72 + 0.20x = x$
$72 = x - 0.20x$
$7200 = 100x - 20x$ [multiply by 100]
$7200 = 80x$
$\$90 = x$

37. **D** Marked price less 20% = selling price (1)
20% of selling price = profit (2)
Cost = \$1.60 (3)
Cost + profit = selling price (4)
Let x = marked price.
$x - 0.20x$ = selling price (1)
$0.20(x - 0.20x)$ or $(0.20x - 0.04x)$ = profit (2)
$1.60 + 0.20x - 0.04x = x - 0.20x$ (4)
$0.20x - 0.04x - x + 0.20x = -1.60$
[multiply by 100]
$20x - 4x - 100x + 20x = -160$
$-64x = -160$
$64x = 160$
$x = \$2.50$

38. **E** Let x = area of top of melted cube in the rectangular solid (in square feet).
Volume in rectangular solid = area of top of melted surface x height $= (x)\left(\frac{1}{8}\text{ foot}\right) = \frac{x}{8}$ cubic feet
Volume of original cube $= 1' \times 1' \times 1' = 1$ cubic foot
Since the amount (volume) of metal cube is equal to melted material,
$\frac{x}{8} = 1$ and
$x = 8$ square feet.

39. **A** The exterior angle of a triangle is equal to the sum of both remote interior angles, or $d = a + b$. Therefore I is correct and II is incorrect. III is incorrect because $d + c = 180$ in various combinations.

40. **D** Let x = size of shadow of the tree.
$$\frac{\text{size of object}}{\text{size of shadow}} = \frac{\text{20-foot pole}}{\text{14-foot shadow}} = \frac{\text{30-foot tree}}{x}$$
$20x = (30)(14)$
$20x = 420$
$x = 21$ feet

41. **D** 1 cup pancake mix = 5 ounces
3 cups pancake mix = 15 ounces
3 ounces oatmeal = 1 cup
$\therefore$ 15 ounces oatmeal = 5 cups

42. **C** $\frac{5}{8}$ of the class consists of boys.
$\frac{3}{8}$ of the class consists of girls.
According to the data, the only ones that may not graduate are the $\frac{1}{10}$ of the boys. They make up $\frac{1}{10}$ of $\frac{5}{8}$ of the class or $\frac{1}{16}$ of the class. Therefore the remaining $\frac{15}{16}$ may graduate.

43. **C** In 5 minutes Abe does $\frac{5}{15}$ or $\frac{1}{3}$ of the lawn.
In 5 minutes Ben does $\frac{5}{20}$ or $\frac{1}{4}$ of the lawn.
In 5 minutes Carl does $\frac{5}{30}$ or $\frac{1}{6}$ of the lawn.
Total done $= \frac{1}{3} + \frac{1}{4} + \frac{1}{6} = \frac{3}{4}$

44. **D** Since the diameter of each circle equals 2 feet, the maximum number of circles along the length is 5 and the maximum number of circles along the width is 2. Total number of circles equals 10.
Area of circle $= \pi r^2$ or area of each circle $= \pi(1)^2 = 3.14$ square feet
Area of all 10 circles = 31.4 square feet
Area of rectangle = bh or $10 \times 4 = 40$ square feet
Area of tin left over $= 40 - 31.4 = 8.6$ square feet
The answer to the nearest square foot is 9.

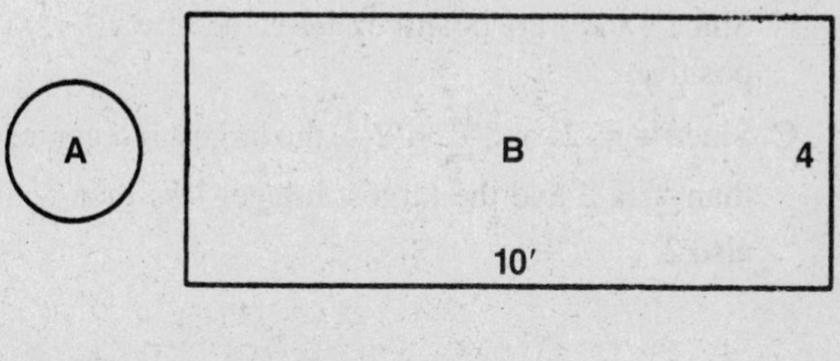

45. D Let x = vertex angle.
Let y = each base angle of the isosceles triangle.

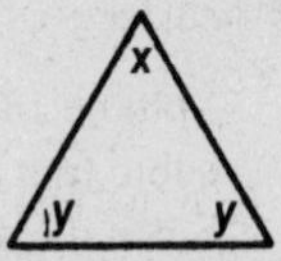

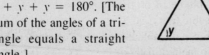

$x + y + y = 180°$. [The sum of the angles of a triangle equals a straight angle.]
$(y + y) = \frac{1}{2}x$ [given]
$2y = \frac{x}{2}$
$4y = x$
$4y + y + y = 180°$ [substitution]
$6y = 180°$
$y = 30°$
$x = 4y = 120°$

46. B Draw $AD \perp BC$.
In $\triangle ABC$, $\angle BAD \overset{\circ}{=} 45$
$\therefore BD = AD$;
$AB = 2\sqrt{2}$ [given]
$\triangle ABD$ is a 45°-45°-90° triangle. The hypotenuse, $a\sqrt{2}$, equals $2\sqrt{2}$, so $a = 2$. Thus, $AD = 2$.

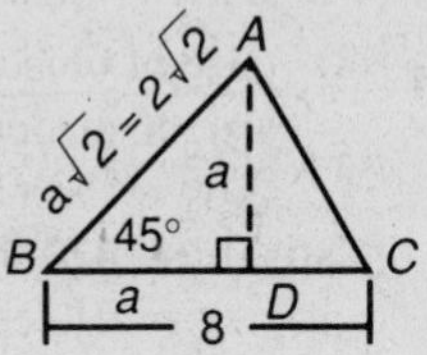

Area of $\triangle ABC = \frac{bh}{2} = \frac{(8)(2)}{(2)} = 8$

47. E Each side $= \frac{x}{3}$
Area = $(\text{side})^2$ or $\frac{x^2}{9}$

48. A If two points have one coordinate the same, the distance between them is the difference between the two other coordinates.
(A) $3 - (-8) \neq 5$; (B) $0 - (-5) = 5$;
(C) $5 - 0 = 5$; (D) $8 - 3 = 5$;
(E) $3 - (-2) = 5$

49. B Area of large circle
$= \pi(\text{radius})^2$
$\pi(2r)^2 = 4\pi r^2$
Area of shaded circle
$= \pi r^2$

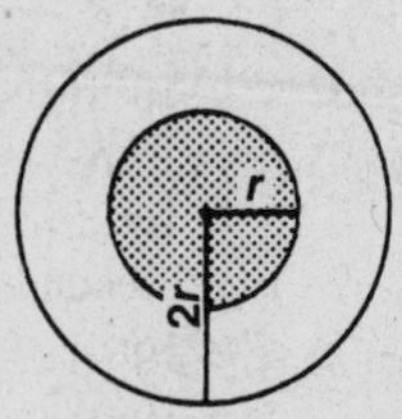

$\frac{\text{shaded circle}}{\text{large circle}} = \frac{\pi r^2}{4\pi r^2}$
$= \frac{\cancel{\pi r^2}}{4\cancel{\pi r^2}} = \frac{1}{4}$

50. A. The resulting solid is a circular cylinder of height a and radius of circular base equal to b. The volume of the cylinder is equal to the area of the circular base multiplied by the altitude.

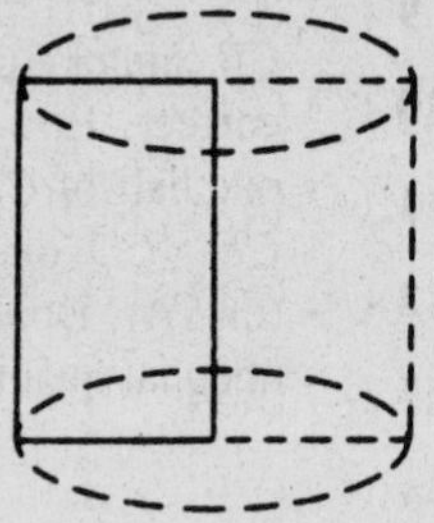

$V = \pi r^2 h$
When $r = b$ and $h = a$,
$V = (\pi)(b^2)(a)$
$V = \pi ab^2$.

PSAT/NMSQT Answer Sheet

TYPICAL TEST J

Verbal Aptitude Section

1 Ⓐ Ⓑ Ⓒ Ⓓ Ⓔ
2 Ⓐ Ⓑ Ⓒ Ⓓ Ⓔ
3 Ⓐ Ⓑ Ⓒ Ⓓ Ⓔ
4 Ⓐ Ⓑ Ⓒ Ⓓ Ⓔ
5 Ⓐ Ⓑ Ⓒ Ⓓ Ⓔ
6 Ⓐ Ⓑ Ⓒ Ⓓ Ⓔ
7 Ⓐ Ⓑ Ⓒ Ⓓ Ⓔ
8 Ⓐ Ⓑ Ⓒ Ⓓ Ⓔ
9 Ⓐ Ⓑ Ⓒ Ⓓ Ⓔ
10 Ⓐ Ⓑ Ⓒ Ⓓ Ⓔ
11 Ⓐ Ⓑ Ⓒ Ⓓ Ⓔ
12 Ⓐ Ⓑ Ⓒ Ⓓ Ⓔ
13 Ⓐ Ⓑ Ⓒ Ⓓ Ⓔ
14 Ⓐ Ⓑ Ⓒ Ⓓ Ⓔ
15 Ⓐ Ⓑ Ⓒ Ⓓ Ⓔ
16 Ⓐ Ⓑ Ⓒ Ⓓ Ⓔ
17 Ⓐ Ⓑ Ⓒ Ⓓ Ⓔ
18 Ⓐ Ⓑ Ⓒ Ⓓ Ⓔ
19 Ⓐ Ⓑ Ⓒ Ⓓ Ⓔ
20 Ⓐ Ⓑ Ⓒ Ⓓ Ⓔ
21 Ⓐ Ⓑ Ⓒ Ⓓ Ⓔ
22 Ⓐ Ⓑ Ⓒ Ⓓ Ⓔ
23 Ⓐ Ⓑ Ⓒ Ⓓ Ⓔ
24 Ⓐ Ⓑ Ⓒ Ⓓ Ⓔ
25 Ⓐ Ⓑ Ⓒ Ⓓ Ⓔ
26 Ⓐ Ⓑ Ⓒ Ⓓ Ⓔ
27 Ⓐ Ⓑ Ⓒ Ⓓ Ⓔ
28 Ⓐ Ⓑ Ⓒ Ⓓ Ⓔ
29 Ⓐ Ⓑ Ⓒ Ⓓ Ⓔ
30 Ⓐ Ⓑ Ⓒ Ⓓ Ⓔ
31 Ⓐ Ⓑ Ⓒ Ⓓ Ⓔ
32 Ⓐ Ⓑ Ⓒ Ⓓ Ⓔ
33 Ⓐ Ⓑ Ⓒ Ⓓ Ⓔ
34 Ⓐ Ⓑ Ⓒ Ⓓ Ⓔ
35 Ⓐ Ⓑ Ⓒ Ⓓ Ⓔ
36 Ⓐ Ⓑ Ⓒ Ⓓ Ⓔ
37 Ⓐ Ⓑ Ⓒ Ⓓ Ⓔ
38 Ⓐ Ⓑ Ⓒ Ⓓ Ⓔ
39 Ⓐ Ⓑ Ⓒ Ⓓ Ⓔ
40 Ⓐ Ⓑ Ⓒ Ⓓ Ⓔ
41 Ⓐ Ⓑ Ⓒ Ⓓ Ⓔ
42 Ⓐ Ⓑ Ⓒ Ⓓ Ⓔ
43 Ⓐ Ⓑ Ⓒ Ⓓ Ⓔ
44 Ⓐ Ⓑ Ⓒ Ⓓ Ⓔ
45 Ⓐ Ⓑ Ⓒ Ⓓ Ⓔ
46 Ⓐ Ⓑ Ⓒ Ⓓ Ⓔ
47 Ⓐ Ⓑ Ⓒ Ⓓ Ⓔ
48 Ⓐ Ⓑ Ⓒ Ⓓ Ⓔ
49 Ⓐ Ⓑ Ⓒ Ⓓ Ⓔ
50 Ⓐ Ⓑ Ⓒ Ⓓ Ⓔ
51 Ⓐ Ⓑ Ⓒ Ⓓ Ⓔ
52 Ⓐ Ⓑ Ⓒ Ⓓ Ⓔ
53 Ⓐ Ⓑ Ⓒ Ⓓ Ⓔ
54 Ⓐ Ⓑ Ⓒ Ⓓ Ⓔ
55 Ⓐ Ⓑ Ⓒ Ⓓ Ⓔ
56 Ⓐ Ⓑ Ⓒ Ⓓ Ⓔ
57 Ⓐ Ⓑ Ⓒ Ⓓ Ⓔ
58 Ⓐ Ⓑ Ⓒ Ⓓ Ⓔ
59 Ⓐ Ⓑ Ⓒ Ⓓ Ⓔ
60 Ⓐ Ⓑ Ⓒ Ⓓ Ⓔ
61 Ⓐ Ⓑ Ⓒ Ⓓ Ⓔ
62 Ⓐ Ⓑ Ⓒ Ⓓ Ⓔ
63 Ⓐ Ⓑ Ⓒ Ⓓ Ⓔ
64 Ⓐ Ⓑ Ⓒ Ⓓ Ⓔ
65 Ⓐ Ⓑ Ⓒ Ⓓ Ⓔ

Mathematical Aptitude Section*

1 Ⓐ Ⓑ Ⓒ Ⓓ Ⓔ
2 Ⓐ Ⓑ Ⓒ Ⓓ Ⓔ
3 Ⓐ Ⓑ Ⓒ Ⓓ Ⓔ
4 Ⓐ Ⓑ Ⓒ Ⓓ Ⓔ
5 Ⓐ Ⓑ Ⓒ Ⓓ Ⓔ
6 Ⓐ Ⓑ Ⓒ Ⓓ Ⓔ
7 Ⓐ Ⓑ Ⓒ Ⓓ Ⓔ
8 Ⓐ Ⓑ Ⓒ Ⓓ Ⓔ
9 Ⓐ Ⓑ Ⓒ Ⓓ Ⓔ
10 Ⓐ Ⓑ Ⓒ Ⓓ Ⓔ
11 Ⓐ Ⓑ Ⓒ Ⓓ Ⓔ
12 Ⓐ Ⓑ Ⓒ Ⓓ Ⓔ
13 Ⓐ Ⓑ Ⓒ Ⓓ Ⓔ
14 Ⓐ Ⓑ Ⓒ Ⓓ Ⓔ
15 Ⓐ Ⓑ Ⓒ Ⓓ Ⓔ
16 Ⓐ Ⓑ Ⓒ Ⓓ Ⓔ
17 Ⓐ Ⓑ Ⓒ Ⓓ Ⓔ
18 Ⓐ Ⓑ Ⓒ Ⓓ Ⓔ
19 Ⓐ Ⓑ Ⓒ Ⓓ Ⓔ
20 Ⓐ Ⓑ Ⓒ Ⓓ Ⓔ
21 Ⓐ Ⓑ Ⓒ Ⓓ Ⓔ
22 Ⓐ Ⓑ Ⓒ Ⓓ Ⓔ
23 Ⓐ Ⓑ Ⓒ Ⓓ Ⓔ
24 Ⓐ Ⓑ Ⓒ Ⓓ Ⓔ
25 Ⓐ Ⓑ Ⓒ Ⓓ Ⓔ
26 Ⓐ Ⓑ Ⓒ Ⓓ Ⓔ
27 Ⓐ Ⓑ Ⓒ Ⓓ Ⓔ
28 Ⓐ Ⓑ Ⓒ Ⓓ Ⓔ
29 Ⓐ Ⓑ Ⓒ Ⓓ Ⓔ
30 Ⓐ Ⓑ Ⓒ Ⓓ Ⓔ
31 Ⓐ Ⓑ Ⓒ Ⓓ Ⓔ
32 Ⓐ Ⓑ Ⓒ Ⓓ Ⓔ
33 Ⓐ Ⓑ Ⓒ Ⓓ Ⓔ
34 Ⓐ Ⓑ Ⓒ Ⓓ Ⓔ
35 Ⓐ Ⓑ Ⓒ Ⓓ Ⓔ
36 Ⓐ Ⓑ Ⓒ Ⓓ Ⓔ
37 Ⓐ Ⓑ Ⓒ Ⓓ Ⓔ
38 Ⓐ Ⓑ Ⓒ Ⓓ Ⓔ
39 Ⓐ Ⓑ Ⓒ Ⓓ Ⓔ
40 Ⓐ Ⓑ Ⓒ Ⓓ Ⓔ
41 Ⓐ Ⓑ Ⓒ Ⓓ Ⓔ
42 Ⓐ Ⓑ Ⓒ Ⓓ Ⓔ
43 Ⓐ Ⓑ Ⓒ Ⓓ Ⓔ
44 Ⓐ Ⓑ Ⓒ Ⓓ Ⓔ
45 Ⓐ Ⓑ Ⓒ Ⓓ Ⓔ
46 Ⓐ Ⓑ Ⓒ Ⓓ Ⓔ
47 Ⓐ Ⓑ Ⓒ Ⓓ Ⓔ
48 Ⓐ Ⓑ Ⓒ Ⓓ Ⓔ
49 Ⓐ Ⓑ Ⓒ Ⓓ Ⓔ
50 Ⓐ Ⓑ Ⓒ Ⓓ Ⓔ

*If there are more answer spaces than you need, leave them blank.

SECTION 1 **Time—50 minutes 65 Questions** For each question in this section, choose the best answer and fill in the corresponding circle on the answer sheet.

Each question below consists of a word in capital letters, followed by five lettered words or phrases. Choose the word or phrase that is most nearly opposite in meaning to the word in capital letters. Since some of the questions require you to distinguish fine shades of meaning, consider all the choices before deciding which is best.

Example:

GOOD: (A) sour (B) bad (C) red (D) hot (E) ugly

Ⓐ ● Ⓒ Ⓓ Ⓔ

1. MUDDLE: (A) wash (B) limit (C) advance (D) clarify (E) change

2. MEDIOCRITY: (A) normality (B) superiority (C) sensitivity (D) vanity (E) stability

3. TAINT: (A) decorate (B) design (C) rejuvenate (D) purify (E) reward

4. INIMITABLE: (A) insignificant (B) predictable (C) avoidable (D) difficult to grasp (E) easy to copy

5. NETTLE: (A) soothe (B) free (C) impress (D) grow (E) desire

6. SUPERFICIAL: (A) profound (B) exaggerated (C) subjective (D) spirited (E) dense

7. DISDAIN: (A) keep (B) discuss (C) endure (D) forbid (E) admire

8. BENEVOLENCE: (A) sameness (B) height (C) descent (D) modernity (E) miserliness

9. AMBIGUOUS: (A) salvageable (B) corresponding (C) responsible (D) clear (E) active

10. VACILLATION: (A) coarseness (B) simplicity (C) retraction (D) firmness (E) tedium

11. COVERT: (A) immutable (B) hostile (C) puzzling (D) generous (E) unconcealed

2. PANDEMONIUM: (A) amusement (B) indolence (C) deceleration (D) tranquillity (E) tolerance

13. ASTUTE: (A) imperceptive (B) affirmative (C) destitute (D) unqualified (E) restrained

14. ARTIFICE: (A) willingness (B) candor (C) incompetence (D) exception (E) loyalty

15. ENERVATE: (A) aggravate (B) stimulate (C) edify (D) applaud (E) disregard

16. DESTITUTION: (A) civilization (B) recompense (C) affluence (D) reformation (E) parsimony

17. RAVENOUS: (A) indifferent (B) colorless (C) sated (D) taciturn (E) contentious

18. ESCHEW: (A) gnaw (B) reproach (C) transform (D) preserve (E) seek

19. ODIUM: (A) monotony (B) irrelevance (C) reticence (D) veneration (E) vigor

20. NEFARIOUS: (A) wanton (B) ephemeral (C) exemplary (D) pusillanimous (E) mortal

Each sentence below has one or two blanks, each blank indicating that something has been omitted. Beneath the sentence are five lettered words or sets of words. Choose the word or set of words that, when inserted in the sentence, best fits the meaning of the sentence as a whole.

Example:

Although its publicity has been ----, the film itself is intelligent, well-acted, handsomely produced, and altogether ----.

(A) tasteless . . respectable (B) extensive . . moderate (C) sophisticated . . amateur (D) risque . . crude (E) perfect . . spectacular

● Ⓑ Ⓒ Ⓓ Ⓔ

21. Concern over the effects of estrogen has ---- in recent weeks as three new studies suggest that birth control pills, which contain estrogen, may increase women's risk of developing breast cancer.
(A) heightened (B) dissipated (C) lapsed (D) suffered (E) alternated

22. Once known only to importers of exotic foreign delicacies, the kiwi fruit has been transplanted successfully to America and is now ---- a much wider market.
(A) accessible to (B) unknown to (C) perplexing to (D) comparable to (E) uncultivated by

23. The debate coach suggested that he eliminate his ---- remarks in his otherwise serious speech because they were inappropriate.
(A) bantering (B) specious (C) solemn (D) tacit (E) perfunctory

24. Measurement is, like any other human endeavor, a complex activity, subject to error, not always used ----, and frequently misinterpreted and ----.
(A) mistakenly . . derided
(B) erratically . . analyzed
(C) systematically . . organized
(D) innovatively . . refined
(E) properly . . misunderstood

25. In one shocking instance of ---- research, one of the nation's most influential researchers in the field of genetics reported on experiments that were never carried out and published deliberately ---- scientific papers on his nonexistent work.
(A) comprehensive . . abstract
(B) theoretical . . challenging
(C) erroneous . . impartial
(D) derivative . . authoritative
(E) fraudulent . . deceptive

26. James Bryce and Harold Laski, household names to intellectuals in another era, appear to have ---- that decent ---- reserved for those whose major works, still in print, are rarely read.
(A) aspired to . . popularity
(B) escaped from . . notoriety
(C) receded into . . obscurity
(D) responded to . . privacy
(E) stumbled upon . . nirvana

27. Her novel published to universal acclaim, her literary gifts acknowledged by the chief figures of the Harlem Renaissance, her reputation as yet ---- by envious slights, Hurston clearly was at the ---- of her career.
(A) undamaged . . ebb
(B) untarnished . . zenith
(C) untainted . . extremity
(D) blackened . . mercy
(E) unmarred . . brink

28 Because he had assumed that the child's first, fierce rush of grief would quickly ----, Murdstone was astonished to find him still ----.
(A) subside . . disconsolate
(B) fade . . irresolute
(C) elapse . . disingenuous
(D) escalate . . forlorn
(E) dwindle . . dormant

29. Glendon provides a dark underside to Frederick Jackson Turner's frontier thesis that saw rugged individualism as the essence of American society—an individualism which she interprets as ---- atomism.
(A) antithetical toward (B) skeptical of
(C) degenerating into (D) aspiring to
(E) renewed by

30. Faced with these massive changes, the government keeps its own counsel: although generally benevolent, it has always been ---- regime.
(A) an altruistic (B) an unpredictable
(C) a reticent (D) a sanguine
(E) an indifferent

Each question below consists of a related pair of words or phrases, followed by five lettered pairs of words or phrases. Select the lettered pair that best expresses a relationship similar to that expressed in the original pair.

Example:

YAWN : BOREDOM : : (A) dream : sleep
(B) anger : madness (C) smile : amusement
(D) face : expression (E) impatience : rebellion

Ⓐ Ⓑ ● Ⓓ Ⓔ

31. CONDUCTOR : ORCHESTRA : :
(A) ballerina : ballet (B) surgeon : hospital
(C) director : cast (D) lawyer : courtroom
(E) tenor : chorus

32. ALPHABET : LETTER : : (A) preface : book
(B) piano : music (C) ruler : distance
(D) deck : card (E) latch : door

33. ESSAYIST : WORDS : : (A) sculptor : chisel
(B) painter : easel (C) soldier : uniform
(D) baker : batter (E) butcher : meat

34. GOLF : LINKS : : (A) baseball : dugout
(B) swimming : laps (C) croquet : mallet
(D) bowling : pins (E) tennis : court

35. SANCTUARY : REFUGE : : (A) oasis : desert
(B) church : pew (C) departure : flight
(D) tree : shade (E) holiday : resort

36. INAUGURATE : PRESIDENT : :
(A) abdicate : king (B) promote : student
(C) campaign : candidate (D) install : officer
(E) succeed : governor

37. RUSTLE : CATTLE : : (A) bleat : sheep
(B) swim : fish (C) pan : gold
(D) speculate : stock (E) hijack : cargo

38. AVARICE : VICE : : (A) charity : virtue
(B) greed : devil (C) motive : suspicion
(D) penury : crime (E) frugality : economy

39. OUTFOX : CUNNING : : (A) outline : thought
(B) outstrip : speed (C) outreach : charity
(D) outrank : bravery (E) outrage : wrath

40. GLINT : LIGHT : : (A) blare : sound
(B) whiff : scent (C) shade : color
(D) glut : food (E) wave : tide

41. EAGER : OVERZEALOUS : :
(A) alluring : repulsive
(B) finicky : fussy
(C) temperate : abstemious
(D) guileless : ingenuous
(E) thrifty : parsimonious

42. MERCURIAL : CONSTANCY : :
(A) sturdy : durability (B) genial : loyalty
(C) ephemeral : permanence
(D) quixotic : idealism (E) diffident : fidelity

43. CACOPHONOUS : HEAR : :
(A) intangible : touch (B) unsavory : taste
(C) olfactory : smell (D) palpable : feel
(E) credulous : believe

44. IMPERTURBABLE : DISCOMPOSE : :
(A) amenable : sway (B) laconic : interpret
(C) boorish : provoke (D) incredulous : convince
(E) egregious : intrude

45. SCOTCH : RUMOR : : (A) divert : traffic
(B) broach : topic (C) suppress : riot
(D) singe : fire (E) spread : gossip

> Each passage below is followed by questions based on its content. Answer the questions following each passage on the basis of what is stated or implied in that passage.

Today, with rare exceptions, these local jails, which are vestiges of a period in which the prison was conceived of as "an antechamber of death," are used to guard persons awaiting trial or sentencing, or serving short sentences, who live in infrahuman conditions, submerged in a state of idleness and corruption.

The penitentiary function that prevails there is one of custody; that is, prevention of escapes or internal disorders. In some the task of production has been added, but only to exploit the free manual labor of the prisoners, who are compelled to render the maximum in collective work, with little or no regard for the process of rehabilitation.

During the last few years isolated attempts have been made to make constructive use of this short period of confinement or, at least, to neutralize its negative influences. We know through the newspapers of the experiment carried out in the local jail by the Chief of Police in the city of Canelones, Uruguay, whose prisoners participate in work projects in the community and enjoy relative liberty while they are at work. In the United States, "juvenile halls" have been built recently in Los Angeles and Denver. Minors detained there participate daily in an intensive vocational program (especially hobbies) of education and recreation while waiting for their cases to come before the Juvenile Court; something similar is being done in houses of detention for adults in Los Angeles County (Rancho Honor Camp).

Other kinds of activities—trade apprenticeships, academic education, and recreation, for example—have been added to those of custody and production, but more as a means of protecting society than of rehabilitating the delinquent. Actually, it has been shown that to submit the penal population to a period of regimented imprisonment, limited to group labor, eating, and sleeping, is ineffectual in changing the antisocial tendencies of the delinquent, who returns to the community with the same or a more dangerous attitude than when he or she committed the crime. To teach delinquents various trades and raise their educational levels would help to convert them into useful persons or, at least, into ones less dangerous to the society into which they will be reintegrated sooner or later.

46. According to the passage, on the whole our present system of imprisonment
(A) does not effectively rehabilitate criminals
(B) deserves to be called an "antechamber of death"
(C) is designed to avenge society on criminals
(D) enables prisoners to live in idleness and corruption
(E) channels prisoners' productivity constructively

47. The primary purpose of this passage is to
(A) denounce the jailing of juvenile offenders in houses of detention
(B) describe the inhumane physical conditions existing in our prisons
(C) compare American penal systems with their foreign counterparts
(D) hypothesize about why some criminals become repeat offenders
(E) explain the ways in which a strictly custodial system has begun to change

48. The author's attitude toward the possibility of turning delinquents into worthwhile citizens can best be described as one of
(A) marked perplexity (B) thoughtless enthusiasm
(C) moral condemnation (D) guarded optimism
(E) cynical disappointment

We still have, in short, all the weapons in the arsenal of satire: the rapier of wit, the broadsword of invective, the stiletto of parody, the Damoclean swords of sarcasm and irony. Their cutting edges are bright and sharp; they glisten with barbs guaranteed to stick and stay stuck in the thickest hide, or stab the most inflated Polonius in the arras. Yet though they hang well-oiled and ready to our hands, we tend to use them separately and gingerly. We are afraid of hurting someone's feelings or of being hurt in a return bout. We tremble at the prospect of treading on someone's moral corns. We are too full of the milquetoast of human kindness. We always see the Other Side of the Case, always remember that our Victim may have a Mom who loves him, always fear that we may be setting him back a few hundred hours in his psychiatric adjustment. Oh, yes. We poke and pry a bit. We pin an errant butterfly to a board or two. But for real lessons in the ungentlest of the arts we must turn back to the older masters.

49. According to the passage, we avoid using satire because we
(A) are apprehensive of its sting
(B) do not comprehend its character
(C) feel inferior to the older masters
(D) are not inquisitive by nature
(E) are too uneducated in its use

50. As used in sentence 3, the word "gingerly" most nearly means
(A) insincerely (B) effectively (C) clumsily
(D) carefully (E) unhappily

51. The passage suggests that modern persons ("we") aspire chiefly to
(A) a sense of emotional security
(B) a feeling of aggressiveness
(C) material wealth
(D) freedom from hunger
(E) protection from satire

52. The tone of the latter part of the passage is one of
(A) outraged dignity (B) pronounced irony
(C) growing distrust (D) calm resignation
(E) happy abandon

The oldest adult human skull yet found belongs to the lowest grade of *Homo erectus*, and to the Australoid line. It is known as Pithecanthropus (Ape-Man) Number 4, because it was the fourth of its kind to be found. All four were unearthed in river banks in central Java. Number 4 is about 700,000 years old, and Numbers 1, 2, and 3 between 600,000 and 500,000. We know this because tektites—small, glassy nodules from outer space—were found in the same beds as the first three, and the beds containing Number 4 lay underneath the tektite bed, along with the bones of a more ancient group of animals. These tektites have been picked up in large numbers in Java, the Philippines, and Australia, where they all fell in a single celestial shower. Their age—approximately 600,000 years—has been accurately measured in several laboratories by nuclear chemical analysis, through the so-called argon-potassium method.

Pithecanthropus Number 4 consists of the back part of a skull and its lower face, palate, and upper teeth. As reconstructed by Weidenreich, it is a brutal-looking skull, with heavy crests behind four powerful neck muscle attachments, a large palate, and large teeth, as in apes. The brain size of this skull was about 900 cubic centimeters; modern human brains range from about 1,450 cc. The brains of apes and Australopithecines are about 350 to 650 cc. So Pithecanthropus Number 4 was intermediate in brain size between apes and living men.

This fragmentary skull was not the only find made in the beds it lay in. Nearby were found the cranial vault of a two-year-old baby, already different from those of living infants, and a piece of chinless adult lower jaw. Two other jaws have been discovered in the same deposits which were much larger than any in the world certainly belonging to *Homo erectus*. They are called Meganthropus (Big Man) and may have belonged to a local kind of Australopithecine, but this is not certain. If so, *Homo erectus* coexisted with, or overlapped, the Australopithecines in Java as well as in South Africa, which implies that man did not originate in either place, but somewhere in between.

53. According to the passage, tektites are
(A) customarily found with the bones of animals
(B) undersized lumps of a glasslike substance
(C) a step in the evolutionary process
(D) equal in age to Ape-Man Number 4
(E) dissolved in a solution of argon-potassium

54. Scientists are certain that Pithecanthropus Number 4 is older than Pithecanthropus Numbers 1, 2, and 3 because
(A) it was discovered later than the others
(B) it was found in the company of tektites
(C) its age was measured by nuclear chemical analysis
(D) it was located below the tektite layer
(E) its skull is larger in cranial capacity

55. According to the passage, archaeological study of Pithecanthropus skulls involves which of the following?
I. Measurement of cranial capacity
II. Piecing together of bone fragments
III. Comparison with analogous primate skulls
(A) I only
(B) II only
(C) I and II only
(D) II and III only
(E) I, II, and III

Mr. Gradgrind walked homeward from the school in a state of considerable satisfaction. It was his school, and he intended it to be a model. He intended every child in it to be a model—just as the young Gradgrinds were all models.

There were five young Gradgrinds, and they were models every one. They had been lectured at from their tenderest years; coursed, like little hares. Almost as soon as they could run alone, they had been made to run to the lecture-room. The first object with which they had an association, or of which they had a remembrance, was a large blackboard with a dry Ogre chalking ghastly white figures on it.

Not that they knew, by name or nature, anything about an Ogre. Fact forbid! I only use the word to express a monster in a lecturing castle, with Heaven knows how many heads manipulated into one, taking childhood captive, and dragging it into gloomy statistical dens by the hair.

No little Gradgrind had ever seen a face in the moon; it was up in the moon before it could speak distinctly. No little Gradgrind had ever learnt the silly jingle, Twinkle, twinkle, little star; how I wonder what you are! No little Gradgrind had ever known wonder on the subject of the stars, each little Gradgrind having at five years old dissected the Great Bear like a Professor Owen, and driven Charles's Wain like a locomotive engine-driver. No little Gradgrind had ever associated a cow in a field with that famous cow with the crumpled horn who tossed the dog who worried the cat who killed the rat who ate the malt, or with that yet more famous cow who swallowed Tom Thumb: it had never heard of those celebrities, and had only been introduced to a cow as a graminivorous ruminating quadruped with several stomachs.

56. The author's tone in describing Thomas Gradgrind's educational methodology is
(A) openly admiring (B) acutely concerned
(C) bitterly scornful (D) broadly satirical
(E) warmly nostalgic

57. The passage suggests that Gradgrind rejects from his curriculum anything that is in the least
(A) analytical (B) mechanical (C) fanciful
(D) dogmatic (E) pragmatic

58. It can be inferred from the passage that the Great Bear and Charles's Wain most likely are
(A) subjects of nursery rhymes
(B) groupings of stars
(C) zoological phenomena
(D) themes of popular songs
(E) popular toys for children

59. Which of the following axioms is closest to Gradgrind's view of education as presented in the passage?
(A) Experience keeps a dear school, but fools will learn in no other.
(B) Let early education be a sort of amusement, that you may be better able to find out the natural bent.
(C) Education is what you have left over after you have forgotten everything you have learned.
(D) A teacher who can arouse a feeling for one single good action accomplishes more than he who fills our memory with rows on rows of natural objects, classified with name and form.
(E) Modern science, as training the mind to an exact and impartial analysis of fact, is an education specially fitted to promote sound citizenship.

60. The author uses all of the following to support the main point of the passage EXCEPT
(A) listing of examples
(B) figurative language
(C) repetition of a phrase
(D) quotations from an authority
(E) allusions to familiar rhymes

Yet, while Darwinian theory extends its domain, some of its cherished postulates are slipping, or at least losing their generality. The "modern synthesis," the contemporary version of Darwinism that has reigned for thirty years, took the model of adaptive gene substitution within local populations as an adequate account, by accumulation and extension, of life's entire history. The model may work well in its empirical domain of minor, local, adaptive adjustment; populations of the moth *Biston betularia* did turn black, by substitution of a single gene, as a selected response for decreased visibility on trees that had been blackened by industrial soot. But is the origin of a new species simply this process extended to more genes and greater effect? Are larger evolutionary trends within major lineages just a further accumulation of sequential adaptive changes?

Many evolutionists (myself included) are beginning to challenge this synthesis and to assert the hierarchical view that different levels of evolutionary change often reflect different kinds of causes. Minor adjustment within populations may be sequential and adaptive. But speciation may occur by major chromosomal changes that establish sterility with other species for reasons unrelated to adaptation. Evolutionary trends may represent a kind of higher level selection upon essentially static species themselves, not the slow and steady alteration of a single large population through untold ages.

Before the modern synthesis, many biologists (see Bateson, 1922, in bibliography) expressed confusion and depression because the proposed mechanisms of evolution at different levels seemed contradictory enough to preclude a unified science. After the modern synthesis, the notion spread (amounting almost to a dogma among its less thoughtful lieutenants) that all evolution could be reduced to the basic Darwinism of gradual, adaptive change within local populations. I think that we are now pursuing a fruitful path between the anarchy of Bateson's day and the restriction of view imposed by the modern synthesis. The modern synthesis works in its appropriate arena, but the same Darwinian processes of mutation and selection may operate in strikingly different ways at higher domains in a hierarchy of evolutionary levels. I think that we may hope for uniformity of causal agents, hence a single, general theory with a Darwinian core. But we must reckon with a multiplicity of mechanisms that preclude the explanation of higher level phenomena by the model of adaptive gene substitution favored for the lowest level.

At the basis of all this ferment lies nature's irreducible complexity. Organisms are not billiard balls, propelled by simple and measurable external forces to predictable new positions on life's pool table. Sufficiently complex systems have greater richness. Organisms have a history that constrains their future in myriad, subtle ways. Their complexity of form entails a host of functions incidental to whatever pressures of natural selection superintended the initial construction. Their intricate and largely unknown pathways of embryonic development guarantee that simple inputs (minor changes in timing, for example) may be translated into marked and surprising changes in output (the adult organism).

Charles Darwin chose to close his great book with a striking comparison that expresses this richness. He contrasted the simpler system of planetary motion, and its result of endless, static cycling, with the complexity of life and its wondrous and unpredictable change through the ages:

> There is grandeur in this view of life, with its several powers, having been originally breathed into a few forms or into one; and that, whilst this planet has gone cycling on according to the fixed law of gravity, from so simple a beginning endless forms most beautiful and most wonderful have been, and are being, evolved.

61. According to the author, many contemporary evolutionists find the Darwinian synthesis
(A) wholly unfounded (B) too restrictive
(C) essentially contradictory (D) sadly confusing
(E) strikingly productive

62. The author does all of the following EXCEPT
(A) denounce an adversary
(B) pose a question
(C) provide an example
(D) use a metaphor
(E) refer to an authority

63. The author's attitude toward the modern synthesis can best be described as
(A) hostile and dogmatic
(B) derisive and scornful
(C) impatient and ruthless
(D) critical but appreciative
(E) indifferent but philosophical

64. In asserting the complexity of nature, the author refers to billiard balls on life's pool table (paragraph 4) as
(A) an illustration of the unpredictable changes of nature
(B) an example of confusion and mobility
(C) an instance of a relatively uncomplicated system
(D) an application of the fixed law of gravity
(E) an accurate model of genetic change

65. It can be inferred that the paragraph immediately preceding this passage most likely discussed
(A) the absence of a unified theory of evolution
(B) individuals challenging the Darwinian synthesis
(C) the expansion of evolutionary theory into new realms
(D) experimental methods of genetic substitution
(E) the place of genetics in the study of natural history

SECTION 2 Time—50 minutes 50 Questions

In this section solve each problem, using any available space on the page for scratchwork. Then decide which is the best of the choices given and fill in the corresponding circle on the answer sheet.

The following information is for your reference in solving some of the problems.

Circle of radius r: Area $= \pi r^2$ Circumference $= 2\pi r$
The number of degrees of arc in a circle is 360.
The measure in degrees of a straight angle is 180.

Definitions of symbols:

- $=$ is equal to
- $\neq$ is unequal to
- $<$ is less than
- $>$ is greater than
- $\leqq$ is less than or equal to
- $\geqq$ is greater than or equal to
- $\parallel$ is parallel to
- $\perp$ is perpendicular to

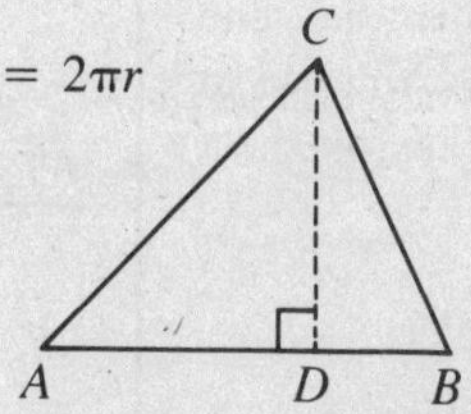

Triangle: The sum of the measures in degrees of the angles of a triangle is 180.

If $\angle CDA$ is a right angle, then

(1) area of $\triangle ABC = \frac{AB \times CD}{2}$

(2) $AC^2 = AD^2 + DC^2$

Note: Figures that accompany problems in this test are intended to provide information useful in solving the problems. They are drawn as accurately as possible EXCEPT when it is stated in a specific problem that its figure is not drawn to scale. All figures lie in a plane unless otherwise indicated. All numbers used are real numbers.

1. $\dfrac{\frac{1}{2} + \frac{1}{3}}{1.2} =$
   (A) $\frac{1}{30}$ (B) $\frac{5}{6}$ (C) $\frac{25}{36}$ (D) 1 (E) $4\frac{4}{5}$

2. Which of the following is largest?
   (A) $\left(\frac{1}{5}\right)^2$ (B) $\frac{5}{0.5}$ (C) 5.5 (D) $\frac{0.5}{5}$ (E) $\sqrt{5}$

3. Which of the following is equal to $\dfrac{(9^{-2}) + (9^{-1})}{(81^0)(9^{-2})}$?
   (A) 0 (B) $\frac{1}{10}$ (C) $\frac{1}{9}$ (D) $\frac{3}{2}$ (E) 10

4. $0.005 =$
   (A) 0.05% (B) $\frac{1}{10}$% (C) $\frac{1}{2}$% (D) 5%
   (E) 50%

5. $\dfrac{x + n}{n}$ equals
   (A) x (B) nx (C) $x + 1$
   (D) $\frac{x}{n} + 1$ (E) $nx + 1$

6. For which of the following values of x and y is $\frac{x}{y} > 1$?
   (A) $x = 0, y = 1$ (B) $x = 1, y = 1$
   (C) $x = 1, y = 2$ (D) $x = 3, y = 2$
   (E) $x = 3, y = 4$

7. Ten years ago I was x years old. How old will I be ten years from now?
   (A) $10x$ (B) $20x$ (C) $x + 10$
   (D) $x + 20$ (E) $2x - 20$

8. How many 4-cent baseball cards can be purchased for $4D$ dollars?
   (A) D (B) $16D$ (C) $400D$ (D) $100D$
   (E) $\frac{16D}{100}$

9. If $n[^{-3}_{+5}$ means that both $n - 3$ and $n + 5$ are divisible by 8, n could have any one of the following values EXCEPT
   (A) 51 (B) 59 (C) 64 (D) 67 (E) 75

10. What is the minimum weight in ounces of 69 eggs taken from a crate containing a grade of eggs weighing 24 to 26 ounces per dozen?
    (A) 115 (B) 137 (C) 138 (D) 139
    (E) 140

11. Martin rides to Cambridge, 30 miles away from home, at the average rate of 10 miles per hour. He returns on a better road that is 50% longer where he can increase his rate by 100%. How much time does he save by taking the better road on his return trip?
    (A) $2\frac{1}{4}$ minutes (B) 15 minutes (C) 45 minutes
    (D) 2 hours 15 minutes (E) 2 hours 45 minutes

12. A man buys a boat for $16,000. He wishes to sell it at a profit of $1000 after paying the legal fees of $100 and a commission of 5% of the selling price. He must sell the boat for
    (A) $17,100 (B) $17,800 (C) $17,900
    (D) $18,000 (E) $18,850

13. At the end of spring training a football coach discharged $\frac{1}{5}$ of his squad and asked the remaining 32 boys to report on Labor Day. The number of boys on the squad at the end of spring training was
    (A) 40 (B) 80 (C) 100 (D) 120 (E) 160

14. A stick 35 inches long is to be cut so that one piece is $\frac{1}{4}$ as long as the other. How many inches long must the shorter piece be?
    (A) 5 (B) 7 (C) 10 (D) 12 (E) 15

15. Formerly, $\frac{1}{6}$ of a pie cost 20¢. Now the price of $\frac{1}{8}$ of a pie is 30¢. The percent increase is
(A) 10% (B) 20% (C) $33\frac{1}{3}$% (D) 50%
(E) 100%

Questions 16-32 each consist of two quantities, one in Column A and one in Column B. You are to compare the two quantities and on the answer sheet fill in circle

A if the quantity in Column A is greater;
B if the quantity in Column B is greater;
C if the two quantities are equal;
D if the relationship cannot be determined from the information given.

Notes:
1. In certain questions, information concerning one or both of the quantities to be compared is centered above the two columns.
2. In a given question, a symbol that appears in both columns represents the same thing in Column A as it does in Column B.
3. Letters such as x, n, and k stand for real numbers.

EXAMPLES

	Column A	Column B	Answers
E1.	2×6	$2 + 6$	● Ⓑ Ⓒ Ⓓ
	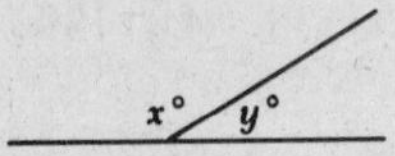		
E2.	$180 - x$	y	Ⓐ Ⓑ ● Ⓓ
E3.	$p - q$	$q - p$	Ⓐ Ⓑ Ⓒ ●

	Column A	Column B
16.	2^3	3^2
17.	$\sqrt{14.4}$	4

$\frac{1}{x} > 1$

18.	x	1

$81 < x < 100$

19.	$\sqrt{x}$	9

The average of 5 and a is 5.

20.	a	5
21.	The square of 0.5	The reciprocal of 4

	Column A	Column B

$3x - 6 = 1$

22.	$x - 2$	$\frac{1}{3}$
23.	$\frac{1}{\sqrt{25}}$	20%

$\frac{a}{3} = b$

24.	$3a$	$9b$

$x < 5$

25.	$(x + 5)(x - 5)$	$x^2 - 25$

$abc = 0$ and $a = 1$

26.	bc	1

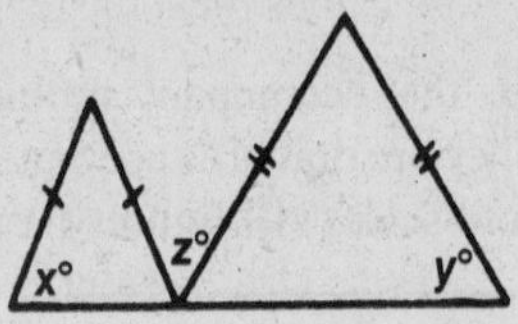

$x = 70$ and $y = 40$

27.	x	z

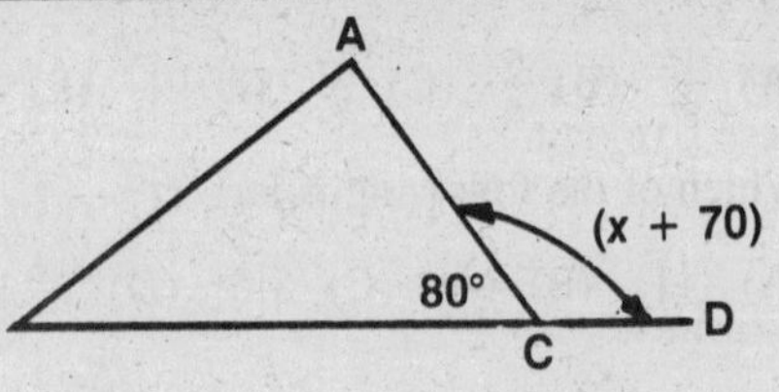

BD is a straight line segment.

28.	x	30

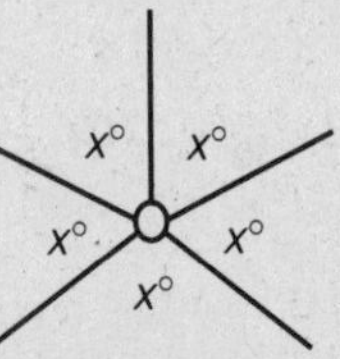

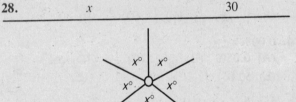

Five line segments meet at point O.

29.	$2x$	72

The operation $\triangle$ is defined by the equation $a \triangle b = a^2 + b^2$.

$xy \neq 0$

30.	$(x \triangle y)^2$	$x^2 \triangle y^2$

$x + 5 = 5 - y$

31.	$x + y$	$x - y$

Judith covered 120 miles in 4 hours and returned over the same route in 3 hours.

32.	The average speed for the entire trip	35 miles per hour

Solve each of the remaining problems in this section using any available space for scratchwork. Then decide which is the best of the choices given and fill in the corresponding circle on the answer sheet.

33. Which of the following is (are) always true for $\triangle ABC$?
I. $AB + BC = AC$
II. $BC + AC > AB$
III. $AB + BC > AC + BC$
(A) I only (B) II only (C) III only
(D) I and II only (E) I, II, and III

34. A baseball team has won 15 games and lost 9. If these games represent $16\frac{2}{3}\%$ of the games to be played, how many more games must the team win to average .750 for the season?
(A) 63 (B) 75 (C) 93 (D) 100 (E) 108

35. The oil burner in a certain house is used to heat the house and to heat the hot water. During the seven cold months when the house is heated, an average of 200 gallons of oil a month is used. In the remaining five months, when the house is not heated, a total of 200 gallons of oil is used. What percentage of the year's oil supply is required to heat water during these five months?
(A) $\frac{1}{8}\%$ (B) 7% (C) 8% (D) $12\frac{1}{2}\%$
(E) 14%

36. $x^2 + y = 9$
$x^2 - y = -1$
$y =$
(A) 1 (B) ± 3 (C) 5 (D) 8 (E) 10

37. $17xy = 22xy - 5$
$x^2y^2 =$
(A) 0 (B) 1 (C) -5 (D) 5 (E) $7\frac{4}{5}$

38. A man pays $8.00 at the box office for 3 adult admission tickets and 4 children admission tickets. If children pay half the admission fee charged for adults, the fee for adults must be
(A) 80¢ (B) $1.00 (C) $1.60 (D) $1.80
(E) $3.20

39. On a rectangular graph, which of the following points will be the same distance from the origin as (3,0)?
I. (0,3)
II. (−3,0)
III. (3,3)
(A) I only (B) II only (C) III only
(D) I and II only (E) I, II, and III

40. If $A = \frac{2}{3}B$, $B = \frac{2}{3}C$, and $C = \frac{2}{3}D$, what part of D is B?
(A) $\frac{8}{27}$ (B) $\frac{4}{9}$ (C) $\frac{2}{3}$ (D) 75 (E) $\frac{4}{3}$

41. Candy formerly sold at $1.76 for a one-pound box is now sold in eight-ounce packages for 96¢. The ratio of the old price to the new price is
(A) 11:6 (B) 6:11 (C) 1.7:1 (D) 11:12
(E) 12:11

42. The number of telephones in a certain town is 48,000. If this represents 12.8 telephones per 100 of population, the population of this town to the nearest thousand is
(A) 128,000 (B) 375,000 (C) 378,000
(D) 566,000 (E) 560,000

43. Find the area of a triangle whose sides are 5, 8, and 5.
(A) 3 (B) 12 (C) 12.5 (D) 20 (E) 24

44. If O is the center of a circle, $AO = 3x + 2$ and $OB = 5x - 4$, find the diameter AOB of the circle.
(A) 3 (B) 6 (C) 9
(D) 11 (E) 22

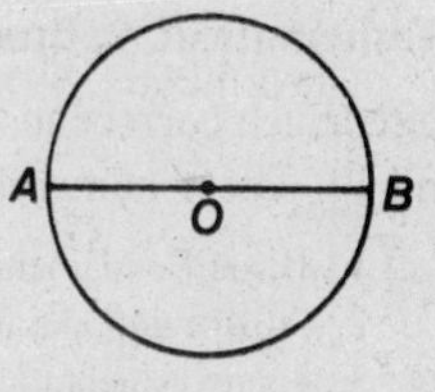

45. AOD is a diameter of circle O. The coordinates of points A and D are $(-11, -5)$ and $(-3, -5)$. Find the area of circle O.
(A) 9π (B) 16π (C) 25π (D) 64π
(E) 116π

46. If the area of a circle is twice the area of a triangle whose base is 4π and whose altitude is 4, the radius of the circle equals
(A) $\sqrt{32}$ (B) 2 (C) 4 (D) 8 (E) 32

47. In parallelogram $ABCD$ $\angle B \stackrel{\circ}{=} \angle A + \angle C$; $\angle D \stackrel{\circ}{=}$
(A) 60 (B) 120 (C) 135 (D) 180 (E) 240

48. In $\triangle ABC$ $AB = 1.37$, $BC = 5.19$; AC may equal
(A) 6.55 (B) 6.57 (C) 6.59 (D) 6.61
(E) 6.63

49. $AB \perp BC$, $BD \perp ADC$. $AD = 9$, $DC = 16$. Find AB.
(A) 7 (B) 12 (C) 15
(D) $\sqrt{237}$ (E) cannot be determined from given information

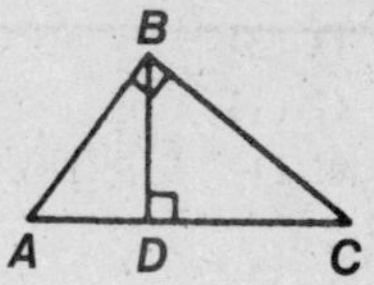

50. Which two of the following are equal?
I. $1 + \dfrac{x}{y}$
II. y
III. $\dfrac{y^2 + 2xy}{xy}$
IV. $\dfrac{y}{x}$
V. $\dfrac{2x + y}{x}$
(A) I and III (B) I and IV (C) I and V
(D) III and V (E) II and V

ANSWER KEY

Verbal Aptitude Section

1. **D**	*11.* **E**	*21.* **A**	*31.* **C**	*41.* **E**	*51.* **A**	*61.* **B**
2. **B**	*12.* **D**	*22.* **A**	*32.* **D**	*42.* **C**	*52.* **B**	*62.* **A**
3. **D**	*13.* **A**	*23.* **A**	*33.* **D**	*43.* **B**	*53.* **B**	*63.* **D**
4. **E**	*14.* **B**	*24.* **E**	*34.* **E**	*44.* **D**	*54.* **D**	*64.* **C**
5. **A**	*15.* **B**	*25.* **E**	*35.* **D**	*45.* **C**	*55.* **E**	*65.* **C**
6. **A**	*16.* **C**	*26.* **C**	*36.* **D**	*46.* **A**	*56.* **D**	
7. **E**	*17.* **C**	*27.* **B**	*37.* **E**	*47.* **E**	*57.* **C**	
8. **E**	*18.* **E**	*28.* **A**	*38.* **A**	*48.* **D**	*58.* **B**	
9. **D**	*19.* **D**	*29.* **C**	*39.* **B**	*49.* **A**	*59.* **E**	
10. **D**	*20.* **C**	*30.* **C**	*40.* **B**	*50.* **D**	*60.* **D**	

Mathematical Aptitude Section

Note: Each correct answer to the mathematics questions is keyed by number to the corresponding topic in Chapters 9 and 10. These numerals refer to the topics listed below, with specific page references in parentheses.

1. Basic Fundamental Operations (155–157)
2. Algebraic Operations (157–160)
3. Using Algebra (160–164)
4. Exponents, Roots and Radicals (159–160)
5. Inequalities (164–165)
6. Fractions (176–178)
7. Decimals (176)
8. Percent (178–180)
9. Averages (180–181)
10. Motion (182–183)
11. Ratio and Proportion (183–185)
12. Mixtures and Solutions (177–178)
13. Work (185–186)
14. Coordinate Geometry (172–173)
15. Geometry (165–172, 173–176)
16. Quantitative Comparisons (189–192)

ANSWER KEY

1. **C** (6,7)	*11.* **C** (8,10)	*21.* **C** (4,6,16)	*31.* **D** (2,16)	*41.* **D** (11)
2. **B** (4,6,7)	*12.* **D** (3,8)	*22.* **C** (2,16)	*32.* **B** (10,16)	*42.* **B** (11)
3. **E** (4,6)	*13.* **A** (3,6)	*23.* **C** (2,4,8,16)	*33.* **B** (15)	*43.* **B** (15)
4. **C** (7,8)	*14.* **B** (3)	*24.* **C** (2,16)	*34.* **C** (8)	*44.* **E** (15)
5. **D** (2,6)	*15.* **E** (8)	*25.* **C** (2,16)	*35.* **D** (8)	*45.* **B** (15)
6. **D** (6)	*16.* **B** (4,16)	*26.* **B** (2,16)	*36.* **C** (2)	*46.* **C** (15)
7. **D** (2)	*17.* **B** (4,16)	*27.* **C** (15,16)	*37.* **B** (2)	*47.* **B** (15)
8. **D** (3)	*18.* **D** (6,16)	*28.* **C** (15,16)	*38.* **C** (3)	*48.* **A** (15)
9. **C** (1)	*19.* **A** (4,16)	*29.* **A** (15,16)	*39.* **D** (14)	*49.* **C** (15)
10. **C** (1)	*20.* **C** (9,16)	*30.* **A** (2,16)	*40.* **B** (1,6)	*50.* **D** (2,6)

SCORING CHART TYPICAL TEST J

Verbal Section		**Mathematical Section***		
No. correct	______	No. correct	(A)	______
No. omitted	______	No. incorrect (# 1-15, 33-50)	(B)	______
No. incorrect	______	No. incorrect (# 16-32)	(C)	______
¼ no. incorrect	______	¼ (B) + 1/3 (C)	(D)	______
Raw Score: (no. correct minus ¼ no. incorrect)	______	*Raw Score* = (A) − (D)		______

* (In the Mathematical section, deduct ¼ of a point for each five-choice question answered incorrectly and 1/3 of a point for each four-choice question answered incorrectly.)

EVALUATION CHART

Study your score. Your raw score on the Verbal and Mathematical Aptitude Sections is an indication of your probable achievement on the PSAT/NMSQT. As a guide to the amount of work you need or want to do, study the following.

Raw Score: *Verbal*	Raw Score: *Mathematical*	Self-rating
58-65	41-50	Superior
46-57	25-40	Very good
40-45	20-24	Satisfactory
36-39	16-19	Average
30-35	10-15	Needs further study
20-29	7-9	Needs intensive study
0-19	0-6	Probably inadequate

ANSWER EXPLANATIONS

Verbal Aptitude Section

1. **D** The opposite of to *muddle* or confuse is to *clarify*. Think of "muddling your brain with a few drinks."
2. **B** The opposite of *mediocrity* (bare adequacy or inferiority) is *superiority*. Think of being unwilling to "settle for mediocrity."
3. **D** The opposite of to *taint* or contaminate is to *purify*. Think of "being tainted with corruption."
4. **E** The opposite of *inimitable* (matchless; impossible to imitate) is *easy to copy*. Context Clue: "Michael Jackson's dancing is inimitable."
5. **A** The opposite of to *nettle* or irritate is to *soothe*. Think of "nettling someone with stinging words."
6. **A** The opposite of *superficial* (shallow; surface) is *profound* or deep. Think of "only a superficial cut."
7. **E** The opposite of to *disdain* or scorn is to *admire*. Think of "disdaining one's inferiors."
8. **E** The opposite of *benevolence* (kindness; generosity) is *miserliness* (stinginess). Think of "admirable benevolence."
9. **D** The opposite of *ambiguous* (uncertain; vague) is *clear*. Think of "puzzling, ambiguous directions."
10. **D** The opposite of *vacillation* (wavering; lack of resolution) is *firmness*. Think of "vacillation between two answer choices."
11. **E** The opposite of *covert* (secret; hidden) is *unconcealed*. Think of "C.I.A. covert operations."
12. **D** The opposite of *pandemonium* or tumultuous uproar is *tranquillity* or calm. Word Parts Clue: *Pan-* means all; *demon-* means evil spirit. Hell or *pandemonium*, the place where all the evil spirits dwell, is a place of noise and uproar. Think of "pandemonium breaking loose."
13. **A** The opposite of *astute* (keen-witted; discerning) is *imperceptive* (undiscerning; dull). Think of being praised for "an astute observation."
14. **B** The opposite of *artifice* (cunning; trickery) is *candor* (frankness; openness). Note this is a less familiar, secondary meaning of *artifice*. Think of "using artifice to deceive."
15. **B** To *enervate* (weaken or enfeeble) is the opposite of to *stimulate* or energize. Think of being "enervated by the heat."
16. **C** The opposite of *destitution* (privation; lack of life's necessities) is *affluence* or wealth. Think of "the poor living in destitution."
17. **C** The opposite of *ravenous* (extremely hungry) is *sated* or satisfied. Beware of eye-catchers. Choice **E** is incorrect. *Contentious* means quarrelsome; it has nothing to do with being satisfied or *content*. Think of "a ravenous appetite."
18. **E** The opposite of to *eschew* or shun is to *seek*. Beware of eye-catchers. Choice **A** is incorrect. *Eschew* is unrelated to chewing or gnawing. Think of "eschewing violence and seeking peace."
19. **D** The opposite of *odium* (detestation; reproach) is *veneration* or honor. Context Clue: "Hitler's crimes against humanity caused him to be held in universal odium."

20. **C** The opposite of *nefarious* or extremely wicked is *exemplary* or extremely good.
Think of "nefarious misdeeds."

21. **A** Logically, such bleak information would make people more worried about using pills containing estrogen. Thus, concern over the effects of estrogen would *heighten*.

22. **A** Because it can now be grown successfully in America, the once-rare fruit is now *accessible* or readily available to American consumers.

23. **A** *Bantering* or joking remarks are inappropriate in a serious speech.

24. **E** The sentence lists negative aspects of measurement. One is that it is *not* always used *properly* or correctly. Another is that it is often *misunderstood*. Note that, while the first missing word must be positive, the second must be negative.

25. **E** Though scientists might be upset by *erroneous* (faulty) or *derivative* (unoriginal) work, the scientific community would be most shocked by *fraudulent* or faked research that was intentionally *deceptive* or deceitful.

26. **C** If Bryce's and Laski's works are now rarely read, these once-prominent figures have *receded into obscurity*. Here *obscurity* is the opposite of *fame*.

27. **B** A writer whose work was universally acclaimed or applauded and whose reputation was not yet *tarnished* or stained would be at the *zenith* or high point of her career.

28. **A** If you expected someone's grief to die down or *subside* quickly, you would be surprised to find that he continued to grieve and was hopelessly unhappy (*disconsolate*).

29. **C** The key phrase here is "dark underside." People usually consider individualism as something positive. Glendon sees its negative side. She interprets it as *degenerating* or disintegrating into atomism—the fragmentation of society into mutually antagonistic units.

30. **C** The key phrase here is "keeps its own counsel." The government is not talking; thus, it can be described as a *reticent* or uncommunicative regime.

31. **C** A *conductor* leads or directs an *orchestra;* a *director* guides or directs a *cast*.
(Function)

32. **D** An *alphabet* is made up of individual *letters;* a *deck* is made up of individual *cards*.
(Part to Whole)

33. **D** *Words* are the medium an *essayist* employs when creating an essay; *batter* is the material a *baker* uses when preparing a cake.
(Worker and Material)

34. **E** *Golf* is played on a golf course or *links; tennis* is played on a *court*.
(Location)

35. **D** A *sanctuary* (place of safety) provides one with shelter or *refuge;* a *tree* provides one with shelter or *shade*.
(Function)

36. **D** To *inaugurate* a *president* is to introduce him or her into office. To *install* an *officer* is to do the same.
(Function)

37. **E** To *rustle cattle* is to steal them. To *hijack cargo* is to steal it.
Note that you are dealing with a secondary meaning of the verb *rustle* here.
(Defining Characteristic)

38. **A** *Avarice* or greed is the name of a particular *vice* (evil quality); *charity* or love is the name of a particular *virtue* (good quality).
(Class and Member)

39. **B** To *outfox* someone is to surpass that person in *cunning;* to *outstrip* someone is to surpass that person in *speed*.
(Defining Characteristic)

40. **B** A *glint* is a small gleam of *light*. A *whiff* is a slight puff of *scent*.
(Degree of Intensity)

41. **E** Someone *overzealous* is excessively *eager;* someone *parsimonious* (stingy) is excessively *thrifty*.
(Degree of Intensity)

42. **C** *Mercurial* (flighty; changeable) by definition means lacking *constancy; ephemeral* (temporary; fleeting) by definition means lacking *permanence*. Beware of eye-catchers. Choice **E** is incorrect. Someone *diffident* by definition lacks faith in himself; he does not necessarily lack *fidelity* or loyalty to others.
(Antonym Variant)

43. **B** Something *cacophonous* (discordant; harsh-sounding) is unpleasant to *hear;* something *unsavory* (unpalatable; disagreeable in taste) is unpleasant to *taste*.
(Defining Characteristic)

44. **D** Someone *imperturbable* (unexcitable; calm) is difficult to *discompose* or agitate; someone *incredulous* (disbelieving) is difficult to *convince*.
(Antonym Variant)

45. **C** To *scotch* or block a *rumor* is to crush it. To *suppress* or quell a *riot* is to crush it.
(Defining Characteristic)

46. **A** Sentence 2 of the final paragraph states that regimented imprisonment "is ineffectual in changing the antisocial tendencies of the delinquent." Thus, our present system *does not effectively rehabilitate* or reform those imprisoned.

47. **E** The author details a variety of reforms, both American and foreign, that show how the present system (whose main aim has been to keep offenders in custody) has begun to change.
Choice **A** is incorrect. While the author mentions that juvenile offenders may be held in houses of detention, he does not condemn or *denounce* this practice. Choice **B** is incorrect. While the author states in passing that prisoners in jails live in "infrahuman conditions," his chief aim is not to describe these conditions. Choice **C** is incorrect. Though the author mentions both American and South American penal systems, he is not making a detailed comparison of the two. Choice **D** is incorrect. The author fails to touch on this topic at all.

48. **D** The author favorably reports on those changes in the penal system that would promote the rehabilitation of offenders. However, he is not totally optimistic that these attempts will turn prisoners into good citizens; his more modest hope is that they will turn prisoners into less dangerous members of society. Thus, his attitude is one of *guarded* (cautious) *optimism*.

49. **A** Sentence 4 indicates that we fail to speak or write satirically because we are afraid or *apprehensive*.

50. **D** The fear of hurting someone's feeling makes us act carefully or *gingerly*.

51. **A** According to the passage, we are afraid of delaying people in their progress toward a perfect psychological readjustment. This suggests that it is of great importance for people to gain such a *sense of emotional security*.

52. **B** The author is clearly mocking the foibles and follies of modern persons. His tone is one of *pronounced* (noticeable; definite) *irony*.

53. **B** *Tektites* are defined in paragraph 1 as "small, glassy nodules from outer space." Note how the phrase defining the new term immediately follows the introduction of the term and is set off by dashes.

54. **D** Paragraph 1 indicates that Pithecanthropus Numbers 1, 2, and 3 lay within the tektite layer, while Pithecanthropus Number 4 lay below it.

55. **E** According to the passage, archaeologists reconstructed or *pieced together* the skull's fragments, measured its brain size (*cranial capacity*), and compared it with the skulls of modern men and apes (*primate skulls*). Thus, archaeological study of the skulls involves all three of the aspects listed.

56. **D** The author is poking fun at Gradgrind's teaching methods and is thus *broadly satirical* (full of ridicule).

57. **C** Gradgrind never introduces his pupils to nursery rhymes or to fantasy creatures such as ogres. This suggests that he rejects from his curriculum anything that is in the least *fanciful* or imaginative.

58. **B** The little Gradgrinds, having studied the Great Bear and Charles's Wain, had never "known wonder on the subject of stars." This suggests that the Great Bear and the Wain are constellations, or *groupings of stars*.

59. **E** Gradgrind's main idea is to fill his pupils full of *facts*, particularly facts about *science* (statistics, constellations, graminivorous quadrupeds, etc.).

60. **D** The author lists examples of the Gradgrinds' studies, uses figurative language (images—being "coursed like little hares" or dragged by the hair into "statistical dens"), repeats a phrase ("No little Gradgrind had ever . . ."), and alludes or refers to well-known nursery rhymes ("Twinkle, twinkle, little star"). He does not quote from an authority.

61. **B** In the third paragraph, the author mentions the "restriction of view" imposed by the modern synthesis, a synthesis he and many of his fellow evolutionists have challenged.
Choice **A** is incorrect. The author states that the "modern synthesis works in its appropriate arena." Choices **C** and **D** are incorrect. It was prior to the modern synthesis that scientists such as Bateson found the proposed mechanisms of evolution confusing and *contradictory*. Choice **E** is incorrect. The author finds the current rethinking of evolutionary theory to be productive; he finds the Darwinian synthesis simplistic.

62. **A** The author poses questions about how well Darwinism works as a model and cites *Biston betularia* as an example of minor, local, adaptive adjustment. He uses the metaphor of the pool table, and refers to Bateson and to Darwin, quoting the latter. He never *denounces* or censures an opponent.

63. **D** The author is both *critical* of the modern synthesis's limitations and *appreciative* of its usefulness in explaining certain phenomena.

64. **C** The movement of billiard balls on a pool table is relatively simple to predict: you can measure the forces involved and figure out where the balls will go. Compared to the complexity of life, the billiard ball provides *an instance of a relatively uncomplicated system*.

65. **C** The opening sentence briefly mentions Darwinian theory's extending its domain, stating that while it has been doing so some problems have arisen. This suggests that the author has just been discussing the *expansion* or extension of evolutionary theory into new fields.

Mathematical Aptitude Section

1. **C** $\frac{1}{2} + \frac{1}{3} = \frac{5}{6}$

$\frac{5}{6} \div 1.2 = \frac{5}{6} \div 1\frac{1}{5} = \frac{5}{6} \div \frac{6}{5} = \frac{5}{6} \cdot \frac{5}{6} = \frac{25}{36}$

2. **B** (A) $\left(\frac{1}{5}\right)^2 = \frac{1}{25}$

(B) $\frac{5}{0.5} = \frac{50}{5} = 10$

(C) 5.5

(D) $\frac{0.5}{5} = \frac{5}{50} = \frac{1}{10}$

(E) $\sqrt{5} = 2+$.

3. **E** $\frac{(9^{-2}) + (9^{-1})}{(81^0)(9^{-2})} = \frac{\frac{1}{9^2} + \frac{1}{9}}{(1)\left(\frac{1}{9^2}\right)} = \frac{\frac{1}{81} + \frac{1}{9}}{\frac{1}{81}} = \frac{\frac{10}{81}}{\frac{1}{81}} = 10$

4. **C** $5\% = \frac{5}{100}$

$0.005 = \frac{5}{1000}$

$0.005 = \frac{0.5}{100} = 0.5\% = \frac{1}{2}\%$

5. **D** $\frac{x + n}{n} = \frac{x}{n} + \frac{n}{n} = \frac{x}{n} + 1$

6. **D** In order for $\frac{x}{y}$ to be greater than 1, x must be greater than y. This is true only in (D).

7. **D** If my age was x years ten years ago, then I am now $x + 10$ years old. In tens year I will be $x + 10 + 10$ or $x + 20$ years old.

8. **D** This is a direct proportion. Let x = number of cards that can be purchased for $4D$ dollars.

$\frac{\text{number of baseball cards}}{\text{dollars}} = \frac{25}{1} = \frac{x}{4D}$

$x = 100D$

9. **C** Notice that 64 is divisible by 8; therefore a number 3 less than 64 or 5 greater than 64 cannot be divisible by 8. You can also test each choice; if you use this strategy, notice that it is necessary to test only one of the requirements, for if $n - 3$ is divisible by 8, then $n + 5$ must also be since it exceeds $n - 3$ by 8.

10. **C** Minimum weight of 1 dozen eggs = 24 ounces
Minimum weight of 1 egg = 2 ounces
Minimum weight of 69 eggs = 138 ounces

11. **C** Distance ÷ rate = time
Trip to Cambridge: 30 miles ÷ 10 miles per hour = 3 hours
Trip from Cambridge: 45 miles ÷ 20 miles per hour = $2\frac{1}{4}$ hours
Saving = $\frac{3}{4}$ hour = 45 minutes

12. **D** Selling price = cost + \$1000 + \$100 + 5% of selling price
Let x = selling price.

$x = \$16{,}000 + \$1000 + \$100 + 0.05x$

$x - 0.05x = 17100$

$0.95x = 17100$

$95x = 1710000$

$x = \$18{,}000$

13. **A** Let x = number of boys on the squad at the end of spring training.

$\frac{4}{5}x = 32$

$x = 40$

14. **B** Let x = length (inches) of shorter piece.
Then $4x$ = length (inches) of longer piece.

$4x + x = 35$

$5x = 35$

$x = 7$

15. **E** Formerly, $\frac{1}{6}$ pie cost 20¢. A pie cost \$1.20
Now $\frac{1}{8}$ pie costs 30¢. A pie costs \$2.40.

$\frac{\text{change}}{\text{original}} = \frac{\$1.20}{\$1.20} = 1 = 100\%$

16. **B** $2^3 = (2)(2)(2) = 8$

$3^2 = (3)(3) = 9$

17. **B** $\sqrt{14.4} = 3+$

18. **D** If x has a negative value, the correct answer would be (B). If x is positive, the correct answer would be (A). Therefore the correct answer is (D).

19. **A** $\sqrt{81} = 9$

$\sqrt{100} = 10$

The square root of x is more than 9 but less than 10.

$9+ > 9$

20. **C** Since the average of these two quantities is 5, the sum of these quantities must be 10. Therefore, $5 + a = 10$ and $a = 5$.

21. **C** $(0.5)^2 = 0.25$
The reciprocal of 4 is $\frac{1}{4}$ or 0.25.

22. **C** $3x - 6 = 1$
Divide each term of the equation by 3: $x - 2 = \frac{1}{3}$.

23. **C** $\frac{1}{\sqrt{25}} = \frac{1}{5} = 20\%$

24. **C** $\frac{a}{3} = b$

$a = 3b$

$3a = 9b$

25. **C** Factor: $x^2 - 25 = (x + 5)(x - 5)$. Even though $x < 5$ makes $x^2 - 25$ negative, the above equation is true.

26. B Since $a = 1$, b and/or $c = 0$.

27. C $x + y + z = 180$
$70 + 40 + z = 180$
$z = 70$

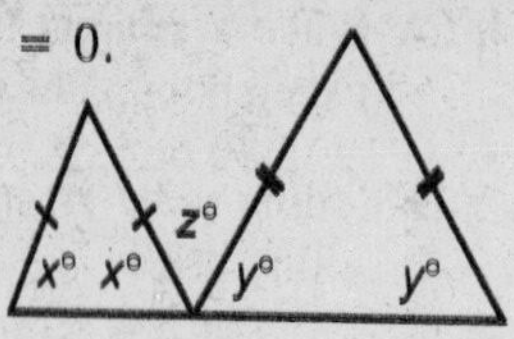

28. C $\angle BCA + \angle ACD \overset{\circ}{=} 180$
$(x + 70)^\circ = 100^\circ$
$x = 30^\circ$

29. A $x = \frac{1}{5}$ of $360^\circ = 72$
$2x = 144$

30. A In Column B, $x^2 \triangle y^2 = x^4 + y^4$
In Column A, $(x \triangle y)^2 = (x^2 + y^2)^2$ or
$(x^2 + y^2)(x^2 + y^2)$ or $x^4 + 2x^2y^2 + y^4$
Since x^2 and y^2 are NOT negative, the value in Column A is greater by $2x^2y^2$; also, $2x^2y^2 \neq 0$ since $xy \neq 0$.

31. D Different values for x and for y produce various relationships. Whereas $x + y$ is always 0, $x - y$ could have any value.

32. B Judith covered 240 miles in 7 hours.
Rate = Distance ÷ Time or
240/7 or $34\frac{2}{7}$ miles per hour.

33. B I is not correct. The sum of two sides of a triangle is greater than the third. Also, recall that a straight line is the shortest distance between two points. Therefore II is correct. III can be reduced to the statement $AB > AC$. This may not be assumed from the information given.

34. C If $16\frac{2}{3}\%$ or $\frac{1}{6}$ of the total = 24 games,
100% = 144 games = total games for season.
.750 average = $\frac{3}{4}(144)$ = 108 games to win
Number of games already won = 15
Games still to win = 108 − 15 = 93

35. D During heating season (200 gallons)(7 months)
= 1400 gallons used
During remaining season amount used
= 200 gallons
Total for year = 1600 gallons
$\frac{200}{1600} = \frac{1}{8} = 12\frac{1}{2}\%$

36. C $x^2 + y = 9$ (1)
$x^2 - y = -1$ (2)
$-x^2 + y = 1$ [divide (2) by −1]
$x^2 + y = 9$ (1)
$2y = 10$ [addition]
$y = 5$

37. B $17xy = 22xy - 5$
$-5xy = -5$
$xy = 1$ [divide by −5]
$x^2y^2 = 1$ [square both sides of equation]

38. C Let x = price for children's admission ticket.
Then $2x$ = price for adults' admission ticket.
$3(2x)$ = cost of 3 adults' tickets
$4(x)$ = cost of 4 children's tickets
$6x + 4x = \$8.00$
$10x = \$8.00$
$x = .80$
$2x = \$1.60$

39. D The distance of (3,0) from the origin is 3 units. This is also true for the coordinates described in I and II. To calculate the distance for the coordinates of III, consider as the distance the hypotenuse of a triangle with legs 3 and 3. It is a 45°-45°-90° triangle, so the hypotenuse = $3\sqrt{2}$.

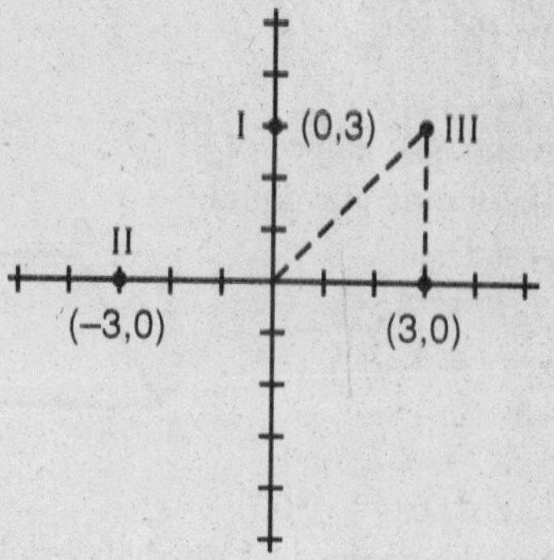

40. B "What part of D is B" means $\frac{B}{D} = ?$
$B = \frac{2}{3}C$
$C = \frac{2}{3}D$
$\frac{3}{2}C = D$
Substitute:
$$\frac{B}{D} = \frac{\frac{2}{3}C}{\frac{3}{2}C} = \frac{2}{3}C \div \frac{3}{2}C = \frac{2}{3} \div \frac{3}{2} = \frac{2}{3}\cdot\frac{2}{3} = \frac{4}{9}$$

41. D Former price was \$1.76 for 16 ounces.
New price is \$1.92 for 16 ounces.
Ratio is $\frac{1.76}{1.92} = \frac{176}{192} = \frac{11}{12} = 11:12$.

42. B Let x = population of town.
$\frac{12.8}{100} = \frac{48000}{x}$
$12.8x = 4800000$
$128x = 48000000$
$x = 375{,}000$

43. B $\triangle ABC$ is isosceles.
Draw altitude AD.
$BD = DC$
$\triangle ABD$ is a 3:4:5 triangle; $AD = 3$.
Area $= \frac{1}{2}(h)(b)$
Area $= \frac{1}{2}(3)(8) = 12$

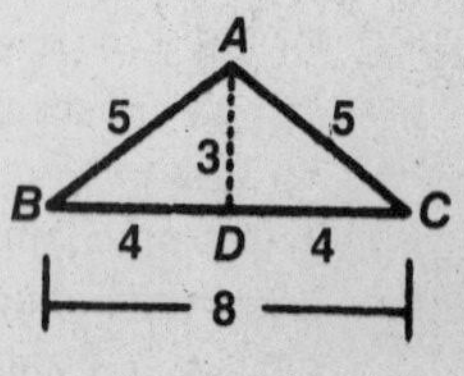

44. **E.** $AO = OB$
$3x + 2 = 5x - 4$
$6 = 2x$
$3 = x$
$AO = 11$ [radius]
Diameter $= 22$

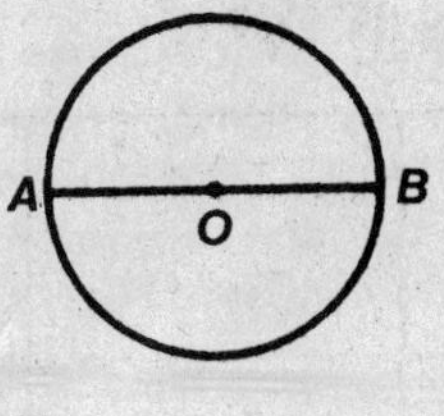

45. **B** Length of $AOD = 8[11 - 3]$
$\therefore$ radius $= 4$
Area $= \pi(4)^2$
Area $= 16\pi$

46. **C** Area of triangle $= \frac{1}{2}$(altitude)(base) or $\frac{1}{2}(4)(4\pi)$ or 8π
Area of circle $= 2(8\pi)$ [given]
Area of circle $= 16\pi$ or πr^2
$\pi r^2 = 16\pi$
$r^2 = 16$
$r = 4$

47. **B** Since opposite angles of a parallelogram are equal,
$\angle B = \angle D$.
$\therefore \angle D = \angle A + \angle C$.
Let $x \overset{\circ}{=} \angle A$.
Then $x \overset{\circ}{=} \angle C$.
Then $2x \overset{\circ}{=} \angle D$ and
$2x \overset{\circ}{=} \angle B$; $6x \overset{\circ}{=} 360$
[sum of the angles of a quadrilaterial $= 360°$].
$x \overset{\circ}{=} 60$, $\angle D$ or $2x \overset{\circ}{=} 120$

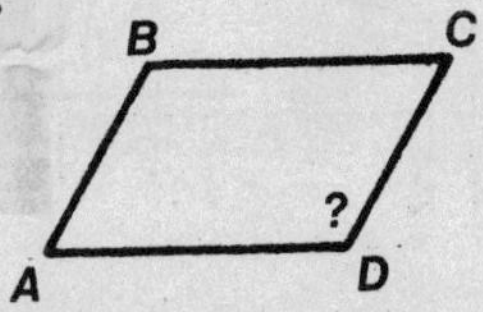

48. **A** Since a straight line is the shortest distance between points, the third side must be less than 1.37 + 5.19 or 6.56. Only choice *A* is less than 6.56.

49. **C** Let $x = AB$.
$\frac{25}{x} = \frac{x}{9}$
[When an altitude is drawn on the hypotenuse, a leg is the mean proportional between the whole hypotenuse and the segment adjacent to it.]
$x^2 = 225$
$x = 15$

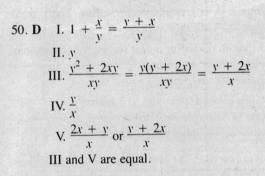

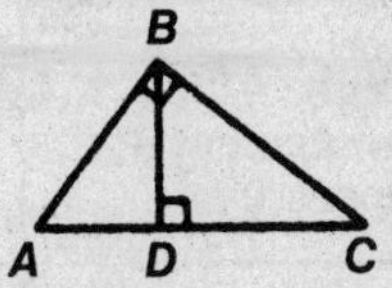

50. **D** I. $1 + \frac{x}{y} = \frac{y + x}{y}$
II. y
III. $\frac{y^2 + 2xy}{xy} = \frac{y(y + 2x)}{xy} = \frac{y + 2x}{x}$
IV. $\frac{y}{x}$
V. $\frac{2x + y}{x}$ or $\frac{y + 2x}{x}$
III and V are equal.

TEST QUESTIONS BY TOPIC

Skill	Pages to Review	Test A	Test B	Test C	Test D	Test E
Basic Fundamental Operations	155–157	2, 6, 8, 15, 17, 21, 23, 39, 48	1, 2, 5, 6, 7, 9, 33, 41, 46, 48	1, 2, 3, 5, 7, 14, 33, 34	4, 7, 17, 36, 37, 38	6, 15, 16, 35
Algebraic Operations	157–160	1, 7, 9, 14, 18, 19, 20, 29, 38, 49	13, 14, 19, 21, 23, 29, 31, 47	8, 10, 17, 18, 20, 28, 31, 37, 38	2, 3, 13, 15, 18, 20, 22, 28 32, 35, 38	2, 4, 19, 20, 21, 23, 28, 29, 31, 34, 36
Using Algebra	160–164	4, 11	3, 15, 43, 45	9, 13, 23, 39, 45	6, 40	10
Roots and Radicals	159–160	3, 5, 16, 23, 32	9, 18, 28, 32	26	16, 30	4, 5, 17, 18, 22, 30
Inequalities	164–165				31	
Fractions	176–178	2, 3, 5, 10, 12, 28, 48	8, 12, 13, 16, 17, 20	1, 2, 6, 19, 21, 32, 35	1, 6, 8, 10,16, 19, 21, 28	1, 5, 7, 9, 11, 17, 21
Decimals	176	2, 3, 5, 6	17	2, 3, 19		5, 17
Percent	178–180	11, 33	15, 22, 33, 35, 36, 45, 49	4, 6, 13, 15, 19, 22, 41, 42	1, 9, 14	10, 11, 13, 37
Mixtures, Motion, and Work	177–178 182–183 185–186	40			34, 39	13
Averages	180–181				33	
Ratio and Proportion	183–185	35, 36, 37	34, 38, 41, 44		11, 12, 14, 23	12, 13, 14, 33
Geometry	165–176	4, 13, 22, 24, 25, 26, 27, 30, 31, 34, 41, 42, 43, 44, 45, 46, 47, 50	4, 10, 11, 24, 25, 26, 27, 30, 37, 39, 40, 42, 50	9, 11, 12, 24, 25, 27, 29, 30, 36, 40, 43, 44, 45, 46, 47, 48, 49, 50	5, 24, 25, 26, 27, 29, 41, 42, 43, 44, 45, 46, 47, 48, 49, 50	3, 8, 24, 25, 26, 27, 32, 38, 39, 40, 41, 42, 43, 44, 45, 46, 47, 48, 49, 50
Quantitative Comparison	189–192	16, 17, 18, 19, 20, 21, 22, 23, 24, 25, 26, 27, 28, 29, 30, 31, 32	16, 17, 18, 19, 20, 21, 22, 23, 24, 25, 26, 27, 28, 29, 30, 31, 32	16, 17, 18, 19, 20, 21, 22, 23, 24, 25, 26, 27, 28, 29, 30, 31, 32	16, 17, 18, 19, 20, 21, 22, 23, 24, 25, 26, 27, 28, 29, 30, 31, 32	16, 17, 18, 19, 20, 21, 22, 23, 24, 25, 26, 27, 28, 29, 30, 31, 32

TEST QUESTIONS BY TOPIC

Mathematical Aptitude

Skill	Pages to study	Test F	Test G	Test H	Test I	Test J
Basic Fundamental Operations	155–157	1, 3, 4, 36	6, 10, 11, 12, 20, 36	1, 5, 35, 37, 40	2, 7, 9, 10, 16, 21, 41	9, 10, 40
Algebraic Operations	157–160	7, 19, 20, 21, 22, 26, 31, 32, 37, 40, 45, 50	2, 3, 4, 5, 11, 17, 18, 23, 30, 34	20, 21, 22, 25, 27, 31, 34, 41, 42	5, 13, 17, 18, 20, 22, 29, 33, 34	5, 7, 22, 23, 24, 25, 26, 30, 31, 36, 37, 50
Using Algebra	160–164		8, 14, 35	8, 9, 13	11, 36, 37	8, 12, 13, 14, 38
Roots and Radicals	159–160	6, 17, 18, 29, 30, 39	5, 16, 21, 31, 48	17, 26, 28, 33	3, 5, 12, 19, 28, 32	2, 3, 16, 17, 19, 21, 23
Inequalities	164–165	28, 38	29, 32	11, 50	35, 39	
Fractions	176–178	1, 2, 3, 8, 12, 16, 17	1, 8, 9, 13, 16, 19, 21, 23, 28, 30	1, 2, 6, 16, 17, 18	1, 2, 3, 8, 19	1, 2, 3, 5, 6, 13, 18, 21, 40, 50
Decimals	176	2, 17, 39	16, 21	16, 17		1, 2, 4
Percent	178–180	5, 9, 10, 33	7, 22, 28, 33, 35	2, 3, 4, 8, 9, 10, 18, 29, 38	4, 6, 36, 37	4, 11, 12, 15, 23, 34, 35
Mixtures, Motion, and Work	177–178 182–183 185–186	34	24	30, 36	43	11, 32
Averages	180–181	14			31	20
Ratio and Proportion	183–185	11, 13, 15, 35, 41	37, 38	6, 7, 14, 15, 19, 32	30, 40, 42	41, 42
Geometry	165–176	23, 24, 25, 27, 42, 43, 44, 46, 47, 48, 49, 50	15, 25, 26, 27, 38, 39, 40, 41, 42, 43, 44, 45, 46, 47, 48, 49, 50	11, 12, 23, 24, 39, 43, 44, 45, 46, 47, 48, 49, 50	14, 15, 23, 24, 25, 26, 27, 35, 38, 39, 40, 44, 45, 46, 47, 48, 49, 50	27, 28, 29, 33, 39, 43, 44, 45, 46, 47, 48, 49
Quantitative Comparison	189–192	16, 17, 18, 19, 20, 21, 22, 23, 24, 25, 26, 27, 28, 29, 30, 31, 32	16, 17, 18, 19, 20, 21, 22, 23, 24, 25, 26, 27, 28, 29, 30, 31, 32	16, 17, 18, 19, 20, 21, 22, 23, 24, 25, 26, 27, 28, 29, 30, 31, 32	16, 17, 18, 19, 20, 21, 22, 23, 24, 25, 26, 27, 28, 29, 30, 31, 32	16, 17, 18, 19, 20, 21, 22, 23, 24, 25, 26, 27, 28, 29, 30, 31, 32

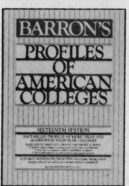

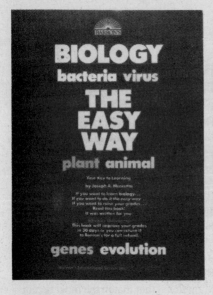

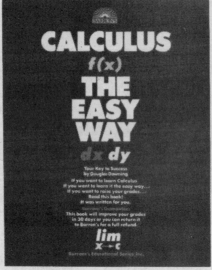